BUDDHA'S WORDS FOR TOUGH TIMES

BUDDHA'S WORDS *for* TOUGH TIMES

AN ANTHOLOGY

Peter Skilling

Foreword by Dzongsar Jamyang Khyentse

Wisdom

Wisdom Publications
132 Perry Street
New York, NY 10014 USA
wisdomexperience.org

Library of Congress Cataloging-in-Publication Data
Names: Skilling, Peter, author.
Title: Buddha's words for tough times: an anthology /
Peter Skilling; foreword by Dzongsar Jamyang Khyentse.
Other titles: Words for tough times
Description: New York, NY, USA: Wisdom Publications, [2024] |
Includes bibliographical references and index.
Identifiers: LCCN 2023017151 (print) | LCCN (ebook) |
ISBN 9781614298892 (acid-free paper) | ISBN 9781614299028 (ebook)
Subjects: LCSH: Buddhism—Doctrines. | Spiritual life—Buddhism. |
Gautama Buddha—Teachings.
Classification: LCC BQ4132 .S55 2024 (print) | LCC BQ4132 (ebook) |
DDC 294.3/444—dc23/eng/20230712
LC record available at https://lccn.loc.gov/2023017151
LC ebook record available at https://lccn.loc.gov/2023017152

ISBN 978-1-61429-889-2 ebook ISBN 978-1-61429-902-8

28 27 26 25 24
5 4 3 2 1

Cover and interior design by Gopa & Ted 2.

Printed on acid-free paper that meets the guidelines for permanence and durability of the Production Guidelines for Book Longevity of the Council on Library Resources.

Printed in the United States of America.

MIX
Paper from responsible sources
FSC® C005010
FSC
www.fsc.org

Please visit fscus.org.

Frontispiece: Colossal statue of the standing Buddha, cast in bronze in about the seventh century. It is 2.3 meters tall and weighs over 500 kilograms, and it must once have been one of the principal cult images at an important monastery lying on the south bank of the Gaṅgā River. There is, however, no inscription to give us any clues to its identity. At some point, we don't know when, the monastery was destroyed or fell into ruins, and the site lay neglected until the nineteenth century, when, in 1862, during the construction of the East Indian Railway, this and other statues and antiquities were uncovered at Sultanganj (सुल्तानगंज , ایک شہر ہے Bhagalpur District, Bihar). The then-resident engineer for the East Indian Railway, E. B. Harris, had the image shipped to Birmingham, and it was donated to the newly opened museum in 1864. It is now on display at the Birmingham Museum and Art Gallery (acc. no. 1885A1116).

Other images from Sultanganj are kept in the British Museum and the Victoria and Albert Museum in London and the Asian Art Museum, San Francisco. See in this volume figures 9, 10, 11, and 53.

Figure 1. Archival photos show, on the left, the frontispiece Buddha after excavation in Sultanganj in 1862 and, on the right, E. B. Harris with some of the Sultanganj images.

Since brass nor stone nor earth nor boundless sea
But sad mortality o'er-sways their power,
How with this rage shall beauty hold a plea,
Whose action is no stronger than a flower?
O, how shall summer's honey breath hold out
Against the wrackful siege of batt'ring days,
When rocks impregnable are not so stout,
Nor gates of steel so strong, but time decays?
O fearful meditation! Where, alack,
Shall Time's best jewel from Time's chest lie hid?
Or what strong hand can hold his swift foot back?
Or who his spoil of beauty can forbid?
O none, unless this miracle have might,
That in black ink my love may still shine bright.

William Shakespeare, Sonnet 65
(RSC, p. 2426)

Although its scent still lingers on
    the form of a flower has scattered away
For whom will the glory
    of this world remain unchanged?
Arriving today at the yonder side
    of the deep mountains of evanescent existence
We shall never allow ourselves to drift away
    intoxicated, in the world of shallow dreams.

Attributed to Kōbō Daishi
(See Abé, *The Weaving of Mantra*, pp. 391–98)

Dedicated to the fond memory of E. Gene Smith
'Jam dbyangs rnam rgyal
འཇམ་དབྱངས་རྣམ་རྒྱལ།

Peerless sage
Powerhouse of wisdom
Omniscient guide
Everlasting inspiration

These translations have no use-by date.

Contents

*Abbreviations identify the language of the principal source text: P = Pāli, S = Sanskrit, T = Tibetan.

Publisher's Acknowledgment

The publisher gratefully acknowledges the generous help of the Hershey Family Foundation in sponsoring the production of this book.

Illustrations

Figures

31. *Dhvajāgra-mahāsūtra*, Peking Kanjur, Sūtra section, Otani cat. no. 959, vol. *lu*, 291b–293a. Page 181.

32. *Dhajaggaparitta*, invocatory stanzas and concluding verses. Pāli language in Thai script, early typeface for Pāli. From the nineteenth-century liturgical collection *Nangsue suatmon*, pp. 34–36. Scan by Fragile Palm Leaves Foundation / Henry Ginsburg Fund. Page 184.

33. The goddess Mahāmantrānusāriṇi, one of the five protection goddesses. Opaque watercolor and ink on palm leaves and wood boards, 2³⁄₁₆ × 23⅝ in. (5.56 × 60.01 cm). San Diego Museum of Art (acc. no. 1990.156.98), Edwin Binney 3rd Collection. Courtesy of Hannah Hyden. Page 190.

34. *Vaiśālipraveśa* from Peking Kanjur, Sūtra section, Otani cat. no. 978, vol. *shu*, fols. 167b–171a. Page 205.

35. Handwritten text of *Svastivākya* in Pracalita script. From Dharmaratna Śākya (ed.), *Svasti bākya va maṃgalāṣṭaba bhābārtha sahita*, Lalitapur, Nepal, Nepal Saṃvat 1112 [1992 CE]. See note at Skilling, *Mahāsūtras*, vol. 1, p. 756. Page 208.

36. *Cakravartin*, wheel-turning emperor, surrounded by his seven "precious treasures." Pillar medallion from Phanigiri archaeological site, Telangana, India. Photo courtesy of John Guy, originally published in his "Dharmachakras," p. 71. Page 214.

37. Tibetan folio of *Cakravartinsūtra* as cited in Tibetan translation in Śamathadeva's *Indispensable Commentary on the Treasury of Abhidharma* (*Abhidharmakośa-upayikāṭīkā*). Peking Tanjur, Abhidharma section, no. 5595, vol. *tu*, 276a–b. Original printing from National Library of Mongolia, Ulaanbaatar, digitized by the Digital Preservation Society (tibet-dps.org). See scans at https://legacy.tbrc.org/#!rid=W1KG26108. Page 216.

38. *Bojjhaṅgaparitta*. The miniatures depict monks chanting with offerings in front. Paper leporello no. 005, Wat Manisathit Kapittharam, Uthai Thani, Thailand. Photo courtesy of Fragile Palm Leaves Foundation/ Henry Ginsburg Fund. Page 218.

39. *Bojjhaṅgaparitta*, Pāli text with invocatory stanzas. Pāli language in Thai script, early typeface for Pāli. *Nangsue suatmon*, 41–42. Scan by Fragile Palm Leaves Foundation / Henry Ginsburg Fund. Page 221.

40. A handsome pair of *kilen* (กิเลน) strut elegantly and birds flutter around fresh crimson blossoms. Paper leporello manuscript, Wat Pak Khlong,

Map

Tables

Boxes

Figure 2. Contemplation of the foul: mural painting with standing gilt Buddha image in foreground. To the left, a monk sits cross-legged with a monastic fan in hand, contemplating a dead body sprawled in front of him. To the right, a monk stands, holding a staff as he gazes down on a corpse. Uposatha hall, Wat Uposatharam, Uthai Thani province, Thailand.

Foreword

As a Buddhist myself for the past half century, I still to this day get surprised and even shocked by how amazingly progressive, accurate, and utterly relevant the Buddha's teachings are in this day and age. The teachings are like perfect acupuncture points, always piercing to the core of what we need to hear and what the world needs, and always completely timely.

In those moments, I can't help thinking—why don't people read this? Why don't people abide by these simple, direct, empirical, hands-on teachings that provide the most practical advice and guidance on how to live our lives?

And in those same moments, I am also totally puzzled why we insist on entangling ourselves and turning our backs ever further on the simple truths that stare us in the face. If only we and the world could learn and deal with those truths that the Buddha taught, we would readily free ourselves from so much unnecessary stress, tension, conflict, and harm.

Peter Skilling has dedicated so much of his life, time, and energy to treasuring these profound wisdom teachings of the Buddha, written down in ancient times on palm leaves and paper in Pāli, Prakrit, Sanskrit, and Tibetan. And for our benefit, he has lovingly and carefully chosen, translated, and presented selections of these teachings for this remarkable anthology—at the just the right time and hour of this difficult period, *Buddha's Words for Tough Times*.

I see it as an encouraging sign that sentient beings must still have some merit if there are people as skilled and dedicated as Peter Skilling doing what he does for the benefit of the world. The release of this remarkable anthology is a sign that the compassion of the Buddha is still with us.

Dzongsar Jamyang Khyentse

Preamble

THIS BOOK IS NONSECTARIAN and at the same time it is polysectarian and pansectarian. It balances on the fine but firm rope of the middle way between all extremes. In Tibetan, it might be described as *rimé* (*ris med*), which means to value all Buddhist traditions and regard them all as worthy of respect and consideration. *Rimé* began in nineteenth-century eastern Tibet as an intellectual and spiritual movement to value and cherish all teachings within the Tibetan tradition and to collect and to preserve them. Today, to suit the expanding horizons of our times, *rimé* goes beyond Tibetan traditions to embrace all forms of Buddhism. At a deeper level, *rimé* means to leave one's identity behind: *urago jiṇṇam iva tacaṃ purāṇaṃ*, as a snake casts off its worn-out skin. This refrain from the ancient *Uragasutta—Sutta on the Serpent*—urges us to leave our shopworn and antiquated identities and agendas behind. Rereading this evergreen two-thousand-year-old poem today reminds me that it is high time for a change.[1]

In the early centuries after Gautama the Buddha passed away in final nirvāṇa, the community of monks and nuns that he had founded developed into eighteen and more orders or schools—as many as twenty, twenty-four, or even thirty over the longue durée.[2] These were not produced by "schisms," and the saṅgha did not split into exclusive and incompatible schools; it was an organic process, more like a banyan tree that sprouts a rich profusion of trunks and branches in all directions.[3] The original schools may have

1. See "The Serpent" in Bodhi, *Suttanipāta*, pp. 157–59. An excerpt is included in the prelude below.

2. Eighteen "was a frequently used number, almost notional, with little attempt at accuracy": Thapar, *The Past before Us*, p. 185, n. 141, with reference to the *Mahābhārata*.

3. *Bheda*, a technical term in Buddhist legal literature, means "split," "break (off)," and in English is usually rendered as "schism." The Sarvāstivāda tradition describes *bheda* as twofold, *cakrabheda* and *karmabheda*. *Cakrabheda* concerns views because it breaks the wheel of

eventually died out in India itself, but what is now "world Buddhism" has transformed into a many-colored array of who knows how many old and new schools, sects, and movements.

The modern study of the eighteen schools has usually been couched in terms of skepticism and a methodological triumphalism that draws up lines of evolution to show what the researcher thinks is the "most authentic" school. But traditional accounts were less exclusive and more tolerant. One example is the *Questions of Mañjuśrī*, a Mahāyāna sūtra translated into Chinese by *Saṅghabhara/Saṅghabhadra, a monk of Funan (Southeast Asia) in 518. Here the bodhisatva Mañjuśrī asks the Buddha:[4]

> World-Honored One, after you enter nirvāṇa, how will your disciples in the future be able to discriminate between the various schools? What will be the fundamental school?

The Buddha tells Mañjuśrī:

> There will be twenty schools that will keep the Dharma in existence for my future disciples. Members of all those twenty schools will attain the four realizations, and their tripiṭakas will be equal, without being inferior, intermediate, or superior. It is like the water of the ocean that is undifferentiated in taste. It is as if a man had twenty sons. This is truly what the Tathāgata has preached! Mañjuśrī, the two original schools derive from the Mahāyāna and from the perfection of wisdom. Mañjuśrī, just as earth, water, fire,

---

the Dharma. In the absence of any contemporaneous records, it is difficult to delineate what really happened or how these concepts were applied in practice, since available documents largely concern the theory and not practice or historical events: see Hong, "Cakrabhedavastu of Guṇaprabha's Vinayasūtra." *Abhidharmakośabhāṣya*, chap. 4, vv. 98–102, gives a detailed explanation of "schism": for *karmabheda*, see Lodrö Sangpo, vol. 2, pp. 1452–56. "Schism connected with formal ecclesiastical actions" (*karmabheda*) is "when, within a single parish or boundary (*sīmā*), the monastics divide themselves in order to perform [separate] ecclesiastical actions, *poṣadha*, etc."

4. Taishō 468 (K 412), *Wen shu shi li weng jing* 文殊師利問經: after John McRae, trans., *The Sutra of Mañjuśrī's Questions*, chap 15, p. 97 = Taishō 14, no. 468, 501a. I first encountered the passage in the excerpt translated by the Rev. Samuel Beal, "The Eighteen Schools of Buddhism," *Indian Antiquary* 9 (1880): 299–302. For a translation from a different part of this interesting sūtra, see Paul Swanson, "*The Questions of Mañjuśrī*," in his *Clear Serenity, Quiet Insight*, vol. 3, pp. 1630–32 (= McRae, pp. 127–31). There is no Tibetan translation.

> wind, and space are that upon which all sentient beings reside, so is the perfection of wisdom. The Mahāyāna is the place from which all the śrāvakas, pratyekabuddhas, and buddhas derive.

Ananda Coomaraswamy quotes from the same passage in Samuel Beal's venerable 1880 translation, remarking, "If these are not the actual words of the Buddha, they testify at least to what the Buddhists at a later period considered that he might well have said."[5] This is an astute assessment. We scholars are too ready to think in terms of an ideal and exclusive authenticity, of what the Buddha "actually said," to champion reality over fiction, defining the terms as we like. But are texts ever fixed and final, or are they creative accomodations and artful interventions that express "what Buddhists at a later period considered that the Awakened One might well have said"? As part of the fabric of Buddhist creativity, are not the "later" texts as worthy of consideration as the "early" ones? And how do we know with any certainty what is early, what is middle, what is later?

In this book, I present translations of texts that were transmitted by several Buddhist orders or schools. These schools were custodians of the Buddha's teachings, which they cherished and polished over the centuries. One result of their editorial care was, naturally enough, that the recensions of the different schools came to diverge. Buddhism is not the voice of any one of the orders. No school, sect, system, or vehicle has any monopoly on the Buddha's teachings. The scriptures—the dharmapadas and dharmaparyāyas, suttas and sūtras, vyākaraṇas and nirdeśas, vepullas and vaipulyas—are not the voice of the Sarvāstivāda, Theravāda, Dharmaguptaka, Sāṃmitīya, Mahāsāṃghika, or Mahāyāna schools: they are the stereophonic multitrack voice of the Awakened One.

The scriptures are products of meditative minds; they were compiled for the benefit and enjoyment of meditative minds. They are uneven in quality as spiritual and literary documents, but the best of them capture the intellectual acumen of Gautama Buddha and his interlocutors. The originality, depth, and energy of the Buddha's thought are preserved in the different recensions. Otherwise, they would have sunk under their dead weight into the slough

5. Coomaraswamy, *Buddha and the Gospel of Buddhism*, p. 156.

of oblivion, as did the teachings of many of Gautama the Buddha's contemporaries, who are active in the early texts but before long disappear from the record.

Dharmaparyāyas are *shared* Dharma. The voice of the Buddha is nonsectarian and unsectarian; it is nondenominational, undenominational, interdenominational, and extradenominational. The Dharma is like the sky, like empty space, and this space cannot be appropriated. The Dharma is nonnational, non-tribal, and non-ethnic; it is public, and open to all. In the same way that you remove your shoes and leave them at the door when you go into a temple, shrine, or home, I hope you will leave your masks, identities, and *-isms* behind when you take this book in your hands.

When Buddhism declined and eventually died out in South Asia—with the important exceptions of Nepal, the Himalayan regions, the Chittagong coast of Bengal, and Sri Lanka—the scriptural collections of most of the schools were lost, many without leaving any trace. The backgound of Buddhist studies is cultural loss: a massive loss of texts, practices, and memory that took place gradually, in stages, over two millennia. Through the nineteenth to twenty-first centuries, experts have tried to reconstruct fragmentary manuscripts with patience and dedication. Buddhist literature may be damaged and fractured, but the Buddhist scriptures are still a stupendous collection. Buddhist literature is alive and well: it is not a dead but a living literature. If I were writing advertising copy, I might write:

> Buddhist literature is a lively living literature that can bring light and life into your living room.

Let us gaze anew at Buddhist literature "with a wild surmise" and silent hearts. Let us let go of the handrails of familiar hermeneutic systems and think afresh. Do we really need to "build on the theories of Z, Y, and X," or to chug along in the wake of the latest trend? Let us remember William Blake's *udāna* of independent thinking: "I must Create a System, or be enslav'd by another Mans. I will not Reason & Compare: my business is to Create."[6]

6. Blake, "Jerusalem: The Emanation of the Giant Albion," p. 153 (chap. 1, plate 10, lines 20–21).

Death's Door Is Always Open

One of the important things in life is to be ready to die. This is hard to see when we're young, but it gets clearer as we grow older. Whether I believe in an afterlife or not, I will die. Whether I believe in an intermediate state between this life and the next—an *antarābhava* or a *bardo*—I will die. Whether I believe that the human (or any other form of) being is annihilated at death, I will die. I may live on for a while as a memory or nebulous presence in the collective *bardo* of family and friends, but this memorialized existence will dissipate sooner rather than later, like a cloud on a windy day. Rituals and prayers guide the collective consciousness through the transition period. When we recognize that, in life and death and in between, our own mind is the star player, this shines a fresh and restorative light on the painful reality of loss. The sincerity of vows and prayers strengthens the living and the dead alike. When personal concern dissolves into love for all beings, it severs the bonds of attachment.

The question is, can I die gracefully and compassionately, without fear? How can I die without fear? We have to confront fear every day, we have to overcome fear every moment, and we have to be ready. Ready, on standby—alert, balanced, and aware. Let us try to be like a Buddha—*akutobhaya*, fearless and unthreatened, with not even a shadow of fear from any quarter. What, after all, is fear? The Abhidharmas do not itemize fear (*bhaya*) as one of the forty-six, fifty-two, seventy-five, or however many mental factors (*caitta*, *caitasika*, or *cetasika*) they may posit in their systems, but nonetheless fear is a state of mind.[7] In the *Sūtra on Multiple Elements*, the Buddha points out that fear arises for the foolish, not for the wise.[8] That is, fear is overcome by cultivating wisdom: to remove, suppress, or avoid external factors is not the solution. Fear arises in the mind, breeds in the mind, and dies away in

7. I often wondered why "fear" (*bhaya* in both Pāli and Sanskrit) does not figure in the lists of mental states drawn up by the masters of Abhidharma, the Ābhidharmikas. When I asked Theravāda masters, some said that it is included under *aversion*, while others told me that it belongs under *attachment*. Indeed, both aversion and attachment do contribute to fear, but fear is a distinctive complex of mental and physical interactions. My understanding may be inadequate: the Abhidharma is, after all, an attempt to strip human experience down to its bare epistemological bones, to its ultimate elements, and perhaps fear vanishes under its stern microscope.

8. *Bahudhātukasutta*, *Majjhimanikāya* no. 115. See further, Giustarini, "The Role of Fear (Bhaya) in the Nikāyas and in the Abhidhamma"; Anālayo, "Overcoming Fear by Recollecting the Buddha: His Role in Early Buddhist Texts."

the mind. Fear of what we have done, fear of what we haven't done, fear of leaving everything behind, fear of not having been to any of the "hundred places to visit before you die"—there are whole industries that exploit the postmodern citizen's anxieties.

Humanity faces a lot of problems, most them self-engineered. Today, might it not make more sense to develop a culture of fearlessness?[9]

> Things fall apart; the centre cannot hold;
> Mere anarchy is loosed upon the world,
> The blood-dimmed tide is loosed, and everywhere
> The ceremony of innocence is drowned;
> The best lack all conviction, while the worst
> Are full of passionate intensity.

One of our main problems is clinging. It is fair to say that clinging, grasping, and attachment lie at the crux of the human problem. Clinging is humanity's hang-up. The Buddha's advice is clear: *let it go*, *let it be*, *drop it*, as he says in this short and succint dictum:

> *Sabbe dhammā nālaṃ abhinivesāya.*

In Pāli the short phrase is transparent and to the point. There are only four words, but I find it hard or impossible to express their message in direct and natural English. It can be, *No thing whatsoever is worth clinging to*. Or, *Nothing whatsoever is worth clinging to*. Or simply, *Don't be attached to anything*. Or, *Don't cling to anything*.

This phrase provides a good example of the vagaries, one might say *caprices*, of translation over a period of nearly a century. One of the earliest renderings, published by Lord Chalmers (1858–1938) in London in 1927, reads, "there should never be an inclination towards any mental states whatsoever."[10] I. B. Horner (1896–1981), president of the Pali Text Society from 1959 to 1981, has, "It is not fitting that there should be inclination towards any (psycho-physical) conditions."[11] For the *Saṃyuttanikāya*, F. L. Wood-

9. William Butler Yeats, *The Second Coming*, after Bloom, *The Best Poems of the English Language*, p. 770. I wonder, though, about the last two lines. I might have written, "The worst lack all conviction, while the best / Are full of passionate intensity."

10. Chalmers, *Further Dialogues of the Buddha*, vol. 1, p. 180.

11. Horner, *Collection of the Middle Length Sayings*, vol. 1, p. 306.

ward (1871–1952) has, "All things ought not to be adhered to"; for the *Aṅguttaranikāya*, E. M. Hare (1893–1955) has, "It befits not to be engrossed in the things of this world."[12] Somehow these all lack punch. Accomplished translator Bhikkhu Bodhi is more to the point with "nothing is worth adhering to"[13] and "nothing is worth holding to."[14] Thai thinker Buddhadāsa Indapañño (1906–93) rendered the phrase in Thai as ธรรมทั้งหลายไม่ควรยึดมั่นถือมั่น, *tham thanglai mai khuan yeutman theuman*. As they stand, the English translations are all correct, but some are more effective than others. The force of the simple admonition gets lost in the fog of rendition. The stumbling block is grammatical: it lies in the expression *nālaṃ* (*na alaṃ*), translated as "should never be," "not fitting that there should be," "not worth," "ought not," "befits not." *Nālaṃ* constructions do not make for comfortable English style.

The notion of nonclinging is difficult to understand. We are conditioned to cling; we are trained to associate our ideas and emotions with our constructed selves, our personalities, our identities. Our ego is our sanctuary, our refuge, our hideout. The Buddha's critique of the self encourages us to let go. Buddhism offers three refuges, the Buddha, the Dharma, and the Saṅgha. Going for refuge to these three is the springboard to realizing emptiness and letting go.

Clinging brings suffering: nonclinging means to not cling to *anything*, even attractive things. We make beautiful things to offer to the Buddha and to deities and spirits, and in the end, when they have served their purposes, we let them go. The beauty is not for us: we dedicate it to the Buddha, the deities, and the spirits. During the autumn Loi Krathong festival in Thailand, we make beautiful floats from segments of banana tree trunks set in banana leaf cups, mostly in the form of a lotus, and place within them flowers, candles, and incense—symbols of offering. We raise our float up to our foreheads, make our prayers, lower them into the water—and let them go. Our lovely and ephemeral offerings float away, bobbing up and down amidst the flotilla of banana floats until they melt away into the darkness.

These are tough times, tossed by turmoil and turbulence. Beset by immense social and ecological change, we are living through an age of angst:

12. Woodward, *Book of Kindred Sayings*, p. 26; Hare, *Book of Gradual Sayings*, p. 53.

13. *Majjhimanikāya*, *Cūlataṇhāsaṅkhayasutta*, no. 37, vol. 1, p. 251.21, trans. Ñāṇamoli and Bodhi, p. 344; *Saṃyuttanikāya*, *Saḷāyatanasaṃyutta*, *Gilānavaggo tatiyo*, vol. 4, p. 50.15; *Aṅguttaranikāya*, *Sattakanipāta*, *Avyākatavagga*, vol. 4, p. 88.12. Bodhi, *Connected Discourses*, p. 1161.

14. Bodhi, *Numerical Discourses*, p. 1061.

the change is flowing and swirling through us, through the collective realities that stream together in the storehouse consciousness of the Anthropocene. We humans face a massive and mind-boggling crisis. We are stumped: planet Earth is lurching into uncharted territories, and nobody knows what is going on. Society, humanity, and the environment are tattered and deeply wounded. To live and die in dignity should be a fundamental human right, but more and more it is honored in the breach.

Figure 3. Buddhadāsa Bhikkhu at Suan Mokkh, 1975.

But haven't we always lived in a state of crisis? Already in the last century, Buddhadāsa Bhikkhu reminded us that crisis is perpetual, permanent, and enduring, using the phrase วิกฤตการณ์ถาวร, *wikritakan thawon*, an expression I describe as hybrid Thai Indic (or hybrid Indic Thai). These are phrases made up of unusual combinations of Indic and Thai elements in fusions you would never find in *pukka* Indic literature. If we transcribe the Thai according to Indic rules, we see that it is made up of two words, *vikṛtakāraṇa* and *thāvara*. The Sanskrit noun *vikṛta* means many things, including transformation and modification as well as apparition, spectre, and product. The words *vikṛta* or *vikṛti* are, however, not used for crisis in Sanskrit, Marathi, or Hindi, in which the most popular words for crisis are *vipadā*, *āpada*, and *saṅkaṭa*. *Vikaṭa*, a Prakritized form of *vikṛta*, is used in the sense of terrible or horrifying.[15] And yes, these are horrifying times.

Kāraṇa is situation or circumstance: *vikṛtakāraṇa* is a state of crisis. *Thāvara* is a Pāli adjective that means standing still, immovable, firm, strong. It is from the root *sthā*, which is cognate with Latin *stō stare*. So here we are: *wikritakan thawon*, a state of standing crisis. Crisis is stable, crisis is our staple fare. Buddhadāsa discusses different aspects of crisis, such as personal crisis, social crisis, and world or universal crisis. He contrasts the crises that humans generate with the natural world, and talks about mental and spiritual disease, which are getting worse, whether they are individual or communal. Because everyone suffers from spiritual illness, the perpetual crisis takes over and usurps the natural space of abiding peace (*santibhāba thāvara*).

We may be in perpetual crisis, but we are not stuck and we are not defenseless. In this age that bristles with weapons, we can take up our own weapons—the instruments of erudition, solitude, and wisdom.[16] Above all, in this age of moral and intellectual bankruptcy, as intolerance rises and the world becomes increasingly polarized, we can cash in on innate goodness and universal buddha nature for the benefit and advantage of all creatures. Buddha nature is our inexhaustible treasure and everlasting endowment.

Freedom from Fear

This book is a collection of translations. The verses and dharmaparyāyas were spoken by Gautama the Buddha over two thousand years ago, but they are anything but inert historical artifacts. (Artifacts are never inert, but that is another tale.) They may well remain in suspended animation for centuries and even millennia, but they spring to life as soon as they are translated or read out or recited. They are undying remedies for spiritual discontents, and they are unfailing aids on the path to liberation.

Liberation: this word has had a checkered history since the nineteenth century, becoming highly charged and increasingly polemical as liberation

15. I thank Mahesh Deokar for his comments on these words in Indian languages.

16. *Saṅgītisutta, Dīghanikāya* vol. 3, p. 219.7, *tīṇ' āvudhāni. Sutāvudhaṃ, pavivekāvudhaṃ, paññāvudhaṃ*. The same three are listed in the Sarvāstivāda *Saṃgītiparyāya*.

movements swirled around the world—liberation from colonialism, liberation from capitalism, liberation from communism, liberation from oppression, liberation from this or that form of domination—and spawned liberation fronts and liberation theologies, to the point that the word "liberation" scares people.[17] Buddhist liberation is even more radical than political or social liberation because it means freedom *within* ourselves and freedom *from* ourselves. Buddhist "liberation theology" is internal and personal; it means freedom of mind and freedom from anguish and discomfort. Freedom of mind is nothing to be afraid of. The first thing to fear is fear itself; the last thing to fear is freedom from fear.

This is an age of demonization and demoralization. We demonize the Other, which is a moving target according to the whim of the week, and cheer each other along. Mob thought swamps individual thought. We are conditioned to blame outsiders and outside forces for our problems, to outsource moral responsibility, and to avoid turning the lens on ourselves. This is an epoch of demoralization. The social environment conditions us to lose faith in humanity, in the dignity of the human spirit, in ideals. A specter looms large over humanity. We are discouraged from having or following moral codes. The result is social and spiritual listlessness, a paralysis of the soul.

Today the world is divided by religion, ideology, social barriers, and entrenched social inequities. Buddhism itself is divided into Buddhisms, schools, and vehicles, into Buddhists, half-Buddhists, and quarter- and quasi-Buddhists. Can a divided Buddhism help us achieve wholeness as individuals? Can a divided Buddhism help a divided world? We say that we are "nonsectarian," but this is an abstract term. For me, nonsectarian means

17. Liberation: for the shifts in meaning of this word, which entered English in the fifteenth century, see Raymond Williams, *Keywords*, pp. 181–83. Ideas of spiritual or psychological liberation are absent from the political and social discourse that Williams describes. Alternate terms like "release" and "emancipation" also seem to have limited horizons in English; spiritual connotations are absent except, it seems, in translations from Indian or Buddhist literature. One might argue that the lack of clear and practical methods of spiritual liberation in Western religious and philosophical systems has encouraged an incremental enthusiasm for Eastern religions, which are perceived to offer attractive techniques to free oneself from the fetters of the materialistic social theologies of the Enlightenment and other Enlightened systems—are these not all what Blake calls "mind-forged manacles"? (Blake, "London," from *Songs of Experience*, after Bloom, *Best Poems*, pp. 310–11). All of this is fraught with faddism and strewn with the pitfalls of self-deception and opportunism.

to recognize the teachings and practices that all Buddhists *share*, no matter what *school* they follow or profess. These are core values, core practices, core meanings because they come from the *coeur*, the heart. They are not dogmas or creeds.

"Nonsectarian" Buddhism is shared Buddhism. Shared Buddhism is cosmopolitan Buddhism, shared by one and all, whatever language they speak, whatever culture they have grown up in, whatever religion they adhere to, whatever religion they don't adhere to. The deepest Dharma goes beyond textbook Buddhism. How can we seek the benefit of all beings (*sabbe sattā*) if we limit the community of beings to "Buddhists," if we exclude some beings on the grounds that they are Muslim, Zoroastrian, Christian, communist, or atheist? *All beings* means *all beings*: it is a universal propostion that is not easy to live out in practice.[18]

We share the air and we share breath. All of us breathe. The breath is central to many contemplative practices: awareness of breath, concentration on breath, control of breath. We humans are breathing machines. Our lives depend on breath and breath depends on the space within and without us. Human space, living space, free space, empty space. This space is emptiness: as breathers we depend on emptiness. When we practice mindfulness of breath, we cultivate emptiness.

As Buddhists, we share. We share anecdotes and stories, stanzas and mantras, gestures and postures, rites and ceremonies. We share dharmaparyāyas, sūtras, jātakas, terminologies, and modes of classification. We share shrines and objects of veneration—icons and images, caityas and sacred sites. At the same time we recognize that our heritage and practices are diverse. Our heritage, our culture, our civilization is an inexhaustible treasure that is as diverse as we are. Human culture is awesome and unimaginably diverse. Isn't it time to celebrate diversities of thought and practice rather than cling to our own limited traditions? Traditions are constructed and concocted, invented and improvised, always on the move. Modern Buddhism seems to be moving towards a soundbite Buddhism, a cuddly "feel-good" Buddhism, a one-size-fits all Buddhism. In academia the Dharma is diluted until it becomes a politically, ecologically, and everything-correct-just-in-case-someone-might-frown-at-us Buddhism, ready to be cut and chopped into easily digestible pieces and fed into the curricula of the knowledge factories. A bite-size, safe,

18. See Skilling, "The Buddhist Cosmopolis."

sterile, and pasteurized Buddhism without much sparkle left. Meanwhile, "Buddhism" and "Buddhists" are being reduced to computer-engineered profiles in the burgeoning marketplace. Buddhist studies aims to cruise along on autopilot.

This book is full of blessings—the blessings of the word of the Buddha. Some readers may balk at this—buy this book and you get bundles of blessings? But where are these blessings? You can't see them, even with a microscope, and you can't hear, taste, smell, or touch them. What good are they? Do blessings work? Subjective questions invite subjective answers, and the answer depends a lot on how you choose to define the word *blessing*. Anyway, to cut this short, the answer is "yes." Blessings are actions: do positive things, do not do negative things, train your mind—this is the teaching of the buddhas, the way to well-being and blessing. This works. Do not scan the skies for signs, hoping for a miracle. Breathing in and out is a miracle, waking up is a miracle, taking a single step is a miracle. Blessings are innate benefits; they sprout within us like miraculous inner gardens of well-being. Well-being cannot be tested externally by gadgets or gizmos, and you can't download it from the web.

It is the message in the miracle that counts; the miracle is the medium. Ask what the miracle means for you. Reading sūtras requires a balanced suspension of disbelief. These ancient texts preserve the teachings of Gautama the Enlightened One, the Awakened One. To read them is to embark on an inner journey, a journey back in time and a grand leap forward in ideas. It is good to sit down and pursue wholeness. By this I mean not to jump from screen to screen, not to change channels every other second. To read whole sūtras, to read whole books, to recite whole sūtras—and, above all, to take your time. Slow cooking, slow reading, and slow practice are the quickest ways to success and satisfaction. Here I am, writing advertizing copy again.

This book is about grave matters like impermanence and death. The Buddha did not invent impermanence: impermanence pervades everything. Insights into impermanence permeate poetry everywhere, as in this seventeenth-century poem:[19]

> The seas are quiet, when the winds give o'er,
> So calm are we, when passions are no more:

19. From *Of the Last Verses in the Book* by Edmund Waller (1606–87): Fowler, *The New Oxford Book of Seventeenth-Century Verse*, p. 403.

For then we know how vain it was to boast
Of fleeting things, so certain to be lost.
Clouds of affection from our younger eyes
Conceal that emptiness, which age descries.

The translations collected here contain some of the most influential ideas and widespread formulas and verses in Buddhist literature. This happened by accident: I did not plan it this way, and I did not have this in mind when I took up my pen forty-odd years ago and began to translate. I translated the texts haphazardly, one by one, without any plan to publish them. Nor did I have this idea in mind when I chose what to include in this volume. I am not sure whether I chose the texts translated here or whether they chose me, but that is another question, and it could not have happened entirely by accident since everything is interrelated and nothing can be utterly random. These widely disseminated passages, these great hits, include the emphasis on heedfulness (translations 1, 2, 3), the stanza on impermanence (translations 4 and 6), the recollection formulas of the Buddha and the Three Precious Gems (translations 12 to 14), the *All you beings gathered here* verses (translations 15 and 16), and the *ye dharmā* stanza, the formula of causation (translation 20).

About This Book

Who is this book for?

This book is a collection of translations and studies. They translate and reflect on a few pages drawn from the great book of the Dharma—they are snapshots of Buddhism's vast scriptural universe. The book is for informed readers who are ready to think outside the box, who have an appetite for the intellectual and spiritual history of Buddhism, India, and the peoples of the world.

This book is for everyone. Everyone means everybody, and everyone includes you. No matter what religion you belong to, no matter whether you are religious or irreligious, it is for you. This is a book is for believers and for nonbelievers. This is a book is for the faithful and the faithless, for the pious and the impious, for the devout and the indevout. This book is for Buddhists, Jains, Parsis, Muslims, Sikhs, Hindus, Jews, and Christians, for devotees, doubters, and disbelievers, for scoffers and skeptics, for freethinkers and latitudinarians. It is for atheists, agnostics, and nullifidians, for nones, nonconformists, and dissenters. This book is nonpartisan, nonconventional, and unconventional. It is a book for the orthodox, the unorthodox, the heterodox, and the allodox, for the orthopraxic and the heteropraxic, for bohemians, offbeats, extraterrestials, poltergeists, malingerers, and heretics. It is for theists, monotheists, pantheists, polytheists, and allotheists; it is for deists, heathens, idolators, and pagans.

I hope I have made my point. This book is for one and all and anyone in between.

The title

The title should be self-explanatory. The past few years have been hard on everyone, owing to the Covid pandemic and the jumble of social and political upheavals that have left the world gasping, almost literally, for breath. I am reminded of the plight of the fish in the "Chapter on Jalavāhana" in the *Sūtra of Golden Light*.[20] In this parable, the disruption of natural resources has caused the waters of the wilds to dry up and left the fish stranded in the shallows, where they gasp for water and breath. The Bodhisatva as Prince Jalavāhana ("Water Carrier") fetches water and food and at the same time he teaches the fish the dharma of conditioned arising.

This book cannot provide material sustenance, but I hope it can offer spiritual sustenance, food for thought and reflection. The texts translated here are not remedies for the rough ride over bumps and brambles that has jolted all of us, but perhaps they can bring needed solace.[21] Our mental worlds are crowded with worry and fear, anxiety and uncertainty; reading opens spaces for thought, reflection, and inspiration. Reading soothes. The resurgence of reading, the realization that reading is a human need, has been expressed in public resistance to the closure of bookstores and the public demand to treat books as essential commodities. These are encouraging signs of intellectual renaissance in the face of the massive onslaught of the monocultural screen culture that is trying to capture human energies and channel them into narrow predetermined paths, drying up the sources of the water of the human spirit. It seems we are losing our ways in the webs of deception, sitting

20. Chap. 17 in Emmerick's translation, pp. 80–88.

21. For an informed presentation of Western writing on consolation across time, see Ignatieff, *On Consolation: Finding Solace in Dark Times*.

blithely in the midst of a wholesale commercial and ideological takeover that is set on scripting the stageplay of human society.

In short, these times are tough and terrible, and humanity is in dire straits.

The structure

This book has four parts. Part I is a general introduction that attempts a brief account of how the Buddhist scriptures were transmitted from the Buddha's time to the present, highlighting the linguistic background and diversity of our scriptural heritage. Part II presents translations of twenty texts of varying length. Part III gives historical and literary studies of each of the texts individually. Part IV is a "Treasury of Terminology"—that is, a glossary of proper names, technical terms, and titles for readers of Buddhist texts. My choice of terminology and my translations of titles (many of which are not especially well known) sometimes differ from mainstream custom, and the glossary is meant to help the reader understand what I write.

I hope the collection will be intellectually stimulating and spiritually uplifting. The translations are the words of the Buddha in English, a (relatively) new language of Buddhism. Texts do not fall from golden lips or float down from the heavens like divine *mandārava* flowers; they are products of the human agency and care that have cherished and transmitted them through the thick and thin of oral, written, print, and digital technologies. The technology of technologies, on which all of these depend, is the awesome craft of our own minds:[22]

> *cittena nīyati loko, cittena parikassati*
> *cittassa ekadhammassa sabbe va vasam-anvagū.*

> The world is led by mind,
> the world is driven by mind;
> everything falls under the sway
> of this one thing, the mind.

22. *Saṃyuttanikāya* vol. 1, p. 39. A Sanskrit version is cited by Yaśomitra in his *Abhidharmakośavyākhyā* (ad *Kośa* 2.1, ed. Wogihara, p. 95.22): *cittena nīyate lokaś cittena parikṛṣyate, ekadharmasya cittasya sarvadharmā vaśānugā.*

They all follow the authority of that one thing: thought or mind. Mind and thought precede the text. Mind and thought are intangible, and texts are their tangible traces.

The studies in part III present glimpses of the individual histories of the chosen texts, and show how both transmission and translation depend on networks of knowledge that extend well beyond the individual textual units. The texts themselves have deep and deeply sedimented histories. Their Dharma is profound, difficult to understand, and difficult to realize (*gambhīro duddaso duranubodho*); this is their spiritual profundity. Historically they are redactions of redactions of redactions: this is their historical depth, their textual stratigraphy. What we read is the *textus receptus*, an end product that depends on the evolution of language and the happenstance of *choice*: the choices of vocabulary and formatting made by redactors through redactions and cross-redactions in conjunction with choice of scripts and technologies of textual preservation. On top of all this, language is ever capricious and delights in taking unpredictable turns.

The pictures

"And what is the use of a book . . . without pictures or conversations?"
—Alice, in Lewis Carroll, *Alice in Wonderland*

This book is filled with conversations and ruminations, and it gives prominence to pictures as well. This is in deference to Alice and in gratitude to David Hockney and Martin Gayford for their conversations in which they point out that "we see with memory" and that "all pictures are, in one way or another, time machines."[23] The pictures are the aesthetic and emotional dimension of the book. They are not illustrations in the conventional sense of narrative representations that the reader is meant to consult. They are "just" pictures—they are statements in their own right, they are visual thoughts, they are channels of aesthetics where the medium is the message, the massage, and the mediator. They are time machines to worlds of past and future imaginings. They augment the contemplative tenor of the volume by reflecting the difficult times in which the book has been written, the long and anxious age of pandemic—of death, disease, dysfunction, and disjuncture. The images are redolent with the *rasa* of calm in the heart of the social

23. Hockney and Gayford, *A History of Pictures*, p. 78.

and spiritual storm, of circumspection and tranquillity in an eternity of protracted tragedy.

Pictures run throughout the volume, interweaving with translation and reflection. The several images of Buddha Śākyamuni include a micro-series in which a stone image of the Master has a carved sketch of a stūpa on the reverse, accompanied by the *ye dharmā* stanza. One might call these "three-in-one" or "trinitarian" images because they unite three aspects of Buddhology: the Buddha is the *rūpa-kāya* or *tathāgata-vigraha*, the physical Buddha, the figure or form of the Buddha; the *stūpa* or *caitya* is the *dhātu-kāya*, the relic embodiment, and the stanza is the *dharma-kāya*, the heart of the teachings. This particular type of image is precious and rare. Not many of them are known to me, and I place them here as icons, as blessings of the integral Buddha.

Most of the paintings are from an illuminated Thai manuscript, a paper leporello or accordion book. Its exact date is not known, but on grounds of style it has been placed in the late Ayutthaya period—that is, the first half of the eighteenth century during the heyday of the kingdom of Siam. The names of the artist(s) and calligrapher(s) are unknown. The manuscript belongs to Wat Pak Khlong in Phetchburi province, central Thailand.[24] It contains Pāli-language liturgical texts written in a calligraphic *khom bali* (ขอมบาลี) script known in Thai as *khom yo* (ขอมย่อ). The paintings are interspersed throughout the manuscript, and they bear no obvious relation to the texts—they are, rather, complementary visual texts—juxtapositions, parallel planes, parallel moments. One series depicts monks engaged in the practice known as "contemplation of the foul" (Pāli: *asubha-kammaṭṭhāna*), of the "repulsive" or, more literally but more mildly, the "ugly," "unattractive," or "unbeautiful"—that is, decomposing corpses in a charnel ground. Another series depicts flowering shrubs and frolicking animals and birds. In this volume, the pictures comment on the theme of tough times and illustrate the mood or *rasa* that is the backdrop of the volume: death, decay, and impermanence. The delicate flowers and delightful creatures point to the beauty and joy that persist in the face of the sorrows of saṃsāra. The artists juxtapose frames of serene contemplation with bright, brisk pastels of blossoming flowers and gamboling creatures, the birds and the bees of the living world. Even the vision of contemplation suggests calm and spirited balance in the midst

24. For the temple and its collection, see Skilling and Santi Pakdeekham, "Manuscripts in Central Thailand."

of inexorable decay and death, exemplified by the radiant demeanor of the contemplative monks and the vibrancy and delicacy of the natural surroundings, and contrasted with the exaggerated ugliness of the corpses, painted in a symbolistic style to the point that they are nearly caricatures. The pictures portray the stages of the meditation on the foul, the stages of decomposition of the human corpse. The frames are not labeled, and I do not introduce any explanations from the classical texts. This, I feel, would be an intrusion.[25]

The presence of the pictures signifies that the material object, the manuscript, is also an icon. The Buddha's words themselves are imbued with protective power, and the pictures augment this power. Frequently depicted are jātakas, which evoke the bodhisatta's *pāramitās* or *barami* (Thai บารมี). In Siamese discourse, these are positive physical-cum-spiritual potencies that enhance an individual's social and spiritual character. The ten and other jātakas permeate the walls of the vihāras and uposatha halls with *barami*. They do the same for the manuscripts.

The pictures are drawn from India, Thailand, Bhutan, and Japan, and from antiquity to yesteryear. They celebrate the universal and nonsectarian nature of the Buddha's teachings.

Ancient Buddhist protocols recognize rules of composition; none of the style sheets survive, but we can recover some of the rules indirectly. Writers of śāstras remark that they will not develop a topic in further detail *bahu-grantha-bhayāt*—for fear the book will get too big ("I'd better shut up now or the book will burst its seams"). In other words, they know when to stop. This protocol holds for formal technical compositions, for authored works, but not for the magnificent arrays of ideas that were called *vaipulya*—for example, the *Perfection of Wisdom*, *Buddhāvataṃsaka*, or *Lotus Flower of the True Dharma*.[26] Best I apply the rules to my own work:

25. Ācariya Buddhaghosa deals in detail with the contemplations in chapter 6 of his *Path of Purification*.

26. There do not seem to have been any similar constraints on nineteenth- and early twentieth-century writers in the West, where works of fiction were often published in installments and ended up as massive tomes, and philosophical and other writings were produced in multi-volume sets. This might have something to do with the invention of leisure and luxury and developments in print technology and commercial entrepreneurship.

Here and now this author takes his leave
to hide behind the folding screen of words.
To all he wishes happy, healthful lives
and a fruitful and instructive read.

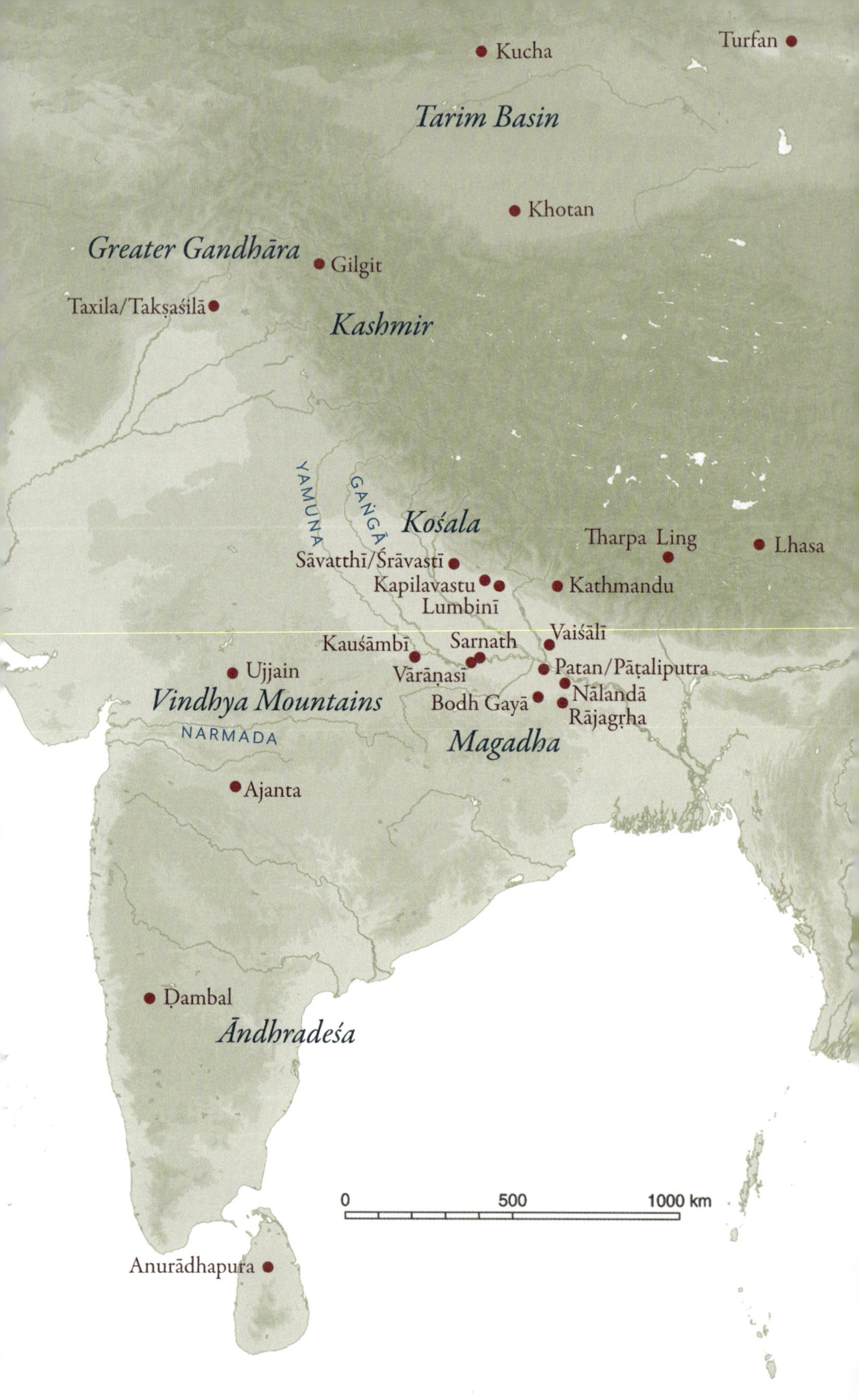

Kucha
Turfan
Tarim Basin
Khotan
Greater Gandhāra
Gilgit
Taxila/Takṣaśilā
Kashmir
YAMUNA
GAṄGĀ
Kośala
Tharpa Ling
Lhasa
Sāvatthī/Śrāvastī
Kapilavastu
Kathmandu
Lumbinī
Vaiśālī
Kauśāmbī
Sarnath
Ujjain
Vārāṇasī
Patan/Pāṭaliputra
Vindhya Mountains
Bodh Gayā
Nālandā
Rājagṛha
NARMADA
Magadha
Ajanta
Ḍambal
Āndhradeśa
0
500
1000 km
Anurādhapura

Beijing
Baodingshan
Uthai Thani
Khu Bua
Wat Pak Khlong
Oc-Eo
Mekong Delta

Map. Places mentioned in the volume.

The map is geographically and temporally hybrid, juxtaposing place names from different periods and different registers of cartographic/historiographic value. It is a conventional tool to help readers identify and locate places mentioned in the different sections and chapters of the book. It does not represent a historical aggregate of sites in geographical or historical/evolutionary trends: it is an aid to orient readers.

Map by Pierre Pichard, March 2022.

Part I

From the Buddha to You: A 2,500-Year Journey

Figures 4 and 5. The image represents the Buddha seated on a lotus. Estimated to date from the seventh century, it comes from an unrecorded site in Bihar, northeast India. The British Museum purchased it in 1854 from Robert Montgomery Martin (ca. 1801–68), an Anglo-Irish British civil servant who published extensively on colonial history and Indian antiquities. On the back of the slab is an outline of a stūpa. Banners, offerings of merit, hang from the topmost parasol. And below the stūpa, the *ye dharmā* stanza is inscribed in Sanskrit (see appendix 2, fig. 54).

The statue was displayed at the exhibition *Buddhism: Art and Faith* at the museum in 1985 and illustrated in the superb catalogue of the same title edited by Wladimir Zwalf, § 141.

Images of the Buddha with a stūpa on the back are known from several sites in Bihar. Three of them are illustrated as icons in this volume: In the Indian Museum (acc. no. 6290) there is a Buddha protected by the serpent king Mucilinda; on the back is a low-relief stūpa with the *ye dharmā* stanza below (below, figs. 6 and 7). The image is from Bodh Gaya, but its precise findspot is not recorded. Asher writes that it is "probably datable just after the middle of the sixth century."[27] There is a standing Buddha with a stūpa and *ye dharmā* inscription on the back in the Asian Art Museum, San Francisco. This is from Sultanganj, probably the site of a monastery, and the same image is in fact seen in the archival photo with the giant Sultanganj Buddha (AAM B60S571) (figs. 9 and 10 below).

27. Asher, *Art of Eastern India*, plates 60 and 61, pp. 42–43.

Figure 4. First sermon: image of the Buddha teaching. He is seated on a throne set on a lotus pedestal and framed by a large halo ringed by flames. Below is a wheel of the Dharma flanked by a pair of deer and a pair of donors. British Museum, no. 1854,0214.1.

Figure 5. On the reverse is an outline of a stūpa, with the *ye dharmā* stanza in the standard Sanskrit recension. For the inscription, see appendix 2, figure 54.

Transmitting the Scriptures

Two thousand and five hundred years ago, Gautama the Buddha taught the middle way for universal benefit in the Deer Park at Sarnath near Vārāṇasī.[28] There he set the wheel of the Dharma rolling, and it is rolling still. By the late nineteenth century, archaeologists had identified and begun to excavate Sarnath, and today it is a spacious park beyond Vārāṇasī's congested urban sprawl. It is a pilgrimage destination and a space for Dharma gatherings; modern paintings often romanticize it by depicting the Buddha amidst bright flowers and shrubs, surrounded by tranquil monks and gentle deer. The multiple layers of meaning are wondrous, but the layers that really count are intangible: the wheel is a metaphor for the realization of Dharma, and the wheel is within us, within the visitors' own minds.[29]

Where do the Buddhist scriptures that we know today come from? Where do the texts that I have translated here come from? How did they get from the Buddha, who lived rather a long while ago, to the pages of this book?

In Thai, quotations of the Buddha's words are sometimes introduced with the elegant expression, "from [the Master's] lips," a phrase popularized by Buddhadāsa Bhikkhu.[30] This raises the question: did the words of Gautama the Buddha that we read in the Tripiṭakas drop directly from the Fortunate One's lips onto the page? Or do they drop discreetly onto the pages of the

28. For Sarnath and its history, see Asher, *Sarnath*.

29. For the Dharma wheel, see further Brunnhölzl, *Gone Beyond*, vol. 1, pp. 679–80, n. 3.

30. จากพระโอษฐ์ *chak phra ōt* : จาก *chak*, Thai preposition, "from"; พระ *phra*, Thai honorific particle prefixed to terms connected with royalty, buddhas, or divine beings; โอษฐ์ *ōt*, Sanskrit *oṣṭha*, "lips" or "mouth," here a loanword from the vocabulary of *rājaśabda* (*ratchasap*), the royal or honorific language register. The beauty of the Central Thai dialect comes from its pedigree as Thai blended with Pāli-Sanskrit, Mon, Khmer, Malay, Southern Chinese, English, and who knows what else. I find it regrettable that so little sustained investigation is being done on this rich hybrid heritage of the Thai language(s).

reader's minds? Or is it more complicated than that? The good news is that "yes indeed, they did." The bad news is that "yes indeed, it is more complicated than that." But perhaps this is good news as well because it encourages us to ponder imponderables like the inconceivable scope of the teachings of the buddhas.

Gautama the Buddha did not write any books or pen any essays. His followers did not take down notes or record his speech. Do the Buddhist scriptures have an author—or are they anonymous? Is it appropriate to classify them as "anonymous literature"? The evolution of Buddhist (and early Indian) literature diverges from the literary practices delineated by modern literary theory. What does "anonymous" mean in this context? Is the word meaningful in ancient South Asian literary practice? What *is* an author? What sort of authorship do we expect to find during a long oral age that took place over two thousand years ago?

Buddhist dharmaparyāyas are complex and layered; they are self-referential structures that respond to the intellectual and spiritual needs and the zeitgeist of the times. The written texts available to us today are artifacts of orality, and their architecture preserves traces of oral composition's craft. We may compare this to the wooden rafters set into the ceilings and facades of the earliest Buddhist rock-cut monuments, or the stone replicas of wooden structural forms that are reproduced in the living rock. Whether made of wood or made of stone, the rafters are structurally redundant, but they do have a function: they cater to the aesthetic needs of designers, patrons, and users. We might compare this to timbered inns or pubs in England or Europe. The timbers are not actual structural elements: they are decorative elements in a nostalgic programme designed to appeal to the public. In the same way, archaism in literature both responds to aesthetic needs and bolsters claims of authenticity.

The written and translated Āgamas/Nikāyas are not anthologies in the latter-day sense of collections of texts authored by a single person or group of people as written documents. They are not "gospels" named after their authors like the four books of the Christian Bible.[31] They are, rather, collective compilations of the words and ideas of Gautama Buddha set within for-

31. The importance of notions of authorship and writing is reflected in the way Christian art depicts the early saints holding or reading books, often pen in hand. This seems to be pervasive: see, for example, Hamburger and O'Driscoll, *Imperial Splendor*, frontispiece and figs. 21–25, 33, 47, 49, 53, 54, et passim.

mulaic narrative and metaphysical frames. They record strands of a grand discourse that originated with the Buddha. As collections, the Āgamas formed gradually and organically within the saṅghas. They could not possibly have been one-time compilations as the time-honored Vinaya accounts would have it. Questions of whether the canons were still open and fluid during the early stages of the transition to writing continue to be debated.[32] How far had the work of editing and structural organization advanced before the collections began to be written down? To what degree did oral and written editorial practices converge and overlap? There can be no definitive answer to questions like these, but they are well worth the asking.

Scriptures before script and vocabularies of transmission

How did Gautama the Buddha's words get from his living teachings to oral collections to manuscripts, from orality to printed books and eventually to translation into the languages of the world? This is a long and complicated story. The resources of transmission are memory, language, letters, and writing. Orality relies on memory, and writing relies on memory and script. A script is an alphabet, a system of notation, a family of letters.[33] The Sanskrit term for "word" is the term for sound, *śabda* (Pāli: *sadda*). Words start as sounds and only later become written signs. Sanskrit, Prakrit, and Pāli developed in the nonliterate, oral period and do not have their "own" scripts. The alphabet is memorized as sounds, not as the visual symbols of written letters.

It is time to reenvision the production of texts to give oral practices due weight. Their original Middle Indic "drafts" were oral recensions agreed upon and recited communally by recitation specialists (*bhāṇaka*). These early versions would have been transmitted by memorization and joint recitations that were orchestrated by individual Buddhist monastic communities. As Buddhism's reach spread and the saṅgha's networks extended, new dialectical influences and editorial tendencies would have led to the periodic need for major recensional overhauls of the received corpora. In order to maintain uniform redactions, the different communities would have had to hold regular recitations or editorial gatherings. The outcome would be

32. See recently Allon, "Formation of Canons," and Bucknell, *Reconstructing Early Buddhism.*
33. *Script* should not be confused with *scripture*, which is a religious composition or sacred text. Technically, *scripture* refers to *written* compositions; nonetheless, the term has come to be used for both oral and written/printed texts.

influenced, as Vinaya master Vinītadeva (late seventh to early eighth century) pointed out, by place or region, by exegesis or interpretation, and by teachers or authorities—that is, leading representatives of the tradition in question—and of course by choice of language.[34]

If all of this took place during the oral period, in the absence of any records how can we know how it happened? We cannot know with any certainty; all we can do is hypothesize based on the rules of linguistic change and on the scrutiny of linguistic stratification embedded in extant written versions. As Allon points out, without agreed, fixed oral texts, communal recitation, memorization, and transmission would not have been possible. This suggests that the formation of individual canons, or distinctive proto-canons, by the different nikāyas must have taken place fairly rapidly, during periods when the different groups were logistically able to assemble together, recite and redact, and agree on the redaction. Otherwise, by the time they were widely dispersed, they would have been unable to agree on and transmit consolidated oral collections. In this context, the idea that there were eighteen or more Tripiṭakas is reasonable and not in the least unlikely. The nikāyas themselves were not stable and unchanging groups, and their editorial activities would have had to keep pace with their own changes and revisions and additions to their canons.

Sūtras were not born in the form that we see today in written or print editions or in modern translations. They have passed through centuries and even two millennia of oral, spoken, and written drafts. The texts we see are palimpsests viewed through a long hall of mirrors. They are not stable texts but "enactments of a mobile consciousness." All texts are works in flux and progress, constantly revised and corrected.[35]

Teams of trained reciters transmitted the "unwritten scriptures," the scriptures before scripts, and consolidated them as mature collections. As noted, there are no such things as Sanskrit, Prakrit, or Pāli scripts. The scriptures can be, and are, written in any script that has a sufficient number and variety of letters to express their sounds. This book, for example, uses the roman script as adapted by Indologists for the writing of Sanskrit, Prakrits including Pāli,

34. *Gzhung tha dad pa rim par klag pa'i 'khor lo las sde pa tha dad par bstan pa bsdus pa* by Ācārya Vinītadeva (Slob dpon dul ba'i lha), Otani no. 5641, 187v7–8, *yul don slob dpon bye brag gis | tha dad rnam pa bco brgyad gsungs |*.

35. To adapt a phrase from Helen Vendler. During her research on Welsh poet Dylan Thomas (1914–53), Vendler found over thirty drafts of his poem "Fern Hill": Helen Vendler interviewed by Corydon Indorf, *Harvard Gazette*, 8 April 2015.

and even for writing non-Indic languages like Tibetan, Burmese, Khmer, Lao, or Thai. Letters or sounds not represented in the standard roman alphabet are indicated through the use of special accents or diacritics. The principles that define the systems of writing are constant through the centuries, but the form and shape of the letters develop across time. How we represent the Indic sounds in the roman alphabet has changed with the evolution of our understanding and of print technologies.

Language and Languages

Does language matter? Yes and no. Yes, language matters because the texts presented here are translated from four languages—Sanskrit, Prakrit, Pāli, and Tibetan—into one very different language, the English of the twentieth to twenty-first centuries, and it is helpful to know something about these languages. No, language does not matter if we maintain that reality transcends speech and realization is inexpressible, and if we adhere to lines of thought like the following:[36]

> Between the night, O Śāntamati, on which the Tathāgata awakened to unsurpassed, true and full awakening, and the night on which he passed away in the remainderless nirvāṇa element—in between the Tathāgata did not utter, announce, or proclaim even a single syllable.

This concept was neatly summarized by Nāgārjuna:[37]

> Not a single syllable has been uttered by you, O Lord,
> [yet] all people fit to be trained
> have been gladdened by the rain of your doctrine.

Here I am translating the language of sūtras, not venturing into the mysteries of the ineffable, so let's stick to language. The languages used by South Asian Buddhist traditions belong to the Indo-Aryan or Indo-Iranian families and

36. *Tathāgataguhyasūtra*, as cited in the *Prasannapadā*: La Vallée Poussin, *Mūlamadhyamakakārikās*, pp. 366.1, 539.3.

37. Nāgārjuna's "Hymn to the Incomparable One" (*Niraupamyastava*), translated from Sanskrit by Mitrikeski, p. 376.

are related to the Indo-European language group—that is, to the same family as most of the languages of Europe, including English.

Early Buddhist texts were preserved in *Indic* languages. "Indic," from Latin *indicus*, Greek *indikos*, means "of or belonging to India; Indian, Hindu. Also, designating the Indian branch of the Indo-Iranian languages, including the dead languages Sanskrit, Prakrit, and Pāli and the living languages Hindi, Bengali, Marathi, etc."[38] Hindi, Bengali, and Marathi are lively living languages, but rumors of the death of Sanskrit, Prakrit, and Pāli are decidedly exaggerated, and the time to publish their necrologies has certainly not yet come.[39] If these languages are dead, then their Buddhist iterations live on not only as "exquisite corpses" (*cadavres exquis*) in the shape of *dharmaśarīra* and *dhammacetiya* but also in the day-to-day liturgies of South and Southeast Asia.

Recognizing diversity: Buddhism and the four scriptural languages

By the Gupta age,[40] the mainstream of north Indian Buddhism recognized four languages used by the four main monastic schools of the time: Sanskrit of the Sarvāstivādins, Hybrid Sanskrit of the Mahāsāṃghikas, Paiśācī of the Sthaviras, and Apabhraṃśa of the Sāṃmitīyas.[41] The first two are Sanskrit or Sanskritic, and the last two are Middle Indic Prakrits. Surviving documentation is insufficient for us to say much about the early literary or canonical

38. OED vol. 7, p. 860, s.v. "Indic." Dictionary definitions are not necessarily reliable; the definition of Pāli at Stevenson, *Shorter Oxford English Dictionary* 2, p. 2078b, is, for example, fair enough until it concludes with "the related language of early Indian inscriptions," invoking a long-abandoned nineteenth-century usage which described *any* Prakrit as "Pāli." The *New Oxford English Dictionary*'s definition is brief and clear (Pearsall, p. 929).
39. Recently Sanskrit has had the honor of joining Ancient Greek, Latin, Old English, Old Irish, and Biblical Hebrew in the elysium of dead languages, but it is (and they are) immediately brought back to life and put to work in Coulter George's engaging book *How Dead Languages Work*. I cannot vouchsafe for the other languages, but I am convinced that Sanskrit and Pāli are both alive and well and that they have not yet checked in at the portals of the *antarābhava* (*bardo*).
40. Mid-to-late third century to 543 CE: the period of the Gupta dynasty's rule over a large swathe of northern and central India. A clumsy term of convenience.
41. See Lin Li-kouang, *Introduction au Compendium de la Loi*, pp. 176–89, for a balanced and comprehensive discussion of the four schools and four languages, a topic first introduced to European scholarship in 1838 by Alexander Csoma de Kőrös, "Notices on the Different Systems of Buddhism, extracted from the Tibetan authorities." See Brunnhölzl, *Gone Beyond*, vol. 1, p. 209 and p. 722, n. 513.

evolution of these languages. The classification reflects contemporaneous Indian ideas of four languages, showing that the Buddhist categorization drew on broader Indian notions of language. Prakrit's role in Indian culture has been obscured by the predominance of Sanskrit.

This includes notions that are widespread in the academy and in general literature, that formal texts *ought* to be in Sanskrit and that the transition from Prakrit to Sanskrit was *inevitable*. Prakrit continued to be a language of literature and culture side by side with Sanskrit well into the late medieval period. This may be seen in works of Sāṃmitīya Buddhist author Sarvarakṣita like the birthstory of Maṇicūḍa, or an anonymous work, a preacher's manual to which Péter-Dániel Szántó assigns the provisional title **Saddharmaparikathā*, that regularly quotes canonical passages in (apparently Sāṃmitīya) Prakrit,[42] or, beyond the Buddhist frame, works like the romance *Lilavai* attributed to the poet Kouhala and written circa 800 CE. At times the same authors composed philosophical and belle-lettristic texts, treatises, and romances, in both Sanskrit and Prakrits including Pāli.[43]

Vedic Sanskrit is said to be the most ancient language of Brahmanic ritual and religion, but its circulation was restricted to limited circles of brahmans. It was not the language of the man in the bazaar, and where and to what degree it was spoken cannot be gauged. For centuries, the mainstream languages used for records, religion, and ritual were Prakrits. The cultural role of Prakrit as the chosen language of early Indian non-Brahmanical religion is increasingly being recognized, and this reflects the role of Pāli in ancient India. Paiśācī has long been seen as having close affinities with Pāli, and modern scholars interpret the Prakrit dialect "Paiśācī" of the Sthavira nikāya in the fourfold grouping as the Pāli of the Theravaṃsa, giving birth to the modern term "Pāli-Paiśācī dialects."[44] The name Pāli is used in Theravāda exegesis, but there is no evidence that the label was current outside of educational circuits or that "Pāli" was a "public" name of the language in either Lanka or India.[45] For centuries Pāli, under the name Paiśācī and doubtless other names, was grouped with the four main languages of Indian Buddhism on

42. Szántó, "Buddhist Homiletics on Grief."

43. For *Maṇicūḍa-jātaka*, see Dimitrov, *Buddhist Indus Script and Scriptures*; for *Lilavai*, see Kouhala; and for other literature, see Ollett, *Language of the Snakes*.

44. Nilakanta Sastri, *Age of the Nandas and Mauryas*, pp. 341–42. Chapter 10 on "Language and Literature" is written by Suniti Kumar Chatterjee and V. Raghavan; the section from which this is drawn is by Raghavan.

45. For more on Pāli, see glossary.

equal terms: the idea of that Pāli was *oldest* or exclusively *original* is absent in the available ancient texts.

I understand the urge, perhaps the passion, to identify the Buddha's language, on the part of both the pious and the curious (sentiments that often mingle). But the long and drawn-out quest to identify and locate the "language of the Buddha" strikes me nonetheless as somewhat misdirected. Do we need to identify a "root language," a *mūlabhāsā*, and raise it up it on a pedestal? Is it not more sensible and more practical to learn to live with the realities of language change? Can we not embrace variety of language as marks of strength, as badges of Buddhism's rich linguistic heritage? Rather than proclaim a single language to be the base or basic language, is it not more meaningful to recognize Buddhism's cultural diversity? The Buddhist schools developed and transmitted several Tripiṭakas. Is there much point, or is there any point at all, in taking one single Tripiṭaka, one single recension in one single language, as genuine or fundamental and relegating the others to the periphery?

Some of the dharmaparyāyas translated here are in the Tibetan language, which belongs to the Trans-Himalayan (Tibeto-Burman, Sino-Tibetan) language family. The Tibetan Kanjur was rendered into Mongolian to make a Mongolian Kanjur, and then, at the behest of the Qianlong emperor, it was translated from Tibetan into Manchu. The large corpus of Buddhist texts in Chinese was translated over more than a thousand years and is still expanding.[46] The characters of written Chinese were adopted as the principal writing system not only of China but also of Korea, Japan, and Vietnam. Chinese translations written in Chinese characters were adopted by Korean, Japanese, and Vietnamese Buddhists as the core corpus of their own canons. The translation and dissemination of Buddhist scriptures is a vast topic, and a great portion of them—the majority?—are found in translation rather than original Indic languages. Often enough the same text survives in one or more translations into Chinese plus a Tibetan version and perhaps others. All I can do here is to attempt a very general sketch that from necessity has to leave out many of the lesser languages and scripts that Buddhists have used for over two millennia.[47]

46. The Kumarajiva Project, established in 2019 by the Khyentse Foundation, is systematically translating into Chinese the texts from the Tibetan canons that "missed the boat" and were never translated into Chinese.

47. In terms of impact and significance to local or historical communities, there is no such thing as a "lesser language," a term that is only a makeshift of convenience.

Pāli and Sanskrit: A long legacy of confusion

Early European research treated Theravāda as "primitive" or "original" Buddhism and Pāli as the language spoken by the Buddha himself. Where, in fact, does Sanskrit stand in the development of Buddhist thought? Decades of misunderstanding have misrepresented Sanskrit's role in the history of Buddhism in general and in Mahāyāna scriptures and śāstras in particular; this has muddled the language question by encouraging the persistent and pervasive idea that the use of Sanskrit signals Mahāyānist, or, if not, then, Brahmanical influence. This line of thought gave rise to the notion that the Mahāyāna is a Brahmanization of primitive Buddhism, an idea coupled with that of the "Mahāyānist divinization" of Gautama the Buddha.

Notions like these have no linguistic or historical basis. Recent evidence shows that some Vaitulya/Mahāyāna texts started out in Prakrit, including Gāndhārī and Prakritized "Buddhist Sanskrit,"[48] and were only gradually made to conform to "proper" or classical Sanskrit norms as part of a broader India-wide movement towards Sanskritization by the third or fourth century CE. Sanskritization was the trend of the times: Prakrits including Pāli were Sanskritized, processed and "smoothed" to approach certain Sanskritic standards; the "intermediate language" or "dialect" (the so-called Buddhist Hybrid Sanskrit) is a product of non-sytematic Sanskritization.[49] Classical Buddhist Hybrid Sanskrit consists of verses in a Prakritic "gāthā language" that are set in a Sanskrit prose, and is really only a recasting of Buddhist Prakrit in syntax and vocabulary.

There is a prevalent notion that Buddhists "adopted" Sanskrit or "switched to" Sanskrit.[50] I find this misleading. Buddhism was never a monolith, and the Sanskrit language itself was never monolithic: rather, it allowed considerable scope for variation and innovation. Two out of the four major Buddhist schools maintained their canons in Middle Indic from the earliest phases of canon formation: these are the Sāṃmitīyas and the Theravāda, who used "Saindhavī" Prakrit and Pāli, respectively. The Mahāsāṃghikas used a

48. Skilling, "Prakrit Prajñāpāramitās"; Eltschinger, "Why Did the Buddhists Adopt Sanskrit?" I write here "started out in," but that is uncertain—we do not know what language or dialect they "started" in. Some Gāndhārī texts may be translations of earlier Middle Indic versions or may have evolved through several Prakrits; some may have been *composed* for the first time in Gāndhārī.

49. "Buddhist Hybrid Sanskrit" is, after all, a curious sort of portmanteau term.

50. On this point see, from a different angle, Bronkhorst, "India's Past Reconsidered."

deeply Prakritic "intermediate language" or "Buddhist Hybrid Sanskrit" that is far from proper or classical Sanskrit. Only, or especially, the Sarvāstivāda or Mūlasarvāstivāda recast their canons in something close to Sanskrit. The (probably) eighth-century master Śākyaprabha's autocommentary on his *Ārya-[mūla]sarvāstivāda-śramaṇera-kārikā*, *Prabhāvatī* (*'Od ldan*), explains this as follows:[51]

> The Sarvāstivādins are like the foundation (*gzhi*, *mūla*: substratum, fundament, basis) . . . because they speak a cultivated language (*legs par sbyar ba'i skad*, Tibetan translation of *saṃskṛta*). In the same way that members of the upper classes, who speak a cultivated language, are like the foundation of the [social] world, because they establish the laws and customary practices, so the Sarvāstivādins are called the foundation—in contrast to the adepts of the other schools, who speak Prakrit, Apabhraṃśa, and the "intermediate dialect" (*bring du 'don pa'i tshig*).

Śākyaprabha goes on to say,

> After King Dharmāśoka died, and the arhats, to curtail the use of Prakrit, Apabhraṃśa, and the intermediate dialect, after resorting to various procedures, made a compilation like those of the sūtrānta and so on redacted in Sanskrit, and from then on Buddhism took on eighteen different forms. In this way the Sarvāstivādins are described as the "foundation."

Śākyaprabha, partisan of the (Mūla)sarvāstivāda, presents an insider's view of the school's adoption of Sanskrit and discounts the Prakrits used by other schools. He directs his criticism at three languages and hence three schools: Prakrit, Apabhraṃśa, and the intermediate dialect, representing the Sthaviras, the Sāṃmitīyas, and the Mahāsāṃghikas. These are the three orders that were active in the northern India of his time. The Sāṃmitīyas were the main school of northern and western India when Xuanzang traveled across India in the first half of the seventh century. There is little epigraphic or other contemporaneous evidence for the presence of the Sthaviras, but the testimony

51. Dating and following translations after Lin Li-Kouang, *Introduction au Compendium de la Loi*, pp. 183–84.

of Xuanzang and other literary sources provide sufficient evidence for them and for the Mahāsāṃghikas as well. Of these three schools, the Sthaviras and the Sāṃmitīyas never turned away from their Middle Indic canonical traditions. The Sthaviras, in the shape of the Theravaṃsa of Sri Lanka and Southeast Asia, continue to maintain a canon in Pāli, to compose literature in Pāli, and to use Pāli daily in liturgy and ritual, in tandem with the vernaculars of South and Southeast Asia. When we count the use of Pāli in daily rituals morning, noon, and night across South and Southeast Asia, this is a massive use of canonical and liturgical Pāli and a monumental use of a Buddhist Prakrit. One may say that by far the largest living use of a classical Prakrit today is that of the Theravāda Buddhists.

The Sāṃmitīyas maintained a Prakrit canon—known so far only through recent manuscript studies—but they also used Sanskrit for scientific and technical compositions such as the cosmological treatise *Mahāsaṃvartanīkathā* by Mahākāvī Sarvarakṣita[52] or the scholastic manual in verse *Abhidharmasamuccaya* by Saṅghatrāta.[53] We know very little about the school because it died out and its scriptures were largely lost.

Sanskrit was an intellectual tool, a vehicle for thought that was used as appropriate to communicate ideas to a broad audience. The idea that the "Buddhists" switched to Sanskrit was based on simplistic notions of a monolithic and ahistorical orthodox Buddhism. The majority of Buddhists did not switch to Sanskrit at all; the majority kept their scriptures in Middle Indic.

What languages didn't Gautama the Buddha speak?

Why do we always ask, "What language did the Buddha speak?" Why don't we ask, "What *languages* did the Buddha speak?" "What languages *didn't* the Buddha speak?" "What languages did the Buddha *use*?" or "What languages *might* Gautama the Buddha *have used* or *might* the Buddha *have spoken*?" Certainly Śākyamuni didn't speak Tibetan or Mongolian or Chinese, Thai, Mon, Lao, or Khmer, and just as certainly he didn't teach the Saddharma in Sanskrit. As far as I know, no nikāya claims that the Buddha spoke Sanskrit. Later works like the Sarvāstivāda or Mūlasarvāstivāda Tripiṭakas or the poems of Aśvaghoṣa portray the Awakened One as speaking Sanskrit—but

52. Okano, *Sarvarakṣitas Mahāsaṃvartanīkathā*.
53. See Sferra, "Pudgalo 'vācyaḥ," and, in general, Skilling, "Rehabilitating the Pudgalavādins."

the texts are composed in Sanskrit, and everyone else is speaking Sanskrit as well.[54] These are literary documents, the work of redactors and poets, who followed linguistic trends and the dictates of literary imagination and catered to the perceived capacities and needs of their audiences. The monastic schools developed consistent and coherent bodies of narrative, liturgical, and philosophical writings as their cultural thought-world, and their chosen language defined their history and marked their heritage and identities. It might be advisable here to speak of *dialect* rather than *language*, since the languages adopted by the schools were all related as dialects or varieties of early Middle Indic. In addition to their canonical dialect, many of the schools—at least those who continued to be active into and beyond the Gupta age—used scholastic Sanskrit to present their doctrinal theories in the public domain. Script choice was another facet of the construction of identity: the schools recorded their texts in the scripts of their chosing, according to their region of activity or to specialized uses like Bhaikṣukī/Saindhavī by the Sāṃmitīyas or the Khom script by the Central Thai. Each school used more than a single script according to circumstances and convenience, to best suit the needs of preservation, education, propagation, and aesthetics.

Language and authenticity

What is the relation between language and authenticity? Does a text have to be in the Buddha's own language to be authentic? If that's the case, is there any point in trying to translate it? If we have a text in several Indic versions, which is the most authentic? Do questions like these make sense? Might it not be better to accept all of them as authentic in their own contexts, within their own school and linguistic and historical communities? From the outset, we need to have a clear idea of what we mean by "authenticity." Is there any such thing as absolute authenticity that stands outside of history? The very idea strikes me as decidedly dubious.

Many early teachings were transmitted in verse (*gāthā*). Different schools may share the same verses, but they often put them to different uses or employ them in different contexts. It seems more rewarding to read variant verses in tandem, to understand their commonalities and differences in terms

54. Buddhist texts do not employ hierarchies of class and language as, for example, does the Sanskrit drama. See Eltschinger, "Why Did the Buddhists Adopt Sanskrit?" and the interesting discussion about Sanskrit and *saṅgīti* in Śrī Puṇḍarīka's *Vimalaprabhā* commentary on the *Kālacakratantra* (see below).

BOX 1. *"Arise, go forth, devote yourselves": comparison of versions*

Each version conveys its meaning in its own context to its own language community.

Udānavarga (Sanskrit)	*Saṃyuttanikāya* (Pāli)	*Dhammapada* (Gāndhārī)
ārabhadhvaṃ niṣkramadhvaṃ yujyadhvaṃ buddhāśāsane dhunidhvaṃ mṛtyunaḥ sainyaṃ naḍāgāraṃ iva kuñjaraḥ.	ārabbhatha nikkhamatha yuñjatha buddhasāsane dunātha maccuno senaṃ naḷāgāraṃ va kuñjaro.	arahadha nikhamadha yujatha budha-sasane dhuṇatha mucuṇo seṇa nadakara ba kuñaru.
yo hy asmiṃ dharmaviṇaye tv apramatto bhaviṣyati prahāya jātisaṃsāraṃ duḥkhasyāntaṃ sa yāsyati.	yo imasmiṃ dhammavinaye appamatto vihessati pahāya jātisaṃsāraṃ dukkhass' antaṃ karissati.	yo imasma dhamaviṇa'i apramatu vihaṣidi praha'i jadi-satsara dukhusada kariṣadi.

Avadānaśataka (Sanskrit)

आरभध्वं निष्क्रामत युज्यध्वं बुद्धशासने | ārabhadhvaṃ niṣkrāmata yujyadhvaṃ buddhaśāsane
धुनीत मृत्युनः सैन्यं नडागारमिव कुञ्जरः || dhunīta mṛtyunaḥ sainyaṃ naḍāgāram iva kuñjaraḥ

यो ह्यस्मिन् धर्मविनये अप्रमत्तश्चरिष्यति | yo hy asmin dharmavinaye apramattaś cariṣyati
प्रहाय जातिसंसारं दुःखस्यान्तं करिष्यति || prahāya jātisaṃsāraṃ duḥkhasyāntaṃ kariṣyati

Tibetan, *Vinayavibhaṅga*

བརྩམ་པར་བྱ་ཞིང་དབྱུང་བར་བྱ། ། brtsam par bya zhing dbyung bar bya ||
སངས་རྒྱས་བསྟན་ལ་འཇུག་པར་བྱ། ། sangs rgyas bstan la 'jug par bya ||
འདམ་བུའི་ཁྱིམ་ལ་གླང་ཆེན་བཞིན། ། 'dam bu'i khyim la glang chen bzhin ||
འཆི་བདག་སྡེ་ནི་གཞོམ་པར་བྱ། ། 'chi bdag sde ni gzhom par bya ||

གང་ཞིག་རབ་ཏུ་བག་ཡོད་པར། ། gang zhig rab tu bag yod par ||
ཆོས་འདུལ་འདི་ལ་སྤྱོད་འགྱུར་བ། ། chos 'dul 'di la spyod 'gyur ba ||
སྐྱེ་བའི་འཁོར་བ་རབ་སྤངས་ནས། ། skye ba'i 'khor ba rab spangs nas ||
སྡུག་བསྔལ་ཐ་མར་བྱེད་པར་འགྱུར། ། sdug bsngal tha mar byed par 'gyur ||

Chinese, *Mūlasarvāstivādavinaya*

汝當求出離，於佛教勤修， Rǔ dāng qiú chū lí, yú fójiào qín xiū,
降伏生死軍，如象摧草舍。 xiángfú shēngsǐ jūn, rú xiàng cuī cǎo shě.

於此法律中，常為不放逸， Yú cǐ fǎlǜ zhōng, cháng wéi bù fàng yì,
能竭煩惱海，當盡苦邊際。 néng jié fánnǎo hǎi, dāng jìn kǔ biānjì.

of philology, rather than to declare a priori that one or the other is original and the rest secondary. It makes more sense to ask whether they convey different meanings, and if so, why, and how? The verses in box 1, above, are available in three Indic versions.[55] I cite them in the order Sanskrit (from the *Udānavarga*), Pāli (from *Saṃyuttanikāya* and *Theragāthā*), and Northwestern Prakrit (from the Khotan *Dharmapada*), followed by their Tibetan and Chinese translations from the *Vinayavibhaṅga*.[56]

Did Gautama the Buddha speak Pāli?

To return to the Buddha. What language did he speak? If you happen to meet the Buddha on the road, don't forget to ask him how many languages he speaks and which he prefers. But don't we know already? Didn't the Buddha speak Pāli? Shouldn't you address him straightaway in Pāli?

This question has been around for a long time, but one crucial point often gets lost. This is that the Buddha himself never tells us what language he is speaking. And why should he?—I ask rhetorically (in English). None of the canonical Pāli texts themselves tell us what language they're in, and the Buddha himself advises us not to get attached to dialects or regional languages.[57] He advises us to adapt our speech to local custom and to express ourselves accordingly without attachment.[58]

We need to wait nearly a thousand years (that is, till around 400 to 500 CE) until the Theravāda commentaries give a name to the language of their collections, and they call it Māgadhī, the "language of Magadha." The idea that Gautama spoke Māgadhī, the language of Magadha, the heartland of his career, is logical. Could he go from place to place and communicate his ideas speaking in an unfamiliar tongue? Schools other than Theravāda may have had the same idea, but their texts are long lost; in the surviving literature the idea that the scriptures were redacted in Māgadhī is rare outside of Theravāda commentarial sources. There are several mentions in Śrī Puṇḍarīka's

55. See translation 3 for an English version (p. 117) and its introduction at pages 279–83.

56. Tibetan, Dergé no. 3, *Vinayavibhaṅga / 'Dul ba rnam par 'byed pa*, 'Dul ba, *ja*, 115a2–3; Chinese, *Mūlasarvāstivādavinaya* 根本說一切有部毘奈耶, translated by Yijing, Taishō 23, no. 1442, 811b21–24.

57. *Janapadaniruttiṃ nābhiniveseyya, samaññaṃ nātidhāveyya*. This is in the *Araṇavibhaṅgasutta* (*Majjhimanikāya, Uparipaṇṇāsa,* no. 139), which shows a fascinating linguistic awareness.

58. Idem, *yathā yathā naṁ tesu tesu janapadesu sañjānanti 'idaṁ kira me āyasmanto sandhāya voharantī'ti tathā tathā voharati aparāmasaṁ*.

Stainless Light (*Vimalaprabhā*) commentary on the *Kālacakratantra*, written perhaps about five hundred years after the Pāli commentaries. Puṇḍarīka follows a very different set of exegetical principles than those of Buddhaghosa and the Aṭṭhakathā masters—that is, he belongs to the transregional intellectual milieu of the *Kālacakratantra*, about 1,500 years after the Buddha's nirvāṇa. Puṇḍarīka is even more elusive than most other premodern South Asian writers: he is said to be the second Kalki king of Shambala, and where and when he lived are not known. He deftly dodges the nets of historicist investigation, but his writing demonstrates that he is an erudite authority with an extraordinarily wide geographical and cultural scope of knowledge.

Puṇḍarīka points out that from the first, in or according to the Śrāvaka system (*śrāvakanaya*), the teaching of the Dharma (*dharmadeśanā*) and the three Piṭakas were in the language of Magadha. Here he quotes, regrettably not completely, the *iti pi so bhagavā* formula in a form that agrees almost perfectly with Pāli: *ityapi so bhagavā sammāsambuddho vijjācaraṇasampanno sugato lokavidū anuttaro ityādinā dharmadeśanā*. Puṇḍarīka's exegetical thought is fascinating but hard to grasp either socially or historically.[59]

Box 2. *The language of Omniscience, by Mattia Salvini*[60]

Introduction

The *Kālacakratantra* is a very extensive system of thought and practice; besides its unique methods of meditation, it offers an entire cosmology of its own, with an astrological landscape that matches the inner physiology of the person.

Amongst the many special features of the Kālacakra is a presentation of the languages of the Buddhist teachings found in its most influential commentary, the "Stainless Light" (*Vimalaprabhā*). Here we find

59. Puṇḍarīka's comments on these and other aspects of the complexities of the language of the Buddhist texts merit careful study: see Upadhyaya ed., *Vimalaprabhāṭīkā Vimalaprabhā*, vol. 1, p. 41.14 = Tanjur, Otani no. 2064, repr. vol. 46, Rgyud 'grel, *ka*-2, 39b4.
60. Introduction and translation from Sanskrit by Mattia Salvini from Śrī Puṇḍarīka's *Vimalaprabhā* commentary on the *Kālacakratantra*, vol. 1, p. 31.29. See also translation in Newman, *Outer Wheel of Time*, pp. 360–63.

a unique distinction between "the language of the Omniscient Ones" (*sarvajña-bhāṣā*) versus the language of sentient beings. The subdivision of different parts of the Buddhavacana into different languages (Magadha, Sanskrit, Prākr̥t, Apabhraṁśa, etc.) is also uncommon, as other Mahāyāna masters offer rather different versions regarding the transmission of the Buddhist teachings. It is also remarkable that the commentary seems to refer to the river Nile, as well as to Persian language, and to Rahya/Rahma language (Arabic?).

"Makers of the communal chanting" here translates *saṁgītikāra*; the term "communal chanting" is more commonly translated as "council," but I prefer a rendering that may better capture what the event was mainly about—i.e., chanting together a set of texts in a form agreed upon by all. The *Vimalaprabhā*, somewhat surprisingly, regards those who translated and collected the teachings into languages beyond "the land of the Noble Ones" as "makers of the communal chanting," which is perhaps not how today's scholars would primarily or usually understand the term (for example: Ārya Ānanda is *the* Saṁgītikāra for the Śrāvaka sūtras).

It is clear that in the following passage "the language of the Omniscient Ones" is not a specific language; language becomes specified only in the process of preserving and transmitting the teachings.

Translation

In these three realms, those Dharmas which have been taught by the Omniscient One in the language of the Omniscient Ones, were written in a book by the makers of the communal chanting in many different languages of sentient beings; they explain the mundane meanings such as the Veda, etc., they explain the meaning of the three vehicles, they are taught in accordance with the truth of worldly conventions and in accordance with ultimate truth, for the sake of all sentient beings' listening and study. Sentient beings who have conviction in regard to these Dharmas, when it comes to the eighty-four thousand Dharma-aggregates taught by the Omniscient One and explaining mundane and supramundane meanings, listen to them, study them, speak of them, retain them in their memory, and elucidate them extensively to others; they establish them, and worship them; with many flowers, with many scents, with many types of incense, with many powders, with many clothes, with many bells, with many standards, with many chowries, with many parasols, with many canopies, with many strings of pearls, with many jewels, with many lamps, with many jewel-ornaments; having worshiped them, they perform five-limbed prostrations towards them.

In this way, the Dharmas taught by the Omniscient One are helpful to others; they have been enjoined or prohibited by the Tathāgata on the basis of convictions, for the sake of helping others, and not on the basis of anyone's birth or lack of a certain birth. Thus, even today, they have not disappeared.

First of all, let alone other countries: here, where the Tathāgata had become a Buddha, in the country of the Noble Ones, once the Buddha had gone into complete nirvāṇa, the three vehicles were written down in a book by the makers of the communal chanting, in accordance with the restrictions laid down by the Tathāgata: the Tripiṭaka in the language of Magadha; the Sūtrānta in the language of Sindhu; in Sanskrit language, the method of the Perfections; as for the Mantra-method, different Tantras were written in Sanskrit language, in Prākṛt language, in Apabhraṁśa language, in the languages of barbarians such as the language of the Śavara—in this way, etc., the Dharma taught by the Omniscient One was written down by the makers of the communal chanting.

In the same way, in the country of Tibet it was written down in Tibetan language, in the country of Cīna it was written down in Cīna language, in the language of Great Cīna it was written down in the language of Great Cīna, in the country of Persia it was written down in the Persian language; above the Śītā river, in the language of the country of Campaka, in the language of the country of Vānara, in the language of the country called Suvarṇa; and above the Nīla river, in the language of the Rahya country, and in the language of the country of Surasmā: in this way, in ninety-six countries consisting of crores and crores of villages, it was written down in the languages of ninety-six countries.

In this way, in twelve parts, in the heaven, the mortal world, and the netherworld, the three vehicles were written down by the makers of the communal chanting, according to the speech of different sentient beings.

The Śrāvaka vehicle was written down by the Śrāvakas; the Pratyeka vehicle, by the Pratyekas; the Mahāyāna of the Perfections and the Mahāyāna of Mantra, having the nature of the cause and having of nature of the result, by the Bodhisattvas—by many makers of the communal chant, in order to guide sentient beings.

When we analyze the Buddha, the Bhagavat, by reasoning that his Textual Tradition has been written down by many different makers of the communal chanting, in the languages of many different countries, it turns out that he is Omniscient, teaching the Dharma in the language of the Omniscient Ones; and this is not the case of others such as Hari, Hara, etc.

On Pāli and Māgadhī, Bhikkhu Bodhi writes,[61]

> The Theravāda tradition identifies Pāli with Māgadhī, the language of the state of Magadha, where the Buddha often stayed. Several of the Buddha's favorite resorts were located in Magadha, amongst them the Bamboo Grove near Rājagaha, mentioned in the suttas as the scene of many discourses. As the language of a powerful and influential kingdom, Māgadhī may well have spread to other states in northeast India and become a prestigious language distinguishing those who used it as persons of culture, somewhat in the way English is used by the educated elite today even in the countries of South Asia. However, while the Buddha himself may have spoken in Māgadhī when teaching in Magadha—and perhaps in other dialects when teaching in other states, such as Kosala—various features of Pāli indicate that it cannot be identified with Māgadhī as we know it from the earliest sources available to us, the edicts of King Aśoka.

61. Bodhi, *Reading the Buddha's Discourses in Pāli*, p. 1.

"Pāli" did not start out as the formal name of a language. As a common noun it means "line of words," a sequence of speech, in the sense of unit of canonical text to be contrasted with and distinguished from exegetical remarks. The word appears in association with language in the Theravāda commentaries, where "Pāli" is the *canonical text citation* and "Aṭṭhakathā," as its name indicates, is the *gloss*. The use of Pāli in this sense seems unique to the Theravaṃsa, as is that of *aṭṭhakāthā*: so far, neither term has been encountered outside of the Lankan Theravāda and its descendants. The usage may have begun as a technical, exegetical term shared by insiders, but it eventually caught on in Theravāda societies as a name of the language itself. The terms *pāli* and *aṭṭhakathā* are found in only the Theravāda commentarial tracts and are not known from the literature of other Buddhist schools.

For nearly a thousand years the "Pāli" texts did not name the language in which they are written, and eventually, the language became known by two different names, the one referring to function and context (Pāli), the other to regional dialect (Māgadhī). For reasons of its own, European scholarship chose to adopt the former and to rather summarily reject the latter. The vernacular imagination of countries where Buddhism prevails saw no harm in keeping the two as alternates. In regular Thai usage, for example, "Pāli" (*phasa bali*/ภาษาบาลี, *bhāṣā pālī*) and "Māgadhī" (*phasa makhot*/ภาษามคธ, *bhāṣā magadha*) can be used interchangeably. So far as we know, the situation was similar in the other orders insofar as their available texts do not have anything to say about the language they are in. To this there is one exception: the Lokottaravāda Mahāsāṃghikas do give a name to the language, not in the body of their texts but in concluding manuscript colophons.

All of this is complicated and controversial. In sum, we do not know the "original" name of Pāli, and we do not know the historical or regional origins of the language, except to say that it is a northern Indian Prakrit, perhaps (probably) western Indian in origin. Behind the story of Pāli is the *storia* of how Pāli grammar and linguistic science evolved, something that remains to be written as a cohesive narrative. (The same is true with other Buddhist languages in which intellectual movements of grammar molded the shape of their canons.)

Some scholars regard Pāli as a hybrid showing features of several Prakrit dialects used around the third century BCE, subjected to a partial process of Sanskritization. According to eminent Indologist Oskar von Hinüber:[62]

62. Von Hinüber, *Handbook of Pāli Literature*, p. 5.

> Pāli has never been a spoken language neither in Magadha nor elsewhere. For it is possible to infer from linguistic peculiarities of this language that it has been created as some kind of *lingua franca* presumably used in a large area at a time considerably later than the Buddha. The evidence, on which these conclusions are based, are the inscriptions of Aśoka (3rd century BC), which allow us to draw a very rough linguistic map of northern India. This map shows that Pāli is rooted in a language spoken in western India far away from the homeland of Buddhism. At the same time certain eastern features embedded in Pāli point to the fact that the texts have been recast from an earlier eastern version into their present western linguistic shape. Therefore, it is evident that the texts as found in the Theravāda canon, though the oldest Buddhist texts surviving, are the result of a lengthy and complicated development.

The language of the available Buddhist Prakrits—Pāli, Gāndhārī, and the Prakrit of the Sāṃmitīyas (known, it seems, as Apabhraṃśa, Saindhavī, and/or Sindhubhāṣā)—is closely related, as is their style, structure, phraseologies, and vocabularies.[63] At one point, all these Tripiṭakas were complete, at least in the eyes of their redactors and users, but today Pāli is the only school for which a complete canon survives. As the sole surviving complete Middle Indic or Indic Tripiṭaka, the Pāli canon is thus a treasure beyond price.

Migrations carried the canonical and commentarial Māgadhī and Pāli languages and textual collections to the isle of Lanka, where new generations of redactors continued to transmit and streamline the texts. Epigraphic and textual evidence shows that the system of trained reciters was established on the island. The texts were eventually recorded in writing, according to legendary history (historical legend) in the first century BCE. The editorial process never stopped and continued under the guidance and influence of new grammatical schools that developed centuries later in Southeast Asia, especially in Pukām (the city of Pagan or Bagan) in Burma. Later, in Thailand, Kaccāyana's grammar was taught and recorded in two languages, Pāli and Thai.

63. Our understanding of regional Prakrits is amplified by the large and growing body of inscriptions in Buddhist contexts, but these are rarely scriptural citations but rather donative and other records.

What is special about Pāli?

For many today, it is an article of faith that Gautama the Buddha's teaching has come down to us unruptured and unbroken. Language does not stand still, however, and we cannot discount the impact of over two millennia, during which editorial practice underwent major shifts in the technologies of storage, reproduction, and communication of knowledge from oral to written media. The various schools redacted and revised their scriptures autonomously and individually. Oral and written practices were subject to the editorial decisions of school-specific redaction committees set up by the individual schools to establish and maintain their chosen standards and their linguistic identities. All this would be enacted by recitation masters and eventually by scribes and readers. The end product is the word of the Buddha, the "holy word" or "holy writ."

Bhikkhu Bodhi goes on to say,[64]

> While the language called "Pāli" is not identical with any that the Buddha himself would have spoken, it belongs to the same broad linguistic family as those he might have used and originates from the same conceptual matrix. The canonical texts preserved in Pāli are not so much translations from more archaic originals into an altogether different language, as a translation from German into English would be, as they are "transfers" or renditions from one Middle Indo-Aryan dialect into another. This language thus reflects the thought-world that the Buddha inherited from the Indian culture into which he was born and captures the nuances of that thought-world without the intrusion of alien influences inevitable in even the best and most scrupulous translations. This contrasts with Chinese, Tibetan, or English translations of Indian Buddhist texts, which inevitably carry over nuances and connotations from those languages.
>
> On this basis we can infer that the language of the Pāli Canon, while likely not identical with the language or languages the Buddha spoke, would be so close as to provide an almost transparent window into the words and expressions he used.

64. Bodhi, *Reading the Buddha's Discourses in Pāli*, p. 2.

Pāli is special: it has an exceptional status amongst Buddhist languages that makes it precious. Pāli is precious as a vehicle for one of the Three Precious Jewels, the Dharma: the Pāli canon is invaluable because out of the Tripiṭakas of the eighteen schools, it is the only Indic-language canon that has survived complete. Pāli is precious because the language is sweet and melodious, rhythmic and resonant, because it is joy to read and a joy to recite.

Received texts are the products of centuries of oral transmission and stages of redaction. When they were written down, they underwent further revision, standardization, and codification according to guidelines set by editorial teams appointed by the different monastic orders. Producing and managing the corpus of Buddhist texts was one of several large projects undertaken in ancient South Asia to manage and maintain bodies of religious literature, conceptually similar to those of the Jains and the brahmans.

Transmission

How did oral transmission work?

The Buddha did not write down his teachings himself, and he did not dictate them directly to scribes. His teachings were received in the memories of his followers: they were redacted orally, and they circulated orally for centuries.

How did the system work? The members of the early saṅgha came from many different backgrounds. Like Śāriputra, celebrated for his wisdom, some of Gautama the Buddha's disciples were brahmans who would have been trained in, or would have at least been closely familiar with, the Brahmanical methods of oral text preservation and transmission that are so highly regarded for their accuracy.[65] The brahmans were an authoritative intelligentsia; in contemporary terms we might compare them to graduates from top universities, with the very significant social advantage that in addition to their educational credentials they enjoyed the privileged status of birth in the "highest" caste.

But the transmission of knowledge was not the domain of the brahmans alone. Some of Gautama's disciples came from Jain communities, and they would have known how the Jains transmitted their literature—and they

65. See Staal, *Discovering the Vedas*, and Bronkhorst, *How the Brahmins Won*. For a general background see Bronkhorst, *Greater Magadha: Studies in the Culture of Early India*, and Bronkhorst, *Buddhism in the Shadow of Brahmanism*.

would have been aware of how the transmission of the Jain scriptural corpus had run into snags from the start. Amongst the Jains themselves, opinions diverged widely as to which scriptures, if any, were authentic, with some holding that Lord Mahāvīra's teachings were lost. The preamble to the canonical Buddhist *Saṅgītisūtras*—shared by the Pāli, Sanskrit, and Chinese versions—reflects the anxieties that arose within the Buddhist saṅgha when it witnessed the turmoil that unsettled the post-Mahāvīra Jains. These relatively recent events warned the saṅgha that regardless of the fact that the Master was still alive, the task of preserving Gautama's teaching was urgent.

In addition to brahmans and Jains, members of the saṅgha from other social or caste groups would have been able to contribute to the preservation of the Master's teachings.[66] Some would have been adept at the transmission of folklore and tribal and regional lore—sagas, myths, poetry, and song; others would have been versed in the knowledge systems of court society. Śramaṇa Gautama's followers did not have to start from scratch—the saṅgha itself was a pool of talent equipped with bodies of knowledge and models that could be put to good use. Each metaphysical system—there were no *religions* as we conceive of them today—had its own Dharma-Vinaya that defined its own identity. The question before the Buddhist saṅgha was this: how to best preserve Śākyamuni's distinctive Dharma-Vinaya now that he had passed away?

This is all hypothesis and speculation. By definition, the oral period, the "classical age of prehistory," did not leave any written records. Can we read through the palimpsest of later written records to the oral records behind them? This is a risky business, and in my effort to understand the architecture of the ancient curricula of the oral Dharma and the libraries of unwritten ideas, I have to grope my way through the ruins of early Buddhist landscapes overgrown with thick tangles of memories and curling creepers of reconceptualizations, revisions, elaborations, and beautifications. I am trying to figure things through, to understand what happened. This book is not a dogmatic tract. I do not pretend to be able to give any sort of definitive account; all I can offer are working models that can be tested, discussed, refigured, and modified—or scrapped. The time has come to rethink yesteryear's religious and scholarly certainties in the light of emerging evidence and fresh understandings. Religious studies depend on our own historical reconstructions of the past. Whether we base our ideas on material culture or on texts, they are

66. For the composition of the early saṅgha, see Anālayo, "Vicissitudes of Memory," p. 14, n. 2.

reenvisionings done now, in the historical present, and they are largely works of the imagination.

The story of the piṭakas

The efforts to preserve and transmit the oral texts led to the formation of *piṭakas*, baskets or containers.[67] The story of the piṭakas is a tale of the formal organization of knowledge—the heritage of Gautama the Buddha's forty-five years of teaching—into sustainable configurations that were designed to endure. It is a tale of the production, preservation, transmission, and communication of large bodies of knowledge, to be reproduced from generation to generation; those who transmitted and managed the corpora were qualified not by dint of birth (as were the brahmans) but by choice and training. To design and launch a new system of knowledge preservation for new corpora or canons of knowledge was a mammoth task; the early saṅghas took up this responsibility with verve, and they maintained their momentum for centuries, well into the period of manuscript production.

The earliest classification of Gautama's legacy seems to have been by genre, itemized as the nine or twelve elements (*aṅga*) of the Buddha's teaching (see glossary under ninefold teaching / twelvefold teaching). These elements are genres, styles, and fluid categories, and they do not constitute a neatly structured collection. The classification is an early one that originated in the oral period, but as the śāsana developed, redactors retained it as a cherished heirloom that stands for the entirety and diversity of the Buddha's teachings. The nine or twelve elements are jumble bags: they are not uniform or systematic lists. They were not used to structure or organize oral or written literary collections as such, although several categories like *Udāna* and *Itivuttaka* were singled out to be edited as distinctive text units, as separate "books," and they are transmitted as books in Pāli and in translation up to today.

The broad category was Dharma-Vinaya, a term also used by other religious groups; these were bodies of principles and practice that as texts and corpora came to be called "Sūtra and Vinaya" and were collected to make the Sūtra and Vinaya Piṭakas. Later on, as the scholastic and theoretical literatures grew into cognate collections of texts, a scholastic corpus was included as Mātṛkā ("Matrixes") and then as Abhidharma to form the Abhidharma

67. For piṭakas, see Skilling, *Questioning the Buddha*, pp. 22–23, 34–35.

Figure 6. The Buddha sits, calm and collected, on the coils of the serpent king Mucilinda, who raises his seven hoods to protect him against a rainstorm.

Figure 7. On the reverse is a stūpa in low relief. The *ye dharmā* stanza is written in Sanskrit below the stūpa. For the text, see appendix 2, figure 55.

Piṭaka.[68] These three categories or collections became the Three Piṭakas, the Piṭakatraya or Tripiṭakas of the various schools.

The scriptures, the Āgamas/Nikāyas, were embedded in the collective memories of the communities. Given that the saṅghas were autonomous and, with time, increasingly dispersed across the broad South Asian landscape, each Buddhist monastic group acted as custodian of the entirety of Buddhist knowledge. They were the guardians of Buddhist cultural memory, and each monastic group processed its own scriptural collection according to its own linguistic and editorial guidelines. The monastic communities were curators and managers, sharing a common intellectual and spiritual inheritance with common values and common aims—for the benefit of the many, the good of gods and humans. There was no single custodian and no orthodox party. The scriptures are reflections of Gautama the Buddha's genius in the net of Indra that shimmers though the long corridors of time and imaginative space.

Crisscrossing the countryside

Gautama the Buddha taught for forty-five years. The Buddha and the saṅghas were regularly on the move. The Master traveled tirelessly on foot from place to place. During the rainy seasons he stayed put, and centers grew up at places that he visited regularly—Rājagṛha, Sarnath, Śrāvastī, Vaiśālī, and Kauśāmbī, for example.

Box 3. *Why the Buddha and the monks traveled*[69]

1. Why the Buddha traveled from place to place

It should be known that buddhas travel and wander for seven reasons:

[1] To "tame" the residents of other or foreign regions (*deśāntara*)

[2] To satisfy the people living there

[3] To keep the hearers/disciples (*śrāvaka*) from staying too long in one place

68. For the nine and twelve *aṅgas* and other categories, see Lamotte on the "formation of the canon of scriptures," *Histoire*, pp. 154–210.

69. Translation after Skilling and Prapod Assavavirulhakarn, "Vasubandhu on Travel and Seclusion," with a few changes.

[4] To demonstrate their freedom from attachment to any particular place
[5] To transform different regions into shrines (*caitya*)
[6] To generate merit (*puṇya*) for numerous beings who would see and visit those [shrines]
[7] To appease disasters such as epidemics (*īti*), drought, and so on

2. Why monks traveled from place to place
It should be known that hearers/disciples (*śrāvaka*) travel for fifteen reasons:

[1] Because five faults (*ādīnava*) have been taught. As the Fortunate One has said (*uktaṃ hi bhagavatā*): "There are five faults in staying too long in one place:
(a) One has many tasks and too many duties (*bahukṛtyaḥ bahukaraṇīyaḥ*)
(b) One accumulates many possessions and objects (*bahubhaṇḍaḥ bahūpakaraṇa*)
(c) One becomes attached to a place and clings to a place
(d) One becomes attached to a home and clings to a home
(e) On leaving one leaves with attachment"
[2] Because of a shortage of robes (*cīvara*) and the like
[3] Because of being tormented by discontent (*arati*)
[4] Because of being afflicted with illness (*roga*)
[5] Because of being afflicted by passion (*rāga*)
[6] Because body and mind are tormented by others, by the deeds of humans and nonhumans
[7] Out of a desire for gain and the like (*lābhādi*)
[8] Out of fondness (*priyatā*) for others
[9] Out of compassion (*anukampā*) for others
[10] Out of respect for a teacher (*gurugaurava*)
[11] To see wonders in [other] lands
[12] To attain to distinction (*viśesa*) in good qualities (*kuśalapakṣa*)
[13] To confess transgressions (*āpatti*)
[14] To worship the Three Jewels (*triratna*)
[15] To pay homage to shrines (*caityavandanā*)

During his lifetime, the monks and nuns of the order that he founded toured the countryside to teach the Dharma, and many of the people who benefited from Gautama's Dharma would have learned directly from his disciples without ever meeting the Master. That the Buddha envisaged teaching as one of the roles of the saṅgha is highlighted by two encounters between Śākyamuni and Māra the Evil One that are related in the *Great Parinibbāna Sutta*. When Śākya successfully achieves awakening, this alarms Māra, who fears that his hold over humankind will diminish. He goes to the Buddha soon after his awakening and suggests that he withdraw from the world:[70]

> [Māra:] "May you pass right away into full nibbāna, respected sir, O Fortunate One: may you pass into nibbāna, O Sugata! The time for your full nibbāna is now, respected sir, O Fortunate One."
>
> The Awakened One's answer is as follows, "I will not pass beyond to full nibbāna, O Wicked One, so long as my monks are not yet sāvakas, skilled, well trained, and confident, so long as they are not yet well versed, Dhamma bearers, practitioners of Dhamma according to Dhamma, correct practitioners, who conduct themselves according to the Dhamma, who grasp their own teacher's thought and then explain, teach, and explicate it, and who, when contention arises with opponents who adhere to other systems, can defeat it according to Dhamma, and teach the Dhamma with its marvels.

The Buddha repeats the same for his nuns, laymen, and laywomen: that is, all of Gautama's followers, regardless of gender or hierarchical status, should share in the dissemination of the Dharma.

Māra then skulks off. Forty-five years later, when the Fortunate One is at the Cāpala Caitya near Vaiśālī, the tenacious Evil One comes back with the same proposal.[71] He recalls the earlier exchange, and says, "Now you've achieved your goal, now the hour has come—time it is for you to quit this world, to extinguish into ineffable nibbāna." And the Buddha replies: "My followers—monks, nuns, laymen, and laywomen—have fulfilled their aims and are accomplished. In three months, O Wicked One, the Tathāgata will pass beyond." At this momentous news, the great earth quakes and trembles.

70. *Dīghanikāya*, vol. 2, p. 112.21.
71. *Dīghanikāya*, vol. 2, p. 104.12.

The *Great Parinibbāna Sutta* is a long and complex document, rich in rhetoric and nuanced in narrative. The two encounters frame the Buddha's final journey, during which he repeatedly instructs his followers,

> Such is moral conduct, such is concentration of mind, and such is wisdom. Concentration fortified by moral conduct leads to formidable results and enormous benefits. Wisdom fortified by concentration leads to formidable results and enormous benefits. A mind imbued with wisdom is naturally freed from the taints—to wit: the taints of sensual desires, of existence, of views, and of ignorance.

We can see the last trip as a final preparation of Gautama's disciples for the tasks they would face after his death. He finds that they are ready, and he announces this to the Wicked One.

In the whole corpus of teachings is no indication that Gautama intended to establish a personality cult. Gautama's aim was to establish the teachings, the Dharma and the Dharma-Vinaya, for the long-term benefit of all humanity and all beings. He taught that a person who sees the Dharma sees the Buddha. In this way, the Buddha was seen by far more people than those who ever met him face to face. And what does seeing the Dharma mean? He explains that it means to see the conditioned nature, the moral and psychological contingency, of all things. This is summed up in the *Rice Stalk Sūtra* (*Śālistambasūtra*): "One who sees dependent arising sees the Dharma, and one who sees the Dharma sees the Buddha."

Transmitting and preserving the Dharma

To return to our question: How was the Dharma preserved and transmitted? The Buddha's disciples taught the Dharma according to the inspiration of the moment through their own insight and eloquence (*pratibhāṇa*). Even a streamwinner, one who has entered the first stage of awakening, understands the teaching on her or his own: she or he does not need to depend on anyone else with regard to the Buddha's teachings.[72] Many dharmaparyāyas relate how Gautama's direct disciples—monks and nuns, laymen and laywomen—interact, exchange insights, and give original teachings. In the *Verses of the*

72. Pāli: *aparapaccayo satthu sāsane.*

Senior Monks (*Theragāthā*) and *Verses of the Senior Nuns* (*Therīgāthā*), his followers express their feelings towards and their insights into the Dharma and give full play to their poetic powers.

Longer prose compositions present the teachings in fixed and modular formulas, such as in ascending numerical groups, and it is likely that even during Gautama's lifetime his followers had begun to organize his teachings so that they could be effectively preserved and transmitted—let us remember that he taught for forty-five years and had a large following in Magadha and Kośala and neighboring regions. Prominent examples are the *Saṃgīti* and *Daśottara* sūtras, which we know in Pāli (Theravāda) and Sanskrit (Sarvāstivāda) recensions, as well as indirectly through a Gāndhārī commentary and through translations into Chinese.[73] These and similar tracts were models, blueprints for organizing the oral teachings of the Buddha. Jains and probably other *śramaṇa* groups developed similar templates, while the brahmans had their own long-standing models and mnemonic techniques for transmitting the Vedas and other sacred lore, including the massive "fifth Veda," the *Mahābhārata* epic.[74] This management of large bodies of spoken literature was an impressive accomplishment of the oral technologies of ancient South Asia.

Shortly after the Buddha's death—after the first rains retreat, according to the shared tradition—a group of monks gathered to recite and codify his teachings. This is known as the first "recitation convocation," *saṃgīti* or *saṅgāyanā*, literally a "reciting" or "intoning together" or a "compilation of the Dharma," *dhamma-saṅgaha*. Reports of the first convocation given in the Vinayas of the different monastic orders are not, however, uniform or consistent but contain many contradictions and anomalies.[75] One of the reasons for this is the fact that when the emergent orders or schools codified their scriptures, roughly during the first and second centuries after the Buddha's nirvāṇa, they were forging their own identities and at the same time trying

73. Modern scholarship presumes that the Gāndhārī version and the Chinese *Dīrghāgama* translation were transmitted by Dharmaguptaka communities. For the importance of the "*Saṃgīti*" sūtras, see Salomon, *Buddhist Literature of Ancient Gandhāra*, chap. 9.

74. The evolution of the epic in relation to orality and recitation, to composition, compilation, and writing, is, to put it mildly, convoluted. For a cogent summary that also addresses the *Rāmāyana*, see Thapar, *The Past before Us*, part 2, "The Embedded Tradition."

75. Some of the accounts preserved in Chinese are collected in the *Forest of Pearls from the Dharma Garden*: see translation in Shinohara, *Forest of Pearls*, vol. 2, pp. 203–26. Classic studies are Przyluski, *Concile de Rājagṛha*, and Bareau, *Les premiers conciles bouddhiques*.

to position themselves within the broader Buddhist ecumene and the greater Indian society. They tailored their narratives to suit their own visions of history and their own perceived needs and aims. That the story is not uniform does not mean that the convocations did not take place, only that they were stages in a long process of negotiation amongst many saṅghas. Modern scholarship has wanted to see a tidy process with clear boundaries, but history's lens refracts events in multiple directions.

The Vinayas of the different schools record two shared or "pan-saṅgha" convocations—the first shortly after the Master's demise, the second about a hundred years later. After this, Gautama's order became plural, spreading geographically and developing into branches that held their own convocations to consolidate their own scriptural traditions and their own individual identities. Originally singular, the saṅgha evolved into a shifting conglomeration of monastic orders. Despite this reality, or, perhaps, to compensate for it, the Buddhist communities maintained a vision of the ideal saṅgha that is expressed in the formula of donation to "the saṅgha of the four directions," or quarters—no matter where they came from, they were still representative of Gautama's saṅgha. The orders evolved and diverged, but they continued to share similar imaginations of continuity: all of them were convinced that their traditions went back to Gautama the Buddha himself through the first two convocations. The early members of Gautama the Buddha's order, the great śrāvakas, figure prominently in the piṭakas of all Buddhist orders as well as in the Vaipulya/Mahāyāna dharmaparyāyas. The shared imaginary of the śāsana starts with the Buddha's life and the first and second convocations.[76]

Where do the texts come from? How were they handed down, and how did they get to us? The process of redaction was a long-term project, continuing for centuries and in most cases never fully completed or finalized. It may be compared with the creation of the rock-cut monasteries and shrines or of the great cathedrals of Europe: monumental projects take monumental time.[77] The early saṅghas redacted Gautama's teachings into distinct collections, settled and ordered their contents, established or streamlined the narrative phraseologies, and set into motion systems of oral transmission by

76. For English translations of the accounts of the first and second convocations, see Kākkāpalliye Anuruddha Thera et al., *The First and Second Buddhist Councils.*

77. Dehejia and Rockwell, *The Unfinished: The Stone Carvers at Work in the Indian Subcontinent.*

trained reciters. When the redactors organized the Buddha's teachings into the broad collections called Āgamas and Nikāyas, texts were classified and placed in the sections that suited them; these were further organized into smaller and more manageable divisions—the *saṃyuktas*, *nipātas*, *vargas*, and so forth. How did the process of classification evolve? From larger collections to smaller units, or from smaller units to larger collections? Or a bit of both? We cannot say, but the last option strikes me as more plausible for a process that continued for centuries. Apart from the four main Āgamas/Nikāyas, smaller collections like the *Udāna*, *Itivuttaka*, and *Dhammapada* gathered together verse teachings. The first two set the verses in relatively brief prose frames, while the last presents the verses alone. One of the most comprehensive verse collections is the *Udānavarga* compiled by Dharmatrāta (see introduction to translation 4).

The Theravāda tradition, as represented by Dhammapāla's commentary, relates that the *Itivuttaka* was memorized by the laywoman Khujjuttarā ("Crooked Uttarā," so called because she was born hunchbacked), who memorized the Buddha's teachings at Kauśāmbī (Pāli: Kosambī) and taught them to the nuns. Later on, they were incorporated into the Dharma-Vinaya at the First Redaction.[78] This account suggests female compilation of a distinctive and coherent regional collection and even that the *Itivuttaka* might be a unique case of a textual collection managed by a differently abled disciple. The story of Khujjuttarā is not, however, confirmed by any sources outside of the Sthavira commentaries.

Dating the Undatable

When and where were the texts composed? Who redacted them? There are no satisfactory answers to these questions—there are no empirical data, only hypotheses. The texts would have been composed and compiled during the oral period, redacted at recitation convocations, and passed down orally until they were written down. After that they would have been copied and recopied, and the culture of orality would have continued as a parallel stream of practice. Orality is an independent dynamic of human intellectual practice.

78. Dhammapāla's commentary gives a long account of Khujjuttarā from a previous life when she aspired to be declared as foremost of the well-versed female disciples in her final existence, going to some lengths to justify the authenticity of the collection and transmission. See translation in Masefield, *Commentary on the Itivuttaka*, pp. 82–94.

It may seem the height of folly to attempt to work out even a relative chronology of all this, let alone to present it as a table, but I take the plunge in table 1. The great nineteenth-century colonial historians of Indian architecture and archaeology, Fergusson and Burgess, once wrote regarding India's rock-cut architecture,[79] "The dates of the various groups of Buddhist caves, especially of the earliest ones, have not yet been ascertained with sufficient precision to admit of their being presented in anything like tabular form . . . It is probable, however, that before long this state of affairs may be altered for the better." The chronology of the rock-cut monuments has indeed become clearer in the last hundred and fifty years, and I hope that that of the monuments of Buddhist literature are also improving, at least incrementally.

The early caves and the early texts are broadly contemporaneous testimonies to the development of early Indian Buddhism, but with a difference: through more than two millennia, hundreds of caves have survived in eastern and western India through centuries of neglect, deterioration, and vandalism—but not a single Indic Buddhist manuscript from the earliest period is extant. Caves are tangible rock-cut monuments; the scriptures are intangible corpora that had oral beginnings and developed as oral literature for more than half a millennium before being recorded in writing. The manuscripts are fragile, written on perishable supports like birchbark scrolls and bundles of palm leaves. The earliest surviving Indic manuscripts come not from India proper, with its hot and humid environment that teems with insect and animal predators, but from cool and arid ecosystems like Afghanistan, Central Asia, and Tibet. In short, beyond hypothetical generalities, we cannot say much at all about the first five or six hundred years, or even the first millennium, of the lives of the texts translated here.

Prehistories and histories

In their received form, the translations published in this volume belong to Āgama collections, but each is an individual and each has its own history. We do not know their prehistories—when and how they entered the Āgama collections, or whether, for example, they were evaluated beforehand according to the "mahāpadeśa model" outlined in the *Mahāparinirvāṇasūtra*. This is an

79. Fergusson and Burgess, *The Cave Temples of India*, p. 181 (brought to my attention by the epigraph in Singh, *Periodisation of Rock-Cut Monuments*, p. 1).

Figure 8. Apsidal caitya cave, Karle, Maharashtra, India. The focus of worship is the stūpa at the end of the nave. The ribs of the rafters and the parasol over the caitya are made of wood.

ancient procedure established to determine whether a teaching attributed to the Buddha was authentic; it goes back to the early oral period, and it continued to be applied in the course of intra-school debates in later periods.[80] Once accepted into an Āgama, texts would have been standardized along with the rest of the collection in question, streamlined according to the "house style" of the saṅgha in question.

The formation and maintenance of the Āgamas was a long-term editorial project of initially oral and, later on, written corpora. Who directed and steered these corpora over the centuries? Who was responsible for this huge and sustained project? Was the project exclusively monastic? Monastics had the scriptural training and expertise as well as the time and the space to assemble and work collectively. The enterprise included the female saṅghas: epigraphic and literary evidence unequivocally shows that nuns had high

80. The classic study is Lamotte's "La Critique d'authenticité dans le bouddhisme." See also Buswell and Lopez, *Princeton Dictionary of Buddhism*, p. 502.

Table 1. *Towards a chronology*

Buddhist Era	Events	Christian Era
	Gautama Buddha • Forty-five years of teaching across northern India • Parinirvāṇa	563–483? 546–483? 483 BCE?
1	First recitation-convocation • Oral transmission of texts in middle Indo-Aryan dialects • Age of reciters (*bhāṇaka*) • Floating *gāthās* and collections of *gāthās*	ca. fifth cent. BCE
100	Second recitation convocation • Formation of proto-collections	ca. fourth cent. BCE
100 to 500	Recitation convocations of the eighteen schools  *The four main monastic orders* Sthavira Mahāsāṃghika Sāṃmitīya Sarvāstivāda	ca. fourth cent. BCE to first cent. CE
400+	Beginnings of manuscript culture	ca. first cent. BCE

standards of scriptural training in the early historical period.[81] The *Chronicle of the Island* describes a large number of nuns who came to Lanka from northern India with Bhikkhunī Saṅghamittā during Aśoka's reign; it lauds their remarkable abilities and concludes the section by stating that at the time of writing, "learned and virtuous, [the nuns] illuminate the earth."[82] The date is

81. See Skilling, "*Eṣā agrā*: Images of Nuns in (Mūla-)Sarvāstivādin Literature" and "Nuns, Laywomen, Donors, Goddesses."
82. Oldenberg, trans., *Dīpavaṃsa*, chap. 18, verse 44.

uncertain, but it should not be later than the end of the sixth century BE (Buddhist era, i.e., first century CE).[83]

The extant accounts of the first two convocations describe them as all-male proceedings: the participants are all arhat monks, five hundred at the first meeting and seven hundred at the second. After the first two gatherings, there were no further pan-Buddhist or "all-India saṅgha" convocations. It is unfortunate that we have very little information about the convocations of the individual schools (for the bulk of them, we have in fact no information whatsoever) and no general or synoptic accounts of the convocations of the eighteen schools as whole. In a word, our documentation for these crucial periods is thin, very thin.

Writing in his *History of the Dharma* in the fourteenth century, Tibetan master Bu ston presents the redactors of the third convocation or "Kaniṣka Council" as a mixed group consisting of Pūrṇika and five hundred arhats, Vasumitra and five hundred bodhisatvas, and an uncertain number of ordinary learned scholars.[84] Whatever the figures or details, this seems more realistic than accounts in which only arhat monks took part. Writing at the beginning of the seventeenth century in his *History of the Dharma*, Tāranātha relates that according to the Tibetans, there were five hundred monks, five hundred bodhisatvas, and five hundred "unrealized experts."[85]

It is rare good fortune that the account of the Sāṃmitīyas, one of the main schools of northern India, is preserved in two versions, both of them produced within the school itself. It mentions five hundred and seven hundred arhat monks for the first and second convocations, but for the three specifically Vātsīputrīya convocations that follow, it does not specify the participants. These accounts report that four hundred years after Tathāgata's parinirvāṇa, the community of ascetics had developed into different saṅghas, each of which evolved as a separate school, and a certain Vātsīputra, about whom nothing is known, collated the Dharma of the Nikāya that became known as the Vātsīputrīya.

83. See Skilling, "A Note on the History of the Bhikkhunī-Saṅgha" (I) and (II).

84. Bu ston gives the variant figures, either 250 or 16,000: *so so skye bo'i paṇḍi ta nyis brgya lnga bcu 'am khri drug stong* ["ordinary learned scholars (**pṛthagjana-paṇḍita*), either 250 or 16,000 in number"]: *Bu ston Chos 'Byung*, Gangs ljongs ed., p. 132.1; translation in Obermiller, *History of Buddhism*, vol. 2, pp. 96–97.

85. Tāranātha, *Rgya gar chos 'byung* (ed. Schiefner, p. 47, lines 20–22): *de la bod rnams ltar na | dgra bcom pa lnga brgya dang | byang chub sems dpa' lnga brgya dang | so so skye bo'i paṇḍi ta lnga brgya 'dus nas bsdus zer*. Cf. translation in Chattopadhyaya, *Tāranātha's History*, p. 93, lines 4–6.

Four hundred years [after the nirvāṇa],
when the community of ascetics had established as individual schools,
the sage Vātsīputra purified the śāsana,
making it pure like the autumn moon.[86]

The Sāṃmitīya account calls this the collecting of the Dharma on five occasions.[87] In other traditions as well, including the Theravāda, to "purify the śāsana" means to edit and revise the Tripiṭaka.

The accounts of the first two convocations are reasonably consistent across canons regarding the circumstances and broad outlines. This is because the different schools transmitted the account in their canonical Vinayas, evidently following a shared template. After the second convocation, the Buddhist order began to divide into an increasing number of distinctive schools, and there were no further pan-Indian councils. This point is too often ignored by modern scholarship, which has treated, and continues to treat, the third Theravāda convocation, which, the school maintains, was held at Pāṭaliputra under King Aśoka's patronage, as the *third Buddhist* convocation, as if it were a pan-Buddhist or pan-saṅgha event. They neglect to note that this convocation is unique and idiosyncratic to the narration of a single school, the Theravāda, and that no comparable account is found in the extant texts of other schools.[88] It is evident that each school counted its convocations in its own way, but almost none of the original sources survive in any form, whether in original Indic languages or in translation, whether in canonical accounts or in post-canonical narratives. Tibetan scholars, using the Indian sources available to them, describe a third convocation held by the Kuṣāṇa king Kaniṣka in the northwest of India, in Kashmir or Gandhāra. The accounts are somewhat muddled, and it looks as if the Tibetan scholars had before them several accounts from disparate sources and tried to collapse them into a single "third council." This Sāṃmitīya

86. "Ascetics": here the Sanskrit has *yāti*, the Tibetan *dka' thub* (normally = *tapasvin*): the reference in either case is to the Buddhist monastic orders.

87. *Chos bsdu ba*, **dharmasaṃgraha*, cp. Pāli *dhammasaṅgaha*: equivalent to *dharmasaṃgīti*, with an emphasis on the idea of collecting and collating the scriptures rather than the method, the collective recitation.

88. There are narratives in other sources that involve Aśoka in some way or another or that take place in Pāṭaliputra, but they do not bring in the Theravaṃsa or resemble the Theravaṃsa account in any way. The latter narrative, a large segment of which draws heavily on the *Brahmajālasutta*, is a markedly artificial exercise in polemics.

account is unique in giving a history in five convocations; unfortunately for us, the account does not specify where the convocations took place.

An important point about the Tibetan sources is that they report that the later convocations decided that the scriptures of the various schools were all *bka'*, "pronouncements of the Teacher." The purpose of the convocations was not one-upmanship: their aim was not to validate the tradition of a single school against all others but to give a seal of approval to plurality by endorsing the variety of scriptural and other traditions that had developed by the seventh or eighth centuries BE (second or third centuries CE).[89] Modern scholarship has tended to marginalize the non-Theravāda sources, dismissing them offhand without seriously evaluating them. The Thera sources are privileged simply because they were written in Pāli in Sri Lanka. More nuanced research is needed to disentangle the significance and implications of non-Theravaṃsa sources.

Who supported the convocations? The standard narratives relate that they were managed by senior monks with the material support of rulers. The convocations were internal saṅgha affairs, or rather, *nikāya* affairs, and decision-making rested with the members of the participating saṅghas. There was no overriding external authority, religious or political. The decisions and redactions made at a particular convocation by a specific saṅgha or group of saṅghas did not apply to, or necessarily even have any impact on, other saṅghas elsewhere in South Asia (or even on non-participating saṅghas in the same area).

The rise of writing

When did the shift from orality to writing begin? For the Theravāda tradition, the *Chronicle of the Island*, composed centuries after the event, devotes three stanzas to the recording of the Pāli texts in writing.[90]

> Vaṭṭagāmani Abhaya ruled as king
> for twelve years . . . .
> Before this time, the text

89. See Skilling, "Redaction, Recitation, and Writing: Transmission of the Buddha's Teachings in India in the Early Period."
90. My translation: chap. 20, vv. 19–21; Pāli, p. 103, translation in Oldenberg, *Dīpavaṃsa*, p. 211. See also *Mahāvaṃsa* (Geiger), chap. 33, v. 101.

> of the Threefold Piṭaka and its commentaries
> had been transmitted orally. Percipient monks
> foresaw the deterioration of beings,[91] and
> with this in mind, they assembled the monks:
> For sake of the long life of the Dharma
> they had it written down in books.[92]

The Theravāda tradition reports that their Tripiṭaka and commentaries were written down as part of a single, coordinated project on the isle of Lanka in the fifth or sixth century BE (first century BCE). None of the sources give any details about the titles of the texts that were written down; nor do they give any indications about their stage of redaction that might help us to compare them with the received versions that we know today. Editorial events were recorded in ideal rather than material terms; we do not see "a Tripiṭaka in the making" but rather ideal piṭakas projected back in time from their much later shapes. Even questions about much more recent editorial projects cannot be answered—for example, the origins of the Pāli manuscripts preserved in Southeast Asia, the origins of the Sanskrit manuscripts preserved in Nepal, or the sources of the manuscripts that were carried from India to Tibet. The only tangible and contemporaneous evidence for the dates of written manuscripts are the Gāndhārī scrolls, which are dated paleographically or by scientific testing, and the texts that were translated into Chinese at certain verifiable dates, although in the latter case only translations and translation records survive: out of the hundreds of texts translated into Chinese over the centuries, out of the thousands of manuscripts recorded as having been brought to China, not a single ancient Indic manuscript is known to survive. Otherwise, we are in the dark about the first five hundred or even one thousand years of transmission for most of the texts that we study. We are lucky when a few scraps of a manuscript survive; these can provide rare snapshots of a text's passage through time.

91. *Hāṇiṃ disvāna sattānaṃ*: the notion of *hāṇi* as a moral degeneration or degradation of beings reminds one of *satva-kaṣāya* (*sems can gyi snyigs ma*), one of the five *kaṣāyas*, for which see Buswell and Lopez, *Princeton Dictionary*, pp. 1075, "five turbidities/degenerations": 424 *kaṣāya*, 787 *sattva-kaṣāya*.

92. "Book," *potthaka*: cp. the use of *postaga* (= Skt. *pustaka*) in two Gāndhārī manuscripts, the "commentary on canonical verses" and the *Perfection of Wisdom*: Salomon, *Buddhist Literature of Ancient Gandhāra*, pp. 311, 358. *Pustaka* is amongst the words connected with writing adopted from Greek: see Tarn, *The Greeks in Bactria and India*, p. 376, n. 2.

From oral to written: Manuscript culture

After about four or five hundred years of oral transmission, the technology of preservation of the Dharma started to shift from orality to writing. This would have been a gradual process across India; texts would have been written down unevenly and unequally even within the same community, let alone in the many communities dispersed across the region. Texts were written down on birchbark scrolls in the northwest and on palm leaves elsewhere on the subcontinent and in Sri Lanka and Southeast Asia. Birchbark was widely used across western Asia and beyond, but the development of a palm-leaf manuscript culture—the preparation and use of the palm leaf as a support for writing—was a distinctive South Asian contribution to the technology of the written word. Indited by hand, texts were literally *manuscripts*. As manuscripts from the earliest period do not survive, we know next to nothing about their physicality—their size, formats, layouts, editorial processing, storage, dissemination, or access. A small number of texts inscribed as "relics of the Dharma" or "memorials of the Dharma" (*dharmaśarīra* or *dhammacetiya*) have been recovered from stūpa complexes, and these give some evidence of how early texts were formatted, but they were produced centuries later, when manuscript culture was already in full swing. Birchbark manuscripts were written in Gāndhārī Prakrit in the Kharoṣṭhī script, and scrolls could run up to five meters long; some of these survive in fragments from the first century CE or even earlier. These are by far the oldest Buddhist manuscripts in existence as well as the oldest Indic manuscripts of any type. As mentioned above, writing did not replace memorization and recitation, which continue up to the present. In Theravāda societies, texts are memorized in Pāli for liturgical, apotropaic, and didactic purposes, and in Tibetan and Himalayan societies, texts are memorized and recited in the Tibetan language for similar reasons. In East Asia they are written in uniform Chinese characters but are remembered and recited with different pronunciations according to dialect area or country, according to the usages of China, Korea, Japan, and Vietnam. Both the person who knows the Dharma and the physical manuscript itself are prized and accorded respect as receptacles of the Dharma.

The notion of a long period of oral transmission challenges received ideas about literacy in ancient south Asia. We have been taught that society (meaning here *people*—mostly, though not exclusively, *males*) has passed through illiterate, preliterate, literate, and postliterate phases, a periodization that reflects and promotes notions that literacy, education, and knowledge are coterminous and that the movement from orality to literacy is an inevitable step forward in human progress. A common conceit is that illiterate people are deprived; that they are incomplete and intellectually inferior to their literate fellows. On the contrary, anthropological and literary evidence demonstrates that while the *illiterate* may be *unlettered*, that does not inhibit them from hosting and passing on sophisticated bodies of knowledge and complex skills. Literacy is irrelevant to many aspects of human culture, science, and technology. The complex protohistoric culture of South Asia included the production and decoration of pottery and the arts and skills of basketry, weaving, and tool making, as well as the technologies of metal working, agriculture, irrigation, architecture, shipbuilding, and navigation. These were all conceived, developed, and maintained by non-literates. The oral period, the age of non- and preliteracy, laid the foundations of many of South Asian civilization's enduring features. The deep origins of the world's mythologies, as proposed by Michael Witzel, go way back to the very beginnings of *Homo sapiens'* history.[93] The nonliterate age was rich and creative; it saw the consolidation of Indian religions, the development of elaborate literary cultures, of sciences and technologies, of city planning, music, dance, and the arts. Even if narratives were not written down in words, they were recorded on the walls of caves and rock shelters or in the decorations of pottery, in the patterns of weaves, in dance, and in song.[94] All of these exercised the human imagination and called for different types of unlettered reading—the deciphering of sounds, patterns, colors, shapes, and figures.

The development of preliterate cultures around the world deserves careful thought and deep consideration.[95] An example of preliterate "high culture" is the well-known 4,500-year-old stone circle of Stonehenge in southwestern England.[96] The huge and heavy stones were transported from Preseli Hills

93. Witzel, *Origins of the World's Mythologies*.

94. For readable and well-illustrated examples of South Asian weaving (from, respectively, the Brahmaputra valley and central India), see Elwin, *Art of the North-East Frontier of India*, and Elwin, *Tribal Art of Middle India*.

95. Like the Buddhist scriptures and culture, the scriptures and culture of the Jains in India and the Zoroastrians in Persia began as oral texts and were gradually recorded in writing. Both religions narrate stories of loss and attempted restitution; in both religions, recitation continues to the present day.

96. Dating is always uncertain in prehistory. The British Museum gives the same date (https://blog.britishmuseum.org, "An Introduction to Stonehenge"), while Fagan, *A Little History of Archaeology*, gives 2,500 years ago. See too Garrow and Wilkin, *The World of Stonehenge*,

in Wales, over three hundred kilometers away. Others, "typically weighing 20 tonnes and standing up to 7 metres tall," were brought from West Woods in Wiltshire[97]—and all of them were arranged according to a sophisticated astronomical plan. Recently a previously unknown structure, made up of twenty or more massive prehistoric shafts, more than ten meters in diameter and five meters deep, has been discovered 1.9 miles northeast of Stonehenge.[98] Excavations conducted in Wales in recent decades suggest that the circle of stones was originally erected in the west of Wales and transported to the Salisbury plains.[99] These massive engineering projects were all conceived and executed not only long before the advent of writing in the British Isles but well before the introduction of the wheel. Questions of literacy are simply not relevant.

The late Janice Stargardt (1936–2020) pointed out how specialists in Southeast Asia have confused "material progress" with the introduction of writing and "Indianization" in Southeast Asia, referencing the construction of Pyu cities like Śrīkṣetra in Burma in the first half of the first millennium.[100] She notes that theorists of Indianizaton assumed that because early states lacked systems of writing, they lacked organized social structures, religions, art, and architecture. Long before the advent of writing, South Asia itself fostered thriving material and intellectual cultures, and this is a remarkably arbitrary and shortsighted assumption. Stargardt challenges the "view that the possession of a system of Indic writing (a) exemplifies Indianization, and (b) that writing is *the* criterion for the emergence of a complex society," and presents compelling supporting evidence from Śrīkṣetra and the Yahanda mound.

During the oral period people were *nonliterate* but they were *lettered.* From the time of Gautama the Buddha, and assuredly long before, an educated person was not "well read" but "well heard": he or she was *bahuśruta*—*bahu* "much" + *śruta* "heard"—one who has listened and learned much, one

which accompanied the exhibition of the same name held at the British Musuem, 17 February–17 July 2022.

97. See Steven Morris, "Archaeologists Discover Likely Source of Stonehenge's Giant Sarsen Stones," *Guardian*, 29 July 2020.

98. Dalya Alberge, "Vast Neolithic Circle of Deep Shafts Found near Stonehenge" and "Scrap Stonehenge Road Tunnel Plans, Say Archaeologists after Neolithic Discovery," *Guardian*, 22 June 2020. What used to be seen as an inert cluster of giant stones was an active cultural center, and new discoveries continue to be made.

99. Pearson et al., "The Original Stonehenge?"

100. Stargardt, "Sri Ksetra," pp. 220–21 et passim.

who is learned, well instructed or, better perhaps, "well versed." As Ananda Coomaraswamy puts it, "From the earliest times, Indians have thought of the learned man, not as one who has read much, but as one who has been profoundly taught."[101] "Well versed" seems a felicitous term when we consider that the greater part of oral literature was in verse—not only in ancient South Asia but worldwide, not only in hoary antiquity but up to the late premodern period. The term is felicitous, however, by association rather than by historical etymology. "Verse" comes through Old English from Latin *versus*, "a turn of the plough, a furrow, a line of writing," while "versed," *versé*, meaning "experienced, practiced, skilled," comes from a different root, Latin *versatus*, past participle of *versari* "be engaged in."[102] The intellectual was not a "man of letters" and India was not an "empire of letters," it was a "land of the well versed," of intelligent and creative people who never held a book in their hands. At the same time, in South Asia the Buddhists were the first religious community to embrace the technology of the written text, already by the first century BCE, so we might say that in South Asia the Buddhists were amongst the first "men and women of letters." The communication of knowledge continued to rely on orality; the consciousness of the "writer" as author or artist does not develop. A "writer" (*lekhaka*) is a scribe, one who indites a manuscript or an inscription; an author is a *śāstrakāra* or *granthakāra*, a "composer of treatises" or a "composer of books." A creative writer is a *kavi*, a poet. In the Āgama/Nikāya literature, the word *kavi* is used unfavorably in connection with the decline of the śāsana in, for example, the *Anāgatabhaya-sutta*. This may reflect a tension between the reciters, whose remit lay in careful memorization and scrupulous recitation of the received texts, and poets, whose talent lay in ornate and expanded creations of their own.

Today even small children trudge to school weighed down by enormous satchels or backpacks stuffed with computers, books, thermos flasks, the costumes of mandatory rituals like sports or scouts—and who knows what else. Oral culture was inclusive and did not require any preparation or props beyond alert minds and bodies. Rabindranath Tagore (1861–1941) notes how the transfer of knowledge, or culture, is instantanteous, and how this ability to absorb is a wonderful faculty not limited by cultural boundaries:[103]

101. Coomaraswamy, "Bugbear of Literacy," p. 41.

102. Pearsall, *New Oxford English Dictionary*, p. 2055b.

103. Citation from Amartya Sen, "Poetry and Reason: Why Tagore Still Matters," *New Republic*, 30 June 2011.

> Whatever we understand and enjoy in human products instantly becomes ours, wherever they might have their origin. . . . I am proud of my humanity when I can acknowledge the poets and artists of other countries as my own. Let me feel with unalloyed gladness that all the great glories of man are mine.

Let us apply Tagore's insights to the Dharma, because he points out how the transfer of culture takes place: *instantly*.[104] Wherever people encountered Gautama the Buddha's Dharma, they understood and benefited according to their own insights and capacities. In the oral period, the transfer was person to person, immediate, instantaneous—to use Tagore's phrasing, the Dharma *instantly* became part of their own thought worlds. Cultural encounter as human exchange is instantaneous; a series of mental instants constitute the processes of localization, translocalization, acculturation, or inculturation—whatever term, fashionable or unfashionable, one may choose. This is one of the reasons why Gautama is depicted as Indo-Greek in the art of Gandhāra, as Chinese in the art of the Middle Kingdom, as Tibetan in the Land of Snows, or as Thai in the art of Siam—to name only a few examples. Otherwise he would be foreign. Otherwise, how could we establish a relationship with him? In the same way, when a translation is vigorous and clear, it engages, captivates, and even bewitches readers—the story and its multiple meanings enter the heart and instantly become the readers' own.

The intellectual significance of writing differs in different cultures and at different points of time. Athenian philosopher Socrates (469–399 BCE) writes that[105]

> The discovery of the alphabet will create forgetfulness for the learners' souls, because they will not use their memories; they will trust to the external written characters and not remember of themselves. . . . You give your disciples not truth but only the semblance of truth; they will be heroes of many things, and will have learned nothing; they will appear to be omniscient and will generally know nothing.

104. I reflected on this theme in the context of narrative in my foreword to Appleton and Shaw, *Ten Great Birth Stories of the Buddha* (vol. 1, pp. xxv–xxvi).
105. Dialogue between Socrates and Phaedrus in Plato's *Phaedrus*, cited in McLuhan, *The Medium Is the Message*, p. 113.

It is only natural that advances in some technologies lead to deterioration in others, and the reliance on written records did contribute to a decline in the cultures of memory, an intellectual devolution that has continued through print and digital technologies. When oral or mnemonic practices are maintained as parallel and complementary technologies to written or digital cultures, they can enrich human experience, but this, it seems, is rarely done or even contemplated. Orality and writing developed as a continuum rather than as successive totalizing phases, in which the oral need necessarily be superseded by the written. The two cooperate in interaction. The written text is not a passive, private artifact but part of a complex and active involvement that includes ritual, recitation/reading, ethical action, and metaphysical reflection and counterreflection. Today the imprudent (and impudent) paradigm is that one technology *should* replace another and the social citizen (read: *consumer*) should be *up to date*, which means nothing much more than that she or he ought to subscribe to the latest product lines. Today the emphasis is on digital literacy, a new and essential "tool for survival" that is rapidly transforming the world's social, technological, and economic fabric.

William Hazlitt (1778–1830) was characteristically blunt about book learning:[106]

> A mere scholar, who knows nothing but books, must be ignorant even of them. "Books do not teach the use of books." . . . The learned pedant is conversant with books only as they are made of other books, and those again of others, without end. He parrots those who have parroted others. He can translate the same word into ten different languages, but he knows nothing of the *thing* which it means in any of them. He stuffs his head with authorities built on authorities, with quotations quoted from quotations, while he locks up his senses, his understanding, and his heart.

Whatever the case, we should use the idea of an "oral period" cautiously. There *was* an oral period (or age, interval, phase). It was coterminous with advanced numeracy and sophisticated skills in the arts of grammar and composition. By no means was it an intellectual, scientific, or cultural *blank* marked simply by the absence of writing—the oral was a complex, innova-

106. Hazlitt, "On the Ignorance of the Learned," p. 150.

tive, and intellectually fecund period in human history. In South Asian history, the oral period coincides with the long Neolithic, Chalcolithic, and Vedic periods. When writing was introduced, it was adopted unevenly, for different purposes, in different regions or areas, and in different circles (urban/rural, court/ascetic). Oral and written practices overlapped just as they overlap to this day. The reason we have textbooks and manuals is that they are the basis of oral instruction and discussion.

Literacy has more than one sense, and different perspectives confuse the discussion unless we are clear about our terminology. In his impassioned and trenchant essay "The Bugbear of Literacy," polymath Ananda Kentish Coomaraswamy (1877–1947) argues strongly for an ideal or idealistic literacy related to the development of human talent and intelligence. He opens his essay by disentangling literacy and culture:[107]

> It was possible for Aristotle, starting from the premise that a man, being actually cultured, may *also* become literate, to ask whether there is a necessary or merely an accidental connection of literacy with culture. Such a question can hardly arise for us, to whom illiteracy implies, as a matter of course, ignorance, backwardness, unfitness for self-government: for us, unlettered peoples are uncivilized peoples, and vice versa.

The savant goes on to say,

> For the sake of brevity we shall assume without argument that "culture" implies an ideal quality and a good form that can be realized by all men irrespective of condition: and, since we are treating of culture chiefly as expressed in words, we shall identify culture with "poetry" . . . with reference to that whole class of prophetic literature that includes the Bible, the Vedas, the Edda, the great epics, and in general the world's "best books," and the most philosophical if we agree with Plato that "wonder is the beginning of philosophy." Of these "books" many existed long before they were written down, many have never been written down, and others have been or will be lost.

107. Coomaraswamy, "The Bugbear of Literacy," p. 33. For Coomaraswamy's fascinating life, see Pal, *Quest for Coomaraswamy*.

This is one literacy. Another is modern pragmatic literacy: the ability to live in today's world, literacy as understood by social scientists, economists, and political analysts.[108] Amartya Sen points out how when Rabindranath Tagore visited Russia in 1930, he was favorably impressed by the expansion of basic education and literacy. Sen comments, "If Tagore were to see the India of today, half a century after independence, nothing perhaps would shock him so much as the continued illiteracy of the masses." He goes on to say that "illiteracy is a deprivation."[109] Literacy in the sense that concerns Sen and many others is the functional literacy that is an indispensable tool for global citizens. This literacy is conceived as a fundamental human right and a foundation for lifelong learning.[110]

> It is widely recognized that mastering literacy is essential for living in a modern society, just as a literate population is essential for a country to compete in a globalized world. Literacy is a human right; it is also key to achieving many development goals, be it improved nutrition and health, increased productivity and poverty reduction, enhanced political participation, conscientization of the poor, empowerment of women, or sensitization to environmental issues. Last, but not least, literacy is necessary to facilitate any further learning.[111]

Coomaraswamy remarks that "to impose our literacy (and our contemporary 'literature') upon a cultured but illiterate people is to destroy their culture in the name of our own." "Barefoot anthopologist" Tom Harrisson (1911–76) would probably have agreed with this assessment; at any rate, he had personal experience of the rich culture of the nonliterate highland Kelabits in northern Borneo during the Second World War and gave an eloquent description of their harvest season,[112]

> All day long, too, as men and women work in lines across the fields, snipping the firm heads of grain—thumb-length knives

108. Sen, *The Argumentative Indian*, pp. 112–13, 115–16.
109. Sen, *The Argumentative Indian*, p. 157.
110. See, for example, Agneta Lind's *Literacy for All: Making a Difference*, with further reference to Sen's ideas.
111. Françoise Caillods, preface to Lind, *Literacy for All.*
112. Harrisson, *World Within*, p. 80.

> worked against thumbs as hard as bone—they will be singing, joking or tirelessly leg-pulling. If one of the older women is in the mood, she may start a song to be carried on all day, unrolling the story of some tremendous hero long ago. These songs would fill many books. In a land without writing they are passed on from generation to generation in gigantic feats of memory, marathon imitation. More often, the men sing stories. Over the fields come their fragments thrown high towards the rains and ranges . . . against the background of windmill groaning, pheasant-cuckoo, bittern and cicada.

This bucolic scene may be far from the presumably sober Buddhist recitations, but it bespeaks a shared orality that is part of the communal lives of social groups. It highlights a salient feature of orality/aurality in general: in non- and preliterate cultures, the act of listening is not the same as it is in manuscript- or book-oriented cultures. Nonliterate listening is unbounded in a way that literate or visual listening is not. Frits Staal (1930–2012) notes how "*we*, readers and writers of books, have little faith in oral traditions. That is our natural and professional opinion, a modern predicament that recent communication technologies have not yet sufficiently challenged. In so far as it derives from ignorance of oral traditions, our opinion is based on prejudice."[113]

To complicate the already complicated, we need to factor resistance to literacy into estimations of the value of literacy.[114] Historically, it is evident that many language groups did *not* embrace literacy and *chose* to remain nonliterate. The reasons for this must have been many, entangled with cultural identity in relation to literacy's association with alien cultures and with the development of urban, court, and mercantile societies. There may have been practices of exclusion like those seen in India, where from antiquity the

113. Staal, *Discovering the Vedas*, p. 32.

114. One might call this *anti-literacy*, but this term has been commonly used for a very different social and historical phenomenon: legal machinations by certain US states to prohibit slaves and free Black people from learning to read and write, aimed to obstruct them from reading laws, documents, or ideas and from achieving independence in the manipulation of written materials. This effort to obstruct access to functional literacy shows how literacy is indeed an indispensable tool for the development of the autonomous and independent intellectual and social self and a tool of empowerment against social injustice. This pertains to literacy *as* resistance rather than resistance *to* literacy—a very different (though not entirely unrelated) topic.

Brahmanical caste denied non-brahmans even oral access to their rituals and scriptures. Literature on literacy is generally couched in triumphalist terms, but resistence to literacy in antique cultures and linguistic societies merits serious reflection: Why did language groups choose to remain nonliterate? In the widespread but disjunctly dispersed Austroasiatic language family, for example, only a handful out of more than one hundred groups, including relatively populous groups like the Munda or Santals, chose to embrace literacy—including the Mon and the Khmer. The Mon and Khmer languages are prominent in the historiography of Brahmanical-cum-Buddhist Southeast Asia, since the arts of writing were disseminated with the knowledge systems of brahmans and Buddhist saṅghas along with those of royal courts and merchants.

Manuscripts and books add elements of visual spatialization, including borders that organize and format ideas. We can even highlight ideas by putting them in boxes.

Box 4. *The very idea of illiteracy*

My computer's dictionary does not have anything good to say about illiteracy. It defines the adjective *illiterate* as "unable to read or write," giving as an example: "his parents were illiterate" (which does not seem especially helpful). It goes on to define the term as

- [with a submodifier,] ignorant in a particular subject or activity: "the extent to which voters are politically illiterate"
- uncultured or poorly educated: "the ignorant, illiterate town council"
- (especially of a piece of writing) showing a lack of education, especially an inability to read or write well

It defines the phrase "functionally illiterate" as "lacking the literacy necessary for coping with most jobs and many everyday situations," and this, perhaps, is the key to the contemporary prejudices packed into the term. Literacy is needed to function in modern society, and there is no question that illiteracy is a liability. The concern of governments and corporations is economic development and the job market—that is, modernity's version of the slave market.

Roget's International Thesaurus gives more depth to the vocabulary:[115] Under heading 476, IGNORANCE, we find "476.4. unenlightenment, benightedness, benightment, dark, darkness" and "476.5. unlearnedness, inerudition, ineducation, unscholarliness, unstudiousness, unletteredness, illiteracy, illiterateness, unintellectuality, unintellectualism." The profusion of terms under "476.15. unlearned" is too long to quote, and it is here that we find "unlettered": "inerudite, unerudite, uneducated, unschooled, uninstructed, untutored, untaught, unedified, unguided, **illiterate, unlettered, grammarless**, unread . . . uncultured, uncultivated, unrefined, rude, Philistine, unintellectual, lowbrow, lowbrowed, lowbrowish."

Under 474, KNOWLEDGE, we find 474.21, "learned, erudite, educated, cultured, lettered, literate," and so on.[116]

If preliterate societies and peoples were really as coarse and lowbrow as these synonyms suggest, they were in a sorry state indeed. On the contrary, however, in ancient times, memory and competence were the marks of intelligence and culture. Illiterate people could not read or write, but they were not unlettered: the Sanskrit alphabet, the "garland of syllables," was mastered as a part of oral education (something that is not especially difficult to do), and complex grammars were compiled and taught orally centuries before the beginning of the Christian era.[117] Prosody and meter were highly developed, and composition was a craft that made use of complex structures, as may be seen in the first Indian writings, those of King Aśoka.

During the several centuries of oral culture that followed the Master's demise, the Buddhist saṅghas supervised a stupendous organization of knowledge that involved "gigantic feats of memory," to borrow Harrisson's words. Although no urcanon (*mūlasaṃgīti*) survives, an early stage in the process must have been the organization of the Dharma into piṭakas. This

115. *Roget's International Thesaurus*, 3rd ed. (Collins 1977), pp. 309–10.
116. *Roget's International Thesaurus*, pp. 308–9.
117. Mentioning the "Christian era" reminds me to note that in Christian circles, the question of whether Jesus was literate continues to be debated, and the friction and heat that the debates generate show how polemically charged is the very idea of literacy.

was facilitated by the use of lists and tables of contents of books, sections, and subsections, precursors of the surviving *uddānas*. Members of the saṅgha had to commit their order's monastic rules to memory and recite them communally each fortnight; these were codified in the Prātimokṣas, with anywhere from two hundred to three hundred rules. Recitation specialists preserved and recited the Āgamas and Vinayas, along with enormous narrative texts in prose and verse like the Pāli Jātakas. As centuries passed, lengthy Abhidharma texts were added to the collections. These burgeoning collections were transmitted orally not by one central or centralized school—South Asian Buddhism never had a center—but by each of a dozen and more schools and monastic centers for their own textual collections, the heritage of their orders. When the Perfection of Wisdom and Vaidalya or Vaipulya sūtras began to circulate, further gigantic texts like the *Large Perfection of Wisdom* and the *Buddhāvataṃsaka* were added to the memory bank.

A lot of Buddhist literature is in verse. Poetry is an oral art, guided by assonance and rhythm. Poets recite: poetry is best when read out loud. Many of the great spiritual masters of India, like Kabir or other saints, are said to have been illiterate, but they expressed their insights in passionate poetry and sonorous song. The relation between the poet and the pen is ambiguous, but it is safe to say that the power of poetry is in the reciting. To read Dylan Thomas's *Under Milk Wood* oneself, alone, whether silently or out loud, is one thing, but to listen to it read by the poet himself or by Richard Burton is quite another. To read *Hamlet* is one thing; to attend a live performance is quite another. To read a Pāli chant from a printed page is one thing, but to hear it chanted by a chapter of monks is yet another. Poetry and sacred literature have been communicated orally since the preliterate age, and they are still communicated orally, around the world, in all its languages, for everyone's ears.

Figure 9. Image of standing Buddha with a stūpa and *ye dharmā* inscription on the back (see fig. 10) in the Asian Art Museum, San Francisco (B60S571). This is from Sultanganj, and the same image is in fact seen in the archival photo with the giant Sultanganj Buddha, figure 1. The statue was displayed at the exhibition *Buddhism: Art and Faith* at the British Museum in 1985 and illustrated in Zwalf's catalogue of the same title, § 139.

Figure 10. Stūpa and *ye dharmā* on back. See appendix 2, figure 56, for the inscription.

Scribbles from a Translator's Notebook

He makes the gift of pens, ink, blank books, and
Dharma thrones in order that all beings may fulfill
the requisite equipment of great wisdom.
Questions of the Bodhisatva Subāhu[118]

THE TRANSLATIONS IN THIS VOLUME are a personal selection of texts that have taken my interest over the years. This interest led me to translate them, and, eventually, to publish them (an illustration of the maxim "interest and inclination are the roots of all mental activity").[119] The selection is not representative of any particular genre, of any particular school, of any particular tradition, or, indeed, of any didactic or ritual collections. They belong to different genres and are brought together here as a group for the first time.

Buddhist texts were not produced for limited use or restricted audiences. Their traditional classification into genres is for practical purposes only, and a single text may often have more than a single identity. Identity depends on context. One member of this anthology, the *Buddha's Visit to Vaiśālī* (translation 15), has multiple identities: Tibetan scholiasts placed it in three sections of the Kanjur—the Sūtra, Tantra, and Dhāraṇī collections. The *Visit to Vaiśālī* is seamlessly incorporated in full in the *Chapter on Medicine* of the Mūlasarvāstivāda *Vinayavastu*, so if we include the Vinaya retelling, the *Visit to Vaiśālī* belongs to *four* sections of the Kanjur. A Sanskrit version with a different title, *Recollector of the Great Mantra* (*Mahāmantrānusāriṇī*), is one

118. *Subāhuparipṛcchā*, Dergé no. 70, Dkon brtsegs, *ca*, 155b6: *sems can thams cad shes rab chen po'i tshogs yongs su bskang bar thob par bya ba'i phyir myu gu dang | snag tsha dang | glegs bu dang | chos kyi khri stan sbyin pa sbyin no* ||. See also Skilling, "Birchbark, Bodhisatvas, and Bhāṇakas."
119. *Chandamūlakā sabbe dhammā*, *Aṅguttaranikāya*, vol. 5, p. 107.6.

of the Five Protections (Pañcarakṣā) that came to be visualized as deities in northern India and Nepal; as a result, the *Buddha's Visit to Vaiśālī* was recast as the "Queen of Spells, Recollector of the Great Mantra" (see figs. 33, 48). In addition, the verses are placed as benedictions (*svastigāthā*) at the end of the Tantra and Vinaya divisions of some Kanjurs and at the end of Tanjurs.[120]

The *Udānavarga* (translation 4) has the distinction of being placed in both parts of the great Tibetan canons, the Kanjur and the Tanjur. It is in the Kanjur because it is, after all, a collection of verses spoken by the Buddha. It is in the Tanjur because, after all, the verses were collected and arranged not by the Buddha himself but by someone else, Dharmatrāta, centuries after the Buddha's demise. Two of the texts (translations 12 and 13) belong to both the Mahāsūtra collection and the Mūlasarvāstivāda *Saṃyuktāgama*. Two other Mūlasarvāstivāda Mahāsūtras that have Pāli counterparts in the *Dīghanikāya* are placed under Sūtra in some Kanjurs, under the Tantra and Dhāraṇī collections in others, and under both or all three in others. These are the *Āṭānāṭīya* and the *Mahāsamāja Mahāsūtras*, not translated here. Translation 9, "King Prasenajit's Grandmother Passes Away," is found in the Āgamas and also in the Mūlasarvāstivāda Vinaya. In short, the classification of texts is conventional and pragmatic; classifications overlap and are neither watertight nor absolute.

As Āgama/Nikāya texts or their offspring, all of the translations in this anthology are *canonical* for the communities that transmitted them, the Mūlasarvāstivāda, Theravāda, and Sāṃmitīya orders. According to their openings, all of the texts were delivered during Śākyamuni's lifetime at north Indian sites that we know today from the archaeological record; the narrative frames of three of them place them during the reign of the historical king Prasenajit (translations 7, 8, 9).[121] In theory, most of the texts translated herein should have been recited and committed to memory at the early convocations. A notable exception to this is the *Udānavarga* (translation 4), which did not yet exist as a collection until five hundred years post-Nirvāṇa—to venture a guess.[122] The *Udānavarga* that we know today did not, as far as we know, exist as a *collection*, but its *components*, the individ-

120. See Skilling, *Mahāsūtras*, vol. 2, pp. 581–85.

121. The interlocutor is King Prasenajit (Pasenadi in Pāli). The Pāli *Sagāthā* section that opens the *Saṃyuttanikāya* dedicates a whole collection, the *Kosala-saṃyutta* with twenty-five suttas, to dialogues between King Pasenadi/Prasenajit and the Fortunate One.

122. We are told that the compiler was named Dharmatrāta, and we conclude that he must have lived several centuries after the Parinirvāṇa.

ual verses and clusters of verses, would have circulated orally for centuries, either individually, incorporated into prose compilations, or included in proto-*Dhammapadas*.

About fifteen of the translations come directly from the Āgamas/Nikāyas, most of them from the *Saṃyuktāgama/Saṃyuttanikāya*, the "Kindred Sayings," "Grouped Sayings," or "Connected Discourses"—a collection organized around themes, practices, and ideas. But the Buddha's teachings were not collected as Āgamas alone. The Āgamas were large and bulky; like big containers (*piṭaka*), they are packed with hundreds and even thousands of sūtras. As oral texts, they took up a lot of memory and storage space, and as written texts they were bulky to transport or to shelve. The saṅghas found it expedient to select important texts and make smaller didactic, homiletic, and ritual collections that were more manageable, more portable, and more convenient to carry, whether mentally as intangible oral collections or physically as tangible written manuscripts. These include the Great Sūtras of the Sarvāstivāda community, the Four Recitations and the Paritta of the Theravāda communities, the Siamese and other chant collections, and the Five Protections of northern India and Nepal, as well as anthologies like the Pāli *Suttasaṅgaha* or the Sanskrit *Tridaṇḍamālā*. Samples from most of these collections are represented here.[123] The only selections that are not strictly from the Āgamas are the Sanskrit Svastivākya (translation 16) and the Pāli Paritta verses (translation 18). Some of the Svastivākya verses are drawn directly from canonical Āgama sources, while amongst the Paritta, the "Protection of the Awakening Factors" is a verse digest of three canonical prose suttas from the Pāli *Connected Discourses*. Whether the category "canonical" applies to this type of text is an open question. They summarize canonical texts, and they invoke the power of the Buddha and the legacy of truth and truth-speaking inherent in his words.

All of the translations in this volume belong to Buddhism's shared heritage. Even if they are classified as "Śrāvaka sūtras," they can still be read and used in the practice of any and all schools and vehicles. All of them are open-source. Open-source is not a new concept: the teachings and practices of ancient Indian *śramaṇa* culture were open to all, without restriction by caste, class, or gender. The Buddha proclaimed that he did not have the "closed

123. On these shorter collections, see Skilling, "The Many Lives of Texts."

fist" of a restrictive or secretive teacher:[124] everyone could have access to his teaching; everyone could benefit from following his practical exposition of the path. The Dharma is for the benefit of all, for the good of all, for the happiness of all. This ideal still sets the standard for Buddhist cultures of knowledge.

Methodology and Technique

When I translate, I try to steer my skiff across the churning sea of words that lies between the precipitous cliffs of "fidelity to the original" and "readability." This means to find a balance, to cleave a middle way through the heaving waters, to pass beyond the scudding clouds of unknowing to the bright clear skies beyond. Literal translations do not translate; they only pretend to say what is written in one language in another "target" language. Literal translation is often impossible, in that it simply misses the mark when attempted. Literal sense—"according to the primitive meaning, not figurative"—can be translated, but to meaningfully translate "following the letter, or exact words" is another matter.[125] These questions are discussed in Buddhist texts as *yathārtha* and *yathāruta* ("according to the sense" and "according to the letter"), *abhiprāya* ("intention"), and *neyārtha/nītārtha* ("provisional and definitive meanings").[126] If I try to translate a word or phrase literally, it may still call for footnotes or exegesis to explain what it actually *means*. So, we learn that the *letter* does not necessarily convey a single *meaning*, a reality of which ancient Indian linguists and philosophers were well aware. Buddhist texts urge us to rely on the meaning, not on the letter. Some writers take "literal" to mean translating every word with a term from an accredited dictionary, and at times translations may seem as if written in dialects of translationese or in ad hoc creoles. Sometimes this may be unavoidable, but it is hardly desirable.

The natural ecologies of language are changing radically, as the way we speak, write, and perceive become increasingly influenced and even dictated

124. For the trope of the closed fist, see Eltschinger, "Aśvaghoṣa and His Canonical Sources," p. 140.

125. Quotes from Johnson in Lynch, *Samuel Johnson's Dictionary*, p. 304, s.v. "literal."

126. No modern scholar has discussed these questions with the breadth, depth, and subtlety as the late and much-lamented David Seyfort Ruegg (1931–2021). See, for example, Seyfort Ruegg, "Purport, Implicature, and Presupposition" and "The Indian and the Indic in Tibetan Cultural History."

by hegemonic electronic media. The undeniable advantages that computers bring to intellectual ventures are overshadowed by regimes of standardization and mechanization and the resultant dehumanization and alienation, along with the corrosion of privacy and dignity. We poor bedraggled humans have all become customers, anonymous users, bald statistics. The four reliances or supports are replaced by new guidelines:[127] rely on a computer, not on your mind; rely on the web, not on the person; rely on the screen, not on inner consciousness; rely on manufactured consensus, not on definitive meanings.

As noted above, words are sounds. I listen to the sound of my translations by reading them out loud to test their cadences. I feel a natural affinity for what Nirad C. Chaudhuri calls "the habit of writing by sounding." Chaudhuri (1897–1999), a master writer of lucid and melodious English prose, was educated in Bengal in the first decades of the twentieth century. He did not learn English from Englishmen and did not hear it "as spoken by natural speakers of the language till late in life." He writes,[128]

> The basic realization which dictates my method [of writing] is that language is something to be heard, not merely to be looked at. Thus I consider what is written by way of literary work to be the exact equivalent of a musical score, and when writing I always behave like a musical composer. I never write without sounding what I am writing in my ear.

Buddhist prose is rhythmic and musical, and I try to adapt my craft to new cadences in English. I can hardly pretend to "behave like a musical composer," but I try to give at least a hint of the majestic sweep of the antique tracts.

Waking and Blossoming: Buddha and Bodhi[129]

Gautama the Buddha-to-be was born into the ruling family at Kapilavastu in today's Nepal.[130] He passed his childhood and young adulthood in comfort,

127. For the four reliances, see Skilling, *Questioning the Buddha*, p. 146.
128. Nirad C. Chaudhuri, "Apologia Pro Scripta Sua," pp. 90–91.
129. See also Skilling, *Questioning the Buddha*, pp. 149–51.
130. This thumbnail account tries to steer clear of the hegemonic historiographies in which Śākyamuni's vita has been cast since the Victorian age. Any version has to face epistemolog-

but at the age of twenty-nine his world was shaken to the foundations when he realized that everyone, himself included, is subject to old age, sickness, and death. He was beset by Angst and overwhelmed by inner turmoil, but just then a renunciant passed before his anguished gaze. Observing the renunciant's serene demeanor, Gautama saw the way out and was moved to leave behind the pleasures of the palace and live beneath the open skies as a wandering ascetic. For six years he unremittingly sought the truth until he discovered a middle way between the two extremes of indulgence and self-torment. It was as if the waters of saṃsāra's ocean had parted, and he sat down beneath a glomerous fig tree until he awakened.

"Awakened" is one of the meanings of *buddha*—an awakened one, one who has woken up from the deep slumber of ignorance. *Buddha* also means blossomed, bloomed, opened up like the petals of a flower. Gautama's awakening is the flower of his insight and knowledge.

For well over a century, *bodhi* has been translated as "enlightenment" and Buddha as "Enlightened One." The European "discovery" of Buddhism came at a momentous juncture when the Enlightenment was, for Western intelligentsia, the cat's pajamas, at least retrospectively: a cherished golden age in the intellectual history of Europe, not to speak of humanity as a whole. Enlightenment's votaries viewed religion with suspicion; superstitious, dogmatic, and backward, religion was seen to be an obstacle to intellectual or scientific progress. This Enlightenment was not value-free; it was not a clean slate or an empty mirror. Dependently originated, it was a reponse to new empirical sciences, including the discovery of continents and cultures quite beyond the narrow biblical compass—but at the same time, biblical beliefs still permeated both private thought and public expression.[131] Even brilliant scholars like proto-orientalist William Jones (1746–94) interpreted the expansive field of Indian knowledge in the light of their own "ancient theologies" (I owe this apt phrase to Urs App).

The fact that state-of-the-art scholarship chose to translate Buddha as

ical and methodological challenges, such as monolithic constructions of the Buddha and Buddhism, the Eurocentric and Christocentric moorings of Western, colonial, and, inevitably, postcolonial studies, the extravagant chauvinism of theocentric and national imaginations, and the dead-end hermeneutics of suspicion trapped in (pseudo-)secular and scientific frameworks.

131. That Enlightenment ideas did not manifest mysteriously on a clean slate is made clear in the superb writings of Urs App—for example, *The Cult of Emptiness* and *The Birth of Orientalism*.

"Enlightened One" was a cultural positive in so far as it elected to situate Gautama within the idealizing frame of the European Enlightenment. Nonetheless, the traditional explanations that evoke wakening and blossoming are meaningful and evocative in themselves, and my personal predilection is to follow these rather than the conceits of Enlightenment polemics.[132]

From Buddhist and humanist perspectives, the Enlightenment was not so very enlightened. In some—or many?—ways it might be described as a benightedment. The colonial adventure was fueled by unjust power relations, militarism, aggression, slavery, and oppression. Eurocentric ideologies dominated discourse, and while philosophers touted high ideals in the metropoles, colonial powers gobbled up resources through sustained daylight robbery across the empire "on which the sun never set" (that is, until the empire itself sank ignominiously through a clutch of clumsy colonial exits to a shambolic Brexit).

The European Enlightenment is ambiguous. There is much to value and celebrate, and there is much to regret or criticize; we must be cautious about either romanticizing or demonizing it. Dr. Johnson's (1709–84) definitions of "to enlighten" in his *Dictionary of the English Language* are full of light, but they do not really suit the Indic notions of *budh*:[133]

> To ENLIGHTEN. v. a. [from *light*.] 1. To illuminate; to supply with light. 2. To quicken in the faculty of vision. 3. To instruct; to furnish with encrease of knowledge. 4. To cheer; to exhilarate; to gladden. 5. To illuminate with divine knowledge.

It is hard to see much resemblance to the Buddha's *bodhi* in the answer that Immanuel Kant (1724–1804) gave to the question "What is Enlightenment?"[134] Kant's musings are thought out in opposition to church and state, and like Europe's Enlightenment in general, is concerned with social

132. See also *Questioning the Buddha*, pp. 149–51. After a careful examination of Pāli sources, Bhikkhu Bodhi argues strongly in favor of "enlightenment" and "enlightened one." He notes, "The choice between the two alternatives—'awakening' vs. 'enlightenment,' and 'awakened one' vs. 'enlightened one'—depends largely on the personal predilection of the translator and the response the rendering is intended to evoke in the reader or listener." See Bodhi, "On Translating 'Buddha'" and "In Defense of 'Enlightenment.'"

133. *Dictionary of the English Language*, 4th ed. (1777), as cited in Puchner, *The Norton Anthology of World Literature*, volume D, p. 104.

134. Immanuel Kant, "What Is Enlightenment?" in Puchner, *Norton Anthology*, vol. D, pp. 105–9.

and political change. Buddhist enlightenment is hard to pin down; it is not opposed to any external structures or explicitly concerned with political action. Its lotus has unfolded in a very different pond.

Europe's Enlightenment was an outward movement, an exploration of the physical universe by exercise of the exact sciences. Buddha's enlightenment, Buddhist enlightenment, the enlightenment sought by Buddhists, is a movement inward; unconditioned and unconditional, it does not depend on cultural, political, or social conditions. It is not a historical or metaphysical reaction or response. Does emptiness respond to emptiness? It is not a response, a dialogue, or a contestation; it unfolds through insight, in silence.

The Buddha's enlightenment was an inward voyage, an inner exploration of the human condition and human spirit by exercise of the natural faculties of mind and body. Europe's encounter with the world was transformational; it brought an enormous strain upon its own thought-world, and this forced open new channels of thought, one of which was the "discovery" of Buddhism. The Enlightenment illuminated Europe with new knowledge and opened new intellectual horizons. Europe's encounter with Buddhism inspired an awareness of Buddhist and non-European thought that would have far-reaching ramifications.

Fast-backward: Gautama remained under or near the Bodhi Tree for several weeks, reflecting on and refining his discoveries. He then set out to teach his Dharma, the truths and realities that he had realized. When we study his earliest teachings carefully, it is clear that his Dharma is not a concoction or a contrived (*parikalpita*) intellectual system, but the product of insight (*jñāna*). It is insight that sets the wheel of Dharma in motion. Gautama compares his experience to that of someone who wanders in the wilderness and stumbles across "an old path, an old course, an old trail that was sought and followed by former men." He follows the path and comes to a city, an ancient and long-abandoned capital. In this parable, the ancient path is the noble eightfold path, and the ancient city is dependent arising.[135]

Translation 11 illustrates how Gautama did not claim to have thought up a new system but rather to have realized or rediscovered the nature of reality, and only then did he set out to teach.

135. *Nagaropamasūtra*: see Bongard-Levin et al., *The Nagaropamasūtra: An Apotropaic Text from the Saṃyuktāgama*; Bodhi, *Reading the Buddha's Discourses in Pāli*, pp. 355–60.

Figure 11. Standing Buddha. See caption on page 90.

Figure 11. Standing Buddha carved in black schist, circa seventh to eighth centuries CE. The Buddha stands on a lotus pedestal. His proper right hand is in the gesture of granting boons (*varadamudrā*), and the whole is surrounded by a flaming halo. To the proper left of the Buddha, a bejeweled Bodhisatva Maitreya (the future Buddha) kneels to venerate his future predecessor. On the inscriptions at the base, see appendix 2, figure 57.

Table 2. *Dependent arising*

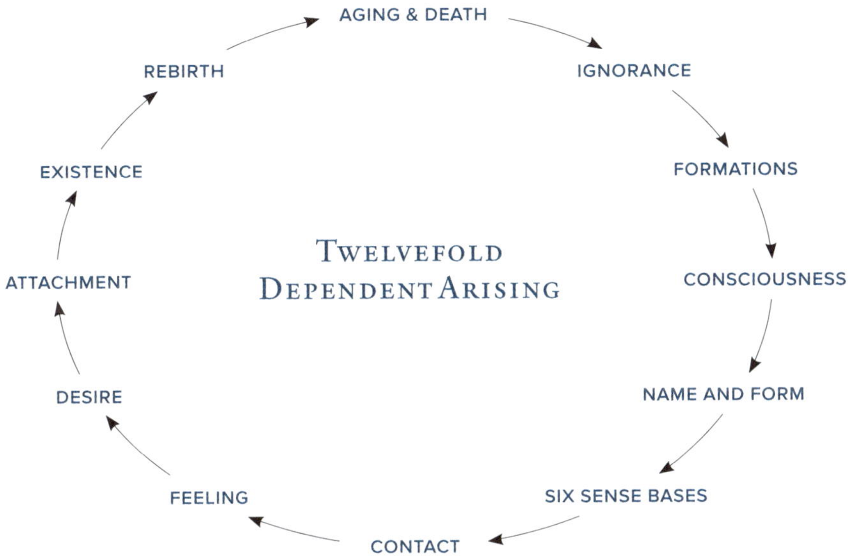

On another occasion, a monk asked the Buddha whether dependent arising "was invented by the Fortunate One or invented by someone else." The Fortunate One replied,[136]

> O monk, dependent arising was not invented by me. Nor indeed was it invented by anyone else. Whether Tathāgatas arise or whether they do not arise, this true nature (*dharmatā*) of phenomena abides—it is the primal element (*dharmadhātu*). When a Tathāgata has known and realized this directly by himself, then he explains it, he teaches it, he analyzes it, he expounds the connections and makes it perfectly clear.[137]

Philology seeks to find out original or ultimate meanings through historical and linguistic analysis—an intellectual exercise vital to the semiotic enterprise. A readable translation takes the text as it stands as the received text and tries to render it in a meaningful and coherent way. As a translator I try to be aware (beware, be wary) of the philological frames, of the multiple

136. Skilling, "Who Invented Dependent Arising? A Short Sūtra from the *Nidānasaṃyukta*."
137. Similar modules are used in translation 11.

complications and latent implications, keeping in mind that the text that lies before me is the product of centuries, indeed millennia, of conscientious editorial work. It is daunting to reflect that I am translating communications that are over two thousand years old, that they are messages from the beyond in both time and space. My task is not to join hands with the bachelors and strip the bride bare but to see the holistic product as it is through the large, shattered glass, even.[138] In these circumstances, it doesn't seem appropriate to set out with the butterfly net of philology and chase after the fast fluttering figments of urtexts. I have it on good report that urtexts are as bashful and elusive as yetis and harder to scoop up than the moon in water.[139]

The translations are from Tibetan, Sanskrit, and Pāli sources. The Tibetan texts are all translations of Sanskrit compositions from India, so when I translate the Tibetan, I have to keep an eye on the Indic palimpsest that shimmers beneath the Tibetic surface—insofar as I can glimpse or imagine it (palimpsests are elusive but not, let us pray, delusive). I generally give technical terms in parentheses in Sanskrit because this is the book's ideal lingua franca. Regardless of the "canonical" or preferred languages of the different monastic orders, Sanskrit was the shared language of Indian Buddhist and South Asian intellectual discourse for well over a thousand years, until emergent vernaculars, first Persian and then English, began to jostle for space. The exception to this is Pāli: in translating Pāli texts, I retain the Pāli forms of proper names and terminology, except for a few instances when it is more practicable to use Sanskrit (for example, Prasenajit rather than Pasenadi).[140] If this seems inconsistent and arbitrary, rest assured that it is. Note also that short Pāli suttas do not have titles, properly speaking; in modern editions and translations, writers have generally drawn titles from the verse keywords that come at the ends of chapters.[141] The keywords can be different in different editions, which means that the short suttas do not necessarily have *single* or *fixed* titles.

Buddhist texts swarm with repetitions. They are repetitive, repeating themselves repeatedly. This is fine for oral and even manuscript culture, but

138. Marcel Duchamp, *The Bride Stripped Bare by Her Bachelors, Even* (*La mariée mise à nu par ses célibataires, même*). For Duchamp's chef d'oeuvre and its meanings, see recently Affron, *The Essential Duchamp*.

139. On urtexts, see Salomon, *Buddhist Literature of Ancient Gandhāra*, pp. 190–91.

140. For the forms of the king's name, including Gāndhārī *prasenao* and Bharhut *rāja pasenaji kosala*, see Allon and Silverlock, "Sūtras in the Senior Kharoṣṭhī Manuscript Collection," p. 13.

141. These keywords are called *uddānas* (see glossary).

repetition doesn't work in English style the way it does in oral or classical styles. Rather than repeat nouns or noun phrases, I change them to pronouns. Isn't this what pronouns are for? In translation 12, rather than repeat "the many merchants of Vaiśālī" ad infinitum, I alternate with "merchants," "merchants of Vaiśālī," "Vaiśālī merchants," or indulge in a plural pronoun.

Regarding the use of plurality, sometimes it makes better English to use plural instead of singular, or vice versa, and I do so when necessary if it does not upset the balance of the passage.

Ancient texts are liberal (to put it mildly) in the use of vocative phrases. *Bhagavā*, "O Fortunate One"; *bhikkhu*, "O monk"; *bhikkhave*, "O monks"; and so on. These usages, courteous reader, are artifacts of the age of oral transmission, when they helped make the who's who of it all clear. In printage English, O esteemed customer, not only is this unnecessary, it clutters the wordscape until it groans under the dead weight of vocative phrases.

There is one school of thought (I confess to being, or having been, an on-and-off member) that says one should translate every word and every repetition. One must, after all, reproduce the *body of the original* in English in order to impart the full effect to the reader. But this often ends up as a parody lampooning a caricature in the theater of the absurd. There is another school, or perhaps it is the same one, that insists that one should always translate the same word the same way regardless of its context. This does not make for very nuanced translations. There are few if any fixed, one-to-one correspondences in translation. Translation requires an extratextual support system, a gallery of ideas beyond the chosen text, a retinue of unrelated relevancies equipped with related irrelevancies—the whole garnished with pinches of irreverance as required.[142] There is much to avoid, cautiously and undogmatically (*appamādena* and *aparāmāsaṃ*: heedfully and without attachment), such as the Christian moorings of European writing and poetry or the brutish usages of contemporary speak. We may use them to our advantage as best we can, and when need be cast them aside, shake free, and explore the profundity of the antique Indian and Buddhist meanings.

Beyond all this, I make small embellishments for rhythm or sonority or to fill in or flesh out implied meanings, especially in lines of verse when the rhythm calls for an extra syllable or two, or when a verse is in want of a trimming. Although I am avowedly following the Tibetan translation that lies before my eyes and not the Sanskrit even when it is preserved, in a few cases

142. To wit: a recipe for mixed metaphors.

I do follow the letter of the latter. In the *Udānavarga*, where the Sanskrit has *martya* (cp. Pāli *macca*), "mortal," the Tibetan simply has *mi*, "man" or "person," perhaps, but only perhaps, reading the term as *manuṣya*, "human being," "personage," I retain "mortal" since the verses are, after all, about our mortality. Where the Sanskrit has "lord of death," the Tibetan simply has "death"; here too I retain the personification of the Sanskrit recension. A translation can be a colonization that imposes the rules of the metropole on hapless native speech habits, as insensitively as might a Macaulay. The gender of the original texts reflects the social hierarchy of ancient India in which the notional or ideal example is the male. I follow this and translate "he" as "he" and "his" as "his," though the exemplary "he" of the ancient texts should not necessarily be read as excluding the silent or unexpressed "she," or "his" as excluding "hers."

Fateful Commas and Unpunctuality

At times I find it helpful to add connecting particles or to change the word order to suit rhetorical needs. Sentence breaks and paragraphing are tailored to English practice—there are few or often none in the original texts. Note also that the originals contain no capitalization and no italicization, and what punctuation there is is thoroughly unpunctual, if it shows up at all. Punctuation does not have the semantic importance that it has in English, something that is neatly demonstrated by the nouveau classic *Eats, Shoots & Leaves*,[143] or by the seasoned saga of "Oscar and the commas."

A recent article in the esteemed *Guardian* opens on an alarming note: "The comma is disappearing, the full stop has come to a full stop, and the semicolon has been repurposed as a pair of winking eyes. While the exclamation mark remains in rude health, the fate of the apostrophe seems especially bleak."[144] In his *Tharoorosaurus!* Shashi Tharoor keeps us up to date on the parlous state of the poor, endangered "humble punctuation mark," the apostrophe.[145]

143. See Truss, *Eats, Shoots & Leaves*.
144. Simon Horobin, "In Our War of Words, Full Stops Are Dying but the Exclamation Mark Is Doing Fine," *Guardian*, 28 December 2021, https://www.theguardian.com/commentisfree/2021/dec/28/punctuation-complicated-full-stop-culture-war.
145. Tharoor, *Tharoorosaurus!* pp. 5–11.

Box 5. *Oscar puts the commas in their place*

There are several conflicting accounts of this event, rather like the accounts of the early Buddhist convocations. The first printed version was published on 8 May 1884, in *The Daily Graphic: An Illustrated Evening Newspaper* of New York City under the title "The Casual Observer" and was quickly reprinted in several other newspapers under different titles, including "Oscar's Morning Work" and "A Fateful Comma." The printed story recapitulates an oral tradition regarding Oscar Wilde (1854–1900).

Once, while on a visit to an English country house, Wilde was much annoyed by the pronounced Philistinism of a fellow guest, who loudly stated that all artistic employment was a melancholy waste of time. "Well, Mr. Wilde," he said one day at lunch, "and pray how have you been passing your morning?"

"Oh! I have been immensely busy," said Oscar with great gravity. "I have spent my whole time over the proof sheets of my book of poems." The Philistine with a growl inquired the result of that. "Well, it was very important," said Oscar. "I took out a comma."

"Indeed," returned the enemy of literature, "is that all you did?"

Oscar, with a sweet smile, said, "By no means; on mature reflection I put back the comma."[146]

The classic punctuational conundrum in Buddhist literature is the sūtra opening "Thus have I heard at one time the Fortunate One was staying at . . . ," which has been variously translated during a century and a half of English-language translation. Red Pine translates, "Thus have I heard. Once the Buddha was staying . . ."[147] Recently Luis Gómez and Paul Harrison have rendered it as "This is what I heard at one time when the Exalted One was staying in Vaiśālī, in the Grove of Āmrapālī."[148] Debate continues to rage about this opening, like a storm in a teacup.[149] Despite the prevalant commentarial interpretation that the "I" is Ānanda—that is, that it is

146. Anecdote as told at the website Quote Investigator, https://quoteinvestigator.com/2015/10/25/comma/.
147. Red Pine, *Why Not Paradise*, pp. 11, 21.
148. Gómez and Harrison, *The Teaching of Vimalakīrti*, p. 3.
149. See Skilling, *Questioning the Buddha*, pp. 133–37.

Śākyamuni's devoted disciple Ānanda who repeats the sūtra—and despite the seemingly widespread acceptance of the chronically faithful and of modern scholars, it is more likely that the statement is the opening formula with which trained reciters introduced their recitations. This idea was proposed by Tominaga Nakamoto (1715–46) in 1744 and belatedly in my own work in 2021.[150]

Readers might also note that the translated languages have no definite or indefinite articles. English translators and editors take it upon themselves to add these niceties, as per regulations, to suit the noble tongue of the small island, which by some curious twist of history has become *the* world language, even as the islet breaks away from the mother continent and floats off into the mists of the vast unknown. *Śubham astu*: May it be well for the brave Britons.

Should I explain my translation decisions, indicating what I have done at every step? Should I straightjacket my changes by confining them in square brackets and annotate every peccadillo committed against the moral code of literalism? Not only would this be pedantic, it would irredeemably tediousize, clumsify, and unnaturalate the translation. I prefer to let the translations open their petals organically, to let them emerge phrase by phrase, gentle into the light of readers' eyes.

From the outset, I tried to avoid annotating the translations proper, to make the translations a note-free zone. For the three Mahāsūtras (translations 12, 13, and 15), the original edition has more than enough notes, even a feast, to satisfy those who hunger for annotations, and the textual studies in my *Mahāsūtras* part 2 wax unpoetic on matters philological, terminological, and historical. The editions of the Sanskrit and Tibetan *Udānavargas* by Bernhard and by Dietz and Zongtse are meticulously annotated, as is Bhikṣuṇī Vinītā's edition of the Potala manuscript. For someone who habitually fills his pages with infinitudes of scarcely intelligible annotations, this was a hard decision. Nevertheless, I gritted my teeth and forged ahead—to quickly find the task insuperable, as the astute reader shall see.

The anti-intellectual lobby has coined "user-friendly" to scare people away from the delights of details and minutiae. Footnotes, foreign words, technical terminology, and diacritics are scorned as user-unfriendly: zeal-

150. Tominaga, "Thus I Have Heard," in *Emerging from Meditation*, pp. 85–88; Skilling, *Questioning the Buddha*, loc. cit. I would be surprised if others have not come to the same conclusion.

ous editors regard them as reprehensible and hence dispensable.[151] This is a wrong dispensation, a wrong direction, that diverts intellectual traffic into a detour for dummies. Publishing should be user-challenging; it should be thought-provoking, and it should inspire readers—whether they are faithful or faithless or agnostic—to develop new patterns of thought and to savor new vocabularies of the imagination. Writing should be simple but not simplistic; it should be chaste but not frigid; it should be deeply rich and not superficially extravagant.

Translation is an art that brings the translator pleasure: it brings the delight of discovering new words and new meanings, it brings the thrill of reading something for the first time ever, and it brings the satisfaction of seeing sentences and thoughts emerge from manuscripts where they have been sleeping for a thousand years and more. This makes one feel "like some watcher of the skies / When a new planet swims into his ken." At times I am inclined to apologize to the texts for waking them up. But I do so to *share* them with my readers.[152]

151. "User-unfriendly," if it really is a word, rubs shoulders with the silly words of newspeak.
152. Reluctant am I indeed to use the word "share," one of the most abused and overused words of the decade, but use it here I must. Here and here only, then I let it loose to graze happily in peace and quiet.

Part II

Twenty Translations for Tough Times

Figure 12. Contemplation of the foul: monks contemplate corpses in the jungle. Wat Naphrathat, Nakhon Ratchasima, Thailand.

Prelude

As a Serpent Sheds Its Worn-Out Skin

One who has neither run too far nor run back,
who has transcended all this proliferation:
that bhikkhu gives up the here and the beyond
as a serpent sheds its old worn-out skin.

One who has neither run too far nor run back,
having known about the world, "All this is unreal":
that bhikkhu gives up the here and the beyond
as a serpent sheds its old worn-out skin.

One who has neither run too far nor run back,
devoid of greed, [knowing] "All this is unreal":
that bhikkhu gives up the here and the beyond
as a serpent sheds its old worn-out skin.

One who has neither run too far nor run back,
devoid of lust, [knowing] "All this is unreal":
that bhikkhu gives up the here and the beyond
as a serpent sheds its old worn-out skin.

One who has neither run too far nor run back,
devoid of hatred, [knowing] "All this is unreal":
that bhikkhu gives up the here and the beyond
as a serpent sheds its old worn-out skin.

One who has neither run too far nor run back,
devoid of delusion, [knowing] "All this is unreal":

that bhikkhu gives up the here and the beyond
as a serpent sheds its old worn-out skin.

One who has no latent tendencies at all,
whose unwholesome roots have been uprooted:
that bhikkhu gives up the here and the beyond
as a serpent sheds its old worn-out skin.

Uragasutta, Suttanipāta verses 8–14, translated by Bhikkhu Bodhi.

1
The Buddha's Teaching in a Single Word

A PRA MĀ DA

Figure 13. Ivory seal from Khu Bua, Ratchaburi province, Thailand. Tracing depicts orientation of seal's impression.

The Buddha's Teaching in a Single Word
An antiquarian mystery

Heedful.

Be heedful.

Take care.

2

The Buddha's Teaching in a Single Verse

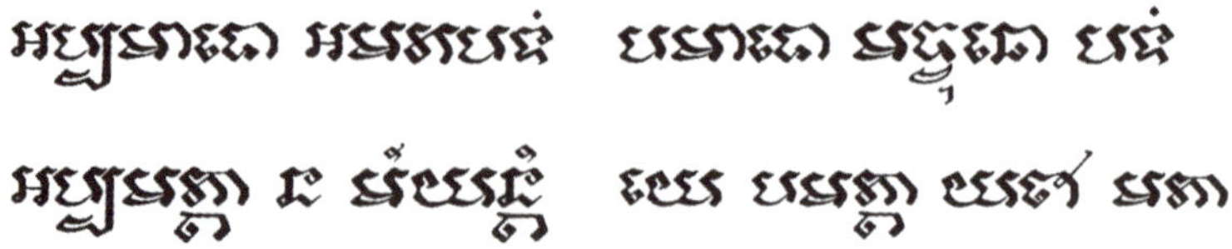

Appamādo amatapadaṃ pamādo maccuno padaṃ
Appamattā na mīyanti ye pamattā yathā matā

Figure 14. *Dhammapada* verse 21 in Khom script. Restoration of damaged inscription from Phra Pathom Chedi gallery by Eng Jin Ooi (August 2021).

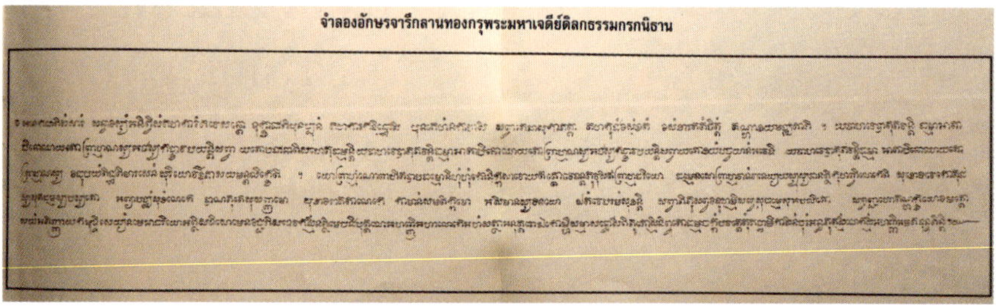

Figure 15. *Appamādavagga* in Khom script. Eye-copy of gold-plate inscription from Wat Pho by Kongkaew Weeraprachak.

The Buddha's Teaching in a Single Verse

DHAMMAPADA 21 AND THE *AṬṬHAKATHĀ*

Dhammapada verse 21:[153]

> Heedfulness is the path to the deathless;
> heedlessness is the path of death.
> They who are heedful do not die;
> they who are heedless are as dead.

The *Commentary on the Dhammapada* (*Dhammapada-aṭṭhakathā*) supplies a short introduction that relates the occasion upon which the Buddha spoke the verse, followed by an explanation of its meaning along with commentaries on the next two verses.[154] Tradition ascribes the commentary to the great Theravādin scholar Buddhaghosa, but many modern scholars question the ascription.

[The occasion]

The Teacher gave this Dhamma teaching when he was staying at Kosambi in the Ghositārāma regarding the tragedy of the death of five hundred women

153. My translation; for another translation, see that by Carter and Palihawadana (*Dhammapada*, pp. 109–11). Note that they translate *appamāda* as "awareness" while I use "heedfulness," and they translate *pamāda* as "unawareness" while I use "heedlessness." Like Carter and Palihawadana, Roebuck also uses "awareness": "Awareness is the place of the deathless; unawareness is the place of death. The aware do not die; the unaware are as though dead already"; Roebuck, *The Dhammapada*, p. 7.

154. *Dhammapada-aṭṭhakathā*, vol. 1, *Appamādavagga* II, *Udenavatthu* 1, pp. 161.4–8, 228.8–229.22.

headed by Sāmāvatī and of Māgandhiyā together with five hundred of her relatives.[155]

[The commentary]

Appamādo, heedfulness: "Heedfulness" indicates a vast topic, and it comprises a huge subject; the entire word of the Buddha included in the Three Piṭakas, when taken up and given articulation, fits into "heedfulness" alone. Therefore it has been said:[156]

> Just as the footprints of all animals that roam on land fit into the footprint of the elephant, and the elephant's footprint is declared foremost amongst them with respect to size, so too, all wholesome qualities are rooted in heedfulness and converge upon heedfulness, and heedfulness is declared foremost amongst them.

Now this [heedfulness] means not being bereft of mindfulness (*sati*); "not being bereft" means that mindfulness is constantly present. It's just that.

Amatapadaṃ, the path to the deathless: "deathless" means nibbāna. Because [nibbāna] is unborn [that is, it is unoriginated and has no beginning], nibbāna does not age or die: therefore it is called "deathless." "Path" means that it is by way of this [heedfulness] that people reach the deathless condition. *Amatapadaṃ* is the path or the place of undying; it is said to be the method by which one realizes the deathless. So is it said.

Pamādo, heedlessness: the state of being heedless. This is a term for the letting go of mindfulness that is counted as muddled awareness.

Maccuno, of death: of the fact of dying.

Padaṃ, the path: the means, the way. A heedless person does not escape birth: one who is born grows old and dies, and thus heedlessness is called the path of death insofar as it leads to death.

Appamattā na mīyanti, the heedful do not die. Heedful beings who possess mindfulness [who are mindful] do not die, but this does not mean that they are free from aging and death, for there is no sentient being whatso-

155. This is an example of the weight of narrative in the *Dhammapada* traditions: the story for this and the following two verses—three verses, twelve lines—runs from page 161 to 227 in the PTS edition—that is, sixty-six pages—before the commentary on the words of the verses, which run from pages 228 to 231, scarcely four pages.

156. I cite Bhikkhu Bodhi's rendering from *Numerical Discourses*, p. 1354.

ever who is beyond aging and death. The cycle [of existence] is not cut off for the heedless, but it is cut off for the heedful. For this reason, because they are not liberated from birth and the rest that follow even when still alive, the heedless are considered to be dead. The heedful, however, having nurtured the quality of heedfulness, quickly realize the paths and fruits and do not produce a second or a third existence (*attabhāva*)—hence while still living it is as if they do not die.

Ye pamattā yathā matā, they who are heedless are as dead: because of the fact that heedless beings are dead through the death of heedlessness, like those who are dead because their life faculty is severed, they are bereft of consciousness like a chunk of wood. As for those who are householders, the thought never comes to them even once that "we will give alms; we will observe the precepts; we will perform the rites of the *uposatha* retreat." As for renunciants, the thought never comes to them even once that "we will perform the duties towards teachers and preceptors; we will undertake the constituents of ascetic practice (*dhutaṅga*); we will develop our spiritual cultivation (*bhāvana*).

[The *Dhammapada* verse that follows celebrates how heedfulness is a source of joy and delight.]

The discerning who have understood
this special feature of heedfulness
find joy in heedfulness,
delighting in the noble ones' domain.[157]

There is no escape from the cycle for the heedless, but there is [a way out] for the heedful; understanding this as a special feature, who is it that undersands the special feature? **The discerning.** . . . Those who are discerning, intelligent, and wise, grounding themselves in heedfulness, cultivate heedfulness—they understand the distinction [between heedfulness and heedlessness] thus. Knowing this, they find joy in their own heedfulness; with smiling faces they are satisfied and joyous. Delighting in the noble ones' domain: they delight in heedfulness, cultivate heedfulness, and delight, rejoice, and celebrate the domain of the noble ones—the buddhas, paccekabuddhas, and sāvakas—the

157. *Dhammapada* chap. 2, v. 2 (Dhp 22), followed by *Dhammapada-aṭṭhakathā* 229.22–230.12.

thirty-seven dharmas conducive to awakening, divided into the four foundations of mindfulness and so on, and the nine transcendent states.

> Those who practice *jhāna*
> are always strong in their efforts.
> The wise touch nibbāna,
> the supreme release from the bonds.[158]

158. *Dhammapada*, chap. 2, v. 3 (Dhp 23). The commentary is rather technical, so I refer the reader to Carter and Palihawadana, pp. 111–12.

3

Getting Off the Wheel of Life

Figure 16. Wheel of life (*bhavacakra*), mural painting, Trongsa Dzong, Bhutan. The Buddha stands outside the wheel in the top right corner and intones the verse translated here. He raises his right hand to point at the inscription. The verses are also lettered below the wheel. Photo courtesy of Eric Huntington, 20 December 2021.

Figure 17. The Buddha intones the verses: detail from figure 16. The pair of verses is on lines 5 to 8. Pada *c* is missing.

Getting Off the Wheel of Life

Two verses from the *Udānavarga/Dharmapada* traditions

Arise, go forth, devote yourself
to the awakened ones' teachings.
Crush the army of death
the way an elephant tramples
a flimsy hut made of reeds.

One who dwells heedful
in this teaching and system of training
leaves rebirth's round behind
and puts an end to pain.

4

Chapter on Impermanence

Figure 18. Meditation on death: a monk sits cross-legged and contemplates a skeleton. Paper leporello manuscript, Wat Pak Khlong.

Chapter on Impermanence

Udānavarga Chapter 1. From the Kanjur (P 992)

Success!
Cast off drowsiness and dullness, gladden your mind, and hearken:
I will proclaim the inspired stanzas uttered by the Victorious One. [1]

The All-Knowing One, the Protector, the Compassionate Sage,
who bears his last body, the Fortunate One, spoke as follows. [2]

Alas! Composite things are impermanent!
It's their character to rise and pass away.
Once they arise, they will surely pass away—
their quieting is happiness.[159] [3]

What pleasure is there, what joy,
in the midst of this blazing fire?
You have plunged into the darkness—
why don't you seek out a lamp? [4]

These pigeon-colored bones
are all that's left behind,
scattered every whichaway—
seeing them, what joy can there be? [5]

159. *Aniccā vata saṅkhārā*, the Pāli counterpart of this verse, is commonly recited at funerals in Thailand and Cambodia to the present day, along with verses 23, 24, and 36.

From the very first night
that a man enters his mother's womb,
he trudges on without respite—
once he sets out, there's no turning back. [6]

Out of the many people we see in the morning,
some won't be seen by nightfall.
Out of the many people we see in the evening,
some won't be seen the next day.[160] [7]

A lot of men, a lot of women[161]
die when they still are young.
How can mortals be so cocky
about life as to think, "I am young"? [8]

Some perish in the womb,
some die at the moment of birth.
Some die when they've just started to crawl,
some die when they've begun to walk. [9]

Some when they're old, some when they're young,
some in the prime of life—
one by one they all pass on,
dropping like ripe fruits.[162] [10]

There's always a risk that well-ripened fruits
will fall from the tree at any time.

160. There is a close parallel in the *Temīya-jātaka*, no. 538, v. 118, vol. 6, p. 28.4. Gāndhārī versions are found in two *Dharmapada* collections: see the Khotan version by Brough, *Gāndhārī Dharmapada*, v. 151, and Falk, "A New Gāndhārī Dharmapada," p. 42.
161. The commentary points out that here the phrase "men and women" is gender-inclusive: Balk, *Udānavargavivaraṇa*, vol. 1, p. 74.1, *skyes pa bud med ces bya ba 'dir ni thams cad 'dus pa yin te | ma ning ni phyogs gnyi ga la brten pa'i phyir gnyi gas gzung ngo || yang na gtso bo yongs su gzung bas gzhan smos mi dgos pa'i phyir ro*. "'Men and women' here includes everyone: non-binary people (*ma ning*, Skt, *napuṃsaka*) are included because they are dependent on the two genders. Another way to explain this is [by the rule that] 'a general statement is inclusive in itself and it is not necessary to mention others.'"
162. This pair of verses is cited in the *Dazhidu lun*: see Lamotte, *Le Traité*, vol. 3, p. 1423, under recollection of death.

Just so there's always a risk
that once a man is born,
he may drop dead any moment.[163] [11]

A potter turns clay into pots,
but in the end they all
shatter and crumble to dust:[164]
like this is the life of mortals. [12]

When the thread of the warp is stretched
and the weft is woven through, back and forth,
in the end the thread runs out;
like this is the life of mortals. [13]

With each and every step he takes,
a prisoner condemned to death
draws closer and closer to the execution ground:
like this is the life of mortals. [14]

As the current of a mighty river
rushes on and never turns back,
just so our human lives
rush on and do not turn back.[165] [15]

Arduous and fleeting,
full of suffering,
life quickly perishes,
like a line drawn in water with a stick. [16]

As with his stick a cowherd
drives cattle to their pens,
so illness and old age
drive men before the lord of death. [17]

163. There is a close parallel in the *Temīya-jātaka*, no. 538, v. 117, vol. 6, p. 28.1.
164. The phrase "and crumble to dust" is a translator's embellishment added for rhythm and effect. The original has one word, *'jig pa* = *bhedana*.
165. There is a close parallel in the *Temīya-jātaka*, no. 538, v. 106, vol. 6, p. 26.19.

Days and nights pass by,
and life draws to a close.
Like water in shallow streams,
the allotted years of mortals
dry up and turn to naught. [18]

Long is the night for the sleepless.
Long is the mile for the weary.
Long is rebirth's round for the fool
who does not know the Saddharma. [19]

"I've got a son, I've got wealth":
so the fool fancies and frets.
When there is no self, within or without,
whose son is it, whose wealth? [20]

Multitudes of men and women
in the hundreds, in the thousands,
amass the goods they yearn to have
then fall under the power of the lord of death. [21]

All that you accumulate
gets used up in the end.
What is raised up falls down in the end.
Meeting ends in separation,
and life ends in death. [22]

All sentient beings will die—
death is indeed the end of life.
Their onward journeys follow their karma
and its fruits, good or bad. [23]

Those who commit evil deeds go to hell.
Those who make merit go to the happy realms.
On the other hand, there are others
who practice the path in this life
and, free of impurities, reach nirvāṇa. [24]

Even the buddhas, the pratyekabuddhas,
and the buddhas' śrāvakas
all have to give their bodies up.
How can it be different for ordinary people? [25]

Not in the sky, not in the ocean deep,
not hidden in a mountain cleft—
there is no spot on this earth
where you might make a stand
and not be touched by death. [26]

Whether in the past, whether in the future,
everyone leaves their body behind and moves on.
Realizing that everything perishes, the wise
stand firm in Dharma and practice the holy life. [27]

Seeing an old man, seeing the pain of the sick,
seeing a corpse bereft of consciousness,
a steadfast one should leave the prison-like household behind—
how can the worldly give sense pleasures up? [28]

Even gorgeous royal chariots wear out;
just so the body succumbs to age.
The Dharma of the virtuous ones is sublime;
they expound it to the righteous so that it doesn't age.[166] [29]

Shame on you, vulgar old age,
you who disfigure us!
You're the one, old age,
who wears our beautiful bodies down. [30]

Even if someone lives a hundred years,
still the lord of death will drag him off.
Still he'll be struck down
by old age, sickness, and death. [31]

166. That is, the Dharma of the teaching does not age because it is transmitted accurately and maintained by righteous people.

Always moving on, never turning back,
degenerating night and day,
those suffering from birth and death
are tormented terribly, like fish in steaming water. [32]

Throughout the day, throughout the night,
whether you move or whether
you stand stock still
like a mighty river current life
rushes on and never turns back. [33]

Days and nights hurtle by,
and our lives grow shorter and shorter,
leaving us stranded like fish in shallow water—
what joy is there in life?[167] [34]

Because the end of life is death,
this nest of old age and disease—
this body—quickly collapses,
and this mass of matter bursts. [35]

Alas! It won't be long before this body,
empty and bereft of consciousness,
lies stretched out on the earth
like a piece of cast-off firewood
in a charnel ground. [36]

Constantly tormented by illness,
perpetually oozing matter,
afflicted by aging and death:
why not let go of this body? [37]

With this very body, leaking pus,
fragile and diseased and as it is,
strive for supreme security,
the unsurpassed accomplishment and joy. [38]

167. There is a close parallel in the *Temīya-jātaka*, no. 538, v. 101, vol. 6, p. 26.9.

"I'll spend the rainy season here,
here the winter, there the summer."[168]
Lost in fantasy, the fool
fails to envisage the dire complications.[169] [39]

The lord of death snatches away
a man whose mind is attached
to sons and wealth, livestock and property,
the way a flash flood sweeps away
a sleeping village. [40]

Nobody can save you
when the hour of death arrives:
your children can't save you,
your father can't save you,
and neither can your relations. [41]

"When I've finished this, I'll get to that.
When I'm done with these things, I take care of that."
We worry ourselves and procrastinate like this
till death along with aging and illness
show up and trample us to smithereens. [42]

Therefore: your mind collected, always delight in meditation,
be ardent and see the last of birth and aging,
vanquish the māras and their troops, O monks,
and cross to the other shore of birth and death.[170] [43]

This completes the Chapter on Impermanence.

168. Rainy season, winter, and summer are the three seasons of the northern Indian year, which determined the periods of residence for ascetics and monastics.
169. *Udānavargavivaraṇa* (see Balk, *Prajñāvarman's Udānavargavivaraṇa*, p. x) remarks that an intelligent person realizes that all sorts of dangers threaten this life and reflects that those who live [long enough] just to breathe in and breathe out are fortunate. This paraphrases a sūtra, the Pāli version of which is found in the *Aṅguttaranikāya*, trans. Sarah Shaw, *Buddhist Meditation: An Anthology of Texts from the Pāli Canon*, pp. 137–39.
170. A Pāli counterpart of this verse occurs in *Itivuttaka, Dukanipāta*, verse 9, pp. 40–41.

5
The Sūtra on Impermanence (1)

Figure 19. Meditation on death: a monk stands, holding a monastic fan, and contemplates a corpse. Mural painting, uposatha hall, Wat Uposatharam, Uthai Thani, Thailand.

The Sūtra on Impermanence (1)

Anityatāsūtra. From the Kanjur (P 975)

This is what I have heard. Once the Fortunate One was staying in Śrāvastī, at Anāthapiṇḍada's Garden in Prince Jeta's Grove, with a large congregation of monks. At that time the Fortunate One addressed the monks.

"Monks, for the entire world four things are sought after but elusive; they are cherished, attractive, and pleasing. What four are these?

"Health, for the entire world, is sought after but elusive; it is cherished, attractive, and pleasing. But health ends in sickness, and for the entire world sickness is undesirable but easy to come by; it is disliked, unattractive, and repugnant.

"Youth, for the entire world, is sought after but elusive; it is cherished, attractive, and pleasing. But youth ends in old age, and for the entire world old age is undesirable but easy to come by; it is disliked, unattractive, and repugnant.

"Good fortune, for the entire world, is sought after but elusive; it is cherished, attractive, and pleasing. But good fortune ends in misfortune, and for the entire world misfortune is undesirable but easy to come by; it is disliked, unattractive, and repugnant.

"Life, for the entire world, is sought after but elusive; it is cherished, attractive, and pleasing. But life ends in death, and for the entire world death is undesirable but easy to come by; it is disliked, unattractive, and repugnant."

The Fortunate One said this. When he had done so, then he, the Well-Farer, the Teacher, uttered these lines:

> Health, youth, good fortune, life:
> not one of these lasts for long.

How can a person besieged by impermanence
delight in the pleasures of the senses?

When the Fortunate One had said this, the monks rejoiced, praising the Fortunate One's words.

This completes the *Sūtra on Impermanence.* It was translated, revised, and established in the new translation terminology by the Indian preceptor Surendrabodhi and the master editor and translator Bhante Zhang Ye shes sde.[171]

171. The chronology of the "new translation terminology" (*skad gsar bcad*) is complicated. For the related royal decrees, see especially the work of Cristina Scherrer-Schaub and Dorji Wangchuk (references in Wangchuk, "The Three Royal Decrees").

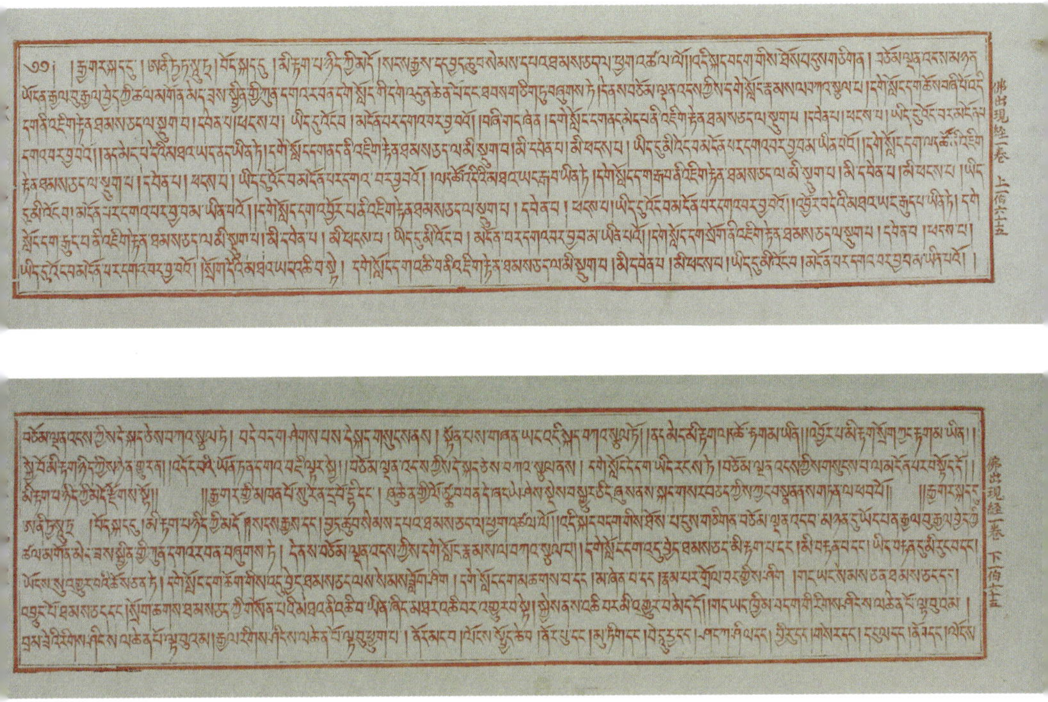

Figure 20. *Sūtra on Impermanence*: Peking Kanjur, Sūtra section (no. 975, fol. 165a1–b3).

6

The Sūtra on Impermanence (2)

Figure 21. Meditation on death: a monk stands in a charnel ground with a staff and a ceremonial monastic fan. He contemplates a dismembered corpse as it is gnawed by animals. Mural painting, uposatha hall, Wat Uposatharam, Uthai Thani, Thailand.

The Sūtra on Impermanence (2)

Anityatāsūtra. From the Kanjur (P 976)

This is what I have heard. Once the Fortunate One was staying in Śrāvastī, at Anāthapiṇḍada's Garden in Prince Jeta's Grove, with a large congregation of monks. At that time the Fortunate One addressed the monks.

"Impermanent are all compounded things, O monks. They are unstable, they are unreliable, they are subject to change—so much so that it is best to turn your minds away from all compounded things. Do not get attached to them, do not cling to them, free yourselves from their grip. For all sentient beings, for all living creatures, for all breathing things, life ends in death and life concludes with death. Once you are born you cannot get away from death.

"There are people who belong to established landowning families, there are people who belong to established brahman families, and there are people who belong to established warrior families.[172] They are well off, wealthy, and prosperous. They have quantities of gems, pearls, beryl,[173] *śaṅkhaśilā*,[174] and coral, and they have plenty of gold, silver, jewels, and possessions. Their storerooms overflow with wealth, grains, and treasure; they have multitudes of male and female slaves, workers, and servants; they have plenty of friends and powerful allies, relatives, and relations. Nonetheless, for them as well,

172. *Mahāśālakula*, "established" means old and long established, like a great *śāla* tree, and well established in wealth and social rank.

173. *Vaiḍūrya*, Tib. *bai dū rya*: debate about whether this is beryl or lapiz lazuli or something else continues.

174. BHSD, p. 522a, *śaṅkhaśilā* "(= Pāli *saṅkhasilā*, conjectured PTSD to mean *mother-of-pearl*, a pure guess) a sort of precious or semi-precious stone, mentioned in rigamarole lists of gems and precious metals, and almost always placed between vaiḍūrya and pravāḍa." The word occurs in the *Lalitavistara*, in the *Mahāvastu*, and in some avadānas and other Mahāyāna sūtras. The Tibetan translations vary. Some treat it as two terms, *dung* = shell and *man shel* = crystal. Modern lexicographers have been unable to decide exactly what sort of precious stone it is.

life ends in death, life concludes with death. Once you are born you can't get away from death.

"There are kings belonging to dynastic lines who are annointed members of the warrior clan. They rule their realms and wield power; they conquer a patch of earth and reign supreme. For them as well, life ends in death, life concludes with death. Once you are born you can't get away from death.

"There are sages who retreat to the forest, where they live on a diet of roots and fruits, where they sustain themselves with roots and fruits, where they keep to a diet of roots and fruits.[175] For them as well, life ends in death, life concludes with death. Once you are born you can't get away from death.

"There are gods who belong to the families of the Four Great Regents, the Thirty-Three gods, the Yāma gods, the Tuṣita gods, the gods who delight in magical emanations, the gods who take control of others' magical emanations. For them as well, life ends in death, life concludes with death. Once you are born you can't get away from death.

"There are gods who belong to the fine-material realm. These include those who have attained the first *dhyāna*: the Brahmakāyikas, Brahmapurohitas, the Mahābrahmās; they include those who have attained the second *dhyāna*: the Parīttābhas, Apramāṇābhas, the Ābhāsvaras. They include those who have attained the third *dhyāna*: the Parīttaśubhas, Apramāṇaśubhas, and Śubhakṛtsnas; and they include those who have attained the fourth *dhyāna*: the Anabhrakas, Puṇyaprasavas, Bṛhatphalas, and the nonpercipient beings the Abṛhas, Atapas, Sudṛśas, Sudarśanas, and the Akaniṣṭha gods. For all of them as well, life ends in death, life concludes with death. Once you are born you can't get away from death.

"There are the gods who belong to the nonmaterial planes: those attained to the sphere of endless space, those attained to the sphere of endless consciousness, those attained to the sphere of nothingness, and those attained to the sphere of neither percipience nor nonpercipience. For them as well, life ends in death, life concludes with death. Once you are born you can't get away from death.

"There are worthy arhats, who have exhausted the corruptions, who have done what is to be done, who have fulfilled their task, who have laid down their burdens, who have realized their own goals, who have exhausted the bonds of existence, who have fully freed their minds by correct insight, who

175. The Sanskrit and Tibetan versions are all phrased differently. The Tibetan version translated here seems somewhat repetitive.

have reached the limit of bringing the mind under their power.[176] They too, by natural law, must lay down their cherished bodies.[177]

"There are pratyekabuddhas, some solitary like a rhinoceros horn and some who live in groups, who tame themselves alone, who calm themselves alone, who go to nirvāṇa themselves alone.[178] They too, by natural law, must lay down their cherished bodies.

"There are tathāgatas, worthy arhats, the fully awakened buddhas who possess the ten powers, who are exalted bulls, who roar the true lion's roar, who are fearless with the four confidences, who nurture Nārāyaṇa's firm energy within their bodies.[179] They too, by natural law, must lay down their cherished bodies.

"To make a simile, O monks: a potter fashions pots, and whether they are fired or whether they are unfired, they all will break in the end, in the end each and every one of them will shatter.[180] In the very same way, O monks, for all sentient beings, for all living creatures, for all breathing things, life ends in death and life concludes with death. Once you are born you can't get away from death."

The Fortunate One said this. When he had done so, then he, the Well-Farer, the Teacher, uttered these verses.

176. For a commentary on these terms, see *Dazhidu lun* in Lamotte, *Le Traité*, vol. 1, pp. 198–219.

177. "Cherished bodies": *de rnams kyang yid du 'ong ba'i lus spong bar byed pa'i chos can no*. The Sanskrit versions quoted by Vinītā all have *teṣām apy ayaṃ kayo nikṣepadharmaḥ* (with small variations). None have any equivalent to *yid du 'ong ba*, which normally translates *manojña* (but there are other possibilities: see TSD, vol. 13, pp. 5811–85, s.v. *yid 'ong*). The same differences in phraseology occur for the arhats, pratyekabuddhas, and samyaksaṃbuddhas.

178. The passage refers to the two types of pratyekabuddha, *khaḍgaviṣāṇopama* (solitary like a rhinoceros horn) and *vargacārī* (who live in groups).

179. Nārāyaṇabala is a measure of immense physical power calculated as "the power of the seventh term of a series that begins with the elephant and in which each term is ten times the preceding" (Gelong Lodrö Sangpo, vol. 3, p. 2225, translating *Kośakārikā*, chap. 7, v. 31). See Chim Jampaiyang, *Ornament of Abhidharma*, pp. 1017–18. See Lamotte, *Le Traité*, vol. 1, p. 269, n. 2; *Kośakārikā*, chap. 7, v. 31, in La Vallée Poussin, *Kośabhāṣya*, vol. 7, pp. 72–74 (Lodrö Sangpo, vol. 3, pp. 2225–26 plus nn. 417–30, p. 2321–22, with references to *Vibhāṣā* and other sources). See Samtani's translation of the *Arthaviniścayasūtranibandhana*, pp. 305–6 and notes, p. 216, and p. 248, n. 248. For references to Pāli *nārāyaṇa-saṅghāṭa-bala*, see DPPN, vol. 2, p. 54; *Vibhaṅga-aṭṭhakathā*, p. 397.

180. The same simile comes at the end of *King Pasenadi's Grandmother Passes Away* (translation 8).

Alas! Composite things are impermanent,
it's their character to rise and pass away.
Once they arise, they will surely pass away—
their quieting is happiness. [1 = Uv 3]

What pleasure is there, what joy,
in the midst of this blazing fire?
You have plunged into the darkness—
why don't you seek out a lamp? [2 = Uv 4]

A potter turns clay into pots,
but in the end they all
shatter and crumble to dust:
like this is the life of mortals. [3 = Uv 12]

There's always a risk that well-ripened fruits
will fall from the tree any time.
Just so, there's always a risk
that once a man's been born
he may drop dead at any moment. [4 = Uv 11]

When the Fortunate One had said this, the monks rejoiced and praised the Fortunate One's words.

This completes the *Sūtra on Impermanence*.

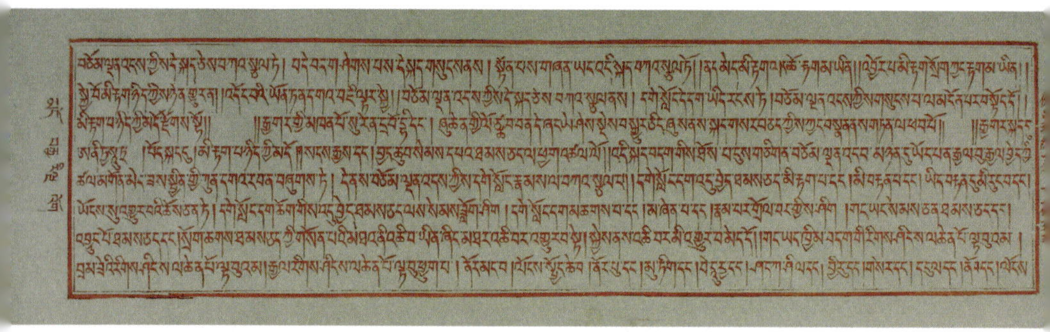

Figure 22. Beginning of the *Anityatāsūtra* from the Peking Kanjur (P 976, fol. 165b, starting in line 3).

7

King Pasenadi Asks about Aging and Death

Figure 23. King Prasenajit goes to pay homage to the Buddha. Bharhut stūpa pillar.

King Pasenadi Asks about Aging and Death

RĀJASUTTA. FROM THE *SAṂYUTTANIKĀYA*

[This is what I have heard. Once the Fortunate One was staying in Sāvatthī at the Jetavana in Anāthapiṇḍika's Garden.[181] At that time King Pasenadi Kosala went to visit the Fortunate One; upon arriving, he exchanged polite and pleasant greetings and sat to the side.][182] When he was seated, King Pasenadi Kosala put this question to the Fortunate One: "Once a person is born, does anything lie ahead apart from aging and death?"

"Great King, once a person is born, nothing lies ahead apart from aging and death.

"There are people who belong to established warrior families and are well off, wealthy, and prosperous, who have plenty of gold and silver, who have plenty of treasures and material possessions, who have plenty of wealth and grain—but even for them, now that they're born, nothing lies ahead apart from aging and death.

"There are people who belong to established brahman families [and are well off, wealthy, and prosperous, who have plenty of gold and silver, who have plenty of treasures and material possessions, who have plenty of wealth and grain—but even for them, now that they're born, nothing lies ahead apart from aging and death.][183]

"There are people who belong to established landowning families and are well off, wealthy, and prosperous, who have plenty of gold and silver, who have plenty of treasures and material possessions, who have plenty of wealth and grain—but even for them, now that they're born, nothing lies ahead apart from aging and death.

181. This translation is from Pāli and therefore uses the Pāli spellings Anāthapiṇḍika, Pasenadi, and Kosala.

182. Syāmaraṭṭha and PTS editions abbreviate the stock opening, given here in square brackets, to *sāvatthiyaṃ*.

183. This rest of the line is abbreviated by a | *pe* | that indicates "abbreviation."

"There are worthy arhants who have extinguished the corruptions, who have lived the life, who have done what is to be done, who have laid down the burden, who have realized their own goals, who have exhausted the bonds of existence, who have freed their minds by correct insight—but for them as well, their bodies will break up by natural law, will be cast aside by natural law."[184]

The Fortunate One said this. [When he had done so, then he, the Well-Farer, the Teacher, uttered these verses.][185]

> The royal chariots are gorgeous
> but even they wear out;
> in the same way, the body succumbs to old age.
> The Dhamma of the virtuous ones is sublime.
> They expound it to the righteous so that it doesn't age.[186] [Uv 29]

184. Pāli: *tesaṃ pāyaṃ kāyo bhedanadhammo nikkhepanadhammo*. Cp. *teṣām apy ayaṃ kāyo nikṣepadharmaḥ* in translation 5.

185. The formula is abbreviated. For the Pāli verse, see *Dhammapada* verse 151.

186. That is, the Dhamma of the teaching does not age because it is transmitted accurately and maintained by righteous people.

8

King Pasenadi's Grandmother Passes Away

Figure 24. Contemplation of the foul: Seated on a platform with almsbowl and water pot before him and sheltered by a parasol as he tells his rosary, a monk contemplates a corpse. Paper leporello manuscript, Wat Pak Khlong, Phetchaburi province, Thailand.

King Pasenadi's Grandmother Passes Away

Ayyikāsutta. From the *Saṃyuttanikāya*

The events take place at Sāvatthī.

[At that time, King Pasenadi Kosala went to see the Fortunate One early in the day. He came before him, paid respects to the Fortunate One, and sat to the side.][187] When the king had taken his seat, the Fortunate One asked him, "What, then, Great King? Where are you coming from so early in the morning?"[188]

"Good sir, my grandmother has just passed away. She was old, aged, burdened with years, advanced in life, come to the last stage, a hundred and twenty years old. My grandmother was dear and beloved to me. If it cost a precious elephant to arrange that my grandmother wouldn't die, I would give away a precious elephant to prevent her death. If it cost a precious horse to arrange that my grandmother wouldn't die, I would give up a precious horse to prevent her death. If it cost a prime village to arrange that my grandmother

187. This opening is abbreviated in the PTS and Syāmaraṭṭha editions of this sutta, but it is part of a standard opening used several times in the second and third chapters of the same *saṃyutta* and given in full on at least three occasions. I have added it from PTS pp. 89.27–29, 91.23–25, and 93.21–23.

188. There is disagreement about the meaning of *divādivassa*, translated here as "early in the day." The Tibetan equivalent *nang par sngar* regularly translates *kālyam eva*: see TSD vol. 7, p. 2813, s.v. *nang pa* (2). DoP, vol. 2, p. 396a, gives two meanings: (1) "in the middle of the day; rather late in the day" (commentaries: *majjhantikasamaye*, *majjhantike kale*), and (2) "early in the day?" PTSD, p. 322b, s.v. *divādivassa* (adv.), has "early in the day, at sunrise, at an early hour." Hartmann concludes that the Sanskrit "*divādivaṃ* must mean something like 'early in the morning' (Ger. *frühmorgen*), at least here. Pāli *divādivassa*, 'early in the day, at sunrise,' confirms it"; see "King Prasenajit Bemoans," p. 98, n. 51. In his translation of a similar question at *Udāna* 14.27, *kin nu tumhe upāsakā allavatthā allakesā idh'upasaṅkamantā divādivassā 'ti*, Ireland notes, "It was the custom to perform a ritual bathing and cleansing after a funeral. 'In the middle of the day' means at an unsuitable, wrong or unusual time to visit"; see Ireland, *The Udāna: Inspired Utterances of the Buddha*, p. 130, n. 4. For an explanation of the commentary, see Masefield, *The Udāna Commentary*, vol. 1, pp. 287–88.

wouldn't die, I would surrender a prime village to prevent her death. If it cost a country district to arrange that my grandmother wouldn't die, I would surrender a country district to prevent her death."

"All beings, Great King, are subject to death; death is their end. They can't get away from death."

"It is marvelous, sir, it is extraordinary, how aptly the Fortunate One expresses this:[189] 'All beings, Great King, are subject to death; death is their end. They can't get away from death.'"

"That's the way it is, Great King, that's the way it is. 'All beings are subject to death and death is their end. They can't get away from death.'

"To make a simile, O Great King: a potter fashions pots, and whether they are fired or whether they are unfired, all of them will break in the end; in the end each and every one of them will shatter.[190] In the same way, 'All beings, Great King, are subject to death, death is their end, and they can't get away from death.'"

All sentient beings will die—
death is indeed the end of life.
Their onward journey is mapped by their deeds
and their fruits, good or bad, as they may be:
the evil doers go to the hells, while those
who made merit go to the happy realms. [1][191]

Therefore do good.
Store up for your future lives.
Merits are a support for breathing beings
in the next world.

189. Cp. the *Rohitassasutta*, *Saṃyuttanikāya*, vol. 1, p. 61, trans. Gethin, *Sayings of the Buddha*, pp. 209–10, "It is remarkable, extraordinary, sir, how this is well put by the Blessed One when you say that. . . ."

190. The same simile comes at the end of the *Sūtra on Impermanence*.

191. *Udānavarga*, chap. 1, vv. 23–24; for a Mahāsāṃghika version, see Karashima, *Die Abhisamācārikā Dharmāḥ*, vol. 1, p. 34.

9

King Prasenajit's Grandmother Passes Away

Figure 25. Contemplation of the foul: Standing in the forest, a monk contemplates a corpse being devoured by birds and giant worms. Paper leporello manuscript, Wat Pak Khlong, Phetchaburi province, Thailand.

King Prasenajit's Grandmother Passes Away

FROM THE MŪLASARVĀSTIVĀDA *VINAYOTTARAGRANTHA* IN THE KANJUR

At Śrāvastī.[192] At that time King Prasenajit Kausala's dear, beloved grandmother had died. He had her body taken out and cremated. After performing the funeral rites, the king went to see the Fortunate One early in the day with his clothes and hair still wet. When he came before him, the king paid respect with his head at the Fortunate One's feet and sat down at the side. When King Prasenjit Kausala was seated, the Fortunate One addressed him.

"Where are you coming from just now, Great King, so early in the morning, your hair and clothes all wet?"

"Good sir, my dear, beloved grandmother just passed away. I had her body taken out and cremated and performed her funeral rites. That's why I've showed up here so early in the day, my hair and clothes all wet."

"Great King, was your grandmother very dear to you?"

"Good sir, she was very dear to me and very beloved. Good sir, if I could revive my grandmother by giving away a parade of elephants from my stables, I would give them away so that she could live. In the same way, [I would give away] a troop of horses, or [I would give away] a convoy of chariots [so that my grandmother could live]. If someone wanted half my kingdom to revive my grandmother, I would give away half my kingdom."

"Good sir, the passing of my grandmother, so dear and so beloved, leaves me so devastated by grief, so anguished, and so riven by sorrow. It came to me that it is marvelous, how well the Fortunate One expressed this, "The lives of all beings, all breathing things, and all creatures end in death. Death is the end of life. For one who is born, the end is death." It is marvelous how the Fortunate One has expressed this."

192. In this Mūlasarvāstivāda version, proper names are given in Sanskrit.

"That's the way it is, Great King, that's the way it is. The lives of all beings, all breathing things, and all creatures end in death. Death is the end of life. For one who is born, there is no escaping death.

"Great King, the people who belong to the great and exalted warrior families, the great and exalted brahman families, the great and exalted landowning families, will all die, in the end they will die. Once one is born there is no escaping death.

"Great King, a member of a dynastic line, an anointed king who rules over the multitudes, powerful and energetic, who dwells having subdued a patch of the wide earth—even for such as these, the end of life is death. For one who is born, there is no escaping death.

"Great King, there are those who relinquish the throne to dwell as sages, eating fruits that fall down by themselves, living on roots and fruits—even for them, the end of life is death. For one who is born, there is no escaping death.

"Great King, there are long-lived and beauteous deities, many of whom dwell in lofty palaces, but their destiny is to fall from those abodes.

"Great King, there are worthy arhats who have exhausted the corruptions, who have accomplished their tasks and laid down their burdens, attained their own goals and exhausted the bonds of existence, their minds liberated through correct understanding[193]—their bodies as well are characterized by decay.[194]

"Great King, there are pratyekabuddhas who live alone, solitary like the horn of a rhinoceros, who train themselves alone, who quiet themselves alone—their bodies as well are characterized by decay.

193. *Yang dag pa'i bka' la sems kyis rnam par grol ba*: I take this to represent *samyag-ājñā-vimukta*, assuming that the translators interpreted *ājñā* in the sense of commandment = *bka'* rather than the usual sense of wisdom, *shes pa*, as at *Mahāvyutpatti* § 1087, *yang dag pa'i shes pas sems shin tu rnam par grol ba*. For an elaborated formula for the arhats, see Lamotte, *Le Traité*, vol. 1, pp. 203–29.

194. Here and in the next two cases—all three for exalted beings—the text has *de dag gi lus kyang rje ba'i chos su 'gyur ro*. This should correspond to the Sanskrit—for example, in the *Anityatāsūtra* (translation 4), *ayaṃ kāyo nikṣepaṇadharmaḥ*—or to the Pāli *nikkhepa-dhamma*. *Rje ba* is an unusual verb and seems to be either an old or an honorific form. TSD, vol. 4, p. 1420a, *rje ba*, gives equivalents *parivarta, parivartana, parivartaka*. See *Encyclopaedic Tibetan-English Dictionary*, p. 1226a, *rje ba*, "to exchange, to change"; Jäschke, *Tibetan-English Dictionary*, p. 180b, "*rje ba*, to change, to shift . . . *tshe*, the life, i.e., to die Cs[oma]"; see also p. 491b, *zla ba* (4) *zlo ba* v. *zla ba* II, "undoubtedly a less correct spelling for *'da ba* . . . to pass, to get beyond . . . *mya-ngán-las zlá-ba* to deliver from pain."

"Great King, the tathāgatas, worthy arhats, correctly and fully awakened ones who possess the ten powers, who are fearless because they possess the four intrepidities, who are superb bulls, who roar the lion's roar—even bodies like theirs are characterized by decay.

"Great King, in this manner everything should be understood like this, that all beings, all living things, and all creatures die at the end of life."

For all beings the end of life is death,
after which they move on to the good or evil fruits
according to the deeds they've done:
evildoers plunge down to the hells
while those who've made merit
go to the happy realms.
As for those who've practiced the path,
they realize nirvāṇa without taints.
Buddhas, pratyekabuddhas, and Buddha's śrāvakas
all have to leave this body behind;
how much more so ordinary people? [1][195]

Then Prasenajit, king of Kausala, delighted by the Fortunate One's words, exhilarated, paid homage with his head to the Fortunate One's feet and took his leave.

195. *Udānavarga*, chap. 1, vv. 23–24; for a Mahāsāṃghika version, see Karashima, *Die Abhisamācārikā Dharmāḥ*, vol. 1, p. 34.

10

Plus ça change: From Araka to Gautama

Figure 26. Rabbits frolic; birds delight in bright blossoms. Paper leporello manuscript, Wat Pak Khlong, Phetchaburi province, Thailand.

Plus ça change: From Araka to Gautama

Arakasutta. From the *Book of the Sevens* in the *Aṅguttaranikāya*

"In ages long past, O monks, there was a teacher named Araka, a religious master[196] who was free of sense pleasures. The teacher Araka had hundreds of votaries, and this is what he taught them:

> Short, O brahmans, is human life: it is insignificant, trifling, fraught with much suffering and tribulation. You should understand this with wisdom. Do good and lead a pure life: once you are born you can't get away from death.
>
> Just as a drop of dew on the tip of a blade of grass will vanish as soon as the sun comes up and will not last long, in the same way, brahmans, human life is like a dewdrop: insignificant, trifling, fraught with much suffering and tribulation. You should understand this with wisdom. Do good and lead a pure life; once you're born you can't get away from death.
>
> Just as when rains pour down from the sky in thick drops, water bubbles form and quickly burst and don't last long: in the same way, brahmans, the life of humans is like a water bubble: insignificant, trifling, fraught with much suffering and tribulation. You should understand this with wisdom. Do good and lead a pure life; once you're born you can't get away from death.
>
> Just as a line drawn with a stick in water quickly vanishes and doesn't last long: in the same way, brahmans, the life of humans is a like a line drawn by a stick on water: insignificant, trifling, fraught with much suffering and tribulation. You should understand this

196. "Religious master" = *titthakara*: see glossary under *tīrthaṃkara*.

> with wisdom. Do good and lead a pure life; once you're born you can't get away from death.
>
> Just as, O brahmans, a river rushes down from the distant mountains and carries everything along with it; it doesn't pause for even an instant, a moment, or a second, but swirls on, moves on, sweeps on: in the same way, brahmans, the life of humans is like a mountain river, fleeting, insignificant, fraught with much suffering and tribulation. You should understand this with wisdom. Do good and lead a pure life; once you're born you can't get away from death.
>
> Just as, O brahmans, a healthy man forms a gob of spittle at the tip of his tongue and spits it out with the utmost ease, in the same way, brahmans, the life of humans is like gob of spittle: insignificant, trifling, fraught with much suffering and tribulation. You should understand this with wisdom. Do good and lead a pure life; once you're born you can't get away from death.
>
> Just as, O brahmans, if somebody drops a lump of meat into an iron pan that has been heated all day long it will quickly dissolve, in the same way, brahmans, human life is like a lump of meat: insignificant, trifling, fraught with much suffering and tribulation. You should understand this with wisdom. Do good and lead a pure life; once you're born you can't get away from death.
>
> Just as, O brahmans, when a cow slated for slaughter is led to the slaughter house, with each step it takes it draws nearer to death, just so human life is like a cow set to be slaughtered: insignificant, trifling, fraught with much suffering and tribulation. You should understand this with wisdom. Do good and lead a pure life; once you're born you can't get away from death.

"In those days, O monks, the life expectancy was sixty thousand years, and maidens were given in marriage when they were five hundred years old. At that time, O monks, humans had six hardships: cold and heat, hunger and thirst, defecation and urination.

"Even when humans had such long lifespans, even when they lived so long, even when they had so few hardships, the teacher Araka taught his votaries, 'Short, O brahmans, is human life: it is insignificant, trifling, fraught with much suffering and tribulation. You should understand this with wisdom.

Do good and lead a pure life; once you are born you can't get away from death.'

"At present, O monks, one might properly say, 'Short is human life: it is insignificant, trifling, fraught with much suffering and tribulation. You should understand this with wisdom. Do good and lead a pure life; once you are born you can't get away from death.'

"These days, O monks, a person who lives a long life lives a hundred years or a little bit more. A person who lives a hundred years lives for three hundred seasons—one hundred winters, one hundred hot seasons, one hundred rainy seasons. Living for three hundred seasons, one lives twelve hundred months—four hundred winter months, four hundred summer months, and four hundred rainy months. Living for twelve hundred months, one lives for 2,400 fortnights—eight hundred of winter, eight hundred of summer, eight hundred of rains. Living for 2,400 fortnights, one lives for 36,000 nights—12,000 in winter, 12,000 in summer, 12,000 in the rains. Living for 36,000 nights, one eats 72,000 meals—24,000 meals in winter, 24,000 meals in summer, and 24,000 meals during the season of rains, all this including breastfeeding and skipped meals. 'Skipped meals' means: you don't eat because you're upset, you don't eat because you're unhappy, you don't eat because you're sick, you don't eat because you're observing a fast, or you don't eat because you've got nothing to eat.

"I have calculated the age of a human who lives a hundred years, I have calculated the span of life, I have calculated the seasons, I have calculated the years, I have calculated the months, I have calculated the fortnights, I have calculated the nights, I have calculated the days, I have calculated the meals, and I have calculated the skipped meals.

"Out of compassion and sympathy I have done what can be done by a teacher who seeks the best for his sāvakas. See here these roots of trees, O monks, see these empty huts: Meditate, O monks, do not be negligent, lest you regret it later. This is my instruction for you all."

11

The Natural Laws of Existence

Figure 27. Squirrels gambol on the ground; birds alight on a graceful tree bright with blossoms. Paper leporello manuscript, Wat Pak Khlong, Phetchaburi province, Thailand.

The Natural Laws of Existence

Dhammaniyāmasutta. From the *Royal Chanting Book*

This is what I have heard. Once the Fortunate One was staying in Sāvatthī at Anāthapiṇḍika's Garden in the Jeta Grove. There the Fortunate One addressed the monks, "O monks." "Sir," the monks replied. The Fortunate One said: "'All compounded things are impermanent.' Whether tathāgatas arise or whether tathāgatas do not arise, this nature stands, this natural state endures, this is a fixed law of nature.[197] The tathāgata awakens to this and understands this; when he has realized and understood this, he announces it, he teaches, proclaims, establishes, discloses, analyzes, and elucidates it:[198] 'all compounded things are impermanent.'

"'All compounded things are unsatisfactory.' Whether tathāgatas arise or whether tathāgatas do not arise, this element stands, this natural state endures, this is a fixed law of nature. The tathāgata awakens to this and understands this; when he has realized and understood this, he announces it, he teaches, proclaims, establishes, discloses, analyzes, and elucidates it: 'All compounded things are unsatisfactory.'

"'All dhammas have no substance.' Whether tathāgatas arise or whether tathāgatas do not arise, this element stands, this natural state endures, this is a fixed law of nature. The tathāgata awakens to this and understands this; when he has realized and understood this, he announces it, he teaches, proclaims, establishes, discloses, analyzes, and elucidates it: 'All dhammas have no substance.'"

Thus spoke the Fortunate One. The monks rejoiced in the Fortunate One's words.

197. See Bodhi, *Reading the Buddha's Discourses*, pp. 315 (translation of the Pāli module as per *Paccayasutta*) and 316–17 (grammatical explanation).

198. For another translation of the string beginning with "The tathāgata awakens to this," see Bodhi, *Reading the Buddha's Discourses*, pp. 314–15.

12

Overcoming Fear through Recollection (1)
The Great Sūtra on the Banner's Crest

Figure 28. Indra rides his white elephant to defend his heaven against the asuras. Detail from a mural painting of the wheel of life, Trongsa Dzong, Bhutan.

Overcoming Fear through Recollection (1)
The Great Sūtra on the Banner's Crest
Dhvajāgra-mahāsūtra. From the Kanjur (P 958)

This is what I have heard. Once the Fortunate One was traveling in the land of Vṛji. When he reached Vaiśālī, he went to stay at the Gabled Hall on the banks of Monkey Pond.

At that time a big group of merchants from Vaiśālī was about to set out for the land of Takṣaśilā to trade. They heard that the Fortunate One was traveling through the land of Vṛji, that he had arrived in Vaiśālī, and that he was staying at the Gabled Hall on the banks of Monkey Pond. When they heard this, they gathered in groups and bunched together in bands and left the city [for the outskirts where the Buddha was staying]. When they came into the Fortunate One's presence, they gathered together, bowed their heads in homage at the Fortunate One's feet, and sat down to the side. Then the Fortunate One instructed, tutored, inspired, and gladdened the big group of merchants from Vaiśālī with talk about the Dharma.

After he had instructed, tutored, inspired, and gladdened them with talk about the Dharma on a variety of themes, the Fortunate One sat in silence. At this point the merchants stood up, arranged their robes over their left shoulders, and bowed before the Fortunate One with palms pressed together. They addressed the Fortunate One:

"We, good sir, are a party of merchants from Vaiśālī. We are about to leave for Takṣaśilā to trade, and we wish to invite the Fortunate One and the order of monks to tomorrow's midday meal."

The Fortunate One signaled his assent by remaining silent.

The merchants of Vaiśālī understood from the Fortunate One's silence that he had agreed, and after praising the Fortunate One's teaching and being satisfied with it, they bowed their heads in homage at the Fortunate One's feet and left his presence.

Then, that very night, the Vaiśālī merchants prepared pure and wholesome food and drink with great care. The next morning they got up early, spread out sitting mats, set out vessels for drinking water, and invited the Fortunate One with this invitation: "Good sir, the meal is ready and the hour approaches. May the Fortunate One know that the time has come."

Then that morning the Fortunate One donned his inner and outer robes and took his almsbowl in hand. Surrounded by a group of monks, at the head of the order of monks, he went to the dining pavilion of the Vaiśālī merchants. He arrived and sat down on the seat that had been prepared for him amidst the order of monks. The merchants of Vaiśālī bowed their heads in homage at the Fortunate One's feet and sat down at the side. The Fortunate One addessed them:

"O merchants: if fear, dread, or horripilation threaten to overwhelm you as you journey through the wilderness tracts, then call me to mind by these attributes:

> This Fortunate One is the Tathāgata. A worthy arhat is he, truly and fully awakened and perfect in knowledge and conduct. A well-farer is he, a knower of the world, an unsurpassed charioteer of people to be tamed, a teacher of gods and humans. He is an awakened one, a fortunate one.

"O merchants, the moment you recollect me by these attributes, all your fear, dread, and horripilation will vanish away.

"If you do not recollect me, then call to mind the Dharma by these attributes:

> The Dharma is well expounded by the Fortunate One: it is verifiable, it is free of defilement's fever,[199] it is not limited by time, it is progressive, it is beneficial here and now, and it is something that intelligent people realize by and for themselves.

199. "Free of defilement's fever," *nad med pa* = *nirjvara*. This epithet for the Dharma is found in Sarvāstivāda traditions but not in those of other schools: see Skilling, *Mahāsūtras*, vol. 2, pp. 414–18. The term is used in the inscription of Senavarman, a gold sheet found in a gilded minature stūpa made of schist found in Swat, Pakistan. See Jongeward et al., *Gandharan Buddhist Reliquaries*, § 24, l. 12, *advarasa*, trans. "without fever," p. 232 (see n. 74). For a related use of the term in Pāli, see Skilling, loc. cit., and Cone, DoP, vol. 2, p. 554b.

"O merchants, the moment you recollect the Dharma by these attributes, all your fear, dread, and horripilation will vanish away.

"If you do not recollect the Dharma, then call to mind the Order by these attributes:

> The Fortunate One's order of *śrāvakas* practices correctly, practices rightly, practices honestly, and practices appropriately; it accomplishes the practices in harmony with the teaching and fares according to the Dharma.
>
> In the Order there are those who progress towards realization of the fruit of stream-entry, and in the Order there are stream-enterers, those who have entered the stream.
>
> In the Order there are those who progress towards realization of the fruit of once-returner, and in the Order there are once-returners, those who will return to this world but one more time.
>
> In the Order there are those who progress towards realization of the fruit of nonreturner, and in the Order there are nonreturners, those who will never return again to this world.
>
> In the Order there are those who progress towards realization of the fruit of arhatship, and in the Order there are worthy arhats.
>
> These are the four pairs of persons, the eight individuals.
>
> The Fortunate One's order of śrāvakas is blessed with virtue, blessed with concentration, blessed with wisdom, blessed with liberation, blessed with the knowledge and vision of liberation.
>
> It is worthy of offerings, it is worthy of gifts, it is worthy of respectful salutation, it is worthy of veneration.
>
> It is an unsurpassed field of merit. It is a receptacle for the world's offerings.

"O merchants, the moment you recollect the Order by these attributes, all your fear, dread, and horripilation will vanish.

"In ages long past, O merchants, when the gods and the asuras were arrayed for battle, then Śakra, lord of the gods, addressed the gods of the Realm of the Thirty-Three:

> 'Dear sirs, if fear, dread, or horripilation threaten to overwhelm you when you enter the fray between the gods and the asuras, then call to mind my glorious Vaijayanta banner. The moment that you

> recollect my Vaijayanta banner, all your fear, dread, and horripilation will vanish away.
>
> 'If you do not recollect my banner, then call to mind the lofty banner of Īśāna, son of the gods.
>
> 'The moment you recollect Īśāna's lofty banner, all your fear, dread, and horripilation will vanish away.
>
> 'If you do not recollect the banner of Īśāna, son of the gods, then call to mind the lofty banner of Varuṇa, son of the gods.
>
> 'The moment you recollect Varuṇa's banner, all your fear, dread, and horripilation will vanish away.'

"O merchants, in just the same way, if fear, dread, or horripilation threaten to overwhelm you as you journey through the wilderness tracts, at that time you should recollect me by these attributes:

> This Fortunate One is the Tathāgata. A worthy arhat is he, truly and fully awakened and perfect in knowledge and conduct. A well-farer is he, a knower of the world, an unsurpassed charioteer of people to be tamed, a teacher of gods and humans. He is an awakened one, a fortunate one.

"O merchants, the moment you recollect me by these attributes, all your fear, dread, and horripilation will vanish.

"If you do not recollect me, then call to mind the Dharma by these attributes:

> The Dharma is well expounded by the Fortunate One: it is verifiable, it is free of defilement's fever, it is not limited by time, it is progressive, it is beneficial here and now, and it is something that intelligent people realize by and for themselves.

"O merchants, the moment you recollect the Dharma by these attributes, all your fear, dread, and horripilation will vanish away.

"If you do not recollect the Dharma, then call to mind the Order by these attributes:

> The Fortunate One's Order of śrāvakas practices correctly, practices rightly, practices honestly, and practices appropriately; it

> accomplishes the practices in harmony with the teaching and fares according to Dharma.
>
> In the Order there are those who progress towards realization of the fruit of stream-entry, and in the Order there are stream-enterers, those who have entered the stream.
>
> In the Order there are those who progress towards realization of the fruit of once-returner, and in the Order there are once-returners, those who will return to this world but one more time.
>
> In the Order there are those who progress towards realization of the fruit of nonreturner, and in the Order there are nonreturners, those who will never return again to this world.
>
> In the Order there are those who progress towards realization of the fruit of arhatship, and in the Order there are worthy arhats.
>
> These are the four pairs of persons, the eight individuals.
>
> The Fortunate One's order of śrāvakas is blessed with virtue, blessed with concentration, blessed with wisdom, blessed with liberation, blessed with the knowledge and vision of liberation.
>
> It is worthy of offerings, it is worthy of gifts, it is worthy of respectful salutation, it is worthy of veneration.
>
> It is an unsurpassed field of merit. It is a receptacle for the world's offerings.

"O merchants, the moment you recollect the Order by these attributes, all your fear, dread, and horripilation will vanish away."

When they saw that the Buddha and the order of monks were seated comfortably, the Vaiśālī merchants fed them well with their own hands and satisfied them with pure and wholesome food and drink.

When they had fed them well with their own hands and had satisfied them with a variety of pure and wholesome food and drink, when they saw that the Fortunate One had finished his meal, set his bowl aside, and washed his hands, they sat down on low seats in front of the Fortunate One to listen to the Dharma.

The Fortunate One celebrated the offerings of the merchants of Vaiśālī with these verses of rejoicing:

> O merchants, you have nourished
> the order of monks with food and drink:

knowing [the benefits] of giving,
the wise imitate the noble ones. [1][200]

The benediction for your benevolence is this:
through the offerings you've made, O merchants,
may your aims and all the goals to which
you rightfully aspire always succeed. [2]

May your two-legged ones be safe;
may your four-legged ones be safe.
may you be safe upon the way;
may you be safe as you return. [3][201]

Be safe by night, be safe by day,
be safe at midday noon:
be everywhere and ever safe—
may no evil befall you. [4]

When healthy seeds are sown
in fertile fields and when
ample rain falls down, then
ample will the harvest be— [5][202]

free of blight or pestilence,
it springs up perfectly
and ripens perfectly:
abundant will the harvest be. [6]

200. My translation of verse 1 is tentative—a guess. I do not understand lines *c* and *d* and their connection to the following verse.

201. Verses 3 and 4 also occur in *Mahāsūtra* 10, §§ 3.14, 15 and 6.14, 15, as well as in the *Mahāvastu* and the *Mahāmāyūrī*: see Skilling, *Mahāsūtras*, vol. 2, pp. 426–27. "Two-legged," "four-legged": *dvipada* and *catuṣpada*, bipeds and quadrupeds. Bipeds are the fellow merchants in the caravan and the merchants' families at home; quadrupeds are the pack animals in the caravan and the livestock at home.

202. Verses 5–8 and 10–12 have Pāli counterparts in the *Khettasutta* of the *Aṅguttaranikāya* (vol. 4, pp. 238–39).

So when good food is offered
to those blessed with virtue,
when this is done for blessing's sake,
then blessing is assured. [7]

Therefore, when a person who
aspires to blessing and aims at blessing
resorts to those blessed with wisdom,
blessings will this person gain. [8]

Therefore, giving birth to firm faith
in the Buddha unsurpassed,
in the Dharma, and in the Order,
one gains blessing of mind. [9]

Having gained blessing of mind (through faith)
in the one blessed with knowledge and conduct,[203]
one performs wholesome deeds—
this is the blessing of deeds. [10]

When you know the world as it is,
you gain the blessing of view;
when the blessing of noble [view] and vision is gained,
the intellect is blessed. [11]

When all faults are overcome,
the blessing of nirvāṇa is gained:
one who puts an end to all pain
accomplishes his aim. [12]

The Fortunate One then instructed, tutored, inspired, and gladdened the big group of merchants from Vaiśālī with talk about the Dharma. When he had instructed, tutored, inspired, and gladdened them with talk about the

203. In my edition of the Pāli (*Mahāsūtras*, vol. 1, p. 287, v. 5), the preferred reading should be *vijjācaraṇa-sampanne* rather than °*sampanno*. The locative suits the context and agrees with the Tibetan *rig dang zhabs su ldan pa la* = **vidyācaraṇa-sampanne*.

Dharma on a variety of themes, the Fortunate One got up from his seat and departed.

This completes the *Great Sūtra on the Banner's Crest*.

It was translated, revised, and established by the Indian preceptors Jinamitra and Prajñāvarman, the master editor and translator Bhante Ye shes sde, and others.

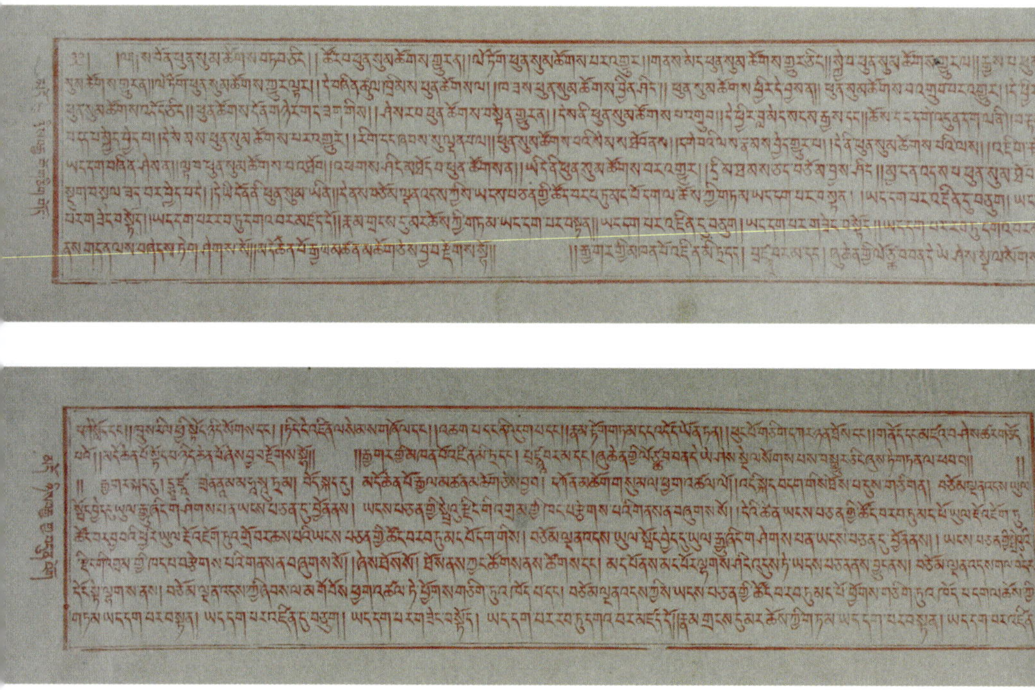

Figure 29. *Dhvajagra-mahāsūtra*, Peking Kanjur no. 958, first and last folios (folios 1 and 8).

13

Overcoming Fear through Recollection (2)
The Great Sūtra on the Banner's Crest

Figure 30. Indra (Jap. Taishakuten) mounted on his elephant, a *vajra* thunderbolt in his right hand. Tōji temple, Kyoto, Japan. Statue carved in 839 CE (Heian era), but head restored in a later period.

Overcoming Fear through Recollection (2)
The Great Sūtra on the Banner's Crest

Dhvajāgra-mahāsūtra. From the Kanjur (P 959)

This is what I have heard. Once the Fortunate One was staying in Śrāvastī, at Anāthapiṇḍada's Garden in Prince Jeta's Grove. At that time the Fortunate One addressed the monks:

"O monks: should fear, dread, or horripilation threaten to overwhelm you when you are staying in a wilderness, at the foot of a tree, or in a deserted building, then call me to mind by these attributes:

> This Fortunate One is the Tathāgata. A worthy arhat is he, truly and fully awakened and perfect in knowledge and conduct. A well-farer is he, a knower of the world, an unsurpassed charioteer of people to be tamed, a teacher of gods and humans. He is an awakened one, a fortunate One.

"The moment you recollect me by these attributes, all your fear, dread, and horripilation will vanish.

"In ages long past, O monks, when the gods and the asuras were arrayed for battle, then Śakra, lord of the gods, addressed the gods of the Realm of the Thirty-Three: 'Dear sirs, if fear, dread, or horripilation threaten to overwhelm you when you enter the fray between the gods and the asuras, then call to mind my glorious Vaijayanta banner. The moment that you recollect my Vaijayanta banner, all your fear, dread, and horripilation will vanish.'

"In the same way, O monks, if fear, dread, or horripilation threaten to overwhelm you when you are dwelling in a wilderness, at the foot of a tree, or in a deserted building, then call me to mind by these attributes:

> This Fortunate One is the Tathāgata. A worthy arhat is he, truly and fully awakened and perfect in knowledge and conduct. A

> well-farer is he, a knower of the world, an unsurpassed charioteer of people to be tamed, a teacher of gods and humans. He is an awakened one, a fortunate one.

The moment that you recollect me by these attributes, all your fear, dread, and horripilation will vanish away.

"O monks: Śakra, lord of the gods, still has desire, still has aversion, and still has delusion. He is not released from birth, aging, and sickness; he is not released from death, sorrow, and lamentation or from suffering, unhappiness, and agitation. He is fearful and frightened, he is afraid and quick to flee—and so at times he is afraid, fearful, and alarmed, and he takes flight.[204]

"O monks: despite the fact that Śakra, lord of the gods, still has desire, aversion, and delusion; despite the fact that he is not released from birth, aging, and sickness, or from death, sorrow, and lamentation, from suffering, unhappiness, and agitation; that he is fearful and frightened; that he is afraid and quick to flee—despite all this, the gods of the Realm of the Thirty-Three still heed his words with faith and follow his commands.

"I, O monks, am the Tathāgata, a worthy arhat, a truly and fully awakened one. I am free of desire, free of aversion, and free of delusion; I am released from birth, aging, and sickness, from death, sorrow, and lamentation, from suffering, unhappiness, and agitation. I am unafraid, fearless, unalarmed, and undaunted.[205]

"This, then, is what you need to do: heed my words and carry out my advice and instruction—for it is that of a tathāgata, a worthy arhat, a truly and fully awakened one who is free of desire, free of aversion, and free of delusion; who is liberated from birth, aging, and sickness, from death, sorrow, and lamentation, from suffering, unhappiness, and agitation; who is unafraid, fearless, unalarmed, and undaunted."

The Fortunate One said this. When he had done so, then he, the Well-Farer, the Teacher, uttered the following verses.

> When in the wilderness, at the foot of a tree,
> or in a deserted building, O monks!—

204. I follow Bhikkhu Bodhi in rendering *palāyin* (Tib. *'bros pa yod*) as "quick to flee."
205. Bhikkhu Bodhi translates the corresponding Pāli terms with positive values: "brave, courageous, bold, ready to stand his place."

bring to mind the Fully Awakened One,
the leader, best of men. [1]

If you don't recollect the Fully Awakened One,
the leader, best of men,
then bring to mind the Dharma,
best of all things free of desire.[206] [2]

If you don't recollect the Dharma,
best of all things free of desire,
then bring to mind the Order,
a field of merit unsurpassed. [3]

When like this you recollect
the Awakened One, the Dharma, and the Order,
then fear, dread, and horripilation
will vanish away, O monks. [4]

Many people run for refuge
to mountains and forest groves,
to parks and sacred trees,
driven there by fear. [5]

But these refuges are not secure;
these are not ultimate refuges.
If for refuge you resort to these,[207]
then from all ill you'll not be freed. [6]

One who has gone for refuge
to the Awakened One, Dharma, and Order
sees correctly with wisdom
the four truths of the noble ones: [7]

206. "Best of all things free of desire" is an epithet of the Dharma as nirvāṇa.
207. Here and in verse 9c the Tibetan uses the collective particle *dag* (for which, see Hahn, "On the Function and Origin of the Particle *dag*"), *skyabs de dag la*, where Sanskrit and Pāli have the singular. The collective must refer to the various refuges mentioned in verse 5.

ill and the arising of ill,
the actual cessation of ill,
and the noble eightfold path
that leads to happiness, to nirvāṇa. [8]

This is the best of all refuges;
this is the ultimate refuge.
If for refuge you resort to these,[208]
then from all ill you'll be freed. [9]

When the Fortunate One had said this, the monks rejoiced and praised the Fortunate One's words.

This completes the *Great Sūtra on the Banner's Crest.*

It was translated, edited, and established by the Indian preceptors Jinamitra and Prajñāvarman and the master editor and translator Bhante Ye shes sde and others.

208. See previous note at verse 6c. Here the collective embraces the classical three refuges and the insight into the four truths of verses 7–8.

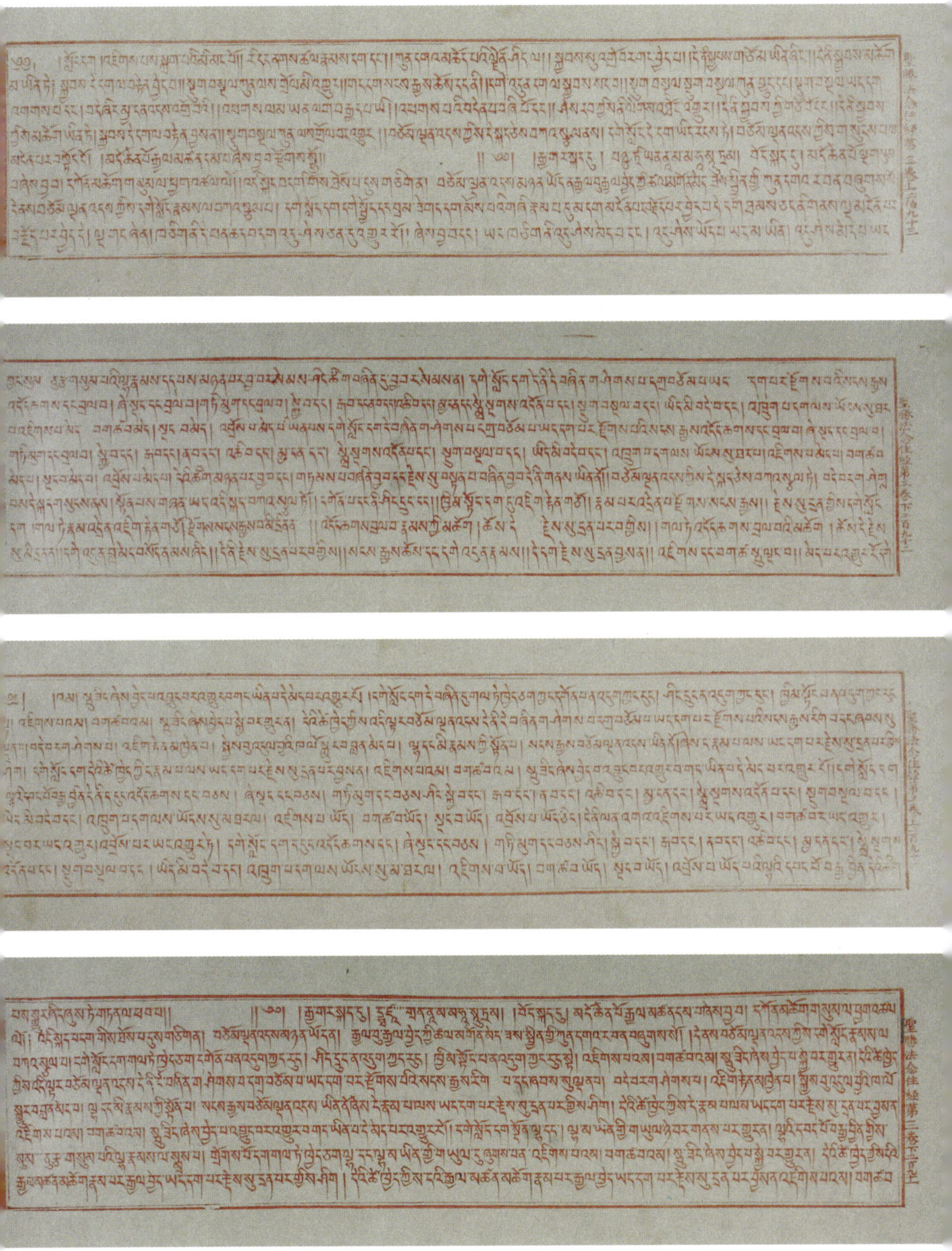

Figure 31. *Dhvajāgra-mahāsūtra*, Peking Kanjur no. 959, folios 1–4.

14

Overcoming Fear through Recollection (3)
The Protection of the Banner's Crest

สิบสองตำนาน

๑ ยัส์สานุส์สรเณนาปิ, อัน์ตลิก์เขปิ ปาณิโน.
ปติฏ์ฐมธิคัจ์ฉัน์ติ, ภูมิยํวิย สัพ์พทา.
สัพ์พุปัท์ทวชาลัม์หา, ยัก์ขโจราทิสัม์ภวา.
คณนา น จ มุต์ตานํ, ปริต์ตัน์ตัม์ภณาม เห.

" อรัญ์เญ รุก์ขมูเลวา, สุญ์ญาคาเรว ภิก์ขโว.
อนุส์สเรถ สัม์พุท์ธํ, ภยํ ตุม์หาก โน สิยา.
โน เจ พุท์ธํ สเรย์ยาถ, โลกเชฏ์ฐํ นราสภํ.
อถ ธัม์มํ สเรย์ยาถ, นิย์ยานิกํ สุเทสิตํ
โน เจ ธัม์มํ สเรย์ยาถ, นิย์ยานิกํ สุเทสิตํ.
อถ สํฆํ สเรย์ยาถ, ปุญ์ญัก์เขต์ตํ อนุต์ตรํ.
เอวัม์ พุท์ธํ สรัน์ตานํ, ธัม์มํ สํฆัญ์จ ภิก์ขโว.
ภยํวา ฉัม์ภิตัต์ตํวา, โลมหํโส น เหส์สติ. "

ธชัค์คปริต์ตํ ธชัค์คสุต์ตํ นิฏ์ฐิตํ ๔ นิคมคาถา

Figure 32. *Dhajaggaparitta*: invocatory stanzas and concluding verses. Pāli language in Thai script. From the nineteenth-century liturgical collection *Nangsue suatmon*.

Overcoming Fear through Recollection (3)
The Protection of the Banner's Crest

DHAJAGGAPARITTA. FROM THE *ROYAL CHANTING BOOK*[209]

Let us recite the protection
that whenever brought to mind
helps beings gain a foothold,
even changing empty space
into solid ground.
Let us intone the protection
that has saved so many people
from the snarls of all sorts of disasters—
from monsters, bandits, and much more—
that they are quite impossible to count.

This is what I have heard. Once the Fortunate One was staying in Sāvatthī in the Jeta Grove in Anāthapiṇḍika's Garden. At that time the Fortunate One addressed the monks, "O monks." "Sir," the monks responded. The Fortunate One then spoke.

"In ages long past, O monks, when the gods and the asuras were arrayed for battle, Sakka, lord of the gods, addressed the gods of the Realm of the Thirty-Three: 'Dear sirs, if fear, dread, or horripilation threaten to overwhelm you when you enter into the gods' battle, at that time you should gaze up at the crest of my banner. When you fix your gaze on my banner's crest, all your fear, dread, and horripilation will vanish.

209. *Suatmon chabab luang*, pp. 17–19. Cp. translation by Bodhi, *Connected Discourses*, pp. 319–21 (without the invocatory stanza, which belongs to the paritta version, not the sutta).

"'If you do not gaze at my banner, then fix your gaze on the banner of the king of the gods Pajāpati. When you fix your gaze on the banner of Pajāpati, king of the gods, all your fear, dread, and horripilation will vanish.

"'If you do not gaze at Pajāpati's banner, then fix your gaze on the banner of the king of the gods Varuṇa. When you fix your gaze on the banner of Varuṇa, king of the gods, all your fear, dread, and horripilation will vanish.

"'If you do not gaze at Varuṇa's banner, then fix your gaze on the banner of the king of the gods Īsāna. When you fix your gaze on the banner of Īsāna, king of the gods, all your fear, dread, and horripilation will vanish.'

"O monks: Gazing on the banner of Sakka, lord of the gods, gazing on banner of Pajāpati, king of the gods, gazing on the banner of Varuṇa, king of the gods, gazing on the banner of Īsāna, king of the gods, any fear, dread, and horripilation that you are experiencing might vanish—but on the other hand, it might not vanish. Why is this? Because Sakka, lord of the gods, still has desire, still has aversion, still has delusion; he is fearful and frightened, he is afraid and quick to take flight.

"O monks, this is what I say:

"Should fear, dread, or horripilation threaten to overwhelm you when you are dwelling in a wilderness, at the foot of a tree, or in a deserted building, then call me to mind:

> This Fortunate One is the Tathāgata. A worthy arhat is he, truly and fully awakened and perfect in knowledge and conduct. A well-farer is he, a knower of the world, an unsurpassed charioteer of people to be tamed, a teacher of gods and humans. He is an awakened one, a fortunate one.

"When you recollect me, all your fear, dread, and horripilation will vanish.

"If you do not recollect me, then call to mind the Dhamma:

> The Dhamma is well expounded by the Fortunate One; it is verifiable, it is not limited by time, it invites people to come and see it, it is progressive, and it is something to be realized directly by intelligent people.

"O monks, when you recollect the Dhamma, all your fear, dread, and horripilation will vanish.

"If you do not recollect the Dhamma, then call to mind the Order:

> The Fortunate One's Order of sāvakas practices correctly, the Fortunate One's Order of sāvakas practices forthrightly, the Fortunate One's Order of sāvakas practices wisely, the Fortunate One's Order of sāvakas practices rightly—this is to say, the four pairs of persons, the eight individuals.
>
> This is the Order of the Fortunate One's sāvakas: it is worthy of offerings, it is worthy of veneration, it is worthy of gifts, it is worthy of respectful salutation. It is an unsurpassed field of merit and a receptacle for the world's offerings.

"O monks, when you recollect the Order by these attributes, all your fear, dread, and horripilation will vanish.

"Why is this? The Tathāgata, the worthy Arhat, the truly and fully awakened Buddha, is free of desire, free of aversion, and free of delusion; he is not fearful or frightened, not afraid or quick to flee."

The Fortunate One said this. When he had done so, then he, the Well-Farer, the Teacher, uttered these verses.

> When in the wilderness, at the foot of a tree,
> or in a deserted building, O monks!—
> bring the Fully Awakened One to mind,
> and your fear will be no more. [1]
>
> If you do not recollect the Awakened One,
> best in the world, bull amongst men,
> then bring to mind the Dhamma,
> which is well taught and brings release. [2]
>
> If you do not recollect the Dhamma,
> which is well taught and brings release,
> then bring to mind the Order,
> a field of merit unsurpassed. [3]
>
> When in this way you recollect
> the Awakened One, Dharma, and Order,

then fear, dread, and horripilation
will be no more, O monks. [4]

This completes the Protection of the Banner's Crest, the *Sutta of the Banner's Crest*.

15

The Buddha's Visit to Vaiśālī

Figure 33. The goddess Mahāmantrānusāriṇī, one of the five protection goddesses. Painting on palm-leaf *Pañcarakṣā* manuscript.

The Buddha's Visit to Vaiśālī

VAIŚĀLĪPRAVEŚA-MAHĀSŪTRA. FROM THE KANJUR (P 978, 142, 714)[210]

This is what I have heard. Once the Fortunate One was staying at Nāḍikā at Kuñjikāvasatha. The Fortunate One said to long-lived Ānanda: "Ānanda, let us go to the city of Vaiśālī."

"Let it be so, sir," assented Ānanda.

Thereupon the Fortunate One set out for the land of Vṛji; when he reached the city of Vaiśālī, he went to stay at the Vaiśālī Āmrapālī Grove. There the Fortunate One addressed long-lived Ānanda:

> Go, Ānanda, to the city of Vaiśālī. When you arrive, press your foot down upon the threshold of the city gate and recite these spells and these verses.[211]
>
> *visarata | visarata | visarata | visarata |*
> *Disperse! Disperse! Disperse! Disperse!*

210. For my 1994 critical edition of the *Vaiśālīpraveśa* (published in Skilling, *Mahāsūtras*, vol. 1) I presented three recensions of the *Vaiśālīpraveśa*. Two are preserved in Tibetan translation: recension A, the *Mahāsūtra* properly speaking, based on twenty-four versions in the Sūtra and Tantra collections of Kanjurs, and recension B, a complete parallel from the *Chapter on Medicine* (*Bhaiṣajyavastu*, *Sman gyi gzhi*) of the Mūlasarvāstivādin Vinaya, based on eleven Kanjurs. A third recension, recension C, is preserved in the Sanskrit *Five Protections* manuscripts. My translation is based on recension A, the *Mahāsūtra*, with occasional reference to B and C. In this translation, I do not give the paragraph numbers; when they are referenced in the notes (§), they follow the edition.

211. The Tibetan translations (both recensions A and B) retain the Sanskrit. The Sanskrit is imbued with the power of the mantras, and I follow suit, even when a translation is possible. For the most part, the long mantras do not have lexical or conventional syntactic meanings: they are configurations of sounds and syllables that are meant to banish evil forces and bring benefits and blessings. Further, the mantras vary in the different versions.

The Buddha, filled with compassion for the world, proclaims:

At the behest of all buddhas,[212] at the behest of all pratyekabuddhas, at the behest of all worthy arhats, at the behest of all trainees, at the behest of all *śrāvakas*, at the behest all truth-speakers, at the behest of the Dharma, at the behest of Brahmā, at the behest of the pratyekabrahmās, at the behest of Kāmeśvara, at the behest of Indra, at the behest of the gods, at the behest of the lord of the asuras, at the behest of all asuras, at the behest of the asura attendants, at the behest of all spirits:

visarata | *visarata* | *visarata* | *visarata* |
Disperse! Disperse! Disperse! Disperse!

The Buddha, filled with compassion for the world, proclaims:

muñcata | *muñcata* |
Be gone! Be gone!

Do not tarry! May the epidemic cease!

nirgacchata | *nirgacchata* | *nirgacchata* | *nirgacchata* |
Depart! Depart! Depart! Depart!

The Buddha, the great god, the god of gods, the teacher of the gods, has arrived. The gods together with Indra, together with Brahmā, together with Īśāna, together with Prajāpati, and the four world guardians have all come. Many hundreds of thousands of gods, the lords of the asuras, and many hundreds of thousands of asuras have all come. Many hundreds of thousands of spirits who have faith in the Fortunate One have all come for the benefit of all sentient beings.

They have come to cause you [demons] great harm:

212. Behest: command, injunction, bidding.

nirgacchata | *nirgacchata* | *nirgacchata* | *nirgacchata* |
Depart! Depart! Depart! Depart!

Hie thee hence! May those amongst you who harbor harmful intentions be vanquished! May those amongst you who foster thoughts of love and wish no harm, who wish to join the protection, remain! May they join in the spirit![213]

The Buddha, filled with compassion for the world, proclaims:

sumu sumu | *sumu sumu* | *sumu* | [1]
sumuru | *sumuru* | *sumuru* | *sumuru* | *sumuru* | *sumuru* |
sumuru | [2]
muru | *muru* | *muru* | *muru* | *muru* | *muru* | *muru* | *muru* |
muru | [3]
miri | *miri* | *miri* | *miri* | *miri* | *miri* | *miri* | [4]
muru miri | *muru miri* | *muru miri* | *muru miri* |
muru miri | *muru miri* | *muru miri* | *muru miri* |
muru miri | *muru miri* | *muru miri* | *muru miri* | [5]
murū rī ti | [6]
ri ri ri ri ri ri | [7]
rī rī rī rī rī rī ti | [8]
miri | *miri* | *miri* | *miri* | *miri* | *miri* | *miri* | *miri ti* | [9]
hasi miri | [10]
mīrī ti | [11]
miti | *si sī si mī* | [12]
kaṅkara | *karakata* | [13]
kaṅkarā | *karakaca* | [14]
kaṅkarā | *kaṅkarā* | *kaṅkarā* | *kaṅkarā* | *kaṅkarā* |
kaṅkarā | *kaṅkarā* | *kaṅkarā* | *kaṅkarā* | *kaṅkarā* |
kaṅkarā | *kaṅkarā* | *kaṅkarā* | *kaṅkarā* | [15]
kaṅkarotī ti | [16]
kuriśo | *kaṅkara* | [17]
kaṅkariśe | [18]
ri ri ri ri ri ri | [19]

213. Recension A has here *lus* ("body," normally standing for Sanskrit *kāya*, *deha*, *ātmabhāva*, etc., which I do not understand in the context. I follow recension B, which has *dgongs pa*, equivalent to the *mata* of the Sanskrit (recension C).

ti re te phu svā | [20]
ripu ripu | *ripu ripu* | *ripu ripu* | *ripu* | [21]
nā thā nā nā thā tha | [22]
ripu ripu | *nā thā tha* | [23]
nirgacchata | [24]
ripu ripu | *nirgacchata* | [25]
palāyāta | *ripū ripū* | *palāyata* | [26]

The Buddha, who has compassion for the world, who seeks the benefit of all sentient beings, who dwells in love, who is endowed with compassion, who dwells in joy, who dwells in equanimity, has arrived:

kṣipraṃ nirgacchata svāhā |
Hie thee hence! Svāhā!

By the supreme knowledge of the Buddha and by the essence of the Dharma may these spell syllables, addressed to all gods and to all spirits, be efficacious! May these verses take effect![214]

He who has overcome and driven off[215]
the entanglements of craving,
his mind at peace, untroubled:[216]
may he bestow well-being upon you! [1]

214. I translate this paragraph (§ 2.10 in the edition [Skilling, *Mahāsūtras I*] after recension A. Recension C gives the section in verse, and in both recensions B and C the sense is somewhat different. Recension B: "The syllables of this successful spell of the knowledge of the essence of Dharma (**dharmatājñāna-mantrapada*)," and "accomplishment verses are spoken by the Buddha, the teacher of all gods (*sarvadeva*) and all spirits (*sarvabhūta*)."

215. "Driven off," Skt. *viralīkṛta*, Tib. B.3.1b, *'bral mdzad pa*, "separate from." Tib. A.3.1b: *dri ma med mdzad*, "made pure." *Vidhvasta* is translated by *rnam bcom* and *rnam par bcom nas*. *Mahāsāhasrapramardanī* (Iwamoto, p. 7.1) describes the driving away of the spirits with *śiṣṭā bhūtagaṇās trastā vikṣiptā* ***viralīkṛtāḥ***, *palāyante daśadiśo mahānādam udīrayan*. Tib., Otani no. 177, repr. vol. 7, Rgyud, *pha*, 67a7: *'byung po'i tshogs ni lhags pa rnams* || *sngangs 'krugs rod rod por gyur nas* || *phyogs bcur rab tu 'byer byed cing* || *sgra bo che yang sgrogs par byed* ||.

216. The two Tibetan translations and the Sanskrit differ on several points. A.3.1ab: ***gang la ser sna rnam chags pa*** || *rnam bcom dri ma med mdzad cing* ||; B.3.1ab: ***gangs gi sred pa'i chags pa dag*** || *rnam par bcom nas 'bral mdzad pa* ||; C.3.1ab: ***viśaktikā yasya tṛṣṇā vidhvastā viralīkṛtāḥ*** |, vl. *visaktikā*. Cp. *Udānavarga* (Bernhard, chap. 3, v. 15a: *tṛṣṇā . . . viṣaktikā*, chap. 29, v. 53a: *yasya jālinī viṣaktikā tṛṣṇā nāsti hi lokanāyinī*. Cp. Pāli *visattikā* (PTSD, p. 639a); Skt. C.3.1c, *śāntacitto hy* ***anāyāsaḥ***; Tib. A.3.1c = B.3.1c: *thugs shi* ***gnod pa mi mnga'*** *de*. Cp.

He, the guide who leads
beings on the path of liberation,
the teacher of all dharmas:
may he bestow well-being upon you! [2]

He, the teacher, resort of errant beings,
the one who brings great happiness[217]
for the benefit of all sentient beings:
may he bestow well-being upon you! [3]

The protector who, with loving heart,
watches over all worldly beings
at all times, as [a parent] an only child:
may he bestow well-being upon you! [4]

For all the sentient beings who circle
in the mill of life and death, he is the resort.
He is an island and a refuge:
may he bestow well-being upon you! [5]

He who has realized all dharmas,
he who is pure and free of deceit,
he whose speech is pure, he whose deeds are pure:
may he bestow well-being upon you! [6]

The great hero, by whose birth
blessings and benefits were accomplished
and a multitude of goals fulfilled:
may he bestow well-being upon you![218] [7]

Theragāthā v. 1008a: ***upasanto anāyāso*** (see Cone, DoP I 102b). I follow recension B and the Sanskrit because *tṛṣṇā/visaktikā* are attested in several sources.

217. I follow recensions B and C: *mang po* = *bahu*.

218. This verse is difficult. Like verses 6–12 of *Mahāsūtra* 5, it uses the word *saṃpadā*, here in connection with the birth of the Buddha (I am not certain whether there are any lists of such *sampadā*). One phrase, *don grub* = *siddhārtha*, is the same as the name given to the infant Bodhisatva; the phrase could be interpreted "Siddhārtha, who perfected the *sambhāra*." "Aims accomplished, the one who has perfected the requisite qualities."

Upon his very birth, this bountiful earth
with its thick forest mantle quivered,
and sentient creatures all rejoiced:
may he bestow well-being upon you![219] [8]

When he reached awakening's heart
the earth trembled six times,
and evil Māra despaired:
may he bestow well-being upon you![220] [9]

When he turned the wheel of Dharma,
he expounded the truths of the noble ones
and gained renown as a sage:
may he bestow well-being upon you![221] [10]

He, the charismatic one, routed
all the sectarians by means of the Dharma
and prevailed over all factions:
may he bestow well-being upon you![222] [11]

May the Buddha bring you blessings:
may the blessings of Śakra and the gods
and the blessings of all spirits
be bestowed upon you at all times. [12]

By the power of the Buddha's merits,
by the wish of all the gods,
may whatever goals you aim for
all be fulfilled this very day. [13]

May your two-legged ones be safe.
May your four-legged ones be safe.

219. Verses 7 and 8 refer to the birth of the Buddha and by association to Lumbinī.
220. Verse 9 has a double sense: it refers to the Buddha's awakening under the Bodhi Tree, and to Awakening's Heart in the sense of the "seat of awakening" (*bodhimaṇḍa*)—that is, Vajrāsana and, by association, Bodh Gayā.
221. Verse 10 refers to the first sermon and by association to the Deer Park at Vārāṇasī.
222. Verse 11 refers to the miracles performed at Śrāvastī. *Yid 'phrog*, found in both Tibetan versions, has no equivalent in recension C, which has *tāyin*.

May you be safe upon the way.
May you be safe upon return. [14]

Be safe by night, be safe by day,
be safe at midday noon.
Be everywhere and ever safe—
may no evil befall you.[223] [15]

Encircled by a thousand gods
the Buddha has arrived:
let all who harbor harmful thoughts disperse,
and may all compassionate souls remain. [16]

By virtue of the truthful speech
of buddhas and pratyekabuddhas,
of worthy arhats and trainees:
let all who harm the world
from this city be gone.[224] [17]

May all sentient beings, all breathing things,
all living beings, and all of you
know naught but happiness.
May all illness disappear;
may all see the auspicious;
may no evil whatsoever befall. [18]

All you beings gathered here,
whether you dwell upon this earth
or in the lofty heavens high:
may you ever and always treat
all humankind with love;
may you practice Dharma night and day.[225] [19]

223. Verses 14 and 15 occur in *Mahāsūtra* 5, § 6.3, 4.
224. Verses 16 and 17, which restate the prose of the beginning of the sūtra, are not included in recension C.
225. Verse 19 occurs at the end of *Mahāsūtra* 9.

When [the Fortunate One] had said this, long-lived Ānanda accepted the Fortunate One's command, replying, "So be it, good sir." He went to Vaiśālī, he set his foot down on the threshold of the city gate, and he recited these spell syllables and these verses.

> *visarata | visarata | visarata | visarata |*
> *Disperse! Disperse! Disperse! Disperse!*
>
> The Buddha, filled with compassion for the world, proclaims:
>
> At the behest of all buddhas, at the behest of all pratyekabuddhas, at the behest of all worthy arhats, at the behest of all trainees, at the behest of all *śrāvakas*, at the behest all truth-speakers, at the behest of the Dharma, at the behest of Brahmā, at the behest of the pratyekabrahmās, at the behest of Kāmeśvara, at the behest of Indra, at the behest of the gods, at the behest of the lord of the asuras, at the behest of all asuras, at the behest of the asura attendants, at the behest of all spirits:
>
> *visarata | visarata | visarata | visarata |*
> *Disperse! Disperse! Disperse! Disperse!*
>
> The Buddha, filled with compassion for the world, proclaims:
>
> *muñcata | muñcata |*
> *Be gone! Be gone!*
>
> Do not tarry! May the epidemic cease!
>
> *nirgacchata | nirgacchata | nirgacchata | nirgacchata |*
> *Depart! Depart! Depart! Depart!*
>
> The Buddha, the great god, the god of gods, the teacher of the gods, has arrived. The gods together with Indra, together with Brahmā, together with Īśāna, together with Prajāpati, and the four world guardians have all come. Many hundreds of thousands of gods, the lords of the asuras, and many hundreds of thousands of asuras have all come. Many hundreds of thousands of spirits who

have faith in the Fortunate One have all come for the benefit of all sentient beings.

They have come to cause you [demons] great harm:

nirgacchata | nirgacchata | nirgacchata | nirgacchata |
Depart! Depart! Depart! Depart!

Hie thee hence! May those amongst you who harbor harmful intentions be vanquished! May those amongst you who foster thoughts of love and wish no harm, who wish to join the protection, remain! May they join in the spirit!

The Buddha, filled with compassion for the world, proclaims:

sumu sumu | sumu sumu | sumu | [1]
sumuru | sumuru | sumuru | sumuru | sumuru | sumuru |
sumuru | [2]
muru | muru | muru | muru | muru | muru | muru | muru |
muru | [3]
miri | miri | miri | miri | miri | miri | miri | [4]
muru miri | muru miri | muru miri | muru miri | muru miri |
muru miri | muru miri | muru miri | muru miri |
muru miri |
muru miri | muru miri | [5]
murū rī ti | [6]
ri ri ri ri ri ri | [7]
rī rī rī rī rī rī ti | [8]
miri | miri | miri | miri | miri | miri | miri | miri ti | [9]
hasi miri | [10]
mīrī ti | [11]
miti | si sī si mī | [12]
kaṅkara | karakata | [13]
kaṅkarā | karakaca | [14]
kaṅkarā | kaṅkarā | kaṅkarā | kaṅkarā | kaṅkarā | kaṅkarā |
kaṅkarā | kaṅkarā | kaṅkarā | kaṅkarā | kaṅkarā |
kaṅkarā | kaṅkarā | kaṅkarā | [15]
kaṅkarotī ti | [16]

kuriśo | *kaṅkara* | [17]
kaṅkariśe | [18]
ri ri ri ri ri ri | [19]
ti re te phu svā | [20]
ripu ripu | *ripu ripu* | *ripu ripu* | *ripu* | [21]
nā thā nā nā thā tha | [22]
ripu ripu | *nā thā tha* | [23]
nirgacchata | [24]
ripu ripu | *nirgacchata* | [25]
palāyāta | *ripū ripū* | *palāyata* | [26]

The Buddha, who has compassion for the world, who seeks the benefit of all sentient beings, who dwells in love, who is endowed with compassion, who dwells in joy, who dwells in equanimity, has arrived:

kṣipraṃ nirgacchata svāhā |
Hie thee hence! Svāhā!

By the supreme knowledge of the Buddha and by the essence of the Dharma may these spell syllables, addressed to all gods and to all spirits, be efficacious! May these verses take effect!

He who has overcome and driven off
the entanglements of craving,
his mind at peace, untroubled:
may he bestow well-being upon you! [1]

He, the guide who leads
beings on the path of liberation,
the teacher of all dharmas:
may he bestow well-being upon you! [2]

He, the teacher, resort of errant beings,
the one who brings great happiness
for the benefit of all sentient beings:
may he bestow well-being upon you! [3]

The protector who, with loving heart,
watches over all worldly beings
at all times, as [a parent] an only child:
may he bestow well-being upon you! [4]

For all the sentient beings who circle
in the mill of life and death, he is the resort.
He is an island and a refuge:
may he bestow well-being upon you! [5]

He who has realized all dharmas,
he who is pure and free of deceit,
he whose speech is pure, he whose deeds are pure:
may he bestow well-being upon you! [6]

The great hero, by whose birth
blessings and benefits were accomplished
and a multitude of goals fulfilled:
may he bestow well-being upon you! [7]

Upon his very birth, this bountiful earth
with its thick forest mantle quivered,
and sentient creatures all rejoiced:
may he bestow well-being upon you! [8]

When he reached awakening's heart
the earth trembled six times,
and evil Māra despaired:
may he bestow well-being upon you! [9]

When he turned the wheel of Dharma,
he expounded the truths of the noble ones
and gained renown as a sage:
may he bestow well-being upon you! [10]

He, the charismatic one, routed
all the sectarians by means of the Dharma

and prevailed over all factions:
may he bestow well-being upon you! [11]

May the Buddha bring you blessings:
may the blessings of Śakra and the gods
and the blessings of all spirits
be bestowed upon you at all times. [12]

By the power of the Buddha's merits,
by the wish of all the gods,
may whatever goals you aim for
all be fulfilled this very day. [13]

May your two-legged ones be safe.
May your four-legged ones be safe.
May you be safe upon the way.
May you be safe upon return. [14]

Be safe by night, be safe by day,
be safe at midday noon.
Be everywhere and ever safe—
may no evil befall you. [15]

Encircled by a thousand gods
the Buddha has arrived:
let all who harbor harmful thoughts disperse,
and may all compassionate souls remain. [16]

By virtue of the truthful speech
of buddhas and pratyekabuddhas,
of worthy arhats and trainees:
let all who harm the world
from this city be gone. [17]

May all sentient beings, all breathing things,
all living beings, and all of you
know naught but happiness.
May all illness disappear;

may all see the auspicious;
may no evil whatsoever befall. [18]

All you beings gathered here,
whether you dwell upon this earth
or in the lofty heavens high:
may you ever and always treat
all humankind with love;
may you practice Dharma night and day. [19]

So Ānanda spoke. There and then, by the buddha power of the buddhas, the fortunate ones, and by the divine power of the gods, the epidemic ended.[226]

This completes the *Exalted Great Discourse on the Buddha's Visit to Vaiśālī.*

It was translated, revised, and established by the Indian preceptor Surendrabodhi and the master editor and translator Bhante Ye shes sde.

226. This concluding prose statement occurs only in recensions B and C: it is not given in A (the Mahāsūtra proper) or the Chinese Vinaya. I translate it after recension B.

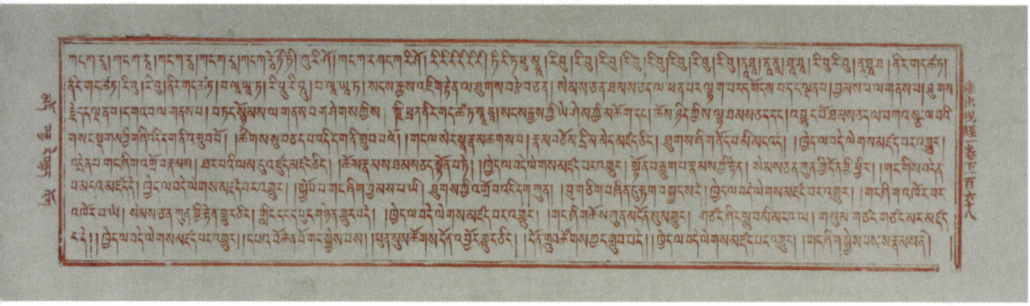

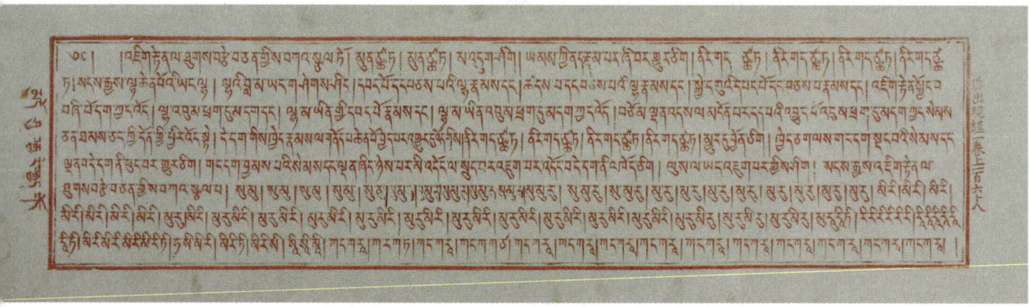

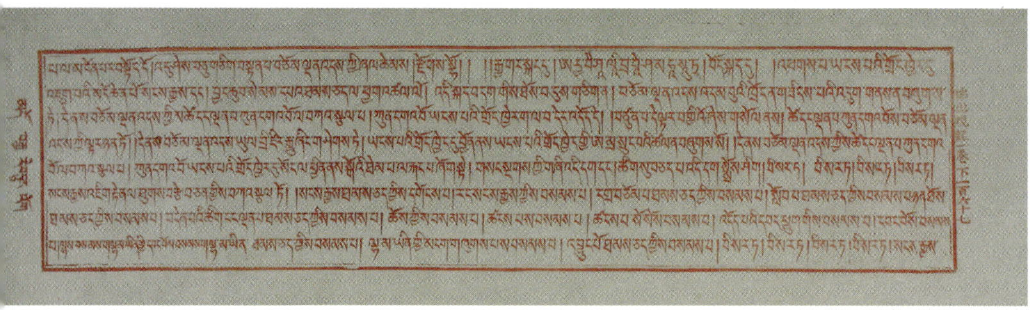

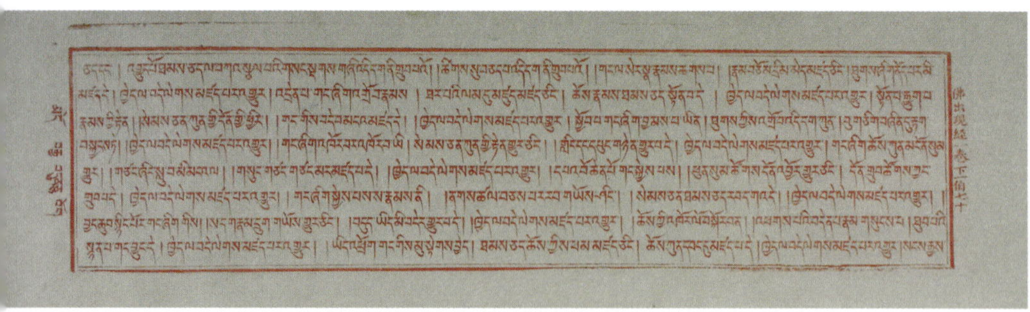

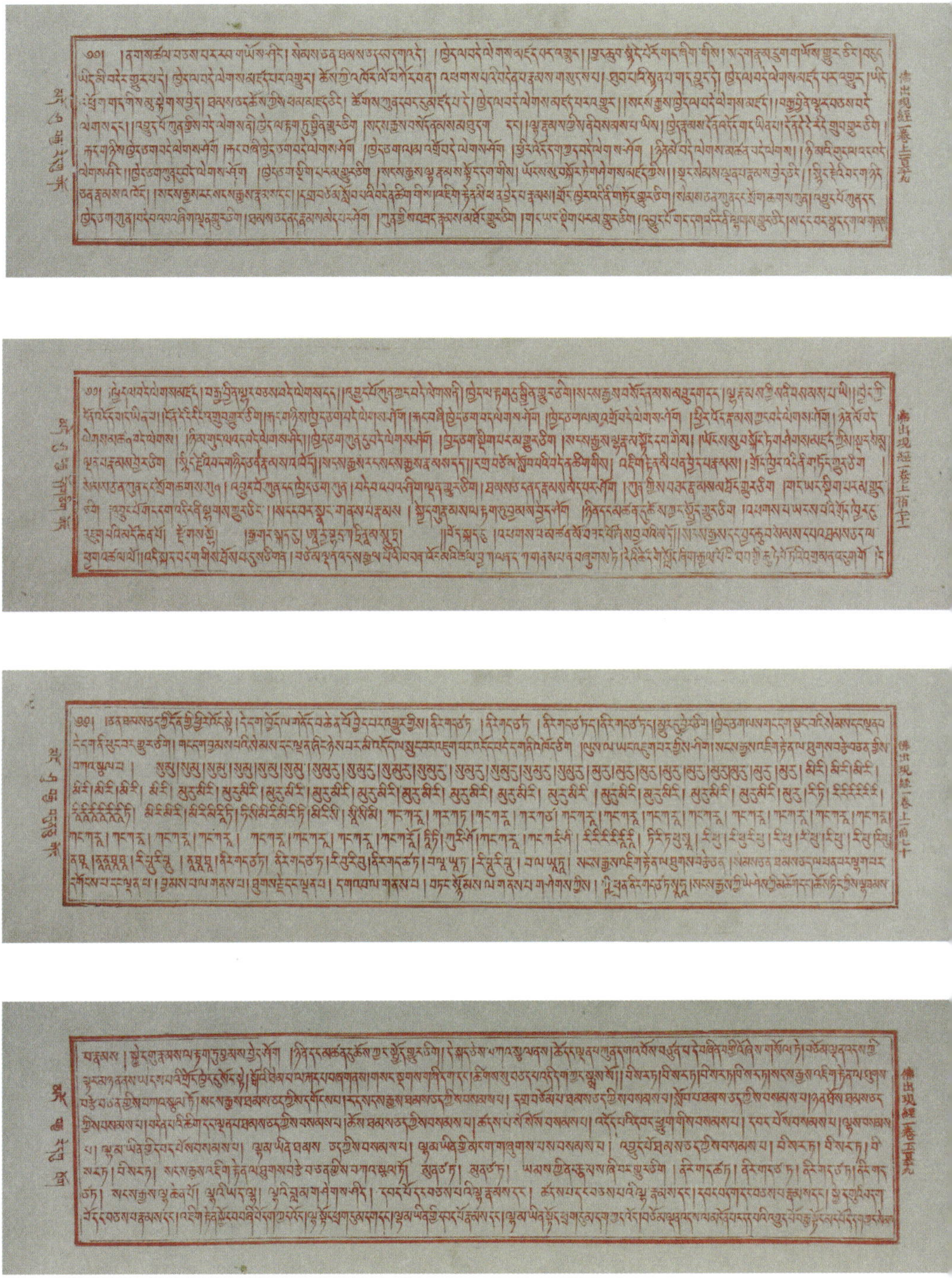

Figure 34. *Vaiśālīpraveśa* from Peking Kanjur no. 978.

16
Verses for Well-Being

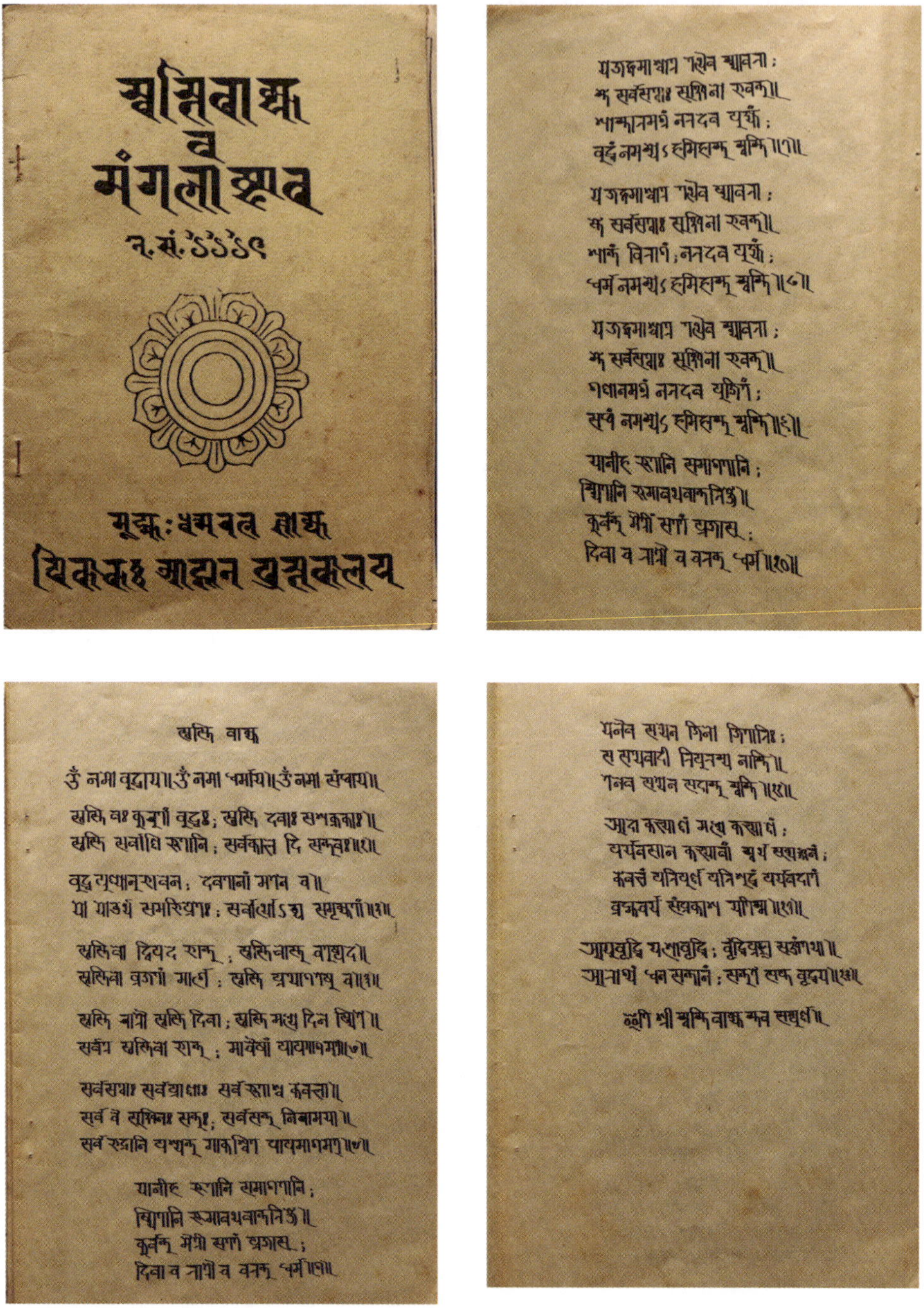

Figure 35. Handwritten text of *Svastivākya* in Pracalita script by Dharmaratna Śākya.

Verses for Well-Being

A Svastivākya Sanskrit Liturgy from Nepal

Oṃ! Homage to the Buddha.
Oṃ! Homage to the Dharma.
Oṃ! Homage to the Saṅgha.

May the Buddha bring you blessings.
May the blessings of Śakra and the gods
and the blessings of all spirits
be with you at all times. [1]

By the power of the Buddha's merits,
by the wish of all the gods,
may whatever goals you aim for
all be fulfilled this very day. [2]

May your two-legged ones be safe.
May your four-legged ones be safe.
May you be safe upon the way.
May you be safe as you return. [3]

Be safe by night, be safe by day,
be safe at midday noon.
Be everywhere and ever safe—
may no evil befall you. [4]

May all sentient beings,
may all breathing things,
may all living creatures,
may every one of you:

may all of you be happy,
may all of you be healthy,
may you all see good things.
May no evil ever
befall you at all. [5]

All you beings gathered here,
whether you dwell upon this earth
or dwell in lofty heavens high,
may you ever and always treat
all of humankind with love.
May you practice the Dharma
by night and by day. [6]

May all beings be happy
whether they move about
or whether they stand still.
Homage I pay to the very best teacher
revered by humans and gods—
may there be well-being here. [7]

May all beings be happy
whether they move around
or whether they stand still.
Homage I pay to the Dharma,
peaceful and free of passion,
revered by humans and gods—
may there be well-being here. [8]

May all beings be happy
whether they move about
or whether they stand still.
Homage I pay to the Order,
the very best of communities,
revered by humans and gods—
may there be well-being here. [9]

All you beings gathered here,
whether you dwell upon this earth
or dwell in lofty heavens high,
may you ever and always treat
all of humankind with love.
May you practice the Dharma
by night and by day. [10]

That truth by which the Conqueror vanquished his foes,
the speaker of truth, who has no enemies—
by that truth may there always be well-being. [11]

Good from the very start,
good in middle, and good till the end;
good in meaning and good in letter;
entire, complete, perfect, and pure:
so the Buddha proclaimed
the holy spiritual life. [12]

May your span of life increase.
May your good name grow.
May your wisdom wax bright.
May your joys all multiply.
May your health and wealth flourish.
May your progeny all prosper.
May these seven things thrive for you. [13]

Complete are the *Glorious Verses of Praise for Well-Being.*

17

The Wheel-Turning King's Treasures and the Seven Awakening Factors

Figure 36. A *cakravartin*, wheel-turning emperor, surrounded by his seven "precious treasures." Pillar medallion from Phanigiri archaeological site, Telangana, India.

The Wheel-Turning King's Treasures and the Seven Awakening Factors

From Śamathadeva's *Upāyikā-ṭīkā* in the Tanjur (P 5595)

At Śrāvastī, the Fortunate One addressed the monks: "O monks, when a wheel-turning king arises in the world, seven precious treasures arise in the world as well. What seven are these? They are the wheel treasure, the elephant treasure, the horse treasure, the gem treasure, the landholder treasure, and the female treasure, with the commanding general as the seventh. O monks, when a wheel-turning king arises in the world, these seven precious treasures arise in the world as well.

"O monks, in the same way, when tathāgatas, worthy arhats, fully and perfectly awakened buddhas arise in the world, seven awakening factors arise in the world as well. What are these seven awakening factors? They are the awakening factor of mindfulness, the awakening factor of scrutiny of dharmas, of energy, of joy, of tranquility, and of equanimity, with the awakening factor of concentration as the seventh. When tathāgatas, worthy arhats, fully and perfectly awakened buddhas arise in the world, these seven awakening factors arise in the world as well."

Figure 37. Tibetan folio of *Cakravartinsūtra* as cited in Tibetan translation in Śamathadeva's *Indispensable Commentary on the Treasury of Abhidharma*. From Peking Tanjur no. 5595.

18

Protective Verses: The Seven Awakening Factors

Figure 38. *Bojjhaṅgaparitta*. The miniatures depict monks chanting on raised benches. In the foreground are candles and incense set up as ritual offerings. Paper leporello no. 005, Wat Manisathit Kapittharam, Uthai Thani, Thailand.

Protective Verses: The Seven Awakening Factors

Bojjhaṅgaparitta. From the *Royal Chanting Book*

These seven dhammas, the awakening factors,
crush Māra's hosts. They're the best way there is
to free oneself from the three worlds.
When they're understood, then beings realize
the unborn, ageless, and illness-free state,
the undying, the fearless.

In order to destroy all the ills
of beings who circle in rebirth's cycle,
let us chant the remedial verses,
the *manta* of the awakening factors[227]
that has such virtues and more
and is a bundle of many good things.

Mindfulness counts as an awakening factor,
as does scrutiny of dhammas.
Energy, joy, and tranquility
are awakening factors as well, as are
the awakening factor of concentration
and that of equanimity.

These seven are rightly expounded
by the All-Seeing One, the Sage;

227. I follow the text, which uses the Pāli form *manta*, related to the Sanskrit term *mantra*, which has become a loanword in English and other European languages.

developed and cultivated they lead on
to direct knowledge, nibbāna, and awakening.
Through the proclamation of this truth
may you be well in every way.

Once upon a time the Protector
saw that Moggallāna and Kassapa
were sick and suffering, and he
expounded the seven awakening factors.
The two monks delighted in this, and
the very moment that they did so
they recovered from their ailments.
Through the proclamation of this truth,
may you be well in every way.

Once when the King of the Dhamma
himself was tormented by illness,
Cunda, the senior monk,
recited these self-same verses
with reverence and care.
In this the Dhamma King rejoiced, and
the very moment that he did so,
he recovered from that illness.
Through the proclamation of this truth,
may you be well in every way.

The illnesses of the three
great sages were all cured,
never to come back again.
Just as when the holy path
eradicates defilements for all time:
through the proclamation of this truth,
may you be well in every way.

๑ สํสาเร สํสรนฺตานํ, สพฺพทุกฺขวินาสเน
สตฺต ธมฺเม จ โพชฺฌงฺเค, มารเสนปฺปมทฺทิโน.
พุชฺฌิตฺวา เยปิเม สตฺตา, ติภวามุตฺตกุตฺตมา.
อชาตึ อชราพฺยาธึ, อมตํ นิพฺภยํ คตา.
เอวมาทิคุณูเปตํ, อเนกคุณสงฺคหํ.
โอสถญฺจ อิมํ มนฺตํ, โพชฺฌงฺคนฺตมฺภณาม เห.

สิบสองตำนาน

ทสมํ โพชฺฌงฺคปริตฺตํ

๑ โพชฺฌงฺโค สติสงฺขาโต, ธมฺมานํ วิจโย ตถา.
วิริยมฺปีติปสฺสทฺธิ, โพชฺฌงฺคา จ ตถาปเร.
สมาธุเปกฺขโพชฺฌงฺคา, สตฺเตเต สพฺพทสฺสินา
มุนินา สมฺมทกฺขาตา, ภาวิตา พหุลีกตา.
สํวตฺตนฺติ อภิญฺญาย, นิพฺพานาย จ โพธิยา.
เอเตน สจฺจวชฺเชน, โสตฺถิ เต โหตุ สพฺพทา.
เอกสฺมึ สมเย นาโถ, โมคฺคลฺลานญฺจ กสฺสป.
คิลาเน ทุกฺขิเต ทิสฺวา, โพชฺฌงฺเค สตฺต เทสยิ.
เต จ ตํ อภินนฺทิตฺวา, โรคา มุจฺจิสุ ตํขเณ.
เอเตน สจฺจวชฺเชน, โสตฺถิ เต โหตุ สพฺพทา.
เอกทา ธมฺมราชาปิ, เคลญฺเญนาภิปีฬิโต.
จุนฺทตฺเถเรน ตญฺเญว, ภณาเปตฺวาน สาทรํ.
สมฺโมทิตฺวา จ อาพาธา, ตมฺหา วุฏฺฐาสิ ฐานโส.
เอเตน สจฺจวชฺเชน, โสตฺถิ เต โหตุ สพฺพทา.
ปหีนา เต จ อาพาธา, ติณฺณนฺนมฺปิ มเหสินํ.
มคฺคาหตกิเลสาว, ปตฺตานุปฺปตฺติธมฺมตํ.
เอเตน สจฺจวชฺเชน, โสตฺถิ เต โหตุ สพฺพทา.

โพชฺฌงฺคปริตฺตํ นิฏฺฐิตํ ๗ คาถากึ่ง

Figure 39. *Bojjhaṅgaparitta*. Pāli text with invocatory stanzas in Thai script. From *Nangsue suatmon*.

19
Blessings and Protective Verses

Figure 40. A handsome pair of *kilen* (กิเลน) strut elegantly, and birds flutter around fresh crimson blossoms. *Kilen* are mythical creatures from China, where they are known as *qilin* 麒; in Japanese *kirin*. At an undetermined point, some of them migrated and settled in Thailand. Paper leporello manuscript, Wat Pak Khlong, Phetchaburi province, Thailand.

Blessings and Protective Verses

Yandunnimittam avamaṅgalañ ca.
From the *Royal Chanting Book*

Unlucky signs, inauspicious portents,
the ominous screeching of birds,
evil stars, unsettling dreams,
and all things unwelcome:
by the power of the buddhas
may they all be eliminated.

Unlucky signs, inauspicious portents,
the ominous screeching of birds,
evil stars, unsettling dreams,
and all things unwelcome:
by the power of the Dhamma
may they all be eliminated.

Unlucky signs, inauspicious portents,
the ominous screeching of birds,
evil stars, unsettling dreams,
and all things unwelcome:
by the power of the Saṅgha
may they all be eliminated.

Indeed, may all beings
who suffer be free from suffering,
who fear be free from fear,
who sorrow be free from sorrow.

Insofar as we've
accomplished the blessing of merits,
may all the gods rejoice.
To succeed in all good things,
be firm in faith and give gifts,
cleave fast to virtue at all times,
rejoice in mental culture,
and fare on to the godly realms.

The powers possessed by all buddhas,
the power of paccekabuddhas,
the ardor of the arhats:
through these do I bind
protection all around.

Just as rivers brimming with water
fill up the oceans deep,
even so does that which we give here
benefit those who've passed away.

Whatever you wish, whatever you aim for,
may it all quickly succeed.
May all your aspirations be fulfilled
like the moon on the fifteenth day,
like a bright and luminous gem.

May all calamities be averted.
May every illness be destroyed.
May no dangers befall you.
May you be happy and may you live long.

May all calamities be averted.
May every illness be destroyed.
May no dangers befall you.
May you be happy and may you live long.

May all calamities be averted.
May every illness be destroyed.
May no dangers befall you.
May you be happy and may you live long.

For one of respectful nature who
constantly honors the worthy,
four dhammas thrive:
long life and beauty,
happiness and strength.

May all good things come to be.
May all the gods stand guard.
By all the Buddha's power,
may you always know well-being.

May all good things come to be.
May all the gods stand guard.
By all the Dhamma's power,
may you always know well-being.

May all good things come to be.
May all the gods stand guard.
By all the Saṅgha's power
may you always know well-being.

ยนฺทุนฺนิมิตฺตํ อวมงฺคลญฺจ
โย จามนาโป สกุณสฺส สทฺโท
ปาปคฺคโห ทุสฺสุปินํ อกนฺตํ
พุทฺธานุภาเวน วินาสเมนฺตุ.
ยนฺทุนฺนิมิตฺตํ อวมงฺคลญฺจ
โย จามนาโป สกุณสฺส สทฺโท
ปาปคฺคโห ทุสฺสุปินํ อกนฺตํ
ธมฺมานุภาเวน วินาสเมนฺตุ.
ยนฺทุนฺนิมิตฺตํ อวมงฺคลญฺจ
โย จามนาโป สกุณสฺส สทฺโท
ปาปคฺคโห ทุสฺสุปินํ อกนฺตํ
สงฺฆานุภาเวน วินาสเมนฺตุ.

๓ คาถา

ทุกฺขปฺปตฺตา จ นิทฺทุกฺขา ภยปฺปตฺตา จ นิพฺภยา
โสกปฺปตฺตา จ นิสฺโสกา โหนฺตุ สพฺเพปิ ปาณิโน
เอตฺตาวตา จ อมฺเหหิ สมฺภตํ ปุญฺญสมฺปทํ
สพฺเพ เทวานุโมทนฺตุ สพฺพสมฺปตฺติสิทฺธิยา
ทานํ ททนฺตุ สทฺธาย สีลํ รกฺขนฺตุ สพฺพทา
ภาวนาภิรตา โหนฺตุ คจฺฉนฺตุ เทวตาคตา.

สพฺเพ พุทฺธา พลปฺปตฺตา ปจฺเจกานญฺจ ยํ พลํ
อรหนฺตานญฺจ เตเชน รกฺขํ พนฺธามิ สพฺพโส.

๔ คาถา

Figure 41. “Unlucky signs, inauspicious portents,” and other chants from the seven protections in the *Royal Chanting Book*. Pāli language in contemporary formal typeface for printed Pāli.

20
Envoi: A Formula of Causation

Figure 42. The bronze-cast crowned and adorned Buddha (held at National Palace Museum, Beijing) sits erect upon a double-lotus throne. His right hand reaches to touch the earth in the *bhūmisparśa mudrā*. His hair is arranged in a high *jāṭā* (chignon), and his crown, ear ornaments, and necklace are inset with turquoise.

Envoi: A Formula of Causation

YE DHAṂMĀ HETUPRABHAVĀ. FROM A PRAKRIT INSCRIPTION

Text

bhagavā āvuso paṭiccasamupādadhaṃmaṃ deseti paṭiccasamupānaṃ ca dhaṃmānaṃ yo nirodho |

> *ye dhaṃmā hetu prabhavā tesaṃ hetuṃ tathāgato avaca*
> *tesaṃ ca yo nirodha evaṃ vādī mahā śramano* ||

Translation

The Fortunate One, sir, teaches the nature of dependent arising and the cessation of dependently arisen dhammas.

> The Tathāgata teaches the cause
> of dhammas that arise from causes
> as well as their cessation.
> Such is the teaching of the Great Ascetic.

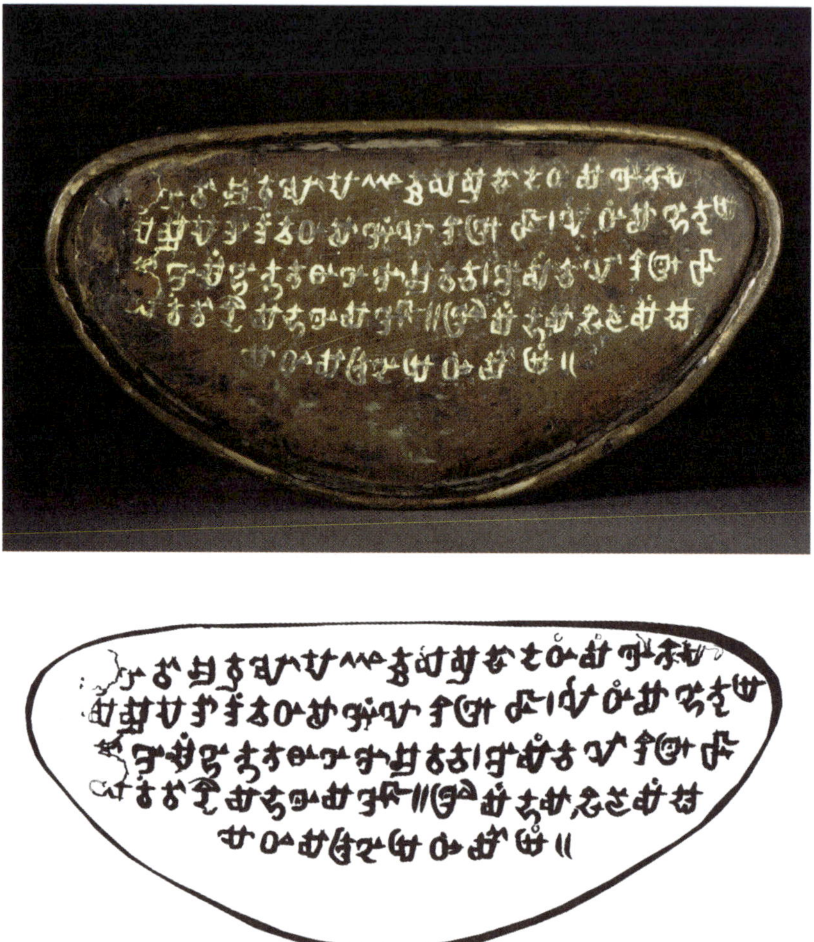

Figure 43. Bottom plate of figure 42 inscribed with *ye dharmā* verse in Prakrit language in Bhaikṣukī/Saindhavī script.

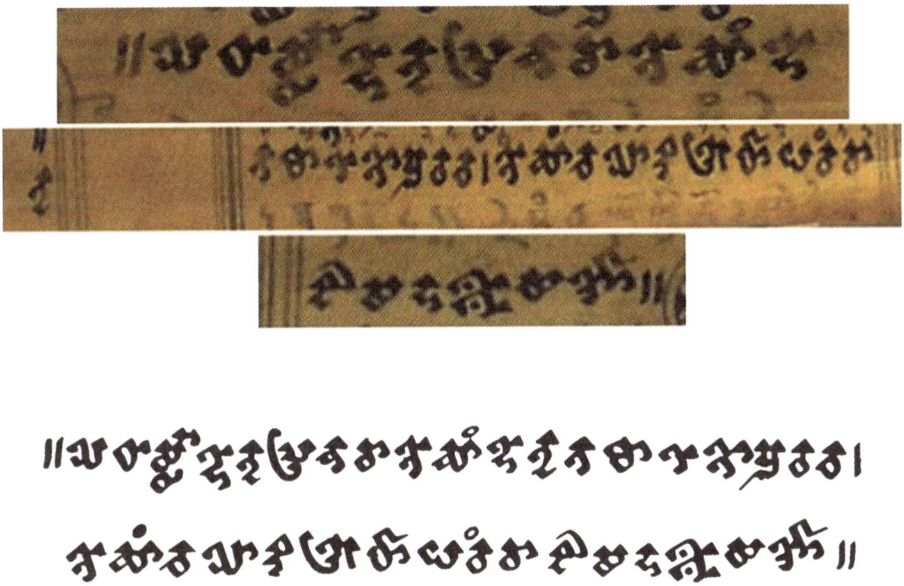

Figure 44. *Ye dharmā* stanza in Prakrit language in Bhaikṣukī/Saindhavī script from the colophon of a palm-leaf manuscript of Saṅghatrāta's *Abhidharmasamuccaya* (fol. 13v8–14r1).

Part III

Textual Studies: Notes on the Translations

EACH OF THE TEXTS translated here has its own unique history. For four or five centuries or more, during the oral period, the texts did not—and could not—leave any material traces. We cannot get even a glimpse of their original faces or of their peregrinations through the unwritten archives of orality. Because the earliest, and even early or middle, Āgamas and Piṭakas do not survive, and their first preserved representatives are late by any standard, it is impossible to determine when and in what shape—in what dialect, in what script—the texts emerged into the written record. Theravaṃsa chronicles report that their Tipiṭaka and commentaries were written down in the fourth century BE (first century BCE). Manuscripts must have been produced in increasing numbers in the centuries that followed, but the earliest Pāli manuscripts that survive today were not produced until at best twenty-one or twenty-two centuries after the Buddha (sixteenth to seventeenth centuries CE), the majority in the twenty-fourth century (nineteenth century CE). Printed editions date to the twenty-fourth and twenty-fifth centuries (late nineteenth and then the twentieth and twenty-first centuries CE). For the Pāli texts quoted in this volume, I use editions of the Pali Text Society (various dates, from the final decades of the nineteenth century on) as well as the Thai-script Syāmaraṭṭha Tepiṭaka (first edition, 1925–28).[228]

As a whole, the Tibetan translations date to a period that begins circa 1300 BE (800 CE), but the oldest extant manuscripts are a few centuries younger. For my translations and research, I consulted a twentieth-century facsimile edition of a xylograph Kanjur carved at Peking in 1737 at the command of the Qianlong emperor (乾隆 1735–96), a great patron of Buddhist scriptures and of the arts. The original xylograph print is preserved at Otani University in Kyoto, one of the oldest centers of modern education in Japan. The facsimile edition, published between 1955 and 1961, was prepared under the aegis of D. T. Suzuki (1870–1966), internationally renowned master of the emergent field of modern Buddhist studies.[229]

228. For these editions, see Bavarian State Library, *Die Worte des Buddha*, §§ 20, 22, pp. 39–42.
229. See Bavarian State Library, *Die Worte des Buddha*, § 85, pp. 116–17. For Suzuki and Buddhist studies, see Mark Blum's introduction to Blum, *Selected Works of D. T. Suzuki*, pp. xi–

This state of affairs is quite normal—I do not believe there is any single Buddhist scripture, let alone any scriptural collection, that we can trace uninterruptedly from its first appearance in writing to the present. We need to mind the gaps and factor them into our narratives. The oldest Buddhist manuscripts are the recently published Gāndhārī texts, which date back to the sixth century BE (first century CE) or even earlier. These new finds have opened startling new perspectives on the development of Buddhism in northwestern India.[230] But the manuscripts to which we have access so far are only a fraction of a once vibrant literature, and this fraction cannot fill in the many blanks in the history of textual evolution. Even if the new discoveries provide invaluable material for the study of the early development of the Dharma, there are still many lacunae and multiple missing links. As far as I know, no Gāndhārī fragments of any of the texts presented in this volume have been identified to date—with the exception of the *Dhammapada* verse on heedfulness (translation 2), the *ārabhatha* verse (translation 3), and counterparts to some of the verses of chapter 1 of the *Udānavarga* (translation 4).

---

xxiv. See also *Questioning the Buddha*, pp. 107–8.

230. For an overview, see Salomon, *Buddhist Literature of Ancient Gandhāra.*

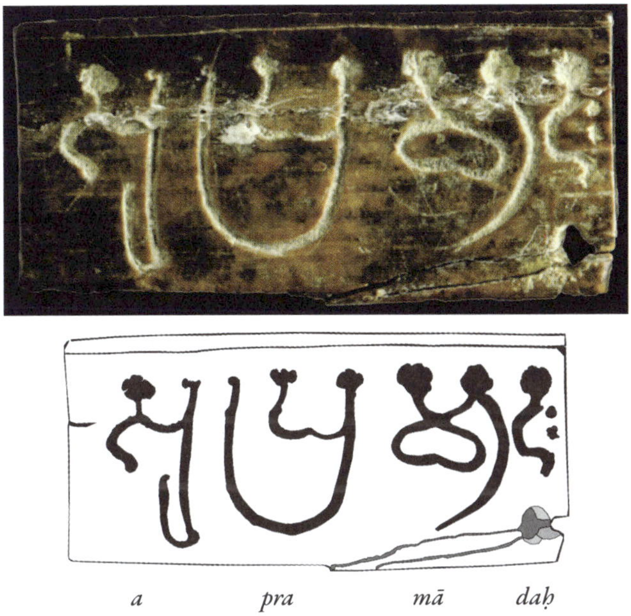

Figure 45. Above: *Apramāda* seal from Khu Bua, Ratchaburi province, Thailand. Front view with Sanskrit inscription in Southeast Asian Brāhmī.

Figure 46. Reverse of figure 45, with flowering vase of plenty.

Apramāda seal from Lower Burma.

Apramāda seal from India.

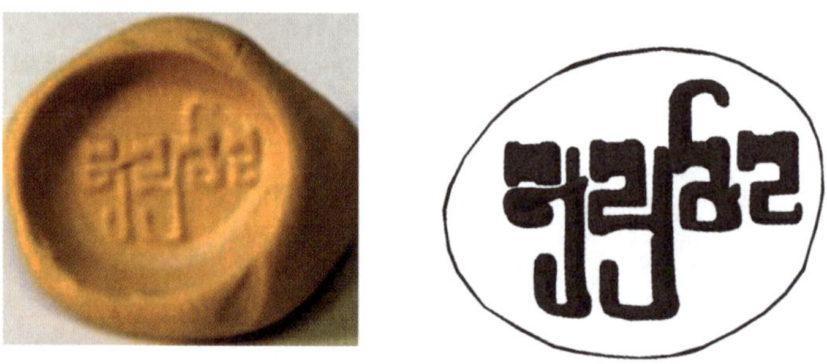

Apramāda seal from India.

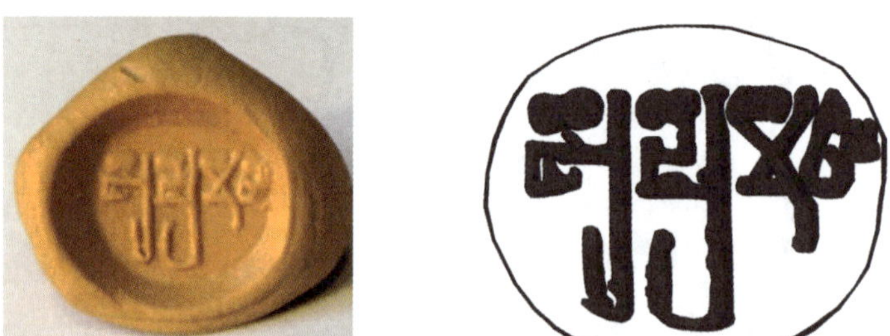

Apramāda seal from India.

Figure 47. Apramāda seals.

Heedfulness

THE FIRST THREE SELECTIONS revolve around *heedfulness*. Heedfulness is a core value in Śākyamuni's philosophy of life. In the introductions that follow, I show how heedfulness has been a central theme in Buddhist literature, epigraphy, and art from the early period of canon formation to the nineteenth century and, indeed, up to the present moment. I try to show how this simple concept—*apramāda* in Sanskrit, *appamāda* in Pāli, and *bag yod* in Tibetan—is a pearl of incalculable price that has been expertly stitched into the rich robes of the Dharma, where it gleams unobtrusively. I also show how this pearl of a word has proven tremendously tricky to capture in translation.

Tracing the textual dynamics of *apramāda* turned out to be a fascinating and meandering anabasis that brought many surprises.[231] I follow this unexpectedly complex adventure through six main themes. The story starts in Siam with the antiquarian mystery of laconic artifacts from the ancient world and ends with the epigraphic wisdom of nineteenth-century Siam's King Mongkut. In between, following *apramāda*'s trail through one of the great monuments of Buddhist literature in its several recensions leads us into a labyrinth. In Sanskrit this is the *Great Parinirvāṇa Sūtra*, in Pāli the *Great Parinibbāna Sutta*—a maze of ideas, a multilayered warren of catacombs of editorial reportage and embellishment.[232] This great work overflows the bounds of conventional literary theory and challenges the specialist's textual acumen. Its complexity is exemplified by the variety of translations of the title, which show a range of interpretations that in part reflect the difficulties

231. An anabasis is a march from a coast into the interior, such as that of the younger Cyrus into Asia in 401 BCE, as narrated by Xenophon in his work *Anabasis*. This is an external journey, while the present anabasis is an intellectual journey into the interior of Buddhist thought.
232. Pāli *Mahāparinibbānasutta*, *Dīghanikāya* 16.

faced in translating the sūtra's main theme—the single word (*pari*)*nibbāna*/*nirvāṇa*.[233] A sampling includes:

Book of the Great Decease
Last Days of the Buddha
Discourse on the Final Nirvana
Discourse about the Great Emancipation
Great Discourse on the Buddha's Extinguishment
Great Total Unbinding Discourse
Das grosse Sutta von Buddhas Tode
Les derniers jours du Bouddha
Soutra de l'ultime voyage ou le dernier discours du Bouddha
Gli ultimi giorni del Buddha
Il libro della totale estinzione del Buddha
Il grande discorso del nibbana definitivo
Het grote heengaan
Discursul Mare despre Completa Dezlegare

At first blush, a reader might think that some of the translated titles refer to different works, but they all stand for the same title, literally the "Grand Nirvāṇa Sūtra." Textual criticism shows that even when the architecture of the individual recensions is internally sound, the final structures are divergent and individual. This architecture is not the object of my study, which is, rather, an attempt to understand several anomalies in the use of *apramāda* in the available recensions. We start out with *apramāda* as "the Buddha's teaching in a single word," but in the end it becomes clear that this single word deserves a monograph or even an extensive tome.

1. The Buddha's Teaching in a Single Word

An antiquarian mystery

Apramāda. Heedfulness: the whole of the Buddha's teaching packed into a single word.

What does tradition tell us about this single word? For this we may con-

233. In the following, to differentiate the versions I refer to the text in general as *Great Parinirvāṇa Sūtra*, to the Pāli version as *Great Parinibbāna Sutta*, and to others by language or school affiliation.

sult commentaries like the *Dhammapada Commentary*, an authoritative testament of Theravādin thought, or Prajñāvarman's magnificent *Udānavarga Commentary* (*Udānavargavivaraṇa*), which was compiled within the Sarvāstivādin tradition. Here the former explains that the word *apramāda* is immensely significant because it sums up the entire Tripiṭaka.[234] This is a remarkable statement because the Tripiṭaka is said to contain 84,000 bundles of teachings. The two commentaries choose to cite one and the same sūtra to illustrate the importance of heedfulness:[235]

> Just as the footprints of all animals that roam on land fit into the footprint of the elephant, and the elephant's footprint is declared foremost amongst them, that is, with respect to size, so too, all wholesome qualities are rooted in heedfulness and converge upon heedfulness, and heedfulness is declared foremost amongst them.

In the eleventh to thirteenth centuries BE (sixth to eighth centuries CE), small, elegantly crafted objects inscribed in Brāhmī letters with the single word *apramāda* were produced throughout South and Southeast Asia. Each of the artifacts found so far has a different design and is inscribed in a different calligraphic script (figs. 13, 45–47). From this I conclude that the objects are not copies of a master model but were conceived and produced independently. Some of the artifacts are seals, some are amulets. We do not know who made them, who used them, or exactly how they were used, but it seems that in some (if not all) cases they were meant to be worn on the body or carried about. Could the designers have taken their cue from the notion that heedfulness sums up the entire Tripiṭaka—that is, the entire teaching of the Buddha? The single word can be a simple reminder, "Be heedful," and at the same time it can stand for the totality of the Buddha's teachings. Perhaps, but these are just guesses, shots in the dark; the *apramāda* artifacts remain an antiquarian mystery.

Illustrated in this volume (figs. 13, 45, 46) are two inscribed objects that were discovered at Khu Bua in Ratchaburi province, Thailand (คูบัว จ. ราชบุรี).[236] Archaeological remains scattered over a wide stretch of the fertile

234. See translation 2 for the full passage.

235. I cite the Pāli version from *Aṅguttaranikāya, Dasakanipāta, Nāthavagga*, no. 15, vol. 5, p. 21.19–25; in Bhikkhu Bodhi's rendering from *Numerical Discourses*, p. 1354. The sutta gives altogether ten comparisons to illustrate how *appamāda* is foremost.

236. For Khu Bua, see Phatcharin Sukpramun, "La ville ancienne de Khu Bua." For examples

rice plain show that Khu Bua was a major urban settlement of the ancient Dvāravatī kingdom that flourished from the eleventh to thirteenth centuries BE (sixth to eighth centuries CE). The two small objects are surface finds from the center of the ancient walled and moated city.[237] Both are fashioned from ivory. One was discovered in 2014, the other in about 2008.[238] Whereas the first is inscribed on one side only with *apramāda* written in reverse, the latter is engraved on both sides: one face has four letters that read *apramādaḥ*, while the second face has a "vase of plenty," an ancient South Asian symbol of fertility and prosperity.

Apramāda artifacts have had a long but not especially dramatic history in South and Southeast Asian archaeology and museology—ever since at least 1892 when two *apramāda* seals collected in India by Alexander Cunningham entered the British Museum (figs. 47b, c). Since then, a variety of artifacts bearing the word *apramāda* have been reported in India, Vietnam (at the Óc Eo conglomeration in the Mekong Delta), Thailand, and Burma (fig. 47a).[239]

The weight of a word

Apramāda is a weighty word.[240]

a + pramāda	Sanskrit
a + ppamāda	Pāli

---

of the masterful stucco work that decorated stūpas and other structures there, see nos. 83–110 in the same volume.

237. In archaeological parlance, a "surface find" is an object found by happenstance rather than through scientifically controlled excavation. Both pieces are now preserved in the collections of the Suthiratana Foundation, Bangkok. I am grateful to Dr. Bunchar Pongpanit (บัญชา พงษ์พานิช, Suthiratana Foundation and Buddhadasa Indapañño Archives) for supplying photographs.

238. The first measures 3 × 2 × 0.6 cm, and the other measures 2.8 × 1.2 × 0.2 cm.

239. For further details, see Skilling, "The Circulation of Artefacts Engraved with '*Apramāda*.'" I had hoped to conduct further research on the *apramāda* artifacts of India and Vietnam but have so far been unable to obtain the necessary photo documentation, a problem aggravated by the travel restrictions imposed by the coronavirus pandemic.

240. *Apramāda* is a significant virtue in Indian religion in general, and a comparative study is a desideratum, but this would lead us too far astray. For a cursory discussion, see Skilling, "Circulation of Artefacts," pp. 72–74.

It is made up of the negative prefix "*a*" before *pramāda*, "heedlessness," "negligence," "carelessness," to make its oppostites, "heedfulness," "non-negligence," "carefulness," "care."[241] Time is precious. Life is short and uncertain, and the Buddha regularly encouraged his followers to make the best of the situation by cultivating their minds through contemplative practices. In this anthology, a verbal form of the word *pramāda/apramāda* occurs in the exhortation *mā pramādetha*, "do not be negligent, "do not be careless"—or, put positively, "be alert," "take care." The Buddha concludes many of his discourses with the admonition "Meditate, O monks; do not be negligent" (see translation 10). He points out suitable spots for meditation in the immediate vicinity.[242] Heedfulness is an open-air, everywhere, and anytime practice; heedfulness is unstructured and does not require any equipment or "how to" manuals.

Apramāda is fundamental to the Buddha's ethical thought, to understanding the mechanics of positive or fruitful behavior, as, for example, when he states, "Whatever positive ideas there may be, all of them are rooted in heedfulness."[243] Ven. Nyanatiloka describes *apramāda* as "the foundation of all progress," and Richard Gombrich singles it out as "the most distinctive contribution of Buddhism to Indian (or the world's) soteriological practice." The Buddha uses the term unobtrusively in many key passages, and it occurs in chants that are recited daily across the Buddhist world like the *Maṅgala* and *Ratana* suttas.

Śāntideva was a philosopher and poet who flourished in northern India around the thirteenth century BE (mid-seventh to mid-eighth centuries CE); his best-known works are the *Guide to the Bodhisatva Practice* (*Bodhisatvacaryāvatāra*, also known as *Bodhicaryāvatāra*), and the *Compendium of Training* (*Śikṣāsamuccaya*). The latter is an anthology of sūtra citations that is structured around a series of root verses that delineate the author's conception of spiritual practice. Root verse 27, the last, gives the factors that lead to success or accomplishment. These are key terms of shared Buddhist practice: *samyakprahāṇa*, *apramāda*, *smṛti*, *saṃprajanya*, and *yoniśaś cintana*

241. See Childers' entry, pp. 323–24, which amongst the examples includes *pamādalekhaṃ*, "errors of transcription, lit. inadvertent writing"—that is, scribal error, which we often meet in manuscripts, or clumsy typing, one of my own unskills.
242. The poet Aśvaghoṣa distills the admonition into two verses of his *Buddhacarita*, chap. 26, vv. 71–72. See further below under translation 10.
243. *Ye keci kusalā dhamma sabbe te appamādamūlakā*: *Appamādasutta*, *Aṅguttaranikāya*, vol. 5, p. 21.16.

(equivalent to *yoniśo manaskāra*). They start with heedfulness and progress to thorough reflection:[244]

> Successful completion comes from not giving up
> heedfulness in the right endeavors
> thorough mindfulness and full awareness
> and thorough reflection.

The sūtra citations that follow mention *apramāda*, and Śāntideva cites a prose passage followed by a verse on *apramāda* from the *Sūtra on the Tathāgata's Secrets* (*Tathāgataguhyasūtra*).[245]

In the Pāli canon, *appamāda* is a profoundly meaningful term. There are chapters or sections (*vagga*) and discourses (*suttas*) on *appamāda*.[246] One of the earliest Pāli-English lexicons is *A Dictionary of the Pali Language* published by Robert Caesar Childers 150 years ago. Childers' definition of *pamāda* shows the scope of the word and gives useful examples. It is still worth reading.[247]

> PAMĀDO, Carelessness, remissness, indifference, sloth, indolence, delay [प्रमाद]. Ab. 173. *Rājapurisānaṃ pamādaṃ disvā*, observing the royal attendants off their guard (Ras. 32). *Yathā bhadro asso pamādam āgamma kasāya niviṭṭho*, like a spirited horse struck with the whip for being lazy (Dh. 310). *Mā pamādena kālaṃ vītināmayittha*, pass not away your time in idleness (Dh. 182). *Pamādo rakkhato malaṃ*, carelessness in one who watches is a blot (Dh. 43, comment says, as if one set to watch cows should go to sleep or play). *Pamādo maccuno padaṃ*, sloth is the way of death (Dh. 5). *Vajjayitvā pamādalekhaṃ*, barring errors of transcription, lit. inadvertent writing. *Pamādacāraṃ carituṃ*, to live a life of sloth (Jāt. 9). Pamādaṭṭhānaṃ = प्रमाद + स्थान, cause

244. Sanskrit text in Harrison, "Case of the Vanishing Poet," p. 242; translated in Harrison, "Verses by Śāntideva," p. 96. For more on the celebrated author and his memorial verses, see Harrison, "Śāntideva: The Author and His Project."

245. *Śikṣāsamuccaya* (ed. Bendall), p. 357.1–14.

246. Malalasekera lists a number of Appamādavaggas in the "Great Chapter" of the *Saṃyuttanikāya* and gives individual entries for eleven appamāda suttas in the *Saṃyuttanikāya* and *Aṅguttaranikāya* (DPPN, vol. 1, pp. 123–24).

247. Childers, *Dictionary of the Pāli Language*, pp. 323–24 (1875 edition).

> or subject of delay or indifference to religion or waste of time. There are several, e.g. *majjapamādaṭṭhānaṃ*, strong drink (Kh. 3), *jūtappamādaṭṭhānaṃ*, gambling. *Idaṃ rajjaṃ nāma mahantaṃ pamādaṭṭhānaṃ kiṃ me rajjena kāritena*, this kingship is very great temptation to me, what is the use of my being a king? (Dh. 406).

Richard Gombrich translates *appamāda* as "diligence." He explains his choice as follows: "The word here rendered as 'diligence,' *appamāda*, could also be translated 'attentiveness'; in psychological terms it is that *awareness* which was the most distinctive contribution of Buddhism to Indian (or the world's) soteriological practice."[248] In the entry for *appamāda* in his *Buddhist Dictionary*, first published in 1952, German bhikkhu-scholar Nyanatiloka (1878–1957) gives "'Zeal,' Non-laxity, Earnestness, Diligence, is considered as the foundation of all progress"; he cites the simile of the elephant's footprint, refers to the "Chapter on Zeal" (*Appamādavagga*) of the *Dhammapada* and "the Buddha's last exhortation: 'Transient are all formations. Strive zealously!'"[249] He adds, "In the commentaries, it is often explained as the presence (lit. 'non-absence') of mindfulness (*satiyā avippavāsa*)." These definitions bring out what is implicit in the term as used in context: *apramāda* and *smṛti* (*sati*) are close cousins. *Sati*, however, has been singled out—dare one say "highjacked"?—to become a secularized, psychological "solution" for a brace of modernity's ills. This curious phenomenon is best viewed *apramādena*.

The Yogācāra school developed a vast and sophisticated technical literature that includes tracts associated with the fourth- to fifth-century masters Asaṅga and Vasubandhu. In Yogācāra Abhidharma, both *apramāda* and *pramāda* are "mental factors" (*caitasikas*); in Asaṅga's *Compendium of Abhidharma* (*Abhidharmasamuccaya*), Rahula translates them as "diligence" and "indolence."[250] The two terms are explained in Vasubandhu's *Treatise on the Five Aggregates* (*Pañcaskandhaprakaraṇa*), the *Introduction to Abhidharma* (*Abhidharmāvatāra*), and other Abhidharma manuals. The Abhidharma is a complex system of ideas and relations, and the various Abhidharma schools developed different criteria of selection and classification. The

248. Gombrich, *Theravāda Buddhism*, p. 78.
249. Nyanatiloka, *Buddhist Dictionary*, p. 19.
250. Rahula, *Abhidharmasamuccaya*, pp. 11, 16.

Theravāda Abhidhamma does not count either *appamāda* or *pamāda* as a mental factor.

Śākyamuni's last words: A textual tangle

TABLE 3. *Some translations of the Mahāparinibbānasutta*

T. W. and C. A. F. Rhys Davids (1910): *The Book of the Great Decease*
A. A. G. Bennett (1964): *Mahāparinibbāna Suttanta*
Sister Vajirā and Francis Story (1964): *Last Days of the Buddha*
Maurice Walshe (1987): *The Great Passing: The Buddha's Last Days*
Yang-Gyu An (2003): *The Buddha's Last Days*

The most widely known use of *appamāda* in Pāli is perhaps that in the *Great Parinibbāna Sutta*, one of the most influential texts of the *Long Discourses* (*Dīghanikāya*)—and of the Pāli canon as a whole. The *Great Parinibbāna Sutta* reports that Śākyamuni's last words were as follows:[251]

> *atha kho bhagavā bhikkhū āmantesi. handa dāni bhikkhave āmantayāmi vo* ***vayadhammā saṃkhārā appamādena sampādethā*** *ti. ayaṃ tathāgatassa pacchimā vācā.*
>
> "Now, O monks, I announce to you: **to pass away is the nature of compounded things. Be heedful and accomplish your aims.**" These were the Tathāgata's last words.

Thomas William Rhys Davids (1843–1922) and his wife Caroline Augusta Foley Rhys Davids (1857–1942) were dedicated scholars who advanced the study of Pāli and Theravāda Buddhism in the British Isles and worldwide enormously—to the extent that one may reasonably ask where Pāli studies would be today were it not for their pioneering efforts. Over a hundred years

251. *Mahāparinibbānasutta*, *Dīghanikāya*, vol. 2, p. 156.1. For the "last exhortation," see following.

ago, in 1910, they published their translation of the *Great Parinibbāna Sutta* as *The Book of the Great Decease*.[252] They rendered the passage as

> Then the Exalted One addressed the brethren, and said:—"Behold now, brethren, I exhort you, saying:—'**Decay is inherent in all component things! Work out your salvation with diligence!**'" This was the last word of the Tathāgata!

Half a century later, in 1964, A. A. G. Bennett published a translation of the first sixteen suttas of the *Dīghanikāya*. He renders the passage like this:[253]

> Then the Exalted One said to the Bhikkhus: "Now, bhikkhus, I call upon you: **Conditioned things are things of decay; with vigilance try to accomplish**." These are the last words of the Tathāgata.

About the same time, Sister Vajirā and Francis Story published their translation in *Last Days of the Buddha*:[254]

> And the Blessed One addressed the bhikkhus, saying: "Behold now, bhikkhus, I exhort you: **Transient are all elements of being! Strive with earnestness!**" This was the last word of the Tathāgata.

In 1987, Maurice Walshe published a new translation of the complete *Dīghanikāya* as *Thus Have I Heard: The Long Discourses of the Buddha*; at the time of writing this is the most recent translation of the long collection into English. Walshe renders the passage as[255]

252. This was in part 2 of their translation of the *Dīghanikāya* as *Dialogues of the Buddha* in the Sacred Books of the Buddhists series edited by none other than F. Max Müller.

253. Bennett, *Long Discourses of the Buddha*, p. 216. The volume was published in Bombay. I do not know how much it circulated outside India or whether Bennett translated or published the rest of the *Dīghanikāya*. Volume 1 of the series was Edward Conze's *A Short History of Buddhism* (1960, since reprinted several times).

254. The translation was first published in 1964, reprinted in 1974, and published in a revised edition in 1988. I cite the revised edition (p. 87) and cannot vouchsafe for the wording of the first edition.

255. Walshe, *Long Discourses*, p. 270. According to wisdomexperience.org, "Maurice Walshe was born in London in 1911 and was an active Buddhist from 1951 until the end of his life in 1998. He served as the Vice-President of the Buddhist Society and Chair of the English

> Then the Lord said to the monks: "Now, monks, I declare to you: **all conditioned things are of a nature to decay—strive on untiringly.**" These were the Tathāgata's last words.

Walshe remarks that "R[hys] D[avid]'s rendering of the latter two words, 'Work out your salvation with diligence' has become too famous.[256] Even Brewster, who normally follows R[hys] D[avids], has changed it to 'Accomplish earnestly!', which is much better."[257]

Thānissaro translates:[258]

> Then the Blessed One addressed the monks, "Now, then, monks, I exhort you: **All fabrications are subject to ending & decay. Reach consummation through heedfulness.**" That was the Tathāgata's last statement.

The variety of translations shows how different translators' choices or preferences reflect their understanding and sensibilities, as well as stylistic change through time.

Redactional labyrinths

The *Great Parinirvāṇa/Parinibbāna* family of texts is one of Buddhist literature's most formidable monuments; I have described it above as a labyrinth, a maze, and a warren of catacombs.[259] This massive compilation survives in two

---

Sangha Trust. A scholar of Pāli and German, his other works include *Buddhism for Today* and translations of the sermons of Meister Eckhart."

256. Walshe, *Long Discourses*, p. 575, n. 453: "Too famous" strikes me as rather an odd turn of phrase. I suspect that Walshe means that the translation "Work out your salvation with diligence" is unjustly famous, overused in English discourse about Buddhism, despite the fact that it is not a good translation. The rendering has a biblical ring that should have appealed to Rhys Davids' post-Victorian/Edwardian readers.

257. Walshe refers to E. A. Brewster, *The Life of Gotama the Buddha, Compiled Exclusively from the Pāli Canon*, London, 1926. Earl Brewster (1878–1957) was an American painter who spent much of his life as a "Himalayan hermit" in Almora, India. He wrote an account of the Buddha's life based on existing translations.

258. Thānissaro Bhikkhu, *The Great Total Unbinding Discourse: Mahā Parinibbāna Sutta* (DN 16), https://www.dhammatalks.org/suttas/DN/DN16.html.

259. There is no English translation of the Sanskrit *Mahāparinirvāṇasūtra*; for German translations, see Weber, *Buddhistische Sutras*, and the synoptic edition/translation by Waldschmidt. For a summary of the Pāli version, see Shaw, *The Art of Listening*, pp. 163–67.

original Indic versions as well as in translations into Chinese and Tibetan. The extant versions were edited and transmitted by several monastic schools. Some schools—for instance, the Mūlasarvāstivāda—transmit the *Great Parinirvāṇa* as a sūtra and also incorporate it in full into their Vinayapiṭaka.

The Pāli *Great Parinibbāna Sutta* has been available in English translation for more than a century and is by far the best known; Buddhaghosa's commentary has been translated and published by the Pali Text Society as *The Buddha's Last Days*.[260] The Rhys Davids' three-volume translation of the *Dīghanikāya* from Pāli published between 1899 and 1921 remains in print,[261] as does Maurice Walshe's version published by Wisdom Publications under the title *The Long Discourses of the Buddha*. In sharp contrast, the versions of schools other than the Theravāda are much less accessible. If translated at all, this has been into languages like French, German, Italian, and Japanese, rather than into today's "universal language of scholarship," English; the versions of other schools reach a limited readership and tend to be overlooked.[262]

As a result, the modern public tends to regard the Pāli *Great Parinibbāna Sutta* alone as the definitive and "authorized version"—as *the* historical account of Gautama the Buddha's final journey and last days. But is the Pāli version really the last word on the Buddha's last words? In the Theravādin *Great Parinibbāna Sutta*, the Buddha's final statement highlights heedfulness: the Buddha's very last words are reported to be *appamādena sampādetha*, "Be heedful and accomplish your aims." This statement is widely, one might say universally, taken as it stands, with no alternate versions.

Can we take this at face value? Are these the Buddha's last words? How do we know this? The answer is "because the sutta tells us so": isn't it right there before our eyes, in the original Pāli? It is probable that most of the Buddhist schools transmitted a version or versions of the *Great Parinirvāṇa Sūtra*.[263] Are the Buddha's last words the same in all of them? It may be better to stand

260. Yang-Gyu An, *The Buddha's Last Days*.

261. Published as *Dialogues of the Buddha*, Sacred Books of the Buddhists, vols. 2–4.

262. For example, Puini's *Mahaparinirvana-sutra ovvero il libro della totale estinzione del Buddha nella redazione cinese di Pe-Fa-Tsu* (Po Fa-tsu, Taishō 5) published in 1919 and reprinted in 2008, or the Chinese *Dīrghāgama* version published in French by Siyan Jin in 2013. The latter is, however, now available in English translations by Ichimura and Anālayo.

263. That *all* schools did this would be an optimistic assumption, but we can never say *all* because some or even many versions are irredeemably lost. We should not say *irredeemably* because some of them may one day turn up.

back and compare the available versions, to ask to what degree the different recensions agree. When we do this, we find that the textual record is far from unanimous.[264] This leads one to wonder: is the statement transmitted in the Pāli *Great Parinibbāna Sutta* really the Buddha's last testament? Or is it a skillful embellishment?

Let us start to examine this by looking at one of the most important non-Pāli recensions, that of the Mūlasarvāstivāda school. The extensive manuscript remains of this version show that it circulated widely in the early and middle periods. Today this recension is available in Sanskrit fragments from several locations in Central Asia and from Gilgit in Kashmir, as well as in a complete Tibetan and several Chinese translations. But to start with, our question seems to lead us straight into a textual *cul de sac*: we find that the *apramāda* phrase is entirely lacking in the Mūlasarvāstivāda *Great Parinirvāṇa Sūtra*. This is nothing new: it has been noted by previous scholars. Walshe, for example, writes:

> Much has been made in some quarters of the fact that the Sarvāstivādin version (and therefore the Tibetan translation) omits these words. But the passage is even expanded in one Chinese version, which makes dubious any conclusions which may have been drawn from the omission elsewhere. However, there does seem to have been an early corruption in the text, as in the parallel passage at *Saṃyuttanikāya* I, p. 158, the order of the two sentences is reversed: *appamādena sampādetha vayadhammā saṅkhārā*. The inference is that the words quoted were lost at an early stage in the Sarvāstivādin tradition. The *Saṃyuttanikāya* passage probably reflects an intermediate stage in that process.

Walshe remarks that the passage in the Chinese *Dīrghāgama* version of the *Great Parinirvāṇa Sūtra* "makes dubious any conclusions which may have been drawn from the omission elsewhere," but on the basis of that sole witness and the *Saṃyutta* passage, Walshe himself concludes that there seems

264. The two scholars who dedicated themselves to the *Great Nirvāṇa Sūtra* were André Bareau and Ernst Waldschmidt. Bareau orchestrates a detailed comparison of sources in *Recherches sur la biographie du Buddha II-II*, pp. 144–50, but even he does not take all of the existing material into account. Waldschmidt presents a Central Asian Sanskrit text alongside the Pāli, the Tibetan translation, and a German translation from the Chinese. See also Nakamura, *Gotama Buddha*, vol. 2, pp. 155–58.

"to have been an early corruption in the text" and speculates about the *Saṃyuttanikāya* (an "intermediate stage") and Sarvāstivāda versions. With regard to the latter, he assumes textual loss—the passage was originally there but "was lost." Walshe's attempt to explain the absence strikes me as hasty and unwarranted, especially in the light of the *Prātimokṣa* passages that I will discuss below.

When he refers to a parallel passage in the *Saṃyuttanikāya*, Walshe is referring to a short account of the Buddha's last moments, the *Parinibbāna-sutta* of the *Brahmasaṃyutta*,[265] which has almost the same title, minus the *mahā-*, as the much longer and better-known *Mahāparinibbānasutta* of the *Dīghanikāya*. The *Brahmasaṃyutta* version reads:

> *atha kho bhagavā bhikkhū āmantesi. handa dāni bhikkhave āmantayāmi vo* ***appamādena sampādetha vayadhammā saṅkhārā*** *ti. ayaṃ tathāgatassa pacchimā vācā.*

The *Dīghanikāya* version, let us recall, reads:

> *atha kho bhagavā bhikkhū āmantesi. handa dāni bhikkhave āmantayāmi vo* ***vayadhammā saṃkhārā appamādena sampādethā*** *ti. ayaṃ tathāgatassa pacchimā vācā.*

That is, the order of the two phrases, "accomplish your aim through heedfulness" (*appamādena sampādetha*) and "compounded things are transient" (*vayadhammā saṅkhārā*) is reversed in these two suttas belonging to the same tectual lineage, the Theravāda.

Bhikkhu Bodhi translates the *Mahāparinibbānasutta* version as follows:[266]

> Then the Blessed One addressed the bhikkhus thus: "Now I address you, bhikkhus: **Formations are bound to vanish. Strive to attain the goal by diligence.**" This was the last utterance of the Tathāgata.[267]

265. *Sagāthavagga, Saṃyuttanikāya*, vol. 1, pp. 157–59. Quote at p. 157.ult.
266. *Connected Discourses*, p. 251.
267. There are several significant differences between the commentary on the *Dīghanikāya* and that on the *Saṃyuttanikāya*. For these see An, *The Buddha's Last Days*, p. 183, nn. 7–9. I follow here the *Saṃyutta* tradition.

Buddhaghosa comments that the last phrase, "This was the last utterance of the Tathāgata" (*ayaṃ tathāgatassa pacchimā vācā*) "was added in the recital":[268] that is, he attributes it to the work of the redactors (of, presumably, the first convocation).

In his two-volume study of the life of Gotama Buddha, accomplished Japanese scholar Hajime Nakamura (1912–99) comments on this topic. He writes,[269]

> Since as the sūtra itself says, "This is the Tathāgata's last teaching [*pacchimā vācā*]," it is easy to imagine how important it was considered. Buddhaghosa wrote: "Thus the Bhagavant lay down on the couch of the great *parinibbāna*, distilled his teachings of forty-five years into the single verse [*pada*, here perhaps better rendered as 'word'] 'Persevere,' and gave it [to the bhikkhus]."

The above is an English translation from Nakamura's Japanese—that is, it is a second-hand rather than a direct translation. I prefer to translate Buddhaghosa's comment as follows:

> "Through heedfulness": accomplish all of your tasks by not neglecting mindfulness (*sati*): in this way, reclining on the divan of his final nirvāṇa, the Fortunate One distilled all of the advice that he had given for forty-five years into the single word *appamāda*.

Buddhaghosa does not equivocate: he presents the phrase as a distillation of the Buddha's life teachings into a momentous single word.

Another twist in the maze

Here the maze takes another twist: according to the Pāli tradition, this is not the first time that the Buddha made this statement. If we give the *Great Parinibbāna Sutta* a close read and go back a few pages to three months

268. An, *The Buddha's Last Days*, p. 184.

269. Nakamura, *Gotama Buddha*, vol. 2, pp. 290–91, n. 104. The commentary in Stede, *Sumaṅgala-vilāsinī*, vol. 2, p. 593.31, reads *appamādena sampādethā ti sati-avippavāsena sabbakiccāni sampadeyatha. iti bhagavā parinibbānamañce nipanno pañcacattārīsa vassāni dinnaṃ ovādaṃ sabbaṃ ekasmiṃ* ***appamādapade*** *yeva pakkhipitvā adāsi.*

before his nirvāṇa, we find that the Buddha foretells his coming death. He assembles the bhikkhus staying at Vesālī and teaches them the core elements of his teaching.[270] He then announces his impending death:[271]

> *atha kho bhagavā bhikkhū āmantesi. handa dāni bhikkhave āmantayāmi vo* ***appamādena sampādetha vayadhammā saṅkhārā*** *na ciraṃ tathāgatatassa parinibbānaṃ bhavissati, ito tiṇṇaṃ māsānaṃ accayena tathāgato parinibbāyassatī ti.*
>
> *paripakko vayo mayhaṃ, parittaṃ mama jīvitaṃ*
> *pahāya vo gamissāmi, katam me saraṇam attano.*
> *appamattā satīmanto susīlā hotha bhikkhavo*
> *susamāhita-saṃkappā sacittam anurakkhatha.*
> *yo imasmiṃ dhammavinaye appamatto vihessati*
> *pahāya jātisaṃsāraṃ dukkhass' antaṃ karissatīti.*[272]
>
> Then the Fortunate One addressed the monks. "I announce to you now, O monks: **accomplish your aim with heedfulness. Transient are compounded things.** It will not be long before the Tathāgata's parinibbāna takes place: three months from now the Tathāgata will pass to parinibbāna.
>
> Ripe is my age, little's left of my life:
> I've made a refuge for myself,
> and soon I'll leave you behind.
> Be heedful, be aware, be virtuous in conduct;
> with thoughts well collected,
> guard over your own mind.
> One who dwells heedful
> in this teaching and system of training
> leaves rebirth's round behind
> and puts an end to pain.

270. See Bareau, *Recherches sur la biographie du Buddha II-I*, pp. 196–207.
271. *Mahāparinibbānasutta, Dīghanikāya*, vol. 2, p. 120.13. For spiritual masters to predict or control their time of death is not uncommon, and the Buddha's prediction is an early literary example of this.
272. For the last verse, see translation 3.

The Rhys Davids' translation reads:

> And the Exalted One exhorted the brethren, and said:—
> "Behold now, O brethren, I exhort you, saying:—
> "**All component things must grow old. Work out your salvation with diligence**. The final extinction of the Tathāgata will take place before long. At the end of three months from this time the Tathāgata will die!"[273]
>
> "My age is now full ripe, my life draws to its close:
> I leave you, I depart, relying on myself alone!
> **Be earnest** then, O brethren, holy, full of thought!
> Be steadfast in resolve! Keep watch o'er your own heart!
> **Who wearies not**, but holds fast to this truth and law,
> Shall cross this sea of life, shall make an end of grief."

Sister Vajirā and Francis Story have:[274]

> Then the Blessed One said to the bhikkhus: "So, bhikkhus, I exhort you: **All compounded things are subject to decay. Therefore strive with earnestness**. The time of the Tathāgata's Parinibbāna is near. Three months hence the Tathāgata will utterly pass away."
>
> And having spoken these words, the Happy One, the Master, spoke again, saying:
>
> "My years are now full ripe, the life span left is short.
> Departing, I go hence from you, relying on myself alone.
> **Be earnest**, then, O bhikkhus, be mindful and of virtue pure!
> With firm resolve, guard your own mind!
> Whoso **untiringly** pursues the Dhamma and the Discipline
> Shall go beyond the round of births and make an end of suffering."

273. For Bareau's rendering of the Pāli, see *Recherches sur la biographie du Buddha II-I*, p. 206. For Nakamura's, see *Gotama Buddha*, vol. 2, p. 102 and p. 263, n. 59.
274. Vajirā and Story, *Last Days of the Buddha*, p. 49.

Maurice Walshe gives the following:[275]

> Then the Lord said to the monks: "And now, monks, I declare to you—**all conditioned things are characterized by decay—strive on untiringly**. The Tathāgata's final passing will not be long delayed. Three months from now the Tathāgata will take his final Nibbāna."
>
> Thus the Lord spoke. The Well-Farer having thus spoken, the Teacher said this:
>
> Ripe I am in years. My life-span's determined.
> Now I go from you, having made myself my refuge.
> Monks, **be untiring**, mindful, disciplined,
> Guarding your minds with well-collected thought.
> He who, **tireless**, keeps to law and discipline,
> Leaving birth behind will put an end to woe.

At this point, a further and perhaps a final turn in the bewildering maze leads us into a cul-de-sac: the passage about the Buddha's last words, so prominent in the Theravāda version with its emphasis on heedfulness, is entirely absent in the Sarvāstivāda version. It seems that the thread of *apramāda* has wound down: has our comparative study of Śākyamuni's last words drawn to a close? Or can it continue in other scriptural collections?

Enter the great disciples: Sāriputta and Revata and the appamāda admonition

To start with, let us note that the *appamāda* admonition of the *Great Parinibbāna Sutta* is not unique but occurs elsewhere in the Pāli collections. In the *Verses of the Senior Monks* (*Theragāthā*), the phrase is presented as the final instruction (*anusāsanī*) spoken individually by two of the Buddha's great disciples, Sāriputta and Revata. In the *Verses*, Sāriputta's final words anticipate those of the Buddha:[276]

275. Walshe, *Long Discourses of the Buddha*, pp. 253–54.
276. *Theragāthā*, v. 1017: Rhys Davids, *Psalms of the Brethern*, p. 349.

> ***sampādeth' appamādena**, esā me anusāsanī*
> *handāhaṃ parinibbissaṃ, vippamutto 'mhi sabbadhī ti.*
>
> **Accomplish your aims through heedfulness:**
> this is my advice.
> Now let me pass to nirvāṇa:
> freed am I in all regards.

C. A. F. Rhys Davids translates the verse with its introductory lines, "And when he [Sāriputta] came to his utter passing away, he thus admonished the brethren assembled around him:

> **Press on with earnestness and win the goal!**[277]
> This the commandment that I give to you.
> Lo! now my going-out complete will be.
> From all am I released and utterly."

K. R. Norman's translation is as follows:[278]

> **Strive with vigilance**, this is my advice; come now, I shall be quenched; I am completely released in every way.

An identical stanza concludes the verses of Revata (*Theragāthā*, v. 658).[279]

I use the word "anticipate" above because Sāriputta died before the Buddha. As we have seen earlier, the Buddha himself anticipates or rather predicts his own last words three months before the nirvāṇa. This and the monks' verses provoke interesting questions about chronology. Whatever chronology we choose, whether literary, historical, or legendary, all of them are decidedly out of sync.

All of this vindicates the idea that *apramāda* was a cardinal teaching of Gautama Buddha, and we will see that it resonates beyond the Pāli canon in the mainstream of Buddhist thought and its literary expressions—in

277. With due respect to the esteemed translator, this rendering invests the spiritual struggle with the spirit of a sports match.
278. Norman, *Elders' Verses I*, v. 1017.
279. For Revata see Revata (3) in Malalasekera, DPPN vol. 2, pp. 752–54.

Aśvaghoṣa's *Buddhacarita*, the Chinese *Dīrghāgama*, and the *Prātimokṣas*.[280] Apramāda was so precious that reciters and redactors took care to weave it into the Buddha's own thought and life story as well as into the thoughts of his prominent disciples.

Box 6. *Aśvaghoṣa's Buddhacarita*

In "The Mahāparinirvāṇa," chapter 26 of his *Career of the Awakened One* (*Buddhacarita*), Aśvaghoṣa relates that not long before his nirvāṇa, the Buddha commended *apramāda*.

de phyir ***bag yod*** *bla ma bzhin du bsnyen mdzod la* ||
bag med dgra bo bzhin du rnam par spongs mdzod dang ||
bag yod pa *las brgya byin gyis ni*[281] *dpal thob cing* ||
bag med pa las lha min khengs rnams rnam par nyams ||

དེ་ཕྱིར་**བག་ཡོད་**བླ་མ་བཞིན་དུ་བསྙེན་མཛོད་ལ། །བག་མེད་དགྲ་བོ་བཞིན་དུ་རྣམ་པར་སྤོངས་མཛོད་དང་། །
བག་ཡོད་པ་ལས་བརྒྱ་བྱིན་གྱིས་ནི་དཔལ་ཐོབ་ཅིང་། །བག་མེད་པ་ལས་ལྷ་མིན་ཁེངས་རྣམས་རྣམ་པར་ཉམས། །

Therefore, respect heedfulness the way you would a teacher (guru),
and avoid heedlessness as you would an enemy.
Through heedfulness Śakra gained his glory, while
through heedlessness the arrogant asuras were undone.
[my translation]

280. The Sanskrit of the *Buddhcarita* does not survive in complete form. The Sanskrit text is preserved only up to verse 14.31; that is, the greater part of chapter 14 (14.32–108) is lost (and there are lacunas in chapter 1 and elsewhere). E. H. Johnston (1885–1952) edited and translated cantos 1 to 14 as available from Sanskrit (Johnston, parts 1 and 2, first published Lahore, 1936) and translated the remainder, cantos 15 to 28, from the Tibetan and Chinese versions (Johnston, part 3, first published in *Acta Orientalia* XV, 1937) under the title *The Buddhacarita: Or, Acts of the Buddha*. Stray verses from the "lost sections" have been periodically retrieved from new sources; most recently Hartmann and Matsuda have identified portions incorporated into the *Tridaṇḍamālā*. Unfortunately, the verses discussed here have not been recovered to date.

281. Reading *gyis ni* with Peking and Narthang against the *gyi na* of other editions (correction with thanks to Saerji, 14 July 2021).

Johnston translates the verse as follows: [282]

> Therefore adhere to heedfulness (*apramāda*) as to a guru, and avoid heedlessness as an enemy. By heedfulness Indra obtained sovereignty, by heedlessness the arrogant Asuras came to destruction.[283] [70]

But Aśvaghoṣa does not describe these as the Buddha's last words, and in fact the verse stands at the beginning of a paraphrase of an exhortation to meditate (see below, translation 10). The Master's last words come further on, in verse 88 (Dergé 93b2):

> *rgyu dang mi rgyu thams cad rnam par 'god pa ste* ||
> *de phyir khyed cag rnams ni legs par bag yod gyis* ||
> *mya ngan 'da' ba'i dus ni yongs su gyur pa ste* ||
> *khyed cag ma smra 'di ni bdag gi phyi ma'i tshig* ||

> རྒྱུ་དང་མི་རྒྱུ་ཐམས་ཅད་རྣམ་པར་འགོད་པ་སྟེ། །དེ་ཕྱིར་ཁྱེད་ཅག་རྣམས་ནི་ལེགས་པར་བག་ཡོད་གྱིས། །
> མྱ་ངན་འདའ་བའི་དུས་ནི་ཡོངས་སུ་གྱུར་པ་སྟེ། །ཁྱེད་ཅག་མ་སྨྲ་འདི་ནི་བདག་གི་ཕྱི་མའི་ཚིག

> Everything, moving or stationary, passes away;
> may you all therefore be well heedful.
> The time has come [for me] to pass fully beyond pain.
> Do not say anything: these are my last words. [my translation]

Johnston translates the verse:[284]

282. Johnston, *Aśvaghoṣa's Buddhacarita*, part 3, canto 26, v. 70 (p. 100). I thank Saerji for sending the Tibetan from Dergé no. 4156, fol. 92b3.
283. Possible parallels for this story are the *Suvīra* and *Susīma* suttas in the *Sakkasaṃyutta* of the *Saṃyuttanikāya*, vol. 1, pp. 466–71, trans. Bodhi, *Connected Discourses*, pp. 317–18. There are parallels in the Chinese *Saṃyuktāgamas*.
284. Johnston, *Buddhacarita*, part 3, canto 26, v. 88 (p. 102).

> Everything, whether moving or stationary, passes away; therefore take ye good heed. The time for My entering Nirvāṇa has arrived. Do not lament: these are My last words.

Aśvaghoṣa's version of the last words gives both ideas: impermanence and heedfulness.

Apramāda and awakening: The Chinese Dīrghāgama

If the *apramāda* exhortation is absent in most recensions of the *Great Parinirvāṇa Sūtra*, apart from the Pāli version, there is, however, one version that does have it. This is the *Great Parinirvāṇa Sūtra* of the Chinese *Dīrghāgama*, a text that contemporary scholarship generally assigns to the Dharmaguptaka school. This version gives even more emphasis to *apramāda* than does the Pāli.

Box 7. *Apramāda and awakening: The Chinese Dīrghāgama*

> 是故，比丘！無為放逸，我以不放逸故，自致正覺，無量眾善，亦由不放逸得，一切萬物無常存者，此是如來末後所說。[285]

In André Bareau's translation, this reads:[286]

> C'est pourquoi, ô moines, n'ayez pas de négligence. C'est parce que je n'ai jamais été négligent que j'ai atteint par moi-même le parfait Éveil. Les innombrables autres biens, c'est aussi par mon absence de négligence que je les ai obtenus. Aucune des innombrables choses qui existent ne dure éternellement: telles sont les dernières paroles de *Tathāgata*.

285. Taishō 1, no. 1, 26b19–21.
286. Bareau, *En suivant Bouddha*, p. 269. Cf. also Siyan Jin, *Soutra de l'ultime voyage*, pp. 631–32.

Bhikkhu Anālayo's English translation is as follows:[287]

> Therefore, monks, do not be negligent. Through not being negligent, I reached right awakening myself. An immeasureable multitude of goodness as well can be attained by not being negligent. All the ten thousand existing things are impermanent. These are the Tathāgata's last words.

Shohei Ichimura translates as follows:[288]

> Therefore, O bhikṣus, be on guard against dissoluteness. It was on the basis of constant vigilance against indolence that I realized perfect enlightenment. An immeasurable number of sentient beings will also realize perfect enlightenment on the basis of constant vigilance against indolence. Of all things in this world, there is nothing whatsoever that exists forever. This is the teaching exhorted by the Tathāgata in his last moment of life.

In his *Research on the Biography of the Buddha*, Bareau compares several accounts.[289] Anālayo, after discussing the various versions, gives a cogent summary:[290] "The main theme underlying these different records of the last words spoken by the Buddha would be that he used his own death as a final illustration of impermanence, and that he encouraged his disciples to devote themselves fully to their practice."

Several points are noteworthy. Firstly, in the Chinese *Dīrghāgama* passage, the order of the two ideas—heedfulness and transience—agrees with that of the Pāli *Brahmasaṃyutta* against that of the Pāli *Great Parinibbāna Sutta*. Secondly, Śākyamuni assigns a prominent role to *apramāda* in his realization of awakening. Thirdly, the sūtra describes the statement as the Tathāgata's last words, as does the Pāli *Great Parinibbāna Sutta*.

287. Anālayo, *Dīrgha-āgama Studies*, p. 227.
288. Shohei Ichimura, *The Canonical Book of the Buddha's Lengthy Discourses*, p. 150.
289. Bareau, *Recherches sur la biographie du Buddha II-II*, pp. 150–51.
290. Anālayo, *Dīrgha-āgama Studies*, p. 233.

I have presented some passages in which Śākyamuni proclaims the prominence of *apramāda* in his system of practice, and I have come across discrepancies in the traditions studied. The instances are "certain," at least as textual artifacts. There may, however, or even certainly, be further instances in recensions of the *Great Parinirvāṇa Sutta* that I have not been able to study owing to my limited language ability. In any case, our records of the *Great Parinirvāṇa Sutta* are incomplete: they are the remains of a robust literary cycle, like the bones of dinosaurs scattered in the bogs and wilds of prehistoric landscapes. There may (should) have been other recensions in the Vinaya and Sūtra piṭakas of the eighteen schools that were lost long ago. Further, to be sound, a theory must take account of the extant Chinese translations; I am unable to do this except vicariously through the work of experts in Chinese translations. When I glance through the English translations of Chinese texts related to the *Parinirvāṇa* cycle, I notice a number of passages that might refer to *apramāda* or express similar ideals.[291] Vaitulya/Mahāyāna texts can by no means be neglected; for example, the *Mahāparinirvāṇa-mahāsūtra*, read in Tibetan translation, offers at least one important case.[292]

Was *appamādena saṃpādetha* indeed Gautama the Buddha's final statement? Textual criticism cannot answer this question: each of us must weigh the evidence and decide, or suspend decision, for ourselves. If the statement's purpose is to assert the deep import of *apramāda*, and if we can grasp this, perhaps doubts about the accuracy or historicity of Gautama's "final exhortation" are beside the point. If we have crossed the river of (conventional) understanding, can we leave the words and letters aside like a raft after crossing a river?

The Sanskrit fragments and the Tibetan translation of the *Mahāparinirvāṇa-mahāsūtra* close with bewildering abruptness. In both of them, the Buddha says, "Sons of good family, be heedful, be heedful!" With these words, the *Mahāparinirvāṇa-mahāsūtra* falls in line with the *Mahāparinirvāṇa* texts that stress heedfulness, but its significance in the overall context of the Buddha's demise and of the recensions and translations of the "Mahāyāna" *Mahāparinirvāṇa-sūtra* needs further exploration.[293]

291. See, for example, the various translations in Numata Center, *Buddha-Dharma*, book VIII, pp. 640–41 (from *Pan-ni-yüan-ching*).

292. Habata, *A Critical Edition of the Tibetan Translation*, § 88, *bag med par ni ma gnas par | bag yod pa la dga' bar gyis*: "Do not pass your time in heedlessness—take delight in heedfulness." For an English translation from the Chinese, see Blum, *Nirvana Sutra*, vol. 1, p. 53.

293. Habata, *Die zentralasiatischen Sanskrit-Fragmente*, 24,13 (p. 101), *apramādam apramādaṃ kulaputrā kuruta*; Habata, *Critical Edition*, § 587, p. 409.5, *rigs kyi bu dag bag yod*

Further afield: Heedfulness and the Prātimokṣas

The alert and heedful life is a cornerstone of Buddhist practice, but Śākyamuni's admontion on *apramāda* is reported only in the Pāli version, where he is presented as speaking it twice, the second time only moments before his conscious and deliberate departure from the mundane plane. The statements are not found in the Mūlasarvāstivāda or other extant versions of the sūtra apart from the Chinese *Dīrghāgama*, which is believed to represent a Dharmaguptaka redaction. Such is the record of the available texts. But the matter does not end here. When we look further afield, we do find the *apramāda* admonition—the "missing last words"—elsewhere, in other non-Pāli canonical collections. They are not presented as the Tathāgata's last words, but they do play a prominent, and even, as in the Chinese *Dīrghāgama*, augmented role. Where can we find them? We do not find them in the Sūtrapiṭakas but in the registers of monks' rules, the *Prātimokṣa Sūtras*. These versions of several north Indian Vinaya schools are preserved in original Indic languages. They report how Śākyamuni urged his monastics to be heedful, without specifying *when* or *where* he did so.

The Sarvāstivāda *Prātimokṣasūtra* preserved in Sanskrit manuscripts from Central Asia places the statement at the end of a stirring passage on impermanence.[294]

> Old age and death bear down, the Teacher's religion is dying out, the life faculty is failing, the True Dharma is being lost . . . the gates to the realms of misery are opening and the doorways to the deathless are drawing shut. The bridge of the Dharma is collapsing, the boat of the Dharma is breaking apart, and the skiff of the Dharma is sinking. The torch of the Dharma is sputtering out, the tree of the Dharma is being uprooted, the banner of the Dharma is tumbling down and Māra's banner is soaring high. The ocean of the Dharma is drying up and the Mount Sumeru of wisdom is imploding . . .
>
> It will not be long before humans look on each other as wild

par gyis shig / bag yod par gyis shig /.

294. Von Simson, *Prātimokṣasūtra der Sarvāstivādins*, vol. 2, pp. 157–58; German translation, pp. 267–68. The manuscripts, from the Turfan collections, are damaged, and there are several lacuna. This and the following passages about impermanence remind one somewhat of the *Śīlasaṃyuktasūtra*, which imparts a sense of urgency to the practice of moral conduct, of which the *Prātimokṣa* is a particular instance. See Vinītā, *Unique Collection*, vol. 1, no. 9.

> beasts [and start to slaughter each other]. . . . Therefore you all, O long-lived ones, should be stirred and moved, and listen to the truthful words—free of falsity, free of spite and harshness—of the unsurpassed Ten-Powered One, the King of the Dharma, the wheel-turning emperor, who is produced by the ripening of his former deeds of good conduct.
>
> O long-lived ones, **make effort with heedfulness**. Through heedfulness the Tathāgatas, the worthy arhats, the truly and fully awakened Buddhas realized awakening along with other wholesome qualities conducive to awakening.

The Mūlasarvāstivāda *Prātimokṣasūtra*, preserved in manuscripts from Gilgit in Kashmir and from Tibet, reads:[295]

> Life moves on and old age and death have arrived. The Teacher's religion is declining: O long-lived ones, **make effort with heedfulness**. Through heedfulness the tathāgatas, the worthy arhats, the truly and fully awakened buddhas realized awakening along with other wholesome qualities conducive to awakening.

The Lokottaravāda-Mahāsāṃghika *Prātimokṣa* from Nepal conveys the same sense of urgency:[296]

> Old age and death bear down, the life faculty is exhausted. The Good Dharma is declining, the torch of the Dharma is flickering out. Capable instructors are passing away and the ranks of practitioners are dwindling. Moments, instants, and seconds, days and

295. Sanskrit manuscript from Gilgit ed. in Banerjee, *Two Buddhist Vinaya Texts*, p. 10.9; Hu-von Hinüber, *Das Bhikṣu-Prātimokṣasūtra der Mūlasarvāstivādins*, p. 5 (see idem., "Some Remarks on the Sanskrit Manuscript of the Mūlasarvāstivāda-prātimokṣasūtra Found in Tibet"); Tibetan trans. from Kanjur ed. and trans. in Vidyabhusana, *So-sor thar pa*, text p. 47.12, Eng. trans. p. 10. Note that the Tibetan translation of the Bhikṣu *Prātimokṣa* was done by Jinamitra, a Vaibhāṣika master from Kashmir. There is a commentary on the passage in the *Prātimokṣapadābhismaraṇa / So sor thar pa'i tshig gi brjed byang*, Otani no. 5610, repr. vol. 122, 'Dul ba'i 'grel pa, *tshu*, 203a8 foll.; passage on *apramāda*, 206b1 foll. The work is ascribed to Dānaśīla, presumably the Indian scholar who worked on translations in Tibet. See also the *Prātimokṣasūtravṛtti / So sor thar pa'i mdo'i 'grel pa*, Otani no. 5608, repr. vol. 121, 'Dul ba'i 'grel pa, *tsu*, 193a7ff. (author and translators not recorded).

296. Tatia, *Prātimokṣasūtram of the Lokottaravādimahāsāṅghika School*, p. 5.20.

> nights, months and fortnights, seasons and years race by.[297] Like the swift and turbulent waters of a stream tumbling down from the mountains, the life forces do not pause for even a second.
>
> O long-lived ones, **you should accomplish your task with heedfulness.** What is the reason? I declare that the awakening of the tathāgatas, the worthy arhats, the truly and fully awakened buddhas was realized through heedfulness; the unsurpassed cessation of the substratum is gained through heedfulness. Therefore, O long-lived ones, you should realize your aims through heedfulness.

Śākyamuni states emphatically that the tathāgatas realize awakening through heedfulness in the Chinese *Dīrghāgama* and in the *Prātimokṣas* of three major Vinaya schools—the Sarvāstivāda, Mūlasarvāstivāda, and Lokottaravāda.[298] But no comparable statement or idea is expressed anywhere in Pāli, whether in the *Pāṭimokkha*, the *Great Parinibbāna Sutta*, or, as far as I know, anywhere else. Amongst the schools that stress this idea, the Sarvāstivāda and Mūlasarvāstivāda are closely related, but they and the other schools are not affiliated. The Dharmaguptaka scriptures are in some cases cognate with those of the Theravaṃsa but they also show their own independent editorial developments. The evidence presented here demonstrates that the connection between heedfulness and awakening was well established in various strands of Buddhist thought across northern India. The redactors of these canons saw fit to emphasize heedfulness: they did not place it in their versions of the *Great Parinirvāṇa Sūtra*; rather they positioned it strategically in the *Prātimokṣa*—a text of cardinal ritual importance that, ideally, was memorized by all the monastics and recited communally every fortnight. In the *Prātimokṣa*, the statement is not specifically connected with the final nirvāṇa but with the basic realities of impermanence and death.

Heedulness and the monks' and nuns' ordination manuals

The connection between ordination and heedfulness is brought out in the Mūlasarvāstivāda "Manual for Bhikṣu Ordination" and "Manual for

297. Compare the passages on the divisions of time in the *Arakasutta* (translation 10) with reference to parallel texts.

298. The Chinese *Dīrghāgama* version reports this in the first person, while the Indic versions give the statement as a general rule for "the tathāgatas" in the third person plural.

Bhikṣuṇī Ordination." The first is preserved in Sanskrit, Tibetan, and Chinese; the second is incompletely preserved in Sanskrit but complete in Tibetan translation. When the ceremony has been completed, the two texts end with these pronouncements:

> You, long-lived one, are [now] fully ordained. Accomplish your aims with heedfulness.[299]

> You, by the name of so-and-so, have now been fully ordained. Conduct yourself heedfully.[300]

"Heedful" in Tibetan is *bag yod par*. That is, *apramāda*.

At the end of the *Pāṇḍulohitakavastu*, the eleventh chapter of the Mūlasarvāstivādin *Vinayavastu*, the saṅgha gives the monk Udāyi the same admonition when he has been freed from a penance: "The saṅgha has lifted your penance. Accomplish your aims with heedfulness."[301] The references quoted here show the importance of the "apramāda admonition" in the ethos of Mūlasarvāstivāda monasticism.

Ācārya Vasubandhu was one of the greatest Indian thinkers of middle-period Buddhism. Immensely learned, he was an unrivaled master of the Āgamas and the Abhidharma who produced intellectually stimulating works like the *Vyākhyāyukti*, the *Karmasiddhiprakaraṇa*, the *Pañcaskandhavivaraṇa*, and the *Pratītyasamutpādanirdeśa*.[302] Evidently Vasubandhu was moved by passages like the ones cited here; he takes them to heart and echoes their sentiments in the concluding verses of his *Treasury of Abhidharma*, up to the final couplet:[303]

299. Chung, *Handbuch für die buddhistische Mönchsordination*. Skt. p. 63: *eṣa tvam āyuṣman upasampanno 'pramādena sampādaya*; Tib. p. 107: *tshe dang ldan pa khyod bsnyen par rdzogs zin gyis | bag yod par sgrubs shig |*.

300. Roloff, *Buddhist Nuns' Ordination*, § IV.v.7 (p. 176): *ming 'di zhes bya ba khyod bsnyen par rdzogs kyis | bag yod par spyod cig |*. My translation; Roloff's translation at p. 272.

301. Yamagiwa, *Das Pāṇḍulohitakavastu*. Skt. p. 140.antepenult: *āvarhitas tvam udāyi saṃghena | apramādena saṃpādaya*; Tib. p. 141: *'char ka khyod dge 'dun gyis phung zin gyis bag yod par sgrubs shig*.

302. Vasubandhu's oeuvre is so extensive and multifaceted that his role in Indo-Tibetan, Central Asian, and East Asian Buddhism is still not adequately understood or appreciated.

303. *Abhidharmakośa*, chap. 8, v. 43. *iti kaṇṭhagataprāṇaṃ viditvā śāsanam muneḥ | balakālaṃ malānaṃ ca na pramādya mumukṣubhiḥ ||*. *de ltar thub pa dag gi bstan pa ni || lkog mar srog phyin 'dra dang dri ma rnams || stobs dang ldan pa'i dus su rig nas ni || thar pa 'dod pa dag gis bag yod gyis ||*.

> Aware that the sage's religion
> is rasping its last gasp
> and that at this time
> negativities wax fierce:
> may those who seek liberation
> not be negligent!

The couplet echoes the words of the two senior monks cited above, which also couple the idea of being liberated (*vippamutto*) with heedfulness, non-negligence, *apramāda*. Scholars in the Land of Snows take the theme up in commentaries on the *Treasury of Abhidharma*, such as that by Mchims 'Jam dpal dbyangs (ca. 1245–1325).[304] The Ninth Karmapa Dbang phyug rdo rje's (1556–1603) commentary on the *Treasury of Abhidharma* explains the verse by citing *Udānavarga*, chapter 3, verse 52, *Suhṛllekha* verse 13, and the *Prātimokṣa*.[305]

Prātimokṣa as the Buddha's successor

We have come to the end of this rather long-winded disquisition on a single word, heedfulness. The Buddha's last words are not the only thing on which the Pāli and other versions of the *Great Parinirvāṇa Sūtra* disagree: there are other discrepancies, some of them major. One weighty point on which the Mūlasarvāstivāda *Great Parinirvāṇa Sūtra* differs from its Pāli counterpart is the question of the Buddha's successor.[306] In the *Great Parinibbāna Sutta*, the Fortunate One declares that after he has passed away the Dhamma and Vinaya will be the monks' teacher. In the Mūlasarvāstivāda version, the Buddha appoints the monastic code, the *Prātimokṣa*, as his successor. This link between the Buddha's passing to final nirvāṇa and the monastic code as his successor is brought out in the opening verses of the Mūlasarvāstivāda *Prātimokṣa* itself:

> When I have passed away, then *this* [the *Prātimokṣa*] will be your teacher.

304. Chim Jampaiyang, *Ornament of Abhidharma*, pp. 1129–30; Tibetan in *Chos mngon pa mdzod kyi tshig le'ur byas pa'i 'grel pa mgnon pa'i rgyan*, pp. 691–92.
305. Tib. text, Karma pa Sku phreng dgu pa Dbang phyug rdo rje, *Chos mngon pa'i mdzod kyi rnam par bshad pa*, p. 578; trans. Choephel, *Jewels from the Treasury*, p. 582.
306. Bareau, *Recherches sur la biographie du Buddha II-II*, pp. 136–37.

2. The Buddha's Teaching in a Single Verse

Introduction

The Buddha's teaching in a single verse, translated here from the Pāli, is the first verse of the "Chapter on Heedfulness" in the Theravāda *Dhammapada*. Four verse collections preserved in Indic languages have a chapter on heedfulness, making the verse available in four Indic versions of the collections of four Buddhist schools:

Chapter 4 of the Sanskrit *Udānavarga*, with 38 verses (ed. Lévi): [Mūla]Sarvāstivāda[307]
Chapter 7 of the Khotan *Dharmapada* with 25 verses (ed. Brough): Dharmaguptaka
Chapter 2 of the Patna *Dhammapada* with 20 verses (ed. Cone):[308] Sāṃmitīya
Chapter 2 of the Pāli *Dhammapada* with 12 verses (many editions): Theravāda

To these we may add a fifth later and independent collection:

Chapter 6 of the *Dharmasamuccaya* with 194 verses (ed. Li-Kouang Lin).

The stanza is also quoted in the *Śarīrārthagāthā*, a collection of verses in the *Yogācārabhūmi*.[309]

307. These verses are all quoted consecutively in section 24.3 of the *Tridaṇḍamālā* (Jens-Uwe Hartmann, emails, 21 February and 2 March 2022).
308. References to Patna *Dhammapada*, passim, are to Margaret Cone's edition as published in Ānandajoti Bhikkhu, *Patna Dharmapada*. I prefer the title *Dhammapada* rather than *Dharmapada*.
309. Texts from Ānandajoti Bhikkhu, *A Comparative Edition of the Dhammapada*.

Box 8. *The apramāda verse: Comparison of sources*

Pāli 21 [2.1] **Appamāda**	**Patna 14 [2.1]** **Apramāda**	**Gāndhārī 115 [7.6]** **Apramadu**
appamādo amatapadaṁ, pamādo maccuno padaṁ, appamattā na mīyanti, ye pamattā yathā matā.	apramādo amatapadaṁ pramādo maccuno padaṁ | apramattā na mrīyanti ye pramattā yathā matā ||	apramadu amudapada pramadu mucuṇo pada apramata na miyadi ye pramata yadha mudu.
Udānavarga 4.1 **Apramāda**	**Śarīrārthagāthā** **vs 16**	**Dharmasamuccaya** **6.4**
apramādo hy amṛtapadaṁ pramādo mṛtyunaḥ padam apramattā na mriyante ye pramattāḥ sadā mṛtāḥ	apramādo 'mṛtapadaṁ pramādo mṛtyunaḥ padaṁ | apramattā na mriyante pramattās tu sadā mṛtāḥ	apramādo 'mṛtapadaṁ pramādo mṛtyunaḥ padam, apramattā na mriyante pramattāstu sadātmṛtāḥ

The first European translation of the verse was published in 1855 by Danish scholar Viggo Fausbøll (1821–1908) in his Latin translation of the *Dhammapada*:

> *vigilantia immortalitatis via (est), socordia mortis via; strenui non moriuntur, qui socordes, quasi mortui (sunt).*[310]

The *Dhammapada* has been translated into English and into many languages since. The translation of the verse given here is,

> Heedfulness is the path to the deathless;
> heedlessness is the path of death.
> They who are heedful do not die;
> they who are heedless are as dead.

The opposites *apramāda* and *pramāda* are frequently paired, and this pair of words is redolent with the flavors of a hundred and eight translations. The number of divergent translations says something about the difficulty of translating the terms. Since the *Dhammapada* is one of the most trans-

310. From the 1855 edition; the edition of 1900 (p. 7) changes *vigilantia* to *strenuitas*.

lated Buddhist works, I draw my examples from a sampling of *Dhammapada* translations.

> vigilantia / socordia (Latin trans. by Fausbøll 1855)
> strenuitas / socordia (Latin trans. by Fausbøll 1900)
> earnestness / thoughtlessness (Max Müller 1881)
> religion / irreligion (Gogerly in Bishop ed. 1908)
> vigilance / negligence (Ananda Maitreya 1978; Fronsdal 2006)
> vigilance / thoughtlessness, sloth, sluggishness, accidia[311] (Radhakrishnan 1950)
> vigilance / heedlessness (Buddharakkhita 1966)
> heedfulness / heedlessness (Buddharakkhita 1996; Thānissaro 1998)
> la vigilance / manque de vigilance (Osier 1997)
> la consapevolezza sollecita / l'incuria (Sferra 2001)
> awareness / unawareness (Carter and Palihawadana 1987; Roebuck 2010)
> mindfulness / unmindfulness (Daw Mya Tin 1993)
> estado de alerta y vigilanci / la desidia (Dragonetti and Tola 2013)
> Strebsamkeit / Nachlässigkeit (Hahn 2007)
> diligence (Malalasekera [1937] 1983)

To these we may add "zeal" (Nyanaponika), "conscientiousness," and Bareau's "absence de négligence" and "négligence,"[312] with Anālayo's "not being negligent" and "negligent," noting that for *pamāda* Childers also has "sloth."

A similar variety is seen in translations of the same terms in Nāgārjuna's celebrated *Letter to a Friend* (*Suhṛllekha*), an epistle that the great master sent to a Sātavāhana king in about the sixth to seventh centuries BE (second century CE):

> carefulness / carelessness (Wenzel 1886; Padmakara 2005)
> concern / unconcern (Karma Thinley 2009)
> heedfulness / heedlessness (Jamspal et al. 1978)
> mindfulness / heedlessness (Tharchin and Engle 1979)

311. For this interesting but somewhat neglected word, see Cassin, *Dictionary of Untranslatables*, pp. 7–8, s.v. *acedia*: "the rich Greek concept of *akâdeia* . . . bearing the twofold meaning of lacking care (negligence) and absence of care (from lassitude or from serenity)."

312. Bareau, *Recherches sur la biographie du Buddha II-II*, p. 140.

carefulness / negligence (Kawamura 1975)
Achtsamkeit / Achlosigkeit (Hahn and Dietz 2008)

Another difficulty in the translation of this deceptively simple *Dhammapada* verse concerns the meaning of *pada*: does it mean "path" or does it mean "place"? Most modern translators choose the former (*path* or *way*; Latin *via*, Italian *sentiero*, French *chemin*), while some choose *place* or *abode*. Michael Hahn has "die Basis" and "das Fundament." The translators into Tibetan chose "place" (*gnas*), probably following Prajñāvarman's exegetical tradition, which has *gnas* and *gzhi* ("base," "basis"), as well as *thabs* (which often translates *upāya*, "means" or "method") because *apramāda* enables one to attain nirvāṇa. In his *Vyākhyāyukti*, Vasubandhu gives nine different meanings of the single word *pada* (Tib. *gzhi*) in a section on "single terms with more than one meaning." The fifth meaning is "basis or foundation," for which Vasubandhu quotes *Udānavarga*, chapter 4, verse 1, lines *a* and *b* as example.[313]

The verse was generally well known, and it is included in all four Indic-language *Dhammapada* collections. Nāgārjuna quotes it as a verse within a verse of his *Letter to a Friend* (see box 9). Until recently the Sanskrit manuscript was not available, but a complete manuscript has recently been published and studied in Tibet by Dngos grub Tshe ring.[314] The citation, even in Sanskrit, does not offer any clues as to which recension Nāgārjuna might have consulted.[315]

313. Vasubandhu, *Vyākhyāyukti / Rnam par bshad pa'i rigs pa*, Otani no. 5562, repr. vol. 113, Sems tsam, *si*, 40a7; Lee, *Vyākhyāyukti*, p. 20.23.

314. Tshe ring, *Ta la'i lo mar bris pa'i rgya dpe bris ma*, p. 138. I am grateful to Saerji for informing me about this publication and to Saerji and the author for sending me a copy of the book.

315. Cf. also Padmakara Translation Group, *Nagarjuna's Letter to a Friend*, v. 13, pp. 30–31, rendering *apramāda* (*bag yod*) as "carefulness." An earlier, Indian commentary is that by Mahāmati (Blo gros chen po): *Vyaktapadā Suhṛllekhaṭīkā / Bshes pa'i spring yig gi rgya cher bshad pa tshig gsal ba*, Otani no. 5690, repr. vol. 129, Gtam yig, *nge*, 333b8–334a6, citing the *Udānavarga* verse at 334a3.

Box 9. *The apramāda verse in Nāgārjuna's Letter to a Friend*

amṛtapadam apramādo mṛtyoḥ padam uktavān pramādam ca
muniḥ |
tat kuśaladharmavṛddhyai tvayādarāt satatam apramādaḥ
kāryaḥ || 14 ||[316]

བག་ཡོད་བདུད་རྩིའི་གནས་ཏེ་བག་མེད་པ།
འཆི་བའི་གནས་སུ་ཐུབ་པས་བཀའ་བསྩལ་ཏེ།
དེ་བས་ཁྱོད་ཀྱིས་དགེ་ཆོས་སྤེལ་སླད་དུ།
གུས་པས་རྟག་ཏུ་བག་དང་བཅས་པར་མཛོད།།

bag yod bdud rtsi'i gnas te bag med pa |
'chi ba'i gnas su thub pas bka' bstsal te |
de bas khyod kyi dge chos spel slad du |
gus pas rtag tu bag dang bcas par mdzod ||

"Heedfulness is the abode of immortality,
while heedlessness is death's abode":
so the Sage [the Buddha] has taught.
Therefore, in order that
your virtuous deeds may grow,
constantly and assiduously be heedful.

A commentary by Nyingma master Kangyur Rinpoche (Klong chen Ye shes rdo rje, 1898–1975) cites *Udānavarga*, chapter 4, verse 1, the source of Nāgārjuna's quote, along with several passages from the *Sūtra on Establishing Awareness of the True Dharma* (*Saddharmasmṛtyupasthānasūtra*).[317] The *Sūtra on Establishing Awareness of the True Dharma* is a voluminous work in prose mixed with verse. Until recently it was not known to survive in Sanskrit, but the verses were available in the *Compendium of Dharma*, an

316. I cite a revised version by Péter-Dániel Szántó (personal communication).
317. Padmakara Translation Group, *Nagarjuna's Letter*, pp. 89–90.

anthology of 2,549 Sanskrit verses in 36 chapters, drawn from the sūtra at an unknown date by a Nepalese monk named Avalokitasiṃha.[318]

The *Compendium of Dharma* (*Dharmasamuccaya*), chapter 6, verse 4 (385), is very close to *Udānavarga*, chapter 4, verse 1 (see box 10).

Box 10. *An apramāda verse in Avalokitasiṃha's Dharmasamuccaya*

apramādo 'mṛtapadam pramādo mṛtyunaḥ padam
apramattā na mrīyante pramattās tu sadā mṛtāḥ

བག་ཡོད་བདུད་རྩིའི་གནས་ཡིན་ཏེ།
བག་མེད་འཆི་བའི་གནས་ཡི་ནོ།
བག་ཡོད་འཆི་བར་མི་འགྱུར་ཏེ།
བག་མེད་པ་ནི་རྟག་ཏུ་འཆི།།

bag yod bdud rtsi'i gnas yin te |
bag med 'chi ba'i gnas yi no |
bag yod 'chi bar mi 'gyur te |
bad med pa ni rtag tu 'chi ||

Heedfulness is immortality's abode,
heedlessness is death's foothold.
The heedful do not die;
the heedless are forever dead.

In 1922, French Indologist Sylvain Lévi was shown a twelfth-century manuscript of the *Compendium of Dharma* in Kathmandu, Nepal; he realized its importance immediately and had it copied. In those days, to copy a manuscript meant to engage a paṇḍita to make a copy by hand, running the risk that he would introduce errors through miscopying, misinterpreting, personal habit, etc.—which frequently enough did happen. Back in Paris, Lévi entrusted the text to Lin Li-Kouang (Lin Liguang 林黎光, 1902–45), a young scholar from Shanghai, to edit. During his stay in Nepal, Italian master of Buddhist and Himalayan studies Giuseppe Tucci arranged for a second

318. For this work, see Barua, "Dharma-samuccaya," and Lin Li-Kouang, *Dharmasamuccaya*. Nothing is known about Avalokitasiṃha. The *Dharmasamuccaya* was translated into Chinese in 1064, so Avalokitasiṃha would have compiled the work some time before that date.

copy to be made. Both copies are poorly executed, and alas, the original manuscript can no longer be traced. Lin Li-Kouang ably edited the *Compendium of Dharma*, and it was published posthumously with the editorial embellishments of some of the greatest masters of European Buddhist studies of the age: André Bareau, J. W. de Jong, Paul Demiéville, and Louis Renou.[319]

"Heedfulness" and the epigraphy of King Mongkut of Siam

Let us jump across the Bay of Bengal to see how "heedfulness" has fared in a region where Theravaṃsa has had a continual living presence.[320] King Rāma IV of Siam (King Mongkut, 1804–68) spent twenty-seven years as a monk before ascending the throne in 1851. A deeply devout Buddhist, he was a profound Pāli scholar in his own right and a master of many genres of writing.[321] A part of his impressive literary legacy is an epigraphic corpus that includes Pāli inscriptions: the king both *composed* Pāli inscriptions and he *chose* Pāli texts to be inscribed by royal command. The king had the "Chapter on Heedfulness" of the *Dhammapada* inscribed on a gold plate to be installed in a stūpa at Wat Pho (Wat Phra Chetuphon: วัดโพธิ์ / วัดพระเชตุพน) in Bangkok. The leaf measures 4.07 × 42.02 cm and is inscribed in five lines on a single side; it gives the complete "Chapter on Heedfulness" in Khom letters.[322] The chapter is followed by a quote from the *Numerical Discourses*:[323]

> Bhikkhus, I do not see a single thing that so causes unarisen wholesome qualities to arise and unwholesome qualities that have arisen to decline as does heedfulness. For one who is heedful, unarisen wholesome qualities arise and arisen unwholesome qualities decline.

319. Lin's model edition gives Sanskrit, Tibetan, and Chinese with French translation for each verse; see his *Dharmasamuccaya: Compendium de la Loi, recueil de stances extraites du Saddharma-smṛty-upasthāna-sūtra par Avalokitasiṃha*.
320. For this idea see Skilling, "The Theravaṃsa Has Always Been Here." I do not mean to propose tidy absolute continuities, only to suggest the persistence and recurrence of ordination lineages and teachings combined with intangible ideals and imaginaires.
321. The king's Pāli writings are collected in King Mongkut, *Prachum Phra Ratchaniphon phasa bali* (in Thai script Pāli and Thai language only).
322. Verse 29 is omitted. I presume this was inadvertent.
323. *Aṅguttaranikāya, Ekanipāta*, vol. 1, p. 11.20–25; trans. Bodhi, *Numerical Discourses*, pp. 98–99; *Dīghanikāya*, vol. 2, p. 156.1.

This is followed by the Buddha's final statement as presented in the *Great Parinibbāna Sutta*. The plate was excavated in 2531 BE (1988 CE) during the course of renovations in the crypt of the Phra Mahachedi Munibatborikhan (Phra Mahācetīya Munīpat-parikhāra พระ มหาเจดีย์ มุนีปัตบริขาร), which had been erected by King Rāma III as the cetiya of his reign in 2376 BE (1833 CE).[324]

King Mongkut's most ambitious epigraphic project was at the great reliquary tower of Phra Pathom Chedi in Nakhon Pathom (then Nakhon Chaisi) west of Bangkok (พระปฐมเจดีย์ นครปฐม / นครชัยศรี = Phra Paṭhama Cetīya, Nagara Paṭhama / Nagara Jayaśrī). The king had revered this cetiya, then in ruins, ever since he visited it when he was a monk; he believed it was the "first cetiya" (*paṭhamacetiya*), erected at the site where the monks Sona and Uttara brought the Buddha's teaching to Suvaṇṇabhūmi when sent by Moggaliputta Tissa during the time of King Aśoka.[325] In this he followed a distinctive Theravāda historiography recounted in middle-period Pāli works like the *Chronicle of the Island of Laṅkā* and the *Vinaya* commentary.[326] The devout King Mongkut had the shrine and its precincts restored, a process that led to the transformation of the area surrounding the deserted jungle ruins into a lively market town. He had Pāli texts inscribed in large calligraphic Khom letters around the entire inner wall of the covered circumambulatory circling the base of the huge cetiya. His choice of texts included the complete *Dhammapada*, the "Chapter of Octads" (*Aṭṭhakavagga*) and "Chapter on the Way to the Beyond" (*Pārāyaṇavagga*) of the *Suttanipāta*, along with several excerpts from the *Sagāthavagga* of the *Connected Discourses*. Included as part of the *Dhammapada*, the "Chapter on Heedfulness" originally occupied bays 5 and 6 out of a total 120 bays that encircle the great stūpa, but at present some portions of texts in bay 5 are damaged, while the writing in bay 6 is entirely effaced.[327]

For the king these were core texts, part of his personal curriculum, but we do not know much more than that: why he undertook the project, how he chose the texts, or what his purpose was beyond spreading the Dhamma. In this unique venture, the king gave a high profile to the Pāli texts by having

324. Wat Phrachetuphonwimonmankhalaram, *Boranawatthu*, pp. 238–39; registration no. กท. ๒๗๕ พช. ๓(๑๓) [*ko.tho* 18, *pho cho* 3(13)].

325. For Suvarṇabhūmi in Southeast Asian epigraphy, see Skilling, "Many Lands of Gold."

326. See Lamotte, *Histoire*, pp. 328–29.

327. "At present" refers to 2020, when a Fragile Palm Leaves / Henry Ginsburg Fund field team photographed the inscriptions.

them inscribed in large Khom letters on the pleasant and spacious grounds of the restored great cetiya.[328] The site was accessible from Bangkok by canals that the king had had built, Mahasawat Canal and Chedi Puja Canal (Canal of Great Auspice and Canal to Worship the Cetiya, คลองมหาสวัสดิ์, คลองเจดีย์บูชา). At some point, the nobility joined in on a related project to sponsor bell shrines around the outer platform and have them inscribed with poems in Thai. Put together, this was a significant cultural project of a reign that saw many innovations in the public face of the Dhamma, including temples, images, inscriptions, and murals. The Pāli inscription around the inner circumambulatory of Phra Pathom Chedi was the biggest Pāli epigraphic undertaking of nineteenth-century Siam.[329]

3. Getting Off the Wheel of Life

Introduction

Heedfulness features in a pair of verses that is widely disseminated not only in texts but in art and epigraphy as well:

> Arise, go forth, devote yourself
> to the Awakened One's teachings.
> Crush the army of death
> the way an elephant tramples
> a flimsy hut made of reeds.
>
> One who dwells heedful
> in this teaching and system of training
> leaves rebirth's round behind
> and puts an end to pain.

These two verses are well represented in literature, where they usually are paired. They conclude the previously mentioned "Chapter on Heedfulness"

328. Note that for the central Thai at the time, Khom (ขอม) was the main option for writing and reading Pāli.
329. Internationally, it was surpassed only by King Mindon's marble Tipiṭaka at Mandalay in neighboring Burma, completed in 1868 and dubbed "the world's largest book." For this see Wiles et al., "The Pāli Tipiṭaka Recension Carved on the Kuthodaw Pagoda Stelae."

of the *Udānavarga*,[330] and are included in the "Heedfulness" (*Apramadu*) chapter of the Khotan *Dhammapada* (verses 123 and 125).

The Pāli *Dhammapada* does not contain the verses, but this does not mean that they are not found in the Pāli canon. The different recensions of the various *Dhammapada*s are independent editorial events, compiled by different redactors belonging to various schools and different times in different places. The redactors drew on pools of verses and did not necessarily choose to include the same texts. Elsewhere in the Pāli Tripiṭaka, the pair occurs two times: once in the *Connected Discourses* and once in the *Verses of the Senior Monks*. In the former, in the *Aruṇavatīsutta*, Gotama the Buddha recites a story that took place in the far distant past in the capital city of Aruṇavatī, during the time of the Buddha Sikhī.[331]

> One day, the Buddha Sikhī traveled to the Brahmā world with one of his "excellent pair of disciples," the brahman monk Abhibhū.[332] At Sikhī's behest, Abhibhū instructed the Brahmā deities and their assembly and performed wondrous feats. Then, with Sikhī's permission, Abhibhū made his voice resound throughout the thousandfold world system, proclaiming the two verses. When he returned to earth, to Aruṇavatī, the Buddha Sikhī asked the monks there whether they on earth had heard the monk Abhibhū intone the verses from the Brahmā world. They replied in the affirmative.

This short sutta becomes the opening for a Pāli cosmological text with the same title, transmitted and perhaps compiled in Siam.[333]

In the *Verses of the Senior Monks*, Abhibhūta (note the similarity of the names) proclaims the couplet to his relatives, prefixing it with a verse of his own.[334]

330. *Udānavarga*, chap. 4, vv. 37–38.

331. *Aruṇavatīsutta*, *Sagāthavagga*, *Brahmasaṃyutta*, *Saṃyuttanikāya*, vol. 1, pp. 155–57. See Skilling, "'Arise, Go Forth, Devote Yourselves.'"

332. According to early Buddhology, all Buddhas share certain qualities or characteristics. One of these is that each Buddha has a pair of outstanding disciples—in Śākyamuni's case, these were Śāriputra and Maudgalyāyana.

333. *Aruṇavatīsutta* in *Lokuppatti Aruṇavatīsūtra Paṭhamamūl Paṭhamakap lae Mūlatantrai*, Pāli pp. 45, 65–66; Thai trans. pp. 73–74, 100–101. The verses occur in several other Thai apocrypha that have not yet been studied or edited.

334. *Theragāthā*, *Tikanipāta*, vv. 255–57; trans. Norman, *Elders' Verses I*, p. 33.

> Listen, kinsmen, as many as are assembled here. I shall teach you the doctrine; rebirth again and again is painful.
>
> Exert yourselves, go forth, devote yourselves to the Buddha's teaching. Knock down the army of death as a kuñjara elephant knocks down a reed hut.
>
> Whoever will dwell vigilant in this doctrine and discipline, eliminating journeying-on from rebirth to rebirth, will put and end to pain.

The second verse occurs in the Pāli *Great Parinibbāna Sutta*.[335]

Mūlasarvāstivāda contributions

The pair of verses is singled out in Mūlasarvāstivāda narratives recounted in the Tibetan translation of the *Chapters on Vinaya* (*Vinayavastu*) and in Sanskrit avadānas preserved in the *Divyāvadāna*. Some stories connect the verses with painting: in one case the wheel of life and in others a portrait of the Buddha on cloth (*paṭa*). According to the *Vinayavastu* and the *Sahasodgata-avadāna*, the verses should be painted alongside the wheel of life in the vestibules of the monasteries.[336] A fragmentary painting of the wheel survives at cave 17 at Ajanta in central India, but if the verses were included at one time, the inscription is now obliterated, and there is no trace of any letters.[337] This is the only known example in India;[338] however, Tibetan and Himalayan Buddhists adhere to the Mūlasarvāstivāda Vinaya tradition and as a result have the custom to paint the wheel at the entrance halls of monasteries, accompanied by the Tibetan translation of the verses. In addition, the verses are lettered on Tibetan scroll paintings (*paṭa*, *thang ka*) of the wheel of life. A rare Chinese example is a wheel of life carved in the rock surface at the Baodingshan cave complex in Sichuan province, southern China; the

335. See introduction to translation 1.

336. *Divyāvadāna* no. 21, *Sahasodgata*, p. 300; trans. Rotman, *Divine Stories: Part 2*, p. 97; Skilling, "'Arise, Go Forth, Devote Yourselves.'" The classic study is Przyluski, "La roue de la vie à Ajanta."

337. Zin and Schlingloff, *Saṃsāracakra*. For a color picture, see Singh, *Ajanta Paintings*, no. 46, pp. 162–63. See also Teiser, *Reinventing the Wheel*, pl. 8, p. 27.

338. Zin and Schlingloff, *Saṃsāracakra*, p. 20, n.81, what was apparently a wheel of life was visible at Kanheri in the nineteenth century. It was described by James Burgess but has been long since obliterated.

two verses in Chinese translation flank the intricately depicted wheel.[339] In all these examples, the positioning of the message like a caption beside the depiction of the Buddha shows that heedfulness is the way out of the whirling rat-race of the wheel of life.

In another narrative, the Buddha explains how to make a portrait of his person for King Bimbisāra to send to King Rudrāyaṇa,[340] or, in the *Adhikaraṇavastu*, to send to a princess on the isle of Laṅkā.[341] The couplet occurs in the well-known episode of the *Great Miracles*, which is found in the "Chapter on Medicine" of the *Vinayavastu*, in the Nepalese *Divyāvadāna*,[342] and is quoted in Śamathadeva's *Upāyikāṭīkā*.[343]

A further connection with monasticism is shown by the placement of the verses at the end of the Mūlasarvāstivāda *Prātimokṣa*,[344] linking them up with the prose pronouncement studied in the introduction to translation 1.

What about India, where the Mūlasarvāstivāda and other Vinaya schools flourished for centuries in well-endowed monasteries? Are there any examples there? Time shows no mercy: long ago the monasteries were destroyed or lapsed into ruin, and as noted, no wall paintings of any extent survive. But a single stone inscription survived at Nālandā, one of the grand monastic centers of medieval northeastern India. There the stanzas are engraved along with a dedicatory inscription and other verses. Archaeologist and epigraphist Hiranand Sastri (1878–1946) describes it as follows:[345] "three fine little stūpas in stone . . . which in all probability were built in the reign of Mahendrapāladeva, who flourished about 896–908 AD and was the son and successor of Bhoja—the well-known Pratihāra king of Kanauj." All bear Sanskrit inscriptions in the Nāgarī script. Inscriptions A and B are citations of a

339. Howard, *Summit of Treasures*, pp. 6–9 with figs. 9, 10.

340. *Divyāvadāna* no. 37, *Rudrāyaṇa*, p. 547; trans. Rotman, *Divine Stories: Part 2*, p. 291. Summarized in the commentary on Mātṛceṭa's *Śatapañcāśatka*: Shackleton Bailey, *Śatapañcāśatka of Mātṛceṭa*, Tibetan text, p. 74, and English summary, p. 202.

341. Gnoli, *The Gilgit Manuscript of the Śayanāsanavastu and the Adhikaraṇavastu*, pp. 65–66, verses at p. 66.8.

342. *Divyāvadāna* no. 12, p. 162, "The Miracle Sūtra," trans. Rotman, *Divine Stories: Part 1*, pp. 279–80. Rotman translates *apramattaś cariṣyati* of line b as "diligently follows."

343. Quotation from the **Mahāprātihāryasūtra / Cho 'phrul chen po'i mdo*, ad *Abhidharmakośabhāṣya*, chap. 4, v. 32, Mngon pa'i bstan bcos, *tu*, verses at 250a2–4.

344. Sanskrit in Banerjee, *Two Buddhist Vinaya Texts in Sanskrit*, p. 56.1–4 (vv. 14, 15); Tib. in Vidyabhusana, *So-sor thar pa*, p. 110.9–16 (vv. 36, 37).

345. Sastri, "Votive Inscription of the Reign of Mahendrapāladeva," pp. 106–7, plate 11, a–c.

verse aspiration from the *Bhadracarīpraṇidhāna*.[346] Inscription C gives the *ye dharmā* stanza in two lines. Inscription D gives the pair of verses.

Occurrences of the pair do not end here. Several apocryphal Pāli suttas transmitted in Thailand cite the verses. The Chinese translation of the *Great Assembly Sūtra* (*Mahāsamājasūtra*, no. 19 in the *Dīrghāgama*) includes the two verses at the end of the sūtra.[347] The Madhyamaka master Bhāviveka cites the two stanzas in his *Jewel Lamp of the Middle Way* (*Madhyamakaratnapradīpa*).[348] Further afield, in chapter 22 of the Khotanese *Book of Zambasta*, Śākyamuni gives a poetic prediction of Maitreya's coming that includes the statement that "three times by night, by day, he will inform beings: . . . 'Begin now to go out! Strive in the Buddha's *śāsana*. Break up the army of death as an elephant a hut of reeds.'" This is clearly parallel to *Udānavarga*, chapter 4, verse 37.

346. Identified in Schopen, "A Verse from the Bhadracārī."

347. Waldschmidt, *Bruchstücke buddhistischer Sūtras*, p. 194; Ichimura, *Canonical Book of the Buddha's Lengthy Discourses*, p. 139.

348. Lindtner, "Materials for the Study of Bhavya," pp. 186–87.

Impermanence

4. Chapter on Impermanence

We have seen that heedfulness is linked to impermanence. Life's transience and instability infuse spiritual practice with urgency, and impermanence is the theme of translations 4 to 11. We open with the "Chapter on Impermanence" of the *Udānavarga*. As universal realities, transience and death are universal themes of philosophy and poetry. In James Shirley's "Dirge" (1659), he reflects on death and impermanence:[349]

> The glories of our blood and state
> Are shadows, not substantial things,
> There is no armour against fate,
> Death lays his icy hand on Kings.
>   Scepter and crown,
>   Must tumble down,
> And in the dust be equal made,
> With the poor crooked scythe and spade.
>
> Some men with swords may reap the field,
> And plant fresh laurels where they kill,
> But their strong nerves at last must yield,
> They tame but one another still.

349. James Shirley (1596–1666), "Dirge"—text and punctuation after Bloom, *The Best Poems of the English Language*, pp. 155–56. Bloom remarks: "I remember Robert Frost, at one of his readings, starting off by reciting Shirley's 'Dirge' from memory, remarking that it was a favorite poem."

Early or late,
They stoop to fate,
And must give up their murmuring breath,
When they, pale captives, creep to death.

The garlands wither on your brow,
Then boast no more your mighty deeds;
Upon death's purple altar now,
See where the victor-victim bleeds,
Your heads must come,
To the cold tomb;
Only the actions of the just
Smell sweet, and blossom in their dust.[350]

Introduction to the Udānavarga

The "Chapter on Impermanence" that opens the *Udānavarga* is not a cheerful chapter; its verses ask us to face what we don't want to face—the stark reality of our mortality.

The *Udānavarga* is a collection of 1050 verses divided into thirty-three chapters. According to Sarvāstivāda tradition, it was compiled by Dharmatrāta (Tib. Chos skyob), about whom little is known.[351] To say that little or nothing is known about an ancient, and even a not so ancient, author is normal in Buddhist and Indian studies. Two thousand years ago and more, hundreds of authors composed and compiled thousands of texts—from poetry to epics, from philosophy to psychology, from medicine to cosmology to grammar. Strictly speaking, they were not writers: they composed their works orally, their works circulated orally, and they were received orally. They were composers, and their poetry was symphonic (but that is another tune). This was an age when records as we conceive of them today were none or scant, and genres like biography and autobiography were not in vogue. Any records or hagiographies that might have existed would have been lost

350. The last two lines bring to mind some of the verses of the "Chapter on Flowers" of the *Dhammapada*: see Roebuck, *Dhammapada*, vv. 54–56.

351. See Lin Li-Kouang, *Introduction au Compendium de la Loi*, appendix 9, especially pp. 314–16, and note on Dharmatrāta by Brough, *Gāndhārī Dharmapada*, pp. 39–41.

during centuries of social change and turbulence—that is, they would have gone the way of impermanence.

Verse collections were cherished sourcebooks, and it is likely that every major Buddhist school would have had at least one. The preface to the Chinese *Faju jing* (法句經, dated 224 CE) reports that śramaṇas of the five schools compiled *Dhammapada* collections, the five schools being interpreted as the Dharmaguptaka, Sarvāstivāda, Kāśyapīya, Mahīśāsaka, and Vātsīputrīya.[352] *Udānavarga* verses are embedded in narrative, homiletic, exegetical, and ritual literature. This wide-ranging intertextuality shows that the *Udānavarga* verses were well known and well used.

The *Udānavarga* was extremely popular in Central Asia, and large numbers of manuscript fragments have been recovered from several sites along the northern Silk Road.[353] There is a detailed and erudite commentary by Prajñāvarman (circa twelfth century BE), *Opening Up the Udānavarga* (*Udānavargavivaraṇa*), a masterpiece of Indian exegetical literature that is preserved in Tibetan translation only—the Sanskrit is no longer extant and there is no Chinese translation. The commentary gives a story for each verse or cluster of verses. Prajñāvarman was a well-versed Sarvāstivādin who had evidently mastered the texts of other Buddhist traditions, and he sometimes supplies two or even three alternate stories for a single verse.[354] It is evident that the verses come first: that it is the verses that count, not their narrative backstories. Different texts give a range of different narratives for the setting of the first verse of the *Udānavarga* alone, a pattern that continues through the thirty-three chapters to the end.[355]

The *Udānavarga* was translated into the Central Asian languages Tocharian A and Tocharian B.[356] The *Ornament of the Udāna* (*Udānālaṃkāra*), or,

352. Lévi, "L'Apramāda-varga," p. 218. Note that the Sthavira, that is the Theravaṃsa, are not mentioned. When we add the Pāli *Dhammapada*, the total becomes six.

353. For a chapter-by-chapter itemization of fragments from the Northern Silk Road preserved in the British Library, see Wille, "Survey of the Identified Sanskrit Manuscripts in the Hoernle, Stein, and Skrine Collections of the British Library (London)," pp. 234–37. For the *Udānavarga* in the Turfan Collection, see Wille, "Survey of the Sanskrit Manuscripts in the Turfan Collection (Berlin)," p. 203; for the French collections, see Hartmann and Wille, "The Central Asian Fragments in the Pelliot Collection (Paris)," pp. 213–22.

354. See Skilling, "Theravādin Literature in Tibetan Translation," § 2.4, pp. 143–53.

355. Lee, *A Study of the Śarīrārthagāthā in the Yogācārabhūmi*, pp. 157–58, n. 495. Some of the narratives overlap while some are quite different.

356. Extracts in Pinault, *Chrestomathie tokharienne*, pp. 37–59. These include five examples from the *Anityavarga*, Skt. verse nos. 12, 16, 17, 28, and 42.

a verse commentary by Dharmasoma, was recovered from Šorčuk and Kizil, and there is also a *Eulogy of the Udāna* (*Udānastotra*) in Tocharian B. In the latter the scribe expresses his wish for benefits and rewards for each chapter that he has written, making it a kind of benedictory exercise in quest of merits and blessings (*anuśaṃsa*).[357] Both texts are fragmentary. There are some folios in Uighur as well.

The deep impact of the *Udānavarga* on the Sarvāstivāda literary legacy is revealed by the prodigious number of Sanskrit manuscripts discovered along the Silk Road in Central Asia, its translation into Tibetan along with Prajñāvarman's commentary, and the translation of the verses into Chinese and Central Asian languages like Tocharian. The prestige that the collection enjoyed in India traveled with it to Tibet, where it was selected for translation in the early period. It was classed as a *śāstra* in the early translation registers the *Lhan dkar ma* and the *'Phang thang ma*, but later it was recognized as *bka'*, word or pronouncement of the Buddha, and the collection was placed in the sūtra section of Kanjurs. Today the *Udānavarga* is preserved in both Kanjurs and Tanjurs. In the former it is available in the two main Kanjur lineages, the Them spangs ma and the Tshal pa, and also in independent and local Kanjurs; in the Tanjur it is placed in the "sūtra commentary section" (*mdo 'grel*), where it is paired with Prajñāvarman's commentary, as Bu ston's catalogue (*dkar chag*) notes.[358]

The *Udānavarga* is one of the "six authoritative treatises of Kadam," a set of curricular works of the Kadampa (Bka' gdams pa), a tradition stemming from the east Indian master Atiśa and established in Tibet by Potowa Rinchen Sal (Po to ba Rin chen gsal, 1027/31–1105):[359]

357. For *anuśaṃsa*, see Skilling, "Ānisaṃsa: Merit, Motivation."

358. See Cordier, *Catalogue du fonds tibétain*, troisième partie, pp. 398–99, "Tome *du*, LXXI, 1," followed immediately by the commentary, *Udānavargavivaraṇa*. Bu ston, *Rgyal ba'i dgongs 'grel bstan 'gyur rin po che'i bzhugs byang dkar chag*, p. 434: *du pa la | ched du brjod pa'i tshoms dgra bcom pa chos skyob kyis bsdus pa . . . 'di bye brag tu smra ba rnams kyis bka' nyid du bzhed do || ched du brjod pa'i tshoms kyi 'grel ba slob dpon shes rab go chas mdzad pa'i stod bzhugs so* ||. Cordier pointed this out in a footnote: "D'après l'I[ndex], (fol. 126^{b}. 2), œuvre considerée comme un Āgama (Bkaḥ) par les Vaibhāṣikas (Bye-brag-tu smra-ba-rnams)." ["According to the Index, the Vaibhāṣikas consider this work to be the authoritative word of the Buddha (*bkaḥ*)."] See also Bu ston's remark at Herrmann-Pfandt, *Die Lhan Kar Ma*, § 309: *'di sngar gyi dkar chag dag las bstan bcos su bgrangs la da lta bkar grags*: "While the earlier registers counted this as a 'treatise,' at present it is consdered to be the word of the Buddha (*bka'*)."

359. Jinpa, trans., *Book of Kadam*, p. 9; Roesler et al. trans, *Stages of the Buddha's Teachings*, p. 633, n. 19. For the history of the Kadam and its distinctive literary traditions, see idem., pp. 1

Bodhisattvabhūmi of Asaṅga
Mahāyānasūtrālaṃkāra of Maitreya
Bodhisatvacaryāvatāra of Śāntideva
Śikṣāsamuccaya of Śāntideva
Jātakamālā of Āryaśūra
Udānavarga

The presence of the *Udānavarga* and the *Jātakamālā* in the curriculum shows how these are shared texts, cherished and consulted by all traditions. The *Udānavarga* is cited in manuals on the stages of the path (*lam rim*) literature and remains popular today.[360] Tsong kha pa Blo bzang grags pa (1357–1419) was trained in the Kadampa tradition; he went on to become one of the most influential figures in Tibetan monasticism, and after his death the spiritual lineage that he established became known as the Gelukpa (Dge lugs pa), today one of the most important Tibetan schools of thought and practice.[361]

The Tibetan title is *Ched du brjod pa'i tshoms*, "Chapter on Significant Sayings." *Brjod pa* means "saying" or "pronouncement," here prefixed by *ched du*. Michael Hahn interpreted *ched du* as follows: "Skt. *udāna* 'solemn uttering (of the Buddha)' becomes *ched du brjod pa* 'that which is spoken in a meaningful manner.' *Ched* 'greatness; importance' is a noun derived from the qualitative verb *che* 'to be great' with the help of the noun suffix *-d*."[362] The *Encyclopaedic Tibetan-English Dictionary* gives several meanings.[363]

As a literary product, as a massive compilation of verses, the *Udānavarga* is closely related to the *Dharmapadas*. At present we have access to four Indic-language *Udānavarga*/*Dharmapadas*:[364]

---

foll., Jinpa's introduction to *Book of Kadam*, and Apple's introduction to *Jewels of the Middle Way*.

360. Gampopa cites the *Udānavarga* by title five times in his chapter 4, "Instruction in the Transitoriness of the Composite" Le'u bzhi pa, 'Dus byas mi rtag pa, in *Dam chos yid bzhin nor bu thar pa rin po che'i rgyan*: see Guenther, trans., *Jewel Ornament of Liberation*, pp. 42, 45, 46, 47.

361. For Tsong kha pa's life and thought, see Jinpa, *Tsongkhapa: A Buddha in the Land of Snows.*

362. Hahn, "Miscellanea Etymologica Tibetica VIII."

363. *Encyclopaedic Tibetan-English Dictionary*, p. 1094 s.v. *ched*; see definitions of *ched du brjod pa'i sde* and *ched du brjod pa'i tshoms*, p. 1095.

364. See Nakatani, "Remarques sur la transmission des Dharmapada," tableau 1, "Versions du Dharmapada." Note that not all versions of the Dharmapada are complete.

Udānavarga in Sanskrit (Sarvāstivāda/Mūlasarvāstivāda)
Dhammapada in Pāli (Theravāda)
Dhammapada in Prakrit (Sāṃmitīya)
Dharmapada in Gāndhārī Prakrit (Dharmaguptaka)[365]

In ancient South Asia, verse collections of known as *Udānas* or *Dhammapadas* were primary sources for learning and teaching the Dharma. They were studied and recited, and they were reflected and commented upon. This was the case until Indian Buddhism declined and the saṅgha system broke down, with the result that the Buddhist Dharma ceased to be a social or intellectual force in mainland South Asia. Its decline and demise had devastating effects: Buddhist texts ceased to be copied, studied, or taught, and the moral and metaphysical spaces once occupied by Buddhism closed down. The result of this was that a significant alternate voice in India's collective spiritual conversation fell silent.

Amongst the various *Dharmapadas*, the Gāndhārī and Prakrit versions were lost when the monasteries that stored them were abandoned or destroyed and the lay and monastic communities that maintained and used them dispersed or died out. They only began to resurface around the end of the nineteenth century—not as living texts but as archaeological booty or bibliographic finds. The Gāndhārī *Dharmapada*—which scholars now prefer to call the "Khotan *Dharmapada*" to differentiate it from other Gāndhārī Prakrit *Dharmapadas* found a century later—was obtained in the last decade of the nineteenth century and studied in Paris and St. Petersburg. The *Dhammapada* of the Sāṃmitīya was unknown until a single manuscript preserved in a Tibetan monastery was photographed in the 1930s, on separate expeditions, by two great twentieth-century cultural explorers, Rahul Sankrityayan (1893–1963) and Giuseppe Tucci (1894–1984). It is in Prakrit and has been known as the "Patna Dhammapada" because the materials collected by Sankrityayan are kept in Patna, the capital of Bihar state in India. There was uncertainty and confusion about the *Dhammapada*'s school affiliation until the 1980s, when researchers began to propose that this was a specific recension, that of the Sāṃmitīya school, and that it was composed in their

365. The last two affiliations are established by hypothesis.

canonical Prakrit. This affiliation is now firmly established, but it is still not widely known, and the text has not yet been translated.[366]

Other recensions of the *Dharmapada* are preserved in Chinese translations, and studying them in tandem with Indic or other versions enables scholars to form a diachronic picture of the development of this family of texts, albeit with many gaps. But this is far afield from our subject here, which is limited to a single chapter of the *Udānavarga*. This section does not pretend to be a comprehensive critical or philological study; it is simply an introduction to a translation of the Tibetan version of the first out of the *Udānavarga*'s thirty-three chapters. The comparative study of the *Udānavarga* was already initiated in 1883 by Rockhill, who refers to parallels in the Kanjur and Tanjur, in Pāli texts such as the *Suttanipāta* and *Mahāparinibbānasutta*, in Vasubandhu's *Gāthāsaṃgraha*, in Beal's translation of the *Dhammapada* from Chinese, and in the *Mānavadharmāśāstra*.

Journey to the West

Out of the many collections of Buddhist verses that once existed and survive in some form today, only two have had an uninterrupted existence as complete, living texts: the Pāli *Dhammapada* and the Tibetan *Udānavarga*. The Pāli *Dhammapada* circulates in lands where Theravāda communities hold sway, and through translation it has become a world classic. Already by 1912 the prescient polymath Sylvain Lévi was able to remark that the *Dhammapada*[367]

> had been translated into all the languages of the Occident and had entered into the literature of humanity. It deserved this honor by virtue of the nobility of its morality and the striking beauty of its imagery which contrasts with the oftentimes plodding allure of the style. India, which has produced many masterpieces

366. The most recent and thorough report on this is Dimitrov, *The Buddhist Indus Script and Scriptures*, especially part 2.

367. Lévi, "L'Apramāda-varga," p. 204: "L'ouvrage a été traduit dans toutes les langues de l'Occident; il est entré dans la littérature de l'humanité. Il méritait cet honneur, par la noblesse de sa morale et par la beauté saisissante des images, qui contraste avec l'allure souvent traînante du style. L'Inde, qui compte tant de chefs-d'œuvre dans la poésie gnomique, n'a rien qui dépasse la Dhammapada, ou même qui l'égale."

of gnomic poetry, has nothing that surpasses, or even equals, the *Dhammapada.*

How did the *Dhammapada* come to be known in Europe and the West? When Buddhism began to attract interest as a field of research, Latin was still a living vehicle of intellectual discourse, and the Pāli *Dhammapada* was published in roman letters with a Latin translation in 1855. This was three decades after the German romanticist A. W. Schlegel (1767–1845) had produced a complete Latin translation of the *Bhagavadgītā* in 1823.[368] In 1836, Indologist Christian Lassen (1800–1876) produced a text edition with Latin translation of a classic of Indian devotional poetry, the *Gītagovinda.*[369] In 1874, Richard Pischel (1849–1908) published his thesis on Prakrit grammar in Latin.[370] This was an age when the learned society of Europe was steeped in Latin; the two living intellectual languages of Sanskrit and Latin met in the early seminars of orientalist learning in the hallowed halls of European universities, which since their foundation had been organs of the church. Now they were branching out towards what would become comparative philology and comparative religion.[371]

That the Pāli text was published in roman script was significant in that the early scholars treated the *Dhammapada* like a European classical work to be studied in the roman script rather than as a local or regional work to be read in Sinhala- or Nāgarī-script editions. Ever since then, Pāli texts have been published in roman letters in the West, and those who wish to study the language are not obliged to learn any "oriental alphabets." This has had the positive effect of making Pāli accessible to European and world scholarship, and the detrimental effect of encouraging scholars to ignore "native" editions in Indic-derived scripts.[372]

368. For reception and research see Malinar, *The Bhagavadgītā*, pp. 17–34.

369. Ramesh, *Light of Asia*, p. 41.

370. It was published at Breslau in Silesia (now Wrocław, Poland) as *De Grammaticis Prâcriticis*, then translated into German as *Grammatik der Prakrit-Sprachen* in 1900, and from German to English in 1955, with a second revised edition in 1981.

371. Earlier orientalist translations of scriptures go back at least to Robert of Ketton's translation of the Qur'an into Latin in 1143.

372. The use of roman letters met, however, some resistance: see Brandt, "Why Dots and Dashes Matter." Danish scholar Viggo Fausbøll had triumphalist notions about not only roman characters but also the English language, writing in the preface to the second edition of the *Dhammapada* (p. ix) that "there can be no doubt about the Roman (Latin) character triumphing at last over all others" and "the English language will in time likewise be the uni-

This was a major phase of transition, an age of interface when information that had been stored in memory and manuscript for centuries was transferred to the printed page and bound in books for the first time. It was the age of manuscript research, and early nineteenth-century scholars worked almost entirely directly from manuscripts, for the simple reason that printed editions scarcely existed at that time. Eugène Burnouf's monumental translation of the *Lotus Sūtra*, 897 pages long and supplemented by twenty-one appendixes, was based on Nepalese manuscripts, and his comparative notes were also drawn directly from manuscripts. For example, for his appendix on the thirty-two characteristics of a great man (appendix 8), Burnouf consulted seven texts: manuscripts of the Sanskrit *Lalitavistara*, the Pāli *Dīghanikāya* (*Lakkhaṇasutta*, *Mahāpadānasutta*), and the Sinhala *Dharmapradīpikā*, along with published versions of the Tibetan *Lalitavistara*, Sanskrit *Dharmasaṃgraha*, and a pentaglot vocabulary.

The *Dhammapada* did not take long to gain the reputation of being a world classic. In 1950, Dr. Sarvepalli Radhakrishnan (1888–1975) published an English translation that included an introductory essay on "Gautama the Buddha," which he had first delivered at the Annual Lecture on a Master Mind at the British Academy in 1938. Radhakrishnan was a world-renowned philosopher, statesman, and teacher: since 1962, his birthday, September 5, has been celebrated as India's Teachers' Day. Radhakrishnan had a distinguished career as professor and chancellor at leading universities in India. At Oxford he was professor of Eastern religions and ethics from 1936 to 1952; from 1952 to 1962 he was vice-president of the Republic of India, and from 1962 to 1967 he was president. For an intellectual of Radhakrishnan's caliber—himself a brahman, a neo-Vedantist philosopher, and a teacher of comparative religion—to have translated the *Dhammapada* testifies to the lasting moral and metaphysical attraction of this slim collection of verses. Although *Dhammapada* translations have continued to appear and now number in the dozens, Radhakrishnan's version remains in print today and counts as a classic translation of this Buddhist masterpiece.

But the *Dhammapada* has its own elaborate history in the East and West; many modern scholars have followed its footprints, and much has been written about it. Let me keep to my subject, the sister (and even near-twin)

versal language of the world, for it is a well known fact that in the beginning the Lord took all languages, boiled them in a pot, and forthwith extracted the English language as the essence of them all."

collection, the *Udānavarga*. If the Pāli *Dhammapada* is world famous, the *Udānavarga*, in any language, is not. The reason for this is simple enough: the *Dhammapada* got there first, a century or more ahead of the *Udānavarga*. Since the two texts overlap and share so much in common, it is pointless to look at them as competitors; they are cognate and complementary, and they both have had long pre- and proto-histories through centuries of orality to written/manuscript culture and then print culture. Each has forged its own distinctive modern trajectory.

The Tibetan *Udānavarga* was confined to the Tibeto-Mongolian cultural regions until the late nineteenth century, when it began to circulate more broadly. Perhaps the first published mention of the *Udānavarga* in modern scholarship was that made by Alexander Csoma de Kőrös in his "Analysis of the Mdo," which appeared in 1839 at Calcutta as part of his path-breaking synoptic study of the Kanjur. Parisian scholar Léon Feer understood the importance of Csoma's work and in 1881, seventy years later, published a French translation.[373] This is an indication of how Buddhist studies were expanding; French was an international language of scholarship, including for "Oriental studies," and Francophone countries were dynamic participants in cutting-edge research. Léon Feer was active in the growing field of Pāli studies (the Pali Text Society was founded in London in 1881), and his accomplishments include a five-volume edition of the Pāli *Saṃyuttanikāya* published by the Society between 1884 and 1898 and still in print.[374] Feer saw the importance of comparative textual studies, publishing articles that collated sūtras in their Tibetan and Pāli versions. Francophone scholars did some of the most brilliant work in early Buddhist studies in the West, and great names of the pantheon like Louis de la Vallée Poussin, Paul Pelliot, Sylvain Lévi, and others all contributed to various aspects of *Udānavarga* studies.[375] Their multilingual and cross-cultural approach to Buddhist studies

373. Csoma de Kőrös, "Analysis of the Mdo," p. 477; Feer, "Analyse du Kandjour," p. 280. Following Csoma, Feer gives Arhan-dharma-rakṣita as author, but he notes that "[V. P.] Vassilief [1818–1900], [in a work published in Russian in 1857, in German in 1860, and in French in 1863], gives the name as Dharmatrāta." The made-up name "Arhan-dharma-rakṣita" is wrong, and the correct form is Dharmatrāta. For Vassilief, see Kapstein, "L'oubli des Russes." Kapstein describes the work in English as "Vasily P. Vasilyev, *Buddhism, Its Dogmatics, History and Literature* (St. Petersburg 1857)." See also Bongard-Levin and Vigasin, *The Image of India*, pp. 79–81.

374. I consulted Feer's editions for translations 7, 8, and 14.

375. For succinct notes on these scholars, see the respective entries in Buswell and Lopez's *Princeton Dictionary of Buddhism*.

often led to exhilarating results; across the channel, British studies tended to be monolingual, cautious, and conservative.

Csoma describes the *Udānavarga* as "reflections on various subjects, in verse, containing many moral and prudential maxims, in thirty-three chapters . . . . These reflections were collected by Dgra bcom pa chos skyob (Sans. *Arhan dharma rakshita*)." The Sanskrit and Tibetan titles and translators' information were published in 1845 by I. J. Schmidt in his transcription of the catalogue (*dkar chag*) of the Kanjur in the Imperial Academy of Sciences in St. Petersburg.[376] The complete Tibetan version was published by Hermann Beckh (1875–1937) in Berlin in 1911. This was an early publication of a Kanjur text in Europe in a Western book format, but not the first. Tibetan Buddhist studies developed in the imperial capitals of St. Petersburg, Berlin, Paris, London, and Tokyo. Tibetan fonts were used for the Bibliotheca Buddhica series published in St. Petersburg, in Sanskrit texts along with other writing systems like Mongolian and Nāgarī. In British India, Tibetan fonts were designed by Baptist missionaries at Serampore in Bengal, and the Asiatic Society of Bengal in Calcutta had already published some texts in the Tibetan script in the series Bibliotheca Indica—A Collection of Oriental Works. For example, Pratápchandra Ghosha published the Tibetan translation of the *Perfection of Wisdom in 100,000 Stanzas* in 1328 pages as *Sher-Phyin or Exposition of the Metaphysical Dogmas Current among the Buddhists of the Maháyána School, Expounded in a Series of Dialogues between S'ákya Sinha and Subhúti Being a Tibetan Translation of the 'Sata Sáhasriká Prajná Páramitá*, printed by the Baptist Mission Press.[377] Even at this length, the text was radically condensed through the use of an innovative system of abbreviation. Moravian missionary Heinrich Jäschke's (1817–83) *Tibetan-English Dictionary*, first published in London in 1881, is handsomely laid out with the key entries in Tibetan script.

A century of translation

Until Sanskrit manuscripts of the *Udānavarga* began to surface at the very end of the nineteenth century, the main source for study of the *Udānavarga*

376. Schmidt, *Der Index des Kandjur herausgegeben von der Kaiserlichen Akademie der Wissenschaften*, p. 50.
377. 1888–1900, 3 vols., not yet complete, but I am not certain any more fascicles were ever published.

was the Tibetan version, which was translated into English in 1883 by pioneering American scholar William Woodville Rockhill (1854–1914). In remarks that reveal the great generosity of his spirit, the great master of the age Sylvain Lévi stated that Rockhill's translation was genuinely admirable.[378]

A second complete English translation was published by one Ayu Subhadra in 1946.[379] In 1959, Edward Conze (1904–79) published translations of two chapters from the Sanskrit—chapter 6, "Śīla," and chapter 9, "Karma"—in his multischool anthology, *Buddhist Scriptures*.[380] Charles Willemen published a complete annotated English translation of a Chinese version in 1978 followed by a revised edition in 2013.[381] In 1983, Gareth Sparham published a complete English translation from the Tibetan, based on the Narthang and Dergé xylographs and done in consultation with Tibetan scholars.[382] In 1986, Raghavan Narasimhan Iyer published a translation of the *Dhammapada* with a complete English version of the Tibetan *Udānavarga* in the same volume.[383] But not until 2007 was a single complete translation of the Sanskrit *Udānavarga* published in a modern European language. This was a German rendition by the enormously talented Indologist Michael Hahn (1941–2014), who found special pleasure in the study and translation of Buddhist verse literature in Sanskrit and Tibetan.[384]

378. Lévi, "L'Apramāda-varga," p. 211: "[M. Rockhill] a pu produire ainsi une œuvre vraiment admirable. Il est facile aujourd'hui, avec les nouveaux matériaux dont nous disposons, d'y relever des erreurs; mais, si on mesure la difficulté de la tâche à l'époque où M. Rockhill l'a entreprise, on est surpris de son courage, et aussi des résultats qu'il a su obtenir." ("Mr. Rockhill was able to produce a work that is genuinely admirable. Nowadays, with the new materials to which we have access, it is all too easy point out mistakes, but when one considers the difficulty of the task at the time that Rockhill undertook it, one can only be amazed at his courage and at the results he was able to achieve.")

379. Published as *The Udanavarga: Verses Collected from the Buddhist Canon, Being the Northern Version of the Dhammapada* in 1946 (not seen). I could not find any information about the publisher, the Universalist Press, London. It appears that Ayu Subhadra was G. W. Reid or George Wilson MacGregor-Reid, dates unknown, who was active in the trade union movement and in Druid spirituality.

380. Conze, *Buddhist Scriptures*, pp. 83–86.

381. Willemen, trans., *The Chinese Udānavarga*; idem, *Collection of Important Odes of the Law*.

382. Sparham et al., *The Tibetan Dhammapada: Sayings of the Buddha*.

383. It is regrettable that Iyer says nothing about the sources of the texts he brings together in the volume. His *Udānavarga* looks as if it is a composite artifact created by rewriting Rockhill's and Sparham's translations (both are listed in his bibliography). In any case, I do not see any evidence that this is an original translation from the Tibetan.

384. Hahn, *Vom rechten Leben: Buddhistische Lehren aus Indien und Tibet*, pp. 9–159; commentary, pp. 368–408; bibliography, pp. 470–72.

In 1970, Lambert Schmithausen (1939–) published an article on the recensions of the *Udānavarga*. He demonstrated that there were two major recensions of the collection: that Bernhard's version represented one of them and the Tibetan translation the other.[385] This explains the noticeable differences between Bernhard's Sanskrit *Udānavarga* and the Tibetan translation, and also some of the differences amongst verses cited in Sanskrit in various sources.

Chapter 1 of a related *Udānavarga* text preserved in Chinese gives some of its verses with stories. Some of the striking similes of the verses occur in a sūtra in the *Aṅguttaranikāya*, in this case spoken by Araka, a religious master who was free of desire for sense pleasures (translation 10 in this volume).

Translation history

The *Udānavarga* was translated by the Indian preceptor Vidyākaraprabha with the Tibetan translator Bhante Rin chen mchog and finalized by the illustrious master editor-translator Dpal brtsegs.

In December 2010, I learned that Gene Smith, peerless master of Tibetan wisdom and scholarship, had died.[386] *Saṃvega*—heartfelt emotion—propelled me to the shrine room, where I sat down and contemplated impermanence: how at any moment death can pounce and take away the best of us. My ruminations inspired me to translate the "Chapter on Impermanence" of the *Udānavarga*. I finished a draft version, but I wanted to compare the Tibetan and Sanskrit versions more closely. My attention turned to other matters, and the translation lay untended. In February 2012, I returned to the verses with David Welsh, then a student at Oslo University. I am grateful to David for his help and his fine sense of the British language, although since then I have reworked the translations so thoroughly that I wonder whether he will be able to recognize much. Again, the translation lay untended. Further *saṃvega* stirred me when Michael Hahn, Hubert Durt, Akira Yuyama, and Seishi Karashima passed away in the intervening years. In August 2019, when I turned seventy, I decided that it was time to finish the translation and publish it before I myself departed for the Elysian Fields. Yet time does not stand still, and on April 30, 2020, news came that Stefano Zacchetti,

385. Schmithausen, "Zu den Rezensionen des Udānavargaḥ."
386. 'Jam dbyangs rnam rgyal, 1936–2010: for a sampling of his oeuvre, see Smith, *Among Tibetan Texts*.

embodiment of generosity, good humor, and deep knowledge, had died in Oxford at the young age of fifty-two. Not long afterward, on May 4, I learned that Kun Sopheap, unsurpassed savant of Khmer Buddhist culture, had passed away in Phnom Penh.[387] My translation of the "Chapter on Impermanence" has been well fueled by impermanence at every step.

Today the world is passing through difficult and uncertain times; disease and unbridled violence make the "Chapter on Impermanence" uncomfortably relevant. Reading the verses encourages us to reflect on how old age and death are part and parcel of life—how they are not taboo topics to fear or avoid but natural inevitabilities to accept and understand. In turn, understanding and wisdom can help us achieve fearlessness and inner balance.

My translation primarily follows the Tibetan Kanjur–Tanjur version in the excellent edition published in 1990 by Siglinde Dietz and Champa Thupten Zongtse, in close comparison with Bernhard's meticulous edition of the Sanskrit fragments. The numbering of the verses follows the Tibetan, which introduces an extra verse (here verse 25).[388]

5. The Sūtra on Impermanence (1)

Introduction

The Tibetan canons contain two texts that bear the same title: in Sanskrit *Anityatāsūtra* and in Tibetan *Mi rtag pa nyid kyo mdo*, or in English, *Sūtra on Impermanence.* I translate both of them here. The first one is brief and to the point. The Buddha speaks directly to the assembled monks about four things that all of us cherish—that is to say, health, youth, good fortune, and life itself. But none of these endure, and life ends in death. The Fortunate One summarizes the teaching with a single verse.

Translation history

The shorter *Anityatāsūtra* was translated from Sanskrit into Tibetan by the Indian preceptor Surendrabodhi and the Tibetan master editor Ye shes sde

387. See the dedication in Skilling, "'Impermanence.'"

388. I do not take into account the Chinese translation, Taishō 213, the *Fa ji yao song jing* 法集要頌經, translated in 985 by the Indian monk Tian xi zai 天息災, for which see Willemen, *A Collection of Important Odes of the Law.*

around the beginning of the ninth century.[389] An extended Sanskrit version is incorporated into the as-yet-unpublished *Tridaṇḍamālā*.[390] This is a "composite sūtra" in which two sūtras are quoted one after the other as if they were only one text.[391] The first corresponds to a sūtra that was translated into Chinese by Yijing 義淨 (635–713 CE) in 701 CE and has been published in English by Charles Willemen.[392] The second corresponds to the *Sūtra on Impermanence* translated here and ends with the same verse.

In the 1970s I translated the *Sūtra on Impermanence* with the help of Ngodup Paljor, using the Otani reprint of the Peking xylograph Kanjur. This was one of my first-ever joint publications.[393] Ngodup was a Tibetan monk studying in Bangkok at the time and staying at Wat Saket. Some years later he moved to Anchorage, Alaska, where he died in an accident in 1988. I dedicate this translation to his kind and cheerful spirit.

6. The Sūtra on Impermanence (2)

Introduction

The second *Sūtra on Impermanence* does not have a translators' colophon.[394] It is broader in scope: it proclaims the impermanence of all sentient beings, all living creatures, and all breathing things. It starts out with the impermanence of the members of high society: the land-owning, priestly, and warrior clans, the ruling class and the religious specialists—the rishis, the sages. It then leaves the human plane behind and goes on to list the whole gamut of gods in ascending hierarchical order, from the four great regents who guard the four quarters of the universe up through the deities of the sensual realm, the fine-material realm, and the nonmaterial realm (see table 8). These are devas, divine beings: each represents a heaven, a divine plane, but at the same

389. Otani no. 975, repr. vol. 39, Mdo sna tshogs, *shu*, 165a1–b3.

390. I thank Jens-Uwe Hartmann for the information about the *Tridaṇḍamālā* in this section. It is based on his and Kazunobu Matsuda's work on this fascinating text and Hartmann's inspiring "Doctrine, Poetry, and Ritual: Did Aśvaghoṣa Author the *Tridaṇḍamālā*?" the 8th Prof. Michael Hahn Memorial Lecture arranged by the Deshana Institute of Buddhist and Allied Studies, Pune, 12 July 2021.

391. I adopt the term *composite sūtra* from Lamotte; see his "Un Sūtra composite de l'Ekottarāgama," translated by Sara Boin-Webb as "A Composite Sūtra from the Ekottarāgama."

392. *Fo shuo wu chang jing* 佛說無常經, Taishō 801, translated and discussed in Willemen, "Yijing's Scriptural Text about Impermanence (T. 801)."

393. Skilling, "The Sūtra on Impermanence."

394. Otani no. 976, repr. vol. 39, Mdo sna tshogs, *shu*, 165b4–169a2.

time they are modalities of mind and spirit that can be reached in this human body through mental cultivation. This interface of the inner and the outer should always be borne in mind with regard to Buddhist cosmology.

In short, the Fortunate One's message is this: there is no life eternal, no heaven everlasting, no comfort zone in the psychophysical system where a sentient being might hope to tuck in cozily for eternity. Returning to the human situation, the Buddha teaches how the situation is the same for the spiritually realized—for the worthy arhats, the autonomous pratyekabuddhas, and even the tathāgatas—all of them have to leave their bodies behind in the end. Our bodies are like clay pots—how can we even dream that they will last forever, that they will not shatter to pieces and crumble to dust? This holds for all beings in the universe. Impermanence is universal: one size fits all.

A number of Sanskrit manuscripts of the *Sūtra on Impermanence* are preserved in various libraries around the world.[395] In addition, one of the texts of the *Ratnamāla-avadāna* collection from Nepal bears the title *Anityatāsūtra*.[396] This is the only text in the collection that is decidedly *not* an avadāna, but it is integrated into the primary narrative frame in which Upagupta relates avadānas to King Aśoka. At the king's request, Upagupta proclaims what has been related by his teacher, the Buddha: the avadāna is a recasting of the *Anityatāsūtra* in verse in the mouth of Upagupta. It opens in the Jetavana at Śrāvastī; it draws on the themes of the longer sūtra with the same progression of thought, but it considerably expands the inventory of beings who are subject to impermanence and death. The verse sūtra is nearly one hundred stanzas long (running from verses 4 to 97); the chapter ends with the brief announcement that people who listen with faith to this well-expounded *Sūtra on Impermanence* will go to the abode of the Sugata—that is, nirvāṇa (verse 98). This version of the *Sūtra on Impermanence* is a good example of the creativity of Buddhist poets in reformulating prose teachings in verse versions.

What about the primary sūtra itself? Where does it fit in the Āgama collections? It appears to me that it was transmitted independently, extra-Āgama, either individually or in small collections like the Potala manuscript.

395. See the list in Vinītā, *Unique Collection of Twenty Sūtras*, vol. 1, p. 170.

396. No. 30 in Takahata, *Ratnamālāvadāna*, pp. 346–50.

Translation history

The Kanjur versions of the long *Sūtra on Impermanence* do not have translators' colophons, but the text belongs stylistically with the early translations. I originally translated this sūtra around the same time as the shorter *Sūtra on Impermanence*, using the Peking Kanjur and one or two earlier printed editions of the Sanskrit, writing it down by hand in a notebook. I have revised the translation on the basis of the Tibetan text edited by Bhikṣuṇī Vinītā, who in 2010 published the sūtra from a Sanskrit manuscript from the Potala in Lhasa. Bhikṣuṇī Vinītā includes an edition of the Tibetan based on the Dergé, Peking, and Stog Palace Kanjurs and compares the Tibetan with published editions of the Sanskrit, an unpublished manuscript from Lhasa, and a Chinese translation done by Fatian (法天) in 984.[397] My translation follows the Tibetan with one exception: the concluding verses. The different versions give different verses at the end, all of which have counterparts in the "Chapter on Impermanence" of the *Udānavarga*. I include all four verses here. This makes my translation a conflation of my sources, but I do so on the precedent of my predecessors, the traditional editors who seem to have enjoyed the freedom to choose what verses to include.

7. King Pasenadi Asks about Aging and Death

Introduction

This short Pāli sutta in the "Collection on Kosala" of the "Chapter with Verses" of the *Connected Discourses* is not, strictly speaking, a parallel to the longer *Sūtra on Impermanence*, but it draws on some of the same ideas and uses a similar phraseology. It concludes with a verse that is included in the "Chapter on Impermanence" of the *Udānavarga* as well as in the "Chapter on Old Age" of both the Pāli *Dhammapada* and the Khotan *Dharmapada*.[398] In his *Udāna* commentary, Prajñāvarman gives two alternative settings for the sūtra:

> This verse was spoken [by the Fortunate One] with reference to King Prasenajit. Others say that it refers to Queen Mallikā, who,

397. *Fo shuo zhu xing you wei jing* 佛說諸行有為經, Taishō 758.
398. *Udānavarga*, chap. 1, v. 28; *Dhammapada*, v. 151; *Gāndhārī Dharmapada*, v. 160.

> intoxicated with the pride of youth, got into a royal chariot and drove it around, hither and thither.[399]

Prajñāvarman explains the verse like this:

> If physical matter and our bodies change because of aging, then what is there that doesn't age? The answer to this is "the Dharma of the good"—that is, the Dharma body (*dharmakāya*) of the buddhas and the *śrāvakas* of the buddhas. The word "but" introduces a qualification, and the verse goes on to explain it: "does not age," there is no chance that it ages—even if everything else is a ground for alteration, there is still one exception, the Dharma body. How do we know that it [the Dharma body] doesn't age? The verse says "the good": because good people (*skyes bu dam pa, satpuruṣa*) understand the Dharma without distortion (*phyin ci ma log pa'i chos, aviparyasta-dharma*) and teach it to others.[400]

That is, the Dharma that is taught does not age because it is preserved and transmitted accurately through the office of good people.

Translation history

I translate the discourse here under the title *King Pasenadi Asks About Aging and Death*. I have consulted the Thai-script Syāmaraṭṭha Tepiṭaka and the Pali Text Society editions.[401] My first translation was written on a foolscap sheet around 1977 or 1978.

399. Balk, *Prajñāvarman's Udānavargavivaraṇa*, vol. 1, p. 120.1–6. An early instance of joy-riding, I suppose. A related story seems to be told in Beal's Cod. iii: see Beal, *Texts from the Buddhist Canon*, p. 31, n. 1, where the reverend author makes the comment, "The sermon was designed to show the comparative worthlessness of all earthly grandeur"—apposite and very Victorian Christian in sentiment. The Rev. Samuel Beal (1825–89) was, after all, an ordained cleric from 1850 on.

400. Balk, *Prajñāvarman's Udānavargavivaraṇa*, vol. 1, p. 121,1–13. For a modern attempt to explain the verse, see Brough, *Gāndhārī Dharmapada*, pp. 227–29.

401. *Rājasutta: Saṃyuttanikāya, Kosalasaṃyutta, Paṭhamo vaggo*, sutta 3: Syāmaraṭṭha, vol. 15, p. 102.3; PTS, vol. 1, p. 71. For Bodhi's English translation, see *Connected Discourses*, p. 167.

8. King Pasenadi's Grandmother Passes Away

Introduction

This sūtra is known from many versions. It is included in the Pāli *Connected Discourses*, in the two Chinese *Saṃyuktāgamas*, and in the Chinese *Ekottarikāgama*,[402] as well as in an independent Chinese translation.[403] Prajñāvarman gives an abbreviated citation in his *Udānavarga Commentary* to introduce his exegesis of *Udānavarga*, chapter 1, verse 25.[404] A version is incorporated into an early *Udānavarga* in Chinese that is accompanied by stories.[405] The sūtra is not only included in the Sūtrapiṭakas, but it is also found in at least one Vinaya: this is the Mūlasarvāstivādin *Vinayottaragrantha*, which includes it in full in the *Muktaka* section (given here as translation 9).

Sanskrit fragments have been identified in the Turfan collection. They are written in the Śāradā script on birchbark, five lines per side. Initially the folios were kept in Berlin, but they were removed for safekeeping during the Second World War along with many other artifacts. They were first identified from reports written by Else Lüders (1880–1945), wife of famed German Indologist Heinrich Lüders (1869–1943), accompanied by photographs of the folios. The identifications were made piece by piece, until what had started with a small section of the single leaf could be almost fully restored. Two rare features helped to identify the scattered fragments: the material and the script. Birchbark manuscripts and the Śāradā script belong to the area of greater Gandhāra in the northwest of the Indian subcontinent (present-day Kashmir, India, Pakistan, and Afghanistan). It is probable that the manuscript originally came from that area and was carried along the Silk Road to the northern Tarim Basin (the exact findspot is not known for certain, but it is likely to have been in the region of Kucha). The first publication was of a single, isolated folio; this was, however, sufficient for Jens-Uwe Hartmann to convincingly identify

402. *Saṃyuttanikāya, Sagāthāvagga, Kosalasaṃyutta*: Syāmaraṭṭha, vol. 15, pp. 141–42; PTS, vol. 1, pp. 96.antepenult.–97.ult. For the Chinese translation, Anālayo lists *Saṃyuktāgama* at Taishō 99, 2, 335b–6; Taishō 100, 2, 392a–c; *Ekottarikāgama* 26.7 at Taishō 125, 2, 638a2, and Taishō 125, 2, 545a24. Anālayo translates the first, *Saṃyuktāgama*, 1227.

403. Taishō 122, 2, 545a24–546a8.

404. Balk, *Prajñāvarman's Udānavargavivaraṇa*, vol. 1, pp. 109.22–110.12.

405. *Fa ju pi yu jing* 法句譬喻經, Taishō 211, trans. Beal, *Texts from the Buddhist Canon*, pp. 31–32; Willemen, *Scriptural Text*, pp. 8–9. This work may be a composite collection compiled from existing translations, but in any case, the materials go back to Indic originals.

the fragment and relate it to the Pāli and Chinese parallels. After further fragments were identified by the academic tertöns Klaus Wille and Hartmann, it became possible to reconstruct more of the Sanskrit text. This was helped by the realization that a close parallel exists in the Tibetan translation of a Mūlasarvāstivāda Vinaya tract, the *Vinayottaragrantha*. In 2017 Hartmann brought all the sources together and published an annotated edition of the Sanskrit fragments with the Tibetan and Chinese texts and an English translation under the title "King Prasenajit Bemoans the Death of His Grandmother: A Study of the Manuscript SHT 7185." Hartmann's publication is an instructive example of how the jigsaw puzzle of manuscript restoration works: how, with care, patience, and skill, fragments of the Buddhist manuscript heritage can be restored over time. In this case the whole process has extended over nearly twenty years—and it is not finished, since further portions of the same text have already come to light.[406]

The colophon to Prajñāvarman's *Commentary* describes the author as a "Sarvāstivāda master (ācārya),"[407] and this leads us to assume that his citation should belong to the Sarvāstivāda tradition—although precisely what "Sarvāstivāda" meant at the time and place that the colophon was penned is open to question. Whatever the case, there are some differences between Prajñāvarman's citation and the Mūlasarvāstivādin Vinaya version: here it is Prasenajit's beloved *wife* who has died;[408] and the word *grandmother* occurs, but the translators into Tibetan construe it as a proper name and transliterate rather than translate it.[409] The mention of "weeping, with wet clothes and hair"[410] places it closer to the Mūlarsarvāstivāda versions (as might be

406. Hartmann has prepared a new edition of the Sanskrit based on the full citation in the *Tridaṇḍamālā*. See Hartmann, "Trauer um die Großmutter und Trost vom Buddha: das *Āryikā-sūtra*."

407. Balk, *Prajñāvarman's Udānavargavivaraṇa*, vol. 2, p. 1055.24: *thams cad yod par smra ba'i slob dpon pra dzñā ba rmma.*

408. Balk, *Prajñāvarman's Udānavargavivaraṇa*, vol. 1, p. 109.22–23: *chung ma sdug cing yid du 'ong ba.*

409. Balk, *Prajñāvarman's Udānavargavivaraṇa*, vol. 1, p. 110.2, 4: *btsun mo a ryi ka.*

410. Balk, *Prajñāvarman's Udānavargavivaraṇa*, vol. 1, p. 109.25: *ngus pas gos dang skra dag gsher bar gyur to*—choosing the variant *ngus*, from *ngu ba*, "weep," over the selected reading *dus*. In the *Sigālovādasutta* of the *Dīghanikāya*, however, we read that the householder Sigālaka "had got up early and left Rājagaha and was honoring each of the directions, bowing with cupped hands to the east, the south, the west . . . his clothes and hair all wet" (*Dīghanikāya*, vol. 3, p. 180.4: *tena kho pana samayena Siṅgālako gahapatiputto kālass'eva vuṭṭhāya rājagahā nikkhamitvā allavattho allakeso pañjaliko puthuddisā namassanti . . .*); see also p. 180.13, 19. Gethin's n. 130, *Sayings*, p. 284 to translation p. 130, says that "his clothes and hair all wet" suggests "that he had gone down into a pool to make his offerings" (see also *Vinaya*

expected), which at least mention "clothes" while the Pāli does not.[411] As in the Pāli, the king states that "the Dharma is well spoken by the Bhagavat";[412] and again as in the Pāli, the Buddha states that "for all sentient beings, all living things, and all creatures the end is death, death is the conclusion: once one is born, there is no avoiding death."[413]

Comparing different editions helps clarify difficult points in the texts we are reading (and just as often helps muddle matters more). In the Pāli version, the king states that he would give away a *hatthi-ratana* or an *assa-ratana* if that would bring his grandmother back. Normally these terms would refer to two of the seven treasures of a *cakravartin*, a "universal emperor" (see translation 17). But King Prasenajit is a historical king: the texts do not portray him as a *cakravartin* or give any hint that he had any such pretensions. Buddhaghosa's commentary interprets *ratana* to mean "precious": "The elephant-gem was an elephant worth 100,000 *kahāpana*, decked with ornaments worth the same amount. The same explanation applies to the horse-gem and the prize village."[414] That is, it is not a question of a *cakravartin* but of a *human* or *earthly* king who is ready to give up a prize elephant or prize horse from the royal stables to bring his grandmother back to life.

Translation history

The Pāli *Sagāthāvagga* version was translated by C. A. F. Rhys Davids with assistance from the Sri Lankan monk Sūriyagoḍa Sumaṅgala Thera (1879–

Cullavagga, vol. 2, p. 126.7). The four Chinese versions show considerable variety: see translations in Bhadanta Pannasiri, "Sigālovādasutta," pp. 165, 173, 188, 204, and general remarks, p. 156. The phrase could also allude to the pouring of lustral water as blessings by priests.

411. See SHT 1586 verso 2, *vastrā*, and n. Parallel phrases occur elsewhere in avadāna and Pāli literature, and further study is needed.

412. The notion that everything spoken by the Buddha is well spoken has a deep history attested by Aśoka's Bhairāṭ inscription and literary texts: see Skilling, *Questioning the Buddha*, pp. 74–77, and the note in Almogi, *Autheticity and Authentication*, pp. 61–62. In Balk, *Prajñāvarman's Udānavargavivaraṇa*, vol. 1, p. 110.5, the phrase is sandwiched in an abbreviation formula (phrases of formula here underlined): *ji srid du bcom ldan 'das kyis* [read *kyis* rather than *kyi*] *legs par gsungs pa'i chos kyi bar du'o*.

413. Balk, *Prajñāvarman's Udānavargavivaraṇa*, vol. 1, p. 110.8: *sems can thams cad dang srog chags thams cad dang byung po thams cad mthar 'chi ba yin zhing 'chi ba mthar 'gag pa yin te | skyes nas mi 'chi ba med do*, for which compare Vinītā's *Anityatāsūtra*, p. 176.4: *sarveṣāṃ sattvānāṃ sarveṣāṃ prāṇināṃ sarveṣāṃ bhūtānāṃ maraṇāntaṃ jīvitaṃ maraṇaparyavasānam, nāsti jātasyāmaraṇam*.

414. Bodhi, *Connected Discourses*, p. 409, n. 251.

1939) and first published in 1917.[415] Bhikkhu Bodhi published a translation in *Connected Discourses of the Buddha* in 2000.[416] The Chinese *Saṃyuktāgama* version has been studied and translated in full by Bhikkhu Anālayo.[417] In translating the Pāli and the parallel Tibetan text, I have benefited from the expert translations of the two bhikkhus.

9. King Prasenajit's Grandmother Passes Away

Introduction

This is a Mūlasarvāstivāda version of the sūtra discussed previously, embedded in the Tibetan translation of the *Vinayottaragrantha*.

Prasenajit's dialogue with the Buddha is incorporated into the *Mahāparinirvāṇa-mahāsūtra*, at least in the Chinese translation by Dharmakṣema,[418] providing an intriguing example of the deep intertextuality of the Buddhist scriptures. The *Mahāparinirvāṇa-mahāsūtra* citation includes the verse:[419]

> As buddhas, pratyekabuddhas, and the assembly of śrāvakas
> Cast off their impermanent bodies:
> How much more so will ordinary people.

The phrasing of the prose is closer to the Mūlasarvāstivāda *Uttaragrantha* and the *Saṃyuktāgama* versions than to the Pāli, and in addition, both of the versions include the same concluding verse, which, again, is not found in the Pāli. That is, the embedded citation in the *Mahāparinirvāṇa-mahāsūtra* bears a closer relation to the greater Sarvāstivāda versions than the Pāli. Its incorporation into the colossal *Mahāparinirvāṇa-mahāsūtra* is a trace of the

415. "Grandmother," in Rhys Davids, *Book of Kindred Sayings*, vol. 1, p. 122. I thank Steve Berkwitz for providing Sumaṅgala Thera's dates (email, 4 February 2021).

416. *Connected Discourses*, pp. 188–89.

417. Anālayo, "The Inevitability of Death," pp. 110–17 in his *Mindfully Facing Disease and Death*.

418. Trans. Blum, *Nirvana Sutra*, vol. 1, 139–40. In English, this text is frequently called the "Mahāyāna *Mahāparinirvāṇasūtra*," but its compilers consistently call it *Mahāparinirvāṇa-mahāsūtra* in Sanskrit and Tibetan and, by process of deduction, in the Chinese translations. This is clearly demonstrated in Habata, "Mahāsūtra and 'Mahāyanasūtra.'" See also Shimoda, "Mahāparinirvāṇamahāsūtra."

419. Translation Blum, *Nirvana Sutra*, p. 139.

short sūtra's circulation and reception, suggesting that it was sufficiently well known to be brought up in the polemics at the time and place the Mahāsūtra was compiled—about which little can be said of any certainty, especially since there seem to have been several recensions in India. A close look at the Mahāsūtra directs our gaze to the fluidity of its textual transmission: the passage in question is not found at all in the Tibetan translation from Sanskrit by Jinamitra, Jñānagarbha, and Devacandra done circa 800 CE. Nor is it found in the extant Sanskrit fragments; no conclusions can be drawn from this beyond that the passage, if it did exist, has not yet turned up amongst known manuscript fragments. At any rate, it could have been included in some recensions but not in others. The relation of the passage to the short sūtra merits further research into the Chinese Āgamas and the other Chinese translations of the Mahāsūtra.

Translation history

For the Chinese *Saṃyuktāgama* and Pāli versions, see preceding. A Sanskrit text restored from Central Asian fragments compared with the Pāli parallel and Tibetan and Chinese translations was published by Jens-Uwe Hartmann in 2017 with an English translation. I translate Hartmann's edition of the Tibetan version from the *Vinayottaragrantha* of the Mūlasarvāstivāda, benefiting from his scholarship.[420]

10. *Plus ça change*: From Araka to Gautama

Introduction

The *Arakasutta* is placed in the "Great Chapter" of the *Book of the Sevens* of the *Numerical Discourses*.[421] Its title comes from Araka, a sage who lived ages before Gautama Buddha's time. I leave the name untranslated, as does Nyanaponika and Bodhi's translation; Hare translates it as Wheel-Wright. Araka is described as a "religious master" (*titthakara* or "ford-maker," "ford-crosser"), which Hare translates as "course-setter" and Bodhi as "founder of a spiritual

420. *Vinayottaragrantha*, *'Dul ba gzhung dam pa*, Otani no. 1037, repr. vol. 45, 'Dul ba, *phe*, 150b3–151b7; Dergé no. 7, 'Dul ba, *pa*, 155a6–b7.

421. *Sattakanipāta*, *Paññāsakāsaṅgahitā Vaggā*, *Mahāvagga*, last sutta: Syāmaraṭṭha, [2471] repr. 2523, vol. 23, pp. 138.ult–142.4; PTS, *Aṅguttaranikāya*, vol. 4, pp. 136.21–139.ult.

sect." Nyanaponika and Bodhi seem to gloss over the term, or perhaps they merge it with "teacher," for which they have "spiritual teacher." I reluctantly translate the term as "religious master," though I am tempted to count it as an untranslatable. *Titthakara*, in Sanskrit *tīrthaṃkara*, refers to an exceptional individual who both crosses the ford and leads others across as well—that is, he is a spiritual leader who crosses from this shore of the ocean or flood of saṃsāra, our everyday world, to the other shore of nirvāṇa. Araka is also described as *kāmesu vītarāgo*, an index of his level of spiritual attainment, translated by Hare as "freed of all lustful passion," by Nyanaponika and Bodhi as "free of sensual lust," and by Bodhi as "one without lust for sensual pleasures."

The Jains call their twenty-four great teachers *tīrthaṃkara*; in Buddhist texts the term refers to non-Buddhist teachers who *claim* to have crossed over but have not reached the true final goal. In the *Book of the Sevens*, the *Arakasutta* follows the *Sunettasutta*, which lists seven such teachers, described in identical terms, from Sunetta to Araka.[422] All of them, including Araka, taught a practice that leads to rebirth in the Brahmā world. Six of these teachers, minus Araka, are mentioned in the *Book of the Sixes*.[423] Each of the seven teachers was in fact Gautama Buddha in a former birth, and most of them feature individually in stories scattered in the Pāli *Jātaka* collection.[424] Sunetta also features in the *Sutta on the Seven Suns* (*Sattasuriyasutta*),[425] well known from citations in cosmological texts.

Araka's teaching is about impermanence and death. He gives seven prose similes for impermanence, and a refrain in his sermon is "there is no escape from death for one who is born," *natthi jātassa amaraṇaṃ*, a frequent theme in teachings on impermanence. Most of the similes are found in the "Chapter on Impermanence" of the *Udānavarga* as well as in a long list of similes in the Chinese *Saṃyuktāgama*.[426]

One of the similes compares human life to a line drawn on water: "Just as a

422. Bodhi, *Numerical Discourses*, p. 1095. The PTS edition treats the section on Araka as a separate sutta, but I wonder whether it really is. It follows immediately and naturally on the *Sunettasutta*, which fits in the *Sevens*. The *uddāna* title seems to be *sunetta-araka*, while in the PTS *Sunetta-Arakena cā ti*, with a number of variant readings that suggest that the line is uncertain. The Rāma V and Mahamakut editions have *sunetta-arakenānusāsanī*.

423. *Aṅguttaranikāya*, vol. 3, pp. 366–74; Bodhi, *Numerical Discourses*, pp. 927–32.

424. See DPPN, vol. 1, pp. 167 (Araka), 170 (Araṇemi), 629–30 (Kuddālaka), 971 (Jotipāla (3)3); DPPN, vol. 2,2, 647–48 (Mūgapakkha), 1213 (Sunetta), 1319–20 (Hatthipāla). For Sunetta (Sunetra) in other sources, see Lamotte, *Le Traité*, vol. 4, pp. 2091–92.

425. *Aṅguttaranikāya*, vol. 4, pp. 100–106.6; Bodhi, *Numerical Discourses*, pp. 1071–75.

426. Anālayo, "On Views and Penetrative Knowledge," p. 91. See Marino, "The Gāndhārī 'Discourse on Pleasure and Pain,'" p. 293 and n. 60.

line drawn with a stick in water quickly vanishes and doesn't last long: in the same way, brahmans, the life of humans is a like a line drawn on water with a stick: it is insignificant and trifling, fraught with much suffering and tribulation." Similar insights are expressed by poets from different times and climes, as, for example, by the immortal bard: "Glory is like a circle in the water, which never ceaseth to enlarge itself, till by broad spreading, it disperse to naught."[427] And it evokes the words that John Keats (1795–1821) "desired . . . to be engraven on his Tomb Stone": "Here lies One Whose Name was writ in Water."[428] In that place of rest lie two celebrated English Romantic poets, John Keats, who died at twenty-five years of age of tuberculosis, and Percy Bysshe Shelley (1792–1822), who drowned at age twenty-nine. Impassioned, young, they lived not the lives that might have been, but they achieved the lasting glory that great poets can claim.

The awareness of impermanence (*anityatā-saṃjñā*) can give rise to a variety of reflections. Seven hundred years after the Buddha, in distant Rome, "the quick and sensitive eye of Marcus Aurelius [121–80 CE] perceived that 'in the ripe olives the very circumstance of their being near to rottenness adds a peculiar beauty to the fruit.'"[429] In the sixteenth and later centuries, European artists painted magnificent bouquets of exquisite colorful flowers, which we know as "still lifes" or, tellingly, in French as "natures mortes." The artists signaled impermanence and death by including an unobtrusive fly or worm.

In his *Udānavarga Commentary*, Prajñāvarman cites the skeleton of a sūtra in which Araṇemi (Rtsibs kyi mu khyud), a master of ages past, teaches five similes of the "Chapter on Impermanence" to his disciples—the similes of the earthenware pot, the woven thread, the man condemned to death, the mountain stream, and the line drawn in water.[430] The setting resembles that of the *Arakasutta*:[431]

427. William Shakespeare, *Henry the Sixth, Part 1*, act 1, scene 2, lines 133–35 (RSC, p. 1096).
428. This is in Rome at the Protestant Cemetery (Cimitero dei Protestanti), also known as Non-Catholic Cemetery or English Cemetery (Cimitero Acattolico, Cimitero degli Inglesi). I thank Giuliano Giustarini for sending photos of the inscription.
429. Nock, *Memoirs of a Superfluous Man*, p. 239.
430. Balk, *Udānavargavivaraṇa*, vol. 1, p. 82.12–83.20. Cp. *Anityavarga* (Tib.) vv. 12–16.
431. Balk, *Udānavargavivaraṇa* vol. 1, p. 82.12.

> In ages long past, O monks, when people lived to eighty thousand years, a cakravartin named *Kuru (Sgra ngan) arose. In his park (*skyed mos tshal*: *udyāna*), at the foot of a king of nyagrodha trees known as Supratiṣṭha (*rab tu gnas pa*), Araṇemi (Rtsibs kyi mu khyud) instructed five hundred young brahmans in mantra (*gsang tshig*)...
>
>> O young brahmans, very short indeed is this human life. Just as potters make different sorts of vessels from clay but they end up being smashed, so human life is like earthenware vessels...

After relating Araka's sermon on impermanence, the Buddha calculates the number of seasons, months, fortnights, days, and meals that a person who lives for a hundred years will experience.[432] Very similar passages are found in the *Sūtra on Lifespans* and the *Sūtra on Conception in the Womb*.[433] In conclusion, the Buddha admonishes the monks to meditate and be heedful:

> What ought to be done by a teacher who seeks benefit for his śrāvakas, out of compassion and grounded in sympathy, this I have done for you. These, O monks, are the wilderness haunts, these are the roots of trees, these are the empty huts. Meditate, O monks, do not be negligent![434] Do not regret later. This is my instruction.

This short but pointed admonition to meditate is frequent, usually as the Buddha's closing statement at the end of sūtras.[435] Aśvaghoṣa presents the

432. See the similar progression of terms in the Lokottaravāda-Mahāsāṃghika *Prātimokṣa* above, p. 267.
433. *Āyuḥparyānta* and *Garbhāvakrānti* sūtras: Matsumura, "Āyuḥparyantasūtra," §§ [15]–[17], Sanskrit, pp. 78–79, Tibetan, p. 92; Kritzer, *Garbhāvakrāntisūtra* §§ 23–24, trans. pp. 83–84, Tibetan pp. 310–11. SHT (V) 1099, vv. 1–3.
434. *Mā pamādatha.*
435. See, for example: (1) *Majjhimanikāya* no. 8, *Sallekhasutta*, vol. 1, p. 46.6–11, trans. by Bodhi in *Middle Length Discourses*, p. 131. (2) Anālayo, *Comparative Study*, vol. 1, p. 66. (3) *Majjhimanikāya* no. 106, *Āneñjasappāyasutta*, vol. 2, pp. 265.35–266.4, trans. by Bodhi in *Middle Length Discourses*, p. 873; parallel at Chinese *Madhyamāgama*, no. 75 (Anālayo, *Comparative Study*, vol. 2, pp. 613–17); cited by Śamathadeva, *Upāyikāṭīkā*, *Mngon pa'i bstan bcos*, *tu*, 263a4–6. (4) *Majjhimanikāya* no. 152, *Indriyabhāvanāsutta*, vol. 3, p. 302.6–10, trans. by Bodhi in *Middle Length Discourses*, pp. 1150–51; citation at Śamathadeva, *Upāyikāṭīkā*, Mngon pa'i bstan bcos, *thu*, 83a5–7. (5) *Aṅguttaranikāya*, *Pañcakanipāta*, *Yodhājīvavagga*, vol. 3, p. 87.25–30; trans. by Bodhi, *Numerical Discourses*, p. 699. (6) *Saṃyuttanikāya*, *Satipaṭṭhānasaṃyutta*, *Ambapālivagga*, vol. 5, p. 157.23–28; trans. by Bodhi, *Connected Discourses*, pp. 1639–40. See also Bodhi, *Reading the Buddha's Discourses in Pāli*, pp. 497–501, for two

passage in two verses of his *Buddhacarita*, in the chapter on the Buddha's last journey, "The Great Parinirvāṇa."[436]

Box 11. *Admonition to meditate from Aśvaghoṣa's Buddhacarita*[437]

[71]
ཕན་པ་དང་ལྡན་རྗེས་སུ་བརྩེ་བ་མངའ་བ་ཡི། །སྟོན་པ་ཐུགས་རྗེ་མངའ་བས་མཛད་བྱ་གང་ཡིན་པ། །
དེ་ནི་བདག་གིས་བྱས་ཤིང་དང་ནི་རབ་བསྡམས་པ། །ཁྱེད་ཅག་རྣམས་ཀྱི་སེམས་ནི་ཞི་བས་བྱས་པའོ། །

phan pa dang ldan rjes su brtse ba mnga' ba yi ||
ston pa thugs rje mnga' bas mdzad bya gang yin pa ||
de ni bdag gis byas shing dang ni rab bsdams pa ||
khyed cag rnams kyi sems ni zhi bas byas pa'o ||

I have done all that should be done by a compassionate sympathetic Master, who aims at others' good; do you apply yourselves (*praṇidha*?) and bring your minds to tranquillity.

[72]
ཅི་སྟེ་རི་རྣམས་དང་ནི་ཁང་པ་སྟོང་པ་དང་། །དགོན་པ་དེ་རྣམས་གང་དང་དེར་ནི་ཡོད་པ་ན། །
རབ་ཏུ་སྦྱོར་ལ་རྟག་ཏུ་འབད་པ་བྱ་བ་སྟེ། །ཕྱི་ནས་ཡོངས་སུ་གདུང་བ་ལྡན་པར་མ་གྱུར་ཅིག

ci ste ri rnams dang ni khang pa stong pa dang ||
dgon pa de rnams gang dang der ni yod pa na ||
rab tu sbyor la rtag tu 'bad pa bya ba ste ||
phyi nas yongs su gdung ba ldan par ma gyur cig |

Then, wherever you may be, on the mountains or in empty dwellings or in the forest, ever be strenuous in religious practice (*prayoga*) and do not give way to remorse (*paścātparitāpa*).

---

suttas from *Asaṅkhatasaṃyutta*. Further Pāli references at Hare, *Gradual Sayings*, vol. 4, p. 94, n. 7. Doubtless there are many more instances in the vast Buddhist canons.

436. Dergé no. 4156, fol. 92b3–4. For the context, see above, p. 252.

437. Chap. 26, vv. 21–22. English translations after Johnston, *The Buddhacarita*.

The Sarvāstivāda tradition uses a longer formula—for example, in the *Arthaviniścayasūtra* (with commentary in the *nibandhana*)[438] and the chapters "Going Forth" and "Bedding and Seats" of the Mūlasarvāstivāda *Vinayavastu*.[439] It gives a longer list of ideal places to meditate—mountain crevices, mountain caves, heaps of straw, open spaces, charnel grounds, forests, remote places—a list that is also found in Pāli in a different though closely related context, the enumeration of remote dwelling places (*vivitta senāsana*).[440]

In the Kanjur, the admonition occurs at the end of the *Sūtra on the Examination of the Good and Bad Karmic Fruits of the Five Classes of Offenses [of the Monastic Code]*, a short sūtra with a long title that is of unknown origin or school affiliation. The intriguing document links the offenses to karmic retribution in the appropriate hells.[441]

The recurrence of this admonition across the scriptures shows how the aim of Gautama the Buddha's sermons went beyond conveying thoughts and ideas, how they were not just templates or homilies. They show that Gautama wanted to inspire his audience to follow through with his ideas—to put them into practice in order to realize, to experience, the truths or realities for themselves through their own introspection.

Translation history

The *Arakasutta* has been translated from Pāli to English by E. M. Hare (1893–1955, published 1935), Bhikkhus Nyanaponika and Bodhi (1999), and Bhikkhu Bodhi (2012).[442]

438. Samtani, *Arthaviniścayasūtra*, p. 67.1–4 (*sūtra*) and pp. 309–11 (*nibandhana*); translation p. 43 (sūtra) and pp. 219–20 (commentary).

439. Dutt, *Gilgit Manuscripts*, III-4, *Pravrajyāvastu*, p. 49.5–8; Gnoli, *Śayanāsanavastu*, pp. 35.18–36.3.

440. See *Pāli Tipiṭaka Concordance*, vol. 3, part 1, p. 210b, s.v. *palāla*.

441. *Pañcāpattinikāyaśubhāśubhaphalaparīkṣasūtra / Ltung ba sde lnga'i dge ba dang mi dge ba'i 'bras bu brtag pa'i mdo*, Otani no. 970, repr. vol. 39, Mdo, *shu*, 136a3 [Dergé 304], trans. Jñānaśrīgupta and Śākya Blo gros.

442. Hare, "Wheel-Wright," in *The Book of Gradual Sayings*, pp. 91–94; Nyanaponika and Bodhi, "Life's Brevity," in *Numerical Discourses of the Buddha*, pp. 193–95; Bodhi, "Araka," in *Numerical Discourses*, pp. 1096–98.

11. The Natural Laws of Existence

Introduction and translation history

This sutta is from a section of the *Royal Chanting Book* that presents "chants in the style of the Dhammayutika order."[443] As the *Chanting Book* notes, it belongs to the *Book of the Threes* in the *Numerical Discourses*.[444] The title in the *Chanting Book* is *Dhammaniyāmasutta*, "Sutta on the Laws of Nature"; the *uddāna* of the *Aṅguttaranikāya* assigns the keyword *uppāda*, "arising."[445]

The short sutta is packed with meaning. In the Jeta Grove, the Buddha makes brief pronouncements about his three iconic teachings: impermanence, suffering, and absence of self. Whether or not tathāgatas appear in the world, these three exist as abiding realities of nature. A buddha "wakes up" to them and then teaches them.

The clause "whether tathāgatas arise or whether tathāgatas do not arise" is a frame that highlights the notion that the true nature of things is something that is independent of tathāgatas or buddhas. A similar frame is used for core teachings like conditioned arising, especially in the Pāli *Nidānasaṃyutta* and the Sanskrit *Nidānasaṃyukta*.[446] These teachings show that from the point of view of Gautama the Buddha and those who compiled the early texts, a buddha does not claim to have *devised* a metaphysical or moral system but to have *understood* things the way they are—the nature of mind, body, and universe, the human condition—and then to have shared their insights to enable and inspire others to realize the truths for themselves.

The sutta may be short, but I find it difficult to translate. The three characteristics or marks of existence (Pāli: *tilakkhaṇa*, Thai: *trailak* ไตรลักษณ์) are a prominent philosophical and motivational category in Theravāda and Thai Buddhism. The first is "All *saṅkhāras* are impermanent," and the second is "All *saṅkhāra*s are *dukkha*." Which meaning(s) of the polyvalent term *saṅkhāra/saṃskāra* fit here? Bhikkhu Bodhi notes that *saṅkhāra* "has been

443. *Suatmon chabap luang*, pp. 279–80.

444. *Aṅguttaranikāya, Tikanipāta, Yodhājīvavagga*: Syāmaraṭṭha, vol. 20, pp. 368.8–369.1; PTS, vol. 1, p. 286. English translation by F. L. Woodward, *Book of Gradual Sayings (Anguttara-nikāya) or More-Numbered Suttas*, vol. 1, pp. 264–65; Nyanaponika and Bodhi, *Numerical Discourses*, p. 77; Bodhi, *Numerical Discourses*, pp. 362–64.

445. *Aṅguttaranikāya*, vol. 1, p. 304.7.

446. See Skilling, "Who Invented Dependent Arising?" See now Chung and Fukita's *New Edition of the First 25 Sūtras of the Nidānasaṃyukta*.

rendered by a bewildering variety of English words: formations, confections, activities, concoctions, preparations, fabrications, and still others. This diversity of renderings has come about because English lacks a concept that exactly corresponds to *saṅkhāra*." Finally, no one seems to agree on how to translate the deceptively simple word *dukkha*. Some translators, like Bhikkhu Anālayo, treat the word as an untranslatable and retain the Pāli. Others use "suffering," "unsatisfactory," "painful," and so on. Bhikkhu Bodhi writes:[447]

> We normally translate this as "suffering," and in certain contexts *dukkha* does mean suffering and painful feeling. But as the theme of the four noble truths, and thus the cornerstone of the Buddha's teaching, "suffering" hardly covers the many nuances and implications of *dukkha*. While for the sake of transparency I render dukkha as "suffering," in doing so I have to acknowledge that this rendering is unsatisfactory and, in some respects, even misleading.

The third mark is "All dhammas are *anatta*." The subject shifts from *saṅkhāra* to *dhamma* because while all *compounded things* are impermanent and unsatisfactory, the *uncompounded* (*asaṅkhata, asaṃskṛta*) nirvāṇa is not. It is therefore incorrect to say all *dhammas* are impermanent or all *dhammas* are suffering. But everything, all *dhammas*, all entities, all phenomena, all moments of existence, are *anatta*: they are nonself, without self, without essence, and insubtantial. There is, perhaps, more disagreement about this single word *anatta* than almost any other concept in Buddhist studies. Our translations seem compelled to use unnatural phraseologies like "all dharmas are suffering" or "all dharmas are nonself."

Sūtra literature frequently uses strings of synonyms or near-synonyms to establish rhythms that reinforce descriptions or set moods. This is a widely recognized artifact of their oral origins. Here the string of verbs for "teach" is challenging to translate naturally. A similar string is used in both Pāli and Sanskrit texts—for example, the Mūlasarvāstivāda *Nidānasaṃyukta* and the *Perfection of Wisdom in Eighteen Thousand Stanzas*:[448]

447. Bodhi, *Reading the Buddha's Discourses*, p. 4.

448. The Gāndhārī *Dhoṇa-sūtra* has three verbs, *akhade vivaḍe s(*)praghaśide*: line 23, p. 124, reconstruction, p. 203. See Allon, *Three Gāndhārī Ekottarikāgama-Type Sūtras*. This may be an earlier version of the formula before it began to be expanded.

Pāli (7 terms total): *abhisambujjhati abhisameti abhisambujjhitvā abhisametvā* ***ācikkhati deseti paññapeti paṭṭhapeti vivarati vibhajati uttānīkaroti.***[449]

Mūlasarvāstivāda texts (8 terms total): *svayam abhijñāyābhisaṃbuddhya* ***ākhyāti prajñapayati prasthāpayati vibhajati vivaraty uttānīkaroti deśayati saṃprakāśayati.***[450]

Prajñāpāramitā (8 terms total): ***ākhyāyanti deśayanti prakāśayanti prasthapayanti vivaranti vibhajanti uttanīkurvanti saṃprakāśayanti.***[451]

449. Bodhi, *Reading the Buddha's Discourses*, p. 314.
450. *Nidānasaṃyukta* §§ 14.3, 5; 17.4; Waldschmidt, *Mahāparinirvāṇasūtra*, § 9.18.
451. Conze, *The Gilgit Manuscript of the Aṣṭādaśasāhasrikāprajñāpāramitā*, pp. 16.10, 20.2, 18, 77.5.

The Practice of Recollection

THE UNIVERSE IS impermanent, painful, and without substance. It is not a comfortable place: this is the message of the *Udānavarga* (translation 4, verses 3–4):

> Alas! Composite things are impermanent,
> it's their character to arise and pass away.
> Once they arise, they will surely pass away—
> their quieting is happiness.
>
> What pleasure is there, what joy,
> in the midst of this blazing fire?
> You have plunged into the darkness—
> why don't you seek out a lamp?

We are beset with uncertainty and insecurity. Apprehensive and afraid, where do we turn? There are several possibilities, several exits, and several lamps. One is the lamp of the Three Precious Gems: Buddha, Dharma, Saṅgha. These are not external lights; rather, they are inner lights powered by the spirit of commemoration and reflection, by the inward turn that leads to confidence and stability. Recollection connects to refuge, which leads, paradoxically, to independence (*aparapratyayatā*).

Overcoming fear through recollection

The next three texts are versions of sūtras with the title *Dhvajāgra*, in Pāli *Dhajagga*, that recommend the recollection of the Buddha or of the Three Precious Gems to overcome fear. The first two texts are Mahāsūtras, "Great Sūtras" (Tib. *mdo chen po*). In 1994 I published an edition of the Tibetan texts of ten Mahāsūtras preserved in the Kanjur, and in 1997 I published introductions to the Mahāsūtras as a group and category as well as to each Mahāsūtra individually. In this volume I translate three of them, according to the numbering of my edition, nos. 5, 6, and 10. The two sūtras that follow here, translations 12 and 13 in this volume, are Mahāsūtras 5 and 6 of that edition. They are closely interrelated: both are Mahāsūtras, and they have the identical Sanskrit title, *Dhvajāgrasūtra*. The Sarvāstivādins placed them together in the same order in their *Saṃyuktāgama* and transmitted them independently as Mahāsūtras.[452] Both of them advocate the practice of commemoration: the first Mahāsūtra the commemoration of the Three Precious Gems and the second the commemoration of the Buddha alone.[453]

Recollection or commemoration was and is a key practice of Buddhist mental culture (*bhāvanā*); that it was an early practice is evident from the fact that the commemorations are largely the same across different schools (including those preserved only in translation), with few variant readings of any significance.[454] Recollection serves many purposes: it gladdens the mind, concentrates the faculties, and establishes an inner relationship between the individual practitioner and the Buddha or the Three Precious Gems. The Sanskrit term for this is *anusmṛti*, which is *anussati* in Pāli and *rjes su dran pa* in Tibetan. I am not certain how to translate it, and I vacillate between "commemoration" and "recollection." Both have their strong points and their weak points, and I will use them interchangeably. At times I find "commemoration" more appropriate in that it evokes the sense of memory and that it gives a better sense of the thick descriptions conveyed by the texts. At

452. *Saṃyuktāgama* = Taishō 99, nos. 980, 981. For bibliography and further post-Waldschmidt Sanskrit fragments, see Chung, *A Survey of the Sanskrit Fragments Corresponding to the Chinese Saṃyuktāgama*, pp. 202–3.

453. For the traditional corpus of commemorations see Lamotte's comprehensive treatment at *Le Traité*, vol. 3, chap. 36, "Les huit commémorations," pp. 1329–1430. For Leon Hurvitz's English translation of this, see Tsukamoto, *History*, vol. 2, pp. 1033ff.

454. For the formula of the recollection of the Buddha, see Skilling, *Mahāsūtras*, vol. 2, pp. 410–13, 429–32, and table 37; for the formula of the recollection of the Dharma, see pp. 413–18 and table 38 in the same volume. For translations of the Pāli formula, see Bodhi, *Connected Discourses*, p. 320; for a translation of a Lokottaravāda formula, see Jones, *Mahāvastu*, vol. 3, p. 196. For the formula of the recollection of the Saṅgha, see *Mahāsūtras*, vol. 2, pp. 418–23 and table 39. The *Arthaviniścayadharmaparyāya* includes here "endowed with faith, endowed with aural learning" (*śraddhā-sampannaḥ śruta-saṃpannaḥ*), which is supported by Vīryaśrīdatta's commentary and Asaṅga's *Commentary on the Recollection of the Saṅgha* (*Saṅghānusmṛti-vyākhyā*). For a sūtra on the six recollections translated from the Chinese *Saṃyuktāgama*, see Eracle, *Paroles du Bouddha*, pp. 191–94 (Taishō 99, from vol. 2, no. 554, 145a–c).

times I feel that "recollection," with its implied sense of "collecting the mind" and "concentration," is called for. The noun *commemoration* has been used in English since about 1384, understood as "a calling to remembrance, in the Wycliffe Bible; borrowed through Old French *commemoration*, or directly from Latin *commemorātiōnem*, from *commemorāre*, commemorate." "Commemorate, v[erb] 1599, to recall, possibly borrowed through Old French *commemorer* or directly from Latin *commemorātus*, past-participle of *commemorāre* bring to remembrance, mention."[455] Recollect means to "call back to one's mind XVI . . . collect again XVI; summon up (one's spirits, courage, etc.) XVII"; while recollection is "concentration of thought; recalling to the memory XVII."[456]

For *anussati*, Venerable Nyanatiloka gives "recollection," "meditation," "contemplation";[457] the last two terms enrich our understanding of the term. *Anu* √ *smṛ* is to recall, to think back, to call or bring to mind. *Anusmṛti* is all of these and more: the hapless translator is obliged to choose a single English term for this spectrum of meanings, and this carries the risk of impoverishing the word by glossing over its multivalence. When all is said and translated, translation remains a tricky craft. As a fundamental spiritual practice, the commemoration of the Buddha inspired a wealth of literature, such as, for example, the *Samādhi of the Direct Encounter with the Buddhas of the Present Time*, a text that is attested in northwestern India by early Gāndhārī fragments and was translated into Chinese seven hundred years after the Parinirvāṇa. The *Samādhi of the Direct Encounter* came to be associated with the Pure Land tradition and in a sense has maintained a degree of living continuity as a contemplation sūtra.[458]

The *Dhvajāgra* sūtras present recitative texts in narrative settings and count amongst the earliest formal Buddhist liturgies to be preserved. The

455. Barnhart, *Chambers Dictionary of Etymology*, pp. 193–94.

456. Onions, *The Oxford Dictionary of English Etymology*, p. 746. The roman numerals indicate "the century in which any word or sense is first recorded" (p. x).

457. Nyanatiloka, *Buddhist Dictionary*, pp. 17–18, s.v. *anussati*.

458. *Pratyutpannabuddha-saṃmukhāvasthita-samādhi*: The text is complete in Tibetan and Chinese translations, the earliest of the latter done by the Indo-Scythian translator Lokakṣema in 179 CE. Damaged paper folios in Sanskrit, recovered in Khadalik, Chinese Central Asia, are preserved in the British Library, and Gāndhārī fragments have recently been identified: see Harrison et al., "Fragments of a Gāndhārī Manuscript"; Harrison, "Remarks on Recently Identified Sanskrit Fragments of the Pratyutpannabuddhasaṃmukhāvasthita-samādhi-sūtra." The editions, translations, and discoveries of new manuscript fragments are markers of the expanding horizons of Buddhist textual studies.

medium for recollection is memory and recitation (and, in some cases, visualization).[459] In the *Dhvajāgra* sūtras, Śakra recommends that the gods of the Realm of the Thirty-Three recollect (or, in the Pāli versions, "gaze on") his *dhvaja* when they are at war with the *asuras*—the titans or antigods. What is a *dhvaja*? It is a banner, standard, flag, or pennant.[460] Triumphal military imagery was popular amongst early Buddhists and must have resonated with other social groups, and the *dhvaja* is a symbol of good fortune, power, victory, and success. The *dhvaja* was one of the lucky signs or *maṅgala* of ancient India. Since the time of the *Mahāvyutpatti*, where the word occurs several dozen times, the chosen Tibetan translation has been not simply "banner" or "flag" but "*victory* banner," or "insignia (*mtshan*) of *victory* (*rgyal*)."

The Mahāsūtra titles use the compound *dhvajāgra* (Pāli: *dhajagga*). In Sanskrit *agra* (Pāli: *agga*) means "tip," "top," "pinnacle," or "summit," but at times it seems justified to translate it adjectively as "lofty." The learned translators of the Tibetan Mahāsūtras render *agra* in a superlative sense but choose different, synonymous words for the two titles: *rgyal msthan* ***mchog*** and *rgyal msthan* ***dam pa***. There is no semantic difference, and the translation team may have decided to use alternate terms simply to differentiate the two Mahāsūtras for ease of reference.[461] Within the text of the two Mahāsūtras themselves, however, the translators chose to use the same translation, *rgyal mtshan* ***mchog***, throughout.[462] Depending on the context, I have translated *dhvajāgra* as "crest of (my) banner," "banner" (when repeated in the same clause), and also "glorious banner" and "lofty banner."

The use of *dhvajāgra* in several of the *Hundred Avadānas* (*Avadānaśataka*) shows that in narrative, the *dhvaja* had ritual functions as a symbol of power and glory. When a king invites a dignitary such as a Buddha to his realm, he has all the thoroughfares cleaned and decorated with flags and banners—perhaps not very different from the modern practice of festooning roads and buildings with national flags to welcome state visitors from abroad.

459. For an overview of early Buddhist meditation and visualization, see Yamabe, "Concentration and Visualization Techniques in Buddhist Meditation."
460. For Śakra's banner (*dhvaja*), see Skilling, *Mahāsūtras*, vol. 2, pp. 424–26.
461. Cp. the titles of the two different translations of the *Vinayottaragrantha* as *'Dul ba gzhung* ***bla ma*** (Otani no. 1036) and *'Dul ba gzhung* ***dam pa*** (Otani no. 1037). This, however, is a case of different renderings of the same word by different translators.
462. See Skilling, *Mahāsūtras*, vol. 2, pp. 444–58.

In the *Avadāna of the Abstinence Rite*,[463] in hope of appeasing a nāga, the king has a basket of gold coins tied to the top of a flagstaff (*dhvajāgra*).[464] He sends out criers to beat drums and announce throughout his realm, "I will give this basket of gold to the person who can teach me the rite of abstinence (*upavāsa*), and I will reward him with great honors."[465] An old woman, a mason's daughter, shows the king a column to which her father had regularly paid worship with fragrances, incense, and flowers and instructs him to have it dug up and examined. The king orders his workers to excavate the pillar, and when they do so, they find beneath it a gold plate inscribed with the *upavāsa* abstinence, the five training rules of the lay follower (*upāsaka*), and the thirty-seven dharmas conducive to awakening (*bodhipakṣya-dharma*). The king has the abstinences written down and gives the document to the nāga and the twelve thousand rishis who reside in the Rishivadana park and they witness the thirty-seven dharmas conducive to awakening.[466] The nāga undertakes the eightfold *upavāsa*; he refrains from taking food and dies along with his retinue of five hundred. They all are reborn amongst the exalted deities of the Realm of the Thirty-Three.

In the *Avadāna of the Epidemic*, the Buddha commands the king:[467] "Great King, attach my outer robe (*saṃghāṭi*) to the tip of a banner and have it carried around your realm with great ceremonial reverence. Hold a grand festival and instruct the great mass of the populace to commemorate the Buddha, and well-being will follow." Feer, in his translation, draws our attention to a parallel in the thirteenth text of the *Garland of Precious Avadānas* (*Ratna-avadāna-mālā*) entitled *Praśāntakaraṇa*, in which a place called Nāḍakanthā (in one place spelled Nāḍakaccha) is disturbed by a series of afflictions. The

463. *Upoṣadha-avadāna*: *Avadānaśataka* no. 59, vol. 1, p. 339.10; Tib. no. 59, *Bsnyen gnas*, pp. 414.3 f.; trans. Feer, pp. 227–29.

464. *Hiraṇyapiṭakaṃ dhvajāgre baddhvā*; *Upoṣadha-avadāna: Avadānaśataka* no. 59, 418. penult, *gser 'bum yod pa'i snod rgyal mtshan gyi rtse mo la btags te*.

465. *Upavāsa*: "The abstinence practiced by lay disciples during the fortnightly *upoṣadha* observance" (*Princeton Dictionary of Buddhism*, p. 942; see also *upoṣadha*, pp. 943–44).

466. How the rishis "witness" the aids to awakening is not clear to me.

467. *Avadānaśataka*, vol. 2, 4 (14), *Īti*; Tib. *Yams kyi nad*, pp. 102.10–109.7; trans. Feer, pp. 64–67. Sanskrit, 82.1: *gaccha mahārājemāṃ saṃghāṭīṃ dhvajāgre baddhvā mahatā satkāreṇa sve vijite paryāṭayāśca mahāntam utsavaṃ kuru sarvañca mahājanakāyaṃ buddhānusmṛtau samādāpaye ti svastir bhaviṣyatīti* ||; Tibetan, 108.7: *nga'i chos gos snam sbyar 'di rgyal mtshan gyi rtse mo la thogs la | bkur sti chen po dang ldan pas | bdag gi yul skor du chug cig 'di la dga' ston chen po yang gyis shig skye bo phal po che thams cad kyang sangs rgyas rjes su dran pa yang dag par 'dzin du chug cig dang | des na khyed bde legs su 'gyur ro* ||.

Buddha is invited, and as soon as he arrives the evil spirits flee, and well-being and prosperity are restored. The Buddha then presents his robe to the people. He relates the story of the past Buddha Candra, who recited a dhāraṇī and a mantra to end a plague. Then the king asks for a means to prevent or to cure disasters like this, and the Buddha gives him his robe to carry in procession throughout the country and drive illness away.[468]

Dhāraṇī texts such the *Mahāsāhasrapramardana*, *Mahāpratisarā*, and the *Ratnaketu* recommend writing down a dhāraṇī, fastening it to the tip of a banner, and then brandishing it in battle or hoisting it up to flutter atop a caitya.[469] A text that was widely disseminated in Tibet—through mass production by blockprinting on "prayer flags"—is the *Dhāraṇī of the Banner and Armband* (*Dhvajāgrakeyūra-dhāraṇī*), the title of which seems to invoke the power of both the lofty banner and the *keyūra*, the upper arm band. In early icons the *keyūra* is one of the adornments of *yakṣas* and bodhisatvas; the former shows that it was already a symbol of power by the fourth century BE (second century BCE). Words like *jaya* and *vijaya* ("victory," "triumph," "success") are perennially popular and used in the names of sūtras and dhāraṇīs or as phrasal elements of dhāraṇīs and mantrapadas. In Thai, "Dhvaja" and "Vijaya/Bijaya" are common male names (ธวัช; วิชัย / พิชัย).

A distinctive feature of the two *Dhvajāgra* Mahāsūtras is the use of the phrase "commemorate or recollect by attribute" (*rnam pa las*, *ākārataḥ*),[470] a usage that seems to be have been introduced, or at least normalized as a standard idiom, by Sarvāstivāda redactors. It is not used in the Lokottaravāda or Theravāda *anusmṛti/anussati* formulas, but is common in Sarvāstivāda texts. The Theravāda exegetical tradition preferred the word *guṇa*, and liturgies, mantras, and yantras proliferated around the Buddhaguṇa (the qualities of the Buddha in *itipiso* formulas) or the 108 syllables of the Buddhaguṇa, Dhammaguṇa, and Saṅghaguṇa combined. A rare use of the word *ākāra* in connection with Pāli recollections is in the title of the *Ākāravattasūtra*, an apotropaic text that circulated widely in Siam.[471]

468. Parallels in Jain stories show a similar practice: see, for example, Woolner, *Introduction to Prakrit*, pp. 139–45, in Jain Mahārāṣṭrī, about an *indraketu*.

469. Hidas, "Rituals in the Mahāsāhasrapramardanasūtra"; Hidas, *Mahāpratisarā-Mahāvidyārājñī*, §§ 27–28, text pp. 142–45, trans. pp. 223–25. See Hidas, *Mahāpratisarā-Mahāvidyārājñī*, pp. 25–26 for more examples.

470. See Skilling, *Mahāsūtras*, vol. 2, pp. 409–10.

471. See Jaini, "(Introduction to and Translation of) Ākāravattārasutta."

12. Overcoming Fear through Recollection (1)

Introduction

The first and longer *Dhvajāgra-mahāsūtra* has no Pāli counterpart, and it is likely that it circulated within Sarvāstivāda communities only.

The Buddha is staying at Vaiśālī in the Gabled Hall (Kūṭāgāraśālā) on the banks of Monkey Pond (Markaṭahrada). Vaiśālī was capital of the Vṛji *janapada* and one of the great cities of northern India during the Buddha's time. According to several traditions, the Gabled Hall stood on the banks of Monkey Pond; according to Mūlasarvāstivāda Vinaya commentaries and to Xuanzang, who visited Vaiśālī in the first half of the seventh century, the pond was so called because it had been dug out by monkeys. The Gabled Hall at Monkey Pond is mentioned in Sarvāstivāda, Mūlasarvāstivāda, and Lokottaravāda texts and in some Vaitulya/Mahāyāna sources as well. Pāli sources, however, do not seem to know Monkey Pond at all; they locate the Gabled Hall in the Great Forest (Mahāvana), as do at least some Vaitulya/Mahāyāna sūtras.[472] The lack of consistency shows that the mainstream tradition was not unanimous on this point. I cannot say whether this means there were two gabled halls, or just one that we, as modern readers, see from different redactional or sectarian angles.

The prose framework of the sūtra is built up from stock phrases or modules, the use of which was a narrative device to facilitate recitation and memorization. Here five hundred merchants of Vaiśālī are about to set out from Śrāvastī for Takṣaśilā—that is, Taxila, one of the leading cities of Gandhāra.[473] In Buddhist narrative, "five hundred" is not meant to be an exact head count or even an approximate figure; it simply means "a large number," just as in English we say "dozens," "scores," or "hundreds," without

472. See further Skilling, *Mahāsūtras*, vol. 2, pp. 406–07, and Lamotte, *Le Traité*, vol. 1, p. 183 and note.

473. For the role of merchants in early Buddhism, see Skilling, *Mahāsūtras*, vol. 2, pp. 428–29. There is a large secondary literature on this topic. Here the number "five hundred" refers to a large group, doubtless including accompanying craftsmen, attendants, servants—not a full five hundred merchants, although the phrase is maintained throughout, with this awkwardly large number of merchants going to see the Buddha at the Gabled Hall, preparing and serving a meal to the Buddha and the saṅgha, listening to his Dharma talk, and, offstage, setting out on the road to Taxila. I do not think we have any statistics for the size of traveling parties and groups (as we do, at least to some degree, for Achaemenid Persia). Buddhist narratives invariably paint the groups as large.

regard for the actual figures.[474] Groups of five hundred merchants feature in the *Hundred Avadānas* in, for example, the *Maitrakanyaka*.[475] Other literary groups of five hundred include musicians (no. 17), gods (no. 59), monks (no. 94), and so on.

Our merchants are about to set out for Taxila. The ancient routes were never entirely secure, and even though traders would have followed the established northern route, this passed through long stretches of uninhabited or sparsely populated wilderness (*araṇya*).[476] Perils included floods, fires, and other natural disturbances; fierce beasts; ruthless dacoits; and rapacious officials. The Buddha's discourse is intended to reassure the traders; he advises them that if they become fearful, they should bring to mind the Buddha, Dharma, and Saṅgha—that is, they should recollect the Three Precious Gems to overcome their fear and to regain calm and confidence. To illustrate his point, he draws on a hoary theme of Indian mythography, the Vedic story of the battle between the gods, the *devas*, and their archrivals, the antigods, the perennially envious *asuras*.[477] When the battle is about to be joined, Śakra, lord of the gods, tells his troops to recollect or gaze on his banner—this will restore their confidence and banish their fears.

Sūtra literature frequently uses strings of synonyms or near-synonyms to reinforce descriptions or set moods. Here a string of three words is used in both of the sūtras: *bhaya*, *chambitatva*, and *romaharṣa* (Tib. *'jigs pa*, *bag tsha ba*, and *spu zing zhes byed pa*; Pāli *bhaya*, *chambhitatta*, and *lomahaṃsa*), which I translate as "fear," "dread," and "horripilation." The last word, *romaharṣa* or *lomahaṃsa*, means "hair raising," rather like our English "hair standing on end." I prefer "horripilation," despite the fact that the *Oxford English Dictionary*'s definition is discouragingly clinical:[478] "Erection of the hairs on the skin by contraction of the cutaneous muscles (caused by cold, fear or other emotion, or nervous affection), producing the condition known as 'goose-flesh'; 'creeping of the flesh.'" The word is an adaptation of late Latin (Vulgate) formed from *horripilāre*, from the stem of *horrēre*, to bristle, plus *pilus*, hair. The earliest reference given by the *Oxford English Dictionary* is from 1656,

474. For groups of five hundred or 1,250 in the āgamas, particularly as attending on the Buddha, see Anālayo, *Comparative Study*, pp. 417–19.

475. *Avadānaśataka* no. 36, p. 199.13, *pañcavāṇikaśataparivāraḥ*; trans. Feer, pp. 133–34, Appleton, *Many Buddhas*, p. 188.

476. Cf. the definition of *araṇya* at *Abhidharmakośa*, chap. 3, end, under *aṅguli*.

477. See Skilling, *Mahāsūtras*, vol. 2, pp. 423–24.

478. Simpson and Weiner, *Oxford English Dictionary*, vol. 7, p. 397a.

when Thomas Blount (1618–79), in his *Glossographia; or, A Dictionary Interpreting the Hard Words of Whatsoever Language, Now Used in Our Refined English Tongue*, defines the word as follows: "Horripilation (horripilatio) the standing up of the hair for fear, a growing rough with hair; a sudden quaking, shuddering or shivering."[479] This fits *romaharṣa* quite nicely.

There are related words like *horripilant* and *horripilate*. Lafcadio Hearn (1850–1904) uses the latter nicely: "Flesh made to creep by the utterance of such words as poets utter—flesh moved by an Idea, flesh horripilated by a Thought!"[480] Now, Orwell's rules include "Never use a long word where a short one will do" and "Never use a foreign phrase, a scientific word, or a jargon word if you can think of an everyday English equivalent." By all rights I should choose an everyday English equivalent, but Orwell also says, "Break any of these rules sooner than say anything outright barbarous." "Hair standing on end" is hardly barbarous, but the aesthetics of speech urge me to choose this wonderful and venerable word *horripilation*.

In his *Commentary on the Arthaviniścayasūtra*, Vīryaśrīdatta states that the three phrases "in a wilderness, at the foot of a tree, or in a deserted building" refer to the state of physical solitude (*kāyavyapakarṣa*): one who dwells alone (*advitīyavihārī*) is physically withdrawn since he is removed from social intercourse (*janasaṃsarga*). The terminology of the practice of withdrawal from social activity—seclusion and retreat—has been integral to Buddhism and śramaṇism since the beginning (and is in certain aspects integral to Indian culture, both social and nonsocial, particularly to Yoga culture). The medical and social crises arising from the spread of the coronavirus pandemic have given new significance to these terms and practices, making them less distant from mainstream social norms than they were in the past.

The verses

After the merchants have offered a meal to the Buddha and the saṅgha, the Fortunate One intones twelve verses to rejoice in the merits they have accrued. Most of the verses have counterparts elsewhere in the scriptures (see table 4). Verses 3 and 4 occur in the *Vaiśālīpraveśa-mahāsūtra* (here translation

479. From reprint of Blount, *Glossographia* (1661; Hildesheim, Germany: George Olms, 1972).
480. *Some Chinese Ghosts*, 1887, vi. 149, from Simpson and Weiner, *Oxford English Dictionary*, loc. cit. Nowadays the very idea of *ideas* or *thoughts* horripilates most social discourse.

15) as well as in the *Mahāvastu* of the Mahāsāṃghika-Lokottaravāda Vinaya and the *Mahāmāyūrīvidyārājñī* of the *Pañcarakṣā*.[481] Verses 5 to 8 and 10 to 12 have Pāli counterparts in the *Field Sutta* of the *Aṅguttaranikāya*.[482] The verses play upon notions formed from the verbal root *sam* √*pad* (indicating success, fulfillment, good fortune, blessing, or perfection; Tib. *phun sum tshogs pa*), forms of which occur in these verses no less than twenty-five times.[483]

Table 4. *Concordance of verses in translation 12*

1. Not traced elsewhere
2. Not traced elsewhere
3. *Dhvajāgra* 2 / *Vaiśālipraveśā* v. 14 / *Mahāvastu* / *Mahāmāyūri*
4. *Dhvajāgra* 2 / *Vaiśālipraveśā* v. 15 / *Mahāvastu* / *Mahāmāyūri*
5. *Khettasutta* v. 1
6. *Khettasutta* v. 2
7. *Khettasutta* v. 3
8. *Khettasutta* v. 4
9. Not traced elsewhere
10. *Khettasutta* v. 5
11. *Khettasutta* v. 6
12. *Khettasutta* v. 7

13. Overcoming Fear through Recollection (2)

Introduction

The second and shorter *Dhvajāgra-mahāsūtra* has counterparts in the Pāli *Saṃyuttanikāya*, the Chinese *Saṃyuktāgama*, and the Chinese *Ekottarikāgama*.[484] The latter is closer to the Pāli than to the Sarvāstivāda (*Saṃyuk-*

481. See Skilling, *Mahāsūtras*, vol. 2, pp. 426–27.

482. *Khettasutta*, *Aṅguttaranikāya* 8:34, vol. 4, pp. 238–39; trans. by Bodhi, *Numerical Discourses*, pp. 1166–68.

483. See Skilling, *Mahāsūtras*, vol. 2, pp. 427–28.

484. *Ekottarikāgama*: Taishō 125, chap. 14. Waldschmidt translates into German the shorter *Saṃyuktāgama* and the *Ekottarikāgama* versions in facing columns: Waldschmidt, *Bruchstücke buddhistischer Sūtras aus dem Zentralasiatischen Sanskritkanon*, pp. [44–51] 240–46. See remarks at Skilling, *Mahāsūtras*, vol. 2, pp. 403–6.

tāgama) version. That is, three versions, in Tibetan, Pāli, and Chinese, are available for comparison. Here I mostly compare the Tibetan and the Pāli.

All three versions give the same setting: Anāthapiṇḍada's Garden in Prince Jeta's Grove at Śrāvastī. This Śrāvastī *nidāna* is one of the most common openings. The *Dazhidu lun* and the Theravāda tradition agree that the Fortunate One spent twenty-five rains retreats at Śrāvastī. According to Buddhaghosa, he passed nineteen of these at the Jetavana.[485] It is natural that many of the Buddha's sermons are located here, to the point that if reciters could not remember where a sermon was spoken, they were encouraged to assume that it took place at Śrāvastī.[486]

TABLE 5. *Concordance of verses in translation 13*

1. Recollection of Sambuddha. Pāli *Dhajagga* v. 1
2. Recollection of Dharma. Pāli *Dhajagga* v. 2
3. Recollection of Saṅgha. Pāli *Dhajagga* v. 3
4. Result: fear will be banished. Pāli *Dhajagga* v. 4
5. Mistaken refuge. *Udānavarga* 27.31; Pāli *Dhammapada* v. 188
6. Mistaken refuge. *Udānavarga* 27.32; Pāli *Dhammapada* v. 189
7. Right refuge. *Udānavarga* 27.33; Pāli *Dhammapada* v. 190
8. Four truths of the noble ones. *Udānavarga* 27.34; Pāli *Dhammapada* v. 191
9. Right refuge. *Udānavarga* 27.35; Pāli *Dhammapada* v. 192

The prose

The introductory part of this short Mahāsūtra is in prose. It opens without fanfare in Prince Jeta's Grove, where the Fortunate One addresses the monks. He recommends the formulaic recollection of himself as Bhagavat and Tathāgata to the monks whenever they become fearful when dwelling alone in remote and wild places. As in the other *Dhvajāgra* sūtras, he compares the

485. Lamotte, *Le Traité*, vol. 1, p. 541 (*juan* 9, p. 125c) and p. 173, n. 3. See also *Le Traité*, vol. 1, p. 94 and n. 1, passage cited in Shinohara, *Forest of Pearls*, p. 209.

486. See, with reference to previous research, Anālayo, *A Comparative Study of the Majjhima-nikāya*, vol. 2, p. 887, n. 138; Anālayo, *Saṃyukta-āgama Studies*, p. 93, n. 10. The idea has been somewhat sensationalized by the title of Gregory Schopen's "If You Can't Remember, How to Make It Up."

recollection of the Buddha to the recollection of Śakra's banner in the war with the asuras. But the Tathāgata is superior to the king of the gods, because he is free from negative mental states and free from fear while Śakra is not.

The verses

The Buddha concludes the sūtra by intoning nine verses.[487] Here as well, most of them have counterparts elsewhere (see table 5). The first four correspond to those at the end of the Pāli counterpart, where they summarize the preceding prose recommendation for meditators to commemorate the Buddha, Dharma, or Saṅgha in moments of stress and need. There is a disjuncture, however, between the verses and the prose: in the Sarvāstivāda versions—found in the *Saṃyuktāgama* and the Mahāsūtra—the prose deals with the recollection of the Buddha alone.[488] The following five verses correspond to five verses of the "Chapter on Seeing" of the *Udānavarga*, where they occur in the same order.[489] These verses occur in other texts, such as the *Sūtra of the Miracles*,[490] and the scholastic literature quotes them to explain the meaning of refuge.

The first four verses are included in the "Chapter on the Buddha" of the Pāli *Dhammapada*[491] and the "Chapter on Refuge" of the Prakrit *Dhammapada* of the Sāṃmitīya school.[492] The verses are not found in the extant portions of the Gāndhārī *Dharmapada*, but this does not mean a great deal since about one third of the manuscript is lost.

A Sanskrit meditation manual from Central Asia has a section on the four commemorations.[493] The manual is largely known from a single manuscript

487. For more about the verses, see Skilling, *Mahāsūtras*, vol. 2, pp. 462–66.

488. Note that there is no sign of abbrevation in the Tibetan (all of the Tibetan Mahāsūtra translations give their texts in full, without abbreviation) or in the Central Asian Sanskrit fragments.

489. Chap. 27, *Paśyavarga*, vv. 31–35.

490. *Prātihāryasūtra*, *Divyāvadāna* no. 12, p. 164.7–16, trans. Rotman, *Divine Stories: Part 1*, p. 282; also in *Vinayakṣudrakavastu*, Otani no. 1035, vol. 44, 'Dul ba, *ne*, 49a8–49b3. Prajñāvarman's primary source for the verses is the "Exposition of the Great Miracle," but he summarizes a *nidāna* related by "others" that closely resembles that of the *Dhammapada* Commentary (Balk, *Prajñāvarman's Udānavargavivaraṇa*, vol. 2, pp. 759.30–760.5).

491. Chap. 14, *Buddhavagga*, vv. 10–14 = *Dhammapada* vv. 188–92. For an English translation of the commentary on the Pāli verses, see Burlingame, *Buddhist Legends*, part 3, pp. 63–67; exegesis at Carter and Palihawadana, *The Dhammapada*, pp. 247–49.

492. Patna *Dhammapada*, vv. 216–19 = chap. 13, *Śaraṇavargga*, vv. 1–4.

493. Schlingloff and Hartmann, *Ein buddhistisches Yogalehrbuch*, § 11, pp. 173–89 (counting *devatānusmṛti*).

(and a few other fragments), and there are no translations into other languages such as Chinese; this is unfortunate because the manuscript is in a fragmentary state. The original title is lost, and the manual has become familiar to scholars under the German title *Yogalehrbuch* since it was retrieved by the Prussian Central Asian expeditions, since it is preserved in the Berlin collections, and since the edition and most literature about it are in German. The fragmentary section on recollection quotes or embeds formulaic passages from the *Dhvajāgrasūtra*. The formulas of the Buddha, Dharma, and Saṅgha, as far as they are preserved, agree with the Sarvāstivāda version, using, for example, the term *ākārataḥ* (at least for the Buddha and the Dharma; the formula on the Saṅgha is not preserved). The quotations contain the verses on the four truths, omitting one of the verses—that is, the itemization of the four truths.

This was an authoritative set of verses. The *Abhidharmakośabhāṣya* and *Vibhāṣāprabhāvṛtti* define *refuge* as "protection" (*trāṇārthaḥ śaraṇārthaḥ*) because "by relying on it one is liberated completely from all suffering"; in illustration they cite verses 7 and 8 "spoken by the Fortunate One."[494] These are Vaibhāṣika glosses; the Mahāsāṃghika *Śrīghanācārasaṅgrahaṭīkā* explains refuge in identical terms and cites verse 5 to illustrate it.[495]

Verses 7 and 8 on the four truths of the noble ones seem to have been added to the set later. Verse 8 has a history of its own, independent of the other verses, in inscriptions in India and Southeast Asia.[496]

Neither the Sanskrit fragments from Central Asia nor the two Chinese *Saṃyuktāgama* translations conclude with verses. The verses occur only in the Tibetan Mahāsūtra and the Pāli versions, but the selection of verses is different.

Translation history

The Mahāsūtras were translated into Tibetan around 800 CE by an accomplished team made up of Jinamitra, Prajñāvarman, and Ye shes sde. I published an edition of the Tibetan text as *Mahāsūtra* 6 in 1994, comparing

494. *Abhidharmaośabhāṣya* ad chap. 4, v. 32 (Pradhan ed. p. 217.7–18) (La Vallée Poussin, vol. 3, pp. 79–80; Lodrö Sangpo, vol. 2, p. 1351. According to La Vallée Poussin the verses are cited in the *Vibhāṣā*, p. 80, n. 1); Jaini, *Abhidharmadīpa*, p. 127.5–14.

495. *Sputārthā Śrīghanācāra* (Singh), p. 49.7, *tatra trāṇārthaḥ śaraṇāthaḥ | tatra evāha bhagavān . . . iti gāthāvacanāt*; Derrett, trans., *A Textbook for Novices*, p. 18.

496. Skilling, "Discourse on the Relative Value of the Varieties of Knowledge," pp. 335–36 and 345, n. 28.

three versions: the Tibetan, the Central Asian Sanskrit, and the Pāli. I translated it by hand in a notebook in the 1970s, and I have revised it repeatedly since.

14. Overcoming Fear through Recollection (3)

Introduction

The two Sarvāstivāda Mahāsūtras have only a single Pāli counterpart: this is the *Dhajaggasutta* in the "Sakka Collection" of the "Chapter with Verses" of the *Connected Discourses*.[497] The etymological root of the Pāli title, *dhaja-agga*, is cognate to that of the Sanskrit title, *dhvaja-agra*. In the Theravāda tradition the *Dhajaggasutta* has the status of a *paritta*—that is, it is separated out from the canonical collection and recited privately or in public ceremonies for protection and blessing. The Pāli commentary credits the *Dhajagga-paritta* with great power. It relates how, when the Dīghavāpi Cetiya was being built in central Sri Lanka, a young monk slipped from high up and tumbled downward. Monks below called out for him to recollect the *Dhajaggasutta*, and he cried out, "May the *Dhajaggaparitta* protect me!" Two bricks issued forth from the body of the cetiya; he landed on them and was saved. This story is summarized in the invocatory verses that introduce the paritta.[498]

Translation history

The Pāli *Sagāthavagga* version was translated as "The Top of the Banner" by C. A. F. Rhys Davids, assisted by the Sri Lankan monk Sūriyagoḍa Sumangala, and first published in 1917.[499] Bhikkhu Bodhi published a translation as "The Crest of the Standard" in *Connected Discourses of the Buddha* in 2000.[500]

497. *Sakkasaṃyutta, Sagāthavagga, Saṃyuttanikāya*; vol. 1, pp. 218–20. Trans. in Rhys Davids, *Book of Kindred Sayings*, vol. 1, pp. 281–83.
498. See Skilling, *Mahāsūtras*, vol. 2, pp. 64–66.
499. C. A. F. Rhys Davids, *Book of Kindred Sayings*, vol. 1, pp. 281–83. According to Rhys Davids, a translation by E. R. Gooneratne was published in the *Ceylon National Review* in 1906 (not seen).
500. "The Crest of the Standard" in Bodhi, *Connected Discourses*, pp. 319–21.

Subduing the Epidemic at Vaiśālī

15. The Buddha's Visit to Vaiśālī

Introduction

The *Vaiśālīpraveśa* is not a member of the set of Mahāsūtras mentioned above (translations 11–12); since, however, its canonical Tibetan translation calls it "Great Sūtra" in its title and closing colophon, I venture to describe it as an "independent Mahāsūtra."[501] The Tibetan Great Sūtras are so great, so beyond normal literary and ritual functionality, that they don't fit comfortably into boxes, and they stretch the standard classifications of the Kanjurs. The *Vaiśālīpraveśa* is a Mahāsūtra in its own right, and Kanjurs preserve it in the Sūtra, Tantra, Dhāraṇī, and Vinaya sections. Under a different title, *Mahāmantrānusāriṇī*, the same sūtra is a member of the Sanskrit *Pañcarakṣā*, or *Five Protections* of northern India and Nepal.[502] As a protection par excellence it is a formidable apotropaic sūtra as defined in the Mūlasarvāstivāda Vinaya commentary.[503]

An epidemic devastates Vaiśālī

The Buddha and Ānanda are staying at the Kuñjikāvasatha in the town of Nāḍikā, which is located across the Ganga River from Pāṭaliputra on the way to Vaiśālī. They go on to Vaiśālī and stay at the Āmrapālī Grove. The *Vaiśālīpraveśa* belongs to a cycle of texts that relate how a terrible epidemic ravaged the northern Indian city of Vaiśālī and how the Buddha assuaged

501. For the title, see Skilling, *Mahāsūtras*, vol. 2, pp. 585–86.
502. For the *Pañcarakṣā* texts and their rituals in Newar society in general, see Lewis, *Popular Buddhist Texts from Nepal*, especially chap. 6, "The Refuge of Recitation: The Pañcarakṣā." For the *Mahāmantrānusāriṇī*, see pp. 152–53.
503. See Skilling, *Mahāsūtras*, vol. 2, pp. 28–31.

Figure 48. Twelve-armed, three-faced Mahāmantrānusāriṇī, from a dhāraṇī manuscript dated 1714 from Patan (Lalitpur), Nepal. 26 × 9.8 cm. Opaque watercolor, ink, and gold on blue paper.

the disease through the incantation of blessings, verses of well-being, and in the present case, spells or *mantrapada*.[504] The background story is that a disaster—an epidemic, a plague of sorts—befell Vaiśālī. We do not know exactly what it was, but whatever the case, people perished in droves. The natural causes of the plague were recognized, but it was blamed on evil spirits or demons as well.

Vaiśālī was an important and well-known city of ancient India. Its remains were identified a century ago by colonial-era archaeologists; further excavations were conducted after India recovered its independence, and the ruins have been restored to turn Vaiśālī into a pilgrim-cum-tourist destination. The Pāli commentary lauds the city in its heyday and then introduces the arrival of the plague:[505]

> By the time the Blessed One arose, Vesālī had become large and successful. It had 7,707 royals, and a similar number of princes, treasurers, and so forth. As it is said, "Now on that occasion Vesālī was successful and prosperous, populous, filled with people, and food was plentiful. It had 7,707 mansions, 7,707 houses with

504. For the broader narrative context, see Skilling, *Mahāsūtras*, vol. 2, pp. 589–93.
505. Translation by Bodhi, *Suttanipāta*, p. 675.

> peaked roofs, 7,707 parks, and 7,707 lotus ponds."[506] Some time later a famine struck, with drought and crop failure. First the poor people died, and their bodies were cast outside. Then, drawn by the smell of the corpses, evil spirits entered the city. Then still more people died, and because of the decay a plague broke out. Thus Vesālī was overrun by three perils: famine, evil spirits, and plague.

A similar description of the city is given in the "Chapter on Bedding and Seats," the *Śayanāsanavastu*, of the Mūlasarvāstivāda *Vinayavastu*.

We do not know when this happened, but the disaster festered in the collective memory and was elaborated by an array of Buddhist texts.[507] The event is associated with the recitation of a particular set of svastigāthā, the intoning of which cured the epidemic. The Pāli version bears the title *Ratanasutta*, the *Discourse on Precious Gems*; it is included in two canonical collections, the *Short Readings* (*Khuddakapatha*) and the *Suttanipāta*, both of which are included in the *Miscellaneous Collection* (*Khuddakanikāya*) of the Tipiṭaka. These two collections give the verses alone without any narrative setting, for which we must turn to the commentary, the *Paramatthajotikā*.[508] Tradition has it that the commentary was composed by the prolific fifth-century scholar Buddhaghosa, but as is often the case, modern scholars have challenged this attribution. Whatever its origin, it is an erudite retelling in Pāli on the basis of earlier materials. Sanskrit verses parallel to those of the Pāli *Ratanasutta* are incorporated into the *Mahāvastu* of the Lokottaravāda Mahāsāṃghika school, where they are called "verses of well-being," *svastyayanagāthā*.[509] Another Sanskrit version of the verses is embedded in a *Pañcarakṣā* text, the *Mahāsāhasrapramardanī*.[510]

506. Here the commentary is citing the *Mahāvagga* of the Pāli *Vinaya* (*Vinaya*, vol. 1, p. 268.4–10).

507. The *Da zhidu lun* mentions that Vaiśālī suffered from frequent famines (*disettes*, *durbhikṣa*): Lamotte, *Le Traité*, vol. 1, p. 189 and n. 2.

508. Translation by Ñāṇamoli, *The Illustrator of Ultimate Meaning (Paramatthajotikā) Part I*, pp. 172–79.

509. The Vaiśālī narrative is in Senart, *Le Mahāvastu*, vol. 1, pp. 253–301; the verses are at p. 290.10. For translations, see Thomas, "Formula of Welfare," pp. 65–69, and Jones, *Mahāvastu*, vol. 1, pp. 208–49.

510. Iwamoto, *Mahāsāhasrapramardanī*, p. 7.1. See Skilling, "Rakṣā Literature of the Śrāvakayāna." A complete English translation of the *Mahāsāhasrapramardanī* under the title "Destroyer of the Great Trichiliocosm" by the Dharmachakra Translation Group (trans. James Gentry) is available at https://read.84000.co/translation/toh558.html.

Invited by the Licchavis to cure the epidemic, the Buddha travels from Rājagṛha to Vaiśālī with Ānanda. When they arrive, he instructs Ānanda to go into the city, place his foot down on the city threshold, and intone a series of commands, *mantrapadas*, and stanzas. Ānanda does this, and this ends the epidemic.[511] The course of events is illustrated in a Tibetan scroll painting (*thangka*) in the collection of the Musée Guimet in Paris, one of a set collected by Jacques Bacot (1877–1965) and donated to the museum in 1912.[512]

Urban pageantry: A Buddha's grand entry to a city

The Buddha's entry into a city was hardly a low-key event; the principles of heroic narration could not permit the royally born mendicant to slip through the gate unnoticed amidst the milling throngs of travelers. The bards who composed the narratives sought to exalt Gautama by celebrating his very special status, elevating him so he would stand out as superhuman, a god above gods. If the Buddha himself did not seek a pedestal in his lifetime, his followers raised him high posthumously, seating him on royal thrones, lion thrones, and capacious cartwheel-sized lotus flowers in full bloom. His arrival in a city is a grand pageant embroidered with marvels and miracles, a powerful metaphor for the transformations that the Buddha and his Dharma effect in places that are in deep distress. The motif of the "entry into the city" is a building block of choice in narrative and avadāna literature: stereotypical descriptions occur in the *Dharmaruci-avadāna*,[513] the *Pāṃśupradāna-avadāna*,[514] the *Ujjvalikadānakathā* (which draws on the *Vaiśālīpraveśa* cycle),[515] and the *Kāśikavastra* of the *Avadānaśataka*,[516] to name but a few of

511. In the *Vaiśālīpraveśa-mahāsūtra* and most versions of the epidemic story, Ānanda is the emissary who recites the words of power at the Buddha's behest.

512. Musée Guimet 16536, cat. no. 58 in Béguin, *Les peintures du bouddhisme tibétain*, pp. 153–55. See Hackin, "Les scènes figurées de la vie du Buddha d'après des peintures tibétaines," pp. 82–87.

513. *Dharmaruci-avadāna*, *Divyāvadāna* no. 18, trans. by Rotman, *Divine Stories: Divyāvadāna, Part 2*, pp. 29–31.

514. *Pāṃśupradāna-avadāna*, *Divyāvadāna* no. 26, trans. by Strong, *The Legend of King Aśoka*, pp. 198–200.

515. *Dvāviṃśati-avadāna*, *Ujjvalikadānakathā*, trans. by Feer, *Fragments extraits du Kandjour*, pp, 544–52.

516. *Kāśikavastra*, no. 19, in Speyer, *Avadânaçataka*, vol. 1, p. 109.1–12; in Vaidya, *Avadānaśataka*, p. 49.19–26; trans. by Feer, *Avadāna-Çataka, Cent légendes bouddhiques*, pp. 83–84; trans. by Appleton, *Many Buddhas*, pp. 133–35.

those that have been translated. The "Chapter on Bedding and Seats" in the Mūlasarvāstivāda *Vinayavastu* gives an elaborate description of the Buddha's arrival in Śrāvastī.[517]

The *King of Samādhis*, a long Vaitulya/Mahāyāna sūtra, portrays the Buddha and his inconceivably vast retinue's arrival in the city of Rājagṛha as a grand and majestic narrative tableau.[518] Another sūtra that celebrates Śākyamuni's entry to the royal capital is the *Splendid Array of Mañjuśrī's Buddhafield*, a longish text that does not survive in Sanskrit but is available in Tibetan and Chinese translations.[519] Here the Fortunate One is residing on Vulture Peak and descends to go to King Ajātaśatru's palace. He is surrounded by a huge retinue, and numerous wonders take place. As he walks, lotuses the size of cart wheels spring up with every step he takes, and in each and every lotus a magically produced bodhisatva sits in meditation. As the Buddha progresses, the bodhisatvas sing verses announcing how he is entering the city. When he steps on the city threshold, further marvels occur, and the populace celebrates his arrival in song. In chapter 22 of the Khotanese *Book of Zambasta*, Śākyamuni gives a detailed prediction of the coming of the future Buddha Maitreya in which he describes Maitreya's triumphal entry to the city of Ketumatī.[520]

The Pāli commentary gives the following account of the happenings at Vesālī:[521]

> Thus the Blessed One spoke this *Discourse on Gems* at the entrance to the city of Vesālī on the very day he arrived there, for the purpose of dispelling those disasters. Having learned it, the Venerable Ānanda, reciting it for the sake of protection, took water in the Blessed One's bowl, and walked around the entire city sprinkling

517. Gnoli, *Śayanāsanavastu*, pp. 25.17–26.27; trans. by Schopen, "Hierarchy and History," pp. 124–25.
518. *Samādhirāja*, trans. by Roberts, *King of Samādhis Sūtra*, https://read.84000.co/translation/UT22084-055-001.html, chap. 10.
519. *Āryamañjuśrībuddhakṣetraguṇavyūha-nāma-mahāyānasūtra* / *'Phags pa 'jam dpal gyi sangs rgyas kyi zhing gi yon tan bkod pa zhes bya ba theg pa chen po'i mdo*, Otani no. 760(15), vol. 23, Dkon brtsegs, *wi*, 282b5–339a4; Toh 59 = Dergé Kanjur, vol. 41 (Dkon brtsegs, *ga*), 248b–297a; *Dpe bsdur ma* CK 71. Trans. by the Dharmachakra Translation Committee, "The Noble Great Vehicle Sūtra 'The Array of Virtues of Mañjuśrī's Buddha Realm,'" available from 84000 at https://read.84000.co/translation/toh59.html.
520. Emmerick, *Book of Zambasta*, vv. 246–66, pp. 326–29.
521. Translation by Bodhi, *Suttanipāta*, pp. 678–79.

> the water. As soon as the elder said, "Whatever" [the first word of the sutta in English translation], those evil spirits who had not already fled—those living off the rubbish heaps, along the walls, and elsewhere—fled through the four gates, so that the gates were crammed. Some, unable to find room at the gates, broke through the walls and fled. As soon as the evil spirits had left, the plague afflicting the people's bodies subsided. Coming out, they made offerings to Ānanda with all sorts of incense, flowers, and other items. The multitude perfumed the meeting hall in the middle of the city with all sorts of incense, erected a canopy, decorated it with all adornments, prepared a seat for the Buddha, and led the Blessed One there. The Blessed One entered the hall and sat down in the seat prepared for him. The Saṅgha of bhikkhus too, as well as the royals and the people, sat down in the appropriate seats. Sakka, the ruler of the devas, drew near together with the assemblies of devas from two deva worlds, and so did other devas. The Elder Ānanda, too, having walked around all of Vesālī and thereby given it protection, came with the residents of Vesālī and sat down to one side. There the Blessed One spoke this *Discourse on Gems* to everyone. But others assert that the Buddha recited only the first five verses and the rest were recited by Ānanda at the time of invoking the protection.

The verses of the *Ratanasutta* preserve an early version of a core protection, but the verses are not identical in the different versions. The commentary reveals that even within the Pāli tradition there was disagreement about the contents of the protection.

Liminality: The threshold at the city gate

A rare and interesting term in the story is *indrakīla*, a compound noun made up of two elements, *indra* (Pāli: *inda*) + *kīla* (Pāli: *khila*), which is variously defined.[522] It is a threshold slab or stone at the gate of a city, royal palace, harem, or house.[523] From the context it is a slab laid flat or a post sunk into

522. See the handful of canonical references at *Pāli Tipiṭakaṃ Concordance*, part 1, p. 362b.
523. BHSD, p. 114b. Tib. *sgo'i them pa*, Pāli *indakhila* (DoP, vol. 1, p. 375a; see also *ummāra*, threshold, p. 506a).

the earth, most commonly used with the verbs "stand" or "step on, put one's foot on."[524] In the Pāli story of the Vesālī epidemic, the Buddha stands at the city gate (*nagaradvāra*) and sends Ānanda into the city to recite the *Ratanasutta*. The *Splendid Array of Mañjuśrī's Buddhafield* (§ 1.21) relates that

> The moment [the Buddha's] right foot touched its threshhold, the entire city shook six times. Hundreds of thousands of divine and human instruments played without being struck, and a rain of divine flowers fell. The blind could see, the deaf could hear, the insane regained their senses, the inattentive became concentrated, the naked received clothes, the hungry received food, and the poor obtained wealth. At that moment, no one was tormented by attachment, aggression, ignorance, jealousy, stinginess, rage, or pride. At that moment, everyone was filled with love and altruism, and they regarded one another as parents.

Outside of the narratives, the word *indrakīla* has a special connection with the *Ratnasūtra* verses themselves, since it occurs in a simile in one of the stanzas shared by the three known Indic versions: the Pāli *Ratanasutta* and the Sanskrit *Mahāsāhasrapramardanī* and *Mahāvastu*. To cite the last named:[525]

> Even as **a pillar at a city's threshold**
> Stands firm in the earth, by the four winds unshaken,
> So, I affirm, is the good man unshaken,
> Who in the Noble Truths is well instructed,
> And pondering their meanings deep perceives them.
> In the Order is this jewel of perfection;
> So through this truth to us may there be welfare,
> Whether from men or superhuman beings.

The Pāli commentary gives a clear definition of how the Sri Lankan Theravāda exegetes interpreted the word *indakhila* towards the end of the first

524. I wonder whether it would be trampled by all and sundry, or whether to step on the *indrakīla* was a deliberate act of subjugation that would be undertaken with reason by only the spiritually, or perhaps the politically, powerful.

525. Trans. by Thomas, "Formula of Welfare," p. 67.

millennium after the Buddha's nirvāṇa.[526] Jones translates the *Mahāvastu* occurrences, including that of the **Ratnasūtra*, as "Indra's column"; Lewis translates in the Newar context as "Indra Pillar." Translations from Pāli include "Inda-wedge" (Jayawickrama), "locking post" (Ñāṇamoli, Norman); *sao kheuan* (เสาเขื่อน, Thai translation, *Suatmon plae*). In a fascicle published in 1971, the *Critical Pāli Dictionary* warns us, however, that the "exact shape and function [remain] doubtful," and today, over fifty years later, the situation hasn't changed.[527] Schlingloff gives a succinct review of the word, largely in terms of definitions given by ancient India's classic legal code, the *Arthaśāstra*, accompanied by plans of gates as prescribed by the text or as uncovered in archaeological excavations.[528] As far as I know, no potential *indrakīla*s have as yet been identified in South Asian excavations, and the question remains: is *indrakīla* a pillar, a post, or a slab?

The sūtra is rich in powerful epithets of the Buddha, a characteristic of devotional and apotropaic verse. The Buddha's presence and his commands attract troops of mighty deities. Notable is that the Buddha intones an exceptionally long string of *mantrapadas* for Ānanda to repeat. The use of *mantrapada* here belies the myth—going back, perhaps, to the Victorian era—that the use of mantras is exclusive to tantric practice and that it is absent in Śrāvaka and even Mahāyāna practice, or that when *mantrapadas* are present, they show "tantric influence." Notions like these were introduced to Buddhist studies early, along with the socio-ideological partitioning that gave rise to separate and incompatible "Buddhisms" and that imagined "Hīnayāna," "Mahāyāna," and "Vajrayāna" as separate "churches." Mantras are used by all schools in ritual practice for protection and prosperity, and do not *necessarily* belong to any school.

The verses

Verses 1 to 13, which seem to be unique to this sūtra, praise the Buddha and invoke his blessings. Verses 7 to 11 commemorate prominent moments in the Master's life—his birth, awakening, defeat of Māra, turning the wheel of the Dharma by expounding the truths of the noble ones, and routing the oppo-

526. *Paramatthajotikā*, vol. 1, p. 185.21–24; trans. by Bhikkhu Ñāṇamoli, *The Illustrator of Ultimate Meaning*, p. 203.

527. *Critical Pāli Dictionary*, vol. 2, fasc. 7, pp. 297–98.

528. Schlingloff, *Fortified Cities of Ancient India*, p. 78 and n. 101; figs. 16–30 and plans at front.

nent teachers through the Great Miracle—events that memorialize Lumbinī, the Heart of Awakening (Bodhimaṇḍa at Vajrāsana / Bodh Gayā), Sarnath, and Vaiśālī, respectively. Verses 14 and 15 are simple but powerful invocations of safety and well-being that are found in the *Dhvajāgra-mahāsūtra* (translation 12 in this volume, verses 3 and 4) and in the *Verses for Well-Being* used to this day by the Newar Buddhists of Nepal (translation 15 in this volume, verses 3 and 4). In the *Mahāvastu*, the recently awakened Buddha recites the two verses in a blessing of the directions for the two paradigmatic merchants, Trapusa and Bhallika.[529] Verses 16 and 17 restate the Buddha's prose proclamation at the beginning of the sūtra.

The last two verses resonate through a range of sources. Verse 18 occurs in several texts, and verse 19, the last, comes at the end of the *Great Sūtra of the Great Assembly* [*of Deities and Supernormal Beings*] (*Mahāsamāja-mahāsūtra*).

Verses like these carried the spirit of blessing and well-being across Asia. There are two epigraphic uses of two of the stanzas, one from South India inscribed on a stone image of Tārā in the Ḍambal fort in Karnataka[530] and one inscribed on gold plates across the seas on the island of Java.[531] The South Indian inscription of the verses was first published in the *Indian Antiquary* in 1881 by John Faithful Fleet (1847–1917), who read it from an ink impression supplied by H. Cousens (1854–1933).[532] The forty-seven-line inscription opens with *namo buddhāya*, "homage to the Buddha"; the body of the inscription is engraved in old Kannada (Old-Kanarese), but around the top of the tablet there are two long lines of writing containing three verses in Sanskrit. The record dates to the time of the Western Chalukya king Tribhuvanamalla (Vikramāditya VI) and bears a date equivalent to 1095–96 CE. It records grants to two *vihāras*, one of the Buddha, the other of Tārādevī.

529. Marciniak, *Mahāvastu*, vol. 3, p. 389.10–13; Tournier, "Protective Verses," p. 426. There are similar lines in *Lalitavistara* but not a complete parallel. Tournier gives a detailed survey of the complex transmission of the set of blessings given to the two merchants. *Lalitavistara* excerpt in Hidas, *Powers of Protection*, § 15, pp. 84–87.

530. Gadag Tālukā, Dhārwād District, north Karnataka: Fleet, "Sanskrit and Old-Canarese Inscriptions"; Tsukamoto (III), Ḍambel 2, p. 394. For Buddhist remains in Karnataka, see Mitra, *Buddhist Monuments*, p. 193, Hiremath, *Buddhism in Karnataka*, and Krishna Murthy, *Buddhist Art and Culture in Karnataka*. Apparently the Tārā image is no longer at the fort and at present cannot be located. I thank Gurudas Shete (email, 9 June and 24 July 2020) and Shrinivas Padigar (email, 8 March 2021) for this information.

531. De Casparis, *Selected Inscriptions*, p. 113 and addenda 1, pp. 338–39.

532. Fleet and Cousens were leading figures in Indian epigaphy and archaeology in the colonial period.

In the following issue of the *Indian Antiquary*, James Burgess (1832–1916) corrected some of Fleet's misinterpretations and noted that Tārā is figured in the Nasik, Aurangabad, and Ellora caves. Closer to hand, a Tārā image was found at Belgami (Dist. Shimoga), and there is other evidence of Tārā worship in Karnataka.[533] All of this shows that Tārā had a presence south of the Narmada River, but normally (as far as we can know) she is not connected with the verse.

Translation history

The translation is based on my edition of the Mahāsūtra (no. 10), published in 1994. I take text A, the Kanjur translation, as primary text, but I also consult text B, the Tibetan Vinaya version, and text C, the Sanskrit *Pañcarakṣā* version. References to paragraph numbers are to those of my published edition. For notes on textual variants in the versions consulted, see the edition in *Mahāsūtras*, vol. 1.

The Sanskrit syllables and phrases of the *mantrapada* are *transliterated* into the Tibetan script but are not *translated* into the Tibetan language. Here I give an English translation from the Sanskrit in italics following each unit of the *mantrapada*. Some phrases are translated into Tibetan—these I give in roman script. *Mantrapadas* are complex liturgical instruments, and it is difficult or impossible to establish a "correct" version.[534]

A fine translation of the *Vaiśālīpraveśa* produced by the Bhaiṣajyavastu Translation Team was published online as "The Noble Mahāsūtra 'On Entering the City of Vaiśālī'" by 84000: Translating the Words of the Buddha in 2020.

533. Burgess, "Ḍambal Buddhist Inscription"; Krishna Murthy, *Buddhist Art and Culture in Karnataka* presents further evidence.

534. For tables of the variants in the versions of the *mantrapada* edited in *Mahāsūtras*, vol. 1, see Skilling, *Mahāsūtras*, vol. 1, pp. 624–738.

Liturgies for Well-Being and Blessing

16. Verses for Well-Being

The remaining texts translated here, with one exception, are liturgical: they are verse texts chanted for well-being and blessing. In all traditions and languages, chants and recitation lie at the heart of Buddhist devotional practice. Here we present a Sanskrit chant of well-wishing from Nepal along with Pāli protective verses that invoke the healing powers of the seven awakening factors. This Sanskrit chant has a deeply intertextual relation with several of the texts translated in this anthology, showing that the lives of these texts are not limited to storage in manuscripts but that they are active in the quotidian world. The exception mentioned is a short sūtra on the wheel-turning king's seven treasures and the seven awakening factors, given here to provide a background to the Pāli chant that follows. Pāli blessings include the protective and auspicious verses that are recited every day throughout Thailand at the conclusion of ceremonies of merit. The anthology closes with the *gāthā* of *gāthās*, the *ye dharmā* stanza or formula of causation.

A Svastivākya from Nepal

An important aspect of Buddhist culture is well-wishing and blessing: there is no justification for ill-will or hatred, which only harm everyone involved. A *Dhammapada* verse declares,

> For never here do hatreds
> ever cease through hatred.
> They cease by power of love:
> this is a truth perennial.[535]

535. *Na hi verena verāni sammant' idha kudācana | averena ca sammanti, esa dhammo*

Svasti means well-being, benefit, safety, blessing. Verses recited for well-being are called *svastigāthā* or, as here, *svastivākya*. *Vāyka* means speech, word, voice: from the root *vac*, it is cognate to Latin *vox*, French *voix*, English *voice*, and so on. These "vocalizations of blessings," verses of well-being, feature in the repertoires of recitation in most or all Buddhist traditions. In Pāli, they are called *sotthigāthā*. There are many types and names: in Sanskrit *svastyayanagāthā* or *maṅgalagāthā*, "auspicious verses" (Tib. *bkra shis kyi tshigs su bcad pa*), and *āśīravāda*, "benediction" (Tib. *shis par brjod pa*).[536] *Svastigāthā* and *maṅgalagāthā* are shared by all Buddhist schools. They are an integral part of rituals, ceremonies, consecrations, and blessings. They are recited in paritta and tantric ceremonies. The Tibetan Kanjur and Tanjur place *maṅgalagāthā* at the end of the main sections and of the whole of each collection. In Tibetan culture, the ceremonial scarves made of fine white cloth that are presented to honor guests or visitors are often woven with auspicious symbols and verses—in particular, two of the verses given here. Svastigāthā, Paritta, and Rakṣā literature are all are deeply intertextual, and three of these verses are also part of the Mahāsūtras translated in this volume.

Translation history

I do not know of any previous European translation. My translation is based on the romanized edition of a Sanskrit *svastivākya* published in *Mahāsūtras*.[537]

---

sanantano: *Dhammapada*, chap. 1, v. 5. For another translation, see Roebuck, *The Dhammapada*. Here I render the negative *a-vera*, "nonhatred," as the positive "love." To translate it as "hatreds cease by nonhatred," or "by absence of hatred," is not wrong but is somewhat tautological.

536. For this type of verse, see Skilling, "Rakṣā Literature," pp. 129–37.

537. Skilling, *Mahāsūtras*, vol. 2, pp. 756–57. This was based on Śākya, *Svasti bākya*: see p. 756, n.

17. The Wheel-Turning King's Treasures and the Seven Awakening Factors

Introduction

This short sūtra draws a parallel between the advent of a wheel-turning king with his seven treasures and the advent of a tathāgata with the seven awakening factors. The pairing up of the two sets of seven illustrates how the awakening factors are treasures of the teaching beyond price. In his *Indispensable Commentary* on Vasubandhu's *Abhidharmakośabhāṣya*, Śamathadeva cites it as "the first sūtra of the Collection on Kings," the *Rājasaṃyuktaka*, of the *Madhyamāgama*.[538] In the Chinese *Middle Collection* the equivalent sūtra is indeed the first text of the "Collection on Kings." The English translation takes up a single page, making it the shortest of the 222 discourses that make up the Chinese *Middle Collection*.[539] The sūtra is also incorporated into the *Kāraṇaprajñapti*, one of the seven books of the Sarvāstivāda *Abhidharma*, which is preserved in Tibetan translation only.[540] The Pāli counterpart is placed in the *Chapter on the Wheel-Turning King* in the "Collection on Awakening Factors" of the *Saṃyuttanikāya*.[541] There is also a parallel in the Chinese *Ekottarikāgama*.[542]

538. Śamathadeva (Zhi gnas lha), *Abhidharmakośa-upāyikāṭīkā / Chos mngon pa'i mdzod kyi 'grel bshad nye bar mkho ba shes bya ba*, Otani no. 5595, vol. 118, trans. Jayaśrī and Shes rab 'od zer, Mngon pa'i bstan bcos, *tu*, 216a8–216b5, *par* (read *rgyal po*, *rājā*, for *rgyas par*, *vistarena*) *dang yang dag par ldan pa'i mdo dang po dang gnyis pa'i mdo dang po las te*. The reference to the "second sūtra" does not seem to fit, since the second sūtra deals with the thirty-two characteristics of the great being (*mahāpuruṣalakṣaṇa*). Admittedly the formula lists the seven treasures near the beginning, but it does not list the seven awakening factors and is not really a source of the citation. Śamathadeva cites the text with reference to Vasubandhu's brief citation: Pradhan, *Abhidharmakośabhāṣya*, chap. 3, v. 96d, p. 186.8: *sūtra uktaṃ rājaś cakravartino loke prādurbhāvāt saptānāṃ ratnānāṃ loke prādurbhāvo bhavati | tadyathā cakraratnasya hastiratnasyāśvaratnasya maṇiratnasya strīratnasya gṛhapatiratnasya pariṇāyakaratnasye ti* |.

539. Chinese *Madhyamāgama* sūtra no. 58, trans. by Shi Chunyin, "The Discourse on the Seven Treasures," in Bingenheimer et al., *Madhyama Āgama*, p. 359.

540. *Kāraṇaprajñapti / Rgyu gdags pa*, trans. Jinamitra, Prajñāvarman, Ye shes sde, etc.: Otani no. 5588, vol. 115, Mngon pa'i bstan bcos, *khu*, 134b5–135a3. For a summary, see La Vallée Poussin, *Bouddhisme. Études et matériaux: Cosmologie*, "Appendice: Analyse du *Kāraṇaprajñaptiçāstra*," p. 328.

541. Sutta 2, *Cakkavattivaggo pañcamo*, *Bojjhaṅgasaṃyutta*, *Saṃyuttanikāya*, vol. 5, p. 99. Trans. by Bodhi, *Connected Discourses*, pp. 1594–95.

542. Taishō 125, vol. 2, 39.7, p. 731b; trans. by Eracle, *Paroles du Bouddha*, pp. 152–53.

The cakravartin is a larger-than-life figure in Buddhist mythology, where he is the paradigm of kingship—possessing royal merit and virtue coupled with the ideals of justice and nonviolent exercise of power.[543] The cakravartin and his seven treasures belong to the shared imaginaire of all known schools. Romila Thapar comments that "the [cakkavatti] king's prime possessions were seven precious objects of sovereignty: the wheel, elephant, horse, gemstone, woman, householder, and councillor, symbolic of law, royalty, force, wealth, fertility, work, and advice."[544] Grand classical texts like the *Lalitavistara*, the *Mahāvastu*, and the Mūlasarvāstivāda *Vinayavastu* incorporate the cakravartin and his seven treasures into their narratives,[545] and Southeast Asian cosmologies like the Pāli *Lokapaññatti* and the Siamese *Traibhūmi* treatises devote considerable space to them.

The Mahāyāna *Kāśyapaparivarta* expands the ideological horizon to include the bodhisatva. It states in prose that when a cakravartin king arises, so do the seven treasures, and wherever a bodhisatva arises, there arise the thirty-seven dharmas conducive to awakening (*saptatriṃśadbodhipakṣyā dharmā*).[546] The verse that immediately follows, however, states,

> Where a cakravartin arises, there the seven treasures arise;
> where a bodhisatva arises, there the seven awakening factors arise.

The verses that follow the prose of Mahāyāna sūtras often summarize the preceding prose. Here there is a discrepancy between the two.[547]

The seven treasures have an early and sustained visual presence, being depicted in painting and sculpture in Āndhradeśa, northeastern India, and Tibet.

543. Note that ***chakkavatti*** and ***chakravartin*** are the same word to be pronounced in the same way, but romanized with *cha* rather than *ca* to make pronunciation easier for those who do not know the rules of Indic spelling and pronunciation.

544. Thapar, *The Past before Us*, p. 403.

545. *Lalitavistara*, pp. 11–12; Senart, ed., *Mahāvastu*, vol. 1, pp. 108–9; *Vinayavastu, Bhaiṣajyavastu*, in Dutt, *Gilgit Manuscripts*, p. 31.12.

546. Pāsādika, *Kāśyapaparivarta*, § 45, p. 40.1.

547. The Chinese versions agree with the Sanskrit and Tibetan, except the Sung dynasty version, which gives "seven" in both the prose and the verse.

Translation history

I do not know of any previous European-language translation.

18. Protective Verses: The Seven Awakening Factors

Verses from the *Seven Awakening Factors* are included under the title *Bojjhaṅgaparitta* in the *Seven Protections* and *Twelve Protections*. These are two of the most popular collections of chants in Thailand, widely disseminated in small booklets. They are a staple of monastic life, and a booklet of one or the other collection is usually presented to a newly ordained novice or monk along with other requisites of the monastic vocation.

Both sets of *Protections* are included in the *Royal Chanting Book*, a comprehensive compendium of chants compiled by the revered master and Pāli scholar Saṅgharāja Pussadeva, who is popularly known by his nickname, Sangkharat Sā (สังฆราช สา, 1819–99).[548] Published in 1880, the *Royal Chanting Book* was one of the earliest Pāli books to be printed in Siam in the modern Thai typographic script. Until then, in the center and in the south, Pāli texts were copied by hand on manuscripts of palm leaf or paper in the special script called *khom bali*, "Khom script for writing Pāli," or in the Mon script. In the north and northeast, they were copied in varieties of the Tham (Dhamma) script. The written culture of Siam used a variety of scripts to match the needs of its linguistic and historical diversity. The introduction of uniform print fonts led to a typographic unification of written language.

The *Seven Awakening Factors* is included at the beginning of both collections, where it follows the *Protection Spoken by the Worthy Arhat Aṅgulimāla* (*Aṅgulimālaparitta*).[549] In the *Royal Chanting Book*, the *Seven Protections* comes first, before the *Twelve Protections*, and as a result, in the latter the *Seven Awakening Factors* is abbreviated with reference to the preceding version.[550] The *Bojjhaṅgaparitta* is sometimes included in old, hand-calligraphed paper leporellos or accordion books but usually in the form of

548. He was appointed Supreme Patriarch of Siam in 1893.

549. *Nangsue suatmon*, p. 16; *Suatmon chabap luang*, p. 44 (introductory verses) and p. 23 (paritta).

550. *Suatmon chabap luang*, p. 44. In *Nangsue suatmon*, pp. 41–42, it is given in full, including the invocatory verses.

the three canonical prose suttas mentioned below rather than the verse version. I illustrate here a sample page from the manuscript collection of Wat Pak Khlong, Phetchaburi province, Thailand (figure 49).

The verses translated here are introduced by a six-line introductory invocation. Invocatory stanzas like these, called *bot khat tamnan* (บทขัดตำนาน) in Thai, are recited to introduce many of the well-known parittas. Here the paritta proper is seventeen lines long; it summarizes three short suttas of the "Chapter on Illness" of the *Collection on the Awakening Factors* in the *Saṃyuttanikāya*.[551] The three consecutive suttas are available in English translation by Bhikkhu Bodhi;[552] they relate how the chanting of the seven factors empowered listeners to overcome illness.[553] In the first, Mahākassapa is gravely ill, in the second, Mahāmoggallāna: the Buddha goes to see them and explains the seven factors of awakening. In the third sutta, the Buddha himself is ill, and Mahācunda Thera goes to him and intones the seven factors. In each case, listening to the seven factors of awakening leads to immediate recovery. The important thing is hearing the Dhamma, listening to it, realizing its scope and potential, and rejoicing. This is not quite the same as listening to the Dhamma as instruction, which also brings joy, but in that case the audience learns something new and is urged to put it into practice. In the three "Illness" suttas, the beneficiaries of the chants are all accomplished arhats who have already developed the seven factors to perfection; it is listening to their positive and uplifting message that does the trick. As a composition, the verse version is noncanonical, although I doubt whether scruples of canonicity mean much in the context of chants. The question reminds me of the simile of the man mortally wounded by a poisoned arrow who refuses to allow the arrow to be extracted until he finds out details like who shot the arrow or the type of bow, bowstring, and arrow.[554] The purpose of the paritta is to heal and protect, and quibbles about origins did not fit in.

551. *Gilānavagga, Bojjhaṅgasaṃyutta, Saṃyuttanikāya*, vol. 5, pp. 79–81, assigned the titles *Gilāna 1, 2,* and *3* after the *uddāna*, p. 83.4, *gilānā apare tayo*.

552. *Connected Discourses of the Buddha*, pp. 1580–82. See Bodhi, *Reading the Buddha's Discourses in Pāli*, pp. 455–58, for a study version of *Gilānasutta*.

553. Bhikkhu Anālayo has translated the three sūtras on the awakening factors and illness, each from a different source: see Anālayo, "The Healing Potential of the Awakening Factors," pp. 14–17. These are pp. 14–15, *Gilāna 1*, trans. from the Tibetan *Gsar 'gyur*; p. 80, *Gilāna 2*, trans. from the Pāli *Bojjhaṅgasaṃyutta*; and p. 81, a counterpart of *Gilāna 3* from the Chinese *Saṃyuktāgama* (also published in Anālayo, *Mindfully Facing Disease and Death*, pp. 43–50).

554. *Cūlamāluṅkyaputtasutta, Majjhimanikāya* no. 63.

One of the three *Saṃyutta* suttas was translated into Tibetan and is included in Kanjurs as one of the thirteen *Gsar 'gyur gyi mdo*, or "newly or recently translated sūtras," so called because they were amongst the last South Asian texts to be translated into Tibetan and included in the Kanjur. The thirteen were translated by Tharpa Lotsāwa and the Sri Lankan master Ānandaśrī at Thar pa gling ("Island of Liberation") in central Tibet. No information is available about why the texts were chosen for translation, but most of the thirteen are parittas. Liturgy lies at the fore of identity and lineage, and perhaps Ānandaśrī wanted to transmit his liturgy to Tibet. For various reasons, the thirteen texts were scarcely studied or recited in Tibet, and they seem to have fallen into neglect not long after they were translated.

The thirteen new translations were placed as a set the end of the Perfection of Wisdom section of the Kanjur. Why were these Theravāda texts placed together with Perfection of Wisdom texts, when the Perfection of Wisdom is an entirely different class of literature with which they have no connection? Their colophons made their origins clear: no one ever connected them with the Perfection of Wisdom, and I suspect that it was largely a question of space. By the time the thirteen texts had been translated, the main divisions of the Kanjur had already been formed and settled (since the age of the imperial registers and the "proto-Kanjurs"): so where to put this new set of translations that did not quite fit anywhere? The last volume of the Perfection of Wisdom section was half empty: there was plenty of space for the thirteen new translations. There they were placed, and there they remain to this day.[555]

Today the Pāli verse version is chanted in Thailand and Burma, while in Sri Lanka the *Bojjhaṅgasaṃyutta* version is chanted, and the verse version does not seem to be transmitted.

19. Protective and Auspicious Verses

In Thai books of chants, the *Seven Awakening Factors* is followed by a set of verses that begins with "unlucky signs, inauspicious portents" (*yandunnimittaṃ*). After this come three verses that start with "Indeed, may all beings who suffer be free of suffering" (*dukkhappattā ca nidukkhā*).[556] These short chants

555. For the "thirteen new translations," see Skilling, "Theravādin Literature in Tibetan Translation."

556. *Nangsue suatmon*, pp. 16–17; *Suatmon chabap luang*, pp. 24–25.

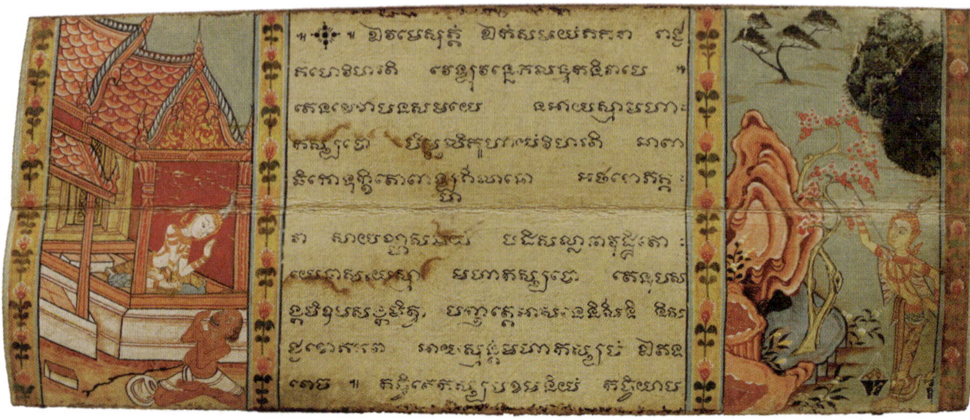

Figure 49. The text is the prose *Bojjhaṅgaparitta* in Khom Bali script. The paintings are from the *Vessantara-jātaka*. Left: the brahman Jūjaka asks the exiled Prince Vessantara for his children. Right: Maddī, the faithful queen, collects fruits in the forest. Paper leporello manuscript, Wat Pak Khlong, Phetchaburi province, Thailand.

do not have formal titles and, like many others, whether or not they have titles, are referred to by their opening lines. *Yandunnimittaṃ* is also known as *Abhayaparitta*, "Fearlessness Paritta," but it is commonly referred to as *Yandun* (ยันทุน, pronounced *yan-thun* in Thai).

The next sets of verses, those beginning "Just as rivers brimming with water" and "May all calamities be averted," are recited by the monks to rejoice in the merit made by those who have made offerings to the saṅgha and to bless and offer protection and security. When those who have participated in an offering hear the Pāli lines *yathā vārivahā* and then *sabbītiyo vivajjantu*, they know that the ceremony is drawing to an end. In the *Royal Chanting Book*, these verses go under the general title "the method of rejoicing."[557] Almost all ceremonies close with the last selection *bhavatu sabbamaṅgalam*, which calls for all good things, the protection of all the devas, and well-being at all times by the power of the Buddha, Dhamma, and Saṅgha. *Bhavatu sabbamaṅgalam.*

My translations are from the Thai-script *Royal Chanting Book*.[558]

557. *Anumodanāvidhī*: *Suatmon chabap luang*, pp. 95–96.
558. *Bhavatu sabbamaṅgalam*: *Suatmon chabap luang*, p. 30.

20. Envoi: A Formula of Causation

The collection closes with the *ye dharmā* stanza. This stanza was widely inscribed throughout the ancient Buddhist world. It is engraved on clay, brick, stone, and metal, and is written in ink on palm leaves, paper, cloth, and walls. It is copied on objects to be installed within stūpas or idols and sacred statues, on the outer surfaces of stūpas and statues (around the base or halo, or on the back), in the colophons of manuscripts, on the front or back of cloth scroll paintings (*thangka*), and so on. It is recited in the consecration rituals for stūpas, buildings, statues, scrolls, and manuscripts.[559] The stanza is known in Prakrit, Pāli, and Sanskrit recensions; the number of inscriptions is immense, and as time passes more continue to be discovered or noted. Beyond the subcontinent, it is usually inscribed in the original Indic language and letters, but sometimes it is translated—for example, into Chinese (see figures 50 and 51).[560] Despite this ubiquity, the function of the stanza is still imperfectly understood. Early ritual was oral, and if any sort of manuals were ever composed when writing came into use, no early examples survive. Manuals and handbooks came much later, especially with the development of tantric ceremonial literature. A curious byproduct of Western or modernist attitudes towards ritual is that from the nineteenth century, the age of "Victorian rationalism," to the present digital age, archaeologists and art historians have dismissed the most widely disseminated stanza in Buddhist history as "the usual Buddhist creed" and misprized it with scarcely any attempt to understand what it means or why it is there.

The stanza was spoken not by Gautama the Buddha but by Aśvajit (Tib. Rta rgyal; Pāli Assaji), one of Śākyamuni's five former companions in self-mortification; after his awakening, Śākyamuni guided the same five, who came to be known as the "happy group," to arhatship at Deer Park near Vārāṇasī.[561] In the second year after the Buddha's awakening, Śāriputra, then a wandering ascetic, saw Aśvajit and was impressed by his calm deportment

559. See "The Heart Formula of Dependent Arising" in Skilling, *Questioning the Buddha*, translation 12.

560. See Wong, *Buddhist Pilgrim-Monks*, pp. 34–39.

561. For this event, see Skilling, *Questioning the Buddha*, pp. 17–19. In the Lokottaravāda *Mahāvastu*, the monk who transmits the *gāthā* is named Upasena rather than Aśvajit.

and radiant demeanor. He asked him who his teacher was and what his teacher taught. Aśvajit replied:[562]

> The Tathāgata proclaims the cause
> of states that arise from causes
> as well as their cessation.
> Such is the teaching of the Great Ascetic.

Upon hearing the verse Śāriputra attained the first stage of realization, the state of *srotāpanna* or "stream winner." Returning to his hermitage, Śāriputra recited the verse in turn to his companion Maudgalyāyana, and the latter attained the first stage as well. This transformative event is narrated once only, in the Vinayas of the various schools. While many verses and prose passages are repeated in different settings within each of the various Tripiṭakas, this verse occurs once only, in this context, and nowhere else.[563] But its importance was such that the verse went on to have a distinguished career, becoming, by the beginning of the Pāla period (about the eighth century CE), if not beforehand, the most inscribed verse in India as well as throughout the Buddhist world. Why was this particular verse selected? Ancient, and even recent, documents do not explain this point, but the answer may lie in the obvious: its direct line of transmission (in Tibetan this might be described as a *lung*) runs from the Buddha himself to Aśvajit to Śāriputra and Maudgalyāyana to the reciter or ritualist. The verse exemplifies the oral circulation of the Dharma.

Here I illustrate and translate an example of the *ye dharmā* stanza that is unusual in that it is introduced by a single line of prose. This particular form of the citation is preserved in about half a dozen exemplars, which suggests that this is a specific canonical version. I illustrate it from an inscription written in the Prakrit language in the Bhaikṣukī script on the bottom plate of a statue of a seated, crowned Buddha that belongs now to the vast collections of the National Palace Museum, Beijing.[564] The version, language, and script are those used by the Sāṃmitīya school. This school, dubbed "personalist" (*pudgalavāda*) by opposing schools of thought, was apparently the largest

562. I translate here from the Pāli version, *Vinaya*, vol. 1, p. 40.28–29. There are no semantic differences amongst the various recensions.

563. For several versions of the narrative see Bareau's account as "La rencontre de Śāriputra et d'Aśvajit," in *Recherches sur la biographie du Buddha* [part I], pp. 343ff.

564. The early history and provenance of the Buddha are not known, and it is not certain that the statue and the base originally belonged together, although they do seem to fit.

monastic order when Chinese monk-scholar Xuanzang visited India in the seventh century.[565] The stanza is semantically equivalent to the other versions, but in Sāṃmitīya epigraphs it is introduced by the line of prose that so far as I know is not found in any other surviving accounts of the momentous encounter.

Until very recently, no original scriptures of the Sāṃmitīya order were known to survive. Scholars have recently identified the "Patna *Dhammapada*," fragments of several long sūtras, and post-canonical poetic works, all in their distinctive Prakrit, as well as an Abhidharma treatise in Sanskrit verse and other materials. The Prakrit prose passage and verse are known from several stone inscriptions from the northeastern Gangetic plain; the verse is attested by the post-colophon of Saṅghatrāta's *Abhidharmasamuccayakārikā*.[566] The entire treatise is in proper Sanskrit; only the *ye dharmā* at the very end is in Prakrit. The Sāṃmitīya Vinayapiṭaka, where, on the example of the piṭakas of other schools, this incident and the stanza would have been recorded, does not survive in the original Prakrit and was never translated into Chinese or Tibetan. The Sāṃmitīya appear to have been flexible about the use of language and script. The "Patna *Dhammapada*" is preserved in Prakrit in a north Indian script. The *Maṇicūḍa-jātaka* is in Prakrit in Bhaikṣukī script. Sarvarakṣita's *Mahāsaṃvartanīkathā* is composed in Sanskrit and preserved in six manuscripts from Nepal on palm leaf and paper, written in Nepalese or north Indian scripts; those that conclude with the *ye dharmā* stanza give it in a standard Sanskrit form, probably as a scribal convention unrelated to the text's school affiliation.

The Sāṃmitīya school accepted the "four seals" of the Buddha's teaching and is therefore counted as Buddhist, and this is indeed confirmed by their adoption of the iconic stanza of causation—*ye dharmā*, the heart of conditioned arising and nonself—in inscriptions and colophons. In respectful homage to this neglected school, I choose to close this volume with their version of the "heart of dependent arising."[567]

565. See Skilling, "Rehabilitating the Pudgalavādins" and "The Vātsīputrīya/Sāṃmitīya: Buddhist Personalism"; Dimitrov, *The Buddhist Indus Script and Scriptures* (reviewed by Vincent Tournier, *Bulletin de l'École française d'Extrême-Orient* 107 (2021).

566. Sferra, "Pudgalo 'vācyaḥ—Apropos of a Recently Rediscovered Sanskrit Manuscript of the Saṃmitīyas," pp. 660–61. Sferra, "The Second Chapter of the *Abhidharmasamuccayakārikā* by Saṅghatrāta."

567. For the "heart of dependent arising" see Skilling, *Questioning the Buddha*, chapters 11 and 12 and p. 264.

Figure 50. Clay tablet of haloed Buddha seated on throne flanked by small stūpas, flowers, and a pair of lissome bodhisatvas. The *ye dharmā* stanza is inscribed below in Chinese, flanked by a pair of lions (or possibly *qilin*).[568]

568. Also illustrated in Forbidden City Publishing House, *Across the Silk Road*, § 243.

Box 12. *Ye dharmā in China*

Figure 51. *Ye dharmā* verse, lower part of north pagoda of Yunju Monastery (雲居寺), Beijing. The bricks with *ye dharmā* are divided into two parts, upper and lower.

Upper Small pagoda with four Chinese characters:

利 法
塔 舍

Below these are two Sanskrit syllables: *oṃ* on the right and *raṃ* on the left. Read from top to bottom, right to left, the inscription reads *fa sheli ta*—that is, *dharma-śarīra-stūpa*, "stūpa of the Dharma relic."

Lower *Ye dharmā* verse, read from top to bottom, right to left:

我 因 我 諸
作 緣 說 法
如 盡 是 因
是 故 因 緣
說 滅 緣 生

That is,
諸法因緣生，我說是因緣，
因緣盡故滅，我作如是說。

The Chinese verse is cited from the *Fo shuo zaota gongde jing* (佛說造塔功德經), *The Sūtra of Virtue of Constructing Stūpas*, which was done by Di po he luo (地婆訶羅) Divākara in the Tang dynasty (680 CE).

The north pagoda was originally built during the Liao dynasty (1111–20 CE), with a total of 176 bricks each bearing the *ye dharmā* verse. When the pagoda was repaired in the 1980s, it was found that most of the *ye dharmā* bricks were broken or damaged, and it was not feasible to make new bricks to replace them. But fortune intervened: by chance the workers found a pit near the pagoda and unearthed 177 duplicate bricks with the *ye dharmā* stanza, which seemed to have been buried there long before. They used these bricks to replace the old ones.

Part IV

A Treasury of Terminology

A Glossary of Proper Names, Technical Terms, and Titles for Sagacious Readers of Buddhist Texts

Figure 52. Flowers, rabbits, and birds. Paper leporello manuscript, Wat Pak Khlong, Phetchaburi province, Thailand.

THIS GLOSSARY is meant to help readers understand the background and literary contexts of terms that are translated herein or that I use in the translator's commentary. For the most part, I limit myself to English-language sources; to draw up glossaries that take into account the array of archaic translation terminologies and informed translations into all available languages would be fascinating and deeply informative but well beyond the scope of this glossary.

The word *glossary* has been around since the mid-sixteenth century. It came through the Middle English noun *gloze*, from Old French *gloser*, from *glose* "a gloss, a comment." This is based on medieval Latin *glossa*, "explanation of a difficult word," from Greek *glōssa*, "word needing explanation, language, tongue." A word of unknown origin that appeared around the same time is *gloss*, "shine" or "luster." *Vocabulary*, a list of words with definitions or translations, from medieval Latin *vocabularius*, from Latin *vocabulum*, belongs to the same period. The glossary that follows attempts to shine some gloss on the vocabulary of the translations.

For further details, readers should consult specialist dictionaries like the *Pali Text Society's Dictionary*, the *Buddhist Hybrid Sanskrit Dictionary*, *A Dictionary of Pāli*, and the *Dictionary of Pāli Proper Names*. For terminology including proper names, the *Princeton Dictionary of Buddhism* is a storehouse of information. The footnotes in the prodigious works of Étienne Lamotte, especially the five monumental volumes of the *Dazhidu lun*, *Le Traité de la Grande Vertu de Sagesse de Nāgārjuna*, are like encyclopedia entries. These are in French, but Lamotte's superbly annotated *Vimalakīrtinirdeśa* and *Śūraṃgamasamādhi* have been published in sympathetic and reliable English translations by Sara Boin-Webb. The indexes in Léon Feer's *Avadāna-Çataka* double as glossaries. See also the glossaries in Edward Conze's *Perfection of Wisdom*; Andy Rotman's *Divine Stories* and *Hungry Ghosts*; Naomi Appleton's *Many Buddhas, One Buddha*; Patrick Carré's *Soûtra de l'entrée dans la dimension absolue*; Luis Gómez's *The Land of Bliss*, and Luis Gómez and Paul Harrison's *Vimalakīrtinirdeśa*, as also the annotations to Karl Brunnhölzl's translations, especially that of the *Ornament of*

Clear Realization (*Abhisamayālaṅkāra*, translated in two volumes as *Gone Beyond*).

It is important to bear in mind that the Pāli lexicons follow Theravaṃsa traditions and are drawn from the Pāli Tipiṭaka and commentaries. The definitions and narratives are not necessarily the same as those of other scholastic traditions. Unfortunately there is no glossary of Buddhist proper names that draws on all traditions.

Dictionaries are wonderful things, the fine products of humankind's ingenuity. Rather than make superficial comments of my own, allow me to cite the comments of earlier and wiser writers. Master of lexicography Eric Partridge noted that "near the end of a not too dull life, Albert Jay Nock proclaimed: 'As sheer casual reading-matter, I still find the English dictionary the most interesting book in our language' and that's as it should be, for what is more fundamental than, what is so indispensable as, a dictionary?"[569] He stated, "For most of us, a dictionary is hardly a book to read; a good dictionary, however, is a book to browse in. Some dictionaries are so well-written that one just goes on and on."[570] Like any other source, dictionaries must be used critically; Partridge notes the "invaluable lexicographical principle: the pundits are not necessarily right even when they're utterly self-confident."[571] In this vein, we must keep in mind that many glossaries and dictionaries on the web are unreliable. They should be used with caution (*apramādena*), if at all. The same holds for what follows here.

569. Nock, *Memoirs of a Superfluous Man*, p. 15, cited in Partridge, *The Gentle Art of Lexicography*, p. 14.
570. Partridge, *The Gentle Art*, p. 14.
571. Partridge, *The Gentle Art*, p. 16.

Figure 53. Head of a Buddha image. See page 360 for caption.

Figure 53. Head of a Buddha image, sandstone, from Sultanganj. The head is severed at the neck; it alone measures 22 cm in height, 14.5 cm in width, and 15 cm in depth, and the original statue would have been larger than life size. The hair, which covers a prominent *uṣṇīṣa*, is in close curls that spiral clockwise, and on the forehead is an *ūrṇā*, or circle of hair. These are all conventional features of a Buddha, here masterfully rendered. An examination of the back reveals that the head once had a nimbus and most probably belonged to a standing Buddha figure. But "nothing beside remains"—no bits or pieces of nimbus or body are known to survive. The head is kept in the South and South East Asia Collection of the Victoria and Albert Museum (accession number IS.171-1949), which assigns the statue to the seventh to eighth century.

The museum's website reports that the Victoria and Albert purchased the head from Ralph Fastnedge, curator of the Holburne of Menstrie Museum in Bath, in 1949 for £40. When the museum acquired it, there was a small paper label stuck on the back of the head, which bore the following history in faded ink: "Found embedded in red clay and dug out during excavations for Sultangange Railway, Bengal, 1862."

The Holburne Museum was established in 1882 and opened in 1893. This raises interesting questions: how did the head get from Sultanganj to England, how and when did it get to the museum in Bath, and how or why was it sold to the Victoria and Albert?

Glossary

THIS GLOSSARY is made up of clusters of related terms, along the lines of the *Mahāvyutpatti* or other thesauri. If the words were lined up in straight alphabetical order, the glossary would lose a lot of its value. The keywords include both Sanskrit and English terms. To locate specific words, consult the index, where page references to glossary entries are given in boldface type.

Numerical Groups

The Buddha taught by organizing his ideas into thematic and numerical groupings. These were adopted and expanded by his followers to become core elements of the scriptures. Useful compendia of numerical lists are given in Dudjom Rinpoche, *The Nyingma School of Tibetan Buddhism*, "Glossary of Enumerations," vol. 2, pp. 103–87, and Buswell and Lopez, *The Princeton Dictionary of Buddhism*, "List of Lists," pp. 1065–1102.

Three Precious Jewels. Tib. *dkon mchog gsum*, Skt. *triratna*. The Buddha, the Dharma, and the Saṅgha are Buddhism's three "gems" or "jewels" (*ratna*) beyond price. Gómez and Harrison, *Vimalakīrtinirdeśa*, pp. 167–68, translate the term as "Three Treasures." I structure the glossary around the Three Jewels. The *Uttaratantra* gives six reasons why they are jewels:[572]

> They are jewels because their appearance is difficult to encounter,
> because they are stainless, because they possess power,

572. Translation in Brunnhölzl, *When the Clouds Part*, ad 1.22. I have added line breaks and numbers in square brackets.

because they are the ornaments of the world,
because they are supreme, and because they are changeless.

In brief, these three that are called "Buddha," "dharma," and "saṃgha" are said to be "jewels" by virtue of their resemblance to a jewel in six ways. That is:

[1] [They are jewels] by virtue of resembling [jewels] in that their appearance is difficult to encounter because those who have not acquired roots of virtue do not get a chance to meet them even during many eons.

[2] [They are also jewels] by virtue of resembling [jewels] in that they are stainless because they are free from all kinds of stains.

[3] [They are furthermore jewels] by virtue of resembling [jewels] in their power because they are endowed with qualities of inconceivable power, such as the six supernatural knowledges.

[4] [They are likewise jewels] by virtue of resembling [jewels] in that they are the ornaments of the world because they are the causes of the splendid intentions of the entire world.

[5] [They are also jewels] by virtue of resembling [jewels] in that they are supreme [compared to] artificial jewels because they are supramundane.

[6] [Finally, they are jewels] by virtue of resembling [jewels] in that they are changeless through praise, blame, and so on, because their nature is unconditioned.

Buddha

Buddha, "Awakened One," is just one of the many epithets used for the Great Sage of the Śākya clan. The sūtra literature, particularly the verses, uses a cornucopia of epithets to celebrate the wisdom, power, and glory of the Omniscient One.[573] Indian lexicons like Amarasiṅha's Sanskrit *Amarakośa* (date uncertain) open with the Buddha's epithets, as does the Pāli *Abhidhānappadīpikā* (perhaps twelfth century CE). The *Mahāvyutpatti*, the bilingual Sanskrit-Tibetan lexicon prepared under imperial patronage as a manual for the grand translation progams of the Dharma kings in eighth- to ninth-century Tibet, opens with a section on names of the Tathāgata with eighty entries.[574] The derivations of fourteen of them are explained in the *Com-*

573. For epithets of "authority and authorization" in Aśvaghoṣa, see Eltschinger, "Aśvaghoṣa and His Canonical Sources," pp. 129–36.
574. Ishihama and Fukuda, *Mahāvyutpatti*, pp. 1–4.

panion to the Mahāvyutpatti.[575] I find it unfortunate that modern translators tend to collapse the rich panoply of epithets (*nāmavyūha*) to the single word "Buddha." This oversimplifies the ancient community's metaphysical, devotional, and mystical images of Gautama: it flattens the poetic depth and obscures the literary vision of the early poets and compilers by reducing the Śākyan sage to a bloodless one-dimensional figure.

In the following, I divide the epithets into "common" or "primary" epithets, found regularly throughout a wide spectrum of texts, and "supplemental" epithets, used more in eulogistic passages. This division is thoroughly arbitrary; the supplemental epithets are regularly used in verse texts, whether for poetic effect or whether to exploit the potential of different metrical forms.

The use of epithets is a feature of oral literature and poetry. The word *epithet* is derived from Greek *epitheton*, and for the Greeks and Romans it means simply "adjective": a word that is placed (*-ject*, *-thet*) next to another word (*ad-*, *epi-*). In the exalted English tongue, *epithet* is more than just a common or garden-variety adjective: it is a word or phrase that has a special or particular association with the noun it modifies.[576]

Common or primary epithets

Strange to say, we do not know the name of the man we call "the Buddha." Modern writers call him Gotama Siddhattha (Pāli) or Gautama Siddhārtha (Sanskrit), as if ancient South Asians had first and last, or given and family, names. They did not. Name depended on context. The "name giving" ceremony is an important event in legendary lives recounted in narrative literature like the avadānas, in which the family bestows an appropriate, and usually auspicious, name upon the child. The protocols of registration of births and deaths with religious or civic authorities were two thousand years in the future. Gautama never had an ID card or passport.

Buddha. Tib. *sang rgyas*. An awakened one, who has woken up from the slumber of ignorance. One who has blossomed, who has opened up like the petals of a lotus flower. Also and often "Enlightened One." See above, pp. 85–88 and *Gone Beyond*, vol. 1, p. 209 and p. 724, n. 516.

575. That is, the *Sgra sbyor bam po gnyis pa* or *Madhyavyutpatti* (Ishikawa, pp. 5–13).
576. George, *How Dead Languages Work*, p. 36.

Saṃbuddha. Tib. *rdzogs sang rgyas*. A fully, completely, thoroughly (*saṃ*, *rdzogs*) awakened one. Also and often "Fully Enlightened One."

Gautama. Tib. *gau ta ma*, Pāli Gotama. The name used for the Buddha by outsiders in the early literature is Śramaṇa Gautama (Pāli: Samaṇa Gotama). Gautama/Gotama is interpreted as his clan name (*gotra*) in exegetical literature. *See also* box 13 for terms of address.

Siddhārtha. Tib. *don grub*, Pāli Siddhattha.[577] Meaning "aims accomplished"; also "Sarvārthasiddha," *don thams cad grub pa*, "all aims accomplished," "all goals fulfilled."[578] Edgerton points out that the latter is commonly used in *Lalitavistara* and *Mahāvastu*, and it is used in the *Saṅghabhedavastu* as well. Modern writers often treat one or the other of these (usually the first) as the Buddha's personal name.

Śākyamuni. Tib. Sha kya thub pa, Pāli Sakyamuni. Śākyan Sage, Sage of the Śākyas. The Buddha was widely known as the "Sage of the Śākya Clan," an epithet attested in the mid-third century BCE inscriptions of the emperor Aśoka. Often used in narratives for the Buddha as a literary figure.

Gautama the Buddha. I use this name in lieu of the modernist term "historical Buddha."

historical Buddha. Gautama the Buddha, Śākyamuni, as conceived or imagined by modern writers from the nineteenth century to today. This "historical Buddha," also called the "mortal" or "human" Buddha, is more properly described as the "**historicist Buddha**": he is a rhetorical figure, a figment, the product of currents of historicist thought that privilege "the historical Buddha" over the "mythical" or "integral" Buddha of the fertile traditional and living imaginaries.[579] It is, however, the **integral Buddha**, the undifferentiated historical-mythical Buddha wreathed in rhapsody, whose activities and teachings have played a transformative role in the history of Asia and the world for 2,500 years.[580] A standard modernist narrative maintains that the

577. See BHSD, p. 596.
578. See BHSD, p. 580.
579. Von Hinüber, "The Buddha as a Historical Person," is a masterful survey of the evidence and some of the debates.
580. See Skilling, "La vie du Bouddha: Traditions et Histoire."

Theravādins or "Hīnayānists" were content with the human "historical Buddha" while Mahāyānists proceeded merrily to "deify" the hapless "genuine Buddha." Contrary to this rhetoric of deification, the evidence of the texts shows that the Theravāda and the known Buddhist schools of thought all shared in the production of rich corpora of legends and myths about Śākyamuni and his wondrous displays of wisdom and power, and it was these that animated the Buddhism that spread across Asia and inspired the masterpieces of Buddhist art that are internationally admired today. Mahāyānists had no monopoly in this; they joined in with the common trend and, as often as not, followed it to its logical conclusions, informed by rhetorics of insubstantiality and emptiness. Texts of all the schools share in the imagination of an integral Buddha, who is neither *this* nor *that* but a complex composite personality who participates in the human and the mythical spheres without conflict or contradiction. These buddhas are all *nirmāṇas*, phantoms of competing imaginaires, from the devoted and credulous to the historicist and skeptical.

Fortunate One. Tib. *bcom ldan 'das*, Skt. *bhagavat*. "Exalted One," per Gómez and Harrison, *Vimalakīrtinirdeśa*, p. 157 and p. 171, n. 1. *Bhagavat* is the most commonly used term for the Buddha in the Āgama/Nikāya literature. In translations from Chinese, *bhagavat* is usually rendered as "World-Honored One," a term with a long history.[581]

Bhagavat is a term of respect widely used in Indian religions, including Jainism and Hinduism, also translated as "Lord": Lord Mahāvīra, Lord Śiva, Lord Krishna, and so on. Readers of Indian religious literature will know the word from the titles of the celebrated and enormously influential Vaiṣṇava works *Bhagavad Gītā*, "Song of the Lord"—Sir Edwin Arnold's "Song Celestial"—and *Bhāgavata Purāṇa*, "Ancient Stories about the Lord." Indian exegetical texts, mainly Buddhist but non-Buddhist as well, regularly cite a stanza that assigns six meanings to *bhagavat*. When *bhagavat* refers to Gautama the Buddha, it has been translated as Lord or Blessed One from the hoary past up to today. "Lord" has its own simple dignity and matches up with *aiśvarya*, one of the six meanings. Another of the six is *bhāgya-vat*, one who possesses good fortune (*bhāgya*). I choose to follow this meaning rather

581. For this and the other epithets in Chinese, see Nattier, "The Ten Epithets of the Buddha in the Translations of Zhi Qian 支謙." For *bhagavat*, see Skilling, *Questioning the Buddha*, p. 150 and n. 315.

than the standard Tibetan translation, *bcom ldan 'das*, which was coined during the reign of the Dharma kings and recorded in the *Companion to the Mahāvyutpatti* and is interpreted as "one who has overcome [enemies] and transcended [the world] / gone beyond [to nirvāṇa]."

Jina. Tib. *rgyal ba*. Conqueror, victor; "victorious one," Gómez and Harrison, *Vimalakīrtinirdeśa*, pp. 169–70. An old epithet for a śramaṇa, an ascetic, who has successfully conquered the forces of evil and all negativities (see translation 16, v. 11). The Jain *tīrthaṅkaras* are also called Jinas, and the name Jain (*jaina*) derives from *jina*.

After his awakening, the Buddha set out on foot for Vārāṇasī. On the way he met a passerby (*upaga*, *upaka*, or, as a proper name, Upaga) who asked him why his demeanor was so bright and pure, saying, "Are you, Long-Lived Gautama, a conqueror?" To this the newly awakened one replied,

> Those like me who attain
> the destruction of the corruptions
> are to be known as jinas, conquerors:
> I have vanquished (*jitā*) evil conditions.
> Therefore, Upaga, I am a conqueror.[582]

Sugata. Tib. *bde bar gshegs pa*. Well-Gone One, one who has realized happiness. "Well-gone . . . epithet of the Buddha who has gone on the right path and to the right place": Conze, *Perfection of Wisdom*, p. 325. "Happy One": Gethin, *Sayings of the Buddha*, p. xlvi; "a fortunate one," Bodhi, *Reading the Buddha's Discourses*, p. 528; "Sublime One," Gómez and Harrison, *Vimalakīrtinirdeśa*, p. 167.

Tathāgata. Tib. *de bzhin gshegs pa*. Bhikkhu Bodhi regards the suttas in which the Buddha speaks of himself as the Tathāgata as "sufficiently impressive to warrant being assigned to a class of their own." He sees the Buddha as "referring to himself not simply as a unique individual but as the latest representative of the 'dynasty' of Buddhas, those extraordinary beings who appear at rare intervals in the cosmic process to rediscover the lost path to nibbāna and teach it to the world."[583] Perhaps we can say that Tathāgata belongs to the

582. Gnoli, *Saṅghabhedavastu*, vol. 1, p. 132.17.
583. Bodhi, *Numerical Discourses*, p. 27. Translation 11 in this anthology belongs very much in

philosophical register of epithets. Gómez and Harrison, *Vimalakīrtinirdeśa*, p. 164, translate it as "Realized One." See also box 13, "Terms of address"; Gethin, *Sayings of the Buddha*, p. xlvi; Skilling, *Questioning the Buddha*, pp. 149–50.

Ten-Powered One. Skt. Daśabala, Tib. *stobs bcu ldan pa*, Pāli Dasabala. Buddhas possess the ten powers of a tathāgata (*tathāgatabala*). These are described in the Sarvāstivāda *Daśabalasūtra*, which, from the number of manuscript fragments retrieved along the northern Silk Road, must have been liturgically and ritually popular in Central Asian Buddhist communities. See Lamotte, *Le Traité*, vol. 3, "Les dix forces du Buddha selon l'Abhidharma," pp. 1505–66.

Buddha Sikhī. Skt. Śikhī, Tib. *gtsug tor can*. A past Buddha. In the *Buddhavaṃsa* system transmitted in the Theravāda canon, Sikhī (the Pāli form) is twentieth in the line of twenty-four past Buddhas.

Poetic or supplemental epithets

Muni. Tib. *thub pa*. Sage, silent one: an ideal figure in ascetic literature.

Devātideva. Tib. *lha'i yang lha*. God beyond gods. The Buddha surpasses and transcends the worldly gods in wisdom and glory. Gods they may be, but they still have desire, aversion, and delusion, which the Buddha has eliminated (see, with regard to Śakra, translations 13 and 14). Worldly gods still circle on the wheel of life.

Devaguru. Tib. *lha'i bla ma*. Teacher of the gods. The Buddha is the teacher not only of humans but also of the gods (*śāstā devamanuṣyānāṃ*), hence he is "teacher of the gods." The gods flock to pay homage to the Buddha and listen to his sermons.

Mahādeva. Tib. *lha chen po*. Great god. As a metaphorical and metaphysical divinity, the Buddha is the "great god," signifying that he is superior to all other gods.

---

this class as does the *Bhikṣusūtra* of the *Nidānasaṃyukta*: see Skilling, "Who Invented Dependent Arising?" for further references.

Mahāvīra. Tib. *dpa' bo chen po*. Great hero: a title that reflects the heroic ideals of the warrior culture to which Gautama belonged. In Jainism, Mahāvīra is a primary epithet for the Tīrthaṅkara known in Buddhist texts as Nirgrantha Nāṭaputra, one of the "six teachers."

Nāyaka. Tib. *'dren pa*. Leader. Also *pariṇāyaka*. The Buddha guides, leads, and directs errant beings to happiness and nirvāṇa.

Śāstṛ. Tib. *ston pa*, Pāli *satthā*. Teacher. In Buddhist texts this almost exclusively refers to *a* or *the* Buddha. However, it can also refer to the paradigmatic "six teachers," *ṣaṭśāstaraḥ*, who were prominent religious and metaphysical masters in Magadha when Gautama began his teaching career.[584] As a group, the six teachers function as narrative paradigms of wrong teachings and methodologies.

Tāyin. (Alt. *trāyin*), Tib. *skyob pa*. One who is like that, one who is thus: a sage or liberated being. Also occurs as *trāyin*, "protector," hence *skyob pa* in Tibetan. The word has a long and tangled history as a Prakrit form reinscribed as Sanskrit; in manuscripts *tāyin* and *trāyin* are regularly used interchangeably. Amongst the versions of the *Visit to Vaiśālī* (translation 15), the Sanskrit *Mahāmantrānusāriṇī* has *tāyin* (C.3.4b, 6.4b), but I would be surprised if all manuscripts of this text maintain the same form, *tāyin*. The two Tibetan versions have *skyob pa*, which translates *trāyin* (A.3.4a, 6.4a; B.3.4a,6.4a). For this word, see the long entry in BHSD, pp. 251–52; de Jong, "Notes on the *Bhikṣuṇī-vinaya*," pp. 69–70, n. 8; and Pecchia and Pierce, *Dharmakīrti on the Cessation of Suffering*, p. 57. See Pāli *tādi(n)* in DoP, vol. 2, p. 302.

Protector. Skt. and Pāli *nātha*. See translation 18. Also translated as "savior."

King of the Dharma. Pāli *dhammarāja*. See translation 18. Regular epithet that reflects on the Buddha's mastery and command of the teaching of the Dharma.

All-Seeing One. Pāli *sabbadassī*. See translation 18.

584. Skilling, "Seeing the Preacher as the Teacher: A Note on *Śāstrasaṃjñā*."

Box 13. *Terms of address*

Literature maps out social distinctions and hierarchies of the time of the Buddha and of the later redactors. This is effected through the careful deployment of terms of address, which mark speakers' identities in both oral and written texts.

The Buddha refers to himself with the first-person singular pronoun *ahaṃ*. In certain contexts he uses the third person singular with Tathāgata; he also makes general statements about the qualities or nature of buddhas, using "tathāgatas" in the third person plural. In some cases, first-person or Tathāgata statements in one school's recension are given as third person singular with Bhagavat in the recensions of other schools. Usage differs in the different redactions, and there is no trans-nikāya uniformity or consistency in usage. One must be wary of drawing broad conclusions from examples that may apply to one nikāya's usage or even one manuscript's habits only.

Aśoka's Lumbinī inscription, for example, records that "Here the Buddha, Śākyamuni, was born," while the Pāli *Great Parinibbāna Sutta* has "Here the Tathāgata was born," and Sanskrit manuscripts associated with the Sarvāstivāda have "Here the Bhagavat was born."[585]

The epithets would have been chosen by different teams of reciters or redactors in different circumstances and progressively edited according to the guidelines of emerging orders with their eyes on desired meaning and perceived impact. Buddha, the most common appellation used in Anglophone and European writing, is used as a nominal agent in narrative writing only infrequently (there are exceptions, as in translation 15 in this collection).[586] The reciters and narrators preferred to use Bhagavat, the common term of respect and reverence in early Indian society.

Social reference and address are complex and relational; whether actual and "live" or reported and narrative, human speech is hierarchical and context bound. Gautama addresses others according to social

585. Skilling, *Questioning the Buddha*, pp. 78–79; von Hinüber, "Buddha as a Historical Person," p. 236.

586. There are always exceptions: the idea of the *exception* is, perhaps, the *product of expectations of uniformity* generated by monolithic paradigms and accentuated by print and even more so pervasive electronic technologies with their inflexible imperatives (*Diktat*) of standardization.

circumstances. When he speaks to a general or predominantly monastic audience, he addresses his listeners as "monks" (Skt. *bhikṣavo*, Pāli *bhikkhave*, Tib. *dge slong dag*). Here the term includes nuns, novices, and everyone else in the assembly. The male gender is used as gender inclusive, rather as in English when (formerly) a male speaker might address a mixed audience of all ages and genders as "fellow countrymen," or when contemporary speakers or texters open communications with "Hey guys," regardless of gender or age groups.

The Buddha addresses individual monks by their names: Ānanda, Śāriputra, and so on. He addresses wanderers and ascetics by their clan names, such as Kāśyapa, Kātyāyana, and so on. He addresses kings as Mahārāja (*rgyal po chen po*), "Great King," brahmans as "Brahman" (*bram ze*), landowners as "Lord of the Household" (*khyim bdag, gṛhapati*), and merchants as "Merchant" (*tshong pa, vaṇij*). I do not mean that Gautama himself *chose* these modes of address; rather, he would have followed contemporary local customs, and this is what the reciters/redactors attempted to record. Customary terms of address were editorially orchestrated to depict the social circumstances of Gautama's encounters and debates.

In the *Mahāparinibbānasutta*, the Buddha tells Ānanda that the monks should address each other according to seniority:[587] "Whereas the monks are in the habit of addressing one another as 'friend,' this custom is to be abrogated after my passing. Senior monks shall address more junior monks by their name, their clan or as 'friend' [*āvuso*], whereas more junior monks are to address their seniors either as 'Lord' [*bhante*] or as 'Venerable Sir' [*āyasmā*]" (for the latter see below, "Long-Lived").

Vocabularies of address are fluid and relational. Outsiders address the Buddha as Śramaṇa Gautama (Pāli: Samaṇa Gotama). His own followers call him Bhagavat or Bhadanta. Some discourses mark an individual's passage from a nonbeliever or even an aggressive opponent to believer by changes in his choice of epithets. An individual might start

587. *Dīghanikāya*, vol. 2, p. 154.9–15, trans. after Walshe, *Long Discourses*, p. 250, with Pāli added in brackets. See DoP vol. 1, pp. 321, s.v. *āyasmā*, and 349, s.v. *āvuso*. See Childers, *Dictionary*, p. 74, s.v. *āvuso*; Bodhi, *Reading the Buddha's Discourses*, p. 182 (trans. "venerable").

out by addressing the Buddha as Śramaṇa Gautama, but his choice of terms changes as his attitude changes, and he begins to address the Buddha as Bhagavat or Bhadanta.

Gethin notes that in the *Bodhirājakumārasutta* (*Majjhimanikāya* no. 85) Prince Bodhi refers to the Buddha as "the Blessed One" (*bhagavat*) when he speaks to the brahman Sañjikāputta, "but when he talks to the Buddha, Sañjikāputta addresses him in characteristic brahman fashion as 'Gotama sir' (*bho Gotama*), indicating that he does not acknowledge the Buddha as his superior."[588]

Long-Lived (One). Tib. *tshe dang ldan pa*, Skt. *āyuṣmat*, Pāli *āyasmā*. The Indian forms and the Tibetan translation mean "possessing age," that is, "longevous" (from Latin *longaevus*), hence, "long-lived." Customarily translated "venerable." Venerable means worthy of veneration or respect, "especially because of age, wisdom, or character: a venerable statesman." As an epithet or title in Western contexts, it can mean (in the Anglican Church) a title given to an archdeacon or (in the Roman Catholic Church) a title given to a deceased person who has attained a certain degree of sanctity but has not been fully beatified or canonized.[589]

Āyuṣmat is sometimes translated as "reverend," from nineteenth-century Christian usage. Most of the early Western translators and scholars of Buddhism had solid Christian backgrounds; some were Christian clergymen whose own names were prefixed with such titles—for example, the Wesleyan Rev. D. J. Gogerly (1792–1862) or the Methodist Rev. Spence Hardy (1803–68), both British missionaries

588. Gethin, *Sayings*, note, p. 287, to translation p. 174.

589. Pearsall, *The New Oxford Dictionary of English*, p. 2051a. The entries and quotations in Simpson and Weiner, *The Oxford English Dictionary*, vol. 19, pp. 498c–499a, show the complex history of the word, which entered English in the first half of the fifteenth century. By at least the mid-eighteenth century, "venerable" was also used as a noun. See also Wyld, *Universal Dictionary*, p. 1351. Today "venerable" (abbr. "Ven.") is widely used by Buddhist monastics of all schools, both as adjective and noun ("She invited three Sri Lankan venerables to *dāna*"). For "longevous," see idem., vol. 8, p. 1133b (and also longeval, longaeval, longeve, longavie, p. 1133a). Often used for plants and animals, "the longevous elephant," 1699. When translating ancient Indic texts, "long-lived" seems to me preferable, though "longevous" does fit nicely.

to Ceylon. Despite the antiquity and patent inappropriateness of these usages, they still have a certain authority and a nice ring—for example:[590]

> Then, the Buddha said to **the venerable** Śāriputra, "Śāriputra, do you see this splendor of the virtues of the buddhafield?"
>
> Śāriputra replied, "I see it, **Lord**! Here before me is a display of splendor such as I never before heard of or beheld!

Sirs, dear sirs. Tib. *grogs po*, Skt. *māriṣa*, Pāli *mārisa*. Friends or sirs: term of address used in a variety of contexts. Śakra uses this term, translated here as "dear sirs," when he addresses the gods of the Realm of the Thirty-Three (translations 12–14).

Buddha image. Tib. *sangs rgyas kyi sku gzugs*, Skt., Pāli *buddharūpa*, *buddhapratimā* (Pāli: °*patimā*). Image, statue, idol: an idealized figure of Śākyamuni or another Buddha.

Dharma

Buddhist heritage is in fragments, crushed, squashed, and mangled by time's relentless engines. We regret and we rue the incalculable loss of canons and even languages over the millennia. But all is not lost, and we can rejoice in what we have: we rejoice in the Piṭakas, the 84,000 clusters of Dharma that are preserved in the Pāli, Tibetan, Mongolian, and Chinese canons. We rejoice in the steady immigration of the 84,000 bundles of Dharma to new language environments and to the nascent English-language canons. We express our utmost respect and gratitude to those who cherish and conserve the Buddha's legacy by preserving manuscripts and by studying, translating, and publishing the texts.

Describing Buddhist literature is not easy. Broadly speaking, it is the

590. Thurman, *Holy Teaching of Vimalakīrti* (1976), p. 19.

product of many schools of thought and individual or independent thinkers, in nearly every conceivable genre over spans of centuries and millennia. Texts fundamental to one school can be unknown to other schools. For example, while today many consider Buddhaghosa's fifth-sixth century *Visuddhimagga* to be a fundamental manual of the Theravāda, the text and even the title appear to have been unknown to Indian Buddhists. That is, its circulation was limited to Sri Lankan Theravāda circles. Tibetans translated a large corpus of middle-period Abhidharma texts, but none of them mention either Buddhaghosa or his opus—the first time they are mentioned in Tibetan is by the savant Gedun Chophel, who traveled to Ceylon in the 1930s. Within Theravāda itself, Steven Collins points out that on the level of popular practice, ritual, and art, the *Vessantara-jātaka* is much more popular than the *Visuddhimagga*. Modern research has been partisan, largely partial to historicist conceptualizations of the Theravāda. Further, it has tended to ignore the great Yogācāra classics, such as that stupendous encyclopedia the *Yogācārabhūmi*, which remains to be translated.

Texts, categories, and genres

Dharma. Tib. *chos*, Pāli *dhamma*. The term *dharma* has many meanings, not only in Buddhism but also in Jainism, Hinduism, the Epics, and contemporary Indian languages (Hindi *dharm*). Whole books are written about this word and idea. As one of the Three Precious Jewels, it means teaching, truth, ideal.

Saddharma. Tib. *dam pa'i chos*, Pāli *saddhamma*. The true or good Dharma, the teaching of a Buddha.

Buddhadharma. Tib. *sangs rgyas kyi chos*, Pāli *buddhadhamma*. The teaching(s) of a Buddha, most frequently of Gautama. The compound may also mean the qualities or characteristics of awakened ones in general.

ninefold teaching of the Buddha. An early term for a Buddha's teachings as constituted by nine genres. See Lamotte, *Histoire*, pp. 157–59; Buswell and Lopez, *Princeton Dictionary*, p. 578, s.v. *navaṅga*[*pāvacana*].

twelvefold teaching of the Buddha. An alternate early classification of a Buddha's teachings as constituted by twelve genres. See Lamotte,

Histoire, pp. 159–61; Buswell and Lopez, *Princeton Dictionary*, p. 276, s.v. *dvādaśāṅga[pravacana]*. See also Lamotte, *Histoire*, pp. 161–62, "Relations entre les Aṅga et le Tripiṭaka"; Buswell and Lopez, *Princeton Dictionary*, p. 44, s.v. *aṅga*.

dharmaparyāya. Tib. *chos kyi rnam grangs*, Pāli *dhammapariyāya*. "Paryāya of the Dharma," a difficult term to translate.[591] Gómez and Harrison's "formulation of the Dharma" (*Vimalakīrtinirdeśa*, p. 158) comes closest to the mark; "configuration of the Dharma" and "presentation of the Dharma" are also suitable. "Figuration of the Dharma," slightly archaic, is nice. Harrison has also rendered the term as "round of teachings." *Dharmaparyāya* seems to mean a self-contained sermon of the Buddha or others that is described internally, in the very text itself, by the Buddha or others as a dharmaparyāya or paryāya. At the end of the *Saṅgītisutta*, the Buddha calls the teaching given by Sāriputta to the monks "Saṅgītipariyāya": "Excellent, excellent, Sāriputta. That you have taught the Saṅgītipariyāya to the monks is excellent."[592] What may be called an autonomous discourse, the *Dhamma-ādāsadhammapariyāya*, is incorporated as a distinct unit in the lengthy Pāli *Mahāparinibbānasutta* as well as in several short suttas.[593] A short sutta in the Pāli *Saṃyuttanikāya* reports that the Fortunate One saw a monk standing and listening to him, and said to him:[594]

> "Did you, monk, hear this dhammapariyāya?"
>
> "Yes, sir, I did."
>
> "Learn, monk, this dhammapariyāya, master this dhammapariyāya, memorize this dhammapariyāya. This dhammapariyāya is full of meaning, it is the basics of the holy life."

What is the difference between a dharmaparyāya and a sūtra? The word *sūtra/sutta* was also current; it stands at the head of the lists of nine or twelve *aṅga*. In manuscripts, *sūtra* is often used in the closing statement that ends the document: "such and such sūtra is finished," but surely such statements

591. See Skilling, *Questioning the Buddha*, pp. 37–38.
592. *Dīghanikāya*, vol. 3, p. 271.17.
593. See Allon and Silverlock, "Sūtras in the Senior Kharoṣṭhī Manuscript Collection," pp. 35–38.
594. *Gahapativagga* 5, *Nidānasaṃyutta*, *Saṃyuttanikāya*: PTS, vol. 2, pp. 74–75; Syāmaraṭṭha, vol. 16, pp. 89–90; translation after Bodhi, *Connected Discourses*, pp. 582–83.

are artifacts of post-oral manuscript culture. That is, they are written editorial or scribal customs and are not an internal or integral part of the discourse. *Sūtra* is rarely used as an internal title,[595] and context suggests that the term *sūtra* refers to the complete package, with the introduction and closing (*nidāna*, *nigamana*) as well as internal narratives, while the dharmaparyāya is the discourse properly speaking, the meat of the matter. But sometimes the term *dharmaparyāya* is used for the entire text, and it is also used for long and expanded Vaitulya/Mahāyāna compilations. Language does not stand still, and the scope and meaning of the two terms changed and expanded with place, time, and circumstance. This is a subject that calls for sustained research in the available canons.

sūtra. Tib. *mdo*, Pāli *sutta*. Generally translated "discourse." I am not certain when this translation became current, but it is already used by Robert Cæsar Childers (1838–76) in his *Dictionary of the Pāli Language*, published in 1875. The words "sermon" and "exposition" were also used. Traditionally, *sutta/sūtra* has been derived from "string" or "thread," but some prefer to see its origin in *sūkta*, "well-spoken," which in Middle Indic languages like Pāli becomes *sutta*. The differentiation is only in Sanskrit: the two Sanskrit terms *sūtra* and *sūkta* both become *sutta* in Pāli and Prakrit, with the result that the absolute derivation (if such a creature exists) is not clear. Childers' comprehensive definition of *sutta* is quite worth reading.[596] In current English usage, a *discourse* is a "written or spoken communication or debate," as a count noun, "a formal discussion of a topic in speech or writing."[597] The term is used to excess in postmodern, well . . . discourse.

Śrāvaka sūtras. This may indicate (1) sūtras handed down by the śrāvakas, who heard them directly from the Buddha, or (2) sūtras recited and transmitted by one or the other of the Śrāvaka schools, for the most part believed to have been recited at the first recitation. The use of this phrase as a category is limited to non-Śrāvaka schools and the Vaipulya/Mahāyāna, since the Śrāvaka schools themselves do not recognize any sūtras outside of their own collections, including even those of other Śrāvaka schools. The Vaitulya and

595. An interesting exception is *some* (later?) versions of the *Bhadrakarātrīsūtra* in which the title *Bhadrarātrīsūtra* is used in conversations within the text itself. See Holz, *Bhadrakarātrīsūtra*, Sanskrit p. 104.1–2; Tibetan translation pp. 101.2, 23–24.
596. Childers, *Dictionary of the Pāli Language*, p. 491b.
597. Pearsall, *New Oxford Dictionary of English*, p. 527a.

Mahāyāna view the scriptures in a broader and less exclusive frame in which there is space for variety and diversity.

Vaitulya, Vaidalya, Vaipulya. Pāli Vetulla, Vedalla, Vepulla. These terms were used for a class or genre of texts, a constituent of the ninefold or twelvefold teaching of the Buddha. The ninefold or twelvefold teachings were *shared*; that is, they were (and are) accepted by all Buddhist schools including Mahāyāna sūtras and śāstras. Nonetheless, the Śrāvaka schools also used the terms to refer to Mahāyānist ideas and texts. The terms are difficult to define because their significations changed with usage and context through the long centuries. It is not easy to choose which of the terms to use in historical writing because the choice of terms shifts with passing scribal and ideological fashion. See Skilling, "Vaidalya, Mahāyāna, and bodhisatva in India," and Skilling, *Questioning the Buddha*, chap. 3.

vaitulya. Pāli *vetulla*. "Unparalleled": *vai-tulya*, without equal or counterpart.

vaidalya. Pāli *vedalla*. Ven. Dhammajoti, "unequalled." *Sarvāstivāda Abhidharma*, p. 3, defines the Pāli counterpart *vedalla* as follows: "*vedalla* . . . the extensive unraveling of the profound doctrinal meanings that have been hidden. In form, it consists of a question-and-answer session on doctrinal matters with a scope apparently broader than that in *abhidhamma-kathā*—either between the Buddha and the fourfold disciples (with others listening) or amongst the disciples themselves."

Dhammajoti's definition is not intended to refer or relate to Mahāyāna, but it is a fair description of many Vaitulya/Mahāyāna sūtras in which "profound doctrinal meanings that have been hidden" are extensively unraveled through questions and answers "between the Buddha and the fourfold disciples, amongst the disciples themselves," and gods and other beings.

vaipulya. Pāli *vepulla*. Extensive, expanded, expansive; "articulated" for the Japanese equivalent *hōdō* in Michael Pye's translation.[598] Of the three terms, in the end Vaipulya seems to have won out and become the term of choice in most extant manuscripts, while the other two terms fell by the wayside.

598. Nakamura, *Emerging from Meditation*, pp. 74–75 and n. 18.

Vaitulya/Mahāyāna. A makeshift term that brings the two ideas together. I use it to open a space for emerging ideas that were only identified as "Mahāyāna" at later periods as they matured and clusters of practices and ideas were assigned distinct identities. My usage is not entirely a personal invention since the terms do appear together in some of the great Vaipulya/Vaitulya/Mahāyāna sūtras—for example, in the *Mahāparinirvāṇa-mahāsūtra*.

muktaka sūtra. "Independent sūtra," a term used in a few middle-period scholastic texts but not defined in any of the sources I have seen. Evidently it refers to a text in sūtra format that was transmitted independently, outside of the Āgamas (cf. the Pāli term *muttaka*, which seems to be limited to Vinaya literature). But how or by whom a muktaka sūtra would have been transmitted is beyond my ken.

stotra. Tib. *bstod pa*. Verses of praise, either independent and freestanding or embedded within longer compilations or sūtras. For the former, see Hartmann, "Poetry: South Asia," and for the latter, Skilling, "Praising the Buddha: *Stotras* in Mahāyāna Dharmaparyāyas."

Dharma-Vinaya. Tib. *chos 'dul ba*. Teaching (*dharma*) and system of training (*vinaya*), a term used to describe religious systems at the time of the Buddha, used by the Buddha and Buddhist literature for his system.

vyākaraṇa. Pāli *veyyākaraṇa*.[599] Vyākaraṇa refers to an explanation or an exposition, or to predictions and prognostications, forecasts of events to come—especially a Buddha's prediction of an individual's or group's realization of buddhahood in the far-away future, sometimes eons hence.

independent Chinese translation. A modern term used for a translation in the Chinese Buddhist canon that was translated and transmitted independently and is not included in any of the known Chinese Āgamas or collections. The school affiliation of such texts needs to be considered case by case.

uddāna (Sanskrit, Pāli). Tib. *sdom*. Also *uddāna-gāthā*, *sdom gyi tshigs su bcad pa*. Table of contents, often, but not exclusively, in verse, listing the

599. For this multivalent term, see Skilling, *Questioning the Buddha*, pp. 39–40.

keywords for a section of a text. In sūtra literature the *uddānas* usually come at the end of a section (*varga, vagga*),[600] but in general they may also come at the beginning of or within texts. *Uddāna* keywords are often adopted as titles.

Manuscript collections

Manuscripts are invaluable records of the breadth and depth of Buddhist thought and practice, but the Buddhist manuscript heritage is scattered across an archipelago of collections and libraries around the world. These institutes, which are far too many to list here, all contribute to the preservation and study of Buddhist documents. The modern provenance of the collections is chequered and complex, but fortunately their importance to world heritage is increasingly recognized, and scholars from around the world study them in international and multidisciplinary collaborations. Noncompetitive cooperation is the keynote, and chauvinistic or nationalistic politics only obstruct progress and disfigure history. For reliable discussions of manuscript finds, see Harrison and Hartmann, *From Birch Bark to Digital Data*, pp. x–xix, and Salomon, "On the Evolution of Written Āgama Collections."

Some Central Asian manuscript collections are known after the names of individuals associated with their early modern history, such as the leaders of the expeditions that retrieved them: Stein (London), Hoernle (London), Pelliot (Paris), Petrovsky (Saint Petersburg), Otani (Japan), and so on. Others are called by the names of the site at which they were found, such as Dunhuang or Turfan. At times they are described by a combination of the two. The first gives a precision to the manuscript's modern history, the second a long-term geographical precision to their locations. Neither of them, however, necessarily relates to the original *manufacture* of the documents, which in many (if not most) cases is unknown. The manuscripts were found at various long-abandoned sites that stretch across the wide swath of western China, from the Hexi corridor through the Tarim Basin to Khotan and Kashgar and beyond. These large collections of manuscripts are in languages of several families, including the transregional languages Sanskrit, Tibetan, and Chinese along with regional languages like Khotanese, Uighur, Toch-

600. *Uddāna* the table of keywords and *Udāna* the genre or specific textual collection (see below) are different terms and not to be confused.

arian, Sogdian, and Tangut. Many are Buddhist, but there are also Daoist, Zoroastrian, Manichean, Christian, and Jewish documents as well as secular records.

Pāli collections. These are preserved in the temples and libraries of Sri Lanka, Burma, Thailand, Laos, and Cambodia. Most of the collections are not catalogued. Important holdings are maintained in European libraries (Berlin, Copenhagen, London, Paris) and elsewhere.

Turfan. Site of an ancient city and cultural center on the northern Silk Road in today's current Xinjiang province, China. Four German (Prussian) expeditions at the beginning of the twentieth century recovered masses of manuscripts and transported them to Berlin, where they have since been conserved and studied. They became known collectively as "Turfan manuscripts" or "Turfan Collections." The series *Sanskrithandschriften aus den Turfanfunden* [*Sanskrit Manuscripts from the Turfan Finds*], under the massive cataloguing project Verzeichnis der Orientalischen Handschriften in Deutschland [Catalogue of the Oriental Manuscripts in Germany], has published twelve volumes to date.

Gilgit. Gilgit in Kashmir, at the confluence of the Hunza and Gilgit rivers, was for centuries a node on the Silk Road and a flourishing center of Buddhist culture. Its complicated history is bound up with the shifting suzerainties in the region through the millennia, starting with local and regional dynasties until 1877, when the British established it as "Gilgit Agency" under Jammu and Kashmir. In 1931, before the traumatic partition of "British India" into India and Pakistan, a trove of Buddhist manuscripts was discovered in a ruined structure, the identity of which remains disputed (was it a library, a residence, a ritual repository, a stūpa?). The manuscripts contain a wide range of texts, including Vinaya, Sūtra, and Perfection of Wisdom, written in ink on birchbark and dating to the tenth to thirteenth centuries BE (fifth to seventh centuries CE). Most of the manuscripts were removed to Shrinagar, capital of Kashmir, but some were taken elsewhere. Known collectively as the "Gilgit Manuscripts," the Indian collection was inscribed in the UNESCO Memory of the World register in 2017.[601] Since the fateful war between

601. "Documentary Heritage Submitted by India and Recommended for Inclusion in the Memory of the World Register in 2017," unesco.org, accessed 24 March 2021.

Pakistan and India in 1947, the main town of Gilgit has been under Pakistani administration, but today the collection is divided amongst the Department of Archaeology in Pakistan and several institutions in India, such as the Sri Pratap Singh Museum in Srinagar, the National Archives in New Delhi, and the Vikram University in Ujjain (Madhya Pradesh). The first edition of the manuscripts was prepared by Nalinaksha Dutt and published in Shrinagar.[602] Important Vinaya manuscripts in the Pakistani collection were published in Rome under a collaboration between Pakistan and Italy. The large collection preserved in the National Archives in New Delhi is being published by the International Research Institute for Advanced Buddhology in Tokyo, in a new series of digital photographs with introductions by leading authorities in the field. The most recent conspectus of the Gilgit collections is published in the volume *From Birch Bark to Digital Data*.[603]

Nepalese collections. Manuscript collections that were historically copied and preserved in northern India and in Nepal, in the monasteries of the Kathmandu Valley and in the royal libraries. Written on palm leaf or paper, they belong to a range of dates, from the beginning of the eleventh century (or earlier) up to the nineteenth, since the copying and reading of manuscripts continued and continues to be a living practice in Newar Buddhist culture.

Schøyen collection. A private collection of manuscripts of all cultures formed by Martin Schøyen of Oslo, Norway, which includes important Buddhist documents from Gandhāra, Bamiyan, and elsewhere. The manuscripts are studied and published in an ongoing series, *Buddhist Manuscripts in the Schøyen Collection*, edited by Jens Braarvig of the University of Oslo.

Tripiṭaka. Tib. *sde snod gsum*, Pāli *tipiṭaka*, *tepiṭaka*, Thai *traipiṭaka* (พระไตรปิฎก). Three (*tri-*) baskets or containers (*piṭaka*), referring to the Vinaya, Sūtra, and Abhidharma as the primary scriptural collections.

602. Nalinaksha Dutt (1893–1973) was a prolific editor of Buddhist texts, especially in Sanskrit, as well as a Congress Party representative for West Bengal in the Rajya Sabha. See necrology by Nirmal C. Sinha, *Sikkim Research Institute of Tibetology*, Gangtok, 1977, pp. 28–29.

603. Oskar von Hinüber, "The Gilgit Manuscripts: An Ancient Buddhist Library in Modern Research," in Harrison and Hartmann, *From Birch Bark to Digital Data*, pp. 79–135.

Vinaya

Vinaya. Tib. *'dul ba*. One of the three divisions that make up the Tripiṭaka, the "three baskets." It contains monastic rules for monks and nuns, exegesis, and narratives that explain the circumstances that led Gautama to promulgate the rules.[604]

Vinayavastu. Tib. *'dul ba gzhi*. A major division of the Mūlasarvāstivāda Vinaya that gives the narrative backgounds of the monastic rules that separately make up the monastic code (*Prātimokṣa*). It contains seventeen chapters (*vastu*, Tib. *gzhi*).[605] Large portions are preserved in Sanskrit in the Gilgit collections, and there are Tibetan and Chinese translations. This book mentions the following chapters:

- **Pravrajyāvastu**. Tib. *Rab tu 'byung ba'i gzhi*. "Chapter on Going Forth" of the *Vinayavastu*. An English translation, "The Chapter on Going Forth from the Chapters on Monastic Discipline," translated by Robert Miller and team, has been published digitally by 84000.co.[606]
- **Bhaiṣajyavastu**. Tib. *Sman gyi gzhi*. "Chapter on Medicine" of the *Vinayavastu*. A long chapter that contains many narratives, including full-fledged jātakas, pūrvayogas, avadānas, and sūtras. An English translation by the Bhaiṣajya Translation Team as "The Chapter on Medicines" has been published digitally by 84000.co.[607]
- **Pāṇḍulohitakavastu**. Tib. *Dmar ser can gyi gzhi*. "The Pāṇḍulohitaka Chapter." Sanskrit and Tibetan edition by Nobuyuki Yamagiwa. Edgerton describes Pāṇḍulohitaka as "a group of troublesome monks."[608]
- **Śayanāsanavastu**. Tib. *Mal cha'i gzhi*. "Chapter on Bedding and Seats."[609]
- **Saṅghabhedavastu**. Tib. *Dge 'dun gyi dbyen gyi gzhi*. "Chapter on Division in the Saṅgha."[610]
- **Adhikaraṇavastu**. Tib. *Rtsod pa'i gzhi*. "Chapter on Disputes."[611]

604. For Vinaya literature, see Clarke, "Vinayas."
605. For an overview of the Mūlasarvāstivāda Vinaya, see Clarke, "Vinayas," pp. 73–81, and the earlier classic, Banerjee, *Sarvāstivāda Literature*, part 2: "An Analytical Study of the Vinayavastu." Chapter enumeration given here is based on the Tibetan Kanjur translation.
606. For an earlier summary, see Banerjee, *Sarvāstivāda Literature*, pp. 101–86.
607. For an earlier summary, see Banerjee, *Sarvāstivāda Literature*, pp. 198–206.
608. Edgerton, BHSD, p. 340; for more on the name see Yamagiwa, pp. 14–15. Summary at Banerjee, *Sarvāstivāda Literature*, pp. 224–29.
609. Banerjee, *Sarvāstivāda Literature*, pp. 234–36.
610. Banerjee, *Sarvāstivāda Literature*, pp. 238–46.
611. Banerjee, *Sarvāstivāda Literature*, pp. 236–38.

Vinayaottaragrantha. Tib. *'Dul ba gzhung bla ma / 'Dul ba gzhung dam pa*. A supplement to the Mūlasarvāstivāda Vinaya, preserved in two different translations (one incomplete) in the Tibetan Kanjur.[612]

Mahāvastu. The *Great Story*, a section of the Vinaya of the Lokottaravāda Mahāsāṃghika school. Compiled in Hybrid Sanskrit, it is preserved in the Kathmandu Valley in palm-leaf and paper manuscripts. There are no translations into either Tibetan or Chinese.

Vinayakṣudrakavastu. Tib. *'Dul ba phran tshegs kyi gzhi*. Section of the Mūlasarvāstivādin Vinaya on "miscellaneous matters." It contains a version of the *Great Parinirvāṇa Sutra* and the account of the first two convocations.[613]

Abhidharma

Abhidharma. Tib. *chos mngon pa*, Pāli Abhidhamma. The third "basket" of the Tripiṭakas, also known as *mātṛkā*, "matrix." Both Theravāda and Sarvāstivāda have seven books in their Abhidharmas. We have surprisingly little information about the Abhidharmas of other schools (often none at all). There is no exact equivalent of the term in English or, I believe, in other European languages, and it has been rendered as "philosophy," "metaphysics," "higher doctrine," and so on.

The Theras have treated their Abhidhamma as *buddhavacana*, or speech of the Buddha, since at least the time of Buddhaghosa. Within the broad band of Sarvāstivāda thought, both over time and across geography, the status of the Abhidharma is debated.

Kāraṇaprajñapti. Tib. *Rgyu gdags pa*. *Expositions on Causes*, translated by Jinamitra, Prajñāvarman, Ye shes sde, and team circa 800 CE.[614] One of the seven books of the Sarvāstivāda Abhidharma. Preserved only in this translation, it is an early treatise that incorporates whole sūtras into its expositions. There are no modern translations; for a summary, see La Vallée Poussin, *Bouddhisme: Études et Matériaux*.

612. See Banerjee, *Sarvāstivāda Literature*, pp. 99–100.
613. See Clarke, "Vinayas," p. 76, and for a detailed summary, Banerjee, *Sarvāstivāda Literature*, pp. 89–99.
614. Otani no. 5588, vol. 115, Mngon pa'i bstan bcos, *khu*.

Abhidharmakośa. Tib. *Chos mngon pa'i mdzod*. *Treasury of Abhidharma*, or *Kośa*, *Mdzod*, or *Treasury* for short. Celebrated and enormously influential treasury of Sarvāstivāda-Vaibhāṣika Abhidharma by fourth–fifth-century northern Indian master Vasubandhu (Dbyig bsnyen). It is organized into eight primary chapters (*kośasthāna*, *mdzod kyi gnas*). The number of commentaries composed over the centuries by Buddhist intellectuals in India, Tibet, and East Asia show how important it has been in Buddhist intellectual history. In Japan the *Kośa* was the focus of one of the six Nara schools, *Kusha shu*. In Tibetan scholasticism it is a key work. The *Kośa* was introduced to Europe by La Vallée Poussin's brilliantly annotated French translation from the Chinese, still an unsurpassed monument in Western Buddhist studies. This version has since been translated into English twice, with a recent monumental version by Gelong Lodrö Sangpo.

Āgamas

Āgama. Tib. *lung*. Literally, that which has come down, has been transmitted, has been handed over (to us): received text or tradition, originally referring to orally transmitted ideas and practices (a general term shared by early Indian knowledge systems) but developing to mean textual heritage. The Buddhist corpus of oral literature was progressively sorted into distinct collections of long, middle-length, connected, and numerically ordered discourses to make four distinct Āgamas. The Pāli counterpart of an *āgama* is called a *nikāya*, a corpus or body of texts, but Pāli tradition also recognized and used the synonym *āgama*. Thus, when we refer to the collections as a whole, regardless of their school affiliations, we can refer to them as Āgamas on the understanding that this includes the Nikāyas. Or we can refer to Āgama/Nikāyas, to make it clear that we mean the collections of the various schools inclusively, regardless of which term the individual schools may have preferred. I follow both practices.

The European-language study of the Āgamas has witnessed extraordinary progress over recent decades, as a result of international and multidisciplinary cooperation and improved methodologies, in part on Indic manuscripts and in part on the Āgamas translated into Chinese in the first half of the first millennium CE. This trailblazing research is presented in two series of four volumes each on the four Āgamas published by the Dharma Drum Institute of Liberal Arts, Taipei: *Dīrgha-āgama Studies* and so on, by Anālayo, and

Research on the Dīrgha-āgama and so on, edited by Dhammadinnā. These are listed in the bibliography under Dhammadinnā and Anālayo.

The four Āgamas are the scriptural foundation of the imposing edifice of developed Buddhist textuality. Some schools transmitted five Āgamas, just as the Theravaṃsa had five Nikāyas.[615] We lack information as to exactly which schools had four and which had five, but we know from passing references that some did have a *Kṣudrakāgama* in addition to the four primary Āgamas. No complete set of the Āgamas of any Buddhist school survives in any language apart from the five Nikāyas transmitted in Pāli by the Mahāvihāravāsin Theravāda tradition. The extant Āgamas have disparate origins: the "four Chinese Āgamas," for example, are not a unitary set but are translated from individual Āgamas of three or four different Indian schools. It is not clear whether any Āgamas were ever translated into Tibetan; there are mentions of an *Ekottarikāgama* translation, but no manuscripts or even quotations from it have been located to date. As it stands, there are no translations of any of the four or five Āgamas in the Tibetan Kanjur. There are, however, miscellaneous Āgama texts in the Multiple Sūtras (Mdo mang) sections of Kanjurs, and there are full sūtras embedded in the Vinaya ('Dul ba) translations. In the Tanjur there are the numerous sūtras cited by Śamathadeva in his commentary on Vasubandhu's *Treasury of Abhidharma* as well as in some other tracts mostly within the broader Sarvāstivāda or Mūlasarvāstivāda fold. That is, the cited texts were extracts from the broader Sarvāstivāda Āgama traditions.

Dīrghāgama. Collection of long discourses. Equivalent in *conception* to the Pāli *Dīghanikāya*, but the arrangement, order, phraseology, and contents differ. See Dhammadinnā, *Research on the Dīrgha-āgama*; Anālayo, *Dīrgha-āgama Studies*; English translation of the Chinese (probably Dharmaguptaka) version by Ichimura, *The Canonical Book of the Buddha's Lengthy Discourses*; English translation of the Pāli counterpart *Dīghanikāya* by Maurice Walshe, *Long Discourses of the Buddha*. The recent retrieval and study of a Sanskrit *Dīrghāgama*, deemed Mūlasarvāstivādin,[616] and of fragments of long discourses in

615. See Lamotte, *Histoire*, pp. 165–81, for the Āgamas and the Nikāyas. Even though by my time of writing this volume, sixty years after Lamotte, the field has been much transformed by new discoveries and research, the Belgian maestro's clear introduction and comprehensive frame of reference remain immensely valuable.

616. Hartmann and Wille, "The Manuscript of the Dīrghāgama and the Private Collection in Virginia."

Gāndhārī[617] are dramatically augmenting our knowledge of this collection. Our image of the synoptic history of the collection of long discourses has been transformed (as, indeed, is the case with all Buddhist scriptural collections).

Madhyamāgama. Collection of discourses of middle or medial length, by definition a subjective and flexible category. Equivalent in conception to the Pāli *Majjhimanikāya*, but the arrangement, order, phraseology, and contents differ. See Anālayo, *Comparative Study of the Majjhima-Nikāya*; Anālayo, *Madhyama-āgama Studies*; Dhammadinnā, *Research on the Madhyama-āgama*; English translation of the Chinese (probably Sarvāstivāda), BDK English Tripiṭaka;[618] English translation of the Pāli counterpart, *Majjhimanikāya*, by Bhikkhu Ñāṇamoli and Bhikkhu Bodhi, *Middle Length Discourses of the Buddha*.

Saṃyuktāgama. Collection of "grouped sayings," "kindred sayings," or "connected discourses." Equivalent in conception to the Pāli *Saṃyuttanikāya*, but the arrangement, order, phraseology, and contents differ. See Dhammadinnā, *Research on the Saṃyukta-āgama*; Anālayo, *Saṃyukta-āgama Studies*. For the Pāli counterpart, the *Saṃyuttanikāya*, see Gethin, *Sayings of the Buddha*, p. 207; English translation by Bhikkhu Bodhi, *Connected Discourses of the Buddha*. The suttas selected by Venerable Bodhi for his recently published resource "to help students of Early Buddhism learn to read the texts of the Pāli Canon," *Reading the Buddha's Discourses in Pāli*, are all from the *Saṃyuttanikāya*.

Ekottarikāgama. The collection of numerically ordered discourses. Equivalent in conception to the Pāli *Aṅguttaranikāya*, but the arrangement, order, phraseology, and contents differ. See Dhammadinnā, *Research on the Ekottarikā-āgama*; Anālayo, *Ekottarikā-āgama Studies*; Palumbo, *An Early Chinese Commentary on the Ekottarika-āgama*. A French translation from the Chinese was published in installments in the *Linh-Son publication d'études bouddhologiques* and the *Buddhist Studies Review* by Ven. Thich Huyen Vi and Bhikkhu Pāsādika. For the Pāli *Aṅguttaranikāya*, see Gethin, *Sayings of the Buddha*, p. 249. English translation by Bhikkhu Bodhi, *Numerical Discourses of the Buddha*. Manuscript fragments of a Gāndhārī and a Sanskrit *Ekottarikā*

617. Salomon, *Buddhist Literature of Ancient Gandhāra*, pp. 96–97.
618. *Madhyama Āgama (Middle-Length Discourses)*, 3 vols. to date: 2013, 2023 (pdf versions 2017, 2020).

have recently come to light.[619] This amplifies our understanding of the nature and importance of the *Ekottarikā* traditions.

Kṣudrakāgama.[620] Miscellaneous collection, containing a variety of canonical texts in different genres. No *Kṣudrakāgama* has come down to us either as Indic manuscripts or translations, and as a result, it is not clear how many schools had a *Kṣudrakāgama* and, when they did have one, what the contents might have been. Titles of texts that could belong to Kṣudraka Piṭakas are listed, sometimes in clusters, in a range of canonical texts of different schools, but they are not associated with or sourced to any named collections.[621] The contents of a *Kṣudrakāgama* are listed in the Chinese translation of the Dharmaguptaka Vinaya. Heinz Bechert hypothesized that a Sanskrit manuscript in the Turfan collection, MS 464, contained five texts and may have been part of a Kṣudrakāgama—but the title is not preserved. In any case, the *Kṣudrakāgama* seems to have been similar in conception but different in contents to the Pāli *Khuddakanikāya*—with some overlaps. That is, in its received form, the Pāli *Khuddakanikāya* is almost cetainly unique as a collection.

Pāli scriptures

Pāli is the canonical and liturgical language of the Theravāda school. Pāli studies have been encouraged by the Pali Text Society since 1881, when the society was founded in England by T. W. Rhys Davids "to foster and promote the study of Pāli texts." It publishes Pāli texts in roman characters and translations for the most part in English. Pāli is taught at leading universities in Europe, the Americas, and East, South, and Southeast Asia. Lately it has gained institutional recognition in the Middle East, at the Hebrew University of Jerusalem in Israel.

There are dozens of books about Pāli and as many conflicting opinions about its relation to Gautama the Buddha: whether it was *the* "language of the Buddha" or whether it was *a* cognate literary language several steps along from the language he spoke. Bhikkhu Bodhi, summarizing the state of schol-

619. See Salomon, "On the Evolution of Written Āgama Collections," pp. 249–51.

620. See Lamotte, *Histoire*, pp. 171–78.

621. See Salomon, "On the Evolution of Written Āgama Collections," p. 249, for "Kṣudraka type" texts in Gāndhārī.

arship, wrote in 2005 that the Middle Indo-Aryan language that we know as Pāli is[622]

> closely related to the language (or, more likely, the various regional dialects) that the Buddha himself spoke. . . . Scholars regard this language as a hybrid showing features of several Prakrit dialects used around the third century BCE, subjected to a partial process of Sanskritization. While the language is not identical to what the Buddha himself would have spoken, it belongs to the same broad linguistic family as those he might have used and originates from the same conceptual matrix. This language thus reflects the thought-world that the Buddha inherited from the wider Indian culture into which he was born, so that its words capture the subtle nuances of that thought-world.

The language and the style of Pāli do reflect the contemporaneous thought-world as well as the Buddha's own usage, as it was codified by the saṅgha, especially the reciters and redactors, but that language itself certainly influenced both the language and style of that thought-world as we see it in the Āgama and Nikāyas. Rather than a simple linear development, evolution of the Āgamas was interactive and multilinear. That it was not a one-way street is seen in word formations, phrasing, vocabulary, and rhetorical styles that are used in the texts of all Buddhist schools but rarely if at all in non-Buddhist literature. That is, Buddhist literary productions have a unique style and flavor (*rasa*).

five Nikāyas. The five Nikāyas correspond in principle to the five Āgamas described above. For the Pāli Nikāyas, see Oskar von Hinüber's *Handbook of Pāli Literature*. Rupert Gethin's *Sayings of the Buddha* is a compendium of English translations with introduction. Bhikkhu Bodhi has published masterful translations of three of the Nikāyas (one conjointly with Bhikkhu Ñāṇamoli), plus the *Suttanipāta* of the *Khuddakanikāya*. Outside of the classical Pāli literature of Sri Lanka, Pāli composition thrived in several genres in Siam, to make up the extensive Pāli literature of Siam/Thailand.[623]

622. Bodhi, *In the Buddha's Words*, pp. 9–10.
623. See Skilling, "Reflections on the Pāli Literature of Siam."

Khuddakanikāya. *Miscellaneous/Heterogeneous Collection* or *Collection of Minor/Lesser Texts*. I prefer to render *khuddaka* as "miscellaneous" rather then "lesser" or "small" because, as von Hinüber puts it, the *Khuddakanikāya* "consists of fifteen very heterogeneous works of widely varying length."[624] The texts that constitute it are not necessarily *minor* or *lesser* either in terms of impact (consider the influence of the *Suttanipāta*, *Dhammapada*, or *Apadāna*) or size (consider the size of the *Jātaka*, *Paṭisambhidāmagga*, *Niddesa*), and I do not think translations like "small" or "lesser" are at all apt. Texts from this collection include:

Verses of the Senior Monks. *Theragāthā*. Verses composed by senior arhat monks, grouped by individual author in ascending order of number of verses from one up, comprising 1,279 stanzas, spoken by 264 monks. The Pāli version is a unique poetic record of early Buddhist spiritual experience. A Sanskrit version is known by name (*Sthaviragāthā*) but, apart from a few small fragments from Central Asia, is not preserved.[625]

Verses of the Senior Nuns. *Therīgāthā*. Verses composed by senior arhat nuns, grouped by author in ascending order of number of verses starting with one, spoken by seventy-three nuns. The Pāli version is a unique poetic record of the spiritual experience of early Buddhist female monastics. A Sanskrit version is known by name (*Sthavirīgāthā*) but is not preserved.

Short Readings. *Khuddakapāṭha*. A collection of nine short texts. The texts are all small, but their impact is not, since several are chanted regularly (*Ratanasutta*, *Maṅgalasutta*) across Theravāda societies.

Sutta Collection. *Suttanipāta*. A collection of texts, mostly in verse, including what are accepted to be amongst the oldest Buddhist works. Several of the chapters were transmitted in the canons or other schools—for example, the *Serpent*, the *Sūtra on Sense Pleasures* (*Kāmasūtra*), the *Rhinoceros Horn*, the *Eights*, and the *Way Beyond*. This shows the importance of these chapters to the compilers of the early canons. The Pāli collection as we know it today, however, seems to be unique to the Theravāda school. Other schools may have had comparable collections with different titles and different contents.

Udāna. Inspired utterance or profound statement, usually in verse. See

624. See von Hinüber, *Handbook*, § II.2.5.

625. See Bechert, *Bruchstücke buddhistischer Verssammlungen*, and Bechert, "On a Fragment of the *Vimānāvadāna*."

Feer, *Avadāna-Çataka*, p. 487. For a succinct description of the Pāli *Udāna* collection, see Anālayo, "Udāna."[626]

Jātaka. Previous birth, past birth, of a Buddha as the Bodhisatva.[627] Jātakas were transmitted by all schools, but the most comprehensive collection of jātakas surviving today is the Pāli corpus, which consists of roughly 2,500 verses divided into 547 separate units, each with an accompanying narrative preserved in the commentary.[628] In the contested terrains of "scriptural authenticity," the status of the jātakas is ambiguous. They are an integral part of the early corpora; they are depicted in the earliest phase of Buddhist art; and through today they are a vital part of popular culture in Theravāda societies. Modern scholarship, however, tends to treat the jātakas as peripheral to early Buddhism and nonauthentic.

Aruṇavatīsutta (1). *Sagāthavagga*, *Brahmasaṃyutta*, *Saṃyuttanikāya*, vol. 1, pp. 155–57. See introduction to translation 2.

Aruṇavatīsutta (2). Expanded Pāli cosmological work based on *Aruṇavatīsutta* (1). Known only in Thailand and probably composed there. See introduction to translation 2.

Other scriptures

Avadāna. Tib. *rtogs par brjod pa*, Pāli *apadāna*. The etymology and meaning of *avadāna/apadāna* is disputed, and the terms resist translation. There are two great Sanskrit collections, the *Divyāvadāna* (translated by Rotman) and the *Avadānaśataka* (translated by Feer, Appleton, and Rotman). In addition there is the *Karmaśataka* (*Las brgya tham pa*), preserved in Tibetan only, with an English translation by Lozang Jamspal and Kaia Tara Fischer as *The Hundred Deeds* published digitally by 84000.[629] An English translation of

626. A much longer Sanskrit collection of verses only is now generally known as the *Udānavarga*.
627. Note the capital here on Bodhisatva, a common English-language usage to indicate that this refers to Gautama in one of his past births.
628. For more on jātakas, see the works of Naomi Appleton listed in the bibilography; Skilling, *Past Lives of the Buddha*, pp. 59–104.
629. See Banerjee, *Sarvāstivāda Literature*, pp. 257–60, for *Avadānaśataka*, 260–62 for *Divyāvadāna*, and 262 for *Karmaśataka*.

the Pāli *Apadāna* by Jonathan S. Walters is available online as *Legends of the Buddhist Saints, Apadānapāli.*

The following avadānas are referred to in this collection:

Prātihāryasūtra, Divyāvadāna no. 12
Dharmaruci-avadāna, Divyāvadāna no. 18
Pāṃśupradāna-avadāna, Divyāvadāna no. 26
Ujjvalikadānakathā a section of the *Dvāviṃśati-avadāna*
Kāśikavastra, Avadānaśataka no. 19
Upoṣadha, Avadānaśataka no. 59
Īti, Avadānaśataka no. 14

Dhvajāgrakeyūra-dhāraṇī. Potent dhāraṇī to be affixed to armband or atop flagstaff; widely blockprinted on cloth and displayed for protection and good fortune throughout Tibetan and Himalayan cultural areas.

Gāndhārī *Dharmapada.* See Khotan *Dharmapada.*

Khotan *Dharmapada*. A birchbark scroll discovered in Khotan containing a Gāndhārī Prakrit *Dharmapada* written in Kharoṣṭhī script. Published by Brough as *Gāndhārī Dharmapada* in 1962, it was one of the first Gāndhārī scrolls to be studied and published, starting with articles and partial editions from the late nineteenth century. Since the discovery of new Gāndhārī *Dharmapada* manuscripts in recent decades, the manuscript published by Brough has been renamed "Khotan Dharmapada" to avoid confusion.

Lalitavistara. Tib. *Rgya cher rol pa. A Detailed Account of the Elegant Sport [of the Buddha]*, a life of the Buddha up to his awakening written in Hybrid Sanskrit. A Tibetan translation is included in the Sūtra section of Kanjurs. After pioneering French translations by Foucaux (from Tibetan, 1848; from Sanskrit, 1884), there have been several English translations, but most recently from the Tibetan at 84000.co as *The Play in Full.*[630]

Samādhirāja. Tib. *Ting nge 'dzin gyi rgyal po. King of Samādhis*, a long Vaipulya/Mahāyāna sūtra in prose and verse, the latter in Buddhist Hybrid

630. See "commentaire" in Ducoeur, *La Vie du Buddha*. For aspects of "Lalitavistara studies," see Silk, "Serious Play: Recent Scholarship on the Lalitavistara."

Sanskrit. Also known as the *Candrapradīpasūtra* (*Zla ba sgron me'i mdo*). A Tibetan translation is included in the Sūtra section of Kanjurs. Complete English translation by Peter Alan Roberts published digitally at 84000.co.

Questions of Mañjuśrī. Skt. *Mañjuśrīparipṛcchā*. Tib. *'Jam dpal gyis dris pa*. A Mahāyāna sūtra preserved in Tibetan and Chinese (Taishō 468) but not known to survive in any Indic version. Translation from Chinese by John McRae, *The Sutra of Mañjuśrī's Questions*.

Other texts

Aṭṭhakathā. Pāli literature boasts a body of learned commentaries on the root texts of the five Nikāyas along with subcommentaries, manuals, and other ancillary texts. The exegetical tradition evolved in India (though *where* in the subcontinent is not clear); it went on to flourish on Sri Lanka's emerald isle and later still in Southeast Asia. Few of the commentaries have been translated into any European language. A complete set of impressive Thai translations of root texts and commentaries has been published by the Mahamakut Foundation, Bangkok. In this volume, reference is made to the following commentaries.

- ***Papañcasūdanī***. *Majjhimanikāya-aṭṭhakathā*. Commentary ascribed to the fifth-century master Buddhaghosa on the 152 suttas of the *Middle Collection*.
- ***Sumaṅgalavilāsinī***. *Dīghanikāya-aṭṭhakathā*. Commentary on the thirty-four suttas of the *Long Collection* ascribed to Buddhaghosa.
- ***Paramatthajotikā***. *Suttanipāta Commentary* held by tradition to be by the scholar Buddhaghosa. English translation in Bhikkhu Bodhi's *Suttanipāta*.
- ***Udānaṭṭhakathā***. Commentary on the *Udāna* by Dhammapāla. English translation by Peter Masefield as *The Udāna Commentary*.

Dazhidu lun 大智度論. Skt. **Mahāprajñāpāramitopadeśa*. A voluminous and encyclopedic commentary on the *Large Perfection of Wisdom* ascribed to Nāgārjuna and translated by the Kuchean master Kumārajīva (344–413). References here are to Lamotte's magistral annotated five-volume French translation as *Le Traité de la Grande Vertu de Sagesse de Nāgārjuna*, the 2,451 pages of which cover only the first of its two sections and chapter 20 of the second. See Buswell and Lopez, *Princeton Dictionary*, p. 227. The *Dazhidu* *lun* may never have existed as an Indian text, but it draws entirely on Indian Buddhist lore.

Yogalehrbuch. A Sanskrit meditation manual unearthed in Central Asia in a fragmentary state. No translations into other languages (Chinese, Tibetan) are known to exist. Edition with German translation by Schlingloff and Hartmann. See Cousins, "A Lost Meditation Tradition from the Silk Road," chapter 7 of his *Meditations of the Pali Tradition*.

Book of Zambasta. A Khotanese poem on Buddhism. Twenty-four chapters have survived; the manuscripts are fragmentary, but large portions are preserved. English study and translation by Emmerick.

Auspicious verses and protections

One of the important hands-on uses of the Buddhavacana is recitation. Recitation is practiced to foster inner balance and social harmony and bring good fortune, spiritual benefits, and protection against calamities. In general, see Skilling, "Rakṣā Literature," and more recently, van Schaik, *Buddhist Magic*.

Svastigāthā. Pāli *sotthi-gāthā*. Verse for well-being, auspicious verse, blessing. Also described in Sanskrit as *svastyāyana-gāthā, maṅgala-gāthā, āśīrvāda*: terms for verse blessings with some nuances according to context.

Ratnasūtra. Pāli *Ratanasutta*. *Discourse on Precious Gems*. A foundational inspirational text that invokes the beneficial power of the Three Precious Gems. The Pāli *Ratanasutta* is placed in two canonical scripture collections, the *Short Readings* and the *Sutta Collection*, both included in the *Miscellaneous Collection*. Sanskrit versions are embedded in the *Mahāvastu* and in several *dhāraṇīs*.

Catubhāṇavāra. *Four Recitations*. A collection of Pāli texts arranged for four recitation sessions, compiled in Sri Lanka at an uncertain, but relatively early, date. A multipurpose collection that is put to didactic, liturgical, and apotropaic ends, it is recited by groups of monastics in auspicious and protective ceremonies. In Southeast Asia, it is transmitted in local scripts in manuscript and printed collections of chants as, for example, the Thai *Suatmon chabap luang*.

Paritta. Protection, safeguard. Pāli chants recited for blessing and protection, arranged in any number of different collections. While the word *paritrāṇa*, "protection," is common in Sanskrit Buddhist texts, especially dhāraṇīs, as far as I know the word is not used independently for protective texts *qua* texts. The use of *paritta* in this sense seems to be unique to the Pāli/Theravāda tradition.

Sattaparitta. *Seven Protections* or *Chet tamnan* (เจ็ดตำนาน), also known as the *Lesser Royal Paritta* (*Cularājaparitta*). Collection of seven chants (with some auxiliary texts) used in Siam from at least the Ayutthaya period to the present (that is, from approximately the seventeenth century onward).

Dvādasaparitta. *Twelve Protections* or *Sipsong tamnan* (สิบสองตำนาน), also known as the *Greater Royal Paritta* (*Mahārājaparitta*). Collection of twelve chants (with some auxiliary texts) used in Siam from at least the Ayutthaya period to the present (that is, from approximately the seventeenth century onward).

Nangsue suatmon (หนังสือสวดมนต์). Thai-script *Book of Chants*: one of the first printed Pāli books of Siam, compiled by Saṅgharāja Pussadeva (Sā).

Suatmon chabap luang (สวดมนต์ฉบับหลวง). Thai-script *Royal Chanting Book*, a revision of *Nangsue suatmon* that continues to be used up to the present. It is published both as a Pāli collection, in Thai script, and as a collection of Thai translations, as *Suatmon plae* (สวดมนต์แปล). The current Pāli version is the twentieth printing; the *Suatmon plae* is the seventeenth printing. There is no complete translation into English, and there have been few comprehensive studies.

Chanting and liturgy inhabit the *bardo* of the oral/print interface and tend to be invisible and inaudible. Academia, tone-deaf, neglects them; nonetheless, chants and liturgies constitute an *audible Buddhism* that resonates throughout Asia and beyond.

dhāraṇī. Tib. *gzungs*. A spell, incantation, or formula to be memorized and recited to enhance the memory, or for blessing, protection, realization of supernormal powers or spiritual goals. See also *mantrapada* below.

mantrapada. Tib. *gsang sngags kyi gzhi / gsang sngags kyi tshig*. Syllables to be recited for protection and success. Mantrapada syllables are often indistinguishable from dhāraṇī syllables, and the two terms are often conjoined as *dhāraṇīmantrapada*. The rich Buddhist apotropaic literature developed over the centuries across a wide region, and it does not privilege any single "official" term.

Five Protections. *Pañcarakṣā*. A collection of five distinctive Sanskrit protections, each represented by a female deity. Especially popular in Newar Buddhist ritual practice and ritual art.

Mahāmantrānusāriṇī. Sanskrit *Pañcarakṣā* version of *Vaiśālīpraveṣa* (translation 15) and a female deity of the same name (see figures 33 and 48).

Mahāsāhasrapramardanī. Tib. *Stong chen mo rab tu 'joms pa*. "Destroyer of the Great Trichiliocosm," one of the *Five Protections* that relates to the Vaiśālī epidemic. English translation by Dharmachakra Translation Committee published digitally by 84000.co.

History and chronicles

Chronicle of the Island [of Lanka]. *Dīpavaṃsa*. Verse chronicle in Pāli that narrates the history of the island of Sri Lanka and the development of Buddhism there.

Great Chronicle. *Mahāvaṃsa*. Pāli chronicle of the island of Sri Lanka from the earliest period, with particular attention to the traditions of the Mahāvihāra Monastery. Periodically updated, it runs up to the twentieth century; a unique document that gives a continuous record of over 2,500 years of legend and history.

History of the Dharma. *Chos 'byung*. See under Bu ston; Tāranātha.

Saṅgha

Roles and ideal figures

The texts translated here were preserved and transmitted orally by Indian Buddhist saṅghas. The saṅgha is an amazing institution that has kept the Buddhadharma alive for well over two thousand years. Buddhists rejoice in the saṅgha's resilience and the benfits it has bestowed to Buddhists and humanity.

The members of the saṅgha listed below are Buddhists through going for refuge in the Three Precious Jewels and through their vows, commitments, and aspirations. In today's individualistic societies, many people shy away from, or actively reject, formal religion or religious commitments. People are no longer ready to answer questionnaires by ticking a box that names their religion. This means that in the current secular age, it is not an easy matter to classify people as "Buddhist" and "non-Buddhist," especially in Western Christian and post-Christian societies.

uncommitted sympathizers. Many people are reluctant and unwilling, or feel morally unable or socially embarrassed to commit themselves to any religion or system of practice. At the same time, some people are attracted to Buddhist thought or praxis and associate themselves with Buddhist teachers or methods, without taking refuge or engaging with the teachings. We might call them "uncommitted sympathizers" or "uncommitted associates."

saṅgha. Tib. *dge 'dun*. The "social saṅgha" is constituted by the Buddhist community as a whole, made up of monks, nuns, and other ordinands, laymen, laywomen, and several other categories. The determining factors are to go for refuge to the Three Precious Jewels and then to undertake to follow a set of vows, precepts, or regulations (*saṃvara*, *sdom pa*). There are seven options:

Monk: *bhikṣu*, *dge slong*, Pāli *bhikkhu*
Nun: *bhikṣunī*, *dge slong ma*, Pāli *bhikkhuni*
Novice: *śrāmaṇera*, *dge tshul*, Pāli *sāmaṇera*
Female novice: *śrāmaṇerikā*, *dge tshul ma*, Pāli *sāmaṇerī*
Layman: *upāsaka*, *dge bsnyen*, Pāli *upāsaka*
Laywoman: *upāsikā*, *dge bsnyen ma*, Pāli *upāsikā*

Trainee (probationary/postulant female ordinand): *śikṣāmāṇā*, *dge slob ma*, Pāli *sikkhāmāṇā*

A male might be a layman, a novice, a monk; a female could be a laywoman, a trainee, a female novice, or a nun. For Pāli usage, see Upasak, *Dictionary*, pp. 209–10.

The "noble" (*ārya*) saṅgha is defined by progress on the path, by spiritual attainment: it consists of "four pairs of persons, the eight individuals," as enumerated in translation 12.

upāsaka. Tib. *dge bsnyen*. Male lay follower. A male who goes for refuge to the Three Jewels and undertakes certain restraints, such as the five precepts. Vasubandhu's *Abhidharmakośabhāṣya* and other Abhidharma or exegetical texts record debates about which vows need to be undertaken and under what circumstances for an individual to count as a "lay follower." It is noteworthy that the emperor Aśoka describes himself as an *upāsaka* in his inscriptions and thereby counts as the earliest recorded "historical" *upāsaka*.

See Buswell and Lopez, *Princeton Dictionary*, p. 941, *upāsaka* and *upāsakasaṃvara*; Upasak, *Dictionary*, pp. 50–51.

upāsikā. Tib. *dge bsnyen ma*. Female lay follower. A female who goes for refuge to the Three Jewels and undertakes certain restraints, such as the five precepts. See Buswell and Lopez, *Princeton Dictionary*, p. 942, *upāsikā* and *upāsikāsaṃvara*; Upasak, *Dictionary*, p. 51.

kulaputra. Tib. *rigs kyi bu*, Pāli *kulaputta*. "Son of good family," a term for an ideal male lay practitioner. Bodhi, *Reading the Buddha's Discourses*, p. 176, gives a literal translation, "family-sons"; he also translates the term as "young people" (p. 178). Gómez and Harrison translate as "gentleman": see note on this and the following at Gómez and Harrison, *Vimalakīrtinirdeśa*, p. 175, n. 40.

kuladuhitṛ. Tib. *rigs kyi bu mo*, Pāli *kuladhītā*. "Daughter of good family," a term for an ideal female lay practitioner. Gómez and Harrison translate as "lady."

bhikṣu. Tib. *dge slong*, Pāli *bhikkhu*. A male mendicant, a renunciant who has left home and family life behind to live in a community of fellow ordinands who seek their daily sustenance through alms. Their lives are regulated by monastic codes that differ for the different orders.

The early Buddhist monastic orders in India followed the monastic codes of the different schools, as many as eighteen in number. Each order's saṅgha was dual or twofold, male and female, to allow for the spititual aspirations of both genders. For a variety of historical and social reasons, the South Asian Buddhist monastic system went though periods of disruption and eventual decline and rupture, and by the fifteenth or sixteenth centuries CE, the monasteries were abandoned, and the monastic lineages, male and female, died out. The monastic orders that survived were all extra-Indian. Three male monastic orders that had been established outside of the subcontinent survived and have remained active up to today. In Lanka and Southeast Asia, the Theravāda saṅghas study and practice their monastic traditions following a canonical and commentarial corpus composed in Pāli and vernacular languages; monastics in the greater Tibeto-Mongolian-Himalayan region study and practice the Mūlasarvāstivāda monastic traditions using a corpus in the Tibetan and Mongol languages, and in East Asia the Dharmaguptaka tradition is practiced following canonical and commentarial literature in Chinese. Thus transregional or international Buddhism is complex, hybrid, and multilingual.

bhikṣuṇī. Tib. *dge slong ma*, Pāli *bhikkhunī*. A female mendicant, a renunciant who has left home and family life behind to live in a community of fellow ordinands who seek their daily sustenance through alms. When the monastic lineages died out in India, a nun's order of hybrid origins that largely uses Dharmaguptaka texts in Chinese translation continued to be active up till today. In Ceylon, Southeast Asia, and greater Tibet, the nun's orders died out or were not soundly established; female renunciant lineages developed and even flourished, but women were precluded from obtaining full ordination as *bhikṣuṇī*. Since the late twentieth century, efforts have been made to establish full *bhikṣuṇī* ordination into the Theravāda and Mūlasarvāstivāda saṅghas with varying degrees of success.[631]

631. I can only give here a summary account—by necessity an oversimplification—of this historically and socially complicated, highly controversial, and emotional topic. For Bhikkhu Anālayo's overview with extensive reference to earlier research, see Anālayo, *Foundation History of the Nuns' Order*.

upādhyāya. Tib. *mkhan po*, Pāli *upajjhāya*. Preceptor, a monk who is qualified to officiate at the ordination of others as monks.

sthavira. Tib. *gnas brtan*. Pāli *thera*. "Senior" or "elder" monk, calculated in years of ordination, not biological age. The feminine forms are *sthavirī* and *therī*, senior or elder nun. *Mahāsthavira*, Pāli *mahāthera* (fem. *mahāsthavirī*, *mahātherī*), great seniors: monastics of over twenty years ordination. All of the monastic orders used this system of monastic ranking by seniority.

arhat. Tib. *dgra bcom pa*, Pāli *arahant*. A worthy one, one who has achieved release. The highest level of accomplishment amongst the eight noble ones. The standard Tibetan translation follows the gloss given in the *Companion to the Mahāvyutpati*, deriving the word from *ari* (enemy) and *han* (eradicate, destroy): one who has eradicated the foe, that is, the defilements—hence sometimes translated "foe destroyer." See Buswell and Lopez, *Princeton Dictionary*, p. 62; Gómez and Harrison, *Vimalakīrtinirdeśa*, pp. 168 and 171, n. 2, "truly worthy one." See Brunnhölzl, *Gone Beyond*, vol. 1, p. 685, n. 32.

śaikṣa. Tib. *slob pa*. Trainee who is already on the path: that is, seven stages from a stream enterer up, excluding the final and eighth stage, the worthy arhat.

pratyekabuddha. Tib. *rang sangs rgyas*, Pāli *paccekabuddha*. A term also used in Jainism. In some early Buddhist texts, especially in verse, also called *pratyayabuddha* or *pratyayajina* (*rkyen rgyal*), and the pratyekabuddha vehicle is called *pratyayayāna*, *rkyen gyi theg pa*. This may have influenced the common gloss that pratyekabuddhas realize conditionality (*pratītyasamutpāda*).[632]

Pratyekabuddha is a term that enjoys a superabundance of translations: autonomous or independent buddha; "single Buddha" (Conze, *Perfection of Wisdom*, p. 321); "self-enlightened being" (Watson, *Lotus Sutra*, p. 335); solitary buddha; hermit buddha; solitary realizer; lonely buddha; lone, private, independent, or silent buddha; *bouddha individuel*, and so on. Candrakīrti and Buddhaghosa describe three types of persons who are awakened ones, buddhas:[633] *samyaksaṃbuddha* (Pāli: *sammāsambuddha*), "truly and fully

632. See Brunnhölzl, *Gone Beyond*, vol. 1, p. 683, n. 17.
633. La Vallée Poussin, "Pratyekabuddha," p. 153.

awakened ones"; *pratyekabuddha* (Pāli: *paccekabuddha*); and (Pāli) *sāvaka-buddha*,[634] "those who achieve awakening through the instruction from a *sammāsambuddha*." The pratyekabuddha is an "individually awakened one" who achieves awakening on his own, in a time period when there are no *samyaksambuddhas* in the world; hence he achieves his goal independently or autonomously, realizing "autonomous awakening" (*pratyekabodhi*) without receiving any instruction from a Buddha. Pratyekabuddhas are superior fields of merit, and they teach and guide in several ways, including through miracles and marvels; but unlike *samyaksambuddhas*, they do not establish a body of teachings or a monastic community. According to an ancient shared doctrine, there can be only one single fully awakened Buddha in a single world system at one time. In sharp contrast, any number of pratyekabuddhas can coexist, and in narratives they appear in groups of, for example, five hundred.[635] In the "vehicle" (*yāna*) system of graded paths, Pratyekabuddha Vehicle is the intermediary path, between the Śrāvaka and Bodhisatva vehicles.

Pratyekabuddha is a fertile term that exercises the dogmatic, literary, and narrative imaginations, and much has been written about the term, although modern scholarship has been unduly suspicious of its significance and value. For modernists, pratyekabuddhas may have the same ontological status as elves—but where would the fairytale be without the wee creatures? Similarly, where would jātakas and avadānas be without pratyekabuddhas?

I shy away from the rendering "independent Buddha" because everything is dependent on causes and conditions and nothing can be literally independent apart from the uncompounded state (*asaṃskṛta*) of nirvāṇa; and because, doctrinally and dogmatically, pratyekabuddhas duly advanced their careers under sammāsambuddhas in past lives, during which they formed the resolution to become a pratyekabuddha. The closest English equivalent might be "autonomous buddha," but in today's English "autonomous" seems to belong more to political than religious discourse.

J. W. de Jong, in his review of Leon Hurvitz's translation of the *Scripture of the Lotus Blossom of the Fine Dharma*, gives an illuminating critical discussion of Chinese translations of pratyekabuddha in relation to Indic terminology.

634. I am not certain whether an equivalent Sanskrit form, *śrāvakabuddha*, is met with in Sanskrit sources. If so, it is rare.
635. See Appleton, "*Jātaka* Stories and *Pacceka Buddhas* in Early Buddhism," with reference to previous scholarship; Buswell and Lopez, *Princeton Dictionary*, p. 673. The main point is that they cannot coexist with a full Buddha.

He remarks that Kumārajīva either transcribed 辟支佛 *pi zhi fo* or translates 緣覺 *yuan jue*, which Hurvitz translates as "condition perceiver." He notes that Paul Demiéville translated the Chinese phrase as "awakened *by* conditions / éveillé *par* les conditions."[636]

śrāvaka. Tib. *nyan thos*, Pāli *sāvaka*. "Advanced disciple," per Gómez and Harrison, *Vimalakīrtinirdeśa*, p. 153. Hearer, auditor, listener, disciple; one who hears or listens to the Dharma from a Buddha or a teacher; in developed Buddhist thought, in contrast to the bodhisatva, a person who aims to become, or becomes, an arhat. Vīryaśrīdatta defines *śrāvakas* as those who are instructed by others—that is to say, they follow the teachings of others.[637] See Buswell and Lopez, *Princeton Dictionary*, p. 850; Brunnhölzl, *Gone Beyond*, vol. 1, p. 683, n. 16. Translations from Chinese use "voice-hearer" (e.g., Watson's *Lotus Sutra*).

The term is also used for non-Buddhists, as in the case of Araka (translation 10, here rendered as "votary").

mahāśrāvaka. Tib. *nyan thos chen po*, Pāli *mahāsāvaka*. Great auditor or hearer. The prominent or best known of Śākyamuni's direct disciples, sometimes listed as numbering sixteen, eighteen, eighty, or five hundred.

śrāvakabodhi. Pāli *sāvakabodhi*. The awakening of a śrāvaka; arhatship, the goal of the śrāvaka path.

Śrāvaka schools. The schools who transmitted, and based their teachings on, the Śrāvaka sūtras. Reference to the eighteen schools, often—but by no means exclusively—from a Mahāyāna perspective.

bodhisatva. Tib. *byang chub sems dpa'*, Pāli *bodhisatta*. A person who is dedicated to the realization of full awakening (*bodhi*) and vows to accomplish this. The undertaking of bodhisatva vows is described in narrative and ritual texts and enacted in ritual practice. The etymology and orthography are contested. Inscriptions and manuscripts are nearly unanimous in spelling the term with a single "t" (the same for *satva* and *mahāsatva*, "being" and "great

636. De Jong, review of Hurvitz, *Scripture of the Lotus Blossom of the Fine Dharma*, pp. 172–73.
637. *Paraiḥ śrāvyanta iti śrāvakāḥ paropadeśānugā ity arthaḥ*: Samtani, ed., *Arthaviniścayasūtranibandhana*, p. 310.1.

being"), and it is this form, *bodhisatva*, that was adopted as a loanword in languages like Tibetan,[638] Khotanese, and Thai (พระโพธิสัตว์). Modern editions and writings usually normalize to *bodhisattva*, with a double "t." For the term in general see Lopez and Buswell, *Princeton Dictionary*, p. 134. For bodhisatva and the Tibetan translation see Brunnhölzl, *Gone Beyond*, vol. 1, p. 209 and pp. 724–26, n. 517.

mahāsatva. Tib. *sems dpa' chen po*, Pāli *mahāsatta*. Great heroic being, great being, great soul, great spirit. Often coupled with bodhisatva: *bodhisatva mahāsatva*. *Mahāsatva* is also used alone as equivalent to bodhisatva.

satva. Tib. *sems can*, Pāli *satta*. One who possesses mind or sentience, "sentient being." What is this curious creature, so frequent in Buddhist literature but not in the least prominent in the annals of science, ethnographies, or demographics? An inclusive nonhumanocentric Indic notion for all orders of sentient existence, the term *sentient being* may have started out as a good example of Buddhist Hybrid English, but it has long been naturalized in English Buddhist discourse.

wanderer. Tib. *kun tu rgyu*, Skt. *parivrājaka*, Pāli *paribbājaka*. Wandering ascetic, with no stated religious affiliation. Perhaps similar in certain regards to the medieval *clerici vagantes* or *vagabundi* (singular *clericus vagans* or *vagabundus*).

Monastic orders and schools

nikāya. Buddhist order, school, or college according to adherence to a particular Vinaya or monastic code.[639] I avoid the word *sect*, which in English seems to most frequently refer to a body or movement of *lay* followers with *lay* leaders (with exceptions) whereas here we are concerned with celibate monasticism.[640] The Buddhist nikāyas were monastic orders; the members

638. This is the spelling, for example, of the Tibetan historical record, *Dba' bzhed*: see Doney, *Bringing Buddhism to Tibet*, pp. xvii and 32, n. 9.
639. For "college," Doctor Johnson gives (1) "A community; a number of persons living by some common rules" and (2) "A society of men set apart for learning or religion," both of which suit the sense of *nikāya* nicely. From Lynch, *Samuel Johnson's Dictionary*, pp. 112–13, s.v. "college."
640. See definition in Wyld, *Universal Dictionary*, p. 1078.

were men and women who took monastic vows and lived apart from society, adhering to a shared system and shared aims and ideals. The Victorian usage *fraternity* doesn't work since both genders actively participated in the monasticism of the known early Buddhist schools. Each school had orders of both nuns and monks, with their own literatures tailored to their status and needs. The members of each nikāya followed distinctive—but historically and ideologically interrelated—sets of rules and regulations. A traditional convention had it that there were eighteen nikāyas, but there is evidence for more, up to twenty or even thirty. The numbers and lists fluctuated in the shifting landscape of South Asian Buddhism as nikāyas died out, merged with other nikāyas, and assumed new identities.

Tibetan tradition, inherited from India, counts four main monastic orders or Vinaya schools plus four schools of philosophical thought. These are regularly referred to in Tibetan manuals and doxographies (table 6).

TABLE 6. *Four Vinaya schools and four philosophical schools*

Four main monastic orders	*Four schools of philosophy*
Sarvāstivāda	Vaibhāṣika
Mahāsāṃghika	Sautrāntika
Sāṃmitīya	Yogācāra
Sthavira	Madhyamaka

The two categorizations had taken shape by the middle of the first millennium CE. The two sets of four are not equivalent; rather, they are distinctly different categories with distinctly different referents.

- The four Vinaya schools are celibate monastic orders. They are the leading representatives of the "eighteen schools" in northern India during the middle period. Each is part of a cluster of historical or doctrinal affiliates.
- The four philosophical schools are four predominant trends in Indian Buddhist philosophy as seen from a particular viewpoint (from northern India, or, more specifically, from Nālandā or Vikramaśīla monasteries) at a particular time.

The fourfold groupings are selective lists. The *first group* highlights the fact that amongst the eighteen Vinaya traditions, the Sarvāstivāda, Mahāsāṃghika, Sāṃmitīya, and Sthavira predominated by mid-millennium CE.

The *second group* lists the four schools of philosophical thought that flourished in northern India at mid-millennium. The four strands—Vaibhāṣika, Sautrāntika, Yogācāra, and Madhyamaka—are mentioned in scholastic literature from the time of the *Mahāvibhāṣā* on, and they were formalized in manuals or textbooks by the middle of the first millennium CE. We know this group from extant (largely north) Indian literature and from the fact that eventually the classifications became part of the curriculum of Tibetan monastic colleges from the turn of the millennium to the present. That is, the classification has been transposed with little change into Tibet's intellectual heritage. Different monastic orders and different philosophical schools would have flourished in regions of India other than the north, and this would have led to different curricular structures and different conversations and debates. But unfortunately, little evidence for the monastic and scholastic makeup of early southern Buddhism survives.

Sarvāstivāda/Mūlasarvāstivāda. A major cluster of northern Indian Vinaya schools that transmitted their scriptures in Sanskrit. These may have (logically, must have) been originally transmitted in Prakrit, but scarcely any information about the early phase survives. Which Prakrit, or which Prakrits, did the early Sarvāstivāda use? Why, when, and where did they begin to redact their texts in Sanskrit? All this remains unknown, although for the first question about which Prakrit was used, Gāndhārī is certainly one candidate for at least some of their scriptures. The school(s) spread widely across Asia, and the Tibetan and Mongolian saṅghas still follow the Mūlasarvāstivāda monastic tradition today. In Tibet, King Khri Ral pa can (alias Khri Gtsug lde btsan, r. 815–36 or 817–38?) decreed that no other nikāya apart from the Mūlasarvāstivāda was permittted, and that translations should be made from the Mūlasarvāstivāda canon only. That is, as a monastic order the Mūlasarvāstivāda lives on, and its literature is studied and commented on, in centers of Himalayan Buddhism. Historian Dung dkar Blo bzang 'phrin las (1927–97) explains that Khri Ral pa can wished to avoid dissension within

TABLE 7. *The panoply of Indian Buddhist schools*

There is no single authoritative list of the Indian Buddhist schools or monastic orders, which over the centuries numbered eighteen or more. The extant enumerations that are scattered in the widely different sources that are available today differ considerably according to period, place of compilation, and the school affiliation of the authors or compilers. For each school to tell its own story was a vital component of its formulation of its identity. This led to different configurations of inter-school relations and chronologies. This table is an approximation that attempts to give an idea of the complexity of Buddhist school development.

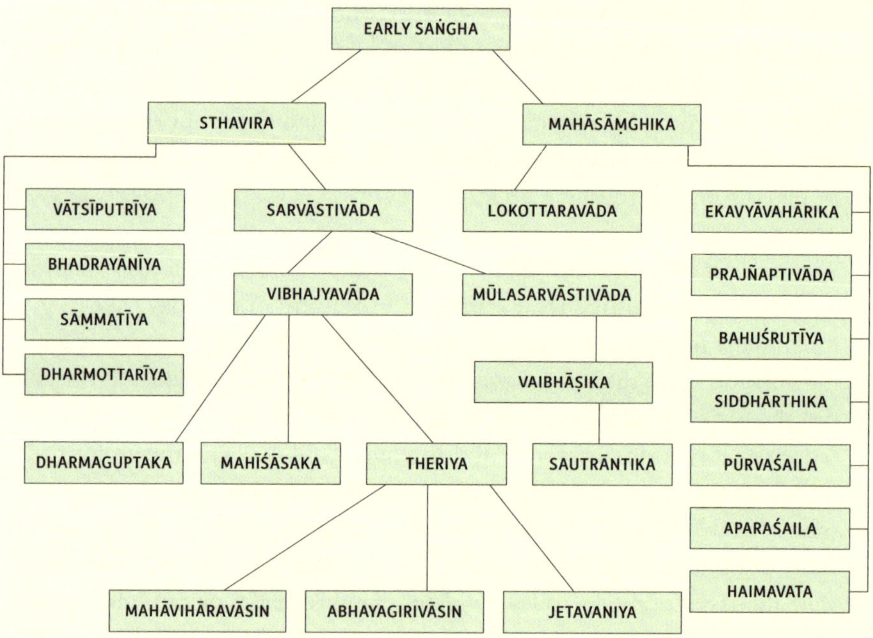

the ordained community so that "the Vinaya practice in Tibet would prevail [without conflict] as one [tradition]."[641]

I use Sarvāstivāda in the broad sense, including related schools like the Mūlasarvāstivāda. The relation between the two *terms*, the question of whether Sarvāstivāda and Mūlasarvāstivāda represent separate ordination lineages—that is, *monastic orders*—that coexisted, or whether they signify phases, regional variations, or repackagings of a single tradition, and whether each had its own distinctive Sūtrapiṭaka, are controversial and much debated. See most recently Hartmann, "Sanskrit Versions of the Āgamas," and Anālayo, "Mūlasarvāstivādin and Sarvāstivādin," both with reference to previous research. A recent publication by Giuseppe Vignato and Satomi Hiyama, *Traces of the Sarvāstivādins in the Buddhist Monasteries of Kucha*, throws new light on the early development of Sarvāstivāda monasteries and art along the northern Silk Road.

Mahāsāṃghika. Early school that transmitted its scriptures in Hybrid Sanskrit. Some sections of their Vinaya are preserved in Chinese translation, but apparently their Sūtrapiṭaka is lost. Apart from the titles of the four Āgamas, not even a list of its contents is known.

Lokottaravāda. A branch of the Mahāsāṃghika noted for its docetic tendencies. Some of the school's Vinaya texts texts survive in Buddhist Sanskrit, notably the *Mahāvastu*, the *Bhikṣuṇīvinaya* (monastic rules for nuns), and the monastic handbook *Abhisamācārikā Dharmāḥ*.

Sāṃmitīya. A branch of the Vātsīputrīya school, the last or last-known form of the complex of schools described by opponents as "personalist" (*pudgalavāda*)[642] By the seventh century, it was the largest monastic order in India. Only a few texts that preserve Indic forms of the name survive. These are specialized tracts produced by different schools in different periods and in different scholastic and linguistic environments, and they spell the name differently; as a result, it is hard to settle on a "correct" or "official" spelling. Attested spellings include at least Sāṃmitīya, Sāṃmatīya, Saṃvidī (*Hevajra Tantra*); epigraphic examples are Samitiya (inscription, second century), Sa[mma]tiya (inscription, fourth century). Pāli has Sammiti (*Dīpavaṃsa*,

641. Translation from Wangchuk, "Three Royal Decrees," p. 951.

642. See Skilling, "Rehabilitating the Pudgalavādins" and "The Vātsīputrīya/Sāṃmitīya: Buddhist Personalism."

Mahāvaṃsa), Sammitiya.[643] The spelling favored by the school itself might be Saṃmatīya. When available, the Tibetan translation is of these different forms is uniformly Mang pos bkur ba'i sde.

Theravāda. A branch of the early Sthavira (Thera) school that developed largely in Sri Lanka, South India, and Southeast Asia and transmitted its scriptures in the Pāli language. The two broad lines of transmission of the Buddhadharma from the early period were the Sthavira (Sthāvira, Theriya, Sthāvarīya) and the Mahāsāṃghika. The Sthavira line is also known as the Theravaṃsa or Theriya. The Theravāda we know today belongs to a lineage associated with the Vibhajyavāda in early India and the Mahāvihāra of Anurādhapura in Sri Lanka. Another important line, the Abhayagirivāsa, died out or was absorbed by the mainstream Mahāvihāra by the medieval period.

Theravaṃsa. Name for the broad Sthavira or Theriya lineage, "the lineage of schools claiming to descend from the early *theras*, the direct followers of Śākyamuni," of which Theravāda is a prominent descendant.

Dharmaguptaka. An early school related to the Vibhajyavāda and Theravāda lines of descent that seems to have flourished in the northwest and greater Gandhāra. Some of its important scriptures are preserved in Chinese translation, and it is generally concluded that many of the Gāndhārī texts studied over the past decades belong to a Dharmaguptaka transmission.

***yāna*.** Vehicle or road or spiritual path. A common classification lists three *yānas*:

> Śrāvakayāna, the vehicle of the disciples
> Pratyekabuddhayāna, the vehicle of the pratyekabuddhas
> Bodhisatvayāna, the vehicle of the bodhisatvas

The first two are subsumed under the name Hīnayāna—Lesser, Smaller, or

643. Śrī Puṇḍarīka's *Vimalaprabhā* commentary on the *Kālacakra* has Sāmmitīya (in a verse list of the four schools): Dwivedi and Bahulkar, *Vimalaprabhāṭīkā*, vol. 3, chap. 5, *Jñānapaṭala*, v. 52 (p. 35.1). On the name, see most recently Tournier, "Buddhist Lineages along the Southern Routes," p. 862, n. 9.

Inferior Vehicle—contrasted with Mahāyāna, the Great Vehicle or Great Way.[644]

The Śrāvaka schools do not recognize the terms Hīnayāna or Mahāyāna, and the yānas are not even mentioned in available Pāli and vernacular scriptures of any period. The Theras did not recognize the Mahāyāna claims, practices, or scriptures; they were unable to accept the very designation Mahāyāna, and their ideological and historiographical strategy seems to have been to ignore it. The few Pāli texts that address Mahāyāna developments use the Pāli terms *vetulla*, *vedalla*, or *vepulla*, three terms that were also used by other schools in their Sanskrit forms *vaitulya*, *vaidalya*, and *vaipulya*.[645]

Modern writings sometimes describe the Mahāyāna as a "movement." The Mahāyāna has been around for about two thousand years, and I do not think that this complex and long-lasting phenomenon fits into the notion of "movement" as generally conceived (and even less so, "reform movement"). Another possibility is "trend," which may seem better, but Mahāyāna thought and practice did not evolve as a single movement or a single trend, or even a conglomerate of trends that stood outside of Buddhism as a whole—and the idea of a two-thousand-year-old trend stretches belief. A variety of innovative and radical ideas and practices went under the banner of "Mahāyāna" and, at the same time, shared trends of thought and practice with the Śrāvaka schools in general, with all forms of Buddhism, including Bodhisatvayāna, and in some cases with South Asian religion in general. Trends—currents of practice and thought—were in constant flux across the subcontinent. Static and extraneous systems of classification only skew the picture.

Buddhism presents a bewildering number of hierarchical models for the paths and attainments. Some of these are historical, some are regional, some are entirely rhetorical. The map of the schools over time and across space is complex and difficult to negotiate. Modern teachers often present their preferred model as exclusive and absolute, while textbooks oversimplify to present classroom-ready versions.

naya. Method or system—for example, *mantra-naya* or *pāramitā-naya*: the system or modality that uses mantras or the system or modality that emphasizes the cultivatation of the pāramitās.

644. See Brunnhölzl, *Gone Beyond*, vol. 1, p. 683, n. 18.
645. See Skilling, "Vaidalya, Mahāyāna, and Bodhisatva in India."

Who's Who

There are two standard reference works for the names of the persons of the Buddha's circle: G. P. Malalasekera's *Dictionary of Pāli Proper Names* (1937) and Nyanaponika and Hecker's *Great Disciples of the Buddha* (English edition compiled from earlier works by the two authors and published in 1997). Both are reliable digests of material from the Pāli canon and commentaries. The explanations of other traditions, such as the Sarvāstivāda, sometimes differ, but regrettably so far there is no dictionary or handbook for the non-Pāli traditions.[646]

Monastics

Ānanda. Tib. Kun dga' bo.[647] Translation 15. A Śākya from Kapilavastu and one of Gautama Buddha's cousins, Ānanda accompanied him for many years as close personal attendant. Ānanda had a phenomenal memory, and Śākyamuni paid tribute to this by pronouncing him "foremost amongst those who are well versed (*bahuśruta*)." He also was known as the "treasurer of the Dharma" (*dhammabhaṇḍāgārika*). In the *Theragāthā* (v. 1031) he is described as

> *bahussuto dhammadharo kosārakkho mahesino*
> *cakkhu sabbassa lokassa pūjaneyyo bahussuto.*
>
> Well versed, bearer of the Dharma,
> guardian of the Great Sage's treasury,
> eye for all the world, worthy of reverence, deeply versed.

C. A. F. Rhys Davids translates the set of verses from the *Theragāthā* about Ānanda as follows:[648]

> Who in the Norm is widely versed,
> And bears its doctrines in his heart,

646. Tola and Dragonetti, "On the Names of Bhiksus and Bodhisattvas in the Lotus Sutra," is of limited use.
647. DPPN, vol. 1, pp. 249–68 (and esp. 262–63); *Encyclopaedia of Buddhism*, vol. 1, fasc. 4 (1965), pp. 529–36; Nyanaponika and Hecker, *Great Disciples of the Buddha*, chap. 4, is a pleasing hagiography compiled from Pāli sources. See especially pp. 150–54, "The Guardian of the Dhamma."
648. Rhys Davids, *Psalms of the Brethern*, p. 353.

Disciple of the Buddha, wise.
Eager to understand the Norm:
Such as he is, him follow ye. [1030]
Who in the Norm is widely versed,
And bears its doctrines in his heart,
Of the great Master's treasure Ward,
An eye is he for all the world,
Whom all should honour and revere
Who in the Norm is widely versed. [1031]
Who in the Norm takes his delight
Doth love and con it over well
And lets it live in memory
That brother from the holy Norm
Will ne'er secede or fall away. [1032]

Kāśyapa. Tib. 'Od srungs, Pāli Kassapa; also **Mahākāśyapa**, *'Od srungs chen po*, Pali *Mahākassapa*.[649] Translation 18. A monk, known by his brahman clan name, who was the foremost authority on the monastic rules.

Mahāmaudgalyāyana. Tib. Maud gal gyi bu chen po, Pāli Mahāmoggallāna.[650] Translation 18. A brahman from the village of Kolita in Magadha. The Buddha pronounced him "śrāvaka foremost in supernormal powers."

Cunda. Tib. Skul byed. Translation 18. A disciple of the Buddha. He appears in a number of sūtras, but there were several monks of this name, and his identity is not clear.[651]

Śāriputra. Sha ri'i bu, Pāli Sāriputta.[652] A brahman from a village in Magadha, near Nālandā, in modern Bihar. The Buddha pronounced him the "śrāvaka foremost in wisdom."

649. DPPN, vol. 2, pp. 476–83, s.v. "Mahā-Kassapa Thera"; Nyanaponika and Hecker, *Great Disciples*, chap. 3.
650. DPPN, vol. 2, pp. 541–47, s.v. "Mahā Moggallāna Thera"; Nyanaponika and Hecker, *Great Disciples*, chap. 2.
651. DPPN, vol. 1, pp. 876–80.
652. DPPN, vol. 2, pp. 1108–18, s.v. "Sāriputta Thera"; Nyanaponika and Hecker, *Great Disciples*, chap. 1. A classic study is Migot's *Un grand disciple du Buddha* (1954).

Abhibhū. Monk of brahman background, one of the past Buddha Sikhī's "excellent pair of disciples."[653]

Abhibhūta. Thera, disciple of Śākyamuni, whose verses are in the *Book of Threes* of the *Verses of Senior Monks*.[654]

Saṅghamittā.[655] Bhikkhunī; according to Sinhalese chronicles, a daughter of Aśoka who became a nun. She carried a sapling of the Bodhi Tree to Sri Lanka, where she was a key figure in the establishment of the order of nuns (*bhikkhunīsaṅgha*) on the island; this earned her the status of one of the foremost nuns in the Theravāda tradition.

Pūrṇika and five hundred arhats. According to Bu ston, members of the third redaction convened by Kaniṣka.

Vasumitra and five hundred bodhisatvas. According to Bu ston, members of the third redaction convened by King Kaniṣka.

Masters

Dates are approximate, given in broad centuries. Even then they may be contested.

Ānandaśrī. Paṇḍita; a Sri Lankan monk who traveled to central Tibet in the fourteenth century and worked at Thar pa gling with Thar pa Lo tsā ba, where they translated the "thirteen new translations," many of them Pāli parittas. See further under Thar pa Lo tsā ba below.

Aśvaghoṣa. Second century. Poet famed for his *Buddhacarita* and *Saundarananda* kāvyas.

Buddhaghosa, Ācariya.[656] Fifth century. Theravāda master who composed his works in line with the thought of the Mahāvihāra, the "Great Monas-

653. DPPN, vol. 1, p. 141.
654. DPPN, vol. 1, p. 142.
655. DPPN, vol. 2, p. 990.
656. DPPN, vol. 2, pp. 306–7.

tery" in Anurādhapura, Sri Lanka. Author of the *Path of Purification* (*Visuddhimagga*) and commentaries on the primary sutta collections of the Pāli canon.

Dharmatrāta. Tib. Chos skyob. Dates unknown. Compiler of the *Udānavarga*. See Lin Li-Kouang, *Introduction au Compendium de la Loi*, appendix 9, especially pp. 314–16.

Prajñāvarman. Tib. Shes rab go cha. Author of the *Udānavargavivaraṇa*, the masterful commentary on the *Udānavarga*, and several important commentaries on stotras. See Hartmann, "Poetry: South Asia."

Śamathadeva. Tib. Zhi gnas lha. Dates unknown. Monk from Nepal (Bal po) who compiled the *Indispensable Companion to the Treasury of Abhidharma*. Lost in Sanskrit and not known to have been translated into Chinese or any language other than Tibetan, this unique work is keyed to sūtra-master Vasubandhu's (frequent) citations of references to his canonical sources in his *Treasury*. Each time Vasubandhu cites or refers to a text, Śamathadeva supplies the source text, either an excerpt or the full text. As a result, this single work is the largest collection of Āgama material in Tibetan translation. See Skilling, "Conjured Buddhas," pp. 711–14.

Vātsīputra. Tib. Gnas ma bu. Founder of the Vātsīputrīya school. Dates or other biographical details are unknown.

Vasubandhu. Tib. Dbyig gnyen. Fourth century. One of the greatest scholars of middle-period Indian Buddhism. Author of the *Treasury of Abhidharma*, *Twenty Verses*, *Thirty Verses*, and commentaries on key texts of the Yogācāra tradition.

Vīryaśrīdatta. Author of the *Arthaviniścayasūtranibandhana*, composed at Nālandā during the reign of King Dharmapāla (ca. 750–800 CE). The work is known only from photos of a Sanskrit manuscript preserved in the K. P. Jayaswal Research Institute, Patna. There is no translation into Tibetan or Chinese.

Bu ston Rin chen grub (1290–1364). Sa skya pa scholar and master of scripture, celebrated inter alia for his *History of the Dharma* (*Chos 'byung*).

Tāranātha (1575–1634). Jo nang pa scholar who compiled a *History of the Dharma* (*Chos 'byung*) on the the basis of original Sanskrit language histories (now lost) and extant Tibetan-language sources.

Thar pa Lo tsā ba (Nyi ma rgyal mtshan dpal bzang po). "Translator from Thar pa," scholar and translator who resided at Thar pa gling Monastery in the fourteenth century. In addition to his translations of tantras, he translated with Ānandaśrī thirteen Theravāda texts, the *Gsar 'gyur gyi mdo*.[657]

Lay followers

Aśoka. Tib. Mya ngan med, Pāli Asoka.[658] King of Magadha in the Maurya dynasty, reigned at Pāṭaliputra. He is known from his own inscriptions, which are the earliest preserved ethical and political writings of India.[659] Otherwise known from legends in the Pāli vaṃsa and Sanskrit avadāna literature. The date and place of his death are unrecorded, and although as a great king he should have deserved a grand funeral and sepulchral monument, there is no record of such in either Indic texts or accounts of the Chinese pilgrim-scholars.

Bimbisāra (also Bimbasāra). Tib. Gzugs can snying po.[660] King of Magadha who reigned at Rājagṛha. He became a devoted disciple of the Buddha but was killed by his ambitious and unscrupulous son Ajātaśatru, who took the throne and himself became a devotee of the Buddha. Sponsor of the first redaction.

Prasenajit. Tib. Gsal rgyal, Pāli Pasenadi.[661] King of Kośala with his capital at Śrāvastī. Contemporary of the Buddha.

Mallikā. Prasenajit's queen, a devotee of the Buddha.[662]

Khujjuttarā. A laywoman who was nicknamed Khujjuttarā "Crooked

657. For Thar pa Lo tsā ba, Ānandaśrī, and Thar pa gling, see Skilling, "Theravādin Literature in Tibetan Translation," pp. 73–135.
658. DPPN, vol. 1, pp. 216–19.
659. See Olivelle, "Ashoka's Writings: New Insights into Ancient Indian Cultural History."
660. DPPN, vol. 2, pp. 285–89.
661. DPPN, vol. 2, pp. 168–74.
662. DPPN, vol. 2, pp. 455–57.

Uttarā" because she was born hunchbacked. She memorized the Buddha's teachings at Kauśāmbī (Pāli: Kosambī) and taught them to the nuns. See above, page 59, and DPPN, vol. 1, pp. 719–21.

Anāthapiṇḍada. Tib. Mgon med zas sbyin, Pāli Anāthapiṇḍika.[663] Various spellings are attested: in Bharhut inscriptions, Anāthapeḍika, and in Gāndhārī manuscripts, Aṇasapiḍia and Anaṣapiḍiga.[664] The name is from *a-nātha-piṇḍa-da*, "giver of food to the needy," or *a-nātha-piṇḍa-ka* with the same meaning, referring to the fabled charity of this wealthy merchant-banker of Śrāvastī. His name was Sudatta, but as he himself explained to the Buddha, "Because I give alms to the needy, people regularly call me 'the landowner Anāthapiṇḍada.'" In the Pāli "Chapter on the Foremost Disciples" of the *Aṅguttaranikāya*, the Buddha states that "foremost amongst donors is the householder Sudatta Anāthapiṇḍika."[665] In chapter 22 of the Khotanese *Book of Zambasta*, Śākyamuni predicts Anāthapiṇḍada's future connection with Maitreya: "he will then be Sudhana by name" and "will at that time buy a garden with clothing for Maitreya."[666]

Deities and supernatural beings

TABLE 8. *Hierarchies of the heavens*

The names and hierarchical position of the deities are cognate but not identical in the canonical and exegetical texts of the different schools. The significations of all the names are not clear, and at times the exegesis does not help much or seems forced. For a tabular presentation with reference to earlier charts, see Rotman, "The Cosmos According to the Divyāvadāna," *Divine Stories, Part 1*, appendix 2. See chap. 3 of *Treasury of Abhidharma* and table at Gelong Lodrö Sangpo, vol. 2, pp. 1078–79. For explanations of some of the complexities, see His Holiness the Dalai Lama, *Science and Philosophy*, vol. 1, especially part 5. Disquistions on the deities often include information about their lifespans or life expectancies. Huntington, *Creating the Universe*, gives vivid illustrations of Himalayan depictions of the realms.

663. DPPN, vol. 1, pp. 67–72; Nyanaponika and Hecker, *Great Disciples*, pp. 335–62.
664. With thanks to Mark Allon, 18 September 2021. For an earlier note on the name, see Lévi, "Observations sur la langue précanonique du bouddhisme," *Journal Asiatique* (July 1912): 495ff. Cf. BHSD, p. 22.
665. Bodhi, *Numerical Discourses*, p. 112.
666. Emmerick, *Book of Zambasta*, v. 209, pp. 318–19.

Sanskrit	Tibetan	Translations
kāmadhātu	**'dod pa'i khams**	**Desire Realm**
bhūta	'byung po	Spirit, ghost. Translation 15.
asura	lha ma yin	Antigod (*a-sura*); powerful, semidivine rivals of the gods who dwell below Mount Meru and periodically launch attacks on Indra's heaven, the Realm of the Thirty-Three. Translation 15.
• asurendra	lha ma yin gyi dbang po	Lord of the asuras. Translation 15.
• asurapreṣya	lha ma yin gyi mngag gzhug	Servant or agent of the asuras. The word seems to be rare. Translation 15.
Kāmeśvara	'dod pa'i dbang phyug	Lord of Desire. This refers to Māra (*bdud*). Lord of the Realm of Desire, the tempter, the Evil One. Māra wants to maintain his sway over the sensual realm and sensual pleasures—therefore he opposes buddhas or anyone who tries to attain or succeeds in attaining awakening. Translation 15, v. [9]; translation 18.
lokapāla	'jig rten skyong ba bzhi po	Four great kings or world guardians, the regents of the four quarters. Translations 12 and 15.
• Dhṛtarāṣṭra (east)	yul 'khor bsrung	
• Virūḍhaka (south)	'phags skye po	
• Virūpākṣa (west)	mig mi bzang	
• Vaiśravaṇa (north)	rnam thos kyi bu	
Trayastriṃśa	sum cu rtsa gsum pa'i lha	The Thirty-Three, referring to the gods and their heaven in Indra's abode atop Mount Meru.

Sanskrit	Tibetan	Translations
• Devendra, Devānāṃ Indra. Pali *devānam inda*	lha'i dbang po	Vedic deity, the lord of the gods who rules over the Realm of the Thirty-Three. Also known as Indra, Śakra, Sahassanaya.
• Śakra	brgya byin	See lha'i dbang po. Translation 13; 14 (Pali: Sakka); 15, v. [12]; 16, v. [1].
• Indra	dbang po	See Devendra.
Yāma	'thab bral ba	"Free of conflict." Name of a heaven.
Tuṣita	dga' ldan	"Contented." Name of a heaven.
Nirmāṇarata	'phrul dga'	Heaven of "gods who find pleasure in magical emanations"
Paranirmitavaśavartin	gzhan 'phrul dbang byed	Heaven of "gods who take control of others' magical emanations"
rūpadhātu	**gzugs kyi khams**	**Fine-Material Realm**
Brahmā	tshang pa	A class of gods on the plane of the first dhyāna. Translation 15.
Brahmāloka	tshang pa'i 'jig rten	World, plane, sphere, inhabited by Brahmā deities. See first dhyāna below.
pratyekabrahma	tshang pa so so	Pali *paccekabrahma*. Rare in the Āgamas, pratyekabrahmas figure in four suttas in the *Brahmasaṃyutta* of *Saṃyuttanikāya* (vol. 1, pp. 146–49). Cf. BHSD p. 379a, s.v. *pratyeka*, and Skilling, *Mahāsūtras* vol. 1, p. 8, § xxviii, pacceka-vasavattino. Lévi, *Mahākarmavibhaṅga*, p. 34.8, yathā Bakapratyekabrahmasūtraṃ.
prathama dhyāna lābhinaḥ	bsam gtan dang po	First Dhyāna
• Brahmakāyika	tshangs ris	Brahmā's Assembly

SANSKRIT	TIBETAN	TRANSLATIONS
• Brahmapurohita	tshangs pa mdun na 'don	Brahmā's Chaplains
• Mahābrahmā	tshangs pa chen po	Great Brahmā
dvitīya dhyāna lābhinaḥ	bsam gtan gnyis pa	Second Dhyāna
• Parīttābha	'od chung	Limited Splendor
• Apramāṇābha	'od tshad med	Immeasurable Splendor
• Ābhāsvara	'od gsal	Radiant
tṛtīya dhyāna lābhinaḥ	bsam gtan gsum pa	Third Dhyāna
• Parīttaśubha	dge chung	Limited Beauty
• Apramāṇaśubha	tsad med dge	Immeasurable Beauty
• Śubhakṛtsna	dge rgyas	Complete Beauty
caturtha dhyāna lābhinaḥ	bsam gtan bzhi pa	Fourth Dhyāna
• Anabhraka	sprin med	Unclouded
• Puṇyaprasava	bsod nams 'phel	Merit-Born
• Bṛhatphala	'bras bu che	Great Result
asaṃjñī		nonpercipient beings
śuddhāvāsa	gnas gtsang ma	pure abodes
• Abṛha	mi che ba	Not Great
• Atapa	mi gdung ba	Serene

Sanskrit	Tibetan	Translations
• Sudṛśa	gya nom pa	Good-Looking
• Sudarśana	shin tu mthong	Clear-Sighted
• Akaniṣṭha	'og min	Supreme
ārūpyadhātu	**gzugs med pa'i khams**	**Nonmaterial Realm**
Ākāśānantya-āyatana	nam mkha' mtha' yas skyed mched	Sphere of Endless Space
Vijñānānantya-āyatana	rnam shes mtha' yas skyed mched	Sphere of Endless Consciousness
Ākiṃcanya-āyatana	ci yang med pa'i skye mched	Sphere of Nothingness
Naivasaṃjñānāsaṃjñā-āyatana	'du shes med 'du shes med min skye mched	Sphere of Neither Percipience nor Nonpercipience
Vedic deities		
Īśāna, devaputra	lha'i bu dbang ldan	Pāli Īsāṇa. Translations 14 (from Pāli) and 15 (from Tibetan and Sanskrit). Īśāna has several roles: as an aspect of Śiva, as one of the eight dikpālakas, the guardian deities of the eight directions, who guards the northeastern direction; one of the eleven rudras of the Vedic pantheon representing the principles of prāṇa or life force.
Varuṇa, devaputra	lha'i bu chu lha	Vedic god of wind and waters. Translations 12, 14, and 15.
Prajāpati	skye dgu'i bdag po	Vedic deity. Translations 14 (Pali: Pajāpati) and 15.

Sanskrit	Tibetan	Translations
Others		
devatā, deva	lha	A god or deity.
devaputra	lha'i bu	Son of the gods. The Sanskrit/Tibetan versions (translation 12) describe Īśāna and Varuṇa as "devaputra."
devarāja	lha'i rgyal po	In the Pāli versions, Pajāpati, Varuṇa, and Īsāna are "devaputta" and Sakka is Devendra, "lord of the gods."
Vasumati		The earth, possessor of wealth. The Sanskrit has Vasumati, but the Tibetan simply sa, "earth." Translation 15.
Vasundharā		The earth, bearer of wealth. The Sanskrit has Vasundharā, but the Tibetan simply sa, "earth." Translation 15.

bhāṇaka. Reciter. One who has memorized and recites sections of scriptures.

dharma-bhāṇaka. Tib. *chos smra ba*. Reciter of the Dharma, preacher, raconteur. See *Questioning the Buddha*, pp. 28, 138–39.

The social landscape: India in Buddha's time

At the time of Gotama the Buddha, Indian society was defined by the interactions between agrarian and urban interests. Social roles were defined and determined by birth status

Vaṇij. Tib. *tshong pa*. Merchant.

brāhmaṇa. Tib. *bram ze*. In English spelled "brahmin" and "brahman." See Onions, *Oxford Dictionary of English Etymology*, p. 113: a "member of the priestly or learned caste of Hindus" by birth. See Yule and Burnell, *Hobson-Jobson*, pp. 111–12, s.v. "Brahmin, Brahman, Bramin." *Oxford English Dictionary*, vol. 2, pp. 477–78, gives a detailed account of the historical evolution of the English forms, explaining that "the form *Brahmin*, a corruption of the Indian vernacular pronunciation, is still all but universal in popular use; during the present [twentieth] century Orientalists have adopted the more correct *Brahman*, which (often written *Brâhman* or *Bráhman*) is employed by most writers in India." Also Barnhart, *Chambers Dictionary of Etymology*, p. 112.

śramaṇa. Tib. *dge sbyong*, Pāli *samaṇa*. Ascetic, recluse, renunciant, including Buddhist and non-Buddhist renouncers, such as followers of the Jain or other systems. Śramaṇas are regularly contrasted with the brahmans, members of the priestly or ritual caste, and the compound *śramaṇa-brāhmaṇa* is used as an inclusive term for the religieux of the time of the Buddha and Aśoka.

Brahmanism. Refers to the ideological-ritual system rather than the brahmans as caste, although the two are often difficult or impossible to disentangle. An important social distinction is that the Brahmanical system was closed to non-brahmans, while the śramanic system was open to all, regardless of birth (although there must have been variations within this general rule). Non-brahmans were effectively barred from practicing or studying within the Brahmanical system, but members of the brahman caste could, and did, participate in the śramaṇa movements. Some of Gautama the Buddha's monastic disciples were caste brahmans, including such prominent figures as Śāriputra, Maudgalyāyana, Mahākāśyapa, and Mahākātyāyana. Early sūtras, especially the long texts of the *Dīrghāgamas*, report dialogues between the Buddha and leading members of the Brahmanical communities of the time. Through discussion and debate, the Buddha convinces his erstwhile opponents of the logic of his ideas and system, and they take refuge in the Buddha, join the Saṅgha, and undertake to practice his Dharma. In the later period, brahmans continued to play an important role in Buddhism: for example, the Great Brahman, Saraha—tantric master, visionary, and composer of enigmatic *dohā* verses.

Caste and other biases were pervasive in Indian society, to the point that relatively early śramaṇa texts specified that members of only two castes, brahmans and kṣatriyas, were able to become buddhas or jinas (in both cases, males only). Narrative texts like jātakas naturalized caste as a social constant that has always existed and will exist even in past and future eons and in different world systems; Buddhist editors took the Indian social system for granted as a universal framework, a kind of perduring cosmic backdrop. On the other hand, admission to the Buddhist monastic order was open to all castes and classes, male or female. The Buddha affirmed that women could reach the highest goal, that of worthy arhat, and literature shows that many of the nuns did just that.

Compromises with the caste system did develop, but the details are unclear owing to the lack of contemporaneous social records. A summarized or standardized description of the four orders or nikāyas relates their leaders to the four castes, but it is impossible to determine what this meant in actual social practice.[667] The ordination lineages that developed in the Sri Lankan saṅgha were determined by local caste, regional, and social status.

tīrthaṃkara. Tib. *mu stegs byed pa*, Pali *titthakara*. In early Buddhist vocabulary, religious specialists ("religieux") are described as "śramaṇas and brāhmaṇas" or "śramaṇas or brāhmaṇas"—a terminology that is attested in the mid-third-century BCE inscriptions of Emperor Aśoka. *Śramaṇa* (Pāli: *samaṇa*, Tib. *dge sbyong*) were men and women who took vows in a range of non-Brahmanical systems. "Brāhmaṇa" (Tib. *bram ze*) here comprises Vedic specialists or ritual masters. They are brahmans by birth and caste, but in this phrase they are not defined by caste alone but by their active participation in the Brahmanical or Vedic knowledge and social system. We know this because caste brahmans could engage in other religious activities and, for example, could become Jain or Buddhist ascetics (see preceding entry).

Amongst the motley crew of religieux seen in Buddhist texts is the *tīrthaṃkara* (Pāli: *titthakara*, Tib. *mu stegs byed pa*). A *tīrthaṃkara* or "ford-crosser," "ford-maker," is an exceptional individual who crosses the ford and leads others across as well. He (all, or nearly all, are males) is a spiritual leader who crosses from this shore of the ocean or flood of saṃsāra, our everyday world, to the other shore of nirvāṇa. Childers defined the term as "a sect-founder, religious teacher"; Edgerton noted that the word is "used by Jains of their own sect-founder; in [Buddhist Hybrid Sanskrit] as in Pali always pejorative, of heretics . . . heretical sectarian, heresiarch, founder of a heresy."[668]

667. One of the early textual studies was in Vassilief, *Le Bouddhisme* (French version, 1863), pp. 270–71, followed nearly a century later by Lin Li-Kouang, *L'aide-mémoire de la vraie Loi* (1949), pp. 176–89.

668. Childers, *Dictionary*, p. 509; Edgerton, BHSD, p. 254, s.v. *tīrtha-kara*. Doctor Johnson explicates *heresiarch* nicely as "the head of a herd of hereticks" in Lynch, *Samuel Johnson's Dictionary*, p. 00.

Tīrthaṃkara/titthakara belongs to a family of terms that derive from *tīrtha* (Tib. *'bab stegs*, Pāli: *tittha*): "ford," *literally* a ford or crossing, a landing, or bathing place, a confluence of rivers and a place of pilgrimage, and *metaphorically* a place of spiritual crossing, a passage across the stream of saṃsāra to the "other shore" of liberation and release.[669] In Hinduism *tīrtha* is a core concept that has animated India's vibrant pilgrimage and spiritual cultures from antiquity to today. Buddhist usage adds the applied sense of *sect*, "always with bad connotation. Promising to lead its votaries over into salvation, it only leads them into error."[670] Cognate terms are **tīrthya**, **tīrthika** (Tib. *mu stegs pa, mu stegs can*, Pāli: *titthika, titthiya*), which refer to certain śramaṇas, both leaders and their followers, and their doctrine and practices.[671]

The use of the term in translation 10 harks back to an age when vocabulary was shared across the broader South Asian society and was not yet partitioned into the exclusive domains of competing religious groups. Foundational terms Dhamma, Vinaya, and Dhamma-vinaya, *karma/kamma* and *saṃsāra*, are shared by all or most śramaṇa groups. Even words for spiritually realized masters like *jina*, "conqueror or victor," and *arhant* (Jain Prakrit *arahant*), "perfected saint," are all shared.

Notions connected with *tīrtha* have specific, and changing, referents. Understanding the ideas and practices of the *tīrthyas* in context helps us understand the social and philosophical dimensions of the Buddhist scriptures. Easy blanket terms like "non-Buddhist" do not produce reflection or lead to knowledge, and I tend towards treating the *tīrthya* family as untranslatables. The identification of Gautama in past lives when he was a bodhisatva with previous teachers like Araka (translation 10), all of them described as *titthakaras*, shows an early Buddhist strand of tolerance and accommodation for at least śramaṇa lineages with similar teachings.

Since the nineteenth-century beginnings of discourse on Buddhism, *tīrthya*, *tīrthika*, and cognate terms have been regularly rendered as "heretic"—a rendering that stands at the top of my list of persistent and pernicious mistranslations in Buddhist contexts. *Heresy* belongs to a cluster of words that

669. See Eck, *India: A Sacred Geography*, pp. 7–11.

670. PTSD, p. 302. See also DoP, vol. 2, pp. 324–26. In Buddhist usage the term is *usually* but *not always* perjorative and does not always "have a bad connotation": see Skilling, "Driving the Heretics Out of Buddhist Translations," in progress.

671. Cone, DoP, vol. 2, p. 325, s.v. *titthiya*, "an adherent of another sect: a non-Buddhist ascetic."

are deeply associated with intolerance—with notions of orthodoxy, unorthodoxy, and apostasy, with dogmatic forms of institutional religion and, historically, with ecclesiastical Catholicism. As out of place as "heathen" or "idolator," "heretic" doesn't even make sense in early South Asian or Buddhist discourse.[672]

Today "heresy" has been secularized and normalized and has gained a thoroughly nonreligious sense, which may refer to religious, political, or social nonconformity or dissidence, to resistance to coercive theological or ideological impositions (*samāropa*).[673]

The Buddhadharma was inclusive and welcoming, and non-Buddhists could play positive literary roles—as, for example, the Nirgrantha Satyaka teaches the Buddhadharma in the *Satyakaparivarta*. From the time of the Master on, some of the leading monastics were brahmans. I wonder whether the notion of "non-Buddhist" existed as a label for *people*, as individuals or as groups, even admitting we have no demographies. Non-Buddhist *views* were many, and sixty-two were catalogued in the *Brahmajālasūtra*, an early text transmitted by several different nikāyas. That the views were "non-Buddhist" was self-evident, but this was not quite the point. They were *wrong* views with specific identities: eternalist views, annihilationist views, hedonistic views, and so on.

Where's Where

For Kumārajīva's conspectus on the places where the Buddha stayed and why he chose them, see, with Lamotte's annotations, *Le Traité*, vol. 1, pp. 169–97. For Kośala, Śrāvastī, and Kapilavastu, see Lamotte, *Le Traité*, vol. 1, pp. 175–79. The module used for Śākyamuni's travels through the countryside is **janapada-cārika** (Tib. *yul rgyu*, *yul ljongs rgyu*), frequent in narrative set-

672. See Doctor Johnson in Lynch, *Samuel Johnson's Dictionary*, s.v. *heathen*: "the gentiles, the pagans; the nations unacquainted with the covenant of grace" (p. 237). For *heresy* he gives "an opinion of private men different from that of the catholick and orthodox church" (p. 240). In later periods, as more exclusivist ideologies took root, it may be possible to speak of heresy and heretics. See Crosby, "The Shared Origins of Traditionalism and Secularism in Theravāda Buddhism," especially pp. 154–59.

673. *Heresy*'s many meanings may be seen by consulting a thesaurus. See, for example, *Roget's International Thesaurus*, 3rd ed. (Collins, 1977): "unconformity," § 83 (p. 39); "apostate," § 626.5 (p. 411); "unorthodoxy," § 1023 (pp. 647–48).

tings of the teachings. For Vasubandhu on why the Buddha and his disciples traveled, see box 3.

Markaṭahrada. Tib. *Spre'u rdzing*. Monkey Pond: a body of water at Vaiśālī said to have been dug by monkeys. Lamotte, *Le Traité*, vol. 1, p. 183.

kūṭāgāra. Tib. *khang pa brtsegs pa'i gnas*. A gabled house: a structure said to exist at several early monastic centers. What kind of building should we expect at the time of Gautama the Buddha? No structures of the period survive, and scarcely even any foundations. The early stone relief carvings do not begin until the fourth century post-nirvāṇa (fourth century BE = second to first century BCE). These may represent "gabled houses," but it is not clear whether the structures depicted would have been the same as those of several centuries earlier.

Śrāvastī. Tib. *Myan yod*, *Mnyan du yod pa*. In present-day Uttar Pradesh, northern India. One of the major cities of northern India at the time of the Buddha. Here the Buddha stayed for many rainy seasons, mostly at the center established by his wealthy supporter, the merchant-banker of Śrāvastī Sudatta, known as Anāthapiṇḍada.

Jetavana. A park outside the city of Śrāvastī that originally belonged to Prince Jeta. *Rgyal bu rgyal byed kyi tshal* became the standard Tibetan translation (see *Mahāvyutpatti*, § 4112), used in hundreds of Kanjur and Tanjur translations. A few texts, such as the *Vinayottaragrantha* and *Vinayakṣudrakavastu*, use instead the transliteration *Dze ta'i tshal* (Jeta + *tshal*, Tibetan for *vana*).

Anāthapiṇḍada's Garden. The garden or park that Anāthapiṇḍada offered to the Buddha as residence and center after he had bought Prince Jeta's Grove at Śrāvastī. *Ārāma*, "pleasance or pleasure garden," Tib. *kun dga' ra ba*, came to mean "monastic center" in Buddhist usage.[674]

The story of how Anāthapiṇḍada first meets the Buddha, invites him to Śrāvastī, purchases a park for an outlandish sum from Prince Jeta, and offers it to the Buddha is told in the *Śayanāsana-* and *Saṅghabheda-vastus* of the

674. See Upasak, *Dictionary of Early Buddhist Monastic Terms*, pp. 30–31.

Mūlasarvāstivāda Vinaya.[675] Malalasekera gives an elaborate description of the Jetavana according to Pāli sources.[676] He notes, "The vihāra is almost always referred to as *Jetavane Anāthapiṇḍikassa Ārāma*. The Commentaries say that this was deliberate, in order that the names of both earlier and later owners might be recorded and that people might be reminded of two men, both very generous in the cause of the Religion, so that others might follow their example."

For Pāli traditions of Anāthapiṇḍika, see Malalasekera, DPPN, vol. 1, pp. 67–72.

Takṣaśilā. Tib. *Yul rdo 'jog*. Modern Taxila, Punjab, Pakistan. A well-known city of ancient times, when it was a center of education, culture, and trade. Excavated by colonial archaeologist Sir John Marshall and later by Pakistani archaeologists. Extensive stūpa and vihāra complexes have been uncovered along with a wealth of Gandhāran art.

Gandhāra. Gandhāra, a region, area, or kingdom in the northeast of ancient India. Situated on the grand trade routes, it was a cosmopolitan center of cultural exchange, which during the Kuṣāṇa era (approximately second century BCE–third century CE) developed a thriving "Indo-Greek" culture incorporating ideas, motifs, and styles from Hellenic Asia.

Lumbinī. Gautama the Buddha's birthplace. Memorialized by King Aśoka with an inscribed stone pillar.

Bodh Gayā. District Gaya, Bihar, India; here Gautama the Buddha awakened beneath the Bo or Bodhi tree.

Uttarāpatha. The "northern route" that led across northern India, linking the major cities of the Ganga plain up to Gandhāra and beyond. It intersected with the Dakṣiṇapatha, the Southern Route that led across the Ganga-Yamuna plains and the Vindhya Range to the south, the Deccan Plateau. The two routes were complex communication networks that carried trade and culture across and beyond the subcontinent.

675. Gnoli, *The Gilgit Manuscript of the Śayanāsanavastu and Adhikaraṇavastu*, pp. 14–27; trans. Schopen, "Hierarchy and History in a Buddhist Monastic Code," pp. 112–26.
676. Malalasekera, DPPN, vol. 1, pp. 963–66.

Gaṅgā River. Skt. Gaṅgānadī, Tib. *gang ga'i klung*. The great river of northern India, anglicized as Ganges. One of the four or five great rivers of Jambudvīpa: see Lamotte, *Le Traité*, vol. 1, p. 385, n. 1. The fine sand of the Gaṅgā River (*gaṅgānadīvālukā*/*-vālikā*, *gang ga'i klung gi bye ma*, or of the Gaṅgā River multiplied many times over, is frequently used as a figure for a vast number or infinitude. See Buswell and Lopez, *Princeton Dictionary*, p. 312.

Vaiśālī. Tib. *Yangs pa'i grong khyer*, *Yangs pa can*.[677] The important ancient city of Vaiśālī often figures into episodes in the Buddha's life. Its site was identified by Alexander Cunningham in the 1840s.[678]

Licchavi. The people of the Vṛji *janapada* (see below).

Vṛji. Tib. *Yul bri dzi*, *Yul spongs byed*. An ancient republic, one of the sixteen *janapada* or *mahājanapada* (polities, states: see Lamotte, *Histoire*, pp. 8–9) of ancient India. Its political center was at Vaiśālī, in modern north Bihar.

Āmrapālīvana. Tib. *A mra srung ba'i tshal*, *Ā mra'i tshal*. Translation 15. Mango grove at Vaiśālī belonging to the famed courtesan Āmrapālī.

Rājagṛha. Tib. *Rgyal po'i khab*, Pāli Rājagaha. The royal citadel, early capital of the kings Śreṇya Bimbisāra and Ajātaśatru, set amidst formidable hills and protected by strong fortifications.[679] Site of the first recitation-convocation after Śākyamuni's death. Modern Rajgir in Bihar state. Mahāsūtra 10.C.1.a only.

- **Veṇuvana**. Monastery donated by King Bimbisāra to the Buddha during the latter's first post-enlightenment visit.
- **Karandakanivāpa**. Another monastery at Rājagṛha.
- **Vulture Peak**. Skt. *Gṛdhrakūṭa*, Tib. *Bya rgod phung po'i ri*, Pāli *Gijjhakūṭa*. A peak in Rājagṛha; Śākyamuni visited several times and delivered important sermons there, including the *Perfection of Wisdom* and the *Lotus Sūtra*. Brunnhölzl, *Gone Beyond*, vol. 1, p. 28, "Vulture Flock

677. Lamotte, *Le Traité*, vol. 1, p. 183 and n. 1.
678. Singh, *Discovery of Ancient India*, pp. 39, 63, 112, 120.
679. For the Buddha's reasons for staying at Rājagṛha and on Vulture's Peak, see Lamotte, *Le Traité*, vol. 1, pp. 179–97.

Mountain"; for traditional explanations of the name, see Brunnhölzl, *Gone Beyond*, vol. 1, p. 685, n. 28.

Patna. Site of ancient Pāṭaliputra on the south bank of the Gaṅgā River; seat of the Maurya dynasty from the time of Ajātaśatru on. Capital of the modern state of Bihar. Located here are the Patna Museum and the K. P. Jayaswal Research Institute, which houses inter alia the archives of manuscripts in Sanskrit, Prakrit, and Tibetan photographed by Rahul Sankrityayan (Rāhula Sāṅkr̥tyāyana, 1893–1963) during his research expeditions to Tibet in the 1930s.

Bihar. Modern state of the Republic of India with its capital at Patna. The name derives from *vihāra*, monastery, reflecting how for centuries this was a center of Buddhist monasticism and activity.

Aruṇavatī. Mythical capital city during the time of the Buddha Sikhī.

Thar pa gling. A monastery in Gtsang, central Tibet, not far south of Zha lu.

Siam. Early offical name of Thailand, up to the mid-twentieth century. Still in use for the area of central Thailand prior to the twentieth century and as a signifier for the historical and cultural entity that is now "Thailand."

Rgya gar. Tibetan term for India.

Kha che. Tibetan term for Kashmir.

What's What

Literary terms

The following terms are not translations from Tibetan or from ancient Indic languages. They are words that exist in their own right in the marvelous and mysterious English tongue. Some are used in Buddhist (and Indian and religious) studies, and others I use throughout the course of the book.

Our daily terminologies teem with multiple meanings. Language and meanings change over time: consider, for example, the passage of material objects like "tablet," "icon," and "notebook" from their pre-computer to their computer-age significations. Words used here like "community" and "culture" become increasingly complicated as different disciplines define, revise, refine, and redefine their technical vocabularies in ways that impact upon the way we speak or are expected to speak. Barbara Cassin's *Dictionary of Untranslatables* devotes over ten pages to "consciousness" (pp. 174–86) without even mentioning the complex and evolving terminologies of Indian and Buddhist philosophy and psychology, which describe assorted *vijñānas* plus a brace of other terms. "Reality" gets just under ten pages (pp. 879–87), but those who are interested in the topic may benefit from recent publications on the topic.[680] A *Dictionary of Buddhist Untranslatables* may not be on anyone's wish list in this age of quick fixes and soundbite solutions, but if one were ever to be made, rather than a slim volume it would be something the size of the *Gaṇḍavyūhasūtra* or Joyce's *Ulysses*.

author, authorship. Notions of author and authorship continue to be under de- and re-construction in the academies. The parameters for authorship in antiquity differ from those of modernity, and the discussions are decidedly Eurocentric: such academic endeavors rarely bring notions of authorship in India or in Buddhism into the picture. Leaving polemics behind, it is safe to say that in writing, or in trying to write, histories of Buddhism, dates and biographical details pose insuperable problems. For most authors we have neither, and we end up comparing one undated author to other undated authors, all from unknown, unidentified, or uncertain places. Because the lack of reliable sources precludes us from writing "a treatise by Devaśarma," we are obliged to be noncommital and write that the treatise is "ascribed" or "attributed" to Devaśarma. Verifying authorship is a general problem in the study of literature and the arts worldwide, to the point that a statement like "After a lifetime of research, the erudite Professors Dupont and Dupond have come to the startling conclusion that the works of Shakespeare were written by someone named Shakespeare" makes perfect, well, sense. Romantic notions of original authorship, the author's formation through social or spiritual struggle, her or his genius and the stamp of the zeitgeist: all play in the imaginations of authorial biographies. Buddhist hagiographies—from the lives of the early saints, to the South and Central Asian siddhas and thaumaturges, to the Tibetan tradition of writing biography as a "tale of liberation" with "inner" and "outer" biographies—follow different parameters of the imagination.

680. For the chimera of "reality," see Westerhoff's *Reality: A Very Short Introduction* and *The Non-Existence of the Real World*.

text. The meaning of the word *text* has changed and changed again with the ineluctable march of time and the mind-boggling somersaults of technology. Raymond Williams did not include *text* in his *Keywords* (1976), but forty years later *Keywords for Today* opens its entry with "In the beginning was the word, now there is [the] text." It goes on to say, "The meanings of this widely used and problematic term follow a media transformation that has taken place over the past century, from script through print to communications by words-on-screen."[681] Text began as scripture, written language with the authority of God. The meaning now is a "text message," as in French *texto*. And *text* has become a verb, an ephemeral instantaneous medium of conversation that now wields a scepter equal to God's word.

I use the word a lot—too much, perhaps, for my liking, for want of any better term or from my native dullness and lack of imagination. In my writing, "text" is a rather staid term meaning simply (as if meaning can ever be simple) "what is on the written, or oral, page."

Box 14. *"Story" by David Crystal*

"People tell stories about their stories at bookfests. It's interesting how the meaning of this word has come full circle. Originally, in the thirteenth century, stories had to be true: the word was a synonym for "history"—indeed, it came from Latin *historia*. But very soon it was applied to stories alleged to be true, and then (by the sixteenth century) to stories that were definitely not true. Today, the original meaning seems to be reasserting itself: I've lost track of the number of historical television programmes called 'The Story of Something-or-Other.' Maybe it's time to resuscitate the verb use too. In the sixteenth century, there was a splendid usage: to story forth, meaning 'to proclaim the story of.'"[682]

This reminds me of the story of the old lady who borrowed a dictionary from her municipal library. She returned it with the comment: "A *very* unusual book indeed—but the stories are extremely short, aren't they?"[683]

681. MacCabe and Yanacek, *Keywords for Today*, pp. 550–55.
682. "David Crystal's Edinburgh Linguistry," *The Times*, 8 August 2007 (written to celebrate the Edinburgh Book Festival in 2007).
683. Eric Partridge, *The Gentle Art of Lexicography*, p. 14.

discourse. Here too is a word with a long history. See glossary under *sūtra*, which has been translated as "discourse" since at least Childers' *Dictionary of the Pāli Language* (1875). See Cassin, *Dictionary of Untranslatables*, pp. 223–24.

scrap. Fragment, shred, remnant. See following snippet.

fragment. Buddhist literature survives in fragments and scraps, as sherds of pots of plenty that in ancient times overflowed with streams of story. This means broken portions of manuscripts that have survived in ruins, caves, or other neglected and unprotected places; in some (most) cases these manuscripts have been shredded, torn, or burnt by accident or design, or have been nibbled at by hungry creatures. This is especially the case with Indic language texts because during Buddhism's long demise in South and Central Asia, no Buddhists were left to care for them. The manuscripts that survived did so because they were protected by the debris of the abandoned monasteries in which they were buried, until such time as they were recovered by treasure hunters or archaeological expeditions. Scholars patiently piece together the jigsaw of fragments, some with only one or two broken letters, and by comparing them to parallel texts in Sanskrit, Pāli, Chinese, or Tibetan—whichever is or are available—try to make sense of and then restore the text. To put the Humpty Dumpty of a Buddhist text back together again is a stimulating and challenging intellectual occupation.

The result of this is that our knowledge is fragmented and scrappy. The objects of knowledge are fragmentary and scrappy. We study manuscript fragments, textual morsels, remnants of murals, statues, and buildings. We reconstruct narratives and histories of the phases of ideas and metaphysical systems from fragments with gaps of whole centuries or for huge areas and regions.

editio princeps. First printed edition of a work that had previously existed only in manuscript form; a Latin term adopted by other disciplines from classical scholarship.

lacuna. A gap, an unfilled space or interval; especially, a missing portion in a manuscript caused by physical damage or errors of copying, translation, printing, and so on. From Latin *lacus*, lake or pool; adopted in English in the seventeenth century. Related to *lagoon*, a different sort of lake.

colophon. A wonderful but elusive thing: a passage, usually at the end of a text, that gives paratextual information—date of composition and/or copying; names of the author, scribes, and/or sponsors; aspirations or intentions of those who produced the manuscript; and the like. In the mainstream Kanjurs (the Tshal pa xylographs and the manuscripts in the Them spangs ma line), most colophons are "translators' colophons" that name the Indian and Tibetan scholars who produced the translation—and not much else. Technical literature, the *śāstra* or *bstan bcos*, is usually authored and hence often has author's colophons. For Indic colophons, see von Hinüber, "On the Early History of Indic Buddhist Colophons." Otherwise, colophonography is sadly neglected.

citation. Quote, quotation: an excerpt from a text or published work. Pearsall, *New Oxford Dictionary of English* (2001), p. 334, "a quotation from or reference to a book, paper, or author, especially in a scholarly work." I use the word in this sense. Latterly it is used to mean the *details* of the source alone (author, title, publisher, date, etc.) and not the *actual quote*. The *contents* of the citations, the quoted material, has become irrelevant as authors line their cloaks with citations to feed the computer-driven rackets that have taken over academia.

typo. Pāli *pamādalekha*. Typographical error: a typing mistake that is invisible until you see it. See above, p. 248 and n. 247.

mainstream. As a lowercase adjective, a practice or concept that is common or shared. *Mainstream* is a word to be used responsibly, with restraint, such as in this quotation from Richard Salomon: "the mainstream sūtras are typically the most stable part of Buddhist canons across space and time."[684]

recitation-convocation. Skt. *saṃgīti*, Pāli *saṃgīti/saṅgīti*, also *saṅgāyanā*. Often translated as "(Buddhist) council." A congregation or assembly of a saṅgha to recite and verify its scriptural tradition. See Edgerton, BHSD, pp. 547–48, s.v, *saṃgīti*; PTSD, pp. 666–67.

collecting of the Dharma. Tib. *chos bsdu ba*, Skt. **dharmasaṃgraha*, cp. Pāli *dhammasaṅgaha*. Editorial convocation equivalent to *dharmasaṃgīti*.

684. Salomon, *Buddhist Literature of Ancient Gandhāra*, p. 364.

Third Theravādin Council. According to middle-period Pāli sources, convocation held at Pāṭaliputra, convened under King Aśoka, presided over by Moggaliputta Tissa Thera. About 210 post-nirvāṇa (circa mid third century BCE).

Third Buddhist Council. According to non-Pāli (Tibetan and Chinese) sources, a convocation held in northwestern India, convened under King Kaniṣka.

redactor. Skt. *saṃgītikāra*. Editor and curator of Buddhist scriptures. Described as *saṃgītikāra-sthaviras*, "senior monks who conducted the redactions," in the Mūlasarvāstivāda *Vinayavastu* (Gnoli, *Saṅghabhedavastu*, vol. 1, p. 181.14); *Śayanāsanavastu*, p. 27.15 (see Schopen, *Buddhist Monks and Business Matters*, pp. 395–407); *Śrāvakabhūmi* (Śrāvakabhūmi Study Group, p. 226.ult). Same form in Pāli; see PTSD, p. 666, s.v. *saṃgīti*; Childers, *Dictionary of the Pāli Language*, p. 450, *saṅgīti*.[685] Salvini translates *saṃgītikāra* as "makers of the communal chanting" (see box 2). That redactors played a major role in the formation and transmission of the Buddha's teachings tends to be ignored by modern scholarship, which treats the received scriptures almost as if they were transcripts of the Master's speech.

Word values change. "Redact" and cognate forms now carry negative implications that I do not think were there when I started my studies half a century ago. "Redaction" has become quite disreputable; it now means an edited, truncated, or censored verson of a testimony or report released by an official body.

scholar. Since Shakespeare's time this word has had several meanings, including "a learned man, erudite person [who knows Latin, the language of exorcism]."[686] C. A. F. Rhys Davids says, "The scholar is a hopeful animal who

685. Some further inchoate notes: PTSD, p. 666, *saṅgahaka*, making a recension; *Jātaka* vol. 1, p. 1, v. 6d, *jātakaṃ nāma saṃgītaṃ dhammasaṃgāhakehi yaṃ*; Trenckner, *Milindapañho*, p. 369.2, *bhāsitam p'etaṃ mahārāja therehi dhammasaṅgāhakehi*; Hardy, *Vimānavatthu-aṭṭhakathā*, p. 169.26, *saṅgītikāle āyasmatā nāradena dhammasaṅgāhakānaṃ ārocito te ca nam tath'eva saṅgahaṃ āropayiṃsu*; p. 172.25, *āyasmā pi vaṅgīso saṅgītikāle dhammasaṅgāhakānāṃ mahātherānaṃ ārocesi, te ca therā naṃ tath'eva saṅgītiṃ āropayiṃsu*; *Chaddanta-jātaka* (*Tiṃsanipāta*, vol. 5, p. 56.9, *imā gāthā dasabalassa guṇe vaṇṇentehi dhamma-saṃgāyika-ttherā ṭhapitā*; Syāmaraṭṭha, vol. 7, p. 254.5, *imā gāthā dasabalassa guṇe vaṇṇentehi dhamma-saṅgāhakattherehi ṭhapitā*.

686. Crystal and Crystal, *Shakespeare's Words*, p. 386.

will accept work he has neither time nor serious intention to take up without delay" ("General Note," introducing G. P. Malalasekera's monumental *Dictionary of Pāli Proper Names*). Related words are "specialist," "authority," "intellectual," "expert," and "pundit." "Scholarly" once carried an aura of "neutral, balanced, unprejudiced," but today this secure status is challenged by the harsh rhetorics of postmodernity. See following.

academic. As a noun, one who works in an academy or institute of higher education. In the eyes of society at large, academics have generally been seen as harmless drudges, but in today's increasingly polarized and politicized world, academics are often viewed with suspicion and treated with aspersion. In the eyes of those who have better things to do (making or spending money, for example), academic endeavor and discussion are a waste of time; hence "academic" has the applied senses of "insignificant," "trivial."

practitioner. This term is widely used in contemporary Buddhist discourse but is rarely defined. Evidently it means a committed individual who engages in some sort of Buddhist praxis, especially meditation or ritual practice, in contrast to scholars or academics who are or profess to be sympathetic to the Buddhadharma but do not follow any of its practices. In traditional terms, to be a *practicing Buddhist* means to take the three refuges and adhere to the five or a certain number of moral codes.

The concept of "practice" has different connotations in different religions. "Catholic practitioner" or "Protestant practitioner," and so on, seem rare, while "practicing Catholic," "practicing Quaker," "practicing Sufi," or, indeed, "practicing Buddhist," have a different sense. In the current discourse of Anglophone Buddhists, the "practitioner" seems to be accorded a high status, below "teachers" but above the larger numbers of uncommitted individuals who are sympathetic to and "interested in" Buddhism. Further precisions as to what this term means, the history of its use in religious studies, and the ways in which it corresponds or does not correspond to the categories of traditional Buddhist and non-Buddhist societies would be useful.[687]

epigraphy. The study and interpretation of inscriptions and lettering systems.

687. The *Oxford Handbook of Buddhist Practice* (2022, edited by Arai and Trainor) may be a step in the right directions. The index does not list "practitioner."

inscription. A statement or record written on a durable support, such as stone or metal.

script. A writing system, a system of letters, an alphabet. (Cp. Skt. *akṣara*, *lipi*, *varṇamālā*.)

paleography. The study of the evolution of ancient scripts or writing systems and the deciphering and dating of historical manuscripts.

archaeology. The study of the past though material remains. Field archaeology is the survey, exploration, and excavation of ancient sites. Archaeology was established and developed worldwide during the high colonial era: imperial Britain introduced archaeological practice to South Asia (present-day India, Pakistan, Bangladesh, Sri Lanka, and the Maldives) and to Southeast Asia (Burma and Malaysia), the French introduced it to Indochina (Cambodia and Vietnam), and the Dutch to the Dutch East Indies (Indonesia), with overlaps and disjunctures following the ebb, flow, and clash of empires. Archaeology in Afghanistan was initiated by the British and continued by the French and Italians, who also work in Pakistan. Because early Indian historical documents have not survived and because the texts that do survive are conceived in mythical frames and dimensions, archaeology is a key science for the understanding of the ancient history of South Asia. This applies very much to the development of Buddhism.

chronology. Periodization. Buddhist (and Indian) studies do not fit in a monochronology. There are many chronologies, and we can look at Buddhism as early, middle, medieval, or late, or as pre-colonial, colonial, or post-colonial, and so on. Chronologies are tools, frames, perspectives.

Buddhology. This word is used in two distinct ways: as (1) the study of the nature of buddhas or of Śākyamuni Buddha (cp. *Christology*), or as (2) the study of Buddhism in its many aspects. I use the term in the first sense. For the second, I prefer the broader term "Buddhist studies."

Indology. The study of Indian languages, history, and culture. An Indologist, one who does research in or is expert in Indology, is an endangered species.

Tibetology. The study of Tibetan language, history, and culture. A Tibetologist is one who does research in or is expert in Tibetology. So for Sinology/Sinologist, Japanology/Japanologist, and so on.

Hodgepodge

Abhisamaya and Dharmacakra. *Abhisamaya* is transformative insight—it is a particular insight or understanding of the four truths of the noble ones that transforms the practitioner into a stream winner, the first stage of spiritual development. When Gautama taught the four truths in the Deer Park at Vārāṇasī, Kauṇḍinya grasped them: it was when insight into the truths turned in his mindstream that the "wheel of the Dharma" (*dharmacakra*) began to turn. The gods realized this and announced that the wheel of the Dharma had begun to turn. This event is described as the *Dharmacakrapravartana*.

I am not comfortable with the usual translation "four noble truths" insofar as it puts "noble," *ārya*, into an adjectival relation to truth, *satya*, and the idea of truth being "noble" seems odd, especially "noble truth of suffering" (and it is the same for renderings like "lofty truth" or "exalted truth"). *Noble truth of suffering* doesn't make much sense except as "the reality of suffering (pain, unsatisfactoriness of life) *understood by* the exalted ones." Sūtra and śāstra passages do in fact interpret *noble* as "noble one," "truth as understood, realized by a noble one." This might seem a bit circular since it is this very realization that transforms an ordinary person into a "noble one," but it makes sense in terms of the logic of the path.

Brunnhölzl argues cogently against the "pervasive and unquestioned, but nonsensical, renderings [of *satya* as "truth" in, for example,] 'the two truths' or 'the four noble truths' in Western Buddhist literature" and prefers to render *satya* as "reality."[688]

antarābhava. Tib. *bardo*. Intermediate state between death and the next rebirth, a transformative phase during which an individual can achieve awakening.

mandārava. The coral tree, Erythrina fulgens. A celestial tree. Divine *mandārava* flowers floated down from the skies when the Buddha lay down

688. Brunnhölzl, *Gone Beyond*, vol. 1, pp. 680–81, n. 4.

on his death bed in the *sālā*-tree grove at Kusinarā (*Dīghanikāya*, vol. 2, pp. 137–38).

robe. Tib. *bla gos*. Lit. "upper cloth," with reference to the robes of the merchants of Vaiśālī, translation 12. From the time of the Buddha until the last century, Indian attire consisted of pieces of cloth that were wrapped around the body, regardless of social roles or gender.

> *Mahāvyutpatti* § 8933 *saṃghāti* = *snam sbyar*. Of the Buddha. Introduction to translation 11.
>
> *Sham thabs dang chos gos gsol te*. When the Buddha leaves his residence to collect alms or to accept and invitation to a meal outside, his departure is described with the module, he "donned his inner and outer robes and took his almsbowl in hand" (see, for example, translation 12; further examples in *Questioning the Buddha*, pp. 280, 280, 336).

Vaijayanta. Tib. *rnam par rgyal byed*. "Victorious," name of Indra's standard or banner in the *Dhvajāgra-mahāsūtras* (translations 12, 13). In Pāli sources, Vejayanta is the name of Śakra's chariot.

ārya. Tib, *'phags pa*. "Exalted," a much-contested term. See Thapar, *The Past as Present*, chapter 3, "Of Histories and Identities."

Indic. Noun, the Indic language group: Sanskrit, Prakrit, and the modern Indian languages that are their descendants. Adj., relating to Indo-European language or to India (via Latin from Greek *indikos*, "from India").

India. In the imaginaire of the translations, what today we call "India" is **Jambudvīpa** (*'dzam bu gling*), the Black Plum Island or continent—the ancient name of the Indian subcontinent used in Buddhist and Indian literature. Formerly this was translated as Rose Apple Continent, and often it still is (for example, Buswell and Lopez, *Princeton Dictionary*, pp. 377–78). Indian medical and other literature show that *jambu* means black plum, *Syzygium cumini* (L.): see Dominik Wujastyk, "Jambudvīpa: Apples or Plums?" Another early term for India is *Bhāratavarṣa*, which is attested in the Prakrit form *Bharatavasa* in the fifth century BE (first century BCE) inscription of King Khāravela.

"India" is an ancient term; it comes via Latin from Greek *India*, from *Indos*, the name of the Indus River, from Persian *Hind*, from Sanskrit *sindhu*, meaning "river," specifically "the Indus," also "the region around the Indus" (compare with Scinde, Sind, Sindh). Both the Greeks and the Persians extended the name to include all the country east of the Indus. More global terms are the Indian subcontinent, the subcontinent, the Indian peninsula: cp. Davies, *Historical Atlas of the Indian Peninsula*.

This is not the place to tell the fascinating and contested story of the naming of the subcontinent; geographical and geopolitical terms of reference have gone through any number of shifts over the millennia. For centuries the region was known as Hindustan.[689] Partition in 1947 brought a radical rupture in the map of South Asia (not to speak of the unspeakable rupture in the subcontinent's human bosom). India's "natural" claim to areas of Assam, the northeast, and the northwest (Aksai Chin) could not be taken for granted post-Partition, nor after 1951, when the People's Republic of China assumed direct control over Tibet, leaving unresolved cartographic conflicts to fester to this day.

As otherwise used in this book, "India" refers to the "Indian subcontinent" as a geographic rather than a geopolitical entity, in the sense of undivided or of pre-Partition (pre-1947) India. It may also mean South Asia, which comprises India, Pakistan, Afghanistan, Nepal, Bhutan, Bangladesh, the Maldives, and Sri Lanka—a congeries of nations that share cognate pasts in which Buddhism is a significant strand.

Indianization. Transfer of culture and technology abroad, from South to (especially) Southeast Asia, with the result that the receiving culture is permeated by Indic "influences." Once taken for granted, the concept has been criticized for multiple reasons.

689. See Eck, *India: A Sacred Geography*, chap. 2, "What Is India?"; also Asif, *The Loss of Hindustan: The Invention of India*; Habib, "The Envisioning of a Nation: A Defence of the Idea of India"; and Habib, "The Formation of India: Notes on the History of an Idea."

Appendix 1. Tibetan, Sanskrit, and Pāli Titles

1. —
2. *Dhammapada* (Pāli)
3. *Udānavarga* (Skt.), *Dhammapada* (Pāli), *Dharmapada* (Gāndhārī)
4. *Udānavarga*, *Anityavarga* (Skt.), *Ched du brjod pa'i tshoms*, *Mi rtag pa'i tshoms* (Tib.)
5. *Anityatāsūtra* (Skt.), *Mi rtag pa nyid kyi mdo* (Tib.)
6. *Anityatāsūtra* (Skt.), *Mi rtag pa nyid kyi mdo* (Tib.)
7. *Rājasutta* (Pāli)
8. *Ayyikāsutta* (Pāli)
9. *Vinayottaragrantha* (Skt.), *'Dul ba gzhung dam pa* (Tib.)
10. *Arakasutta* (Pāli)
11. *Dhammaniyāmasutta* (Pāli)
12. *Dhvajāgra-nāma-mahāsūtra* (Skt.), *Mdo chen po rgyal mtshan mchog ces bya ba* (Tib.)
13. *Dhvajāgra-nāma-mahāsūtra* (Skt.), *Mdo chen po rgyal mtshan dam pa shes bya ba* (Tib.)
14. *Dhajaggaparitta* (Pāli)
15. *Vaiśālīpraveśa-mahāsūtra* (Skt.) *Yangs pa'i grong khyer du 'jug pa'i mdo chen po* (Tib.)
16. *Svastivākya* (Skt.)
17. *Cakkavattisutta* (Tib.). From Śamathadeva's Upāyikā-ṭīkā.
18. *Bojjhaṅgaparitta* (Pāli)
19. *Yandunnimittaṃ avamaṅgalañ ca* (Pāli)
20. *Ye dhaṃmā hetuprabhavā* (Prakrit)

Appendix 2. Texts of the Inscriptions[690]

The most common epigraphic form is this:[691]

> ye dharmmā hetuprabhavā, hetuṃ teṣāṃ tathāgato hy avadat |
> teṣāñ ca yo nirodha, evaṃ vādi mahāśramanaḥ ||

Figure 54. **Inscription on reverse side of image of seated Buddha from Bihar, now in the British Museum. See figures 4 and 5 (pp. 25 and 26).**

The stanza is written in Sanskrit in three lines:

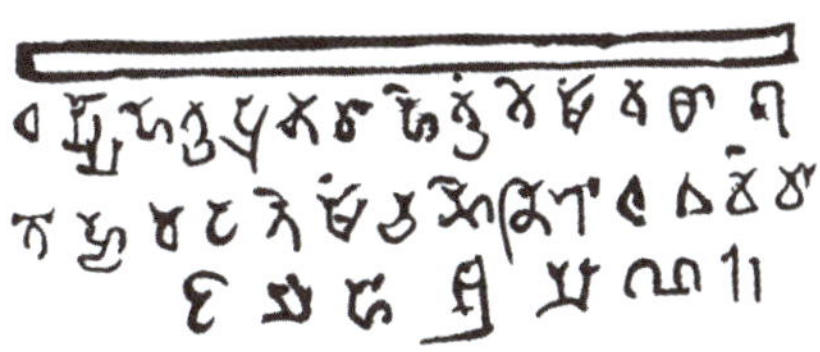

690. In the inscriptions in this appendix, letters in parentheses are partly visible, and letters in square brackets are conjectural.

691. There is no absolutely standard form. This is a common form found in inscriptions and manuscript colophons.

[ye] dha rmmā he tu pra bha vā he tuṃ te ṣaṃ ta thā ga
to hya va da te ṣāṃ ca yo ni ro dha e vaṃ vā
di ma hā śra ma ṇa ||

Figure 55. Inscription on reverse of Buddha seated on serpent king, Indian Museum, Kolkata. See figures 6 and 7 (pp. 51 and 52).

The stanza is somehat effaced after the first line. It seems to be in three lines, but there may have been more writing below that is now effaced or chipped off.

ye dha rmmā he tu pa bha vā he tu te (ṣaṃ?) ta thā
e vaṃ vā di . . .
. . . . śa . . . .

Figure 56. Inscription on reverse of standing Buddha, Asian Art Museum, San Francisco. See figures 9 and 10 (pp. 79 and 80).

The stanza is neatly written in Sanskrit in four lines:

[ye] dha rmmā he tu pra bha vā he tu[ṃ]te(ṣ)aṃ? ta thā ga
to hya va dat te ṣām ca to ni ro dha e vaṃ vā
di mahā śra ma ṇo ||

Figure 57. Sanskrit inscriptions on front of base of standing Buddha from Sultanganj in British Museum. See figure 11 (p. 90).

1. Donative inscription on base beside proper right foot:

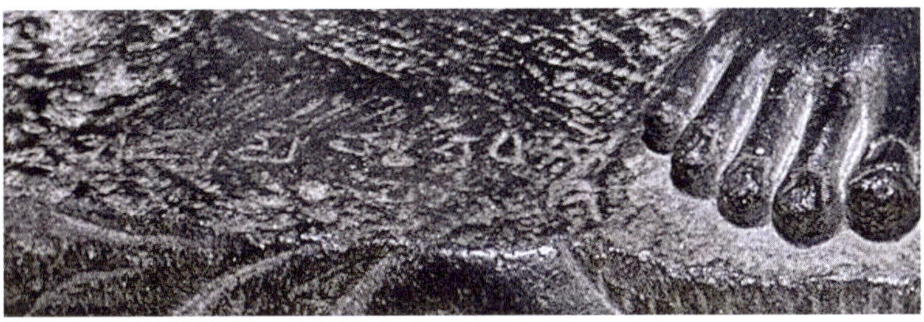

(de) (ya) (dha) rmmo ya[ṃ] . . . .

2. *Ye dharmā* on petals of lotus base (the strokes indicate the individual petals):

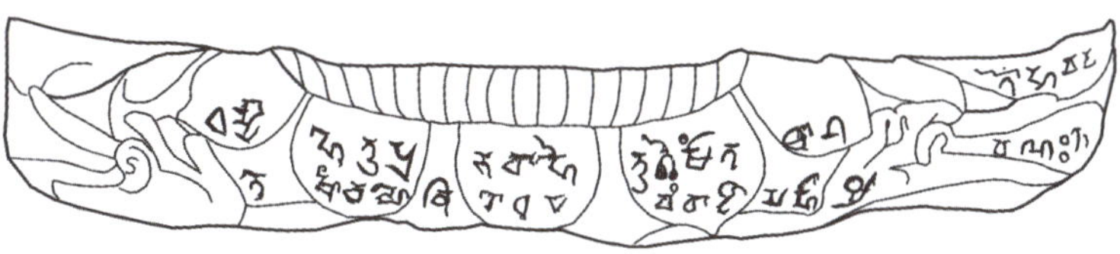

[ye] dha rmmā / he tu pra / bha vā he / tu nte ṣāṃ ta / thā ga / to hya va da /
te ṣāṃ ca yo / ni / ro dha e / vaṃ vā dī / ma hā / śra? / [ma] ṇaḥ ||

Figure 58. Bee, birds, blossoms, and boars. Paper leporello manuscript, Wat Pak Khlong, Phetchaburi province, Thailand.

Notes on Style

Spelling and pronunciation

English is the accepted lingua franca of our drastically globalizing world. In addition to English (to my good fortune my own native tongue), this book uses three other languages for technical terminologies, proper names, titles, and text citations. They are Pāli, Sanskrit, and Tibetan, along with desultory dashes of Prakrit and Thai. With some exceptions, these are presented in roman letters with appropriate diacritics. The diacritics are not difficult to learn and are useful for other languages as well. Pāli, Sanskrit, and Prakrit are transliterated according to standard contemporary romanization systems; Tibetan is given in the basic Wylie system.[692]

For those who know English or European languages, the three Indic alphabets are relatively easy to pronounce, despite the fact that speakers of different language groups pronounce the Indic alphabets differently, in ways that reflect their received historical pronunciation. Contemporary "international academic" pronunciation claims to follow current South Asian pronunciations, in particular those of northern India and Sri Lanka. There are inevitable discrepancies—for example, in the pronunciation of the Sanskrit dipthong *jña* and its Pāli counterpart *nya*,[693] or the pronunciation of the semivowel *ṛ*, in simplified romanization "ri" or "ru" (*tṛpti*, *tripti*, *trupti*).

Tibetan is a bit more of a challenge for untutored tongues. Its orthography is, to put it mildly, conservative, and is not much different from the orthography of the first translations a millennium ago. But if spelling has not changed much, pronunciation has, to evolve in many directions into different dialects

692. See also the Tibetan and Himalayan Library's Extended Wylie Transliteration Scheme at www.thlib.org.

693. To see just how complicated this can be, see "On the Pronunciation of Jña," *Jayarava's Raves* (jayarava.blogspot.com), 15 March 2020. In Thai *ña* becomes "ya" (for example, *ñāṇa* is pronouced "yāna").

and registers.[694] The written language does not account for the variety of pronunciation.

A diacritical question

Some years ago, I decided not to use the diacritics that indicate the long vowels in the romanizations of Pāli and Gāndhārī: that is, to write Pali instead of Pāli (or Pālī or Pāḷī, as it may also be written), Gandhari instead of Gāndhārī. My reasoning in these two cases was that to use diacritics is inconsistent with the standard European usage that, almost universally, writes *Sanskrit* for *Saṃskṛta* and *Prakrit* for *Prākṛta*. Hybrid usages like "the text survives in Pāli and Sanskrit versions" made me uncomfortable. But I found that my decision made editors uneasy, and they would automatically "correct" my spelling to "Pāli" (without, it seems, ever thinking of "correcting" Sanskrit to Saṃskṛt or Prakrit to Prākṛt). This reminded me that convention sometimes outweighs logic and consistency, and in this book I spell the two words Pāli and Gāndhārī with diacritics side by side with the nondiacritic Sanskrit and Prakrit.

We note that the official name of the venerable Pali Text Society is just that: without the diacritic. To add to the confusion, some editors choose to capitalize the "the" in mid-sentence to make, for example, "a work published by The Pali Text Society," while others prefer to *decapitalize* it as "published by the Pali Text Society." Common translations of *duḥkha* include "unsatisfactory" and "painful." This, and other, editorial inconsistencies are *unsatisfactory* but not exactly *painful*. They are all part of broader ambiguities in the rules of the great world language. French is more sensible: it does not capitalize language names and has particular spellings for Prakrit and Sanskrit: *le pāli, le pracrit, et le sanscrit*.[695]

Conventions

Typographic practices like italicization, hyphenation, or complex punctuation and formatting (formatization, to join the club) are not used in the writing systems of the languages translated here (Sanskrit, Pāli, Prakrit, and Tibetan); these practices have evolved over centuries of European manu-

694. For spelling and pronunciation guides, see www.thlib.org.

695. English has a historical use of "Sanscrit," still given as the key entry in Wyld, *Universal Dictionary*, p. 1049 ("Sanscrit, Sanskrit" followed by "Sanscritic").

script and book production from its calligraphic beginnings to the age of print. The print customs and aesthetic imaginary of each language (Italian, French, German, etc.) have developed according to their own impetus, with the result that today customs differ considerably across the map. English-language practice changes over time according to editorial and typographic fashion, and differs between Great Britain, her former colonies, and the innovative and betimes abrasive United States. When transferring terms from the original Sanskrit, Pāli, or Tibetan texts and inducting them as "loan" or "foreign" words into English language contexts, we subject them to the rules of English syntax, grammar, and typography. This raises questions that are not always straightforward or consistent, and it can be difficult to decide what to do: To italicize or not italicize? To hyphenate or not to hyphenate?[696] To capitalize or not to capitalize? One stylist says "yes," another says "no," and yet another, "wait, let's give it some thought." Circumstances often force writers to make ad hoc decisions, and one writer's choices might not agree with what others expect or with those solemnly sanctioned by consensus (a mythical deity who haunts academia's hallowed halls). I apologize for any inconsistences and hope, above all, that what I write is clear.[697]

Several of the Kanjur texts begin with an expression of homage. Translations 5, 6, and 15 have "Homage to the Three Precious Gems" (*namo ratnatrayāya*). Translations 12 and 13, the Mahāsūtras have "Homage to all buddhas and bodhisatvas." These are found in Tibetan and Sanskrit manuscripts, where they are added by the scribes. I have omitted them here.

This book is written in Buddhist time: dates of Buddhist history are given in the Buddhist era (BE), with Christian era (CE) dates in parentheses. I use the Thai Buddhist era. Early Buddhism stands outside the antique and discredited periodization of Indian history into an artificial progression of Buddhist–Hindu–Muslim–British eras.[698] Early Buddhism flourished in a period of diversity and experimentation, neither the idealized Axial Age nor the hubristic Anthropocene.

696. The sixth edition of the *Shorter Oxford English Dictionary* appeared in 2007. In it 16,000 words lost their hyphen; according to the editor, Angus Stevenson, this was because "People are not confident about using hyphens anymore, they're not really sure what they are for." Its researchers reviewed a corpus of 2 billion words (in newspapers, books, websites, and blogs from 2000). Bumble-bee is now bumblebee, ice-cream is ice cream, and pot-belly is pot belly. Conventions change, sometimes rapidly.

697. For more ruminations on conventions, see Skilling, *Questioning the Buddha*, appendix 2, "Conventions."

698. See Skilling, *Questioning the Buddha*, appendix 1, "Vacillations of Dating."

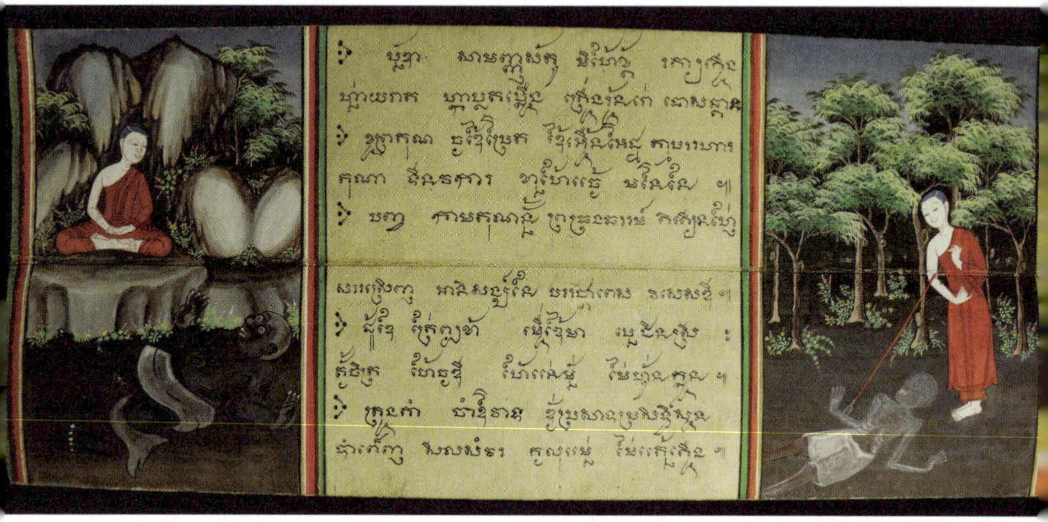

Figure 59. Contemplation of the foul. Text: story of Phra Malai in Thai language in Khom Thai letters. Left: a monk sits cross-legged in meditation, contemplating a swollen corpse. Right: a monk stands, contemplating a skeletal corpse. Paper leporello no. 004, Wat Manisathit Kapittharam, Uthai Thani, Thailand.

Remerciements

I am grateful to the council of the Pali Text Society for its support and encouragement throughout my research on the Mahāsūtras, with especial thanks to former presidents K. R. Norman, Richard Gombrich, and Lance Cousins and to current president Rupert Gethin and the current council. A long-time supporter on the council was the late and deeply esteemed David Seyfort Ruegg, who encouraged my work on the Mahāsūtras from the outset.

I offer my deep thanks to the late E. Gene Smith for his warm and omniscient guidance across the valleys, peaks, and plains of Kanjur research. I offer sincere thanks to Dzongsar Khyentse Rinpoche for his dynamic vision of how the translation of Buddhist texts is essential for the sustainable long-term development of the Dharma worldwide; for the way in which he has tirelessly fostered public awareness of this; for his inspiration and support for the 84000 and Kumārajīva projects; for his *rimé* support of Pāli studies and of the preservation of Southeast Asian Pāli manuscripts; and, last but by no means least, for his gracious encouragement of my own recondite efforts. I weave garlands of gratitude for Rinpoche and the Khyentse Foundation for their unstinting support.

The following roll call of those who have inspired my practice and my research along the way through their teaching, personal example, and enthusiasm is necessarily incomplete owing to the passage of time and the vagaries of memory. To meet a sage even for a moment stamps the lasting impression of the great seal of wisdom on even the most vagabond of minds. I am thankful to them all.

> S. N. Goenka, Anāgārika Munindra, Kalu Rinpoche, Alak Zenkar Rinpoche (A lags gzan dkar rinpoche Thub bstan nyi ma), Tulku Urgyen Rinpoche, Chökyi Nyima Rinpoche, John Blofeld, A. K. Warder, and the Venerables Dhammagutto, Khantipālo,

Kittisubho, Dhammadharo, Vimalo, Jamnian Sīlaseṭṭho, Buddhadāsa Indapañño, Ñāṇasaṃvaro, Ānanda Maitreya, Vipassī Dhammārāmo, Sugandho, Singthong Dhammavaro, Paññavaṃso, Minyak Tulku, Doboom Tulku, Payutto, Jayasāro, Dhammananda, Nāgasena, Ghosānanda, Dhammasāmi, Pāsādiko, Dhammajoti, and Dhammadinnā.

I thank the abbots and communities of the temples who have generously permitted the Fragile Palm Leaves / Henry Ginsburg Fund team to photograph their manuscripts and visual treasures. Special thanks go to Phra Khru Sophit Wachara Chot, abbot of Wat Pak Khlong, for his gentle humor and warm hospitality.

I am grateful to the libraries, publishers, printers, and distributors around the world who keep intellectual discourse alive, and to booksellers and antiquariats the world over whose premises are quiet islands of refuge from the brash and busy highstreets of commerce.

The translations and studies published here depend on the work of over two millenia of scholarship in South and Southeast Asia, the Himalayas, Tibet, and East Asia and more than two centuries of research in the West: the debt I owe to the lineage of scholars is inestimable. For their kind help during the preparation of this book, I salute Bhikkhu Anālayo, Mark Allon, Arthid Sheravanichkul, Nalini Balbir, Olivier de Bernon, Mark Blum, John Canti, Chanwit Tudkaeo, Natchapol Sirisawad, Claudio Cicuzza, David Crystal, Mahesh Deokar, Eng Jin Ooi, John Guy, Kengo Harimoto, Oskar von Hinüber, Hudaya, Iyanaga Nobumi, Janice Leoshko, Todd Lewis, Christian Lammerts, Christian Luczanits, Forrest McGill, Pairot Singbun, Prapod Assavavirulhakarn, Alexander von Rospatt, Saerji, Mattia Salvini, Somneuk Hongprayoon, Martin Straube, Péter-Dániel Szántó, Trent Walker, Vesna Wallace, and Songwut Boonmak. Many thanks to all my helpful friends at Chulalongkorn University Book Centre (CUBC),[699] especially to Laksana (Kung) Janechang for being always ready to solve problems and to Thidarat (Nok Khonsuay) for efficiently supplying the books needed for my research. I thank Jinah Kim for her advice and for guiding me to the manuscript images of the goddess Mahāmantrānusāriṇī. My warm thanks go to Dr. Wasan Udayachalerm for gently leading me along the path to health. It is my pleasure to thank Arun and Suriya for their care and Nong Pooh for his

699. Not to be confused with the Cambridge University Boat Club.

exuberant challenges. All of them have helped me to make up for my many inadequacies and the deeply furrowed *vāsanās* of my inefficiency.

I am especially indebted to Jens-Uwe Hartmann for his close reading of the manuscript and his perspicuous comments.

I thank the Fragile Palm Leaves / Henry Ginsburg Fund field team for their patient and careful photography in the provinces around Bangkok: Santi Pakdeekham, Somneuk Hongprayoon, Phongsathorn Buakhampan, Wisitthisak Sattaphan, and Natthawat Janngam. I thank John Guy for the image of the cakravartin from Phanigiri, Gudrun Melzer and Monika Zin for the Bharhut photo, and the San Diego Museum of Art for the photo of glorious goddess Mahāmantrānusāriṇī. Thanks go to Buddhadāsa Indapanno Archives for the photograph of Ven. Buddhadāsa (figure 3), through the courtesy of Kittisak Rungrueangwatthanachai, head of archives, 17 September 2021.

I am grateful to David Kittelstrom and Brianna Quick for their insights, adjustments, and corrections to my sprawling manuscript

Apologies

Despite the support of those who, like throngs of beneficent deities, have encouraged and aided me, many blemishes remain in this book. For these I alone am responsible and for these I apologize. Eric Partridge notes that "He who never makes mistakes makes nothing":[700] aware of the chance and even likelihood of mistakes, what else can one do but blunder on? My interpretations and ideas tend to differ from current received ideas; I hope they are based on a careful examination of the evidence and are worthy of consideration. For Buddhist studies to progress we need to reexamine old ideas and develop new ones in accordance with the principle of change (*vipariṇāmadharmatā*). In 1941, Ananda Coomaraswamy wrote that "we must not shrink from the truth that all education implies revaluation."[701] What he wrote about museums equally applies to ideas and books: "It is not the function of a museum or of any educator to flatter and amuse the public." He notes that the cultural value of the exhibition of works or art or the reading of books is

700. *Gentle Art*, p. 32; Partridge goes on to say, "Yes; I know that, in 1899, Edward John Phelps, who died a year later, said that 'A man who makes no mistakes does not usually make anything.' Egotistically, I prefer the modified form." This is a good example of Partridge's quest for perfection.

701. Coomaraswamy, "Why Exhibit Works of Art?" p. 22.

to "nourish and make the best part of us grow, as plants are nourished and grow in suitable soils."[702] The same is to be said for the translation and publication of spiritual classics. The field of Buddhist studies has altered radically in the last twenty years, especially as a result of new manuscript and archaeological discoveries; we have to take this in our intellectual stride and move ahead. We need to experiment, to break down the old boxes and compartments, and to propose new frames of reference and visions for Buddhism and its history.

I am somewhat unlocated (*aniketacārī*) in what appears to me to be the overdetermined disciplines of today's Buddhist studies. I do not feel comfortable in any of its narrow niches. As a result, I may not satisfy expected standards of romanization, reference, and resource set by the specialists. For this I apologize. I cannot compete with the omniscience of the field, and I am deeply suspicious of the much-vaunted digital omniscience.

702. Coomaraswamy, "Why Exhibit Works of Art?" p. 20. Nock, *Memoirs of a Superfluous Man*, p. 258, cites Henry Adams, "Nothing in education is so astonishing as the amount of ignorance it accumulates in the form of inert facts."

Abbreviations

The observant reader may notice that I am not fond of abbreviations. I follow *pūrvācāryas* like Lamotte who rarely used them. I limit myself to a few standard abbreviations that "everybody knows" and generally use them only in the footnotes and references. To use abbreviations in the body of the text is unsightly.

ARIRIAB	*Annual Report of the International Research Institute for Advanced Buddhology at Soka University*
BHSD	Ed Abbgerton, *Buddhist Hybrid Sanskrit Dictionary*
DoP	Cone, *A Dictionary of Pāli*
DPPN	Malalasekera, *Dictionary of Pāli Proper Names*
JIABS	*Journal of the International Association of Buddhist Studies*
JPTS	*Journal of the Pali Text Society*
OED	Simpson and Weiner, *The Oxford English Dictionary*
PED	*Pali-English Dictionary*, parts 1–3, edited by Margaret Cone. The Pali Text Society.
PTS	Edition or publication by the Pali Text Society, UK.
PTSD	*The Pali Text Society's Pali-English Dictionary*. Edited by T. W. Rhys Davids and William Stede. London: Pali Text Society, 1972 [1921–25].
RSC	Bate and Rasmussen et al., *William Shakespeare Complete Works*
SHT	Sanskrithandschriften aus den Turfanfunden
TSD	Negi, *Tibetan-Sanskrit Dictionary*
P	Peking Tanjur
Uv	Udānavarga

References

References to Pāli texts are to the editions of the Pali Text Society (PTS, UK), unless otherwise noted. I started my research using the Thai-script Syāmaraṭṭha Tepiṭaka and, somewhat later, the Nalanda Devanagari editions. Eventually I began to use the roman-script Pali Text Society editions.

I do not hesitate to use Pāli, Sanskrit, Tibetan, or Chinese terms when appropriate or attractive—I give the original language to make it easier for readers who have these languages to consult and to check the original texts, as well as to inspire those who do not have the languages to learn them.

I have not tried to seek out and give all possible references, especially to secondary sources. I try my best to cover relevant primary material.

I regret that I have been unable to consult East Asian scholarship except in translation.

Translations are my own unless otherwise noted.

Abé, Ryūichi. *The Weaving of Mantra: Kūkai and the Construction of Esoteric Buddhist Discourse*. New York: Columbia University Press, 1999.

Ackroyd, P. R., and C. F. Evans, ed. *The Cambridge History of the Bible*. Vol. 1, *From the Beginnings to Jerome*. Cambridge: Cambridge University Press, 1970.

Affron, Matthew, et al. *The Essential Duchamp*. New Haven and London: Philadelphia Museum of Art in association with Yale University Press, 2018.

Allon, Mark. *The Composition and Transmission of Early Buddhist Texts with Specific Reference to Sutras.* Hamburg Buddhist Studies 17. Bochum/Freiburg: projekt-verlag, 2021.

———. "The Formation of Canons in the Early Indian Nikāyas or Schools in the Light of the New Gāndhārī Manuscript Finds." In *Buddhist Path, Buddhist*

Teachings: Studies in Memory of L. S. Cousins, edited by Naomi Appleton and Peter Harvey, 249–68. Sheffield and Bristol: Equinox, 2019.

———. *Three Gāndhārī Ekottarikāgama-Type Sūtras: British Library Kharoṣṭhī Fragments 12 and 14*. Seattle: University of Washington Press, 2001.

Allon, Mark, and Blair Silverlock. "Sūtras in the Senior Kharoṣṭhī Manuscript Collection with Parallels in the Majjhima-nikāya and/or the Madhyama-āgama." In *Research on the Madhyama-āgama*, edited by Dhammadinnā, 1–54. Taipei: Dharma Drum Publishing, 2017.

Almogi, Orna. *Authenticity and Authentication: Glimpses behind the Scenes of the Formation of the Tibetan Buddhist Canon*. Indian and Tibetan Studies 9. Hamburg: Department of Indian and Tibetan Studies, Universität Hamburg, 2020.

An, Yang-Gyu, trans. *The Buddha's Last Days. Buddhaghosa's Commentary on the Mahāparinibbāna Sutta*. Oxford: Pali Text Society, 2003.

Anālayo, Bhikkhu. "Awakening or Enlightenment? On the Significance of *Bodhi*." *Mindfulness* 12 (2021): 1653–58. https://doi.org/10.1007/s12671-021-01628-2.

———. "The Buddha as a Supreme Physician." In Anālayo, *Mindfully Facing Disease and Death: Compassionate Advice from Early Buddhist Texts*, 9–16. Cambridge: Windhorse Publications, 2017.

———. *A Comparative Study of the Majjhima-nikāya*. 2 vols. Taipei: Dharma Drum Publishing, 2011.

———. *Dīrgha-āgama Studies*. Taipei: Dharma Drum Publishing, 2017.

———. *Ekottarika-āgama Studies*. Taipei: Dharma Drum Publishing, 2016.

———. *The Foundation History of the Nuns' Order*. Hamburg Buddhist Studies 6. Bochum: Projektverlag, 2016.

———. "The Four Levels of Awakening." *Mindfulness* 12 (2021): 831–40. https://doi.org/10.1007/s12671-020-01530-3

———. "The Healing Potential of the Awakening Factors in Early Buddhist Discourse." In *Buddhism and Medicine*, edited by C. Pierce Salguero, 14–17. New York: Columbia University Press, 2019.

———. *Madhyama-āgama Studies*. Taipei: Dharma Drum Publishing, 2012.

———. "'Mūlasarvāstivādin and Sarvāstivādin': Oral Transmission Lineages of Āgama Texts." In *Research on the Saṃyukta-āgama*, edited by Dhammadinnā, 387–426. Taipei: Dharma Drum Publishing, 2020.

———. "On Views and Penetrative Knowledge: A Translation of *Saṃyukta-āgama* Discourses 139 to 187 (Fascicle 7)." *Dharma Drum Journal of Buddhist Studies* 17 (December 2013): 43–99.

———. "Overcoming Fear by Recollecting the Buddha: His Role in Early Buddhist Texts." *Mindfulness* 12 (2021): 594–603. https://doi.org/10.1007/s12671-020-01518-z.

———. *Saṃyukta-āgama Studies*. Taipei: Dharma Drum Publishing, 2015.

———. "Udāna." In *Encyclopaedia of Buddhism*, edited by W. G. Weeraratna, vol. 8, fasc. 2, 375–84. [Colombo:] Department of Buddhist Affairs, Ministry of Religious Affairs, Sri Lanka, 2008.

———. "The Vicissitudes of Memory and Early Buddhist Oral Transmission." *Canadian Journal of Buddhist Studies* 5 (2009): 5–19.

———. *Vinaya Studies*. Taipei: Dharma Drum Publishing, 2017.

Ananda Maitreya, Ven. B., trans. *Dhammapada (Law Verses) Freely Rendered into English*. Colombo: Metro Printers, 1978.

Ānandajoti Bhikkhu. *A Comparative Edition of the Dhammapada with Parallels from Sanskritised Prakrit, Edited together with A Study of the Dhammapada Collection*, 4th rev. ed. ancient-buddhist-texts.net (April 2020).

———. *Patna Dharmapada as Transcribed by Margaret Cone (1989) with Pāḷi Parallels, Metrical Commentary, Notes and Indexes compiled by Ānandajoti Bhikkhu* (2007). http://bit.ly/ABT-PDhp-Text.

App, Urs. *The Birth of Orientalism*. Philadelphia: University of Pennsylvania Press, 2015.

———. *The Cult of Emptiness: The Western Discovery of Buddhist Thought and the Invention of Oriental Philosophy*. Wil, Switzerland: UniversityMedia, 2014.

Apple, James, trans. *Jewels of the Middle Way: The Madhyamaka Legacy of Atiśa and His Early Tibetan Followers*. Studies in Indian and Tibetan Buddhism. Somerville, MA: Wisdom Publications, 2018.

Appleton, Naomi. "*Jātaka* Stories and *Paccekabuddhas* in Early Buddhism." In *Buddhist Path, Buddhist Teachings: Studies in Memory of L. S. Cousins*, edited by Naomi Appleton and Peter Harvey, 305–18. Sheffield: Equinox, 2019.

———. *Jātaka Stories in Theravāda Buddhism: Narrating the Bodhisatta Path*. Aldershot and Burlington, VT: Ashgate Publishing, 2010.

———. *Many Buddhas, One Buddha: A Study and Translation of Avadānaśataka 1–40*. Sheffield: Equinox, 2020.

———. *Narrating Karma and Rebirth: Buddhist and Jain Multi-life Stories*. Cambridge: Cambridge University Press, 2014.

———. *Shared Characters in Jain, Buddhist and Hindu Narrative: Gods, Kings and Other Heroes*. Dialogues in South Asian Traditions: Religion, Philosophy, Literature and History. Abingdon: Routledge, 2016.

Appleton, Naomi, and Sarah Shaw, trans. *Ten Great Birth Stories of the Buddha: The Mahānipāta of the Jātakatthavaṇṇanā*. 2 vols. Chiang Mai and Bangkok: Silkworm Books and Chulalongkorn University Press, 2015.

Appleton, Naomi, Sarah Shaw, and Unebe Toshiya. *Illuminating the Life of the Buddha: An Illustrated Chanting Book from Eighteenth-Century Siam*. Oxford: Bodleian Library, 2013.

Arai, Paula, and Kevin Trainor, eds. *Oxford Handbook of Buddhist Practice*. Oxford: Oxford University Press, 2022.

Asher, Frederick M. *The Art of Eastern India, 300–800*. Delhi: Oxford University Press, 1980.

———. *Sarnath: A Critical History of the Place Where Buddhism Began*. Los Angeles: Getty Research Institute, 2020.

Asif, Manan Ahmed. *The Loss of Hindustan: The Invention of India*. Cambridge, MA: Harvard University Press, 2020.

Balk, Michael. *Prajñāvarman's Udānavargavivaraṇa: Transliteration of Its Tibetan Version (based on the xylographs of Chone/Derge and Peking)*. 2 vols. Indica et Tibetica, Arbeitsmaterialien A. Bonn: Indica et Tibetica Verlag, 1984.

Banerjee, Anukul Chandra. *Sarvāstivāda Literature*. Calcutta: World Press Private Limited, 1979 [1957].

———, ed. *Two Buddhist Vinaya Texts in Sanskrit: Prātimokṣa Sūtra and Bhikṣukarmavākya*. Calcutta: World Press, 1977.

Bareau, André. *En suivant Bouddha*. [1985] Repr. Paris: Éditions du Félin, Philippe Lebaud, 2000.

———. *Les premiers conciles bouddhiques.* Annales du Musée Guimet, Bibliothèque d'études 60. Paris: Presses Universitaires de France, 1955.

———. *Recherches sur la biographie du Buddha dans les Sūtrapiṭaka et les Vinayapiṭaka anciens: de la quête de l'éveil à la conversion de Śāriputra et de Maudgalyāyana*. Publications de l'École française d'Extrême-Orient 73. Paris: École française d'Extrême-Orient, 1971.

———. *Recherches sur la biographie du Buddha dans les Sūtrapiṭaka et les Vinayapiṭaka anciens: II. Les derniers mois, le parinirvāṇa et les funérailles*. Tome II. *De la quête de l'éveil à la conversion de Śāriputra et de Maudgalyāyana*. Publications de l'École française d'Extrême-Orient 53. Paris: École française d'Extrême-Orient, 1963.

Barnhart, Robert K, ed. *Chambers Dictionary of Etymology*. New York: Chambers, 1988.

Barua, B. M. "Dharma-samuccaya [The latest recension of the Dhammapada]." *Indian Culture*, 3.2 (October 1936): 366–69.

Bate, Jonathan, and Eric Rasmussen, eds., with Ian De Jong and Molly G. Yarn. *William Shakespeare Complete Works* (= RSC). 2nd ed. New York: Modern Library, 2022.

Baums, Stefan. *A Gāndhārī Commentary on Early Buddhist Verses: British Library Kharoṣṭhī Fragments 7, 9, 13 and 18*. PhD dissertation. University of Washington, 2009.

Bavarian State Library. *Die Worte des Buddha in den Sprachen der Welt / The Words of the Buddha in the Languages of the World: Tipiṭaka, Tripiṭaka, Dazangjing, Kanjur.* Edited by Günter Grönbold et al. Munich: Bayerischen Staatsbibliothek, 2005.

Bays, Gwendolyn, trans. *The Voice of the Buddha: The Beauty of Compassion*. 2 vols. Berkeley, CA: Dharma Publishing, 1983.

Beal, Samuel. "The Eighteen Schools of Buddhism." *Indian Antiquary* 9 (1880): 299–302.

———, trans. *Texts from the Buddhist Canon Commonly Known as Dhammapada with Accompanying Narratives*. The English and Foreign Philosophical Library 20. [Boston: Houghton, Osgood, 1878] San Francisco: Chinese Materials Center, 1977.

Bechert, Heinz, ed. *Bruchstücke buddhistischer Verssammlungen aus zentralasiatischen Sanskrithandschriften: 1. Die Anavataptagāthā und die Sthaviragāthā*. Sanskrittexte aus den Turfanfunden 6. Berlin: Akademie Verlag, 1961.

———. "On a Fragment of the *Vimānāvadāna*. A Canonical Buddhist Sanskrit Work." In *Buddhist Studies in Honour of I. B. Horner*, edited by L. Cousins, A. Kunst, and K. R. Norman, 19–25. Dordrecht: D. Reidel, 1974.

Béguin, Gilles. *Les peintures du bouddhisme tibétain: Musée National des Arts Asiatiques–Guimet*. Paris: Réunion des Musées Nationaux, 1995.

Bendall, Cecil, ed. *Çikshāsamuccaya: A Compendium of Buddhistic Teaching Compiled by Çāntideva Chiefly from Earlier Mahayana-sūtras.* Bibliotheca Buddhica 1. St. Pétersbourg: Commissionnaires de l'Académie Impériale des Sciences, 1897–1902. Note that the title of this important wok has suffered from the vagaries of romanization practices: *Çikshāsamuccaya*, *Śikshā-samuccaya*, and, correct by current standards, *Śikṣāsamuccaya*. The use of the hyphen is arbitrary and optional.

Bennett, A. A. G., trans. *Long Discourses of the Buddha*. The Buddhist Library, edited by Bhikshu Sangharakshita, vol. 3. Bombay: Chetana, 1965.

Bernhard, Franz, ed. *Udānavarga*. 2 vols. Sanskrittexte aus den Turfanfunden 10. Göttingen: Vandenhoeck & Ruprecht, 1988 [1965].

———. "Zum Titel des sogenannten *Udānavarga*." In *ZDMG-Supplementa 1*, 872–81. Wiesbaden, 1969.

Bingenheimer, Marcus. *Studies in Āgama Literature: With Special Reference to the Shorter Chinese Saṃyuktāgama*. Dharma Drum Buddhist College Special Series 1. Taipei: Dharma Drum Publishing, 2011.

———, trans. "Two Sūtras on Healing and Healers from the Chinese Canon." In *Buddhism and Medicine*, edited by C. Pierce Salguero, 163–69. New York: Columbia University Press, 2019.

Bingenheimer, Marcus, Bhikkhu Anālayo, and Roderick S. Bucknell, eds. *The Madhyama Āgama (Middle Length Discourses)*, vol. 1. Berkeley, CA: Bukkyo Dendo Kyokai America, 2013.

Blake, William. "Jerusalem: The Emanation of the Giant Albion" [1804]. In *The Complete Poetry and Prose of William Blake*, new rev. ed., edited by David V. Erdman, commentary by Harold Bloom, 144–71. Berkeley: University of California Press, 2008.

Bloom, Harold. *The Best Poems of the English Language*. New York: HarperCollins, 2004.

Blum, Mark L., trans. *The Nirvana Sutra (Mahāparinirvāṇa-sūtra)*, vol. 1. BDK English Tripiṭaka Series. Berkeley, CA: Bukkyo Dendo Kyokai America, 2013.

———, ed. *Selected Works of D. T. Suzuki*. Vol. 4, *Buddhist Studies*. Berkeley: University of California Press, 2021.

Bodhi, Bhikkhu, trans. *The Connected Discourses of the Buddha: A New Translation of the Saṃyutta Nikāya. Translated from the Pāli.* 2 vols. Boston: Wisdom Publications, 2000.

———. "In Defense of 'Enlightenment': Ven. Bhikkhu Bodhi in Conversation with Matthew Abrahams." *Tricycle: The Buddhist Review* (Summer 2021).

———, trans. *In the Buddha's Words: An Anthology of Discourses from the Pāli Canon*. Boston: Wisdom Publications, 2005.

———, trans. *The Numerical Discourses of the Buddha: A Translation of the Aṅguttara Nikāya*. Boston: Wisdom Publications, 2012.

———. "On Translating 'Buddha.'" *Journal of the Oxford Centre for Buddhist Studies*, 19 (2020): 52–78.

———. *Reading the Buddha's Discourses in Pāli: A Practical Guide to the Language of the Ancient Buddhist Canon*. Somerville, MA: Wisdom Publications, 2020.

———, trans. *The Suttanipāta: An Ancient Collection of the Buddha's Discourses Together with Its Commentaries Paramatthajotikā II and Excerpts from the Niddesa*. Somerville, MA: Wisdom Publications, 2017.

Boin-Webb, Sara, trans. to English from French trans. by Etienne Lamotte. *Śūraṃgamasamādhisūtra: The Concentration of Heroic Progress: An Early Mahayānā Buddhist Scripture*. Honolulu: University of Hawai'i Press, in association with the Buddhist Society, 2009.

———, trans. to English from French trans. by Etienne Lamotte. *The Teaching of Vimalakīrti (Vimalakīrtinirdeśa): from the French Translation with Introduction and Notes (L'Enseignement de Vimalakīrti)*. Bristol: Pali Text Society, 2011.

Bongard-Levin, G[regory], and A. Vigasin. *The Image of India: The Study of Ancient Indian Civilisation in the USSR*. Moscow: Progress Publishers, 1984.

Bongard-Levin, Gregory, Daniel Boucher, Takamichi Fukita, and Klaus Wille. *The Nagaropamasūtra: An Apotropaic Text from the Saṃyuktāgama: A Transliteration, Reconstruction, and Translation of the Central Asian Sanskrit Manuscripts. Sanskrit-Texte aus dem buddhistischen Kanon: Neuentdeckungen und Neueditionen III*. Sanskrit-Wörterbuch der buddhistischen Texte aus den Turfan-Funden 6. Göttingen: Vandenhoeck & Ruprecht, 1996.

Boyer, A. M., E. J. Rapson, and E. Senart. *Kharoṣṭhī Inscriptions Discovered by Sir Aurel Stein in Chinese Turkestan*, parts 1 and 2; part 3 transcribed and edited by E. J. Rapson and P. S. Noble. New Delhi: Cosmo Publications, 1997 [1920–29].

Brandt, Carmen. "Why Dots and Dashes Matter: Writing Bengali in Roman Script." In *"Das alles hier": Festschrift für Konrad Klaus zum 65. Geburtstag*, edited by Ulrike Niklas et al., 23–54. Heidelberg and Berlin: CrossAsia-eBooks, 2021.

Brewster, E. A. *The Life of Gotama the Buddha, Compiled Exclusively from the Pāli Canon*. London: Kegan Paul, Trench-Trubner, 1926.

Bronkhorst, Johannes. *Buddhism in the Shadow of Brahmanism*. Handbook of Oriental Studies, Section 2 South Asia, vol. 24. Leiden: Brill, 2011.

———. *Greater Magadha: Studies in the Culture of Early India*. Handbook of Oriental Studies, Section 2 South Asia, vol. 19. Leiden: Brill, 2007.

———. *How the Brahmins Won: From Alexander to the Guptas*. Handbook of Oriental Studies, Section 2 South Asia, vol. 30. Leiden: Brill, 2016.

———. "India's Past Reconsidered." In *"At the Shores of the Sky": Asian Studies for Albert Hoffstädt*, edited by Paul W. Kroll and Jonathan A. Silk, 12–22. Leiden and Boston: Brill, 2020.

Brough, John, ed. *The Gāndhārī Dharmapada*. London Oriental Series 7. London: Oxford University Press, 1962.

Brunnhölzl, Karl, trans. *Gone Beyond: Prajñāpāramitā Sūtras, The Ornament of Clear Realization, and Its Commentaries in the Tibetan Kagyü Tradition*, vol. 1. Ithaca, NY: Snow Lion Publications, 2010.

———, trans. *When the Clouds Part: The Uttaratantra and Its Meditative Tradition as a Bridge between Sūtra and Tantra*. Boston: Snow Lion Publications, 2015.

Bu ston Rin chen grub. *History of the Dharma. Rgyal ba'i dgongs 'grel bstan 'gyur rin po che'i bzhugs byang dkar chag ces bya be bzhugs so*. Si khron dpe skrun tshogs pa, si khron mi rigs dpe skrung khang, 2011. For translation, see Obermiller, *History of Buddhism*.

Bucknell, Roderick S. *Reconstructing Early Buddhism*. Cambridge: Cambridge University Press, 2023.

Buddharakkhita Thera, Venerable Ācharya, trans. *Dhammapada: A Practical Guide to Right Living (Text and Translation)*. Bangalore: Buddha Vacana Trust, Maha Bodhi Society, 1966.

———, trans. *The Dhammapada: The Buddha's Path of Wisdom*. 2nd ed. Kandy: Buddhist Publication Society, 1996.

B[urgess], J[ames]. "Ḍambal Buddhist Inscription of Ś. 1017." *Indian Antiquary* 10 (September 1881): 273–74.

Burlingame, Eugene Watson, ed. *Buddhist Legends: Translated from the Original Pāli Text of the Dhammapada Commentary*. 3 vols. Harvard Oriental Series 28–30. London: Pali Text Society 1979 [1921].

Burnouf, Eugène. *Introduction à l'histoire du Buddhisme indien*. 2nd ed. Bibliothèque orientale vol. 3. Paris: Maisonneuve et Cie, [1844] 1876. English edition, *Introduction to the History of Indian Buddhism*, translated by Katia Buffetrille and Donald S. Lopez Jr. Chicago: University of Chicago Press, 2015.

Buswell, Robert E., Jr., and Donald S. Lopez. *The Princeton Dictionary of Buddhism*. Princeton: Princeton University Press, 2014.

Carré, Patrick, trans. *Soûtra de l'entrée dans la dimension absolue: extrait du grand*

"Soûtra des ornements de Bouddha" dans la traduction chinoise de Śiksānanda. Gandavyuhasutra avec le commentaire de Li Tongxuan. Plazac: Éditions Padmakara, 2019.

Carter, John Ross, and Mahinda Palihawadana. *The Dhammapada: A New English Translation with the Pāli Text and the First English Translation of the Commentary's Explanation of the Verses with Notes Translated from Sinhala Sources and Critical Textual Comments.* New York and Oxford: Oxford University Press, 1987.

de Casparis, J. G., ed. *Selected Inscriptions from the 7th to the 9th century AD.* Prasasti Indonesia 2. Bandung: Masa Baru, 1956.

Cassin, Barbara, ed. *Dictionary of Untranslatables: A Philosophical Lexicon.* Princeton and Oxford: Princeton University Press, 2004.

Chakravarti, Niranjan Prasad. *L'Udānavarga Sanskrit, Text sanscrit en transcription, avec traduction et annotations, suivi d'une étude critique et de planches.* Mission Pelliot en Asie Centrale, Série Petit in-Octavo 4. Paris: Librairie Orientaliste Paul Geuthner, 1930.

Chalmers, Lord [Robert]. *Further Dialogues of the Buddha.* Translated from the Pāli of the Majjhima Nikāya, vol. 1. Delhi: Sri Satguru Publications, 1988 [1926].

Chattopadhyaya, Debiprasad, ed. *Tāranātha's History of Buddhism in India.* Translated from the Tibetan by Lama Chimpa and Alaka Chattopadhyaya. Calcutta: K. P. Bagchi, 1980 [1970].

Chaudhuri, Nirad C. "Apologia Pro Scripta Sua." In *The Book of Indian Essays: Two Hundred Years of English Prose*, edited by Arvind Krishna Mehrotra, 88–94. Delhi: Black Kite/Ashoka University, 2020. Originally published in *Granta: Special Indian Number* (May 1997).

Chet Prichanon. *Chareuk thi ong Phra Pathom Chedi.* Bangkok: Chudarat Kanphim, 2528 [1985].

Childers, Robert Caesar. *A Dictionary of the Pāli Language.* London: Trübner, 1875. Repr. New Delhi and Madras: Asian Educational Services, 1993.

Chim Jampaiyang (Mchims 'jam dpal dbyangs). *Chos mngon pa mdzod kyi tshig le'ur byas pa'i 'grel pa mgnon pa'i rgyan.* Bod kyi gtsug lag zhib dpyod khang. Bod kyi gtsug lag bces btus pod phreng 23. New Delhi: Institute of Tibetan Classics, 2009.

———. *Ornament of Abhidharma: A Commentary on Vasubandhu's Abhidharmakośa.* Translated by Ian James Coghlan. Library of Tibetan Classics 23. Somerville, MA: Wisdom Publications, 2018.

Choephel, David Karma, trans. *Jewels from the Treasury: Vasubandhu's Verses on the Treasury of Abhidharma and Its Commentary Youthful Play by the Ninth Karmapa Wangchuk Dorje.* Woodstock, NY: KTD Publications, 2012.

Chung, Jin-il. *A Survey of the Sanskrit Fragments Corresponding to the Chinese Saṃyuktāgama.* Tokyo: Sankibō Busshorin, 2008.

———, ed. *Handbuch für die buddhistische Mönchsordination bei den Mūlasarvāstivādins* = 根本說一切有部出家授近圓羯磨儀範 [Gen ben shuo yi qie you bu chu jia shou jin yuan jie mo yi fan]. Gimpo-si: Institute for Buddhist Scriptures in Korean Translation, Joong-Ang Sangha University, 2011.

Chung, Jin-il, and Takamichi Fukita, eds. *A New Edition of the First 25 Sūtras of the Nidānasaṃyukta*. Tokyo: Sankibobusshorin, 2020.

Clarke, Shayne. "Vinayas." In *Brill's Encyclopedia of Buddhism*. Vol. 1, *Literature and Language*, edited by Jonathan A. Silk, 60–87. Leiden and Boston: Brill, 2015.

Cone, Margaret, ed. *Patna Dhammapada*. See under Ānandajoti.

———. *A Dictionary of Pāli*. Published by the Pali Text Society, 3 parts to date (December 2022): part 1, Oxford, 2001; part 2, Bristol, 2010; part 3, Bristol, 2020.

Conze, Edward. *Buddhist Scriptures*. Harmondsworth: Penguin Books, 1959.

———, ed. and trans. *The Gilgit Manuscript of the Aṣṭādaśasāhasrikāprajñāpāramitā, Chapters 55 to 70 Corresponding to the 5th Abhisamaya*. Serie Orientale Roma 26. Rome: Istituto Italiano per il Medio ed Estremo Oriente, 1962.

———, trans. *The Perfection of Wisdom in Eight Thousand Lines and Its Verse Summary*. Delhi: Sri Satguru Publications, 1994. [Bolinas: Four Seasons Foundation, 1973.]

Coomaraswamy, Ananda. *Buddha and the Gospel of Buddhism*. London: George G. Harrap, 1916.

———. *The Bugbear of Literacy*. Bedfont, Middlesex: Perennial Books, 1979 [1949].

———. "Why Exhibit Works of Art?" In *Christian and Oriental Philosophy of Art*, 7–22. Mineola, NY: Dover Publications, 1956. Address first delivered before the American Association of Museums at Columbus, OH, and Newport, RI (May and October 1941), and printed in the *Journal of Aesthetics* (Fall 1941).

Cordier, P. *Catalogue du fonds tibétain de la Bibliothèque nationale*, troisième partie: *Index du Bstan-ḥgyur (Tibétain 180–332)*. Paris: Imprimerie nationale, 1915.

Cousins, L. S. *Meditations of the Pali Tradition: Illuminating Buddhist Doctrine, History, and Practice*, edited by Sarah Shaw. Boulder: Shambhala Publications, 2022.

Cox, Collett. "Whether Buddhas Arise or Do Not Arise: The Variant or Invariant Nature of Dependent Origination (*pratītyasamutpāda*)." In *Abhidharma and Indian Thought: Essays in Honour of Professor Doctor Junsho Kato on his Sixtieth Birthday*, [31]–[47]. Tokyo: Shunju-sha, 2000.

Crosby, Kate. "The Shared Origins of Traditionalism and Secularism in Theravāda Buddhism." In *Secularizing Buddhism: New Perspectives on a Dynamic Tradition*, edited by Richard K. Payne, 135–61. Boulder: Shambala Publications, 2021.

Crystal, David, and Ben Crystal. *Shakespeare's Words: A Glossary and Literary Companion*. London: Penguin Books, 2002.

Csoma de Kőrös, Alexander. "Analysis of the Mdo," section of "Analysis of the Sher-chin—P'hal-ch'hen—Dkon-séks—Do-dé—Nyáng-dás—and Gyut; Being the

2nd 3rd, 4th, 5th, 6th, and 7th Divisions of the Tibetan Work, Entitled the Kahgyur by Mr. Alexander Csoma Kőrösi, Siculo-Hungarian of Transylvania." Originally published in *Asiatic Researches* 20 (1836): 393–552. Reprinted in *Tibetan Studies: Being a Reprint of the Articles Contributed to the Journal of the Asiatic Society of Bengal and Asiatic Researches by Alexander Csoma de Kőrös*, edited by E. Denison Ross, 265–424. Calcutta, 1912 [repr. New Delhi: Gaurav Publishing House, 1991].[703]

———. "Notices on the Different Systems of Buddhism, Extracted from the Tibetan Authorities." Originally published in *Journal of the Asiatic Society of Bengal* 7.1 (1838). Reprinted in *Tibetan Studies: Being a Reprint of the Articles Contributed to the Journal of the Asiatic Society of Bengal and Asiatic Researches by Alexander Csoma de Kőrös*, edited by E. Denison Ross, 73–79. Calcutta, 1912 [repr. New Delhi: Gaurav Publishing House, 1991].

Dalai Lama, His Holiness the, et al. *Science and Philosophy in the Indian Buddhist Classics.* Vol. 1, *The Physical World.* Edited by Thupten Jinpa, translated by Ian Coghlan. Somerville, MA: Wisdom Publications, 2017.

Davies, C. Collin. *An Historical Atlas of the Indian Peninsula.* 2nd ed. London: Oxford University Press, 1959 [1949].

Dehejia, Vidya, and Peter Rockwell. *The Unfinished: The Stone Carvers at Work in the Indian Subcontinent.* New Delhi: Roli Books, 2016.

de Jong, J. W. "Notes on the *Bhikṣuṇī-vinaya* of the Mahāsāṃghikas." In *Buddhist Studies in Honour of I. B. Horner*, edited by L. Cousins et al., 63–70. Dordrecht and Boston: D. Reidel, 1974.

———. Review of *Scripture of the Lotus Blossom of the Fine Dharma (The Lotus Sūtra).* Translated from the Chinese of Kumārajīva by Leon Hurvitz. *The Eastern Buddhist*, new series, 10.2 (October 1977): 169–74.

Derrett, J. Duncan M., trans. *A Textbook for Novices: Jayarakṣita's "Perspicuous Commentary on the Compendium of Conduct by Śrīghana."* Turin: Indologica Taurinensia, 1983.

Deshpande, Madhav M. "From Orality to Writing: Transmission and Interpretation of Pāṇini's Aṣṭādhyāyī." In *Travaux de Symposium international: Le Livre, la Roumanie, l'Europe: troisième édition—20 à 24 septembre 2010*, edited by Florin Rotaru. Vol. 3, *La troisième section—Études Euro- et Afro-Asiatiques.* Bucharest: Bibliothèque Métropolitaine Bucarest / Bibliothèque de Bucarest, 2011.

Dhammadinnā, ed. *Research on the Dīrgha-āgama.* Dharma Drum Institute of Liberal Arts Research Series 1. Taipei: Dharma Drum Publishing, 2014.

703. *Asiatic Researches* was reprinted as *Asiatic Researches*, vol. 23, New Delhi: Cosmo Publications, 1980 [1839]. This rather shoddy reprint omits some parts such as tables of contents; therefore I rely on the Denison Ross version, referring to the original pagination as given in the upper headers. Distinguished Orientalist and linguist E. Denison Ross (1871–1940) was the first director of the School of Oriental Studies (now SOAS) at the University of London.

———, ed. *Research on the Ekottarika-āgama (Taishō 125)*. Dharma Drum Buddhist College Research Series 6. Taipei: Dharma Drum Publishing, 2013.

———, ed. *Research on the Madhyama-āgama*. Dharma Drum Institute of Liberal Arts Research Series 5. Taipei: Dharma Drum Publishing, 2017.

———, ed. *Research on the Saṃyukta-āgama*. Dharma Drum Institute of Liberal Arts Research Series 8. Taipei: Dharma Drum Publishing, 2020.

Dhammajoti, K. L. *Sarvāstivāda Abhidharma*. Hong Kong: Buddha-Dharma Centre of Hong Kong, 2015.

Di Crocco, Virginia McKeen. *Footprints of the Buddhas of This Era in Thailand and the Indian Subcontinent, Sri Lanka, Myanmar*. Bangkok: Siam Society, 2004.

Dietz, Siglinde, and Champa Thupten Zongtse, eds. *Udānavarga*. Vol. 3, *Der tibetische Text*. Abhandlungen der Akademie der Wissenschaften in Göttingen, Philologisch-historische Klasse 3. Folge, no. 187; Sanskrittexte aus den Turfanfunden 10. Göttingen: Vandenhoeck & Ruprecht, 1990.

Dimitrov, Dragomir. *The Buddhist Indus Script and Scriptures: On the So-Called Bhaikṣukī or Saindhavī Script of the Sāṃmitīyas and Their Canon*. Veröffentlichungen der Fächergruppenkommission für Außereuropäische Sprachen und Kulturen: Studien zur Indologie. Wiesbaden: Harrassowitz Verlag, 2020. (Review by Tournier, q.v.)

Doney, Lewis. *Bringing Buddhism to Tibet: History and Narrative in the Dba' bzhed Manuscript*. Beyond Boundaries 10. Berlin: Walter De Gruyter, 2021.

Dragonetti, Carmen, and Fernando Tola, trans. *Dhammapada: La Esencia de la Sabiduria Budista*. 8th ed. Hillsborough, NJ: Dharma Translation Organization (Buenos Aires: Fundación Bodhiyāna), 2013.

Ducœur, Guillaume. *La Vie du Buddha: Lalitavistara sūtra ou Sūtra des jeux [du Bodhisattva], IIe–VIIe siècle après J.-C.* Strasbourg: Presses Universitaires de Strasbourg, 2018.

Dudjom Rinpoche. *The Nyingma School of Tibetan Buddhism*. Translated and edited by Gyurme Dorje and Matthew Kapstein. Boston: Wisdom Publications, 1991.

Dutt, Nalinaksha. *Gilgit Manuscripts*. 4 vols. Delhi: Sri Satguru Publications, 1984 [1939].

Dwivedi, Vajravallabh, and S. S. Bahulkar, eds. *Vimalaprabhāṭīkā of Kalkin Śrīpuṇḍarīka on Śrīlaghukālacakratantrarāja by Śrīmañjuśrīyayaśas*, vol. 3. Rare Buddhist Texts Series 13. Sarnath, Varanasi: Central Institute of Higher Tibetan Studies, 1994.

Eck, Diana L. *India: A Sacred Geography*. New York: Harmony Books, 2012.

Eltschinger, Vincent. "Aśvaghoṣa and His Canonical Sources: 4. On the Authority and the Authenticity of the Buddhist Scriptures." In *Archaeologies of the Written: Indian, Tibetan, and Buddhist Studies in Honour of Cristina Scherrer-Schaub*, edited by Vincent Tournier, Vincent Eltschinger, and Marta Sernesi, 127–69. Naples: Università degli Studi di Napoli "L'Orientale," 2020.

———. "Why Did the Buddha Come to Earth? Monastic Lineage, Interreligious Polemics, and Philosophy." In *Reasons and Lives in Buddhist Traditions: Studies in Honor of Matthew Kapstein*, edited by Dan Arnold, Cécile Ducher, and Pierre-Julien Harter, 293–306. Somerville, MA: Wisdom Publications, 2019.

———. "Why Did the Buddhists Adopt Sanskrit?" *Open Linguistics* 3 (2017): 308–26.

———. "The Yogācārabhūmi against Allodoxies (*paravāda*): 1. Introduction and Doxography." *Wiener Zeitschrift für die Kunde Südasiens* 55 (2013–14 [appeared in 2015]): 191–234.

Elwin, Verrier. *The Art of the North-East Frontier of India*. Shillong: North-East Frontier Agency, 1959.

———. *The Tribal Art of Middle India: A Personal Record*. London: Geoffrey Cumberlege, Oxford University Press, 1951.

Emmerick, R. E., ed., trans. *The Book of Zambasta: A Khotanese Poem on Buddhism*. London Oriental Series 21. London: Oxford University Press, 1968.

———, trans. *The Sūtra of Golden Light: A Translation of the Suvarṇbhāsottamasūtra*. Delhi: Motilal Banarsidass Publishers Private Limited, 2016 [1970].

An Encyclopaedic Tibetan-English Dictionary: A Revised Version of Bod rGya Tshig mdzod chen mo. Vol. 1, *ka–nya*. Translated by Gyurme Dorje and Tudeng Nima. Editor of the Tibetan text, Tudeng Nyima. Executive Editor Tadeusz Skorupski. Beijing and London: Nationalities Publishing House / School of Oriental and African Studies, 2001.

Eracle, Jean. *Paroles du Bouddha: tirées de la tradition primitive*. Paris: Éditions du Seuil, 1991.

Fagan, Brian M. *A Little History of Archaeology*. New Haven and London: Yale University Press, 2018.

Falk, Harry. "A New Gāndhārī Dharmapada (Texts from the Split Collection 3)." *ARIRIAB* 18 (2015): 23–62

Fausbøll, Viggo, ed. and trans. *Dhammapadam: Ex tribus codicibus Hauniensibus Palice edidit, Latine vertit, Excerptis ex commentario Palico Notisque illustravit V. Fausbøll*. Copenhagen, 1855.

———, ed. and trans. *The Dhammapada: Being A Collection of Moral Verses in Pali. Edited a Second Time with a Literal Latin Translation and Notes for the Use of Pali Students*. Repr. Secunderabad, Telangana: Ananda Buddha Vihara Trust, 2000.

Feer, Léon. *Analyse du Kandjour*. Annales du Musée Guimet 2. Lyon: Imprimerie Pitrat Ainé, 1881.

———, trans. *Avadāna-Çataka: Cent légendes bouddhiques*. Annales du Musée Guimet 18. Amsterdam: Oriental Press, 1979 [Paris: Ernest Leroux, 1891].

———, trans. *Fragments extraits du Kandjour*. Annales du Musée Guimet 5. Paris: Ernest Leroux, 1883.

Fergusson, James, and James Burgess. *The Cave Temples of India*. Cambridge: Cambridge University Press, 2013 [1880].

Fleet, J. F. "Sanskrit and Old-Canarese Inscriptions." *Indian Antiquary* 10 (July 1881): 185–90.

Forbidden City Publishing House. *Across the Silk Road: Gupta Sculptures and Their Chinese Counterparts during 400–700 AD*. Compiled by the Palace Museum, the Fujian Museum, the Zhejiang Museum, and the Sichuan Museum. 2 vols. Beijing: Forbidden City Publishing House, 2016.

Foucaux, Philippe Edouard, trans. *Le Lalitavistara: L'histoire traditionelle de la vie du Bouddha Çakyamuni*. Paris: Les Deux Océans, 1988 [1884].

———, trans. *Rgya tch'er rol pa ou développement des jeux contenant l'histoire du Bouddha Çakya-mouni*. Paris: L'Imprimerie Royale, 1848.

Fowler, Alastair, ed. *The New Oxford Book of Seventeenth Century Verse*. Oxford: Oxford University Press, 1991.

Francis, H. T., trans. *The Jātaka or Stories of the Buddha's Former Births*. Translated from the Pāli by various hands under the editorship of Professor E. B. Cowell. Vol. 6. London: Pali Text Society, 1981 [1895].

Garrow, Duncan, and Neil Wilkin. *The World of Stonehenge*. London: British Museum, 2022.

Geiger, Wilhelm. *The Mahavāmsa or the Great Chronicle of Ceylon*. English translation assisted by Mabel Haynes Bode. London: Pali Text Society, 1912.

George, Coulter H. *How Dead Languages Work*. Oxford: Oxford University Press, 2020.

Gethin, Rupert. *Sayings of the Buddha: New Translations by Rupert Gethin from the Pāli Nikāyas*. Oxford: Oxford University Press, 2008.

———. "Tales of Miraculous Teachings: Miracles in Early Indian Buddhism." In *The Cambridge Companion to Miracles*, edited by G. H. Twelftree, 216–34. Cambridge: Cambridge University Press, 2011.

Giustarini, Giuliano. "The Role of Fear (Bhaya) in the Nikāyas and in the Abhidhamma." *Journal of Indian Philosophy* 40 (2012): 511–31.

Gnoli, Raniero. *The Gilgit Manuscript of the Śayanāsanavastu and the Adhikaraṇavastu: Being the 15th and 16th Sections of the Vinaya of the Mūlasarvāstivādin*. Serie Orientale Roma 50. Rome: Istituto italiano per il Medio ed Estremo Oriente, 1978.

Gnoli, Raniero, ed., with T. Venkatacharya. *The Gilgit Manuscript of the Saṅghabhedavastu: Being the 17th and Last Section of the Vinaya of the Mūlasarvāstivādin*. 2 parts. Serie Orientale Roma 49, 1, 2. Rome: Istituto Italiano per il Medio ed Estremo Oriente, 1977, 1978.

Gombrich, Richard. *Buddhism and Pāli*. Oxford: Mud Pie, 2018.

———. *Theravāda Buddhism: A Social History from Ancient Benares to Modern Colombo*. London: Routledge & Kegan Paul, 1988.

Gómez, Luis O., trans. *The Land of Bliss, The Paradise of the Buddha of Measureless Light: Sanskrit and Chinese Versions of the Sukhāvatīvyūha Sutras*. Honolulu: University of Hawai'i Press, 1996.

Gómez, Luis, and Paul Harrison, with the Mangalam Translation Group, trans. *Vimalakīrtinirdeśa: The Teaching of Vimalakīrti. An English Translation of the Sanskrit Text Found in the Potala Palace, Lhasa*. Berkeley, CA: Mangalam Press, 2022.

Goswami, Bijoya, trans. *Lalitavistara: English Translation with Notes*. Bibliotheca Indica 320. Kolkata: Asiatic Society, 2001.

Grünbold, Günter, et al., ed. *Die Worte des Buddha in den Sprachen der Welt / The Words of the Buddha in the Languages of the World: Tipiṭaka, Tripiṭaka, Dazangjing, Kanjur*. Munich: Bayerische Staatsbibliothek, 2005.

Guenther, Herbert V., trans. *The Jewel Ornament of Liberation*. London: Rider and Company, 1959.

Guenther, Herbert V., and Leslie Kawamura, trans. *Mind in Buddhist Psychology: A Translation of Ye-shes rgyal-mtshan's "The Necklace of Clear Understanding."* Emeryville, CA: Dharma Publishing, 1975.

Guy, John. "Dharmachakras, Yashtis and Yakshas with Special Reference to Phanigiri." In *Phanigiri: Interpreting an Ancient Buddhist Site in Telangana*, edited by Naman P. Ahuja, 66–91. Mumbai: Marg Publications / Department of Heritage Telangana, 2021.

Habata, Hiromi. *A Critical Edition of the Tibetan Translation of the Mahāparinirvāṇa-mahāsūtra*. Wiesbaden: Dr. Ludwig Reighert Verlag, 2013.

———. "Mahāsūtra and 'Mahāyānasūtra.'" *Hōrin: Comparative Studies in Japanese Culture* 20 (2019): 132–51.

———. *Die zentralasiatischen Sanskrit-Fragmente des Mahāparinirvāṇa-mahāsūtra. Kritische Ausgabe des Sanskrittextes und seiner tibetischen Übertragung im Vergleich mit den chinesischen Übersetzungen*. Indica et Tibetica 51. Marburg: Indica et Tibetica Verlag, 2007.

Habib, Irfan. "The Envisioning of a Nation: A Defence of the Idea of India." *Social Scientist* 27.9/10 (September–October 1999): 18–29.

———. "The Formation of India: Notes on the History of an Idea." *Social Scientist* 25.7/8 (July–August 1997): 3–10.

Hackin, Joseph. "Les scènes figurées de la vie du Buddha d'après des peintures tibétaines." In *Mémoires concernant l'Asie Orientale (Inde, Asie Centrale, Extrême-Orient)*, publiés par l'Académie des inscriptions et belles-lettres sous la direction de MM. Senart, Chavannes, Cordier, vol. 2, pp. 1–112 + tables and plates. Paris: Ernest Leroux, Éditeur, 1916.

Hahn, Michael. "Miscellanea Etymologica Tibetica VIII. Ting nge 'dzin et alia." In *Chomolangma, Demawend and Kasbek. Festschrift für Roland Bielmeier zu seinem 65. Geburtstag*, edited by Brigitte Huber, Marianne Volkart, and Paul

Widmer, Band 1, pp. 107–18. Beiträge zur Zentralasienforschung 12. Halle: International Institute for Tibetan and Buddhist Studies, 2008.

———. "On the Function and Origin of the Particle *dag*." In *Tibetan Studies Presented at the Seminar of Young Tibetologists, Zurich, June 26–July 1, 1977*, edited by Martin Brauen and Per Kvaerne, 137–47. Zürich: Völkerkundemuseum der Universität Zürich, 1978.

———, trans. *Vom rechten Leben: Buddhistische Lehren aus Indien und Tibet*. Aus dem Sanskrit und aus dem Tibetischen übersetzt und herausgegeben von Michael Hahn. Frankfurt am Main and Leipzig: Verlag der Weltreligion, 2007.

Hahn, Michael, and Siglinde Dietz, trans. *Wege zur rechten Erkenntnis: buddhistische Lehrbriefe*. Frankfurt am Main: Verlag der Weltreligionen, 2008.

Hamburger, Jeffrey F., and Joshua O'Driscoll. *Imperial Splendor: The Art of the Book in the Holy Roman Empire, 800–1500*. New York: Morgan Library and Museum, 2021.

Hare, E. M., trans. *The Book of Gradual Sayings (Anguttara-Nikāya) or More-Numbered Suttas*. Vol. 4, *The Books of the Sevens, Eights and Nines*. London: Pali Text Society / Luzac, 1965 [1935].

Harris, E. B. *Description of Buddhist Remains Discovered at Sooltangunge, on the River Ganges, 1862–63*. London: A. Williams, 1864.

Harrison, Paul. "The Case of the Vanishing Poet: New Light on Śāntideva and the Śikṣā-samuccaya." In *Indica et Tibetica: Festschrift für Michael Hahn, Zum 65. Geburtstag von Freunden und Schülern überreicht*, edited by Konrad Klaus and J.-U. Hartmann, 215–48. Vienna: Arbeitskreis für tibetische und buddhistische Studien Universität Wien, 2007.

———. "Remarks on Recently Identified Sanskrit Fragments of the *Pratyutpanna-buddhasaṃmukhāvasthitasamādhi-sūtra*." In *Archaeologies of the Written: Indian, Tibetan, and Buddhist Studies in Honour of Cristina Scherrer-Schaub*, edited by Vincent Tournier, Vincent Eltschinger, and Marta Sernesi, 269–85. Naples: Università degli Studi di Napoli "L'Orientale," 2020.

———. "Śāntideva: The Author and His Project." In *Readings of Śāntideva's Guide to Bodhisattva Practice (Bodhicaryāvatāra)*, edited by Jonathan C. Gold and Douglas S. Duckworth, 27–44. Columbia Readings of Buddhist Literature. New York: Columbia University Press, 2019.

———. "Verses by Śāntideva in the 'Śikṣāsamuccaya': A New English Translation." *Bulletin of the Asia Institute*, new series 23 (2009): 87–103.

Harrison, Paul, and Jens-Uwe Hartmann, eds. *From Birch Bark to Digital Data: Recent Advances in Buddhist Manuscript Research*. Papers Presented at the Conference "Indic Buddhist Manuscripts: The State of the Field," Stanford, June 15–19, 2009. Beiträge zur Kultur- und Geistesgeschichte Asiens 80, Denkschriften der philosophisch-historischen Klasse 460. Vienna: Österreichische Akademie der Wissenschaften, 2014.

Harrison, Paul, Timothy Lenz, and Richard Salomon. "Fragments of a Gāndhārī Manuscript of the *Pratyutpannabuddhasaṃmukhāvasthitasamādhisūtra* (Studies in Gāndhārī Manuscripts 1)." *Journal of the International Association of Buddhist Studies* 41 (2018): 117–43.

Harrisson, Tom. *World Within: A Borneo Story*. Singapore: Oxford Unversity Press, 1986 [1959].

Hartmann, Jens-Uwe. "King Prasenajit Bemoans the Death of His Grandmother: A Study of the Manuscript SHT 7185." *International Journal of Buddhist Thought and Culture* 27.1 (June 2017): 73–105.

———. "Poetry: South Asia." In *Brill's Encyclopedia of Buddhism*, vol. 1, edited by Jonathan A. Silk, 532–40. Leiden: Brill, 2016.

———. "Sanskrit Versions of the Āgamas: Schools, Regions and Editors." In *Research on the Saṃyukta-āgama*, edited by Dhammadinnā, 359–86. Taipei: Dharma Drum Publishing, 2020.

———. "Trauer um die Großmutter und Trost vom Buddha: das *Āryikā-sūtra*." In *Connecting the Art, Literature, and Religion of South and Central Asia: Studies in Honour of Monika Zin*, edited by Ines Konczak-Nagel, Satomi Hiyama, and Astrid Klein, 153-60. New Delhi: Dev Publishers, 2022.

Hartmann, Jens-Uwe, and Klaus Wille. "The Central Asian Fragments in the Pelliot Collection (Paris)." In *From Birch Bark to Digital Data*, edited by Paul Harrison and Jens-Uwe Hartmann, 213–22. Vienna: Österreichische Akademie der Wissenschaften, 2014.

———. "The Manuscript of the Dīrghāgama and the Private Collection in Virginia." In *From Birch Bark to Digital Data*, edited by Paul Harrison and Jens-Uwe Hartmann, 137–55. Vienna: Österreichische Akademie der Wissenschaften, 2014.

Hazlitt, William. "On the Ignorance of the Learned." In *A Book of English Essays*, edited by W. E. Williams, 144–55. London: Penguin Books, 1978 [1942].

Hidas, Gergely, ed., trans. *Mahāpratisarā-Mahāvidyārājñī, The Great Amulet, Great Queen of Spells: Introduction, Critical Editions and Annotated Translation*. Śatapiṭaka Series 636. New Delhi: International Academy of Indian Culture and Aditya Prakashan, 2012.

———. *Powers of Protection: The Buddhist Tradition of Spells in the Dhāraṇīsaṃgraha Collections*. Beyond Boundaries, edited by Michael Willis, Sam van Schaik, and Lewis Doney, vol. 9. Berlin and Boston: Walter de Gruyter, 2021.

———. "Rituals in the Mahāsāhasrapramardanasūtra." In *Puṣpikā: Tracing Ancient India through Texts and Traditions, Contributions to Current Research in Indology, 1*. Proceedings of the First International Indology Graduate Research Symposium, September 2009, Oxford, edited by Nina Mirnig, Péter-Dániel Szántó, Michael Williams, 225–40. Oxford and Oakville: Oxbow Books, 2013.

Hikata, Ryusho, ed. *Suvikrāntavikrāmi-Paripṛcchā-Prajñāpāramitā-Sūtra*. Kyoto: Rinsen, 1983 [1958].

von Hinüber, Oskar. "The Buddha as a Historical Person." *JIABS* 42 (2019): 231–64.

———. *A Handbook of Pāli Literature.* Indian Philology and South Asian Studies 2. Berlin and New York: Walter de Gruyter, 1996.

———. "On the Early History of Indic Buddhist Colophons." *International Journal of Buddhist Thought and Culture* 27.1 (June 2017): 45–72.

von Hinüber, Oskar, and Peter Skilling. "Two Buddhist Inscriptions from Deorkothar (Dist. Rewa, Madhya Pradesh)." In *Annual Report of the International Research Institute for Advanced Buddhology at Soka University for the Academic Year 2012*, vol. 16, pp. 13–36, plates 4–11. Tokyo: International Research Institute for Advanced Buddhology, Soka University, 2013.

Hiremath, R. C. *Buddhism in Karnataka.* New Delhi: D. K. Printworld, 1994.

Hôbôgirin: Dictionnaire encyclopédique du bouddhisme d'après les sources chinoises et japonaises, fascicules 1 to 8. Edited by Paul Demiéville, Sylvain Lévi, J. Takakusu, et al. Publié par Tokyo: L'Académie des Inscriptions et Belles-Lettres Institut de France avec le concours de L'Académie du Japon et de la Maison Franco-Japonaise, 1929–2003.

Hockney, David, and Martin Gayford, *A History of Pictures: From the Cave to the Computer Screen.* New ed. London: Thames & Hudson, 2016.

Holz, Kathrin. *The Bhadrakarātrī-sūtra: Apotropaic Scriptures in Early Indian Buddhism.* Monographien zur indischen Archäologie, Kunst und Philologie 27. Heidelberg University Library: CrossAsia-eBooks, 2021.

Hong, Luo. "The Cakrabhedavastu of Guṇaprabha's *Vinayasūtra.*" *Journal of Indian and Tibetan Studies* 24 (March 2021): 49–56.

Horner, I. B., trans. *The Collection of the Middle Length Sayings (Majjhima-Nikāya).* 3 vols. London, Luzac for the Pali Text Society, 1967–75 [1954–59].

Howard, Angela Falco. *Summit of Treasures: Buddhist Cave Art of Dazu, China.* Bangkok: Orchid Press, 2001.

Hu-von Hinüber, Haiyan, ed. *Das Bhikṣu-Prātimokṣasūtra der Mūlasarvāstivādins anhand der Sanskrit-Handschriften aus Tibet und Gilgit sowie unter Berücksichtigung der tibetischen und chinesischen Übersetzungen kritisch herausgegeben.* Freiburg: Freiburg Universität, 2003.

———. "Some Remarks on the Sanskrit Manuscript of the Mūlasarvāstivāda-Prātimokṣasūtra Found in Tibet." In *Jaina-itihāsa-ratna: Festschrift für Gustav Roth zum 90. Geburtstag*, edited by Ute Hüsken, Petra Kieffer-Pülz, and Anne Peters, 283–337. Indica et Tibetica 47. Marburg: Indica et Tibetica, 2006.

Ichimura, Shohei, trans. *The Canonical Book of the Buddha's Lengthy Discourses*, vol. 1. Berkeley, CA: BDK America, 2015.

———, trans. *The Canonical Book of the Buddha's Lengthy Discourses*, vol. 2. Moraga, CA: BDK America, 2016.

Ignatieff, Michael. *On Consolation: Finding Solace in Dark Times.* New York: Metropolitan Books, 2022.

Ireland, John D., trans. *The Udāna: Inspired Utterances of the Buddha*. Kandy: Buddhist Publication Society, 1990.

Ishihama Yumiko and Fukuda Yoichi, ed. *A New Critical Edition of the Mahāvyutpatti: Sanskrit-Tibetan-Mongolian Dictionary of Buddhist Terminology*. Studia Tibetica 16 / Materials for Tibetan-Mongolian Dictionaries 1. Tokyo: Toyo Bunko, 1989.

Ishikawa Mie, ed. *A Critical Edition of the sGra sbyor bam po gnyis pa, An Old and Basic Commentary on the Mahāvyutpatti*. Studia Tibetica 18 / Materials for Tibetan-Mongolian Dictionaries 2. Tokyo: Toyo Bunko, 1990.

Iwamoto, Yutaka, ed. *Mahāsāhasrapramardanī*. In *Kleinere Dhāraṇī Texte*. Beiträge zur Indologie Heft 1: Pañcarakṣā 1. Kyoto: Shobundo Shoten, 1937.

Jaini, Padmanabh S, ed. *Abhidharmadīpa with Vibhāṣāprabhāvṛtti*. Tibetan Sanskrit Works 4. Patna: Kashi Prasad Jayaswal Research Institute, 1977.

———. "(Introduction to and Translation of) Ākāravattārasutta: An 'Apocryphal' Sutta from Thailand." In *Collected Papers on Buddhist Studies*, 535–57. Delhi: Motilal Banarsidass, 2001.

Jamspal, Lozang, Ngawang Samten Chophel, and Peter Della Santina, trans. *Nāgārjuna's Letter to King Gautamiputra with Explanatory Notes Based on Tibetan Commentaries and a Preface by His Holiness Sakya Trizin*. Delhi: Motilal Banarsidass, 1978.

Jayawickrama, N. A. *Suttanipāta: Pali Text with Translation into English and Notes*. Kelaniya, Sri Lanka: Post-Graduate Institute of Pali and Buddhist Studies, University of Kelaniya, 2001.

Jin, Siyan, trans. *Soutra de l'ultime voyage ou le dernier discours du Bouddha: Mahā-Parinibbāna-Sutta*. Paris: Éditions You Feng, 2013.

Jinpa, Thupten, trans. *The Book of Kadam: The Core Texts*. Attributed to Atiśa and Dromtönpa. The Library of Tibetan Classics 2. Somerville, MA: Wisdom Publications, 2008.

———. *Tsongkhapa: A Buddha in the Land of Snows*. Lives of the Masters. Boulder: Shambala Publications, 2019.

Johnston, E[dward] H[amilton], ed. and trans. *Aśvaghoṣa's Buddhacarita or Acts of the Buddha: Complete Sanskrit Text with English Translation: Cantos I to XIV Translated from the Original Sanskrit Supplemented by the Tibetan Version together with an Introduction and Notes*. Delhi: Motilal Banarsidass, 2007.

Jones, J. J., trans. *The Mahāvastu*. 3 vols. London: Pali Text Society, 1973–78 [1949–56].

Jongeward, David, Elizabeth Errington, Richard Salomon, and Stefan Baums. *Gandharan Buddhist Reliquaries*. Gandharan Studies 1. Seattle: University of Washington Press, 2012.

Kākkāpalliye Anuruddha Thera, Mary M. Y. Fung, and S. K. Siu, trans. *The First and Second Buddhist Councils: Five Versions: English Translations from Pāli and Chinese*. Hong Kong: Chi Lin Nunnery, 2008.

Kapstein, Matthew T. "L'oubli des Russes: An (Almost) Forgotten Chapter in the History of 19th-Century Orientalism." *Revue internationale de philosophie* 1.287 (2019): 79–90.

Karashima, Seishi, ed. *Die Abhisamācārikā Dharmāḥ: Verhaltensregeln für buddhistische Mönche der Mahāsāṃghika-Lokottaravādins, herausgegeben, mit der chinesischen Parallelversion verglichen, übersetzt und kommentiert*. Bibliotheca Philologica et Philosophica Buddhica 13. Tokyo: International Research Institute for Advanced Buddhology, Soka University, 2012.

Karma Thinley Rinpoche. *The Telescope of Wisdom: A Condensed Interlinear Commentary on the Great Master Nagarjuna's The Letter to a Friend*. Bristol: Ganesha Press, 2009.

Karma pa Sku phreng dgu pa Dbang phyug rdo rje. *Chos mngon pa'i mdzod kyi rnam par bshad pa chos mngon rgya mtsho'i snying po mkhyen brtse'i zhal lung gzhon nu rnam rol legs bshad chos mig rnam 'byed grub pa'i shing rta*. Sarnath: Vajra Vidya Institute, 2003.

Karttunen, Klaus. *Persons of Indian Studies*. https://whowaswho-indology.info/.

Kawamura, Leslie, trans. *Golden Zephyr: Instructions from a Spiritual Friend by Nagarjuna and Lama Mipham*. Emeryville, CA: Dharma Publishing, 1975.

Kim, Jinah, and Todd Lewis, ed. *Dharma and Puṇya: Buddhist Ritual Art of Nepal*. Leiden and Boston: Hotei Publishing, 2019.

Kloppenborg, Ria. *The Paccekabuddha: A Buddhist Ascetic*. A study of the concept of the paccekabuddha in Pāli canonical and commentarial literature. Orientalia Rheno-Traiectina 20. Leiden: E. J. Brill, 1974. Repr. as Wheel Publication 305/306/307. Kandy: Buddhist Publication Society, 1983.

Kolb, Anne, ed. *Literacy in Ancient Everyday Life*. Berlin: De Gruyter, 2018.

Kouhala. *Lilavai*. Edited and translated by Andrew Ollett. Murty Classical Library of India 29. Cambridge, MA: Harvard University Press, 2021.

Krishna Murthy, M. S. *Buddhist Art and Culture in Karnataka–India*. Mysuru: Department of Archaeology, Museums and Heritage, 2019.

Kritzer, Robert, ed. and trans. *Garbhāvakrāntisūtra: The Sūtra on Entry into the Womb* Studia Philologica Buddhica Monograph Series 31. Tokyo: International Institute for Buddhist Studies of the International College for Postgraduate Buddhist Studies, 2014.

La Vallée Poussin, Louis de. *L'Abhidharmakośa de Vasubandhu*. 5 vols. Paris: Paul Geuthner, 1923–31.

———. *Bouddhisme. Études et matériaux: Cosmologie: le monde des êtres et le monde-réceptacle. Vasubandhu et Yaçomitra, troisième chapitre de l'Abhidharmakoça: Kārikā, Bhāsya et Vyakhyā. Avec une analyse de la Lokaprajnápti et de la Kāranaprajñāpti de Maudgalyāyana. Versions et textes établis d'après les sources sanscrites et tibétaines*. Académie royale de Belgique, Classe des Lettres et des Sciences morales et politiques et Classe des Beaux-Arts: Mémoires, Collection in 40, Deuxiéme série—Tome VI, janvier 1919. Brussels: Hayez, Imprimeur de l'Académie Royal.

———. "Documents sanscrits de la seconde collection M. A. Stein." *Journal of the Royal Asiatic Society* (April 1911): 759–77.

———. "Documents sanscrits de la seconde collection M. A. Stein. Fragments de l'Udānavarga de Dharmatrāta." *Journal of the Royal Asiatic Society* (April 1912): 355–77.

———. "Pratyekabuddha." In *Encyclopaedia of Religion and Ethics*. Edited by James Hastings. Vol. 10, 152–54. Edinburgh: T. & T. Clark, 1918.

———, ed. *Mūlamadhyamakakārikās (Mādhyamikasūtras) de Nāgārjuna*. Bibliotheca Buddhica 4. Osnabrück: Biblio Verlag, 1970.

Lamotte, Étienne, trans. *Abhidharmakośa de Vasubandhu*. Nouvelle édition anastatique présentée par Étienne Lamotte, Tome I. Brussels: Institut Belge des Hautes Études Chinoises, 1971.

———. "La Critique d'authenticité dans le bouddhisme." In *India Antiqua: A Volume of Oriental Studies Presented by His Friends and Pupils to Jean Philippe Vogel, C.I.E., on the Occasion of the Fiftieth Anniversary of His Doctorate*, 213–22. Leyden: E. J. Brill, 1947.

———. *Histoire du bouddhisme indien, des origines à l'ère Śaka*. Publications de l'Institut Orientaliste de Louvain 14. Louvain-la-Neuve: Université de Louvain, Institut Orientaliste, 1976 [1958].

———. "Un Sūtra composite de l'Ekottarāgama." *Bulletin of the School of Oriental and African Studies* 30.1 (February 1967): 105–16; English translation by Sara Boin-Webb as "A Composite Sūtra from the Ekottarāgama" in *Buddhist Studies Review*, 1995.

———. *Le Traité de la Grande Vertu de Sagesse de Nāgārjuna (Mahāprajñāpāramitāśāstra)*. 5 vols. Louvain: Institut Orientaliste, Université de Louvain, 1976.

Lee, Hsu-Feng. *A Study of the Śarīrārthagāthā in the Yogācārabhūmi*. PhD dissertation. University of Sydney, 2017.

Lefman, S., ed. *Lalita Vistara*. Erster Teil. Halle: Verlag der Buchhandlung des Waisenhauses, 1902.

Lévi, Sylvain. "L'Apramada-varga: Étude sur les recensions des Dharmapadas." Documents de L'Asie Centrale (Mission Pelliot). *Journal Asiatique* (September–October 1912): 203–94.

———. "Observations sur la langue précanonique du bouddhisme." *Journal Asiatique* (July 1912).

Lewis, Todd T. *Popular Buddhist Texts from Nepal: Narratives and Rituals of Newar Buddhism*. Translations in collaboration with Subarna Man Tuladhar and Labh Ratna Tuladhar. Albany: State University of New York Press, 2000.

Lin Li-Kouang. *Dharmasamuccaya: Compendium de la Loi, recueil de stances extraites du Saddharma-smṛty-upasthāna-sūtra par Avalokitasiṃha, chapitres VI–XII*. Texte sanskrit édité avec la version tibétaine et les versions chinoises et traduit en français par Lin Li-Kouang, Révision de André Bareau, J. W. de Jong et Paul Demiéville avec des Appendices par J. W. de Jong. Paris: Librairie d'Amérique et d'Orient, Adrien-Maisonneuve, 1969.

———. *Introduction au Compendium de la Loi (Dharma-Samuccaya). L'Aide-Mémoire de la Vraie Loi (Saddharma-smṛtyupasthāna-sūtra): Recherches sur un Sūtra Développé du Petit Véhicule*. Publications du Musée Guimet, Bibliothèque d'Études, 54. Paris: Librairie d'Amérique et d'Orient, Adrien-Maisonneuve, 1949 [repr. Shanghai 2014].

Lind, Agneta. *Literacy for All: Making a Difference*. Paris: UNESCO, 2008. https://www.iiep.unesco.org/en/publication/literacy-all-making-difference.

Lindtner, Christian. "Materials for the Study of Bhavya." In *Kalyāṇamitrārāgaṇam: Essays in Honour of Nils Simonsson*, edited by Eivind Kahrs, 179–202. Oslo: Norwegian University Press, Institute for Comparative Research in Human Culture, 1986.

Lodrö Sangpo, Gelong, trans. *Abhidharmakośa-Bhāṣya of Vasubandhu: The Treasury of the Abhidharma and Its (Auto) Commentary*. 4 vols. English translation of the French translation of Louis de La Vallée Poussin. Delhi: Motilal Banarsidass, 2012.

Lokuppatti Aruṇavatīsūtra Paṭhamamūl Paṭhamakap lae Mūlatantrai. Bangkok: Ho samut haeng chat krom sinlapakon [National Library Fine Arts Department], 2533 (1990).

Lynch, Jack, ed. *Samuel Johnson's Dictionary: Selections from the 1755 Work That Defined the English Language*. London: Atlantic Books, 2004 [2002].

MacCabe, Colin, and Holly Yanacek, eds. *Keywords for Today: A 21st Century Vocabulary*. New York: Oxford University Press, 2018.

McLuhan, Marshall, and Quentin Fiore. *The Medium Is the Message*. New York: Bantam Books, 1967.

McRae, John, trans. *The Sutra of Mañjuśrī's Questions*. Berkeley, CA: Numata Center for Buddhist Translation and Research, 2016.

Mahāvyutpatti. See Ishihama and Fukuda, *A New Critical Edition of the Mahāvyutpatti*.

Malalasekera, G. P. *Dictionary of Pāli Proper Names*. 2 vols. New Delhi: Munshiram Manoharlal Publishers, 1983 [1938].

Malinar, Angelika. *The Bhagavadgītā: Doctrines and Contents*. Cambridge: Cambridge University Press, 2007.

Marciniak, Katarzyna, ed. *The Mahāvastu: A New Edition*, vol. 3. Bibliotheca Philologica et Philosophica Buddhica 14.1. Tokyo: International Research Institute for Advanced Buddhology Soka University, 2019.

Marino, Joseph. "The Gāndhārī 'Discourse on Pleasure and Pain': Some Thoughts on Similes and Textual Variation in the Connected Discourses." In *Research on the Saṃyukta-āgama*, edited by Dhammadinnā, 259–300. Taipei: Dharma Drum Publishing, 2020.

Masefield, Peter, trans. *The Commentary on the Itivuttaka, The Itivuttaka-aṭṭhakathā (Paramatthadīpanī II) of Dhammapāla*, vol. 1. Oxford: Pali Text Society, 2008.

———, trans. *The Udāna Commentary (Paramatthadīpanī nāma Udānāṭṭhakathā) by Dhammapāla*. 2 vols. Oxford: Pali Text Society, 1994, 1995.

Matsuda Kazunobu. "Sanskrit Fragment of the Udānavarga (Recension 2) from Gilgit." *Bukkyōgakubu Ronshu* (*Journal of School of Buddhism*, Bukkyo University) 95 (March 2011): 17–32.

Matsumura Hisashi. "Ayuḥparyantasūtra: Das Sūtra von der Lebensdauer in der verschiedenen Welten. Text in Sanskrit und Tibetisch, nach der Gilgit-Handschrift herausgegeben." In *Sanskrit-Texte aus dem buddhistischen Kanon: Neuentdeckungen und Neueditionen*, edited by Fumio Enomoto, Jens-Uwe Hartmann, and Hisashi Matsumura, 69–100. Sanskrit-Wörterbuch der buddhistischen Texte aus den Turfan-Funden 2. Göttingen: Vandenhoeck & Ruprecht, 1989.

Migot, André. *Un grand disciple du Buddha: Sáriputra*. Paris: Ecole française d'Extrême-Orient / Librairie d'Amérique et d'Orient, Adrien-Maisonneuve, 1954.

Mirsky, Jeannette. *Sir Aurel Stein: Archaeological Explorer*. Chicago: University of Chicago Press, 1977.

Mitra, Debala. *Buddhist Monuments*. Calcutta: Sahitya Sasmad 1980 [1971].

Mitrikeski, Drasko, trans. "Hymn to the Incomparable One." In *The Norton Anthology of World Religions: Buddhism*, edited by Donald S. Lopez Jr., 376–78. New York and London: W. W. Norton, 2015.

Mongkut, King (Rama IV). [*Prachum Phra Ratchaniphon phasa bali nai ratchakan thi 4: Corpus of Royal Writings in Pali, the Fourth Reign*]. 2 parts. Bangkok: Mahamakut University Press, 2515 (1972) / ประชุมพระนิพนธ์ภาษาบาลีในรัชกาลที่ 4 ภาค 2. คณะธรรมยุต พิมพ์โดยเสด็จพระราชกุศล ในงานพระเมรุพระศพ สมเด็จพระสังฆราช สกลมหาสังฆปริณายก ณ พระเมรุวัดเทพศิรินทราวาส วันที่ 17 มิถุนายน พุทธศักราช 2515. กรุงเทพฯ: โรงพิมพ์มหามกุฏราชวิทยาลัย, 2515.

Mukherjee, P[rabhat] K[umar]. "The Dhammapada and the Udānavarga." *Indian Historical Quarterly* 11 (1935): 741–60.

Mya Tin, Daw, trans. *The Dhammapada*. Yangon: Department for the Promotion and Propagation of the Sāsanā, 1993 [1986].

Nakamura, Hajime. *Gotama Buddha: A Biography Based on the Most Reliable Texts*, translated by Gaynor Sekimori. 2 vols. Tokyo: Kosei, 2005.

Nakatani, Hideaki. "Remarques sur la transmission des Dharmapada." *Bulletin d'Études Indiennes* 2 (1984): 135–51.

———, ed. *Udānavarga de Subaši. Édition critique du manuscrit sur bois provenent de*

Subaśi. Bibliothèque Nationale de Paris, Fonds Pelliot. 2 vols. Paris: Collège de France, Institut de Civilisation Indienne, 1987.

Ñāṇamoli, Bhikkhu, trans. *The Illustrator of Ultimate Meaning (Paramtthajotikā): Part I, Commentary on the Minor Readings by Bhadantācariya Buddhaghosa*. In *The Minor Readings (Khuddakapāṭha), The First Book of the Minor Collection (Khuddakanikāya)*. Oxford: Pali Text Society, 1991 [1960].

Ñāṇamoli, Bhikkhu, and Bhikkhu Bodhi, trans. *The Middle Length Discourses of the Buddha: A New Translation of the Majjhima Nikāya*. Boston: Wisdom Publications, 1995.

Nangsue suatmon ruam phra sut lae phra parit tang tang (หนังสือสวดมนต์รวมพระสูตรแลพระปริตรต่างๆ) [*Book of Chants containing a Variety of Suttas and Parittas*]. [Bangkok:] Rongphim Luang nai Phra Borommaharachawang, C.S. 1242 / BE 2423 [1880], repr. Bangkok: Amarin Printing and Publishing, 2551 [2008].

Nattier, Jan. "The Ten Epithets of the Buddha in the Translations of Zhi Qian 支謙." *ARIRIAB* 6 (2003): 207–50.

Naudou, Jean. *Les bouddhistes Kaśmīriens au Moyen Age*. Paris: Presses Universitaires de France, 1968.

Newman, John Ronald. *The Outer Wheel of Time: Vajrayāna Buddhist Cosmology in the Kālacakra Tantra*. PhD dissertation. University of Wisconsin–Madison, 1987.

Nilakanta Sastri, K. A., ed. *Age of the Nandas and Mauryas*. 2nd ed. Delhi: Motilal Banarsidass, 1967.

Nock, Albert Jay. *Memoirs of a Superfluous Man*. New York and London: Harper & Brothers, 1943.

Norman, H. C., ed. *The Commentary on the Dhammapada: Dhammapada-aṭṭhakathā*. 5 vols. London: Pali Text Society, 1970 [1906].

Norman, K. R., trans. *The Elders' Verses I: Theragāthā*. 2nd ed. Lancaster: Pali Text Society, 2007.

———. *Pali Literature: Including the Canonical Literature in Prakrit and Sanskrit of All the Hīnayāna Schools of Buddhism*. Wiesbaden: Otto Harrassowitz, 1983.

Numata Center for Buddhist Translation and Research. *Buddha-Dharma*. 2nd ed. Berkeley, CA, 2003 [1984].

Nyanaponika Thera and Hellmuth Hecker. *Great Disciples of the Buddha: Their Lives, Their Works, Their Legacy*. Boston: Wisdom Publications, 1997.

Nyanaponika Thera and Bhikkhu Bodhi, trans. *Numerical Discourses of the Buddha: An Anthology of Suttas from the Aṅguttara Nikāya*. Walnut Creek, CA: Altamira Press, 1999.

Nyanatiloka. *Buddhist Dictionary: Manual of Buddhist Terms and Doctrines*. 3rd ed., edited by Nyanaponika. Colombo: Frewin, 1972 [1952].

Obermiller, E., trans. *History of Buddhism (Chos-ḥbyung) by Bu-ston*. 2 vols. Materialien zur Kunde des Buddhismus 18/19. Tokyo: Suzuki Research Foundation, 1964 [Heidelberg: O. Harrassowitz, 1931–32].

Okano, Kiyoshi, ed., trans. *Sarvarakṣitas Mahāsaṃvartanīkathā: Ein Sanskrit-Sāṃmitīya-Schule des Hīnayāna-Buddhismus*. Sendai: Seminar of Indology, Tohoku University, 1998.

Oldenberg, Hermann, ed. and trans. *The Dīpavaṃsa: An Ancient Buddhist Historical Record*. New Delhi: Asian Educational Services, 1982 [1879].

Olivelle, Patrick. "Ashoka's Writings: New Insights into Ancient Indian Cultural History." In *Questioning Paradigms Constructing Histories: A Festschrift for Romila Thapar*, edited by Kumkum Roy and Naina Dayal. New Delhi: Aleph in association with The Book Review Literary Trust, 2019.

Ollett, Andrew. *Language of the Snakes: Prakrit, Sanskrit, and the Language Order of Premodern India*. South Asia across the Disciplines. Oakland: University of California Press, 2017.

Onions, C. T., with G. W. S. Friedrichsen and R. W. Burchfield, eds. *The Oxford Dictionary of English Etymology*. Oxford: Clarendon Press, 1967 [1966].

Pachow, W. *A Comparative Study of the Prātimokṣa on the Basis of Its Chinese, Tibetan, Sanskrit and Pāli Versions*. Buddhist Tradition Series 31. Delhi: Motilal Banarsidass Publishers Private Limited, 2000 [1955].

Padmakara Translation Group, trans. *Nagarjuna's Letter to a Friend with Commentary by Kangyur Rinpoche*. Ithaca, NY: Snow Lion Publications, 2005.

Pal, Pratapaditya. *Quest for Coomaraswamy: A Life in the Arts*. Calgary: Bayeux Arts, 2019.

Palumbo, Antonello. *An Early Chinese Commentary on the Ekottarika-āgama: The Fenbie gongde lun and the History of the Translation of the Zengyi ahan jing* Dharma Drum Buddhist College Research Series 7. Taipei: Dharma Drum Publishing, 2013.

Pannasiri, Bhadanta, trans. "Sigālovādasutta." *Visva-Bharati Annals* 3 (1950): 150–228.

Papañcasūdanī Majjhimanikāyaṭṭhakathā of Buddhaghosâcariya. 5 parts. London: Pali Text Society 1977 [1922–38].

Partridge, Eric. *The Gentle Art of Lexicography as Pursued and Experienced by an Addict*. London: Andre Deutsch, 1963.

Pāsādika, Bhikkhu, ed. and trans. *The Kāśyapa-parivarta*. New Delhi: Aditya Prakashan, 2015.

Pearsall, Judy, ed. *The New Oxford Dictionary of English*. Oxford: Oxford University Press, 2001 [1998].

Pearson, Mike Parker, et al. "The Original Stonehenge? A Dismantled Stone Circle in the Preseli Hills of West Wales." *Antiquity* 95.379 (12 February 2021): 85–103. Published online by Cambridge University Press.

Pecchia, Cristina, with Philip Pierce, eds. and trans. *Dharmakīrti on the Cessation of*

Suffering: A Critical Edition with Translation and Comments of Manorathanandin's Vṛtti and Vibhūticandra's Glosses on Pramāṇavārttika II.190–216. Leiden and Boston: Brill, 2015.

Pinault, Georges-Jean. *Chrestomathie tokharienne: Textes et grammaire*. Leuven-Paris: Peeters, 2006.

Pischel, Richard. "Die Turfan Recensionen des Dhammapada." In *Sitzungsberichte der Königlich Preussischen Akademie der Wissenschaften zu Berlin* 39 (July 1908): 968–85.

Pradhan, P., ed. *Abhidharma Kośabhāṣya of Vasubandhu*. Tibetan Sanskrit Works Series 8. Patna: K. P. Jayaswal Research Institute, 1967.

Prebish, Charles S. *Buddhist Monastic Discipline: The Sanskrit Prātimokṣa Sūtras of the Mahāsāṃghikas and Mūlasarvāstivādins*. University Park: Pennsylvania State University Press, 1975.

Przyluski, Jean. "La roue de la vie à Ajanta." *Journal Asiatique* 11.16 (1920): 313–31.

———. *Le Concile de Rājagṛha: Introduction à l'histoire des canons et des sectes bouddhiques*. Buddhica: série 1, tome 2. Paris: Paul Geuthner, 1927.

Puchner, Martin, general editor. *The Norton Anthology of World Literature*, vol. D. 4th ed. New York and London: W. W. Norton, 2018.

Puini, Carlo, trans. *Mahaparinirvana-sutra ovvero il libro della totale estinzione del Buddha nella redazione cinese di Pe-Fa-Tsu*. Lanciano: R. Carabba Editore, 2008 [1919].

Rahula, Walpola, trans. *Abhidharmasamuccaya: The Compendium of the Higher Teaching (Philosophy) by Asaṅga*. English version from French by Sara Boin-Webb. Fremont, CA: Asian Humanities Press, 2001.

Ramesh, Jairam. *The Light of Asia: The Poem That Defined the Buddha*. New Delhi: Penguin Books, 2021.

Red Pine, trans. *Why Not Paradise: The Pure Land of Amitabha Buddha*. Anacortes, WA: Empty Bowl Press, 2019.

Rhys Davids, C. A. F., assisted by Sūriyagoḍa Sumangala Thera, trans. *The Book of Kindred Sayings (Sanyutta-Nikāya) or Grouped Suttas: Part 1, Kindred Sayings with Verses (Sagāthā-vagga)*. Pali Text Society Translation Series 7. London: Luzac, 1971 [1917].

———, trans. *Psalms of the Early Buddhists, Part II: Psalms of the Brethren*. London: Pali Text Society / Henry Frowde, 1913.

Rhys Davids, T. W., and C. A. F. Rhys Davids, trans. "Mahâ Parinibbâna Suttanta-"/"*Book of the Great Decease*." In *Dialogues of the Buddha*, part 2: 71–191. 4th ed. Sacred Books of the Buddhists 3. London: Pali Text Society / Routledge & Kegan Paul, 1977 [1910].

Roberts, Peter Alan, trans. *The King of Samādhis Sūtra*. Taipei: Corporate Body of the Buddha Educational Foundation, 2018. Also available at 84000.co.

Rockhill, William Woodville, trans. *Udânavarga: A Collection of Verses from the*

Buddhist Canon Compiled by Dharmatrâta Being the Northern Buddhist Version of Dhammapada. Translated from the Tibetan of the Bkaḥ-ḥgyur, with Notes and Extracts from the Commentary of Pradjnâvarman. London: Trübner, 1883.

———. *The Life of the Buddha and the Early History of His Order Derived from Tibetan Works in the Bkah-Hgyur and Bstan-Hgyur Followed by Notices on the Early History of Tibet and Khoten.* Trübner's Oriental Series 30. London: Kegan Paul, Trench, Trübner, 1907.

Roebuck, Valerie, trans. *The Dhammapada.* London: Penguin Books, 2010.

Roesler, Ulrike, Ken Holmes, and David P. Jackson, trans. *Stages of the Buddha's Teachings: Three Key Texts.* Library of Tibetan Classics 10. Somerville, MA: Wisdom Publications, 2015.

Roget's International Thesaurus. 3rd ed. London and Glasgow: Collins, 1977 [1963].

Roloff, Carola. *The Buddhist Nuns' Ordination in the Tibetan Canon: Possibilities of the Revival of the Mūlasarvāstivāda Bhikṣuṇī Lineage.* Hamburg Buddhist Studies 15. Hamburg: Projektverlag, 2020.

Rotman, Andy, trans. *Divine Stories: Divyāvadāna, Part 1.* Boston: Wisdom Publications, 2008.

———, trans. *Divine Stories: Divyāvadāna, Part 2.* Somerville, MA: Wisdom Publications, 2017.

———. *Hungry Ghosts.* Somerville, MA: Wisdom Publications, 2021.

Roy, Kumkum, and Naina Dayal, eds. *Questioning Paradigms, Constructing Histories: A Festschrift for Romila Thapar.* New Delhi: Aleph in association with The Book Review Literary Trust, 2019.

Saito, Akira, editor in chief. *Buddhakośa: A Treasury of Buddhist Terms and Illustrative Sentences.* Vol. 2, *The One Hundred Elements (dharma) of Yogācāra in the Abhidharmasamuccaya and Pañcaskandhaka.* Bibliotheca Indologica et Buddhologica 16. Tokyo: Sankibo Press, 2014.

Śākya, Dharmaratna, ed. *Svasti bākya va maṃgalāṣṭaba bhābārtha sahita.* Lalitpur, Nepal Saṃvat 1112 (1992).

Salguero, C. Pierce, ed. *Buddhism and Medicine: An Anthology of Premodern Sources.* New York: Columbia University Press, 2017.

Salomon, Richard. *The Buddhist Literature of Ancient Gandhāra: An Introduction with Selected Translations.* Somerville, MA: Wisdom Publications, 2018.

———. *Indian Epigraphy: A Guide to the Study of Inscriptions in Sanskrit, Prakrit, and the Other Indo-Aryan Languages.* Oxford: Oxford University Press, 1998.

———. "On the Evolution of Written Āgama Collections in Northern Buddhist Tradition." In *Research on the Madhyama-āgama,* edited by Dhammadinnā, 239–68. Dharma Drum Institute of Liberal Arts Research Series 5. Taipei: Dharma Drum Publishing, 2017.

Samtani, N. H., ed. *Arthaviniścaya-sūtra and Its Commentary (Nibandhana) (Writ-*

ten by Bhikṣu Vīryaśrīdatta of Śrī-Nālandāvihāra). Tibetan Sanskrit Works Series 13. Patna: K. P. Jayaswal Research Institute, 1971.

———., trans. *Gathering the Meanings: The Compendium of Categories. The Arthaviniścaya Sūtra and Its Commentary Nibandhana.* Berkeley, CA: Dharma Publishing, 2002.

Sastri, Hirananda. "Votive Inscription of the Reign of Mahendrapāladeva." In *Nalanda and Its Epigraphic Material.* Memoirs of the Archaeological Survey of India 66. New Delhi, 1999 [1942].

van Schaik, Sam. *Buddhist Magic: Divination, Healing, and Enchantment through the Ages.* Boulder, CO: Shambhala Publications, 2020.

Schlingloff, Dieter, and Jens-Uwe Hartmann. *Ein buddhistisches Yogalehrbuch.* Buddhismus-Studien 5. Munich: Iudicium, 2006.

———. *Fortified Cities of Ancient India: A Comparative Study.* London: Anthem Press, 2014.

Schmidt, I. J. *Der Index des Kandjur herausgegeben von der Kaiserlichen Akademie der Wissenschaften.* Osnabrück: Biblio Verlag, 1988 [1845].

Schmithausen, Lambert. "Zu den Rezensionen des Udānavargaḥ." *Wiener Zeitschrift für die Kunde Südasiens* 14 (1970): 47–124.

Schneider, Johannes, ed. and trans. *Der Lobpreis der Vorzüglichkeit des Buddha: Udbhatasiddhasvāmins Viśeṣastava mit Prajnāvarmans Kommentar.* Indica et Tibetica 23. Bonn: Indica et Tibetica Verlag, 1993.

———, ed. and trans. *Eine buddhistische Kritik der indischen Götter: Śaṃkarasvāmins Devātiśayastotra mit Prajñāvarmans Kommentar.* Wiener Studien zur Tibetologie und Buddhismuskunde 81. Vienna: Universität Wien, Arbeitskreis für Tibetische und Buddhistische Studien, 2014.

Schopen, Gregory. *Buddhist Monks and Business Matters: Still More Papers on Monastic Buddhism in India.* Studies in the Buddhist Traditions. Honolulu: University of Hawai'i Press, 2004.

———. "Hierarchy and History in a Buddhist Monastic Code." In *Buddhist Literature* 2 (2000): 92–196.

———. "A Verse from the Bhadracārī." *JIABS* 12.1 (1989): 149–57.

Sen, Amartya. *The Argumentative Indian: Writings on Indian Culture, History and Identity.* London: Penguin Books, 2005.

Senart, Émile, ed. *Le Mahâvastu.* 3 vols. [Paris: L'Imprimerie Nationale, 1882–97]. Repr. Tokyo: Meicho-Fukyū-Kai, 1977.

Seyfort Ruegg, David. *The Buddhist Philosophy of the Middle: Essays on Indian and Tibetan Madhyamaka.* Studies in Indian and Tibetan Buddhism. Boston: Wisdom Publications, 2010.

———. "The Indian and the Indic in Tibetan Cultural History, and Tsoṅ Kha Pa's Achievement as a Scholar and Thinker: An Essay on the Concepts of Buddhism in Tibet and Tibetan Buddhism." *Journal of Indian Philosophy* 32.4 (August 2004): 321–43 (repr. in Seyfort Ruegg, *Buddhist Philosophy of the Middle*, as essay 15).

———. "Purport, Implicature, and Presupposition: Sanskrit *abhiprāya* and Tibetan *dgongs pa / dgongs gzhi* as Hermeneutical Concepts." *Journal of Indian Philosophy* 13 (1985): 309–25 (repr. in Seyfort Ruegg, *Buddhist Philosophy of the Middle*, as essay 7).

Sferra, Francesco, trans. "Parole di Dhamma." In *La Rivelazione del Buddha, vol. 1: I testi antichi*. Rome: Arnoldo Mondadori Editotre, 2001.

———. "Pudgalo 'vācyaḥ—Apropos of a Recently Rediscovered Sanskrit Manuscript of the Saṃmitīyas. Critical Edition of the First Chapter of the Abhidharmasamuccayakārikā by Saṅghatrāta." In *Archaeologies of the Written: Indian, Tibetan, and Buddhist Studies in Honour of Cristina Scherrer-Schaub*, edited by Vincent Tournier, Vincent Eltschinger, and Marta Sernesi, 647–710. Naples: Università degli Studi di Napoli "L'Orientale," 2020.

———. "The Second Chapter of the Abhidharmasamuccayakārikā by Saṅghatrāta." In *"Verità e bellezza": Essays in Honour of Raffaele Torella*, edited by Francesco Sferra and Vincenzo Vergiani, 1145–66. Dipartimento Asia, Africa e Mediterraneo Università degli Studi di Napoli "L'Orientale" Series Minor 97.2. Naples: Universitá degli Studi di Napoli "L'orientale" / University of Cambridge; UniorPress 2022.

Shackleton Bailey, D. R., ed. *The Śatapañcāśatka of Mātṛceṭa: Sanskrit Text, Tibetan Translation and Commentary and Chinese Translation*. Cambridge: Cambridge University Press, 1951.

Shaw, Sarah. *The Art of Listening: A Guide to the Early Teachings of Buddhism. Exploring the Dīghanikāya—the Long Discourses of the Buddha*. Boulder, CO: Shambala Publications, 2021.

———. *Buddhist Meditation: An Anthology of Texts from the Pāli Canon*. London: Routledge, 2006.

Shimoda, Masahiro. "*Mahāparinirvāṇa-mahāsūtra*." In *Brill's Encyclopedia of Buddhism*. Vol. 1, edited by Jonathan A. Silk, 158–70. Leiden: Brill, 2016.

Shinohara, Koichi, trans. *A Forest of Pearls from the Dharma Garden*. Vol. 2. Moraga, CA: BDK America, 2019.

Silk, Jonathan A. "Serious Play: Recent Scholarship on the Lalitavistara." *Indo-Iranian Journal* 65 (2022): 267–301.

Simonsson, Nils. *Indo-tibetische Studien*: *Die Methoden der tibetischen Übersetzer, untersucht im Hinblick auf die Bedeutung ihrer Übersetzungen für die Sanskritphilologie*, vol. 1. Uppasala: Almqvist & Wiksells, 1957.

Simpson, J. A., and E. S. C. Weiner, eds. *The Oxford English Dictionary*, 2nd ed. Oxford: Clarendon Press, 1989.

von Simson, Georg, ed. *Prātimokṣasūtra der Sarvāstivādins*, Teil 2. *Kritische Textausgabe, Übersetzung, Wortindex sowie Nachträge zu Teil 1*. Abhandlungen der Akademie der Wissenschaften zu Göttingen, Philologisch-Historische Klasse, Dritte Folge, Nr. 238 / Sanskrittexte aus den Turfanfunden 11. Göttingen: Vandenhoeck & Ruprecht, 2000.

Singh, Rajesh Kumar. *Ajanta Paintings: A Compilation of 84 Abridged Narratives*. Ajanta Mahāpiṭaka 6-1. Baroda: Hari Sena Press, 2018.

———. *Periodisation of Rock-Cut Monuments of India*. Ajanta Mahāpiṭaka I-3. Baroda: Hari Sena Press, 2020.

Singh, Saṅghasen, ed. *A Study of the Sphuṭārthā Śrīghanācārasaṅgraha-ṭīkā*. 2nd ed. Tibetan Sanskrit Works Series 24. Patna: K. P. Jayaswal Research Institute, 1983.

Singh, Upinder. *The Discovery of Ancient India: Early Archaeologists and the Beginnings of Archaeology*. Delhi: Permanent Black, 2004.

———. *Inscribing Power on the Realm: Royal Ideology and Religious Policy in India c. 200 BCE–300 CE*. 28th J. Gonda Lecture 2022. Amsterdam: Royal Netherlands Academy of Arts and Sciences.

Sinha, Nirmal C. *Sikkim Research Institute of Tibetology*. Gangtok, 1977.

Skilling, Peter, trans. "The Sūtra on Impermanence." *World Fellowship of Buddhists Review* 13.6 (November–December, BE 2519 [1976]): 15–16.

———. "Ānisaṃsa: Merit, Motivation and Material Culture." *Journal of Buddhist Studies Sri Lanka* 14 (2017): 1–56.

———. "'Arise, Go Forth, Devote Yourselves . . .': A Verse Summary of the Teaching of the Buddhas." In *Socially Engaged Buddhism for the New Millennium: Essays in Honor of the Ven. Phra Dhammapitaka (Bhikkhu P. A. Payutto) on His 60th Birthday Anniversary*, edited by Purob Udomittipong and Chris Walker, 440–44. Bangkok: Sathirakoses-Nagapradipa Foundation, 1999.

———. "Birchbark, Bodhisatvas, and Bhāṇakas: Writing Materials in Buddhist North India." In *Lecteurs et copistes dans les traditions manuscrites iraniennes, indiennes, et centrasiatiques / Scribes and Readers in Iranian, Indian and Central Asian Manuscript Traditions*, edited by Nalini Balbir and Maria Szuppe, 499–521. Eurasian Studies 12/1–2. Rome: Istituto per l'Oriente.

———. "The Buddhist Cosmopolis: Universal Welfare, Universal Outreach, Universal Message." *Journal of Buddhist Studies* 15 (2018): 55–80.

———. "The Circulation of Artefacts Engraved with '*Apramāda*' and Other Mottos in Southeast Asia and India: A Preliminary Report." *Annual Report of the International Research Institute for Advanced Buddhology at Soka University for the Academic Year 2014*, vol. 18. Tokyo: International Research Institute for Advanced Buddhology, Soka University, 2015.

———. "Conjured Buddhas from the *Arthavargīya* to Nāgārjuna." In *Archaeologies of the Written: Indian, Tibetan, and Buddhist Studies in Honour of Cristina*

Scherrer-Schaub, edited by Vincent Tournier, Vincent Eltschinger, and Maria Sernesi, 711–51. Series Minor 89. Naples: Università degli Studi di Napoli "L'Orientale" / École française d'Extrême-Orient / Université de Lausanne, 2020.

——— (Bhadra Rujirathat). "'Discourse on the Relative Value of the Varieties of Knowledge' (*Vidyāsthānopama-sūtra*): A Translation." In *Research on the Saṃyukta-āgama* (雜阿含經研究論文集), edited by Dhammadinnā, 327–55. Taipei: Dharma Drum Publishing, 2020.

———. "Driving the Heretics out of Buddhist Translations: Tirtha and Its Derivatives." *Journal of Buddhist Studies* 19 (forthcoming).

———. "*Eṣā agrā*: Images of Nuns in (Mūla-)Sarvāstivādin Literature." *JIABS* 24.2 (2001): 135–56.

———. "'Impermanence': A Translation of the First Chapter of the Tibetan Udānavarga." *Buddhist Studies Review* 37.1 (2020): 15–25.

———. "La vie du Bouddha: Traditions et Histoire." *Religions et Histoire* 8 (May–June 2006): 18–23.

———, ed. *Mahāsūtras: Great Discourses of the Buddha*. Vol. 1, *Texts*. Critical editions of the Tibetan Mahāsūtras with Pāli and Sanskrit counterparts as available. Sacred Books of the Buddhists 44. Oxford: Pali Text Society, 1994.

———. *Mahāsūtras: Great Discourses of the Buddha*. Vol. 2, Parts 1 and 2. Sacred Books of the Buddhists 46. Oxford: Pali Text Society, 1997.

———. "Many Lands of Gold." In *Suvarnabhumi, the Golden Land: The New Finding for Suvarnabhumi Terra Incognita*, edited by Bunchar Phongpanich and Somchet Thinapong, 191–217. Bangkok: GISTDA (Geo-Informatics and Space Technology Development Agency) and BIA (Buddhadasa Indapanno Archives), 2019.

———. "The Many Lives of Texts: The *Pancatraya and* the *Mayajala Sutras*." In *Research on the Madhyama-agama*, edited by Dhammadinnā, 269–326. Taipei: Dharma Drum Publishing, 2017.

———. "A Note on the History of the Bhikkhunī-Saṅgha (I): Nuns at the Time of the Buddha." *WFB Review* 31.2–3 (April–September 2537/1994): 47–55.

———. "A Note on the History of the Bhikkhunī-Saṅgha (II): The Order of Nuns after the Parinirvāṇa." *WFB Review* 30.4–31.1 (October–December 2536/1993—January–March 2537/1994): 29–49.

———. "Nuns, Laywomen, Donors, Goddesses: Female Roles in Early Indian Buddhism." *JIABS* 24.2 (2001): 241–74.

———, ed. *Past Lives of the Buddha: Wat Si Chum: Art, Architecture and Inscriptions*. Bangkok: River Books, 2008.

———. "Praising the Buddha: *Stotras* in Mahāyāna Dharmaparyāyas." *Journal of Buddhist Studies* 12 (2014–15): 1–61. Centre for Buddhist Studies, Sri Lanka and The Buddha-Dharma Centre of Hong Kong.

———. "Prakrit Prajñāpāramitās: Northwest, South, and Center: Gleanings from Avalokitavrata and Haribhadra." In *Evo suyadi: Essays in Honor of Richard Salomon's 65th Birthday*, edited by Carol Altman Bromberg, Timothy J. Lenz, and Jason Neelis. *Bulletin of the Asia Institute*, new series 23 (2009) 199–208.

———. *Questioning the Buddha: A Selection of Twenty-Five Sutras*. Classics of Indian Buddhism. Somerville, MA: Wisdom Publications, 2021.

———. "The Rakṣā Literature of the Śrāvakayāna." *JPTS* 16 (1992): 109–82.

———. "Random Jottings on Śrīghana: An Epithet of the Buddha." *ARIRIAB for the Academic Year 2003*, vol. 7, 147–58. Tokyo: International Research Institute for Advanced Buddhology, Soka University, 2004.

———. "Redaction, Recitation, and Writing: Transmission of the Buddha's Teachings in India in the Early Period." In *Buddhist Manuscript Cultures: Knowledge, Ritual, and Art*, edited by Stephen C. Berkwitz, Juliane Schober, and Claudia Brown, chap. 4. London: Routledge, 2009.

———. "Reflections on the Pāli Literature of Siam." In *From Birch Bark to Digital Data: Recent Advances in Buddhist Manuscript Research* edited by Paul Harrison and Jens-Uwe Hartmann, 347–66. Beiträge zur Kultur- und Geistesgeschichte Asiens, 80; Denkschriften der philosophisch-historischen Klasse 460. Vienna: Österreichische Akademie der Wissenschaften, 2014.

———. "Rehabilitating the Pudgalavādins: Monastic Culture of the Vātsīputrīya-Sāṃmitīya School." *Journal of Buddhist Studies* 13 (2016): 1–53. Centre for Buddhist Studies, Sri Lanka, and The Buddha-Dharma Centre of Hong Kong.

———. "The Sambuddhe Verses and Later Theravādin Buddhology." *JPTS* 22 (1996): 151–83.

———. "Seeing the Preacher as the Teacher: A Note on *Śāstrasaṃjñā*." *Annual Report of the International Research Institute for Advanced Buddhology at Soka University for the Academic Year 2008*, vol. 12, 73–100. Tokyo: International Research Institute for Advanced Buddhology, Soka University.

———. "The Theravaṃsa Has Always Been Here: K. 1355 from Angkor Borei." *Journal of the Siam Society* 107.2 (2019): 43–62.

———. "Theravādin Literature in Tibetan Translation." *JPTS* 19 (1993): 69–201.

———. "Vaidalya, Mahāyāna, and Bodhisatva in India: An Essay towards Historical Understanding." In *The Bodhisattva Ideal: Essays on the Emergence of the Mahāyāna*, edited by Bhikkhu Nyanatusita, 69–162. Kandy: Buddhist Publication Society, 2013.

———. "The Vātsīputrīya/Sāṃmitīya: Buddhist Personalism as a Mainstream School of Thought." *Routledge Handbook of Indian Buddhist Philosophy*, edited by Sara McClintock, Pierre-Julien Harter, and William Edelglass, 188–203. New York: Routledge, 2022.

———. "Who Invented Dependent Arising? A Short Sūtra from the *Nidānasaṃyukta*." In *Saddharmāmṛtam: Festschrift für Jens-Uwe Hartmann zum*

65. Geburtstag, edited by Oliver von Criegern, Gudrun Melzer, and Johannes Schneider, 441–58. Vienna: Arbeitskreis für Tibetische und Buddhistische Studien (WSTB 93), 2018.

Skilling, Peter, with Prapod Assavavirulhakarn. "Vasubandhu on Travel and Seclusion." *Manusya: Journal of Humanities* (Chulalongkorn University) 2.1 (March 1999): 13–24.

Skilling, Peter, with Santi Pakdeekham. "Manuscripts in Central Thailand: Samut Khoi from Phetchaburi Province." *Manuscript Studies: A Journal of the Schoenberg Institute for Manuscript Studies* (University of Pennsylvania Libraries) 2.1 (Spring 2017): 125–50.

Smith, E. Gene. *Among Tibetan Texts: History and Literature of the Himalayan Plateau*. Studies in Indian and Tibetan Buddhism, edited by Kurtis R. Schaeffer. Boston: Wisdom Publications, 2001.

Sparham, Gareth, with guidance from Lobsang Gyatso and Ngawang Thekchok. *The Tibetan Dhammapada: Sayings of the Buddha, a translation of the Tibetan version of Udānavarga compiled by Dharmatrāta*. London: Wisdom Publications, 1986.

Speyer, J. S., ed. *Avadānaçataka. A Century of Edifying Tales Belonging to the Hînayâna*. 2 vols. Bibliotheca Buddhica 3. Osnabrück: Biblio Verlag, 1970 [St. Petersburg: Imperial Academy of Sciences, 1902–6].

Śrāvakabhūmi Study Group, ed. *Śrāvakabhūmi: Revised Sanskrit Text and Japanese Translation: The First Chapter*. Taishō University Sōgō Bukkyō Kenkyūjo Series 4. The Institute for Comprehensive Studies of Buddhism, Taishō University. Tokyo: Sankibo Press, 1998.

Śrīpuṇḍarīka. *Vimalaprabhāṭīkā*: see Upadhyaya, ed., and Dwivedi and Bahulkar, ed.

Staal, Frits. *Discovering the Vedas: Origins, Mantras, Rituals, Insights*. New Delhi: Penguin Books, 2008.

Stadtner, Donald M. *Sacred Sites of Burma: Myth and Folklore in an Evolving Spiritual Realm*. Photos by Phaisān Pīammēttāwat. Bangkok: River Books, 2015.

Stargardt, Janice. "Sri Ksetra, 3rd Century BCE to 6th Century CE: Indianization, Synergies, Creation." In *Primary Sources and Asian Pasts*, edited by Peter C. Bisschop and Elizabeth A. Cecil, 220–65. Beyond Boundaries 8. Berlin and Boston: De Gruyter, 2021.

Stede, W., ed. *The Sumaṅgala-vilāsinī: Buddhaghosa's Commentary on the Dīgha-nikāya*, part 2. London: Luzac , 1971 [1931].

Stein, Marc Aurel. *Ancient Khotan: Detailed Report of Archaeological Explorations in Chinese Turkestan*. Repr. 2 vols. in one. Bangkok: SDI Publications, 2001 [1907].

———. *An Archaeological Tour in Upper Swāt and Adjacent Hill Tracts*. Memoirs of the Archaeological Survey of India 42. Delhi: Swati Publications, 1991 [Calcutta: Government of India Central Publication Branch, 1930].

Stevenson, Angus, ed. *Shorter Oxford English Dictionary*. 6th ed. 2 vols. Oxford: Oxford University Press, 2007.

Strong, John. *The Legend of King Aśoka: Study and Translation of the Aśokāvadāna*. Princeton: Princeton University Press, 1983.

Subhadra, Ayu. *The Udanavarga: Verses Collected from the Buddhist Canon, Being the Northern Version of the Dhammapada*. London: Universalist Press Limited, 1946.

Sukpramun, Phatcharin. "La ville ancienne de Khu Bua." In *Dvāravatī—aux sources du bouddhisme en Thaïlande*, edited by Pierre Baptiste and Thierry Zéphir. Paris: Réunion des Musées Nationaux / Établissement Public du Musée des Arts Asiatiques Guimet, 2009.

Swanson, Paul. "*The Questions of Mañjuśrī*." In *Clear Serenity, Quiet Insight*. Honolulu: University of Hawai'i Press, 2017.

Syāmaraṭṭha Tepiṭaka. Thai-Script Pāli Tipiṭaka in 45 volumes, published by the Mahamakuta Printing Press, Bangkok. See Bavarian State Library, *Die Worte des Buddha*, § 22, pp. 41–42.

Szántó, Péter-Dániel. "Buddhist Homiletics on Grief (**Saddharmaparikathā*, ch. 11)." *Indo-Iranian Journal* 64 (2021): 291–347. doi:10.1163/15728536-06403001.

Takahata, Kanga, ed. *Ratnamālāvadāna: A Garland of Precious Gems or a Collection of Edifying Tales, Told in a Metrical Form, Belonging to the Mahāyāna*. Oriental Library Series D 3. Tokyo: Toyo Bunko, 1954.

Tāranātha. *Rgya gar chos 'byung*. Edited by Antonius Schiefner, Târanâthae de doctrinae buddhicae in india propagatione narratio. Contextum tibeticum e condicibus petropolitanis edidit. [Petropoli (St. Petersburg) 1868.] Repr. in Reprint Series 2. Tokyo: Suzuki Research Foundation, 1965.

Tarn, William Woodthorpe. *The Greeks in Bactria and India*. 2nd ed. Cambridge: Cambridge University Press, 2010 [1966].

Tatia, Nathmal, ed. *Prātimokṣasūtram of the Lokottaravādimahāsāṅghika School*. Tibetan Sanskrit Works Series 16. Patna: Kashi Prased Jayaswal Research Institute, 1976 [1975].

Teiser, Stephen F. *Reinventing the Wheel: Paintings of Rebirth in Medieval Buddhist Temples*. Seattle and London: University of Washington Press, 2006.

Thānissaro Bhikkhu, trans. *The Great Total Unbinding Discourse: Mahā Parinibbāna Sutta* (DN 16). Dhammatalks.org accessed 21 July 2021.

Thapar, Romila. *The Past as Present: Forging Contemporary Identities Through History*. New Delhi: Aleph Book Company, 2014.

———. *The Past before Us: Historical Traditions of Early North India*. Ranikhet: Permanent Black in Association with Asoka University, 2013.

Tharchin, Geshe Lobsang, and Artemis B. Engle. *Nāgārjuna's Letter: Nāgārjuna's "Letter to a Friend" with a Commentary by the Venerable Rendawa Zhön-nu Lodrö*. Dharamsala: Library of Tibetan Works and Archives, 1979.

Tharoor, Shashi. *Tharoorosaurus!* Gurgaon: Penguin/Viking, 2020.

Thomas, E. J., trans. "The Formula of Welfare." In *The Quest of Enlightenment: A Selection of the Buddhist Scriptures Translated from the Sanskrit*, edited by J. L. Cranmer-Byng, 65–69. Wisdom of the East Series. London: John Murray, 1950.

Thurman, Robert A. F., trans. *The Holy Teaching of Vimalakīrti: A Mahāyāna Scripture.* University Park: Pennsylvania State University Press, 1976. See also online version: *Teaching of Vimalakīrti (Vimalakīrtinirdeśa)*, edited by 84000: Translating the Words of the Buddha, 2017. https://read.84000.co/translation/toh176.html.

Tola, Fernando, and Carmen Dragonetti. "On the Names of Bhiksus and Bodhisattvas in the Lotus Sutra." *Journal of Institute for the Comprehensive Study of Lotus Sutra (Hokekyō Bunka Kenkyūjo)* 22 (March 1996): 95–123.

Tominaga Nakamoto. *Emerging from Meditation.* Translated by Michael Pye. London: Duckworth, 1990.

Tournier, Vincent. "Buddhist Lineages along the Southern Routes: On Two Nikāyas Active at Kanaganahalli under the Sātavāhanas." In *Archaeologies of the Written: Indian, Tibetan, and Buddhist Studies in Honour of Cristina Scherrer-Schaub*, edited by Vincent Tournier, Vincent Eltschinger, and Marta Sernesi, 859–912. Naples: Università degli Studi di Napoli "L'Orientale," 2020.

———. "A 4th/5th-Century Sūtra of the Saṁmitīya Canon? On the So-Called 'Continental Pāli' Inscription from Devnimori (Gujarat)." In *Proceedings of the Third International Pali Studies Week—Paris 2018*, edited by Claudio Cicuzza. Bangkok and Lumbini: Fragile Palm Leaf Foundation; Lumbini International Research Institute, forthcoming.

———. "Protective Verses for Travellers: A Fragment of the Diśāsauvastika-gāthās Related to the Scriptures of the Mahāsāṃghika-Lokottaravādins." In *Buddhist Manuscripts*, vol. 4, edited by Jens Braarvig, 407–37. Manuscripts in the Schøyen Collection. Oslo: Hermes Publishing, 2016.

———. "Review of Dimitrov 2020." *Bulletin de l'École française d'Extrême-Orient* 106. Forthcoming.

Trautmann, Thomas R. *Languages and Nations: The Dravidian Proof in Colonial Madras.* New Delhi: Yoda Press, 2006.

Trenckner. V. *The Milindapañho: Being Dialogues between King Milinda and the Buddhist Sage Nāgasena.* London: Royal Asiatic Society, 1928.

Tripāṭhī, Candrabhāl, ed. *Fünfundzwanzig Sūtras des Nidānasaṃyukta.* Berlin: Akademie Verlag, 1962.

Truss, Lynne. *Eats, Shoots & Leaves: The Zero Tolerance Approach to Punctuation.* New York: Gotham Books, 2003.

Tshe ring, Dngos grub. *Ta la'i lo mar bris pa'i rgya dpe bris ma bshes spring skor gyi dpe bsdur zhib 'jug* [Comparative Textual Study of the Indian Palm-Leaf Manuscript of the Suhṛllekha]. Lhasa: Bod ljongs bod yig dpe rnying dpe skrun khang, 2020.

Tsukamoto Keisho. *A Comprehensive Study of the Indian Buddhist Inscriptions*. 2 parts. Kyoto: Heirakuji Shoten, 1996–98.

Tsukamoto Zenryū. *A History of Early Chinese Buddhism from Its Introduction to the Death of Hui-yüan*. 2 vols. Trans. from the Japanese by Leon Hurvitz. Tokyo: Kodansha International, 1985.

Upadhyaya, Jagannatha, ed. *Vimalaprabhāṭīkā of Kalki Śrī Puṇḍarīka on Śrī Laghukālacakratantrarāja by Śrī Mañjuśrīyaśa*, vol. 1. Bibliotheca Indo-Tibetica 11. Sarnath, Varanasi: Central Institute of Higher Tibetan Studies, 1986.

Upasak, C. S. *Dictionary of Early Buddhist Monastic Terms (Based on Pāli Literature)*. Varanasi: Bharati Prakashan, 1975.

Vaidya, P. L., ed. *Avadānaśataka*. Buddhist Sanskrit Texts 19. Darbhanga: Mithila Institute, 2000 [1958].

———, ed. *Lalita-vistara*. Buddhist Sanskrit Texts 1. Darbhanga: Mithila Institute, 1958.

Vajirā, Sister, and Francis Story. *Last Days of the Buddha: The Mahā Parinibbāna Sutta*. Kandy: Buddhist Publication Society, 1988 [1964].

Vassilief, V. [Vasilyev]. *Le Bouddhisme, see dogmes, son histoire et sa littérature. Première partie: Aperçu Général*. Translated from the Russian by G. A. La Comme. Paris: Auguste Durand, 1863.

Verardi, Giovanni, with appendices by Federica Barba. *The Gods and the Heretics: Crisis and Ruin of Indian Buddhism*. New Delhi: Aditya Prakashan / Buenos Aires: Fundación Bodhiyāna, 2018.

Vidyabhusana, Satis Chandra, ed. and trans. *So-sor thar pa (Khrims): Vol. V of the Dulwa Portion of the Kangyur (Leaves 1–29 and Top Line of Leaf 30)*. Calcutta: R. N. Bhattacharya, 2000. From the *Journal and Proceedings, Asiatic Society of Bengal*, new series 11.3–4 (1915).

Vignato, Giuseppe, and Satomi Hiyama, with appendices by Petra Kieffer-Pülz and Yoko Taniguchi. *Traces of the Sarvāstivādins in the Buddhist Monasteries of Kucha*. Leipzig Kucha Studies 3. New Delhi: Dev Publishers, 2022.

Vinītā, Bhikṣuṇī (Vinita Tseng), ed. and trans. *A Unique Collection of Twenty Sūtras in a Sanskrit Manuscript from the Potala*. Sanskrit texts from the Tibetan Autonomous Region 7/1. Beijing and Vienna: China Tibetology Publishing House and Austrian Academy of Sciences Press, 2010.

Waldschmidt, Ernst, ed. *Bruchstücke buddhistischer Sūtras aus dem Zentralasiatischen Sanskritkanon*. Kleinere Sanskrit-Texte 4 [Leipzig, 1932], repr. Monographien zur indischen Archäologie, Kunst und Philologie 2. Wiesbaden: Franz Steiner Verlag, 1979.

———. *Die Überlieferung vom Lebensende des Buddha: Eine vergleichende Analyse des Mahāparinirvāṇasūtra und seiner Textentsprechungen*. 2 vols. Abhandlungen der Akademie der Wissenschaften in Göttingen. Phil.-hist. Klasse. Folge 3. no. 29, 3. Göttingen, 1944–48.

Walker, Annabel. *Aurel Stein: Pioneer of the Silk Road*. London: John Murray, 1995.

Walshe, Maurice, trans. *The Long Discourses of the Buddha: A Translation of the Dīgha Nikāya*. Boston: Wisdom Publications, 1995 [1987].

Wangchuk, Dorji. "The Three Royal Decrees (bka' bcad gsum) in the History of Tibetan Buddhism." In *Archaeologies of the Written: Indian, Tibetan, and Buddhist Studies in Honour of Cristina Scherrer-Schaub*, edited by Vincent Tournier, Vincent Eltschinger, and Marta Sernesi, 943–75. Naples: Università degli Studi di Napoli "L'Orientale," 2020.

Wat Phrachetuphonwimonmangkhalaram. *Boranawatthu chak phra mahacedi 4 rachakan Wat Phra Chetuphonwimonmangkhalaram* [Antiquities from the Great Chedi of Four Reigns in Wat Phra Chetupon Wimonmangkhalarama]. Bangkok: 2541 (1998).

Watson, Burton, trans. *The Lotus Sutra*. New York: Columbia University Press, 1993.

Webb, Sara (Boin), trans. "Udānavarga I." *Pāli Buddhist Review* 6.1 (1981–82): 1–4.

Weber, Claudia. *Buddhistische Sutras: Das Leben des Buddha in Quellentexte*. Munich: Diederichs, 1999.

Wenzel, Heinrich, trans. "Bçes pai phrin yig ('Friendly Epistle')." *JPTS* (1886) 1–32.

Westerhoff, Jan. *The Non-Existence of the Real World*. Oxford: Oxford University Press, 2020.

———. *Reality: A Very Short Introduction*. Oxford: Oxford University Press, 2011.

Wiles, Royce et al. "The Pāli Tipiṭaka Recension Carved on the Kuthodaw Pagoda Stelae and Its Relation to Other Burmese Versions." *Journal of the Pali Text Society* 34 (2021): 155–226.

Wille, Klaus. "Survey of the Identified Sanskrit Manuscripts in the Hoernle, Stein, and Skrine Collections of the British Library (London)." In Harrison and Hartmann, *From Birch Bark to Digital Data*, 223–46.

———. "Survey of the Sanskrit Manuscripts in the Turfan Collection (Berlin)." In Harrison and Hartmann, *From Birch Bark to Digital Data*, 187–211.

Willemen, Charles, trans. *The Chinese Udānavarga: A Collection of Important Odes of the Law, Fa Chi Yao Sung Ching*. Mélanges chinois et bouddhiques 19. Brussels: Institut Belge des Hautes Études Chinoises, 1978.

———, trans. *A Collection of Important Odes of the Law: The Chinese Udānavarga, Fa Chi Yao Sung Ching (Taishō 213)*. Berkeley, CA: Institute of Buddhist Studies and BDK America, 2013.

———, trans. *The Scriptural Text: Verses of the Doctrine with Parables*. Translated from the Chinese of Fa-li and Fa-chü. Taishō 4, no. 211. BDK English Tripiṭaka 10-II. Berkeley, CA: Numata Center for Buddhist Translation and Research, 1999.

———. "Yijing's Scriptural Text about Impermanence (T. 801)." In: *Methods in Buddhist Studies: Essays in Honor of Richard K. Payne*, edited by Scott A. Mitchell and Natalie Fisk Quli, 67–76. London: Bloomsbury Academic, 2019.

Williams, Raymond. *Keywords: A Vocabulary of Culture and Society*. Rev. ed. New York: Oxford University Press, 1983 [1976].

Witanachchi, C. "Udānavarga." *Encyclopaedia of Buddhism*, vol. 8, fasc. 2 (2008): 384–86.

Witzel, Michael. *The Origins of the World's Mythologies*. New York: Oxford University Press, 2012.

Wogihara, U, ed. *Sphuṭârthā Abhidharmakośavyākhyā: The Work of Yaśomitra*. Tokyo: Sankibo Buddhist Book Store, 1989 [1936].

Wong, Dorothy C. *Buddhist Pilgrim-Monks as Agents of Cultural and Artistic Transmission: The International Buddhist Art Style in East Asia, ca. 645–770*. Singapore: NUS Press, 2018.

Woodward, F. L., trans. *The Book of Kindred Sayings (Saṃyutta-nikāya) or Grouped Suttas*, Part 4. London: Pali Text Society, 1972 [1927].

———, trans. *The Book of Gradual Sayings (Anguttara-nikāya) or More-Numbered Suttas*. 5 vols. London: Pali Text Society, 1932–36.

Woolner, Alfred C. *Introduction to Prakrit*.Delhi: Motilal Banarsidass, 1996 [1928].

Wujastyk, Dominik. "Jambudvīpa: Apples or Plums?" In *Studies in the History of the Exact Sciences in Honor of David Pingree*, edited by Charles Burnett, Jan P. Hogendijk, Kim Plofker, and Michio Yano, 287–301. Leiden and Boston: Brill, 2004.

Wyld. *Universal Dictionary*.

Yamabe, Nobuyoshi. "Concentration and Visualization Techniques in Buddhist Meditation." In *The Oxford Handbook of Meditation*, edited by Miguel Farias, David Brazier, and Mansur Lalljee, chap. 15. Oxford University Press, 2021.

Yamagiwa, Nobuyuki, ed. *Das Pāṇḍulohitakavastu: Über die verschiedenen Verfahrensweisen der Bestrafung in der buddhistischen Gemeinde: Neuausgabe der Sanskrit-Hanschrift aus Gilgit, tibetischer Text und deutsche Übersetzung*. Indica et Tibetica 41. Marburg: Indica et Tibetica Verlag, 2001.

Yule, Henry, and A. C. Burnell. *Hobson-Jobson: A Glossary of Colloquial Anglo-Indian Words and Phrases, and of Kindred Terms, Etymological, Historical, Geographical and Discursive*. New edition edited by William Crooke, New Delhi: Munshiram Manoharlal, 1984 [London: John Murray, 1903].

Zin, Monika, and Dieter Schlingloff. *Saṃsāracakra: Das Rad der Wiedergeburten in der indischen Überlieferung*. Buddhismus-Studien / Buddhist Studies 6. Düsseldorf: Ekō Haus, 2007. English translation: *Saṃsāracakra: The Wheel of Rebirth in the Indian Tradition*. New Delhi: Dev Publishers, 2022.

Zinn, Katharina. "Literacy in Pharaonic Egypt: Orality and Literacy between Agency and Memory." In *Literacy in Ancient Everyday Life*, edited by Anne Kolb, 67–97. Berlin and Boston: De Gruyter, 2018.

Zwalf, Wladimir. *Buddhism: Art and Faith*. London: British Museum, 1985.

Index

Page locators in boldface indicate glossary entries.

C

Z

About the Author

PETER SKILLING is a special lecturer at Chulalongkorn University, Bangkok, and an honorary associate, Department of Indian Subcontinental Studies, University of Sydney, Australia. Until his retirement in 2017, he was a professor at the French School of Asian Studies (École française d'Extrême-Orient) based in Bangkok. He was awarded an honorary doctorate in the humanities by Chulalongkorn University in 2020.

He is an honorary member of the Siam Society, Bangkok, and in 2017 he was elected an honorary fellow of the Asiatic Society of Mumbai. He has been visiting professor at Harvard University (2000), the University of California at Berkeley (2001), Oxford University (2002), Sydney University (2009), Soka University (2009), and Savitribai Phule Pune University (2016–17).

His main field of research is the epigraphy, archaeology, history, and literature of Buddhism in South and Southeast Asia according to Sanskrit, Pali, Thai, and Tibetan sources.

yathā pattharacuṇṇamhi jātarūpaṃ na dissati
parikammena tad diṭṭhaṃ evaṃ loke tathāgatā

EVAṂ

Figure 60. Contemplation of the foul: mural painting with standing gilt Buddha image in foreground. Uposatha hall, Wat Uposatharam, Uthai Thani province, Thailand.

What to Read Next from Wisdom Publications

Rebirth in Early Buddhism and Current Research
Bhikkhu Anālayo

A fascinating investigation of what we can—and cannot—know about the impact of oral transmission on the development of early Buddhist texts.

Questioning the Buddha
A Selection of Twenty-Five Sutras
Peter Skilling

"In this volume, prose and verse join beautifully to celebrate the Dharma. The selections show how rich, how diverse, and how wonderful the Kangyur is—and how little we know about it."—from the foreword by Dzongsar Jamyang Khyentse

Early Buddhist Oral Tradition
Textual Formation and Transmission
Bhikkhu Anālayo

A fascinating investigation into the formation and transmission of the early Buddhist oral tradition.

Noble Truths, Noble Path
The Heart Essence of the Buddha's Original Teachings
Bhikkhu Bodhi

"A precious and reliable guide to a vast spiritual domain, and I cannot recommend it too highly."—Ven. Ajahn Amaro, Abbot, Amaravati Buddhist Monastery, UK

About Wisdom Publications

Wisdom Publications is the leading publisher of classic and contemporary Buddhist books and practical works on mindfulness. To learn more about us or to explore our other books, please visit our website at wisdomexperience.org or contact us at the address below.

Wisdom Publications
132 Perry Street
New York, NY 10014 USA

We are a 501(c)(3) organization, and donations in support of our mission are tax deductible.

Wisdom Publications is affiliated with the Foundation for the Preservation of the Mahayana Tradition (FPMT).